THE MOST ENORMOUS PUB QUIZ BOOK EVER! 2

This edition published in 2002

Previously published as *The Biggest Pub Quiz Book Ever 2!*

1 86200 107 3

Editor: Kerrin Edwards
Designer: Vaseem Bhatti
Production: Lisa French

Questions set by The Puzzle House

Printed and bound in Great Britain

THE MOST ENORMOUS PUB QUIZ BOOK EVER! 2

SEVENOAKS

Contents

MEDIUM

HARD

Introduction

Quizzes are a strange thing. If you were to stroll up to some poor bloke on the street – let's say it's a Saturday lunch time, and he's out with the wife doing the weekly shopping, trying to get it over and done with so he can make it back home for kick-off – and started firing questions at him, one after the other, he'd probably take it pretty badly. He'd be nervous, irritated, and looking for quick ways to escape the maniac that's latched on to him. If you take a moment to picture it ("Quick, mate, what would you ride in a velodrome? What colour is an aubergine?"), you'll see how ludicrous it sounds. If he doesn't lamp you one, he'll probably run off screaming in terror.

However, get the same bloke later on the same Saturday, down the pub with his mates after the match, and then you leap up and start firing the same questions at him, at the very least he's going to rise to the challenge and prove he's the equal of your questions. If you've taken the time to sort things out with the landlord in advance, and you're asking the whole pub, you'll have a crowd of people enthralled, hanging on your every word, and not just our bloke. Even if – and this is the best part – there's absolutely no prize at the end of it. We all love glory, after all, and what could be more glorious than proving you've got the keenest mind in the bar? It beats getting onto a horse and charging at a cannon hands down.

This is the second bumper volume of *The Biggest Pub Quiz Book Ever!* and it keeps getting better and better. Inside these hallowed covers, you'll find more than 16,000 questions covering a stunning range of topics, divided into laughably easy, reasonably medium, and brain-shreddingly hard. At the back, you'll also find a comprehensive set of guidelines on how to prepare for and run a successful quiz of your own down the local, and some handy answer sheet templates to photocopy and give out to contestants. There is one important thing you have to remember though, and that is never, ever, under any circumstances, give out your own pens.

The aim of this fine tome is to guide you through the pitfulls of pub quizzardry to the land of Pub Facts (and I'm not talking warm beer) where you can safely head up a quiz at your local hostelry and thereby gain the undying gratitude of the stout yeoman of the bar and the love of the locals.

It may be wise in fact to talk the idea through with your landlord or landlady and have the quiz at your local where you know everyone and everyone knows you. Start slowly and build up your quiz nights carefully, controlling and feeding the voracious appetites of the regulars until you have them eating quiz out of the palms of your hands. Finally and quite seriously. No, really.

More important than that, though, is that when you are going to be running a quiz, prepare properly beforehand. Don't just take this book along and read out of it (because apart from anything else, some other wise guy might have bought a copy too, and be checking the answers). Note down all the questions and all the answers, and make sure you've got everything. If an answer makes you think "hang on a moment, is that right?" then double-check it to make sure that it is not only correct, but it is the only correct answer. While every possible effort has been undertaken to make absolutely sure that every answer is accurate, there is a slight possibility that an error may have crept in and the answer is wrong. Nothing is more humiliating than telling people who are right that they are wrong, in front of a lot of other people who will remember it and tease you about it mercilessly for the next three years. If you've made sure of your answers, you'll be absolutely 100% safe, not just 99.99% safe.

So, there you go. Wade in, and have fun. After all, that's what it's all about.

Easy Questions

"Easy! Easy!" It's no good putting these questions near the end when everyone's well into their stride (there's an outside chance they may even be a little tipsy too) and they're knocking the questions down like it's nobody's business. Except that, as the boozer's esteemed Quizmaster (or perhaps someone else has helpfully volunteered you), it is very much *your* business. So it's probably best, as you may well imagine, that these come at the start of a quiz – bowl these mostly harmless questions rather gently at the teams, underarm so to speak, while they find their bearings.

Moreover, at this point in the evening, most of your jolly quizzers should still be relatively sober, so that the kind of ridiculously childish chanting warned of earlier ought not to be taking place. In short, there should be plenty in here that quite a lot of people ought to know – so these questions will be good to get everyone nicely in the mood!

Quiz 1 The Movies: Actresses

Answers - see Quiz 2, page 12

1 In which film did Uma Thurman play Emma Peel?
2 What part of her did Demi Moore remove completely for G.I.Jane?
3 How many films had Barbra Streisand been in before being the star of Funny Girl?
4 Which crime writer did Vanessa Redgrave play in Agatha?
5 Is Nicole Kidman shorter or taller than husband Tom Cruise?
6 Which Sandra starred in Speed and The Net?
7 What is the name of Audrey Hepburn's cat in Breakfast at Tiffany's?
8 Which blonde was the star of Some Like It Hot?
9 Which English actress was the first to play M in the Bond movies?
10 During which war was Land Girls with Anna Friel set?
11 Which Audrey played Eliza Doolittle in My Fair Lady?
12 Which Tallulah was known for calling everyone "Dahling"?
13 Who played Rita in Educating Rita?
14 Which Ms Foster had a son Charles in 1998?
15 Which actress Vanessa is Natasha Richardson's mother?
16 Ingrid Bergman and Judy Garland had what type of flower named after them?
17 What was the nationality of Ingrid Bergman?
18 What was Julie Andrews' first film, about a nanny?
19 Is Shirley MacLaine left or right handed?
20 Which Ursula co starred with Elvis in Fun in Acapulco?
21 Which blonde French actress's real name is Camille Javal?
22 Which Jane was one of the first actresses to produce fitness videos?
23 Which item of Madonna's underwear made £4,600 at auction in '97?
24 Brigitte Bardot had a theatre named after her in which French city?
25 Which Marlene said, "I acted vulgar, Madonna IS vulgar"?
26 Which Irish TV personality was named after Gloria Swanson?
27 Which actress Debra served in the Israeli army?
28 Which Christina played the sinister Wednesday in the Addam Family films?
29 What is Goldie Hawn's real name?
30 Catherine Zeta Jones supports which South Wales soccer side?

Answers

Nature: Animal World (see Quiz 2, page 12)
1 (African) elephant. **2** Wolf. **3** Warm blooded. **4** Tooth. **5** Voice box. **6** Alone. **7** Primate. **8** Duck. **9** Dog. **10** Sheep. **11** Sight. **12** Offensive smell. **13** Brown. **14** (South) America. **15** Eye. **16** Hare. **17** Its ears. **18** Alaska. **19** Warm. **20** Carnivorous. **21** Cows. **22** Chimpanzee. **23** Neck. **24** Invertebrates. **25** One. **26** Tail. **27** Polar bear. **28** Milk. **29** Fingerprints. **30** Southern.

Quiz 2 Nature: Animal World

Answers - see Quiz 1, page 11

1 Which land mammal has the largest ears?
2 Which wild animal is the domesticated dog descended from?
3 Are mammals warm blooded or cold blooded?
4 Which part of the body has a crown and a root?
5 What is another name for the larynx?
6 Do tigers hunt in packs or alone?
7 Which group of animals shares its name with an archbishop?
8 What type of creature is an Aylesbury?
9 What was the first animal to be domesticated?
10 Cheviot and Suffolk are both types of what?
11 Shrews have acute sense of smell and hearing to compensate for which weak sense?
12 The opossum and the skunk are famous for what?
13 What colour is a grizzly bear?
14 The llama is native to which continent?
15 Which part of a human's body has a cornea?
16 A leveret is a young what?
17 What part of a Basset Hound is particularly long?
18 Which northerly US state is famous for the brown bear?
19 Does the moose live in a warm or cold climate?
20 Are crocodiles carnivorous or herbivores?
21 Which farm animals chew the cud?
22 Which primate species is the closest genetic cousin to humanity?
23 Where is a human's jugular vein?
24 Are most animals vertebrates or invertebrates?
25 How many young does a kangaroo usually produce at any one time?
26 What part of the body of a Manx cat is missing which is present on most other cats?
27 Which bear is the largest meat-eating land animal?
28 What do all mammals feed their babies on?
29 Which part of a human includes loops and whorls?
30 In which hemisphere do penguins live in the wild?

Answers

The Movies: Actresses (see Quiz 1, page 11)
1 The Avengers. **2** Her hair. **3** None. **4** Agatha Christie. **5** Taller. **6** Bullock. **7** Cat. **8** Marilyn Monroe. **9** Judi Dench. **10** Second World War. **11** Hepburn. **12** Bankhead. **13** Julie Walters. **14** Jodie Foster. **15** Redgrave. **16** Rose. **17** Swedish. **18** Mary Poppins. **19** Left. **20** Andress. **21** Brigitte Bardot. **22** Fonda. **23** Black bra. **24** Paris. **25** Dietrich. **26** Gloria Hunniford. **27** Winger. **28** Ricci. **29** Goldie Hawn. **30** Swansea City.

Quiz 3 TV: Cops & Robbers

Answers - see Quiz 4, page 14

1 What is the surname of cop Maisie played by Pauline Quirke?
2 Michael French left which soap to become a Crime Traveller?
3 Who replaced Sue Cook as co presenter of Crimewatch UK?
4 Which series featured Eddie "Fitz" Fitzgerald?
5 Which early police serial is found at the end of the alphabet?
6 Which Yorkshire police series did Nick Berry leave in 1997?
7 In which US city was Cagney and Lacey set?
8 Dangerfield deals with what type of police personnel?
9 David Suchet played which Belgian Agatha Christie detective?
10 In which English county does Wycliffe take place?
11 Which assistant to Morse was missing from the show in 1998?
12 Michael Gambon played which French detective in the 90s?
13 How was The Bill's DC Lines, played by Kevin Lloyd, better known?
14 Which Glasgow detective was played by Mark McManus?
15 Which Hetty has a sidekick called Geoffrey?
16 What is the surname of detective Jack played by David Jason?
17 Which police station's blues were led by Captain Frank Furillo?
18 What is the first name of Commander Dalgliesh, created by PD James?
19 Which Jimmy starred in Evita and played Geordie Spender?
20 Which Victorian sleuth from Baker Street was played by Jeremy Brett?
21 In "Pie in the Sky", which profession did Henry combine with policing?
22 In which northern city was City Central set?
23 How is Cordelia Gray's creator Baroness James better known?
24 Which bald TV cop was Friends' Jennifer Aniston's godfather?
25 Where was the police sitcom Duck Patrol set?
26 Where did Sonny Crockett aka Don Johnson sort out Vice?
27 Who has played Jack Regan and Morse?
28 In which city was Cagney and Lacey set?
29 Which crime buster show shared its name with insects?
30 In which city did Maigret operate?

Answers

Pot Luck 1 (see Quiz 4, page 14)
1 Drinks. **2** Bread & cheese. **3** American. **4** The Sun. **5** Romantic. **6** Paris. **7** The Mouse Trap. **8** Waterloo. **9** Pyramids. **10** Sheep. **11** Gates. **12** Christmas. **13** Nile. **14** Dog. **15** October. **16** Lancashire. **17** Association. **18** Thistle. **19** Cattle. **20** 80s. **21** Travel. **22** Wight. **23** Game. **24** Royals. **25** Hong Kong. **26** London. **27** Mont Blanc. **28** Pancakes. **29** 29th. **30** Beijing.

Quiz 4 Pot Luck 1

Answers - see Quiz 3, page 13

1 What is usually sold at reduced prices during a happy hour?
2 What are the two main ingredients of a ploughman's lunch?
3 What was Martina Navratilova's nationality when winning her last Wimbledon title?
4 Which UK daily newspaper has the shortest name?
5 Dame Barbara Cartland is famous for what type of fiction?
6 In which city is the Louvre Museum?
7 Which Agatha Christie play has run in the West End for over 45 years?
8 From which London railway station do Eurostar trains depart?
9 Which surviving tombs were built for the Pharaohs of Egypt?
10 What type of animal was the first successful adult cloning?
11 Which Bill is the world's richest businessman?
12 Twelfth Night marks the end of which festive season?
13 On which river does Cairo stand?
14 What type of animal is a Chihuahua?
15 In which month did the 1987 hurricane take place in the UK?
16 Which county does TV detective Hetty Wainthropp come from?
17 In motoring terms, what does the second A in AA stand for?
18 What is the national emblem of Scotland?
19 What type of animal does BSE affect?
20 In which decade of the 20th century was Prince William born?
21 What sort of tickets would a bucket shop sell?
22 On which Isle is Parkhurst prison?
23 What is hopscotch?
24 Which family receives a payment from the Civil List?
25 Which British colony returned to China in July 1997?
26 In which city did rhyming slang originate?
27 Which alpine peak's name means White Mountain?
28 Which food is traditionally eaten on Shrove Tuesday?
29 If August 31st was a Wednesday what date would August Bank Holiday Monday be in England?
30 In which city is Tiananmen Square?

Answers

TV: Cops & Robbers (see Quiz 3, page 13)

1 Raine. **2** Eastenders. **3** Jill Dando. **4** Cracker. **5** Z Cars. **6** Heartbeat. **7** New York. **8** Police surgeon. **9** Poirot. **10** Cornwall. **11** Lewis. **12** Maigret. **13** Tosh. **14** Taggart. **15** Wainthropp. **16** Frost. **17** Hill St. Blues. **18** Adam. **19** Nail. **20** Sherlock Holmes. **21** Chef. **22** Manchester. **23** P.D. James. **24** Kojak (Telly Savalas). **25** River Thames. **26** Miami. **27** John Thaw. **28** New York. **29** Bugs. **30** Paris.

Quiz 5 Rich & Famous: Names

Answers - see Quiz 6, page 16

1 How is Jeremy John Durham Ashdown better known?
2 Raymond Blanc is famous for being what?
3 Which Betty became the House of Commons' first woman Speaker?
4 Which Melvyn stopped starting the week when he became a peer?
5 Which one time husband and wife actors were dubbed Ken and Em?
6 Which trendy homeware store did Terence Conran found in the 60s?
7 Which part of you would you ask Nicky Clarke to cut off?
8 How was Yorkshire based murderer Peter Sutcliffe better known?
9 Which celebrity daughter was named after the song Chelsea Morning?
10 Who released an album in 1975 called Uri Geller?
11 Which 90s PM was in a university pop group called Ugly Rumours?
12 Who is taller, Kylie Minogue or Naomi Campbell?
13 Who launched Virgin Cola and Virgin PEPs ?
14 Which singer Sarah was once Mrs Andrew Lloyd Webber?
15 Who is Michelle Lineker's famous husband?
16 Which Monica was intimately associated with Bill Clinton?
17 Was Joan Collins born in the 1920s, 1930s or the 1940s?
18 Which British Party leader has the same first names as Bill Clinton?
19 Which model Jerry had a cameo role in Batman?
20 What colour is Dame Edna Everage's hair?
21 Which London football club does David Mellor famously support?
22 Which Scot Andrew was the Sunday Times editor from 1983 to 1994?
23 John Prescott is Deputy Leader of which political party?
24 Which Prime Minister had twins called Mark and Carol?
25 The names Saatchi and Saatchi are associated with which industry?
26 Which Rolling Stone Bill was 34 years older than bride Mandy Smith?
27 What title does the brother of the late Princess Diana have?
28 What type of shops did Tim Waterstone found?
29 Which designer Vivienne is famous for her outrageous clothes?
30 What is the nickname of Royal 'nanny' Alexandra Legge-Bourke?

Answers

Pot Luck 2 (see Quiz 6, page 16)
1 Donkey. **2** Italy. **3** Tipperary. **4** White. **5** Poppy. **6** 48. **7** Lah. **8** A calf. **9** China. **10** Frank Sinatra. **11** Chequered. **12** Japan. **13** C. **14** Bach. **15** HM Customs & Excise. **16** Orange. **17** 11. **18** Blue. **19** Dublin. **20** Florence Nightingale. **21** Pumpkin. **22** Bill Haley & the Comets. **23** London. **24** Hans Christian Andersen. **25** The twins. **26** Shropshire. **27** Grapes. **28** Tennis. **29** Sound and noise. **30** One.

Quiz 6 Pot Luck 2

Answers - see Quiz 5, page 15

1 What kind of animal is Eeyore in the children's classic?
2 Which country produces Parmesan cheese?
3 Where, according to the song, is it a long way to in Ireland?
4 What colour were all guests asked to wear at Mel B's wedding?
5 Which flower is linked with Remembrance Sunday?
6 How many sides are there in a dozen quadrilaterals?
7 Which note follows the musical note 'soh'?
8 What name is given to a young elephant?
9 In which country was acupuncture developed?
10 Which singer was known affectionately as 'Old Blue Eyes'?
11 Which flag in motor racing signals the end of the race?
12 In which country is the yen the unit of currency?
13 Which vitamin is found in oranges and lemons?
14 Which composer had the forenames Johann Sebastian?
15 Which Government department collects V.A.T?
16 What kind of fruit is a satsuma?
17 How many players are in a hockey team?
18 What colour is the shade of cobalt?
19 The Abbey Theatre is in which Irish city?
20 Which nurse was called 'The Lady with the Lamp'?
21 What was Cinderella's coach made from?
22 Who rocked around the clock in 1955?
23 Which zoo is found in Regent's Park?
24 Who wrote The Ugly Duckling?
25 What is the Zodiac sign Gemini also called?
26 Shrewsbury is the county town of which county?
27 Which fruit when dried produces raisins?
28 In which sport did Ivan Lendl achieve fame?
29 What is measured in decibels?
30 How many horns was a unicorn supposed to have?

Answers

Rich & Famous: Names (see Quiz 5, page 15)
1 Paddy Ashdown. **2** Chef/Restaurateur. **3** Boothroyd. **4** Bragg. **5** Kenneth Branagh and Emma Thompson. **6** Habitat. **7** Hair. **8** Yorkshire Ripper. **9** Chelsea Clinton. **10** Uri Geller. **11** Tony Blair. **12** Naomi Campbell. **13** Richard Branson. **14** Brightman. **15** Gary. **16** Lewinsky. **17** 1930s. **18** William Jefferson Hague. **19** Hall. **20** Mauve. **21** Chelsea. **22** Neil. **23** Labour. **24** Margaret Thatcher. **25** Advertising. **26** Wyman. **27** Earl Spencer. **28** Bookshops. **29** Westwood. **30** Tiggy.

Quiz 7 Sport: Football UK

Answers - see Quiz 8, page 18

1 Messrs Docherty, Atkinson and Ferguson have all managed which team?
2 Who was the first football boss to marry one of her former players?
3 Which Arsenal player's autobiography was called Addicted?
4 Which Stanley was first winner of the European Footballer of the Year award?
5 Which was the first Rovers side to win the Premiership?
6 Graham Taylor was likened to a turnip after a defeat in which Scandinavian country?
7 Who did Ruud Gullit replace as manager of Newcastle Utd?
8 In which Asian country did Gary Lineker play club soccer?
9 What colour are the stripes on Newcastle Utd's first choice shirts?
10 Which side moved from Roker Park to the Stadium of Light?
11 Was Alan Shearer sold to Newcastle for £5 million, £15 million or £25 million?
12 In which country was George Best born?
13 What is the nationality of Dennis Bergkamp?
14 Which ex Anfield goalie Bruce was charged with match fixing in '95?
15 How many clubs were in the Premier league in 1997/8?
16 Which Yorkshire side was involved in a plane crash in March 1998?
17 Which Paul was the first black player to captain England?
18 Who was known as El Tel when he managed Barcelona?
19 Who in 1997 became Arsenal's all-time leading goal scorer?
20 How is the Football Association Challenge Cup better known?
21 Which Welshman Ian said living in Italy was like "living in a foreign country"?
22 Which club Charlton were promoted to the Premier League in 1998?
23 Which colour links shirts at Liverpool, Middlesbrough and Southampton?
24 Which Brian managed Notts Forest for 18 years?
25 At which international stadium were the 1993/4 FA Cup semis held?
26 Which Charlton brother was the first to be knighted?
27 Which Eric was the first overseas PFA Player of the Year winner?
28 Who was dubbed Duncan Disorderly?
29 Which London side does ex PM John Major support?
30 From which group of islands does Graeme Le Saux hail from?

Answers

Pot Luck 3 (see Quiz 8, page 18)

1 Austria. **2** Fawn. **3** Plums. **4** Heel. **5** Granddad. **6** Me. **7** Sand. **8** Beatrix Potter. **9** Hampshire. **10** La Marseillaise. **11** Lion. **12** Ebony. **13** Ireland. **14** Golf. **15** Big Ben. **16** Bull. **17** Bayeux. **18** Beef. **19** Lira. **20** Prince Edward. **21** Eight. **22** An angle. **23** Boyzone. **24** Bury its head. **25** Or Nearest Offer. **26** A clear soup. **27** Purplish red. **28** Apple. **29** West Ham. **30** Nottinghamshire.

Quiz 8 Pot Luck 3

Answers - see Quiz 7, page 17

1 Vienna is the capital of which European country?
2 What name is given to a young deer?
3 Which fruit when dried produces prunes?
4 Where was Achilles hit with a fatal arrow?
5 Which relation gave actor Clive Dunn a hit?
6 Which musical note follows ray?
7 What do you find in a bunker on a golf course?
8 Who wrote The Tale of Peter Rabbit?
9 Winchester is the county town of which county?
10 What is the name of the French National Anthem?
11 Which animal was Androcles very friendly with?
12 Which black wood is used for piano keys?
13 Which island is affectionately called the Emerald Isle?
14 In which sport is the Ryder Cup competed for?
15 What is the clock tower in the Houses of Parliament usually called?
16 Which animal is linked with the Zodiac sign Taurus?
17 Which town is home to the Bayeux Tapestry?
18 What kind of meat can be silverside and topside?
19 What is the unit of currency in Italy?
20 What is the name of the Queen's youngest son?
21 How many notes are there in an octave?
22 What do you measure with a protractor?
23 Ronan Keating heads which boy band?
24 What is it said an ostrich does, if it thinks it is in danger?
25 After a selling price, what do the initials O.N.O stand for?
26 Which type of soup is a consomme?
27 What colour is magenta?
28 What type of fruit is an Orange Pippin?
29 Which London based football club are known as 'The Hammers'?
30 In which county is Sherwood Forest?

Answers

Sport: Football UK (see Quiz 7, page 17)
1 Manchester Utd. **2** Karren Brady. **3** Tony Adams. **4** Matthews. **5** Blackburn. **6** Sweden. **7** Kenny Dalglish. **8** Japan. **9** Black & white. **10** Sunderland. **11** £15 million. **12** Northern Ireland. **13** Dutch. **14** Grobbelaar. **15** 20. **16** Leeds Utd. **17** Ince. **18** Terry Venables. **19** Ian Wright. **20** FA Cup. **21** Rush. **22** Charlton Athletic. **23** Red. **24** Clough. **25** Wembley. **26** Bobby. **27** Cantona. **28** Duncan Ferguson. **29** Chelsea. **30** Channel Islands.

Quiz 9 Hobbies and Leisure 1

Answers - see Quiz 10, page 20

1 The art of self defence aikido originated in which country?
2 Which Bank Holiday comes immediately before Easter Day?
3 Pools is a gambling game based on which sport?
4 Where might you be entertained by a redcoat?
5 Which reptiles feature in a popular board game?
6 Which is bigger Disneyland or Disneyworld?
7 What do you play baccarat with?
8 Which leisure park Towers are near Stoke on Trent?
9 In which game is the object to gain checkmate?
10 What is the minimum number of players in a cribbage game?
11 Which quiz board game involves the collection of coloured wedges?
12 Brass rubbing usually takes place in what type of building?
13 How much is it for one game in the weekly national Lottery draw?
14 In which English city could you watch Rovers and City play soccer?
15 Which part of a pub shares its name with an area of a law court?
16 Which End of London is famous for its theatres?
17 Microlighting takes place in what sort of craft?
18 What name is given to the hours that a pub can open to sell alcohol?
19 Which property board game had a World Cup version in 1998?
20 What colour is the L on a normal learner driver's L plate?
21 What sort of accommodation is provided in a B & B?
22 Knitting needs needles, what does crochet need?
23 Which pier is to the north of Blackpool's central pier?
24 What type of castle do young children enjoy jumping up and down on?
25 'The dogs' involves races of which breed?
26 What colour are the segments on a roulette wheel?
27 Which Planet is a celebrity-founded restaurant chain?
28 What colour are Scrabble tiles?
29 Which gambling game's best hand is Royal flush?
30 What colour is the M on the McDonalds logo?

Answers

Pot Luck 4 (see Quiz 10, page 20)
1 Green. **2** Fish. **3** Friar Tuck. **4** Coal. **5** Leo. **6** Motor racing. **7** Public Limited Company. **8** Switzerland. **9** Bear. **10** Alexandra. **11** April. **12** 76. **13** Pancakes **14** On board ship. **15** A snake. **16** Linda McCartney. **17** Yellow/orange. **18** Apple. **19** George Orwell. **20** Isle of Wight. **21** 60s. **22** Before they're hatched. **23** Holland. **24** Saturday. **25** A pup. **26** Malta. **27** Bill Clinton. **28** Eucalyptus leaves. **29** White coffee. **30** The Tower of London.

Quiz 10 Pot Luck 4

Answers - see Quiz 9, page 19

1. If you mix blue and yellow paint what colour is made?
2. What is usually eaten with Tartare Sauce?
3. Who was Robin Hood's priest?
4. What is normally kept at home in a bunker?
5. Which sign of the Zodiac is normally shown as a lion?
6. Which sport is associated with Silverstone and Brands Hatch?
7. What do the initials plc stand for after a company name?
8. Berne is the capital of which European country?
9. What type of creature was Baloo in The Jungle Book?
10. Which London palace is also called 'Ally Pally'?
11. St George's Day is in which month?
12. How many trombones led the big parade according to the song?
13. What are Crepes Suzettes a type of?
14. Where does a purser usually work?
15. What is a black mamba?
16. Which member of Wings died in 1998?
17. What colour is ochre?
18. What kind of fruit is a russet?
19. Who wrote Animal Farm?
20. On which island is Osborne House, home of Queen Victoria?
21. In which decade did Yuri Gagarin become the first man in space?
22. When must you not count your chickens, according to the proverb?
23. Which country makes Gouda cheese?
24. What day of the week is the Jewish Sabbath?
25. What name is given to a young seal?
26. Which island was awarded the George Cross in 1942?
27. Kenneth Starr produced a report about which famous American?
28. What does a koala have for its main source of food?
29. What is cafe au lait?
30. Where are the Crown Jewels kept?

Answers

Hobbies and Leisure 1 (see Quiz 9, page 19)
1 Japan. **2** Good Friday. **3** Football. **4** Holiday camp (Butlin's). **5** Snakes (& ladders). **6** Disneyworld. **7** Cards. **8** Alton Towers. **9** Chess. **10** Two. **11** Trivial Pursuits. **12** Churches. **13** £1. **14** Bristol. **15** Bar. **16** West End. **17** Plane. **18** Licensing hours. **19** Monopoly. **20** Red. **21** Bed & breakfast. **22** Hook. **23** North pier. **24** Bouncy castle. **25** Greyhounds. **26** Red, black. **27** Hollywood. **28** Cream. **29** Poker. **30** Yellow.

Quiz 11 Pop: Musical Babes

Answers - see Quiz 12, page 22

1 Which Spice Girl advertised Milky Bars as a child?
2 Was Billie Piper 10, 15 or 20 when she first went to No 1?
3 Which Tina sang the title song from Whistle Down the Wind?
4 Who put her famous Union Jack dress up for auction?
5 What is singing babe PJ Harvey's first name?
6 How many girls make up N-Tyce?
7 Janet and La Toyah are from which famous family?
8 What is the first name of the welsh babe from Catatonia?
9 Whose album Always and Forever gives a clue to their name?
10 Which 60s babe's first hit was written by the Rolling Stones?
11 Heather Small found fame with which band?
12 What is the surname of sister Kylie and Dannii?
13 How many girls make up Alisha's Attic?
14 Which Michelle left EastEnders to pursue a pop career?
15 Where do Scary Spice and Princess Anne's daughter have a stud?
16 Who share their name with an Egyptian queen?
17 Which Aussie soap did Natalie Imbruglia appear in?
18 How many babes make up B*witched?
19 How did the Bangles Walk?
20 Shaznay is in which all girl band?
21 Which 60s singer now hosts Surprise Surprise?
22 Which Capstan sang with the B52s and guested with REM?
23 Which babe was the lead singer for Blondie?
24 Which musical instrument is Vanessa Mae famous for?
25 Wendy James was the lead singer with which Vamp band?
26 Alanis Morissette and Celine Dion are from which country?
27 Who sang about Baboushka and Wuthering Heights?
28 In which decade did Bananarama have their first hit?
29 Miss Nurding dropped her surname and became known as whom?
30 Tracy Shaw's pop career began when she was in which soap?

Answers

Pot Luck 5 (see Quiz 12, page 22)
1 July. **2** Bull/cow. **3** Cider. **4** Peru. **5** A savoury snack. **6** 1969. **7** Venice. **8** Mount Ararat. **9** Forbidden fruit. **10** A will. **11** France. **12** Norwich City. **13** Vincent van Gogh. **14** Aries. **15** Calligraphy. **16** Harley Street. **17** Pinocchio. **18** Tanks. **19** Friday. **20** A bird. **21** Caernarvon. **22** Cherry. **23** 17. **24** September. **25** Devon. **26** Baptism. **27** Bee Gee. **28** A.A. Milne. **29** Hippopotamus. **30** Sausage.

Quiz 12 Pot Luck 5

Answers - see Quiz 11, page 21

1 St Swithin's Day is in which summer month?
2 Who or what is an Aberdeen Angus?
3 What drink did writer Laurie Lee share with Rosie?
4 Where did Paddington Bear originally come from?
5 What are pretzels?
6 Did man first land on the moon in 1966, 1969 or 1972?
7 In which Italian city is St Mark's cathedral?
8 On which Mount is the resting place of Noah's Ark?
9 Which fruit tastes sweetest according to the proverb?
10 What does a testator make, in law?
11 Which country produces Camembert cheese?
12 Which football team is known as 'The Canaries'?
13 Which Dutch painter cut off his ear?
14 Which Zodiac sign is normally associated with the ram?
15 What is the study of handwriting called?
16 Which London street is associated with the medical profession?
17 Which wooden puppet was written about by Carlo Collodi?
18 Shermans, Grants and Cromwells are all types of what?
19 Which day of the week is the Muslim Holy Day?
20 What is a quail?
21 In which castle was the investiture of the Prince of Wales?
22 Which fruit is used to make kirsch?
23 How old should you be to apply for a car driving licence in the UK?
24 In what month is Michaelmas Day?
25 Which county has Exeter as its county town?
26 For which religious ceremony is a font normally used?
27 Was Lulu's first husband a Beatle or a Bee Gee?
28 Who wrote about Tigger, Eeyore and Piglet?
29 Which animal has a name which means 'river horse'?
30 What would you be eating if you ate a saveloy?

Answers

Pop: Musical Babes (see Quiz 11, page 21)
1 Emma (Baby Spice). **2** 15. **3** Tina Arena. **4** Geri Halliwell. **5** Polly. **6** Four. **7** Jackson. **8** Nerys. **9** Eternal. **10** Marianne Faithful. **11** M People. **12** Minogue. **13** Two. **14** Gayle. **15** Tongue. **16** Cleopatra. **17** Home & Away. **18** Four. **19** Like an Egyptian. **20** All Saints. **21** Cilla Black. **22** Kate. **23** Debbie Harry. **24** Violin. **25** Transvision Vamp. **26** Canada. **27** Kate Bush. **28** 80s. **29** Louise. **30** Coronation Street.

Quiz 13 The Movies: Blockbusters

Answers - see Quiz 14, page 24

1 Which early Spielberg blockbuster was about a shark?
2 Who played the title role in the Orson Welles directed Citizen Kane?
3 In which 90s musical film did Madonna change costume 85 times?
4 What was the name of the movie based on TV's The X Files?
5 Scarlett O'Hara was heroine of which Atlanta based epic?
6 Who was the star of the Western The Alamo?
7 Which musical about Danny and Sandy was re-released in 1998?
8 Which creatures dominated Jurassic Park?
9 What was Crocodile Dundee's homeland?
10 Hook was based on which children's book?
11 Which lizard-like monster's name is a mix of the Japanese words for gorilla and whale?
12 Who left Kramer in the 70s movie with Hoffman and Streep?
13 From Here To Eternity is set before the Japanese attack on where?
14 Raging Bull was about which sport?
15 Which film was an abbreviation of Extra Terrestrial?
16 The Empire Strikes Back was a sequel to what?
17 Raiders of the Lost Ark was about which Mr Jones?
18 Robin Hood was Prince of what in the 1991 blockbuster?
19 Was Snow White and the Seven Dwarfs released before or after World War II?
20 Where was Gary Oldman Lost in the 1998 hit movie?
21 Which Caped Crusader was the subject of one of the top 80s films?
22 Which watery film succeeded Waterworld as the most costly to make?
23 Gene Kelly was An American ... where in the Vincente Minnelli movie?
24 Which star of Grease and Saturday Night Fever is a qualified pilot?
25 Was The Sting a hit in the 50s, 70s or 90s?
26 Which Disney animal movie was a 1994 blockbuster set in Africa?
27 Amadeus told the story of which composer?
28 Home Alone shot which child star to fame?
29 Was Schindler's List in colour or black and white?
30 Which Kevin played Mariner in Waterworld?

Answers

Pot Luck 6 (see Quiz 14, page 24)
1 Switzerland. **2** Charles. **3** Golden Hind. **4** The Gondoliers. **5** Thrillers.
6 Fleet Street. **7** Suffolk. **8** V-shaped. **9** St Patrick. **10** Pisces. **11** Beetroot soup.
12 16 years. **13** 4. **14** A Question of Sport. **15** Reindeer. **16** Golf. **17** Astronomy.
18 Rome. **19** Alpha. **20** A dog. **21** France. **22** Lawn. **23** Herbs. **24** Green.
25 Katrina and the Waves. **26** A newspaper. **27** Eel. **28** Seaweed.
29 The Sound of Music. **30** Dorchester

Quiz 14 Pot Luck 6

Answers - see Quiz 13, page 23

1 Which country produces Gruyere cheese?
2 Who was invested as Prince of Wales in 1969?
3 Francis Drake's ship Pelican was renamed what?
4 Which opera by Gilbert and Sullivan is set in Venice?
5 Did John Le Carre write thrillers or romantic fiction?
6 Which London Street was home to several British newspapers?
7 Which county has Ipswich as its county town?
8 What shape are the teeth on pinking shears?
9 Which Saint is commemorated on the 17th of March?
10 Which Zodiac sign is normally associated with two fishes?
11 What kind of food is borscht?
12 What is the minimum age for leaving school in England?
13 In snooker, how many points is the brown ball worth?
14 Which TV programme has the logo QS?
15 What kind of animals were Cupid, Donner and Blitzen?
16 In which sport would you use a caddie?
17 Which science looks at the planets and the stars?
18 According to the proverb, which Italian city was not built in a day?
19 What is the first letter of the Greek alphabet?
20 What is a Shih-Tzu?
21 Which country does the wine claret come from?
22 In tennis, what does the initial L in LTA stand for?
23 What kind of plants are sage, lovage and basil?
24 Which London park is the name of a colour?
25 Who were the UK's first Eurovision winners after Bucks Fizz?
26 If you bought Le Figaro in France what would you be buying?
27 An elver is a young what?
28 What is kelp?
29 Which film featured the Von Trapp Family?
30 What is the county town of Dorset?

Answers

The Movies: Blockbusters (see Quiz 13, page 23)
1 Jaws. **2** Orson Welles. **3** Evita. **4** The X Files. **5** Gone With the Wind.
6 John Wayne. **7** Grease. **8** Dinosaurs. **9** Australia. **10** Peter Pan. **11** Godzilla.
12 Kramer. **13** Pearl Harbor. **14** Boxing. **15** E.T. **16** Star Wars. **17** Indiana Jones.
18 Thieves. **19** Before. **20** Space. **21** Batman. **22** Titanic. **23** Paris.
24 John Travolta. **25** 70s. **26** The Lion King. **27** Mozart. **28** Macaulay Culkin.
29 Black & white. **30** Costner.

Quiz 15 TV: Quiz & Game Shows

Answers - see Quiz 16, page 26

1 On which channel is Countdown broadcast?
2 What is the version of 100 Per Cent for the over 50s called?
3 Which show does Dale Winton present from a supermarket?
4 Eric Knowles is the resident expert on which antiques quiz?
5 Which game show with Jim Davidson is based on snooker shots?
6 Who was the first 'female' presenter of Blankety Blank?
7 Which Noel Edmonds show was originally called Telly Quiz?
8 What completes the culinary challenge show Can't Cook,_______?
9 Through the Keyhole looks at which celebrity possessions?
10 How many students make up one University Challenge team?
11 In Blind Date a choice is made from what number of the opposite sex?
12 Which Ms Jonsson was the first female presenter of Gladiators?
13 Which darts based show offered losers a 'bendy Bully'?
14 Who hosts Bruce's Price is Right?
15 In the first Blockbusters were the contestants students or OAP's?
16 In which show do celebrities try to find True and Bluff?
17 Who presented the celebrity version of Countdown?
18 Which half of Richard and Judy hosted Cluedo?
19 Who was the only presenter of Mastermind on TV?
20 Which Angus says Have I Got News For You??
21 Does Carol adjudicate over letters or numbers in Countdown?
22 What night of the week is the National Lottery midweek draw?
23 Which Des hosted Take Your Pick in the 90s?
24 How many people start out on William G Stewart's afternoon quiz?
25 Which Frank was a team captain on Call My Bluff?
26 Which Gaby offered contestants Whatever You Want?
27 Who would have fulfilled your request to "Give me a K please, Bob?"
28 Which magician first presented Wipeout?
29 Which show had a Big Ticket challenge with Anthea Turner and Patrick Kielty?
30 What were contestants Going For in Henry Kelly's TV quiz show?

Answers

Pot Luck 7 (see Quiz 16, page 26)
1 Tax. **2** Insects. **3** The Boy Scout Movement. **4** Shrove Tuesday. **5** Pink. **6** Sagittarius. **7** Aylesbury. **8** Badger. **9** Liam Gallagher. **10** Romeo and Juliet. **11** England. **12** Egypt. **13** Little Acorns. **14** Nazareth. **15** A tutu. **16** Take Your Pick. **17** Clouds. **18** In water. **19** Wood. **20** John Cleese. **21** Ontario. **22** Adolf Hitler. **23** Chelsea. **24** Blood. **25** Venice. **26** Silence. **27** Warwickshire. **28** A toad. **29** Gladys Knight. **30** Aldershot.

Quiz 16 Pot Luck 7

Answers - see Quiz 15, page 25

1 What does T stand for in the initials V.A.T?
2 What does a Venus fly-trap trap?
3 Which movement was founded by Lord Baden-Powell?
4 What day precedes Ash Wednesday?
5 In snooker, is the pink ball or the brown ball of higher value?
6 Which sign of the Zodiac is pictured by an archer?
7 What is the principal county town of Buckinghamshire?
8 Which animal is often given the name Brock?
9 Who was Patsy Kensit's third husband?
10 Which Shakespeare play features the Capulets and Montagues?
11 Which country was called Albion by Greeks and Romans?
12 In which country is the battle site of El Alamein?
13 Great oak trees grow from what, according to the proverb?
14 Which town did Jesus grow up in?
15 What is the name of the dress worn by a ballerina?
16 Which TV show features the Yes/No Game?
17 Stratus, Cirrus and Cumulus are all types of what?
18 Where do mosquitoes lay their eggs?
19 What are clogs traditionally made from?
20 Which actor played Basil Fawlty in Fawlty Towers?
21 Toronto is the capital of which Canadian province?
22 Who wrote Mein Kampf?
23 Which football team plays at Stamford Bridge?
24 What do your arteries carry from your heart?
25 In which northern Italian city is the Doge's Palace?
26 If speech is silver, what is golden according to the proverb?
27 Which county cricket team plays at Edgbaston?
28 What is a natterjack?
29 Which Gladys sang the theme song to the 007 movie Licence to Kill?
30 Which Hampshire town has England's largest military camp?

Answers

TV: Quiz and Game Shows (see Quiz 15, page 25)
1 Channel 4. **2** 100 Per Cent Gold. **3** Supermarket Sweep. **4** Going For A Song. **5** Big Break. **6** Lily Savage. **7** Telly Addicts. **8** Won't Cook. **9** Houses. **10** Four. **11** Three. **12** Ulrika. **13** Bullseye. **14** Bruce Forsyth. **15** Students. **16** Call My Bluff. **17** Richard Whitely. **18** Richard. **19** Magnus Magnusson. **20** Deayton. **21** Numbers. **22** Wednesday. **23** O'Connor. **24** 15. **25** Muir. **26** Roslin. **27** Bob Holness. **28** Paul Daniels. **29** National Lottery. **30** Gold.

Quiz 17 Leisure: Books

Answers - see Quiz 18, page 28

LEVEL 1 

1 Which detective did Dr Watson assist?
2 Which egg shaped nursery rhyme character appears in Alice Through the Looking Glass?
3 Mrs Beeton was most famous for writing on what subject?
4 Are Penguin books hardbacks or paperbacks?
5 Was St Trinian's a school for boys or girls?
6 What type of animal is Winnie the Pooh?
7 What relation was Charlotte to Emily and Anne Bronte?
8 Who is Agatha Christie's most famous female detective?
9 Which ex MP Edwina wrote A Parliamentary Affair?
10 How is crime writer Baroness James better known?
11 Who's Winter Collection of recipes sold 1.5 million copies in just eight weeks?
12 What sort of Factory is associated with Roald Dahl's Charlie?
13 In which book are there four accounts of Jesus's life called gospels?
14 Which African president's autobiography was called Long Walk to Freedom?
15 Which animal was Beatrix Potter's Mrs Tiggywinkle?
16 What was Schindler's Ark renamed when it was made into a film?
17 Where was Douglas Adams' Hitchhiker's Guide to?
18 What type of tales did the Grimm brothers write?
19 What is the nationality of novelist Maeve Binchy?
20 Which novelist Dame Catherine died in 1998?
21 Which Jilly penned The Man who Made Husbands Jealous?
22 Who was Ian Fleming's most famous secret agent creation?
23 Who did Laurie Lee write of Cider with...?
24 Which soccer coach's World Cup Story 1998 caused an outrage over breaches of confidentiality?
25 Which Stephen is famous for horror writing such as The Shining?
26 What was Dick Francis's profession before he turned to writing?
27 What was Bram Stoker's most famous monstrous creation?
28 In which century did Charles Dickens live?
29 Which comedian Ben wrote Gridlock and Popcorn?
30 Which Frederick's first success was The Day of the Jackal?

Answers

Pot Luck 8 (see Quiz 18, page 28)

1 November. **2** The tail. **3** Oprah Winfrey. **4** An alkali. **5** A small wood. **6** Hamlet. **7** Angels. **8** Conservatives. **9** Afrikaans. **10** Kenya. **11** Willow. **12** Seven. **13** An eyrie. **14** Threadneedle Street. **15** Doncaster. **16** Goodbye Yellow Brick Road. **17** £1. **18** Ballet. **19** Violet. **20** Adder. **21** Nepal. **22** Agoraphobia. **23** Mercury. **24** Pasta. **25** Spencer. **26** A Minister/Clergyman. **27** Norwich. **28** A News agency. **29** Mars. **30** Four.

Quiz 18 Pot Luck 8

Answers - see Quiz 17, page 27

1 In which month is Thanksgiving celebrated in America?
2 Where is the rattle in a rattlesnake?
3 Which talk show hostess looks back on founding Harpo Productions?
4 What is the opposite of an acid?
5 What is a spinney?
6 Who said, "To be or not to be, that is the question"?
7 In The Bible, what were seraphim and cherubim?
8 Which political party had Benjamin Disraeli as a leader?
9 Which South African language derives from the Dutch settlers?
10 Which country has Nairobi as its capital?
11 Cricket bats are traditionally made from which wood?
12 How many colours are in the spectrum?
13 What name is given to the home of an eagle?
14 On which Street is the Bank of England?
15 The St Leger is run at which Yorkshire race course?
16 The original Candle in the Wind was on which album?
17 Which coin was first introduced in the UK in 1983?
18 For what type of dancing did Anna Pavlova achieve fame?
19 What colour is an amethyst?
20 What is the only poisonous snake in Britain?
21 Which country is native homeland to the Gurkha troops?
22 Which phobia is the fear of open spaces?
23 Which chemical is also known as quicksilver?
24 Penne, rigatoni and tagliatelle are all types of what?
25 What did the initial 'S' stand for in Winston S Churchill?
26 Who lives in a Manse?
27 Which Norfolk city stands on the River Wensum?
28 What is Reuters?
29 Who was god of war in Roman mythology?
30 How many times does the letter 'S' appear in Mississippi?

Answers

Leisure: Books (see Quiz 17, page 27)
1 Sherlock Holmes. **2** Humpty Dumpty. **3** Cooking. **4** Paperbacks. **5** Girls. **6** Bear. **7** Sisters. **8** Miss Marple. **9** Currie. **10** P.D. James. **11** Delia Smith. **12** Chocolate. **13** Bible. **14** Nelson Mandela. **15** Hedgehog. **16** Schindler's List. **17** The Galaxy. **18** Fairy tales. **19** Irish. **20** Cookson. **21** Cooper. **22** James Bond. **23** Rosie. **24** Glenn Hoddle. **25** King. **26** Jockey. **27** Dracula. **28** 19th. **29** Elton. **30** Forsyth.

Quiz 19 Sport: Record Breakers

Answers - see Quiz 20, page 30

1 Mark Spitz won seven Olympic golds at record speeds doing what?
2 Which South American soccer team has won most World Cups?
3 Was Tessa Sanderson competing in her second, fourth or sixth Olympics in 1996?
4 Lyn Davies broke the British record in which jump event?
5 David Campese was leading try scorer for which country?
6 Which Sally was a world record hurdler and '92 Olympic champion?
7 Who was made England's youngest ever football coach in 1996?
8 Did Roger Bannister run the first four minute mile in Oxford or Cambridge?
9 Was Martina Hingis 13, 15 or 17 when she first won Wimbledon doubles?
10 Which ice dancers won a record six successive British championships between 1978 and 1984?
11 Which Nigel was the first to win both F1 and Indy Car world championships?
12 Which record breaker Sebastian went on to become a Tory MP?
13 Which Tony made the first televised hole in one in Britain?
14 Who won the 100m in Seoul in record time before being disqualified?
15 Which Steve was six times World Snooker Champion in the 80s?
16 For which former Iron Curtain country did Marita Koch break records?
17 Which English Steve won four Olympic golds between '84 and '96?
18 How many events were in Daley Thompson's speciality event?
19 Which Pete equalled Borg's five Wimbledon singles wins in 1998?
20 Which Gareth became Wales youngest ever Rugby captain in 1968?
21 Alain Prost was the first to win the F1 world title for which country?
22 Bob Beaman held which Olympic jump record for over 20 years?
23 Who was Britain's only Men's 100m world record holder between 1983 and 1993?
24 Which David did Graham Gooch overtake to become England's highest scoring Test player?
25 World record breaker Kip Keino is from which continent?
26 Did Nadia Comaneci first score a perfect Olympic 10 at 14, 18 or 21?
27 Which two Steves were record breaking middle distance runners of the 70s and 80s?
28 Colin Jackson was a world record holder in which event?
29 Who was the first player to score 100 goals in the Premiership?
30 Duncan Goodhew held British records in which sport?

Answers

Pot Luck 9 (see Quiz 20, page 30)
1 Oliver Twist. **2** Gin. **3** Taj Mahal. **4** Dingoes. **5** Actor/Actress. **6** Violins. **7** Greece. **8** June. **9** Bridges. **10** May. **11** Rumpelstiltskin. **12** A stipend. **13** Red. **14** Kite-mark. **15** New York. **16** Albatross. **17** Barrels. **18** Sherry. **19** The worm. **20** Paul McCartney. **21** Bread. **22** 45. **23** In the mouth. **24** Andrew Lloyd Webber. **25** St Paul's Cathedral. **26** Vertical. **27** Theatres. **28** Sugar, almonds. **29** Evangelism. **30** Magpie.

Quiz 20 Pot Luck 9

Answers - see Quiz 19, page 29

1 In which Dickens' novel is the character Bill Sikes?
2 Which alcoholic drink contains juniper as a flavour?
3 By what name is the mausoleum at Agra, India normally known?
4 Which dogs are a serious pest in Australia?
5 What would your profession be if you were a member of Equity?
6 Which instruments did Antonio Stradivari produce?
7 Which country is famous for moussaka?
8 In which month is Father's Day in the UK?
9 Pontoon and suspension are both types of which construction?
10 What did the 'M' stand for in Louisa M. Alcott's name?
11 Which name did a fairytale Queen have to guess or lose her child?
12 What is a salary paid to a clergyman called?
13 What colour is cochineal?
14 The British Standards Institute uses what mark as a sign of approval?
15 Which American city is served by Kennedy Airport?
16 Which bird has the largest wing span?
17 What does a cooper make?
18 What kind of drink is Amontillado?
19 What does an early bird catch, according to the proverb?
20 Which Beatle's daughter is a dress designer?
21 Bloomers and baps are both types of what?
22 How many years are there in four and a half decades?
23 Where are your incisors?
24 Who, together with Tim Rice, wrote Evita?
25 Where is Lord Nelson buried?
26 On a staircase are the risers flat or vertical?
27 The Cambridge, Adelphi and Lyric in London are all what?
28 What are the two ingredients of marzipan?
29 Billy Graham is famous for which branch of Christianity?
30 Which black and white bird is usually accused of stealing?

Answers

Sport: Record Breakers (see Quiz 19, page 29)
1 Swimming. **2** Brazil. **3** Sixth. **4** Long jump. **5** Australia. **6** Gunnell. **7** Glenn Hoddle. **8** Oxford. **9** 15. **10** Torvill & Dean. **11** Mansell. **12** Coe. **13** Jacklin. **14** Ben Johnson. **15** Davis. **16** East Germany. **17** Redgrave. **18** Ten. **19** Sampras. **20** Edwards. **21** France. **22** Long jump. **23** Linford Christie. **24** Gower. **25** Africa. **26** 14. **27** Ovett & Cram. **28** Hurdles. **29** Alan Shearer. **30** Swimming.

Quiz 21 Science: Communication

Answers - see Quiz 22, page 32

1 Is 020 the dialling code for Manchester or London?
2 Which mobile phone company shares its name with a fruit?
3 If you dial 1471 whose number are you given?
4 Which four letters preface access to an Internet website?
5 What is the normal size of a floppy disk?
6 What sort of cards can you use in a cardphone?
7 What is held in the hands to communicate through semaphore?
8 The fingertips represent which five letters in sign language?
9 112 is an alternative to which number?
10 A modem connects a computer to what?
11 Qantas Airways originated in which country?
12 Which cross Channel link has its French terminus at Coquelles?
13 Tresco airport links which Isles to the UK?
14 What is the regulatory body of the telecommunications industry called?
15 What did Le Shuttle change its name to in 1998?
16 What does the second D stand for in IDD?
17 Which character divides the person from the place in an email address?
18 Which type of clock works from shadows?
19 Numbers beginning with 0800 usually cost how much to the caller?
20 What do Demon and AOL offer access to?
21 Combinations of which two signs are used in Morse code?
22 What country are PanAm based in?
23 Before '81, telecommunications were under the authority of which Office?
24 Which number do you ring to contact a BT operator?
25 Which country's airline has the code PK?
26 What is the American version of the British post code?
27 With BT calls when does daytime end Monday to Friday?
28 What does 'I' stand for in IT?
29 Which two digits are the first to dial for an international number?
30 Ryan Air is a budget airline from which country?

Answers

Pot Luck 10 (see Quiz 22, page 32)
1 Pastry. **2** Mr Hyde. **3** Jewellery. **4** Red. **5** Loudspeakers. **6** Marriage. **7** Flamingo. **8** Table Mountain. **9** The Rank Organisation. **10** China. **11** Senorita. **12** Russia. **13** Hudson (Butler). **14** Disraeli. **15** Dame Edna Everage. **16** Hong Kong. **17** Church/Cathedral. **18** Agenda. **19** Andrew. **20** Three. **21** Pears. **22** Shrew. **23** The Mayflower. **24** Oil Rigs. **25** Green. **26** Wuthering Heights. **27** Bridgetown. **28** Sultana. **29** Penultimate. **30** Fern Britton.

Quiz 22 Pot Luck 10

Answers - see Quiz 21, page 31

1 Choux, puff and short are all types of what?
2 Who was the more unpleasant - Dr Jekyll or Mr Hyde?
3 Generally what is Hatton Gardon in London famous for?
4 What colour is carmine?
5 What are tweeters and woofers?
6 Which ceremony is associated with orange blossom?
7 Which pink bird sleeps on one leg?
8 Which mountain overlooks Cape Town, South Africa?
9 Which British film company used a symbol of a man striking a gong?
10 Which country is renowned for sweet and sour cooking?
11 What is the Spanish word for a young or single lady?
12 Where was the news agency Tass based?
13 Which part did Gordon Jackson play in Upstairs, Downstairs?
14 Who was the first Jewish Prime Minister in Britain?
15 Comedian Barry Humphries plays which female character?
16 Which colony ceased to be British in June 1997?
17 Where would you be if you were in a transept?
18 What is the list of the subjects to be discussed at a meeting called?
19 Which Prince served in the Falklands War?
20 In the old saying, how many makes a crowd if two are company?
21 Conference and Cornice are types of which fruit?
22 Which animal needs 'Taming' in the title of the Shakespeare play?
23 Aboard which ship in 1620 did the Pilgrim Fathers sail to America?
24 What type of rigs are Ekofisk, Forties and Frigg?
25 What colour is angelica?
26 What connects singer Kate Bush with novelist Emily Bronte?
27 What is the capital of Barbados?
28 What is a wife of a sultan called?
29 What word describes something being next to last?
30 Who first presented Ready Steady Cook?

Answers

Science & Nature: Communication (see Quiz 21, page 31)
1 London. **2** Orange. **3** Last person to have called you. **4** http (not all have www). **5** 3.5ins. **6** Phone cards and credit cards. **7** Flags. **8** Vowels. **9** 999. **10** Telephone. **11** Australia. **12** Channel Tunnel. **13** Scilly Isles. **14** Oftel. **15** Eurotunnel. **16** Dialling. **17** @. **18** Sundial. **19** Nothing. **20** The Internet. **21** Dots & dashes. **22** USA. **23** Post Office. **24** 100. **25** Pakistan. **26** Zip. **27** 6 pm. **28** Information. **29** 00. **30** Ireland.

Quiz 23 Pop: 70s

Answers - see Quiz 24, page 34

1 Which country did Abba come from?
2 Which 70s pop movie with John Travolta was re-released in 1998?
3 Which band did Diana Ross leave at the start of the decade?
4 T Rex was led by which singer?
5 What colour was Debbie Harry's hair which named her band?
6 Maggie May provided who with his first No 1?
7 Kiki Dee's biggest 70s hit was with whom?
8 Where did Supertramp have Breakfast in 1979?
9 Who was lead singer with the Boomtown Rats?
10 Who cleaned Wimbledon Common and cleaned up in the charts in '74?
11 What went with Peaches in the 70s charts?
12 Who had a posthumous hit with Way Down?
13 Song for whom was Elton John's first instrumental hit?
14 Which World Cup football squad did Rod Stewart have a hit with?
15 Which Rollers had two No 1's in 1975?
16 Who had a single hit from the album Bat Out of Hell?
17 Izhar Cohen and Alphabeta won Eurovision for which country?
18 Which brothers included Wayne, Donny and Little Jimmy?
19 Whose first hit was Wuthering Heights?
20 Which 70s B side for Queen became a football anthem?
21 Which Abba hit became the name of an Alan Partridge spoof?
22 Which Gary's first hit was as Tubeway Army?
23 Which hostel did the Village People visit in the 70s?
24 How many performers made up The Carpenters?
25 Which soccer side had a hit with I'm Forever Blowing Bubbles?
26 Tubular Bells is credited with establishing which record label?
27 Which band were Part of the Union?
28 Which Bryan founded Roxy Music?
29 Who celebrated his Ding-A-Ling in song?
30 Who had the last 70s Xmas No 1 with Another Brick in the Wall?

Answers

Pot Luck 11 (see Quiz 24, page 34)
1 The Jungle Book. **2** Cumberland. **3** Michael Jackson. **4** Tailoring. **5** Yellow. **6** Two. **7** Swan. **8** Elvis Presley. **9** Otters. **10** Ballet. **11** Portugal. **12** Tenor. **13** White. **14** Open University. **15** Attila. **16** Louis Braille. **17** Stephen. **18** Carrot. **19** Count. **20** Julie Andrews. **21** The Sound of Music. **22** South America. **23** Eight. **24** Johann Strauss. **25** Ginger Rogers. **26** Cheese. **27** Monopoly. **28** Gordonstoun. **29** Red. **30** Asia.

Quiz 24 Pot Luck 11

Answers - see Quiz 23, page 33

LEVEL 1 

1 Which Disney film is I Wanna be Like You from?
2 Which British sausage is traditionally sold in a coil?
3 Which pop megastar celebrated his 40th birthday on 29th August 1998?
4 Which profession is associated with Savile Row?
5 What colour is the flower of an oil seed rape plant?
6 How many packs of playing cards are needed to play Canasta?
7 Bewick, Black and Whooper are all types of what?
8 Which pop star is linked with blue suede shoes?
9 Which animals live in a holt?
10 With which type of dance was Nijinsky famous?
11 In which country is the Algarve Coast?
12 Which voice is higher - a tenor or a baritone?
13 What colour is the St Andrew's cross on the Scottish flag?
14 Which University is based in Milton Keynes?
15 Who in AD 434 was King of the Huns?
16 Who invented the dot system with which the blind can read by touch?
17 On whose feast day did King Wenceslas look out?
18 Which vegetable are people told to eat to help them see at night?
19 An abacus helps you do what?
20 Which actress sang A Spoonful of Sugar in Mary Poppins?
21 Which musical does Climb Every Mountain come from?
22 The anaconda is native to which continent?
23 How many legs does a spider have?
24 Who wrote the waltz called The Blue Danube?
25 Who was the most famous dancing partner of Fred Astaire?
26 What are Gorgonzola, Dolcelatte and Pecorino?
27 On which board game are The Strand, Mayfair and Park Lane?
28 At which Scottish school was Prince Charles educated?
29 What colour is the spot on the Japanese flag?
30 Which continent is native home to the tiger?

Answers

Pop: 70s (see Quiz 23, page 33)
1 Sweden. **2** Grease. **3** The Supremes. **4** Marc Bolan. **5** Blonde. **6** Rod Stewart. **7** Elton John. **8** America. **9** Bob Geldof. **10** The Wombles. **11** Herb. **12** Elvis Presley. **13** Guy. **14** Scottish. **15** Bay City Rollers. **16** Meat Loaf. **17** Israel. **18** Osmond. **19** Kate Bush. **20** We Are the Champions. **21** Knowing Me Knowing You. **22** Numan. **23** YMCA. **24** Two. **25** West Ham. **26** Virgin. **27** Strawbs. **28** Ferry. **29** Chuck Berry. **30** Pink Floyd.

Quiz 25 TV: Sitcoms

Answers - see Quiz 26, page 36

LEVEL 1

1 What is the profession of Geraldine Grainger of Dibley?
2 How do Men Martin Clunes and Neil Morrissey behave in the sitcom?
3 Which Scottish pop star played Adrian Mole's mum?
4 Which Duchess made a cameo appearance in Friends as herself?
5 Whatever Happened to the Likely Lads? was the sequel to what?
6 Which sitcom classic was about self sufficiency in Surbiton?
7 How did Hyacinth pronounce 'Bucket' in Keeping Up Appearances?
8 Which show about Grace Brothers' store had a rerun in 1998?
9 What was the sequel to Yes Minister?
10 Which sitcom about the Trotters was originally to be called Readies?
11 Craig Charles was Dave Lister in which sci fi sitcom?
12 Which Penelope alias Audrey was To the Manor Born?
13 How many children feature in the sitcom about Bill and Ben Porter?
14 Which Ronnie played Arkwright in Open All Hours?
15 Ian McShane starred in which sitcom about a shady antiques dealer?
16 In which historical sitcom did Baldrick first appear?
17 Which show was originally to have been called Your Bottom?
18 Which Felicity was the star of Solo?
19 In which sitcom did Joanna Lumley play champagne swilling Patsy?
20 What are the names of the Birds in Birds of a Feather?
21 In Dad's Army, who called Sgt. Wilson Uncle Arthur?
22 Frasier was a spin off from which series based in a Boston bar?
23 What was the occupation of the stars of Common as Muck?
24 Which wartime sitcom featured Rene and Edith Artois?
25 Who played Jean, husband of Lionel, in As Time Goes By?
26 Goodnight Sweetheart is set in the 40s and which other decade?
27 Which series was based on Butlin's and Pontin's?
28 What was Anton Rodgers' legal job in May to December?
29 Which Family is a sitcom with ex Mrs Merton Caroline Aherne?
30 What is Mrs Victor Meldrew's first name?

Answers

Pot Luck 12 (see Quiz 26, page 36)

1 Butterflies. **2** Pork Pie. **3** The Sahara. **4** Horse racing. **5** Wright Brothers. **6** John Ridd. **7** Medicines/Drugs. **8** Pinocchio. **9** Fox. **10** Red/green. **11** Asp. **12** Three. **13** Evita. **14** Small pieces of wood. **15** Haricot. **16** Flower/Shrub. **17** Otter. **18** Flanders. **19** Baloo and Mowgli. **20** Pepsi Cola. **21** Four. **22** 1970s. **23** Italy. **24** Stamps. **25** Blue. **26** Peppermint. **27** Dove. **28** Aintree. **29** Soprano. **30** The English Channel.

Quiz 26 Pot Luck 12

Answers - see Quiz 25, page 35

1 Red Admirals, Fritillaries and Tortoiseshells are all what?
2 Which pie is Melton Mowbray renowned for?
3 Which has more rainfall the Sahara or Antarctica?
4 Which sport would you see at Chepstow?
5 Which brothers made the first manned powered aero flight in 1903?
6 Who is the main male character in the novel Lorna Doone?
7 What was sold in an apothecary?
8 From which Disney film is Give a Little Whistle from?
9 Which animals live in an earth or lair?
10 Along with white, what colours appear on the Italian flag?
11 Which snake is it said Cleopatra used to poison herself?
12 How many ships came sailing by according to the carol?
13 Which musical does Don't Cry for Me, Argentina come from?
14 What is chipboard made from?
15 What bean is made into a baked bean?
16 What is a poinsettia?
17 In the novel what kind of animal was Tarka?
18 Bruges is the capital of which part of Belgium?
19 Which characters sang The Bare Necessities in the Jungle Book?
20 Madonna's Like A Prayer advertised which soft drink?
21 How many wings does a bee have?
22 In which decade did Britain convert to decimal currency?
23 Sardinia is part of which country?
24 What are collected by a philatelist?
25 What colour is the background of the Scottish flag?
26 What flavour is creme de menthe?
27 What type of bird are Ring, Turtle and Collared?
28 On which horse race course are Becher's Brook and the Chair?
29 Which is the highest female singing voice?
30 Which sea is called La Manche by the French?

Answers

TV: Sitcoms (see Quiz 25, page 35)
1 Vicar. **2** Badly. **3** Lulu. **4** Duchess of York. **5** The Likely Lads. **6** The Good Life. **7** 'Bouquet'. **8** Are You Being Served? **9** Yes Prime Minister. **10** Only Fools and Horses. **11** Red Dwarf. **12** Keith. **13** 2 Point 4. **14** Barker. **15** Lovejoy. **16** Blackadder. **17** Bottom. **18** Kendall. **19** Absolutely Fabulous. **20** Sharon & Tracy. **21** Pike. **22** Cheers. **23** Dustmen. **24** Allo Allo. **25** Judi Dench. **26** 90s. **27** Hi-De-Hi! **28** Solicitor. **29** Royle. **30** Margaret.

Quiz 27 The Movies: Comedies

Answers - see Quiz 28, page 38

1 Which Rowan played a vicar in Four Weddings and a Funeral?
2 Which Carry On film was set on board the SS Happy Wanderer?
3 Who played the bowler hatted Tramp in The Kid?
4 Addams Family Values was the follow up to what?
5 Which west London borough is associated with classic comedies?
6 What age group are the performers in the gangster film Bugsy Malone?
7 Which cartoon set in Bedrock starred John Goodman in the human version?
8 What type of Adventure did Bill and Ted have?
9 What sort of farm animal was Babe?
10 Which Tom starred in Jerry Maguire?
11 What type of animals were Lady and the Tramp?
12 Who's World did Mike Myers and Dana Garvey live in?
13 A Fish Called ... what was a John Cleese & Jamie Lee Curtis classic?
14 What was Whoopi Goldberg disguised as in Sister Act?
15 Which group sang the theme song for Four Weddings and a Funeral?
16 Which Jim was the shy bank clerk in The Mask?
17 Forrest Gump said life was like a box of what?
18 Which Julia was the Pretty Woman in the film's title?
19 Which British comedy duo were the stars of The Magnificent Two?
20 What did Robin Williams in Mrs Doubtfire and Dustin Hoffman in Tootsie have in common?
21 What unusual handicap did Bernie have as a host in A Weekend at Bernie's?
22 Which film of a Book featured The Bare Necessities?
23 Which Sid's first Carry On was Carry On Constable?
24 To whom did someone say 'I Shrunk The Kids' in the film title?
25 Which spinach-loving cartoon character was played by Robin Williams?
26 Which 1980 film title suggests normal working hours?
27 Was Patrick Swayze or Demi Moore the Ghost in the 1990 film?
28 Look Who's Talking Too was the sequel to what?
29 Who was the Queen of the Desert in the transvestite comedy?
30 Which Inspector played by Peter Sellers was in The Pink Panther?

Answers

Pot Luck 13 (see Quiz 28, page 38)
1 Red/Yellow. **2** Stop bleeding. **3** The King and I. **4** Canada. **5** Sir Cliff Richard. **6** Tower of London. **7** Blue/violet. **8** Suffolk. **9** General Strike. **10** Cricket. **11** Russian. **12** Australia. **13** 24. **14** Sturgeon. **15** Heart. **16** White. **17** Manchester City. **18** Spirit level. **19** Anna Sewell. **20** Maundy money. **21** Kayaks. **22** Oranges. **23** All for one and one for all. **24** Doncaster. **25** Windsor. **26** A Sharp. **27** Rolf Harris. **28** Cambridge. **29** Red/white. **30** Amy Johnson.

Quiz 28 Pot Luck 13

Answers - see Quiz 27, page 37

1 Along with black which colours appear on the German flag?
2 What is a tourniquet used for in First Aid?
3 Which musical is based on a book called Anna and the King of Siam?
4 The chipmunk is native to America and which other country?
5 Who was pop's first Knight?
6 Where in London is the ceremony of the keys held each night?
7 What colour is indigo?
8 Which East Anglian county is often called "Constable Country"?
9 In 1926 which General crisis happened in England?
10 Which sport links Ted Dexter, Peter May and Ray Illingworth?
11 What was the nationality of composer Rimsky-Korsakov?
12 Budgerigars are native to which country?
13 How many carats in pure gold?
14 Caviar comes traditionally from which fish?
15 What does a cardiologist study?
16 What colour are Aylesbury ducks?
17 Which football team plays at Maine Road for its home matches?
18 What is used to check something is level by a builder?
19 Who wrote Black Beauty?
20 What does the Queen give out on the day before Good Friday?
21 What are the sealskin boats used by Eskimos called?
22 What did Nell Gwyn sell when Charles II first saw her?
23 What was the motto of the Three Musketeers?
24 On which course is the horse race the St Leger run?
25 Which castle is in the royal county of Berkshire?
26 If a musical note is lowered by a flat, what raises it?
27 Who was the first presenter of Animal Hospital?
28 In which city is the River Cam?
29 Apart from blue, what two other colours appear on the Dutch flag?
30 In 1930 which female aviator flew from England to Australia?

Answers

The Movies: Comedies (see Quiz 27, page 37)
1 Atkinson. **2** Cruising. **3** Charlie Chaplin. **4** The Addams Family. **5** Ealing. **6** Children. **7** The Flintstones. **8** Excellent. **9** Pig. **10** Cruise. **11** Dogs. **12** Wayne's. **13** Wanda. **14** Nun. **15** Wet Wet Wet. **16** Carrey. **17** Chocolates. **18** Roberts. **19** Morecambe & Wise. **20** Dressed in drag. **21** Dead. **22** The Jungle Book. **23** James. **24** Honey. **25** Popeye. **26** Nine to Five. **27** Patrick Swayze. **28** Look Who's Talking. **29** Priscilla. **30** Clouseau.

Quiz 29 Geography: The UK

Answers - see Quiz 30, page 40

1. Is Holy Island off the east or west coast of England?
2. What is a native of Aberdeen called?
3. Is London's Docklands, north, south, east or west of the city?
4. Where do people go to spot Nessie?
5. Which English gorge takes its name from a nearby village famous for its cheese?
6. Which county has the abbreviation Beds?
7. St Anne's lies to the south of which British seaside resort?
8. Which Royal residence stands by the river Dee?
9. In which country is the UK's highest mountain?
10. What sort of an institution in London is Bart's?
11. On a London Tube map the Central Line is what colour?
12. In which Scottish city did you find the Gorbals?
13. Where is London's most famous Dog's Home?
14. Which Isle off the south coast of England is a county in its own right?
15. What is Britain's most southerly country?
16. Norwich is the administrative centre of which county?
17. In which city did the National Trust buy the childhood home of Paul McCartney?
18. Which motorway runs almost parallel to the A4?
19. With which profession is London's Harley Street associated?
20. What is Britain's largest international airport?
21. In which county is Land's End?
22. Would a Scotsman wear a sporran at the front or at the back of a kilt?
23. Which motorway goes from Lancashire to Yorkshire east to west?
24. In Ireland what is a lough?
25. In which part of the UK is Land of My Fathers a traditional song?
26. Winchester is the adminstrative seat of which county?
27. Aston University is near which Midlands city?
28. Most of the Lake District is in which county?
29. What red flower does Lancs have?
30. In which city is the Barbican Centre?

Answers

Pot Luck 14 (see Quiz 30, page 40)

1 101 Dalmatians. **2** Mozart. **3** A peach. **4** Sark. **5** Brown. **6** He who laughs last. **7** 1953. **8** Carpets. **9** Diagonally. **10** Spain. **11** Charles Dickens. **12** Black/Yellow. **13** A vixen. **14** Cakes. **15** Pinocchio. **16** Fencing. **17** Colour. **18** Isle of Wight. **19** A fish. **20** 39. **21** Blackberry. **22** Zambezi. **23** Herring. **24** Marie Antoinette. **25** Spam. **26** Victor Hugo. **27** Puffin. **28** Red, yellow & blue. **29** Four. **30** Italy.

Quiz 30 Pot Luck 14

Answers - see Quiz 29, page 39

1 Pongo and Perdita appear in which canine film?
2 Who composed the opera The Marriage of Figaro?
3 What type of fruit is a nectarine?
4 Which of the four Channel Islands is the smallest?
5 What colour is sepia?
6 Who, according to the proverb, laughs longest?
7 In which year was Everest conquered?
8 Which house furnishing is associated with the town of Kidderminster?
9 How does a bishop move in chess?
10 The drink sangria comes from which European country?
11 Who wrote The Old Curiosity Shop?
12 What two colours other than red appear on the Belgian flag?
13 What is a female fox called?
14 What is sold in a patisserie?
15 When You Wish Upon A Star comes from which Disney film?
16 In which sport would you need a foil or epee?
17 What can a chameleon lizard change?
18 The rocks called The Needles are close to which island?
19 What is a barracuda?
20 How many steps were there in the title of the novel by John Buchan?
21 A loganberry is a cross between a raspberry and what?
22 Which river are the Victoria Falls on?
23 Sardines and pilchards are part of which fish family?
24 Which French Queen was executed in the French Revolution?
25 What name was spiced ham given during wartime?
26 Who wrote The Hunchback of Notre Dame?
27 Which seabird is associated with Lundy Island?
28 What are the three primary colours in art?
29 How many wings does a moth have?
30 From which country does the football team Juventus come from?

Answers

Geography: The UK (see Quiz 29, page 39)
1 East. **2** Aberdonian. **3** East. **4** Loch Ness. **5** Cheddar. **6** Bedfordshire. **7** Blackpool. **8** Balmoral. **9** Scotland. **10** Hospital. **11** Red. **12** Glasgow. **13** Battersea. **14** Isle of Wight. **15** England. **16** Norfolk. **17** Liverpool. **18** M4. **19** Medical profession. **20** Heathrow. **21** Cornwall. **22** Front. **23** M62. **24** Lake. **25** Wales. **26** Hampshire. **27** Birmingham. **28** Cumbria. **29** Rose. **30** London.

Quiz 31 Sport: Who's Who?

Answers - see Quiz 32, page 42

1 Who was tennis star Martina Hingis named after?
2 Which lauded soccer-star was born Edson Arantes do Nascimento?
3 Which French footballer David advertised L'Oreal hair products?
4 Golfer Ernie Els is from which African country?
5 Which British tennis player was born on Greg Rusedski's first birthday?
6 Jonah Lomu plays for which international side?
7 Athlete Kelly Holmes was formerly a member of which armed service?
8 Which swimmer Sharron is married to athlete Derek Redmond?
9 Which snooker champ Ray was nicknamed Dracula?
10 What sort of eye accessory does Chris Eubank wear?
11 Who replaced David Coleman on A Question of Sport?
12 Which Monica was stabbed in the back by a fanatical Graf supporter?
13 Was tennis's Michael Chang from Hong Kong or the USA?
14 Which Irishman Alex won his last World Snooker Championship in 1982?
15 Which TV presenter ended her relationship with Stan Collymore during France 98?
16 Which four legged, three times Grand National winner died in 1995?
17 Which Greg rejected a maple leaf for a Union Jack in the 90s?
18 Who founded the book known as the cricketer's Bible?
19 Rachel Hayhoe Flint is a famous name in which sport?
20 Who was Ben Johnson running for when disqualified in Seoul?
21 Which Princess won the '71 European Three Day Event?
22 Who replaced Mike Atherton as England cricket captain?
23 Which temperamental tennis player was dubbed Superbrat?
24 Which Jenny was the first woman to train a Grand National winner?
25 Who was John Fashanu's late brother?
26 Which boxer's catchphrase was "Know what I mean 'Arry"?
27 Which disappearing horse last won the Derby in 1981?
28 Who founded the Stewart motor racing team?
29 What was cricket umpire Harold Bird's nickname?
30 Who became the first black manager of a Premiership club when he took over at Chelsea in 1996?

Answers

Pot Luck 15 (see Quiz 32, page 42)

1 Four. **2** Loire. **3** Kristin Scott Thomas. **4** Cornwall. **5** South-south-east. **6** Thomas Hardy. **7** Slavery. **8** King. **9** Red/White. **10** USA. **11** Seven. **12** Kew. **13** Hadrian's Wall. **14** Purple. **15** Mont Blanc. **16** Venice. **17** June. **18** Malta. **19** Blue Peter. **20** Apple. **21** Queen's Counsel. **22** The Black Death/Bubonic Plague. **23** New Orleans. **24** A spring tide. **25** Argentina. **26** Daisy. **27** Shropshire. **28** Pigeon racing. **29** Melon. **30** Switzerland.

Quiz 32 Pot Luck 15

Answers - see Quiz 31, page 41

1 How many wings does a butterfly have?
2 Which river is the longest in France?
3 Who is older – Kristin Scott Thomas or Kate Winslet?
4 In which county is Bodmin Moor?
5 Which compass point is opposite North-north-west?
6 Which Thomas wrote The Mayor of Casterbridge?
7 Which trade was abolished in 1807 in the British Empire?
8 Which chess piece should be protected at all costs?
9 What two colours are on the Austrian flag?
10 In which country was there a North v South civil war from 1861-65?
11 How many players are in a netball team?
12 Where in Britain are the Royal Botanic Gardens?
13 Which ancient wall crosses England from Wallsend to Solway?
14 What colour is an aubergine?
15 Which mountain is the highest in the Alps?
16 The artist Canaletto was associated with which Italian city?
17 In which month is the Trooping of the Colour?
18 Which island is also called the George Cross Island?
19 Which children's show did Anthea Turner present?
20 Cox, Braeburn and Gala are all kinds of which fruit?
21 In legal terms, what do the initials QC stand for?
22 Which disaster struck England in the 1340s?
23 Where, in America, is jazz supposed to have been born?
24 What is the opposite of a neap tide?
25 Which country lies immediately east of Chile?
26 Who was asked to ride "a bicycle made for two" in the song?
27 In which English county is the town of Telford?
28 The National Homing Union is involved with which leisure pursuit?
29 What kind of fruit can be cantaloupe?
30 Which country as well as France is Lake Geneva in?

Answers

Sport: Who's Who? (see Quiz 31, page 41)
1 Martina Navratilova. **2** Pele. **3** Ginola. **4** South Africa. **5** Tim Henman. **6** New Zealand. **7** Army. **8** Davies. **9** Reardon. **10** Monocle. **11** Sue Barker. **12** Seles. **13** USA. **14** Higgins. **15** Ulrika Jonsson. **16** Red Rum. **17** Rusedski . **18** Wisden. **19** Women's cricket. **20** Canada. **21** Anne. **22** Alec Stewart. **23** John McEnroe. **24** Pitman. **25** Justin Fashanu. **26** Frank Bruno. **27** Shergar. **28** Jackie Stewart. **29** Dickie Bird. **30** Ruud Gullit.

Quiz 33 Pop: The 80s

Answers - see Quiz 34, page 44

1 Who went straight to No 1 in 81 with Stand and Deliver?
2 What colour Door gave Shakin' Stevens an 80s hit?
3 Which ex Beatle had a hit with Stevie Wonder in 1982?
4 Whose album Thriller provided several hit singles?
5 Who was KC's backing Band?
6 Which Scot had chart success after Esther Rantzen's The Big Time?
7 Which BBC Radio station banned Relax?
8 Ravel's Bolero charted because of which skaters' Olympic success?
9 Which actor Robert was named in a Bananarama song title ?
10 Which Superstar Rat sang Love Me Tender?
11 Which Alison's nickname was Alf?
12 Which Elaine and Barbara topped the charts in 1985?
13 Which Mrs Andrew Lloyd Webber had a hit with Pie Jesu?
14 David Bowie and Mick Jagger had a hit after which Concert?
15 Elton John charted with Nikita at the same time as Sting had which coincidental hit?
16 Who had hits as part of Visage and Ultravox?
17 Who told you that you were In The Army Now?
18 Who fronted Culture Club?
19 Graham McPherson of Madness was known as what?
20 Which Kim reached No 2 in 1981, 24 years after dad Marty?
21 Which Spanish singer had the UK's first chart topper in Spanish?
22 David Sylvian was part of which Asian sounding band?
23 Who was the first ventriloquist in the charts with Orville?
24 Who teamed up with Annie Lennox in The Eurythmics?
25 Who was the then oldest man in the charts with New York New York?
26 Who joined Cliff Richard for his 80s Living Doll?
27 Which TV puppets sang The Chicken Song?
28 Which red haired Royal liked Lady in Red?
29 Which future England coach joined Waddle on Diamond Lights?
30 Who had a Xmas No 1 in 88 after 30 year in the charts?

Answers

Pot Luck 16 (see Quiz 34, page 44)
1 Ian McCaskill. **2** Raymond Briggs. **3** 13. **4** Soft fruit. **5** Surrey. **6** A monologue. **7** Isle of Man. **8** Queen Victoria. **9** Oranges. **10** French. **11** Horse Guards Parade. **12** Drugs. **13** Your Old Kit Bag. **14** Hats. **15** Honey. **16** Five. **17** Distillery. **18** His tools. **19** The Jordan. **20** Needles. **21** Blackbird. **22** Richard I. **23** Whales. **24** American Football. **25** Capricorn. **26** Pears. **27** November. **28** Agatha Christie. **29** Boxing. **30** Harp.

Quiz 34 Pot Luck 16

Answers - see Quiz 33, page 43

1 Which weatherman featured in a BT ad with the song Bring Me Sunshine?
2 Which cartoonist was the creator of The Snowman?
3 How many are there in a baker's dozen?
4 What would you find in a punnet?
5 In which county are Britain's Royal Botanic Gardens?
6 What is a speech or scene with only one actor called?
7 Douglas is the capital town of which Isle?
8 Who was wife to Prince Albert of Saxe-Coburg and Gotha?
9 The Spanish city of Seville is famous for which fruit?
10 What is the nationality of pianist Richard Clayderman?
11 Where does the Trooping of the Colour take place in London?
12 Pharmacology is the study of what?
13 Where, according to the song, should you pack up your troubles?
14 What is usually kept in a band-box?
15 What is the main ingredient in the drink mead?
16 In music, how many lines are there in a stave?
17 What name is given to the building where whisky is made?
18 According to the proverb, a bad workman always blames what?
19 Jesus Christ was baptised in which river?
20 What are inserted into the body during acupuncture?
21 According to rhyme which bird pecked off the maid's nose?
22 Which King was known as the 'Lionheart'?
23 Beluga, Sperm and Blue are all types of what?
24 Which sport is played on a grid iron?
25 Which Zodiac sign is known as the sign of the goat?
26 What is perry made from?
27 In which month is the State Opening of Parliament in England?
28 Who created sleuth Miss Marple?
29 With which sport do we associate Larry Holmes?
30 Which musical instrument is a national emblem of Ireland?

Answers

Pop: The 80s (see Quiz 33, page 43)
1 Adam and the Ants. **2** Green. **3** Paul McCartney. **4** Michael Jackson. **5** Sunshine Band. **6** Sheena Easton. **7** Radio One. **8** Torvill & Dean. **9** Robert de Niro. **10** Roland. **11** Moyet. **12** Paige, Dickson. **13** Sarah Brightman. **14** Live Aid. **15** Russians. **16** Midge Ure. **17** Status Quo. **18** Boy George. **19** Suggs. **20** Kim Wilde. **21** Julio Iglesias. **22** Japan. **23** Keith Harris. **24** Dave Stewart. **25** Frank Sinatra. **26** The Young Ones. **27** Spitting Image. **28** Duchess of York. **29** Hoddle. **30** Cliff Richard.

Quiz 35 Leisure: Food & Drink 1

Answers - see Quiz 36, page 46

1 Which batter mix is an accompaniment to roast beef?
2 Which blackcurrant drink was advertised by Michael Portillo when he was a child?
3 What colour wine is Beaujolais Nouveau?
4 What colour is the flesh of an avocado?
5 What is the traditional colour for the outside of a stick of rock?
6 Would you eat or drink a Sally Lunn?
7 What type of egg is covered in sausage meat?
8 Scrumpy is a rough form of what?
9 Which mashed vegetable tops a shepherd's pie?
10 Which food has given its name to a road network near Birmingham?
11 Is a Spotted Dick a first course or a pudding?
12 Which fruit is associated with tennis at Wimbledon?
13 Champagne originated in which country?
14 Is a Melton Mowbray pie sweet or savoury?
15 What is a pistachio?
16 What sort of fruit is in a teacake?
17 What is a slice of bacon called?
18 Which is more substantial, afternoon tea or high tea?
19 If you ate al fresco would you be indoors or out of doors?
20 What is the usual shape of a Camembert cheese?
21 Which soft pulpy peas are eaten with fish and chips?
22 What type of food may be served clotted?
23 What would you make in a cafetiere?
24 What type of drink is Bristol Cream?
25 Is chowder a soup or a pudding?
26 A 'pinta' is usually a pint of what?
27 Should red wine normally be drunk chilled or a room temperature?
28 Is there milk in a cappuccino coffee?
29 Are you more likely to eat a croissant at breakfast or supper?
30 A gateau is a creamy type of what?

Answers

Pot Luck 17 (see Quiz 36, page 46)
1 Edward. **2** Staff/stave. **3** Everton. **4** Films. **5** Drowning Men. **6** Hillary Clinton. **7** Eyes. **8** A fool. **9** 101 Dalmatians. **10** Baghdad. **11** B. **12** Four years. **13** Portugal. **14** Damon Hill. **15** Wood. **16** Fish. **17** Beta. **18** Ear, Nose & Throat. **19** Assisi. **20** Stitches. **21** Cancer. **22** Tammy Wynette. **23** Brown. **24** New Zealand. **25** St Bernard. **26** California. **27** 21. **28** Michael and John. **29** Norway. **30** Roald Dahl.

Quiz 36 Pot Luck 17

Answers - see Quiz 35, page 45

1 Which English King was also called 'The Confessor'?
2 What are the lines called on which music is written?
3 Which football team play their home games at Goodison Park?
4 PG, 15 and 18 are all classifications for what?
5 According to the proverb, who clutches at straws?
6 How is US lawyer Hillary Roddam better known?
7 In Cockney rhyming slang, what are your mince pies?
8 According to the proverb, who is soon parted from his money?
9 From which Disney film does Cruella De Vil come from?
10 What is the capital of Iraq?
11 Which letter describes a soft lead pencil?
12 How long is an American president's term of office?
13 The Azores are a part of which European country?
14 Who, surprisingly, won the 1998 Belgian Formula 1 Grand Prix?
15 What are the bars on a xylophone made from?
16 What is a mud skipper?
17 What is the second letter of the Greek alphabet?
18 In medicine, what do the initials ENT stand for?
19 With which Italian town is Saint Francis linked?
20 Blanket, back and buttonhole are all types of what?
21 Which Zodiac sign is known as the sign of the crab?
22 Whose life story was called Stand By Your Man?
23 Which wire is live in modern three core electric cable?
24 From which country other than Australia did Anzac troops come from?
25 Who is the patron saint of mountaineers?
26 In which state of the US is the resort of Palm Springs?
27 How many consonants are in the English alphabet?
28 In Peter Pan what are names of Wendy's brothers?
29 The port of Bergen is in which European country?
30 Who wrote the original Tales of the Unexpected?

Answers

Leisure: Food & Drink 1 (see Quiz 35, page 45)
1 Yorkshire pudding. **2** Ribena. **3** Red. **4** Green. **5** Pink. **6** Eat. **7** Scotch egg. **8** Cider. **9** Potato. **10** Spaghetti (junction). **11** Pudding. **12** Strawberries. **13** France. **14** Savoury. **15** Nut. **16** Currants and/or other dried fruit. **17** Rasher. **18** High tea. **19** Out of doors. **20** Round. **21** Mushy peas. **22** Cream. **23** Coffee. **24** Sherry. **25** Soup. **26** Milk. **27** Room temperature. **28** Yes. **29** Breakfast. **30** Cake.

Quiz 37 TV: Soaps

Answers - see Quiz 38, page 48

1 Which Coronation Street character had the names Fairclough and Sullivan?
2 In which country is The Sullivans set?
3 Characters from which UK soap went to the '98 World Cup Final?
4 What was Channel 5's first major soap called?
5 Which soap sparked the campaign to 'Free the Weatherfield 1'?
6 Lisa Riley was in which soap before You've Been Framed?
7 Danielle Brown of Emmerdale has a sister in which pop band?
8 In which soap were the Battersbys introduced as the family from hell?
9 In Albert Square did Sharon marry Grant or Phil Mitchell?
10 In which northern city was the docu soap Hotel set?
11 In Coronation Street is Spider a pet or an eco warrior?
12 Which soap has an omnibus edition on Sunday afternoons?
13 Gillian Taylforth's sister Kim joined which northern soap in 1998?
14 In which soap did Bobby come back from the dead?
15 The docu soap Lakesiders took place in what type of venue?
16 Which soap has featured aristocrat Lady Tara?
17 Who started soap life as Alma Sedgewick?
18 Which soap has a car repair business at The Arches?
19 What sort of road is Brookside?
20 What time does Coronation Street usually start?
21 Which actress Anna found fame as Beth Jordache in Brookside?
22 Who is Nick Cotton's long suffering mum in Albert Square?
23 How had the Carringtons made their money in Dynasty?
24 What is the first name of Phil and Grant Mitchell's mum?
25 Which Baldwin in Coronation Street hasn't a northern accent?
26 Which Jack and Vera took over the Rovers from the Bet Gilroy?
27 Which Ken has been in Coronation Street from the start?
28 Which soap is the BBC's most watched programme?
29 Which southern hemisphere country did Kathy go to when she left Albert Square?
30 In which city is Brookside set?

Answers

Pot Luck 18 (see Quiz 38, page 48)
1 Fishermen. **2** Doctor. **3** Nothing. **4** Siam. **5** H. **6** Scorpio. **7** Bones.
8 In your mouth. **9** Paul Young. **10** You spoil the child. **11** Violin.
12 A backbone or spinal column. **13** Bean. **14** Queen of Sheba. **15** John Prescott.
16 J.R.R. Tolkien. **17** The Shannon. **18** 30th November. **19** Double bass. **20** Dr Zhivago.
21 Radio 2. **22** The Mall. **23** Islam. **24** Dick Emery. **25** Wiltshire. **26** A thief.
27 Brown. **28** Shakespeare. **29** Knots. **30** A long spoon.

Quiz 38 Pot Luck 18

Answers - see Quiz 37, page 47

1 What job was done by Peter and Andrew before they were disciples?
2 Ex MP David Owen previously followed which profession?
3 If you are in your birthday suit, what are you wearing?
4 Thailand was formerly known by what name?
5 Which letter describes a hard leaded pencil?
6 Which Zodiac sign is usually shown as a scorpion?
7 Osteoporosis affects which part of the body?
8 Where would you find an incisor?
9 Whose first UK No. 1 hit was Wherever I Lay My Hat?
10 According to the proverb, what happens if you spare the rod?
11 Stephane Grapelli is associated with which musical instrument?
12 What do vertebrates have that invertebrates do not?
13 Which vegetable can be dwarf, runner and broad?
14 Which Queen made a visit to Solomon in The Bible?
15 Who was Tony Blair's first Deputy PM?
16 Who wrote Lord of the Rings?
17 Which river is the longest in the British Isles?
18 On which date is Saint Andrew's Day?
19 Which is largest - cello, viola or double bass?
20 Which epic film had the theme tune Somewhere My Love?
21 Terry Wogan's daily show is on which radio station?
22 Buckingham Palace is at the end of which famous London road?
23 A muezzin is an official of which religion?
24 Who used the catch phrase, "Ooh, you are awful, but I like you"?
25 In which county is Salisbury Plain?
26 In Cockney rhyming slang, what is a tea leaf?
27 What colour is the skin of a kiwi fruit?
28 What does 'S' stand for in RSC?
29 What can be granny, sheepshank and bowline?
30 What do you need to sup with the devil, according to the proverb?

Answers

TV: Soaps (see Quiz 37, page 47)
1 Rita. **2** Australia. **3** EastEnders. **4** Family Affairs. **5** Coronation Street. **6** Emmerdale. **7** The Spice Girls. **8** Coronation Street. **9** Grant. **10** Liverpool. **11** Eco warrior. **12** EastEnders. **13** Brookside. **14** Dallas. **15** Shopping centre. **16** Emmerdale. **17** Alma Baldwin. **18** EastEnders. **19** Close. **20** 7.30 p.m. **21** Friel. **22** Dot. **23** Oil. **24** Peggy. **25** Mike. **26** Duckworth. **27** Barlow. **28** EastEnders. **29** South Africa. **30** Liverpool.

Quiz 39 Nature: Living World

Answers - see Quiz 40, page 50

1 Glaucoma affects which part of the body?
2 Which flightless bird lays the world's largest egg?
3 What is a puffball?
4 What happens to a female butterfly after it has laid its eggs?
5 In what type of environment do most crustaceans live?
6 Which natural disaster is measured on the Richter scale?
7 What is the main ingredient of glass?
8 Does a millipede have more, less or exactly 1,000 feet?
9 An ore is a mineral which contains a what?
10 Is the whale shark a mammal like the whale, or a fish like the shark?
11 Which bird is the symbol of the USA?
12 Are butterflies more colourful in warmer or cooler countries?
13 What sort of rock is lava?
14 Which is larger, the dolphin or the porpoise?
15 Which organ of the body has the aorta?
16 How many bones does a slug have?
17 Are worker ants male or female?
18 Altocumulus is a type of what?
19 What is the main source of energy in our ecosystem?
20 Which name for remains of plants and animals which lived on Earth means 'dug up'?
21 On which continent is the world's largest glacier?
22 Kelp is a type of what?
23 What order of mammals does the gibbon belong to?
24 What is the staple food of over half of the world's population?
25 Which creatures are larvae and pupae before being adults?
26 Are most bats visible at night or by day?
27 Which part of a jellyfish has stinging cells?
28 Natural rubber is obtained from what?
29 What is the mother of all the bees in a colony called?
30 The giant sequoia is the largest living what?

Answers

Pot Luck 19 (see Quiz 40, page 50)
1 Jane MacDonald. **2** Egg whites. **3** Betjeman. **4** Liquid or gas. **5** Motor racing. **6** 18. **7** Gabriel. **8** Mods. **9** Drei. **10** Winnie The Pooh. **11** Canute. **12** Victor. **13** Bruce Forsyth. **14** Snap-dragon. **15** Sheffield. **16** Quickly. **17** Fountain pen. **18** Italy. **19** Estimated Time of Arrival. **20** Wine. **21** A-Team. **22** Loch Ness Monster. **23** Seven. **24** The All Blacks. **25** The sparrow. **26** Brazil. **27** James Herriot. **28** Poland. **29** Play. **30** Dallas.

Quiz 40 Pot Luck 19

Answers - see Quiz 39, page 49

1 Who appeared on The Cruise and became famous for her singing?
2 What is sugar added to, to make meringues?
3 Which poet laureate Sir John died in 1984?
4 What can pass through something if it is porous?
5 For which sport is Eddie Irvine famous?
6 How old should you be to marry without parental permission?
7 In The Bible, which angel foretold of the birth of Jesus?
8 What youth group took to wearing parkas?
9 What is the German word for the number three?
10 Which children's favourite bear said he had "very little brain"?
11 Which English king reputedly commanded the sea to retreat?
12 What is the letter "V" if A is Alpha and B is Bravo?
13 Whose is famous for saying, "Nice to see you, to see you nice"?
14 What is a popular name for the flower the antirrhinum?
15 Which Yorkshire city were Pulp from?
16 In music what does presto mean?
17 What object was invented by Lewis Waterman in 1884?
18 Tuscany is in which European country?
19 In the world of flying, what do the initials ETA stand for?
20 What is retsina?
21 Which Team featured Hannibal Smith?
22 Which monster first hit the headlines in 1933?
23 How many edges are there around a 20 pence coin?
24 What are the New Zealand rugby union team called?
25 According to the rhyme, who killed Cock Robin?
26 The Samba originated in which South American country?
27 Who wrote It Shouldn't Happen to a Vet?
28 The port of Gdansk is in which country?
29 Would you eat, play or sit on a sitar?
30 Which TV series included Sue Ellen and Miss Ellie?

Answers

Nature: Living World (see Quiz 39, page 49)
1 Eyes. **2** Ostrich. **3** Fungus. **4** It dies. **5** Water. **6** Earthquake. **7** Sand. **8** Less. **9** Metal. **10** Fish. **11** Eagle. **12** Warmer. **13** Volcanic rock. **14** Dolphin. **15** Heart. **16** None. **17** Female. **18** Cloud. **19** Sun. **20** Fossil. **21** Antarctica. **22** Seaweed. **23** Primates (also accept apes). **24** Rice. **25** Insects. **26** At night. **27** Tentacles. **28** Rubber Tree. **29** Queen. **30** Tree.

Quiz 41 The Movies: Who's Who?

Answers - see Quiz 42, page 52

1 Which ex James Bond has 'Scotland Forever' tattooed on his arm?
2 Which Jools starred in Spiceworld: The Movie?
3 Which Irish born 007 starred in Tomorrow Never Dies?
4 Which Grease actor danced with Princess Diana at the White House?
5 Which sleuth did Albert Finney play in Agatha Christie's Murder on the Orient Express?
6 Which Attenborough brother is a film actor and director?
7 Who was the star of Moonwalker after being in The Jackson Five?
8 Which bespectacled US actor/director directed the musical Everyone Says I Love You?
9 What type of hat was Charlie Chaplin most famous for?
10 Who is Emma Forbes' actor/director dad?
11 Who was named after her home town of Winona?
12 Which knighted pop singer wrote the music for The Lion King?
13 Hayley Mills is the daughter of which knighted actor?
14 Who separated from husband Bruce Willis in 1998?
15 Which newspaper magnate bought 20th Century Fox in 1985?
16 Who was Sid played by Gary Oldman in Sid and Nancy?
17 What name usually associated with a schoolbag did Woody Allen give his son?
18 Which Welsh actor Sir Anthony bought part of Mount Snowdon in 1998?
19 Which pop star Tina starred in Mad Max Beyond the Thunderdome?
20 Which Ms Foster swapped her real first name from Alicia?
21 In rhyming slang what financial term is Gregory Peck?
22 Which child star was Shirley MacLaine named after?
23 Who appeared first at Madame Tussaud's, Harrison Ford or Hugh Grant?
24 Who starred as Steed in the film version of The Avengers?
25 Which boxer played himself in The Greatest?
26 Film buff Barry Norman is a member of which club with the same name as a Marx brother?
27 Who sang It's Not Unusual in Mars Attacks!?
28 Which racing driver Moss starred in Casino Royale?
29 Who are Cary, Katharine and James in The Philadelphia Story?
30 Whose real name is James Baumgarner?

Answers

Pot Luck 20 (see Quiz 42, page 52)
1 Samantha Janus. **2** Ian Fleming. **3** Cornwall. **4** Skeleton. **5** Oporto. **6** Green. **7** Diamond. **8** Pirates. **9** Deux. **10** August. **11** Wrestling. **12** Buttocks. **13** Antonio Banderas. **14** Spain. **15** Rice. **16** Indianapolis. **17** Sylvester. **18** Dover. **19** Deer. **20** Light. **21** Blair. **22** 42. **23** BBC. **24** Delta. **25** Japan. **26** Horse racing. **27** Orange/Yellow. **28** An elephant. **29** Lighthouse Family. **30** Par.

Quiz 42 Pot Luck 20

Answers - see Quiz 41, page 51

1. Which actress plays Ruth in the TV comedy Babes In The Wood?
2. Who wrote the novel You Only Live Twice?
3. Which English county has a border with only one other county?
4. What collective name is given to the structure of bones in the body?
5. The drink port takes its name from which town?
6. What colour is normally associated with ecological groups?
7. What is the hardest substance known to man?
8. Which people are associated with the Jolly Roger flag?
9. What is the French word for the number two?
10. Alphabetically, which is the second of the 12 calendar months?
11. With which sport do we associate a half nelson?
12. Which muscle is the largest - heart, biceps or buttocks?
13. Which actor played Che in Evita when Madonna was Eva Peron?
14. Which country did the paso doble dance originate in?
15. What type of food can be pilau?
16. In which American city is a 500 mile motor race run annually?
17. Which cartoon cat never manages to catch Tweetie Pie?
18. What is Britain's busiest ferry passenger port?
19. What kind of animal is a hind?
20. What can pass through something if it is translucent?
21. Which Tony first became MP for Sedgefield in 1983?
22. How many sides do seven hexagons have?
23. Was Crackerjack shown on BBC or ITV?
24. What is the letter "D" if A is Alpha and B is Bravo?
25. Which country does the drink sake come from?
26. For which sport is Pat Eddery famous?
27. What colour is saffron?
28. In children's books and on TV, what kind of animal is Babar?
29. Which group entered the UK charts in 1995 with Lifted?
30. What term is used in golf to indicate the stroke rating for each hole?

Answers

The Movies: Who's Who? (see Quiz 41, page 51)

1 Sean Connery. **2** Holland. **3** Pierce Brosnan. **4** John Travolta. **5** Poirot. **6** Richard. **7** Michael Jackson. **8** Woody Allen. **9** Bowler. **10** Bryan Forbes. **11** Winona Ryder. **12** Sir Elton John. **13** Sir John Mills. **14** Demi Moore. **15** Rupert Murdoch. **16** Vicious. **17** Satchel. **18** Hopkins. **19** Turner. **20** Jodie Foster. **21** Cheque. **22** Shirley Temple. **23** Harrison Ford. **24** Ralph Fiennes. **25** Muhammad Ali. **26** Groucho. **27** Tom Jones. **28** Stirling Moss. **29** Grant, Hepburn, Stewart. **30** James Garner.

Quiz 43 Hobbies & Leisure 2

Answers - see Quiz 44, page 54

1 What is a bookmaker's licensed premises called?
2 What shape is the target in archery?
3 Where on a dartboard is the bull?
4 Which cubes are necessary for a game of craps?
5 Which direction do you go if you are abseiling?
6 What sort of Park is at Whipsnade?
7 Which locomotive identification hobby shares its name with a controversial 90s movie?
8 In which game do you aim to call "House!"?
9 Yoga was developed from which nation's religion?
10 Is scuba practised above or below the water's surface?
11 From which part of a vehicle might you sell goods to raise cash?
12 What name is given to a small piece of land rented for growing food?
13 In the UK most Bank Holidays fall on which day of the week?
14 Which commodities would you buy at a PYO centre?
15 What does E stand for in NEC?
16 What colour is the baize on a snooker table?
17 Which word precedes sport to describe killing animals for recreation?
18 What type of weapon is used in fencing?
19 What is the name of a coach trip where few know the destination?
20 If you practised on a pommel horse where would you probably be?
21 The Chamber of Horrors is in which London waxworks museum?
22 Which weekly draw is run by Camelot?
23 Are bonsai trees smaller or larger than average?
24 Which club moved to The Riverside in the 1990s?
25 What sort of establishment is a greasy spoon?
26 Who is a tied house usually tied to?
27 What is the type of billiards played in pubs called?
28 The Summer Bank Holiday takes place in which month in the UK?
29 Which name for an expert in a particular hobby is the same as a padded jacket?
30 What does Y stand for in DIY?

Answers

Pot Luck 21 (see Quiz 44, page 54)
1 70s. **2** Middlesbrough. **3** Cuba. **4** Springfield. **5** Seven. **6** Toboggan. **7** Goliath. **8** On water - it's a boat. **9** Costner. **10** Elephant. **11** Tower Bridge. **12** Their gills. **13** Meat. **14** Six. **15** Possession. **16** Green & Yellow. **17** Nephews. **18** Eins. **19** James Herriot. **20** Catherine Wheel. **21** Victoria. **22** Canaveral. **23** Mineral water. **24** Baldrick. **25** Pounds. **26** 650. **27** Rome. **28** Yellow. **29** Moses. **30** Six.

Quiz 44 Pot Luck 21

Answers - see Quiz 43, page 53

1 Did Britain join the EEC in the 60s, 70s or 80s?
2 At which club did Gazza and Paul Merson play in the same team?
3 The Rumba originated in which country?
4 Where do the cartoon Simpsons live?
5 How many edges are there around a 50 pence coin?
6 What type of vehicle is seen on the Cresta Run?
7 Which Biblical giant was killed by David?
8 Where would you find a useful junk?
9 Which Kevin was Wyatt Earp in the 1994 movie?
10 Which animal does ivory predominantly come from?
11 Which London bridge opens upwards to let tall ships through?
12 Fish breathe through what?
13 What was sold at London's Smithfield market?
14 How many noughts are there in the written number one million?
15 According to the saying, what is "nine points of the law"?
16 What colour is earth in modern three core electric cables?
17 What relation are Huey, Dewey and Louie to Donald Duck?
18 What is the German word for the number one?
19 Who wrote the novel All Creatures Great and Small?
20 Which firework is named after a saint?
21 Which Queen became Empress of India in 1876?
22 From which cape is the American Space Shuttle launched?
23 Vichy is famous for which drink?
24 Which Blackadder character had a fascination for turnips?
25 According to the saying, which money will look after itself?
26 How many centimetres are there in six and a half metres?
27 The Vatican City is within which other capital city?
28 What colour is the shade of jonquil?
29 In The Bible, who was found in the bulrushes?
30 How many points does a snowflake have?

Answers

Hobbies & Leisure 2 (see Quiz 43, page 53)
1 Betting shop. **2** Circular. **3** Centre. **4** Dice. **5** Downwards. **6** Animal Park. **7** Trainspotting. **8** Bingo. **9** Indian. **10** Below. **11** Car boot. **12** Allotment. **13** Monday. **14** Fruit and vegetables (Pick Your Own). **15** Exhibition. **16** Green. **17** Blood. **18** Sword. **19** Mystery tour. **20** Gym. **21** Madame Tussaud's. **22** The National Lottery. **23** Smaller. **24** Middlesbrough. **25** Cafe. **26** Brewery. **27** Bar billiards. **28** August. **29** Anorak. **30** Yourself.

Quiz 15 Sporting Chance 1

Answers - see Quiz 46, page 56

1 Which ice dance pair have the freedom of the city of Nottingham?
2 Which Frank Sinatra classic did Geoff Boycott choose on Desert Island Discs?
3 What sort of animal takes part in a point-to-point?
4 In snooker what colour ball scores least?
5 In which country did sumo wrestling originate?
6 What was the name of Damon Hill's racing driver father?
7 Mike Tyson was suspended for biting off which part of Evander Holyfield?
8 In which sport did Justin Rose become a pro after the '98 British Open?
9 In which Channel does the Admiral's Cup take place?
10 Which Scot Stephen won five successive snooker world championships in the 90s?
11 What do Redgrave and Pinsent race in?
12 Which Walter won the Derby on Lammtara in 1995?
13 In athletics what is the shortest outdoor track race?
14 What is the national sport of Spain known as corrida de toros?
15 How often is the Grand National normally run?
16 What would you ride in a velodrome?
17 Which sport has Australian Rules?
18 Which golfer Jack was known as the Golden Bear?
19 How long does the annual motor race at Le Man last?
20 The 'Golden Gloves' championship is in which sport?
21 The Fastnet Race is competed for on what type of surface?
22 Which youngsters run between the ends of the net during a tennis match ?
23 How does soccer player Dennis Bergkamp refuse to travel?
24 In which sport do you try to play below par?
25 Which Frankie had seven wins at Ascot at odds of 25,095 to 1?
26 How was Sir Garfield St Auburn Sobers known as a player?
27 Which sport do The Barbarians play?
28 Which game can be lawn or crown green?
29 Which two continents compete for the Ryder Cup?
30 Which jockey was jailed in the 80s for tax evasion?

Answers

Pot Luck 22 (see Quiz 46, page 56)
1 Greendale. **2** Bruce Forsyth. **3** 25. **4** Hutchence. **5** Banned from British racecourses. **6** Travel agents. **7** Liver. **8** Grasshoppers. **9** Roberts. **10** Oldest university. **11** Great Britain. **12** Heart. **13** Birds. **14** Peter Gabriel. **15** No. **16** Blue. **17** Two. **18** Glasgow. **19** Lancashire. **20** Roxy Music. **21** Stripes. **22** Delilah. **23** Canada. **24** Italy. **25** The Lone Ranger. **26** East. **27** Lewinsky. **28** 16. **29** Gallagher. **30** Guernsey.

Quiz 46 Pot Luck 22

Answers - see Quiz 45, page 55

1 Where are you if Mrs Goggins serves you in the post office?
2 Whose catchphrase was, "Didn't they do well"?
3 What percentage is half of a half?
4 Which late Michael was lead singer with INXS?
5 What happens if a bookie is "warned off Newmarket Heath"?
6 ABTA is concerned with which group of people?
7 In the body, which organ secretes bile?
8 In Switzerland, which famous soccer club has an insect name?
9 Which Julia starred as a waitress in Mystic Pizza?
10 What will Harvard University always be in America?
11 Which country was the first to use postage stamps?
12 Which part of his anatomy did Tony Bennett leave in San Francisco?
13 What does Bill Oddie like to go outside to watch?
14 Which Peter made the album Solsbury Hill?
15 Was the great racehorse Red Rum coloured red?
16 Traditionally, what colour is willow pattern?
17 How many members were there in the group The Carpenters?
18 Sauciehall Street is in which city?
19 Wasim Akram first played County Cricket for which county?
20 Which group was fronted by Bryan Ferry?
21 What is the distinctive pattern on Dennis The Menace's shirt?
22 In The Bible, who cut off Samson's hair?
23 The province of Manitoba is in which country?
24 Was Gazza's first foreign club based in France, Italy or Spain?
25 Which cowboy had a horse named Silver?
26 Is St Andrew's golf course on the east or west coast of Scotland?
27 Which Monica became intimately associated with Bill Clinton?
28 How many sides would four trapezium's have?
29 Which Liam married Patsy Kensit in 1997?
30 St Peter Port is on which island?

Answers

Sporting Chance 1 (see Quiz 45, page 55)

1 Torvill & Dean. **2** My Way. **3** Horse. **4** Red. **5** Japan. **6** Graham. **7** Ear. **8** Golf. **9** English Channel. **10** Hendry. **11** Boat. **12** Swinburn. **13** 100m. **14** Bull fighting. **15** Once a year. **16** Bicycle. **17** Football. **18** Nicklaus. **19** 24 hours. **20** Boxing. **21** Water. **22** Ballboys/ballgirls. **23** By air. **24** Golf. **25** Dettori. **26** Gary Sobers. **27** Rugby. **28** Bowls. **29** Europe & America. **30** Lester Piggott.

Quiz 47 TV: Famous Faces

Answers - see Quiz 48, page 58

1 Who travelled from Pole to Pole and Around the World in 80 Days?
2 Which Newsnight interrogator has the nickname Paxo?
3 Clive James hails from which Commonwealth country?
4 Who was born John Cheese and changed his name by one letter?
5 Which Magnusson was given the first TV interview by Earl Spencer after his sister's death?
6 Which David and Jonathan hosted the 1998 Election coverage?
7 Which Gardener's World presenter wrote a novel Mr MacGregor?
8 Which Kate won an OBE for her reporting in Beijing and the Gulf?
9 Which famous part of her did Friends' Rachel advertise?
10 Anthony Worrall Thompson replaced Michael Barry on which food magazine show?
11 Which Sir David's catchphrase is "Hello, good evening and welcome"?
12 After 25 years at the BBC which football pundit went to Sky in 1998?
13 Which Paula gave interviews on her bed in The Big Breakfast?
14 Which Irishman has presented The Eurovision Song Contest?
15 Which practical joke Jeremy first hosted You've Been Framed?
16 Which 'big name' moved her talk show from ITV to BBC in 1998?
17 Is Paul Ross the brother, son or no relation of Jonathan Ross?
18 Whose catchphrase was 'Awight!'?
19 Which stock cube did Lynda Bellingham advertise?
20 How are TV cooks Clarissa and Jennifer better known?
21 What is Anthea Turner's TV presenter sister called?
22 Who was the footballing team captain on They Think It's All Over?
23 Who is actor Tony Britton's TV presenter daughter?
24 Ian McCaskill retired from presenting what in 1998?
25 Which Gloria presented an Open House on Channel 5?
26 In Ground Force is it Charlie or Tommy who has long red hair?
27 What are the first names of Reeves and Mortimer?
28 Which Judith did Anthea Turner replace on Wish You Were Here?
29 Which Match of the Day presenter took on a Radio 2 show in 1998?
30 What is Prime Suspect actress star Helen Mironoff's real name?

Answers

Pot Luck 23 (see Quiz 48, page 58)
1 Wherever I Lay My Hat. **2** 13. **3** Hip. **4** Black Sea. **5** Carbon dioxide. **6** Hamlet. **7** Basketball. **8** Richard Branson. **9** Mary Poppins. **10** Seven. **11** June. **12** Gideons. **13** Shakespeare. **14** Member (of the Order) of the British Empire. **15** Country. **16** Jonah. **17** Motorcycling. **18** Louis Armstrong. **19** Primer. **20** Ludo. **21** Truro. **22** Anatomy. **23** Farming & Agriculture. **24** Time. **25** West Sussex. **26** Sherry. **27** Actual Bodily Harm. **28** Matador. **29** House of Commons. **30** Funf.

Quiz 48 Pot Luck 23

Answers - see Quiz 47, page 57

1 What was Paul Young's only UK No. 1 hit in 1983?
2 How many players are on a cricket field during normal play?
3 What fruit comes from the rose?
4 The River Danube flows out into which Sea?
5 Which gas puts the bubbles into bottled fizzy drinks?
6 Which Shakespeare character gave the "To be or not to be" speech?
7 The Harlem Globe Trotters are famous in which sport?
8 Who is older Richard Branson or William Hague?
9 "Supercalifragilisticexpialidocious" comes from which Disney movie?
10 How many noughts are there in the written number ten million?
11 Which month of the year in Britain includes the longest day?
12 Copies of The Bible are left in hotel rooms by which religious organisation?
13 Who wrote the play A Winter's Tale?
14 What do the initials M.B.E. stand for?
15 What have you betrayed if you commit treason?
16 Who was swallowed by a whale in The Bible?
17 For which sport is Mick Doohan famous?
18 Which musician had the nickname 'Satchmo'?
19 When decorating what name is given to the first coat?
20 What is the children's version of backgammon called?
21 What is the administrative headquarters of the county of Cornwall?
22 Which scientific word deals with the structure of the body?
23 The Royal Smithfield Show is connected to which industry?
24 What does a chronometer measure?
25 Chichester is the county town of which county?
26 Jerez in Spain is famous for which alcoholic drink?
27 In crime what do the initials A.B.H. stand for?
28 In a bull fight, what name is given to the person who kills the bull?
29 Which is the Lower House in British politics?
30 What is the German word for the number five?

Answers

TV: Famous Faces (see Quiz 47, page 57)
1 Michael Palin. **2** Jeremy Paxman. **3** Australia. **4** John Cleese. **5** Sally. **6** Dimbleby. **7** Alan Titchmarsh. **8** Adie. **9** Hair. **10** Food & Drink. **11** Frost. **12** Jimmy Hill. **13** Yates. **14** Terry Wogan. **15** Beadle. **16** Vanessa. **17** Brother. **18** Michael Barrymore. **19** Oxo. **20** Two Fat Ladies. **21** Wendy. **22** Gary Lineker. **23** Fern Britton. **24** Weather forecasting. **25** Hunniford. **26** Charlie. **27** Vic & Bob. **28** Chalmers. **29** Desmond Lynam. **30** Helen Mirren.

Quiz 49 Celebs

Answers - see Quiz 50, page 60

1 Which pop band did Geri Halliwell leave in Spring 1998?
2 What is the married name of Cherie Booth QC?
3 Who was the fiancee of Michael Hutchence at the time of his death?
4 What is Caroline Aherne's showbiz pensioner persona?
5 Which London store did Mohammed Al-Fayed buy in 1985?
6 What is the first name of politician turned author Lord Archer?
7 Who is the man behind the Virgin group?
8 What type of adviser was subsequent bankrupt John Bryan to Fergie?
9 Which footballer married Sheryl and had a son called Regan?
10 Which Tory politician did Ffion Jenkins marry?
11 Which rock star did Texan model Jerry Hall marry in 1990?
12 In which country was Ulrika Jonsson born?
13 Which radio DJ has his own company, Ginger Productions?
14 Who left husband Peter Powell for Grant Bovey in 1998?
15 How is former Royal girlfriend Kathleen Stark better known?
16 Who founded the London nightclub Stringfellow's?
17 Which country did Earl Spencer move to in the mid 1990s?
18 Which Royal was Lord Snowdon married to?
19 What was Liz Hurley's infamous Versace dress held together with?
20 Which millionairess cook is a director of Norwich City Football Club?
21 Which chain of cosmetics shops did Anita Roddick found?
22 What was the sporting profession of Jemima Khan's husband?
23 What is Camilla Shand's married name?
24 What is Simon Le Bon's model wife called?
25 Which celebrity actor Grant's middle name is Mungo?
26 Which nightclub was named after Lady Annabel Goldsmith?
27 What does John Galliano design?
28 Which Nigel writes about celebs in his Daily Mail diary?
29 Which Foreign Secretary did Gaynor Regan marry in 1998?
30 What is the first name of PR man Mr Clifford?

Answers

Pot Luck 24 (see Quiz 50, page 60)
1 Athletics. **2** Champion. **3** James Herriot. **4** Joseph. **5** Grievous Bodily Harm. **6** Like a lamb. **7** Snow White & the Seven Dwarfs. **8** Five. **9** Caribbean. **10** India. **11** Growing of crops. **12** Mae West. **13** On the shoulder. **14** King Charles. **15** Military policeman. **16** Animal. **17** Boutique. **18** Member of the European Parliament. **19** Grand National. **20** Mg. **21** 2000. **22** December. **23** David. **24** Leather. **25** Five. **26** John Lennon. **27** Democrats & Republicans. **28** Trowbridge. **29** Dix. **30** Harry Corbett.

Quiz 50 Pot Luck 24

Answers - see Quiz 49, page 59

1 For which sport is Paula Radcliffe famous?
2 In the TV song, who was the 'Wonder Horse'?
3 Who wrote the novel "Let Sleeping Vets Lie"?
4 Which of Jacob's sons had a coat of many colours, in The Bible?
5 In crime what do the initials G.B.H. stand for?
6 According to the saying, how will March go out if it comes in like a lion?
7 Which Disney movie includes the song Whistle While You Work?
8 After how many years must an election be held in Britain?
9 Jamaica is in which sea?
10 Which country does the musical instrument the sitar come from?
11 Which kind of farming is arable farming?
12 Which famous film star gave her name to a life jacket?
13 Where would you wear an epaulette?
14 Which kind of spaniel was named after a king?
15 In the army what is an MP?
16 Is a jellyfish a mineral, vegetable or animal?
17 In the Sixties what was Biba?
18 In politics, what do the initials M.E.P. stand for?
19 In 1993, which horse race was made void after a false start?
20 Which two letters form the symbol for the element magnesium?
21 How many centimetres are there in twenty metres?
22 Which month of the year in Britain includes the shortest day?
23 Who killed the giant Goliath?
24 What is prepared in a tannery?
25 How many lines are there in a limerick?
26 Which member of the Beatles sang Imagine?
27 Which are the two main political parties in America?
28 What is the administrative headquarters of the county of Wiltshire?
29 What is the French word for the number ten?
30 Did Harry Corbett, Harry H Corbett or Ronnie Corbett work with Sooty?

Answers

Celebs (see Quiz 49, page 59)

1 The Spice Girls. **2** Blair. **3** Paula Yates. **4** Mrs Merton. **5** Harrods. **6** Jeffrey. **7** Richard Branson. **8** Financial. **9** Paul Gascoigne. **10** William Hague. **11** Mick Jagger. **12** Sweden. **13** Chris Evans. **14** Anthea Turner. **15** Koo Stark. **16** Peter Stringfellow. **17** South Africa. **18** Princess Margaret. **19** Safety pins. **20** Delia Smith. **21** Body Shop. **22** Cricketer. **23** Parker-Bowles. **24** Yasmin. **25** Hugh Grant. **26** Annabel's. **27** Clothes. **28** Dempster. **29** Robin Cook. **30** Max.

Quiz 51 Children's TV

Answers - see Quiz 52, page 62

1 What mighty hero did Prince Adam turn into with the aid of Greyskull castle?
2 Where is Grange Hill Comprehensive?
3 What was the follow up to How!?
4 Tom Baker was the longest serving Doctor in which sci fi series?
5 Which children's favourite has the number plate PAT 1?
6 Which Linford presented Record Breakers?
7 Which Engine's friends were Terence the Tractor and Bertie the Bus?
8 Does Tom or Jerry have the furrier coat?
9 What cuddly creatures are Uncle Bulgaria and Orinoco?
10 What was Worzel Gummidge?
11 Are Smurfs blue or orange?
12 Which Street teaches about letters and numbers?
13 What sort of creature is Pingu?
14 Which family is headed by Homer?
15 What colour is Teletubby Laa Laa?
16 Which Bear was found in a London railway station?
17 What is Popeye's occupation?
18 What sort of creature is Children's BBC's Otis?
19 What is the most number of presenters Blue Peter has at once?
20 Matthew Corbett said goodbye to which puppet companion in 1998?
21 What sort of animal was Huckleberry?
22 Which Grove is a children's drama series?
23 Who is Dastardly's canine sidekick?
24 On Your Marks and Art Attack are about what subject?
25 Spot is chiefly what colour?
26 Which heroic earth organisation fought Spectra in Battle of the Planets?
27 What sort of animal is Garfield?
28 What is Casper?
29 What Sentinels were Mercury, Hercules and Astria?
30 What kind of prehistoric creature is Dink?

Answers

Pot Luck 25 (see Quiz 52, page 62)
1 Butterfly. **2** Two. **3** The eye. **4** Red rose. **5** Jamaica. **6** Tom Hanks. **7** Lisa Riley. **8** Alcohol. **9** Trois. **10** Animal. **11** Motor racing. **12** Fire. **13** Reveille. **14** Limerick. **15** John Smith. **16** Max Bygraves. **17** K. **18** Greece. **19** Mrs Laurence. **20** A brush. **21** El Salvador. **22** Etc. **23** A jellyfish. **24** Zoos. **25** A Tap. **26** U. **27** Tom. **28** Ulrika Jonsson. **29** Not speaking to them. **30** Three.

Quiz 52 Pot Luck 25

Answers - see Quiz 51, page 61

1 Which swimming stroke was introduced in the 1956 Olympics?
2 What's the greatest number of consecutive calendar months with 31 days?
3 What name is given to the calm area at the centre of a hurricane?
4 Which flower is the symbol of the Labour Party in Britain?
5 Kingston is the capital of which island nation?
6 Who played Forrest in the 1994 film Forrest Gump?
7 Who replaced Jeremy Beadle to present You've Been Framed!?
8 Complete the Oasis song title "Cigarettes and ....?
9 What is the French word for the number three?
10 Are sponges mineral, vegetable or animal?
11 For which sport is Jean Alesi famous?
12 According to the proverb, there's no smoke without what?
13 Which army bugle call is played to wake up the troops?
14 Which Irish town gives its name to a five line humorous verse?
15 Who preceded Tony Blair as Labour Party leader?
16 Who is renowned for saying, "I wanna tell you a story"?
17 Which letter of the alphabet is used as a measure of the size of a computer's memory?
18 Which country produces the pine scented wine called retsina?
19 What is the Princess Royal's married name?
20 What name is given to a fox's tail?
21 San Salvador is in which country?
22 Which abbreviation means "and so on"?
23 What is a Portuguese Man-o'-War?
24 What do Whipsnade, Chessington and London have in common?
25 What is the English equivalent of the American 'faucet'?
26 Alphabetically, which letter is the last of the vowels?
27 Which name links golfers Kite and Watson?
28 Who presents Gladiators with Jeremy Guscott?
29 What are we not doing if we send someone to Coventry?
30 How many balls are used in billiards?

Answers

Children's TV (see Quiz 51, page 61)
1 He-Man. **2** London. **3** How 2. **4** Doctor Who. **5** Postman Pat. **6** Christie. **7** Thomas the Tank Engine. **8** Tom. **9** Wombles. **10** Scarecrow. **11** Blue. **12** Sesame Street. **13** Penguin. **14** The Simpsons. **15** Yellow. **16** Paddington. **17** Sailor. **18** Aardvark. **19** Four. **20** Sooty. **21** Hound. **22** Byker Grove. **23** Muttley. **24** Art & crafts. **25** Yellow. **26** G-Force. **27** Cat. **28** Ghost. **29** The Space Sentinels. **30** Dinosaur.

Quiz 53 Leisure: Food & Drink 2

Answers - see Quiz 54, page 64

LEVEL 1

1 Tikka is a dish in which country's cookery?
2 A strudel is usually filled with which fruit?
3 What relation is Albert to fellow chef and restaurateur Michel Roux?
4 Which pasta sauce originated in Bologna in Italy?
5 What is a frankfurter?
6 How are eggs usually cooked in the breakfast dish bacon and eggs?
7 What is fromage frais a soft type of?
8 Does an Italian risotto contain rice or pasta?
9 Over what would you normally pour a vinaigrette dressing?
10 Rick Stein's restaurant and cooking specialises in what?
11 What colour wine is a Valpolicella?
12 In which country did Chianti originate?
13 What is the main filling ingredient of a quiche?
14 Is a poppadum crisp or soft?
15 What sort of drink is espresso?
16 Is brioche a type of bread or a fruit?
17 What shape is the pasta used to make lasagne?
18 What is mozzarella?
19 What colour is fudge?
20 Which north of England county is famous for its hotpot?
21 Do you eat or drink a loyal toast?
22 What type of meat is found in a cock-a-leekie soup?
23 Which food links Gary Lineker and The Spice Girls?
24 What is the alcoholic ingredient of Gaelic coffee?
25 Which fruit is usually used in marmalade?
26 At what age can you legally drink alcohol in an pub?
27 What does G stand for in G and T?
28 What are the two main colours of liquorice Allsorts?
29 Would you eat or drink schnapps?
30 A Conference is what type of fruit?

Answers

Pot Luck 26 (see Quiz 54, page 64)
1 The mice. **2** Sport's trophy (golf). **3** American Indians. **4** Queen Mother. **5** Spanish. **6** 1997. **7** Perry Como. **8** Six. **9** Advent. **10** A kimono. **11** Mount Sinai. **12** Worzel Gummidge. **13** Althorp Park. **14** Quotient. **15** Hiroshima. **16** Tottenham Hotspur. **17** Tomorrows World. **18** Germany. **19** Boxing. **20** Neuf. **21** Tiger. **22** Tuxedo. **23** Battle of Hastings. **24** Rabbit. **25** Terry Waite. **26** Yellow. **27** Victory in Europe. **28** 168. **29** The eye. **30** Anne Frank.

Quiz 54 Pot Luck 26

Answers - see Quiz 53, page 63

1 According to the proverb, what plays when the cat's away?
2 Did Harry Vardon give his name to a disease, a sport's trophy or a fruit?
3 Which people wore moccasins originally?
4 Which Royal was born in 1900?
5 What is the main spoken language in Mexico?
6 In which year did Hong Kong revert to being part of China?
7 Who had hits with Magic Moments and Catch a Falling Star?
8 How many noughts are there in the written number fifty two million?
9 Which season comes just before Christmas in the Christian calendar?
10 Which long dress is traditionally worn by Japanese women?
11 In The Bible, on which mountain was Moses told the commandments?
12 Actor John Pertwee played which TV scarecrow?
13 At which Park is Princess Diana buried?
14 What does the Q stand for in IQ?
15 Where was the first atomic bomb dropped on 6th August 1945?
16 White Hart Lane is home to which football club?
17 Philippa Forrester and Peter Snow co-hosted which science based TV programme?
18 Hanover, Westphalia and Bavaria are all parts of which country?
19 For which sport is Chris Eubank famous?
20 What is the French word for the number nine?
21 Which animal in the poem by Blake was described as "burning bright"?
22 What do Americans call a dinner jacket?
23 In which battle was King Harold killed?
24 What type of animal can be Dutch, Angora and Chinchilla?
25 Who was a Beirut hostage with John McCarthy and Brian Keenan ?
26 What colour was the "itsy bitsy teeny weeny bikini" in the pop song?
27 What do the initials VE stand for in VE Day?
28 How many hours are there in a week?
29 Which part of the body can suffer from an astigmatism?
30 Which Jewish girl kept a diary whilst hidden in Amsterdam in 1942?

Answers

Leisure: Food & Drink 2 (see Quiz 53, page 63)
1 India. **2** Apple. **3** Brothers. **4** Bolognaise. **5** Sausage. **6** Fried. **7** Cheese. **8** Rice. **9** Salad. **10** Fish. **11** Red. **12** Italy. **13** Eggs. **14** Crisp. **15** Coffee. **16** Bread. **17** Rectangular. **18** Cheese. **19** Light brown. **20** Lancashire. **21** Drink (toast to the queen). **22** Chicken. **23** Walker's crisps. **24** Whiskey. **25** Oranges. **26** 18. **27** Gin. **28** Black and white. **29** Drink. **30** Pear.

Quiz 55 The Movies: Greats

Answers - see Quiz 56, page 66

1 Which great screen dancer is on the cover of Sgt Pepper?
2 Which wartime classic starred Ingrid Bergman and Humphrey Bogart?
3 Who is Jamie Lee Curtis's actor father?
4 Cary Grant was born in which west country port?
5 Was Rita Hayworth a blonde or a redhead?
6 Was it Bob Hope or Bing Crosby who was born in south London?
7 Which monster was arguably Boris Karloff's most famous role?
8 How was dancer Eugene Curran Kelly better known?
9 Who was the original Candle in the Wind dedicated to?
10 Which Anthony starred as the lead character in Psycho?
11 Which Sir Alec starred in, and had a share of the profits of, Star Wars?
12 Who was taller, Rock Hudson or Mickey Rooney?
13 Which James starred in Harvey and The Philadelphia Story?
14 Which Italian born actor is best known for silent movies such as The Sheikh?
15 Which Citizen was the subject of Orson Welles' first film?
16 Lauren Bacall was the wife of which Humphrey?
17 Tough guy Frank J Cooper adopted which first name?
18 Which Joan starred in Whatever Happened to Baby Jane?
19 How was Ruth Elizabeth Davis better known?
20 Which Charlie was a founder of the film studio United Artists?
21 Bing Crosby had just finished a round of which game when he died?
22 William Claude Dunkenfield used his first two initials to become who?
23 Jane and Peter are the children of which screen great Henry?
24 Which Katharine enjoyed a long on and off screen relationship with Spencer Tracy?
25 Which Doris enjoyed popularity in films with Rock Hudson?
26 He was born John Uhler Lemmon III but how is he known in films?
27 Who is Michael Douglas's famous actor father?
28 In which German capital was Marlene Dietrich born?
29 Did Clark Gable die during his last film in the 40s, 50s or 60s?
30 Greta Garbo was born in which Scandinavian capital?

Answers

Pot Luck 27 (see Quiz 56, page 66)
1 Italy. **2** An ill wind. **3** Aladdin. **4** Beef cattle. **5** Windsor. **6** Runnymede. **7** Washington. **8** Around your waist. **9** Neun. **10** Egypt. **11** J. **12** Jack. **13** Origami. **14** Circus. **15** Germany. **16** Krypton. **17** Trousers. **18** The teeth. **19** Spain. **20** 900. **21** Jennifer Aniston. **22** Computer Languages. **23** Cavalier. **24** Easter. **25** Pink. **26** France. **27** Arachnophobia. **28** The skin. **29** Horses. **30** Rugby League.

Quiz 56 Pot Luck 27

Answers - see Quiz 55, page 65

1. Sicily, Lombardy and Tuscany are all parts of which country?
2. What kind of wind blows no good according to the proverb?
3. Which Disney movie includes the song A Whole New World?
4. What type of animal can be Charolais, Galloway and Simmental?
5. Which is the largest castle in Britain?
6. Where did King John sign the Magna Carta?
7. In which capital is the Capitol Building?
8. Where would you wear a cummerbund?
9. What is the German word for the number nine?
10. Which country had eleven kings called Rameses?
11. What appears most as the initial letter in calendar month names?
12. According to the rhyme, who fixed his head with vinegar and brown paper?
13. What name is given to the Japanese craft of paper folding?
14. Billy Smart and Chipperfields provided what type of entertainment?
15. In which country was Cabaret set?
16. What was the name of Superman's home planet?
17. Who or what are Oxford Bags?
18. What part of your body is covered by orthodontics?
19. Paella is a traditional dish from which country?
20. How many seconds are in a quarter of an hour?
21. Which Friends star has advertised L'Oreal?
22. What are COBOL, FORTRAN and ALGOL?
23. What type of person was Laughing in the famous portrait?
24. Which festival follows Lent in the Christian calendar?
25. What colour is the Financial Times?
26. Brittany and Picardy are parts of which country?
27. Which phobia describes the fear of spiders?
28. In medicine, what does a dermatologist specialise in?
29. Suffolk Punch, Shires and Clydesdales are all types of what?
30. For which sport are Robbie and Henry Paul famous?

Answers

The Movies: Greats (see Quiz 55, page 65)

1 Fred Astaire. **2** Casablanca. **3** Tony Curtis. **4** Bristol. **5** Redhead. **6** Bob Hope. **7** Frankenstein. **8** Gene Kelly. **9** Marilyn Monroe. **10** Perkins. **11** Guinness. **12** Rock Hudson. **13** Stewart. **14** Rudolph Valentino. **15** Citizen Kane. **16** Bogart. **17** Gary. **18** Crawford. **19** Bette Davis. **20** Chaplin. **21** Golf. **22** W.C.Fields. **23** Fonda. **24** Hepburn. **25** Day. **26** Jack Lemmon. **27** Kirk Douglas. **28** Berlin. **29** 60s. **30** Stockholm.

Quiz 57 Geography: Euro Tour

Answers - see Quiz 58, page 68

1 In which country would you find Jerez?
2 How would you travel if you left for France from a hoverport?
3 Eurostar trains run from London to which Belgian city?
4 In which country is Cologne?
5 Does London or Rome have the higher population?
6 The province of Flanders is in which country?
7 Which landlocked country is divided into cantons?
8 In which city would you find the Parthenon?
9 Bohemia is part of which Republic, formerly part of Czechoslovakia?
10 Is Schiphol an airport or a river in the Netherlands?
11 In which country is Estoril?
12 Where is the Black Forest?
13 What type of country is Monaco?
14 Andorra lies between France and which other country?
15 In which Sea does Cyprus lie?
16 Belarus and Ukraine were formerly part of which huge republic?
17 What is the English name for the city known to Italians as Venezia?
18 Is Sweden a kingdom or a republic?
19 Vienna lies on which river?
20 Is Ibiza part of the Canaries or the Balearics?
21 In which Circle does about a third of Finland lie?
22 The Hague is the seat of government of which country?
23 Crete and Corfu belong to which country?
24 Which Scandinavian country is opposite Norway and Sweden?
25 Is Europe the second largest or the second smallest continent?
26 Which country marks the most westerly point of mainland Europe?
27 The Iberian Peninsula consists of Portugal and which other country?
28 Which French city is Europe's largest?
29 What are the Balkans, the Apennines and the Pyrenees?
30 Which island is known to the French as Corse?

Answers

Pot Luck 28 (see Quiz 58, page 68)
1 Film. **2** Born. **3** Brian Johnston. **4** Reed. **5** 60s. **6** Muslim. **7** Michael Heseltine. **8** Enfield. **9** Bees. **10** Four. **11** Falk. **12** Golf. **13** Provence. **14** Devon. **15** Greek gods. **16** Flint. **17** John Le Mesurier. **18** Irish. **19** Noddy. **20** Triangular. **21** England. **22** Furniture. **23** Witch. **24** Harmonica. **25** Sport. **26** Keystone. **27** Forty. **28** Meat Loaf. **29** Celtic. **30** Dog.

Quiz 58 Pot Luck 28

Answers - see Quiz 57, page 67

1 Which came first the film or stage show of Phantom Of The Opera?
2 In Bruce Springsteen songs what goes before In The USA and To Run?
3 Which famous cricket commentator died of a heart attack in January 1994?
4 Which Lou wrote and sang A Perfect Day?
5 Was Liz Hurley born in the 50s, 60, or 70s?
6 Which religion has people called to prayer by a muezzin?
7 Which Tory MP earned the name Goldilocks?
8 Which Harry created the character of Frank Doberman?
9 Which insects include drones, queens and workers?
10 Has a violin four, six or eight strings?
11 Which actor Peter played crumple coated cop Columbo?
12 Fuzzy Zoeller was linked with which sport?
13 Where did Peter Mayle spend a year of his life?
14 In which county was the Plymouth Brethren founded?
15 Athena, Nike and Zeus were all what?
16 Which Keith is lead singer with the Prodigy?
17 As what name did John Elton Halliley act in Dad's Army?
18 Which Derby is run at the Curragh?
19 Who had a best friend with the politically incorrect name of Big Ears?
20 A lateen sail is what shape?
21 Revie, Robson, and Taylor have all managed which team?
22 Which valuable things were made by Thomas Sheraton?
23 On TV, Sabrina is the name of the Teenage... what?
24 Which musical instrument does Larry Adler play?
25 Tony Banks was Minister for what in Tony Blair's first Cabinet?
26 What type of crazy cops were created by Mack Sennett?
27 What do XL stand for in Roman numerals?
28 What's the foodie stage name of sizeable singer Marvin Lee Aday?
29 Brady, Macari and Stein have managed which Scottish soccer club?
30 What kind of animal is a fox terrier?

Answers

Geography: Euro Tour (see Quiz 57, page 67)
1 Spain. **2** Hovercraft. **3** Brussels. **4** Germany. **5** London. **6** Belgium. **7** Switzerland. **8** Athens. **9** Czech Republic. **10** Airport. **11** Portugal. **12** Germany. **13** Principality. **14** Spain. **15** Mediterranean. **16** USSR. **17** Venice. **18** Kingdom. **19** Danube. **20** Balearics. **21** Arctic Circle. **22** Netherlands. **23** Greece. **24** Denmark. **25** Second smallest. **26** Portugal. **27** Spain. **28** Paris. **29** Mountain ranges. **30** Corsica.

Quiz 59 Nature: Plant World

Answers - see Quiz 60, page 70

1 Where is water stored in a cactus plant?
2 Are most conifers evergreen or deciduous?
3 Ceps and chanterelles are types of what?
4 Flax is grown to produce which fabric?
5 Which drug is obtained from the coca plant?
6 Bamboo is the tallest type of what?
7 Which Mexican drink comes from the agave plant?
8 Is it true or false that laurel has poisonous leaves?
9 The petiole is on which part of a plant?
10 What colour is cuckoo spit?
11 Juniper is the flavouring in which drink?
12 What colour are oil seed rape flowers?
13 What goes before lavender and holly to make another plant's name?
14 What can be obtained from the cassava plant which would have gone in a typical school dinner pudding?
15 Harebells are usually what colour?
16 Does a polyanthus have a single or several blooms?
17 Which ingredient in tonic water comes from the bark of the cinchona?
18 Which plants would a viticulturist grow?
19 Wild cornflowers are usually what colour?
20 Which paintbrush cleaner is found in the resin of a conifer?
21 Which pear has the most protein?
22 In the garden what would you use secateurs for?
23 Do peanuts grow on trees or low plants?
24 What colour is chlorophyll?
25 In which Gardens is the Princess of Wales Conservatory?
26 Cacti are native to which continent?
27 What would you find in an arboretum?
28 Which fast grower is nicknamed the mile-a-minute vine?
29 Which yellow flower is nicknamed the Lent lily?
30 Which trees carry their seeds in cones?

Answers

Pot Luck 29 (see Quiz 60, page 70)
1 A will. **2** Four. **3** Warwick. **4** Lewis Collins. **5** Zwanzig. **6** Bryan Adams. **7** A cactus. **8** Brazil. **9** Street-Porter. **10** Australia. **11** Eight. **12** Black. **13** Landscape Gardening. **14** A size of paper. **15** Edward Woodward. **16** A herb. **17** River Niagara. **18** Snow White. **19** Horse racing. **20** Beef. **21** Purple. **22** Three. **23** Alaska. **24** Val Doonican. **25** Simple Simon. **26** Luke and Matt Goss. **27** A kind of plum. **28** Fourteen. **29** Lizzie. **30** Flattery.

Quiz 60 Pot Luck 29

Answers - see Quiz 59, page 69

1 If you die intestate you have not made what?
2 What's the least number of Mondays that can occur in July?
3 Which Derek partnered John Cleland at the Vauxhall Touring Cars Team?
4 In the TV series The Professionals, who played Bodie?
5 What is the German word for the number twenty?
6 Who had a No. 1 UK hit with Everything I do, I do it for You?
7 What is a prickly pear?
8 Romario starred in the 1994 World Cup for which country?
9 Media person Janet Bull changed her last name to what in her search for 'yoof'?
10 Bob Hawke was prime minister of which country?
11 How many coins of different denominations does Great Britain have?
12 What colour is sable in heraldry?
13 For what was Capability Brown famous?
14 What is foolscap?
15 On TV who played the Equaliser?
16 What kind of plant is marjoram?
17 On which River are the Niagara Falls?
18 Which Disney movie includes the song Heigh-Ho?
19 For which sport is Willie Carson famous?
20 Sirloin, Rump and Topside are all joints of which meat?
21 What colour is Tinky Winky in the Teletubbies?
22 How many leaves are on a shamrock?
23 Which American state is the largest in area?
24 Which singer was associated with a rocking chair?
25 According to the nursery rhyme, who met a pieman going to the fair?
26 Which two brothers made up the group Bros?
27 What is a bullace?
28 How many lines are in a sonnet?
29 A Model T Ford was nicknamed Tin what?
30 According to the proverb, imitation is the sincerest form of what?

Answers

Nature: Plant World (see Quiz 59, page 69)
1 Stem. **2** Evergreen. **3** Fungi. **4** Linen. **5** Cocaine. **6** Grass. **7** Tequila. **8** True. **9** Leaf stalk. **10** White. **11** Gin. **12** Yellow. **13** Sea. **14** Tapioca. **15** Blue. **16** Several. **17** Quinine. **18** Vines. **19** Blue. **20** Turpentine. **21** Avocado. **22** Cutting, pruning. **23** Low plants. **24** Green. **25** Kew. **26** America. **27** Trees. **28** Russian Vine. **29** Daffodil. **30** Conifers.

Quiz 61 Sporting Chance 2

Answers - see Quiz 62, page 72

1 What type of sport is eventing?
2 Which international side did Diego Maradona play for?
3 Phidippides was the first runner of which 26 mile race?
4 Which Stephen was the then youngest ever winner of a professional snooker title in 1987?
5 Did Evander Holyfield box at heavyweight or welterweight?
6 Which country did Virginia Leng represent at the Olympic Games?
7 FC Porto play football in which country?
8 At the USA PGA Championships, what game is played?
9 If you saw Benny the Dip win, what would you be watching?
10 At which sport might you see the American Williams sisters play?
11 Does the Le Mans 24 hour race take place in summer or winter?
12 In swimming, is freestyle usually performed on the back or front?
13 Which country won the first 25 America's Cup trophies in yachting?
14 In which sport is there a Foil discipline?
15 How was boxer Rocco Francis Marchegiano better known?
16 Caber tossing is native to which country?
17 What is the slowest swimming stroke?
18 For which national rugby side did Gavin Hastings play?
19 Magic Johnson found fame at which US sport?
20 Which horse race is sometimes called just The National?
21 What was tennis's Billie Jean Moffitt's married name?
22 Which Jackie's record of Grand Prix wins did Alain Prost pass in '87?
23 Which heavyweight Mike knocked out 15 of his first 25 pro opponents in the first round?
24 Which first name is shared by jockeys Carson and Shoemaker?
25 In which sport is a ball hit through a hoop with a mallet?
26 What is Scottish long distance runner Liz Lynch's married name?
27 What does the first F in FIFA stand for?
28 F1 driver Jacques Villeneuve is from which country?
29 Which winter sport can be alpine or Nordic?
30 Is the Oaks a race for colts or fillies?

Answers

Pot Luck 30 (see Quiz 62, page 72)

1 Two. **2** Mean. **3** Lettuce. **4** A flag. **5** An even number. **6** Fan-dabi-dozi. **7** Avocado pear. **8** The mirror. **9** Half a pound of tuppenny rice. **10** Eight. **11** A Watermelon. **12** Penny Black. **13** Judas. **14** Half a crown. **15** Zulu. **16** One. **17** The Alps. **18** Gold. **19** Pepper. **20** Westminster Abbey. **21** A knot. **22** Coffee. **23** Victory. **24** Bread. **25** Green. **26** The harp. **27** Blue. **28** White Star Line. **29** An element. **30** Queen Victoria.

Quiz 62 Pot Luck 30

Answers - see Quiz 61, page 71

1 How many people perform a pas de deux in a ballet?
2 If T is time what is M in G.M.T.?
3 Cos and Iceberg are varieties of which salad plant?
4 As well as being a TV programme, what is a Blue Peter?
5 What type of number will you always get if you add two odd numbers together?
6 What was the phrase associated with the duo the Krankies?
7 Which pear is usually served as a starter and is not sweet?
8 Who told the Queen that Snow White was the "fairest of them all"?
9 What is mixed with half a pound of treacle in Pop goes the Weasel?
10 How many furlongs are there in a mile?
11 Which melon has black pips and red juicy flesh?
12 What was the common name for the first postage stamp?
13 Which biblical character had the second name Iscariot?
14 What was the name for two shillings and sixpence?
15 What is the letter "Z" if A is Alpha and B is Bravo?
16 How many hooks do you use for crochet?
17 The Matterhorn is in which European mountain range?
18 What did Fort Knox originally store?
19 Steak au poivre is steak covered in what?
20 Where did the Queen's Coronation take place?
21 If you asked a Scout to make a sheep-shank, what would he make?
22 What drink is the main export from Brazil?
23 What was the name of Admiral Nelson's ship?
24 Chapatti is a kind of Indian what?
25 What colour is the door of the pub the Rovers Return?
26 Which stringed instrument has the most strings in an orchestra?
27 What colour is connected with the River Danube?
28 Which shipping line did Titanic belong to?
29 What is the name of the glowing curly wire in a light bulb?
30 At the start of the 20th century who was Queen of England?

Answers

Sporting Chance 2 (see Quiz 61, page 71)
1 Equestrian. **2** Argentina. **3** Marathon. **4** Hendry. **5** Heavyweight. **6** Great Britain. **7** Portugal. **8** Golf. **9** Horse racing. **10** Tennis. **11** Summer. **12** Front. **13** USA. **14** Fencing. **15** Rocky Marciano. **16** Scotland. **17** Breast stroke. **18** Scotland. **19** Basketball. **20** Grand National. **21** King. **22** Stewart. **23** Tyson. **24** Willie. **25** Croquet. **26** McColgan. **27** Federation. **28** Canada. **29** Skiing. **30** Fillies.

Quiz 63 Pop: Karaoke

Answers - see Quiz 64, page 74

1 Which Grease classic begins "I got chills, they're multiplyin'"?
2 What's the title of The Spice Girls hit which begins "I'll tell you what I want, what I really really want"?
3 What is the first line of Nessun Dorma?
4 What did Tina Turner sing after "Do I love you my oh my"?
5 What follows the Beatles "will you still need me, will you still feed me"?
6 Which song begins, "I feel it in my fingers, I feel it in my toes"?
7 In Candle in the Wind 98 " how are England's hills described?
8 How many times is "submarine" sung in the chorus of Yellow Submarine?
9 Which hit began "Oh my love, my darlin', I hunger for your touch"?
10 Which song's second line is "and so I face the final curtain"?
11 Which song begins "First I was afraid I was petrified"?
12 In which song did Tammy Wynette bemoan "Sometime it's hard to be a woman"?
13 Which Slade Xmas hit has the line "Everybody's having fun"?
14 In the Titanic song what follows, "Near, far, wherever you are, I believe..."?
15 What follows Bryan Adams "Everything I do"?
16 Which Dire Straits hit begins "Here comes Johnny"?
17 What follows "Two little boys had two little....."?
18 Which charity hit has the line "Feed the world"?
19 What follows The Spice Girls "swing it, shake it, move it, make it"?
20 Which Abba hit states "I was defeated you won the war"?
21 What do neighbours become in the Neighbours theme song?
22 What follows "I believe for every drop of rain that falls"?
23 Which football anthem speaks of "Jules Rimet still gleaming"?
24 Which song's second line is "I just called to say I care"?
25 Which Evita song begins, "It won't be easy, you'll think it strange"?
26 What did Boy George sing after singing karma five times?
27 Which Lion King song began "From the day we arrive on the planet"?
28 Which Simon & Garfunkel hit begins "When you're weary, feeling small"?
29 Which traditional song has the line, "The pipes, the pipes are calling"?
30 What are the last three words of Queen's We Are the Champions?

Answers

Pot Luck 31 (see Quiz 64, page 74)
1 The Peril. **2** Jennifer Paige. **3** Mint. **4** Soldier Sailor. **5** Calais. **6** Horse racing. **7** August. **8** Berkshire. **9** Trombone. **10** Tuesday. **11** VAT. **12** Bulb. **13** Yellow. **14** Cricket. **15** Andrew Lloyd Webber. **16** A constellation or galaxy. **17** Minestrone. **18** Champagne. **19** Little girls. **20** Patience. **21** They are poisonous. **22** Silver. **23** Ganges. **24** Tannic/Tannin. **25** Boots. **26** A house. **27** Please. **28** Red. **29** Norfolk. **30** Sherry.

Quiz 64 Pot Luck 31

Answers - see Quiz 63, page 73

1 If Dennis is the Menace what is Beryl?
2 Who had a huge UK hit in September 1998 with Crush?
3 Which sweet flavoured herb is often used to accompany roast lamb?
4 According to the rhyme, which two characters followed Tinker Tailor?
5 Which French port is closest to Britain?
6 To see which sport could you go to Towcester?
7 Lammas Day is in which month?
8 In which county is the Royal Military Academy at Sandhurst?
9 Which brass instrument has a sliding, adjustable tube?
10 Which day's child is "full of grace" according to the traditional rhyme?
11 Which current day tax replaced Purchase tax in 1973?
12 Is a snowdrop grown from a bulb or seed?
13 What colour is Laa Laa in the Teletubbies?
14 For which sport is David Gower famous?
15 Who composed the music for Cats?
16 What do we call a group of stars?
17 Which soup is made from a variety of vegetables and pasta?
18 What sort of drink is Moet & Chandon?
19 Maurice Chevalier "thanked heaven" for what?
20 Which has smaller cards, an ordinary pack or a patience pack?
21 What gives cause for concern about the seeds of a laburnum tree?
22 What colour is argent in heraldry?
23 The city of Calcutta stands on which river?
24 Tea contains which acid?
25 Which High Street chemists shop opened its first store in 1877?
26 What are you probably buying if you are gazumped?
27 What does the Italian "per favore" mean?
28 What colour, together with yellow, is the Spanish flag?
29 In which county was Lord Nelson born?
30 What kind of drink can be Bristol Cream?

Answers

Pop: Karaoke (see Quiz 63, page 73)
1 You're the One That I Want. **2** Wannabe. **3** Nessun dorma, nessun dorma. **4** River deep mountain high. **5** When I'm sixty four. **6** Love Is All Around. **7** Greenest. **8** Six. **9** Unchained Melody. **10** My Way. **11** I Will Survive. **12** Stand By Your Man. **13** Merry Christmas Everybody. **14** That the heart does go on. **15** I do it for you. **16** Walk of Life. **17** Toys. **18** Do They Know It's Christmas? **19** Who do you think you are? **20** Waterloo. **21** Good friends. **22** A flower grows. **23** Three Lions. **24** I Just Called to Say I Love You. **25** Don't Cry For Me Argentina. **26** Chameleon. **27** Circle of Life. **28** Bridge Over Troubled Water. **29** Danny Boy. **30** Of the world.

Quiz 65 TV Times 1

Answers - see Quiz 66, page 76

1 Which is the female half of Mulder and Scully?
2 What is the profession of TV's Two Fat Ladies?
3 What is the subject of the Channel 4 show Hooked?
4 Football Focus is a part of which Saturday sports programme?
5 What colour is Channel 5's logo?
6 Which Ally is a zany US TV lawyer?
7 What would Peter Cockcroft talk about on TV?
8 Who took over Gardener's World from the late Geoff Hamilton?
9 Which Australian co presents Animal Hospital?
10 Maureen Rees found TV fame at what type of School?
11 GMTV is usually seen at what time of day?
12 Which letters does TV's Kavanagh have after his name?
13 What sex is the audience of Chris Tarrant's show Man O Man?
14 Who first presented the celebrity version of Ready Steady Cook?
15 Which TV presenter is Johnny Ball's daughter?
16 Which Mary founded the Clean Up TV campaign in 1964?
17 Which female pop quintet launched Channel 5?
18 Does Food & Drink's Oz Clarke specialise in food or drink?
19 Which Jerry hosts a controversial talk show?
20 In which work location was the series The Hello Girls set?
21 Which Carol took over from Anne Robinson on Points of View?
22 What links Terry Wogan, Les Dawson and Lily Savage?
23 Which part of the country is served by Anglia Television?
24 Ground Force offered a viewer a makeover in which part of the home?
25 Who is presenter Julia Carling's ex-husband?
26 'It's good to talk' was the ad slogan of which phone company?
27 Who is taller, Michael Barrymore or Ronnie Corbett?
28 Which broadcasting corporation is known as Auntie?
29 On which channel is Panorama broadcast?
30 Who is the human half of Wallace and Gromit?

Answers

Pot Luck 32 (see Quiz 66, page 76)
1 Darts. **2** The farmer's wife. **3** Organ. **4** Diamonds. **5** Broken. **6** All Saints. **7** 1984. **8** Apples. **9** Rutland. **10** Lady and the Tramp. **11** Blue Peter. **12** Hops. **13** Pears. **14** Saviour's Day. **15** Paul Merton. **16** White. **17** He was married. **18** Torvill & Dean. **19** Eight. **20** Dance steps. **21** A plant. **22** Richard. **23** Red. **24** Birmingham. **25** Three. **26** Bank of England. **27** Goodwood. **28** Champagne. **29** A bulb. **30** New York.

Quiz 66 Pot Luck 32

Answers - see Quiz 65, page 75

1 For which sport is Eric Bristow famous?
2 According to the nursery rhyme, who cut off the three mice tails?
3 Which is the largest musical instrument which has a keyboard?
4 What is mined at Kimberley in South Africa?
5 What does a German mean if he says something is "kaput"?
6 Who had a No. 1 UK hit in September 1998 with Bootie Call?
7 Which George Orwell novel has a year as its title?
8 Cider is made from which fruit?
9 What was the smallest county in England until 1974?
10 Which Disney movie includes the song He's A Tramp?
11 Which children's TV series was forty years old in October 1998?
12 What is dried in Kentish oast houses?
13 Which fruit can be served Belle Helene?
14 Which Day gave Cliff Richard a No. 1 for Christmas 1990?
15 Who is older Paul Merson or Paul Merton?
16 What colour along with red and blue is the Luxembourg flag?
17 What happened to Solomon Grundy on Wednesday, according to the rhyme?
18 Which Olympic ice skating duo danced to Ravel's Bolero?
19 On the Union Jack, how many blue triangles are there?
20 What does a choreographer plan?
21 What is a yucca?
22 In pop music, who is Jagger's long time writing partner?
23 What colour is Po in the Teletubbies?
24 Crossroads was set near which major city?
25 How many people are in a boat in a rowing coxed pair race?
26 What is sometimes called the 'Old Lady of Threadneedle Street'?
27 Which race meeting is known as 'Glorious'?
28 What was invented by Dom Peter Perignon, a French monk?
29 Is a tulip grown from seed or a bulb?
30 Which American city has the Yankees and Mets baseball teams?

Answers

TV Times (see Quiz 65, page 75)
1 Scully. **2** Cooks. **3** Fishing. **4** Grandstand. **5** Yellow. **6** McBeal. **7** Weather. **8** Alan Titchmarsh. **9** Rolf Harris. **10** Driving School. **11** Morning. **12** QC. **13** Female. **14** Fern Britton. **15** Zoe Ball. **16** Whitehouse. **17** The Spice Girls. **18** Drink. **19** Springer. **20** Telephone Exchange. **21** Vorderman. **22** Blankety Blank. **23** East Anglia. **24** Garden. **25** Will Carling. **26** BT. **27** Michael Barrymore. **28** BBC. **29** BBC 1. **30** Wallace.

Quiz 67 Sporting Chance 3

Answers - see Quiz 68, page 78

1 What is the surname of German F1 drivers Ralph and Michael?
2 Which jump event did Carl Lewis specialise in as well as sprinting?
3 What colour is the cover of the Rothman's Football Yearbook?
4 Is professional badminton an indoor or outdoor game or both?
5 What was the professional name of boxer Joe Louis Barrow?
6 Who won the European Cup-winner's Cup in 1998?
7 Of the 197 teams invited to the 1996 Olympics, how many accepted?
8 At which sport did suspended Irish Olympic gold medal winner Michelle de Bruin compete?
9 Which horned animal name does Leeds' Rugby Super League team have?
10 In which sport might you hit another living thing with a crop?
11 Peter O'Sullevan commentated on which sport?
12 Which Rugby side shares its name with stinging insects?
13 Which red flower is the emblem of the England Rugby Union team?
14 In which country is the golfing venue Valderrama?
15 Which motoring Grand Prix is held at the Hungaroring?
16 What's the highest score in darts from three different doubles?
17 In which country is the oldest football league in the world?
18 Which area of New York has a Globetrotters basketball team?
19 Which Bin was introduced for Rugby League players in 1983?
20 How many disciplines are there in a biathlon?
21 In which Sheffield theatre were the World Snooker Championships first held in 1977?
22 In which country was judo coincidentally added to the Olympic programme?
23 In badminton what were goose feathers used for?
24 What is the usual surface of the lane in ten pin bowling?
25 Which German Men's Wimbledon champion was born on Billie Jean King's 23rd birthday?
26 Which positive statement did Magic Johnson make prior to temporary retirement?
27 On what surface is curling played?
28 Which animal is on top of Rugby's Calcutta Cup?
29 In which sport would you wear a judogi?
30 What type of sporting event was The Rumble in the Jungle?

Answers

Pot Luck 33 (see Quiz 68, page 78)
1 Red. **2** A hat. **3** Liver. **4** Julie Walters. **5** The Severn Estuary. **6** Music. **7** Swimming. **8** Tower of London. **9** Peter Sellers. **10** New York. **11** A beetle. **12** Isle of Dogs. **13** Hastings. **14** African. **15** Dudley Moore. **16** Robson and Jerome. **17** Antelope. **18** Linen. **19** Red. **20** The Bill. **21** Saddam Hussein. **22** Spitting Image. **23** Vauxhall. **24** A bull. **25** Four. **26** Sheffield. **27** Chippendale. **28** None. **29** Trotters. **30** Australia.

Quiz 68 Pot Luck 33

Answers - see Quiz 67, page 77

1 What colour is Michael Aspel's book on This is your Life?
2 What is a tam-o'-shanter?
3 Which organ is particularly affected by hepatitis?
4 Who played the title role in the film Educating Rita?
5 On which river estuary does Swansea stand?
6 The letters F.R.A.M. mean a Fellow of which Royal Academy?
7 For which sport was Duncan Goodhew famous?
8 The raven is traditionally associated with which Tower?
9 Who played Inspector Clouseau in the Pink Panther films?
10 In which country is the Big Apple?
11 What is a cockchafer?
12 Which animal isle is in the River Thames?
13 Where did a famous battle take place in 1066?
14 Which elephants are the largest - African or Indian?
15 Which English musician and comedian married Tuesday Weld?
16 Who released I Believe coupled with Up On The Roof?
17 What kind of mammal is a chamois?
18 Which fabric is produced from flax?
19 Does coq au vin contain red or white wine?
20 Which TV series is set in Sun Hill police station?
21 During the Gulf War, who was the leader of Iraq?
22 Which TV puppet programme makes fun of politicians?
23 Which car maker has the same name as a London bridge?
24 Which animal should you take by the horns, according to the proverb?
25 How many pins are in the back row of a ten pin bowling triangle?
26 Which city is furthest North - Bristol or Sheffield?
27 Which of Chippendale, Ming and Wedgwood is not a type of pottery?
28 How much gold is there in a one pound coin?
29 What are a pig's feet called?
30 Of which country's coast is the world's largest coral reef?

Answers

Sporting Chance 3 (see Quiz 67, page 77)
1 Schumacher. **2** Long jump. **3** Blue. **4** Indoor. **5** Joe Louis. **6** Chelsea FC. **7** 197. **8** Swimming. **9** Rhinos. **10** Equestrianism. **11** Horse racing. **12** Wasps. **13** Rose. **14** Spain. **15** Hungarian. **16** 114. **17** England. **18** Harlem. **19** Sin bin. **20** Two. **21** Crucible. **22** Japan. **23** Shuttlecock. **24** Wood. **25** Boris Becker. **26** First basketball player to say he was HIV positive. **27** Ice. **28** Elephant. **29** Judo. **30** Boxing match.

Quiz 69 Movies: The Brits

Answers - see Quiz 70, page 80

1 What was the Spice Girls' first film?
2 Who with The Shadows starred in The Young Ones?
3 Which movie told of redundant steel workers becoming strippers?
4 The Bridge on the River Kwai prisoners are imprisoned by whom?
5 Nick Hornby's Fever Pitch is about which game?
6 Which Kenneth directed and starred in Hamlet?
7 The Blue Lamp preceded which TV series about PC George Dixon?
8 A BAFTA is a British Award for film and what?
9 What nationality was The...Patient in the 1996 Oscar winner?
10 Which US food expert Loyd is the son in law of David Puttnam?
11 Mrs Blake Edwards won an Oscar for Mary Poppins; who was she?
12 What is the nationality of Sir Anthony Hopkins?
13 In which part of the UK was Trainspotting set?
14 Which British Transport Minister twice won an Oscar?
15 Which Sir Richard directed Chaplin?
16 Which 1994 British hit shot Hugh Grant to superstardom?
17 Which Emma wrote the screenplay for Sense & Sensibility?
18 Jenny Agutter found fame in which movie about an Edwardian family?
19 Is Helena Bonham Carter a British Prime Minister's or a US President's grand daughter?
20 Elizabeth Taylor was twice married to this Welsh actor; who was he?
21 Who was born Maurice Micklewhite but is perhaps best known as Alfie?
22 Which Julie was Oscar nominated in 1998?
23 Which Ewan plays the young Obi Wan Kenobi in Episode I of Star Wars
24 In which film did Tom Conti play Pauline Collins' Greek lover?
25 Which blonde bombshell was born Diana Fluck?
26 Linus Roache's father has played which Coronation Street character since the soap began?
27 Who or what was the film Wilde with Stephen Fry about?
28 In which film did Joanna Lumley play Shirley's old school friend?
29 In which part of the UK was Robert Carlyle born?
30 Hot Chocolate's You Sexy Thing was the theme for which 1997 film?

Answers

Pot Luck 34 (see Quiz 70, page 80)

1 France. **2** Windsor Castle. **3** Yogi Bear. **4** Lime. **5** Badminton. **6** Oysters. **7** Norman Watts. **8** Five. **9** Four. **10** Coronation. **11** Flock together. **12** Poet. **13** Ten shilling note. **14** Javelin. **15** Cornwall. **16** A catamaran. **17** Eeyore. **18** L. S. **19** An apple. **20** Europe, Asia. **21** Elizabeth I. **22** Yachting. **23** Yugoslavia. **24** Goat. **25** Leeds. **26** Peppermint. **27** The humming bird. **28** Cricket. **29** Michael & Janet. **30** Bottom.

Quiz 70 Pot Luck 34

Answers - see Quiz 69, page 79

1 The Dauphin was heir to which European throne?
2 Which castle was partly damaged by fire in 1992?
3 Which bear had a friend called Boo Boo?
4 What is the another name for a linden tree?
5 Which sport is named after a place which is famous for horse trials?
6 The precious stone, a pearl, can be found in what?
7 What is Curly's proper character name in Coronation Street?
8 How many senior titles (excluding over 35 events) are contested each Wimbledon?
9 How many passenger terminals does Heathrow Airport have?
10 At which ceremony is a Monarch given their crown?
11 According to the saying, what do birds of a feather do?
12 Was Ted Hughes a dancer, painter or poet?
13 Which British bank note stopped being available in 1970?
14 For which sport is Tessa Sanderson famous?
15 Prince Charles is Duke of which English county?
16 What is a yacht with two hulls called?
17 Which character from Winnie The Pooh lost his tail?
18 What two initials did northern artist Lowry have?
19 What did William Tell shoot from his son's head with a crossbow?
20 Which continents are separated by the Urals?
21 Who was England's Queen when Shakespeare was alive?
22 Cowes on the Isle of Wight is famous for which sport?
23 Which country was formerly ruled by President Tito?
24 Which animal's milk is used to make cheese called Chevre?
25 Which city is furthest North – Lincoln or Leeds?
26 What flavour is Kendal's most famous cake?
27 Which is the only bird that can fly backwards?
28 What is John Major's favourite sport?
29 Which Jacksons recorded Scream?
30 Which part of your body is a character in Shakespeare's A Midsummer Night's Dream?

Answers

Movies: The Brits (see Quiz 69, page 79)
1 Spiceworld The Movie. **2** Cliff Richard. **3** The Full Monty. **4** Japanese. **5** Football. **6** Branagh. **7** Dixon of Dock Green. **8** Television. **9** English. **10** Grossman. **11** Julie Andrews. **12** Welsh. **13** Scotland. **14** Glenda Jackson. **15** Attenborough. **16** Four Weddings and a Funeral. **17** Thompson. **18** The Railway Children. **19** British Prime Minister's. **20** Richard Burton. **21** Michael Caine. **22** Christie. **23** McGregor. **24** Shirley Valentine. **25** Diana Dors. **26** Ken Barlow. **27** Oscar Wilde. **28** Shirley Valentine. **29** Scotland. **30** The Full Monty.

Quiz 71 Leisure: Home & D-I-Y

Answers - see Quiz 72, page 82

1 What sort of security device is a Chubb?
2 An Entryphone would normally be found at the entrance to what?
3 What in the bedroom would have a TOG rating?
4 What colour is Copydex adhesive?
5 What is the abbreviation for volt?
6 Is pine a soft or hard wood?
7 Which machine tool is used for turning wood?
8 Do weft fibres run across the width or the length of a fabric?
9 What goes between a nut and the surface to protect it?
10 Soldering joins two pieces of what?
11 Cushions, curtains etc. are referred to as what sort of furnishings?
12 Should silk be washed in hot or cool water?
13 Which tool can be band, hand or hack?
14 E numbers refer to additives to what?
15 Is an emery cloth rough or smooth?
16 Which device turns off an appliance when a temperature is reached?
17 A rasp is a type of what?
18 Is Araldite a strong or light glue?
19 In which sort of bank would you deposit waste glass?
20 Canning, bottling and freezing are types of what?
21 What would a bradawl produce in wood?
22 Batik is a type of dyeing on what?
23 What would you normally make in a percolator?
24 Where is the door on a chest freezer?
25 A bedsit usually consists of how many rooms?
26 What type of electrical devices are 'white goods'?
27 Is a kilogram less or more than two pounds in weight?
28 What colour does silver turn when it is tarnished?
29 Which wood is darker, mahogany or ash?
30 What does the ply of a yarn refer to?

Answers

Pot Luck 35 (see Quiz 72, page 82)
1 George Bush. **2** Sheffield. **3** Dock. **4** North Sea. **5** Angela Lansbury. **6** China. **7** Lines of longitude. **8** Scotland. **9** Glasgow. **10** Furniture. **11** Buttons. **12** Red Rum. **13** Daisy. **14** De Lorean. **15** Blubber. **16** Red. **17** Bob Dylan. **18** Birds of a Feather. **19** Chocolate. **20** Roy Rogers. **21** Decathlon. **22** King John. **23** Scotland. **24** Erasure. **25** A crop. **26** White. **27** At the beginning. **28** Sand. **29** Four. **30** Train.

Quiz 72 Pot Luck 35

Answers - see Quiz 71, page 81

1 Who was the last President of the USA elected in the 1980s?
2 Which city is furthest North – Cardiff or Sheffield?
3 Which plant helps to take away the sting of a stinging nettle?
4 The River Forth flows into which Sea?
5 Which actress plays Jessica Fletcher in Murder She Wrote?
6 Which country was ruled by Chairman Mao?
7 What name is given to the imaginary lines drawn from north to south on a map?
8 Where in Britain can you spend paper £1 notes?
9 What is Rab C. Nesbitt's city?
10 Thomas Sheraton was a designer and manufacturer of what?
11 Which came first, zips, velcro or buttons?
12 Which horse named after a drink won the Grand National three times?
13 What was the name of Donald Duck's girlfriend?
14 What make of car was featured in the movie Back to the Future?
15 What is the fat of a whale called?
16 Which is the warmest sea in the world, The Red, Med or Dead?
17 Who wrote the pop anthem Knockin' On Heaven's Door?
18 Who or what flock together according to the saying?
19 What is the flavour of a Devil's Food Cake?
20 Which cowboy had a horse called Trigger?
21 For which sport is Daley Thompson famous?
22 Which King put his seal on the Magna Carta?
23 Which is nearest to Ireland, England, Scotland or Wales?
24 Abba-Esque wasn't a No. 1 for Abba, but it was for which group?
25 What is a horse rider's whip called?
26 What colour balls were used at Wimbledon before yellow balls?
27 Where would you expect to hear the prologue in a play?
28 Which of the following will not dissolve in water, salt, sugar or sand?
29 How many teats does a cow have normally?
30 Was the Flying Fortress a plane or a train?

Answers

Leisure: Home & D-I-Y (see Quiz 71, page 81)
1 Lock. **2** Block of flats. **3** Duvet. **4** White. **5** V. **6** Soft. **7** Lathe. **8** Width. **9** Washer. **10** Metal. **11** Soft furnishings. **12** Cool. **13** Saw. **14** Food. **15** Rough. **16** Thermostat. **17** File. **18** Strong. **19** Bottle bank. **20** Preserving. **21** Hole. **22** Fabric. **23** Coffee. **24** Top. **25** One. **26** Large kitchen appliances, such as freezers and washing machines. **27** More. **28** Black. **29** Mahogany. **30** Its thickness.

Quiz 73 Pop: The 90s

Answers - see Quiz 74, page 84

1 Which football anthem was co written by Skinner and Baddiel?
2 What is the surname of Oasis brothers Noel and Liam?
3 Who was Candle in the Wind 1997 dedicated to?
4 Which Zoo sang Spaceman in 1996?
5 In which drama series did chart toppers Robson & Jerome find fame?
6 Isaac, Taylor and Zac make up which boy band?
7 Who said 'Eh Oh' on the their first smash hit?
8 Whose album of Urban Hymns hit the top spot?
9 Which 90s band were named after an area of London?
10 Knockin' On Heaven's Door was released after which 1996 tragedy?
11 Which single was released by Robson & Jerome and two years later by The Three Tenors?
12 Who was 'Older' in the 90s after a long running battle with Sony?
13 Who were Back For Good in 1995 before disbanding altogether?
14 Whose death propelled Bohemian Rhapsody back to the charts?
15 Which Peter had a No 1 with Flava?
16 Who had a No 1 with Nilsson's Without You?
17 Who backed Katrina on her 1997 Eurovision winner?
18 Which Damon fronted Blur?
19 Who starred in and sang on the soundtrack of The Bodyguard?
20 In September '98 Celine Dion released an album in which language?
21 Which toy provided Aqua with a No 1?
22 Which country singer John died flying his plane in 1997?
23 Who had a daughter Lourdes Maria in 1996?
24 Which band's name is a US emergency number?
25 Dana International won Eurovision 98 for which Middle East country?
26 Oasis were formed in which UK city?
27 Who had a huge hit with Drop Dead Gorgeous?
28 Which Darren appeared in the 90s version of Summer Holiday?
29 In which county were Blur formed?
30 My Heart Will Go On came from which smash hit film?

Answers

Pot Luck 36 (see Quiz 74, page 84)
1 Tasmania. **2** Balsawood. **3** Tennis. **4** The candlestick maker. **5** Up. **6** Roald Dahl. **7** Hindu. **8** St. David. **9** USA. **10** 1940s. **11** Davy Crockett. **12** Polo. **13** Shoes. **14** South Pacific. **15** George Bush. **16** Silver. **17** A stone. **18** Sweets. **19** St Ives. **20** 240. **21** Four. **22** Jacobites. **23** Touché. **24** Rainbow. **25** Avon. **26** Boots. **27** Black and yellow. **28** Javelin. **29** One. **30** Chester.

Quiz 74 **Pot Luck 36**

Answers - see Quiz 73, page 83

1 Which Australian state is named after its discoverer Abel Tasman?
2 Which very soft wood is popular with model makers?
3 Which sport was played by Gabriela Sabatini?
4 According to the nursery rhyme, who joined the butcher and baker?
5 Do bananas grow pointing up or down?
6 Who wrote Charlie and the Chocolate Factory?
7 The River Ganges is sacred to the people of which religion?
8 Which Saint is the patron saint of Wales?
9 Which country was the 1994 football World Cup Final played in?
10 Was Terry Venables born in the 1940s, 1950s or the 1960s?
11 Which American hero wore a hat with a racoon tail hanging from the back?
12 Which sport is played on the largest pitch: cricket, football or polo?
13 What are or were winkle pickers?
14 Which part of an ocean shares its name with a musical?
15 Who was American president immediately before Bill Clinton?
16 Which metal is the FA Cup made from?
17 What did David throw from his sling to kill Goliath?
18 What do American children mean if they ask for candy?
19 Where was the person going, who met a man with seven wives?
20 Electricity comes into our homes at how many volts?
21 In the neck of a violin how many tuning pegs are there?
22 What were supporters of James II and his Stuart descendants called?
23 What is shouted by people when they make contact in fencing?
24 Which children's TV programme featured Bungle and Zippy?
25 Which English county shares its name with a beauty products range?
26 Which is the largest chain of chemist shops in the world?
27 What colour is Rupert the Bear's scarf?
28 For which sport was Fatima Whitbread famous?
29 How many players take part in a game of patience at any one time?
30 Which city is furthest north – Bristol or Chester?

Answers

Pop: The 90s (see Quiz 73, page 83)
1 Three Lions. **2** Gallagher. **3** Diana, Princess of Wales. **4** Babylon Zoo. **5** Soldier Soldier. **6** Hanson. **7** Teletubbies. **8** The Verve. **9** East 17. **10** Dunblane. **11** You'll Never Walk Alone. **12** George Michael. **13** Take That. **14** Freddie Mercury. **15** Andre. **16** Mariah Carey. **17** The Waves. **18** Albarn. **19** Whitney Houston. **20** French. **21** Barbie. **22** Denver. **23** Madonna. **24** 911. **25** Israel. **26** Manchester. **27** Republica. **28** Day. **29** Essex. **30** Titanic.

Quiz 75 People & Places

Answers - see Quiz 76, page 86

1 In which World War was the Home Guard founded?
2 In which country were the Borgias a powerful family?
3 Benazir Bhutto was Prime Minister of which Muslim state?
4 Which Al was crime boss of Chicago during the Prohibition?
5 Which South African shared the Nobel Peace Prize with FW de Klerk in 1993?
6 What was President John F Kennedy's wife called?
7 What did Anthony Wedgwood Benn become known as?
8 In which country was Terry Waite imprisoned?
9 Roman Emperor Hadrian gave his name to what in Britain?
10 Which animals did Hannibal use to frighten the Romans?
11 Hirohito was Emperor of which country during WWII?
12 Which Russian word for Caesar was used by Russian monarchs?
13 Where was T.E. Lawrence involved in an independence struggle?
14 Which Russian revolutionary took his name from the River Lena?
15 When did Columbus discover America?
16 Which 11thC Scottish king was the subject of a Shakespeare play?
17 In which country of the UK was David Livingstone born?
18 Which British admiral Horatio was born in Norfolk?
19 Where is Botany Bay?
20 Which country put the first woman in space?
21 Which journalist John was imprisoned in Beirut with Brian Keenan?
22 What was Argentinean vice president Eva Duarte's married name?
23 Ho Chi Minh founded the Communist Party in which country?
24 Which English Quaker founded the colony of Pennsylvania?
25 Which African country was bombed on the orders of Ronald Reagan in 1986?
26 In which country was Joan of Arc born?
27 Where was the tomb of Tutankhamun discovered in 1922?
28 Which famous Indian monument was built by Shah Jahan?
29 Zulu leader Buthelezi became a government minister where?
30 Which nurse is famous for her work during the Crimean War?

Answers

Pot Luck 37 (see Quiz 76, page 86)
1 Golf. **2** Marzipan. **3** Rural England. **4** Two. **5** 22. **6** Putty. **7** Roger Bannister. **8** Ballet. **9** Glasgow. **10** Eleven. **11** Des O'Connor. **12** A skateboard. **13** Carrot. **14** Gymnasts. **15** Billy Butlin. **16** The sea. **17** A fiddle. **18** Cookery. **19** Canada. **20** 19th. **21** Collar bone. **22** Victoria. **23** The service. **24** Forget. **25** Grass. **26** Kill You. **27** A Swiss cheese. **28** Spain. **29** The knight. **30** Red and black.

Quiz 76 Pot Luck 37

Answers - see Quiz 75, page 85

1 Which sport is Sandy Lyle famous for playing?
2 What name is given to the almond coating often on a Christmas cake?
3 C.P.R.E. is the Council for the Protection of what?
4 How many Bank Holidays are there in May?
5 How many yards are there between the wickets in cricket?
6 What sticky paste usually holds glass in a window?
7 Who was the first person to run a mile in under four minutes?
8 What is performed by the Russian Bolshoi company?
9 Which Scottish city has the biggest population?
10 How many players can a team have on the field in American football?
11 Which Des invited contestants on the TV programme to Take Your Pick?
12 What has a kicktail and four wheels?
13 Which vegetable, high in vitamin A, is said to be good for the eyes?
14 What kind of athletes perform a flic-flac?
15 Who set up England's biggest chain of holiday camps?
16 Neptune was the god of what?
17 According to the saying, which instrument can you be as fit as?
18 What type of TV programmes are presented by Keith Floyd?
19 Which is biggest – the USA, Germany or Canada?
20 Was basketball developed in the 17th, 18th or 19th century?
21 What is the common name for the clavicle?
22 Africa's biggest lake is named after which British queen?
23 What is the name given to the first hit in a game of tennis?
24 What do elephants never do according to the saying?
25 Bamboo is a very large variety of what?
26 What will too much love do, according to Brian May?
27 What is Emmenthal?
28 In which country were the 1992 Summer Olympic Games held?
29 Which chess piece is shaped like a horse's head?
30 What two colours are Dennis the Menace's sweater?

Answers

People & Places (see Quiz 75, page 85)
1 Second. **2** Italy. **3** Pakistan. **4** Capone. **5** Nelson Mandela. **6** Jackie. **7** Tony Benn. **8** Lebanon. **9** Hadrian's Wall. **10** Elephants. **11** Japan. **12** Tsar. **13** Arabia. **14** Lenin. **15** 1492. **16** Macbeth. **17** Scotland. **18** Nelson. **19** Australia. **20** USSR. **21** McCarthy. **22** Peron. **23** Vietnam. **24** Penn. **25** Libya. **26** France. **27** Egypt. **28** Taj Mahal. **29** South Africa. **30** Florence Nightingale.

Quiz 77 TV Times 2

Answers - see Quiz 78, page 88

1 On which type of show is Ainsley Harriott most likely to appear?
2 Which Carol was the first presenter of Changing Rooms?
3 Which washing up liquid did Nanette Newman famously advertise?
4 Which programme is often referred to simply as Corrie?
5 Which Zoe succeeded Gaby Roslin on The Big Breakfast?
6 Which impersonator Rory starred in Who Else?
7 Who is Mrs Richard Madely who appears on This Morning?
8 Which Fiona succeeded Anthea Turner on GMTV's morning sofa?
9 In which country is Ballykissangel set?
10 Scriptwriter Carla Lane is famous for campaigning on whose behalf?
11 Who was the BT housewife in the ads as played by Maureen Lipman?
12 In which show did David Jason call Nicholas Lyndhurst a plonker?
13 Which Rik was involved in a quad bike accident in 1998?
14 Which Have I Got News For You? star's real name is Paul Martin?
15 Which Helen appeared nude on the cover of Radio Times to celebrate her 50th birthday?
16 Who was the taller in the Peter Cook and Dudley Moore partnership?
17 Did Bob Monkhouse celebrate his 60th, 70th or 80th birthday in a TV special in 1998?
18 Who is Paul O'Grady's blonde, cigarette smoking alter ego?
19 What is the occupation of Bramwell in the TV series?
20 Who was the regular presenter of The Cook Report?
21 Who is Reeves' TV comedy partner?
22 In which show would you see the neighbour-from-hell Dorien Green?
23 Which TV cook went on tour on The Rhodes Show?
24 What is the first name of Prime Suspect writer La Plante?
25 Which morning show did Chris Evans and Gaby Roslin present?
26 Which TV astronomer was born Patrick Caldwell-Moore?
27 What is the surname of sister presenters Anthea and Wendy?
28 Who presented The Full Wax?
29 Which Victorian drama series has a hospital called The Thrift?
30 Laurence Llewelyn-Bowen is a TV expert on what?

Answers

Pot Luck 38 (see Quiz 78, page 88)

1 Hovercraft. **2** Three. **3** A mole. **4** Makepeace. **5** Jersey. **6** George Graham. **7** Rats. **8** The Bermuda Triangle. **9** Wheel clamps. **10** Maple. **11** Guinevere. **12** Newcastle. **13** Hiawatha. **14** A gas. **15** Four. **16** Peacocks. **17** Enid Blyton. **18** A harmonica. **19** Debbie McGee. **20** The bully-off. **21** Yellow. **22** Coca-Cola. **23** Golf. **24** A river. **25** Roller skates. **26** Boxing. **27** Squirrel. **28** Brown. **29** Three. **30** The Muppets.

Quiz 78 Pot Luck 38

Answers - see Quiz 77, page 87

1 In 1959, what kind of vehicle crossed the Channel for the first time?
2 How many minutes are there per round in professional boxing?
3 Which animal built the hill that William III's horse stumbled on?
4 Which is female, Dempsey or Makepeace?
5 Which Channel Isle is famous for very creamy milk?
6 Which soccer boss left Arsenal following 'bung' allegations?
7 Which animals do sailors say desert a sinking ship?
8 Which triangle are ships and planes said to disappear in?
9 What were used on illegally parked cars for the first time in 1983?
10 The leaf from which tree is a logo for Air Canada?
11 Who was the legendary King Arthur's wife?
12 The TV series Byker Grove is set in which city?
13 Which Red Indian married Laughing Water?
14 What does a liquid turn into if it is heated up?
15 How many people take part in each heat of Blind Date?
16 A muster is a collection of what type of birds?
17 Who wrote about Noddy and Big Ears?
18 What is the proper name for a mouth organ?
19 Who is Paul Daniels' wife?
20 What is the start of a hockey match called?
21 What colour was Bobby Shafto's hair in the nursery rhyme?
22 Which popular drink was invented by Dr John Pemberton?
23 Which sport did Sam Snead play?
24 What is the Tigris?
25 In Starlight Express what do the performers wear on their feet?
26 Which sport is featured in the Rocky movies?
27 Which animal family do chipmunks belong to?
28 What colour is umber?
29 How many of Henry VIII's wives were called Catherine?
30 Which puppet show has two old men called Statler and Waldorf?

Answers

TV Times 2 (see Quiz 77, page 87)

1 Cookery. **2** Smillie. **3** Fairy liquid. **4** Coronation Street. **5** Ball. **6** Bremner. **7** Judy Finnegan. **8** Phillips. **9** Ireland. **10** Animals. **11** Beattie. **12** Only Fools and Horses. **13** Mayall. **14** Paul Merton. **15** Mirren. **16** Peter Cook. **17** 70th. **18** Lily Savage. **19** Doctor. **20** Roger Cook. **21** Mortimer. **22** Birds of a Feather. **23** Gary Rhodes. **24** Lynda. **25** The Big Breakfast. **26** Patrick Moore. **27** Turner. **28** Ruby Wax. **29** Bramwell. **30** Home decorating.

Quiz 79 Summer Sports

Answers - see Quiz 80, page 90

1 Which sport are the Lord's Taverners famous for playing?
2 Which Denise won European gold in the heptathlon in '98?
3 Who was the last British Wimbledon champion?
4 Sergey Bubka has set a world record in which field event over 30 times?
5 Which British tennis star reached the Wimbledon semi finals in 1998?
6 Which summer sport did Kerry Packer revolutionise in the 70s?
7 Who has won more Major golf titles than any other player?
8 Chris Boardman suffered an accident riding what in summer 1998?
9 Which country staged the summer Olympics in 1984 and 1996?
10 Between 1990 and 1998 all Ladies Wimbledon Singles champions were born in which continent?
11 The summer Olympics are held every how many years?
12 In cricket, what must a ball not do to score six runs?
13 Jonathan Edwards specialises in what type of jump?
14 For which international side did Shane Warne play cricket?
15 Which golfer is known as the Great White Shark?
16 Which Martina did Martinez beat in the 1994 Wimbledon final?
17 Which Tour is the world's premier cycling event?
18 Which German tennis player's father Peter was jailed for tax fraud?
19 Sonia O'Sullivan races for which country?
20 How many runners are there in the 400m relay team?
21 Which Jana won Wimbledon 98 after her third final?
22 You would do a Fosbury flop in which athletics event?
23 Which country has the oldest cricket competition in the world?
24 How many balls an over are there in cricket?
25 Who told a Wimbledon umpire "You cannot be serious!"?
26 Which West Indian cricketer was called Vivian?
27 Who shattered Roger Maris's all-time Baseball home run record in '98
28 Which Jimmy won Wimbledon doubles with Ilie Nastase?
29 What was the nationality of tennis pin up Gabriela Sabatini?
30 Which team competes against America in the Ryder Cup?

Answers

Pot Luck 39 (see Quiz 80, page 90)
1 Wrestling. **2** Stirrups. **3** Dogger Bank. **4** Nine. **5** US President. **6** Perception. **7** Scandinavia. **8** One. **9** He was bald. **10** Animated cartoons. **11** A reservoir. **12** A spider. **13** The 1812 Overture. **14** 14th February. **15** Hundred Acres Wood. **16** Victoria. **17** Four. **18** Moses. **19** The Pacific Ocean. **20** Teeth. **21** Harvey. **22** The maiden all forlorn. **23** Arms. **24** Show jumping. **25** Worms. **26** Four. **27** Jade. **28** Four. **29** A collage. **30** Sixpence.

Quiz 80 Pot Luck 39

Answers - see Quiz 79, page 89

1 With which sport is Hulk Hogan associated?
2 What are the metal loops that you place your feet in when horse riding?
3 Which bank is a dangerous sand bar in the North Sea?
4 How many players are there in a rounders team?
5 Whose official plane is Air Force One?
6 What does the letter P stand for in ESP?
7 Which group of countries did the Vikings come from?
8 How many Popes have been English – one, two or three?
9 What colour was Kojak's hair?
10 What kind of programmes are Hanna and Barbara famous for?
11 What is a man-made lake in which water is stored called?
12 What type of creature is a Black Widow?
13 Which overture has a date in its title and includes cannons and bells?
14 On what date did the St. Valentine's Day Massacre take place?
15 Winnie the Pooh lived in which wood?
16 Melbourne is the capital of which Australian State?
17 How many walls surround a squash court?
18 In The Bible, who parted the sea?
19 Fiji is in which ocean?
20 Which part of your body has a coating of enamel?
21 Which Mr Goldsmith promotes rock concerts?
22 Who milked the cow with the crumpled horn, in the rhyme?
23 Which part of the Venus de Milo's body are missing?
24 In which sport are Michael and John Whitaker famous?
25 Would a vermicide be used to kill worms or mice?
26 How many presidents' faces are carved into Mount Rushmore?
27 Which green stone was buried by the Chinese with their dead?
28 How many New Testament Gospels are there?
29 What word describes a picture made from sticking scraps onto a background?
30 Which English coin was nicknamed the tanner?

Answers

Summer Sports (see Quiz 79, page 89)
1 Cricket. **2** Lewis. **3** Fred Perry. **4** Pole vault. **5** Tim Henman. **6** Cricket. **7** Jack Nicklaus. **8** Bicycle. **9** USA. **10** Europe. **11** Four. **12** Bounce. **13** Triple jump. **14** Australia. **15** Greg Norman. **16** Navratilova. **17** Tour de France. **18** Steffi Graf. **19** Ireland. **20** Four. **21** Novotna. **22** High jump. **23** England. **24** Six. **25** John McEnroe. **26** Viv Richards. **27** Mark McGwire. **28** Connors. **29** Argentinean. **30** Europe.

Quiz 81 Science & Nature: Space

Answers - see Quiz 82, page 92

1 What force makes the Earth orbit the Sun?
2 What colour is the Great Spot on Jupiter?
3 Is Jupiter larger or smaller than Earth?
4 Which gas is present in the Earth's atmosphere which is not present on any other planet?
5 A solar eclipse occurs when the Moon gets between Earth and what?
6 Which is the seventh planet from the Sun?
7 What is the layer around the Earth called?
8 What is the name given to matter so dense that even light cannot escape its pull?
9 Which planet's name comes nearest the end of the alphabet?
10 Herschel planned to name Uranus after the King; which one?
11 What would you find on a celestial map?
12 Is the science of celestial bodies, astrology or astronomy?
13 Which colour in the rainbow has the shortest name?
14 Which TV programme called space The Final Frontier?
15 Were the first US Shuttle flights in the 50s, 60s, or 80s?
16 Which show with Reeves & Mortimer shares its name with another term for meteors?
17 What is a group of stars which make a recognisable pattern called?
18 What does 'S' stand for in NASA?
19 In which decade was the US's first satellite launched?
20 What is the English name for the lunar sea Mare Tranquillitas?
21 Castor and Pollux are two stars in which constellation?
22 John Young ate which item of fast food in space in 1968?
23 Was Apollo a US or USSR space programme?
24 Prior to being an astronaut was John Glenn in the Air Force or the Marines?
25 How long does it take the Earth to orbit the Sun?
26 Mishka, the 1980 Olympic mascot was the first of which toy in space?
27 How is Ursa Major better known?
28 How many times did Gagarin orbit the Earth on his first space flight?
29 What travels at 186,272 miles per second?
30 Edward White was the first American to walk where?

Answers

Pot Luck 40 (see Quiz 82, page 92)
1 Nora Batty. **2** Green. **3** An earthquake. **4** Tennis. **5** Monday. **6** Barber. **7** Peron. **8** A sword. **9** West Ham. **10** Oxford. **11** Boxing Day. **12** Nine. **13** A bird (falcon). **14** Mo Mowlam. **15** Blue and White. **16** Boyzone. **17** Clint Eastwood. **18** A cherry. **19** Chess. **20** Nuclear. **21** Methane. **22** Nick Leeson. **23** Cain. **24** BSkyB. **25** Ena Sharples. **26** Annie. **27** Venice. **28** Eight. **29** Eiffel Tower. **30** Strawberry.

Quiz 82 Pot Luck 40

Answers - see Quiz 81, page 91

1 In Last of the Summer Wine, which part was played by Kathy Staff?
2 What colour is Dipsy in the Teletubbies?
3 An aftershock can sometimes follow what natural disaster?
4 For which sport was Sue Barker famous?
5 Which day's child is "fair of face" according to the traditional rhyme?
6 Which tradesman from Seville is featured in the title of an opera?
7 Which Argentinean president had wives called Eva and Maria Estela?
8 In legend, who or what was Excalibur?
9 Which London club did soccer's Ian Wright join from Arsenal?
10 Which university is the oldest in England?
11 St Stephen's Day is generally known by what other name?
12 How many players are in a baseball team?
13 What is a peregrine?
14 Who was Tony Blair's first Northern Ireland Minister?
15 What are the two main colours of the Argentinean flag?
16 Who had a No. 1 UK hit in September 1998 with No Matter What?
17 Which actor links Play Misty For Me and Pale Rider?
18 What type of fruit is a morello?
19 With which board game are Karpov and Kasparov associated?
20 Sizewell in Suffolk is associated with which form of power?
21 Which gas is the full name for marsh gas?
22 Who was Lisa Leeson's notorious husband?
23 In The Bible, who was Adam and Eve's firstborn son?
24 Which company acquired Manchester United Football Club in September 1998?
25 Which character in Coronation Street was played by Violet Carson?
26 The song Tomorrow comes from which musical?
27 In which Italian city is the Rialto Bridge?
28 How many noughts are in the written number one hundred million?
29 What is the most lasting symbol of the French Exhibition of 1889?
30 Royal Sovereign is a type of which soft fruit?

Answers

Science & Nature: Space (see Quiz 81, page 91)
1 Gravity. **2** Red. **3** Larger. **4** Oxygen. **5** The Sun. **6** Uranus. **7** Atmosphere. **8** Black Hole. **9** Venus. **10** George. **11** Stars. **12** Astronomy. **13** Red. **14** Star Trek. **15** 80s. **16** Shooting Stars. **17** Constellation. **18** Space. **19** 1950s. **20** Sea of Tranquillity. **21** Gemini. **22** Burger. **23** USA. **24** Marines. **25** A year. **26** Teddy bear. **27** Great Bear. **28** Once. **29** Light. **30** Space.

Quiz 83 The Movies: The Oscars

Answers - see Quiz 84, page 94

1 Which Oscar winner became a Labour MP?
2 Which sea disaster movie swept the Oscars at the 1998 ceremony?
3 Which Plasticine pair had six Oscar nominations by 1998?
4 Which Kevin won Best Director and starred in Dances With Wolves?
5 Braveheart was set in which country?
6 Who won Best Actor for The Silence of the Lambs?
7 Who directed Schindler's List?
8 Which British actor Jeremy was a winner with Reversal of Fortune?
9 Was it Tom Hanks or Tom Cruise who won in 1993 and again in '94?
10 Sonny's ex wife won Best Actress in Moonstruck; who was she?
11 Which Susan won for Dead Man Walking?
12 Which foot is named in the title of the movie with Daniel-Day Lewis?
13 Was Clint Eastwood Best Actor or Best Director for Unforgiven?
14 How often are the Oscars presented?
15 Which keyboard instrument gave its name to a film with Holly Hunter?
16 Kathy Bates won with Misery based on which Stephen's novel?
17 Which Kate was Oscar-nominated for Titanic?
18 Did Madonna receive one, two or no nominations for Evita?
19 What was Best Picture when Tom Hanks won Best Actor for Forrest Gump?
20 Which Al was Best Actor for Scent of a Woman?
21 Which Shirley won an Oscar at the age of five?
22 For which film did James Cameron win a 1997 Oscar?
23 Which British movie about the 1924 Olympics was an 80s winner?
24 Which Oscar winner based in India holds the record for most extras?
25 Which son of Kirk Douglas won for Wall Street?
26 Platoon was about which Asian war?
27 Which Ralph was an English Patient winner?
28 Talk To The Animals came from which movie about a Doctor?
29 When did the English Patient win Best Picture?
30 Dances With Wolves was the first film of what type to win Best Picture for 60 years?

Answers

Pot Luck 41 (see Quiz 84, page 94)

1 Lean. **2** Anglesey. **3** A hop, a step and a leap. **4** Gondolas. **5** Canaries. **6** Greece. **7** Red. **8** Milky Way. **9** Motor racing. **10** Green (the Incredible Hulk). **11** Six. **12** Its age. **13** A flower. **14** A fish. **15** Table tennis. **16** High jumping. **17** Universe. **18** A monkey. **19** Beatrix Potter. **20** Spain. **21** In your bones. **22** Apple trees. **23** The Flintstones. **24** A Christmas Carol. **25** Falkland Islands. **26** White. **27** Ireland. **28** Dick Turpin. **29** Scotland. **30** Six.

Quiz 84 Pot Luck 41

Answers - see Quiz 83, page 93

1 Which David directed the epic movie Lawrence of Arabia?
2 Which island is off the north-western tip of Wales?
3 The triple jump involves a run and then which three movements?
4 Which black boats sail along the canals of Venice?
5 Which bird was taken to work by miners to test for gas?
6 Mount Olympus is in which European country?
7 What colour hat is worn by Papa Smurf?
8 Which chocolate sweet bar is named after our galaxy?
9 For which sport was Gilles Villeneuve famous?
10 What colour did Dr. Banner become when he got angry?
11 How many legs does a fully grown insect have?
12 What can be discovered by counting the rings in a tree trunk?
13 Who or what is Sweet William?
14 What kind of creature is an anchovy?
15 What game are you playing if you hold a bat in a penholder grip?
16 In which sport would you see a Fosbury Flop?
17 Which word collectively describes all the stars and planets?
18 Which has the longer tail, a monkey or ape?
19 Who wrote the Peter Rabbit novels?
20 Which country produces Valencia oranges?
21 Where in your body would you find marrow?
22 Which tree does mistletoe grow on?
23 Who live at 342 Greasepit Terrace, Bedrock?
24 In which Dickens' novel does Jacob Marley's ghost appear?
25 Which islands were invaded in 1982 by the Argentineans?
26 What colour are the stars on the American flag?
27 In which country would you visit to kiss the Blarney Stone?
28 Which highwayman had a horse called Black Bess?
29 The TV series Take the High Road is set in which country?
30 How many strings are there on a Spanish guitar?

Answers

The Movies: The Oscars (see Quiz 83, page 93)
1 Glenda Jackson. **2** Titanic. **3** Wallace & Gromit. **4** Costner. **5** Scotland. **6** Anthony Hopkins. **7** Steven Spielberg. **8** Irons. **9** Hanks. **10** Cher. **11** Sarandon. **12** Left Foot. **13** Director. **14** Once a year. **15** The Piano. **16** King. **17** Winslet. **18** None. **19** Forrest Gump. **20** Pacino. **21** Temple. **22** Titanic. **23** Chariots of Fire. **24** Gandhi. **25** Michael. **26** Vietnam. **27** Fiennes. **28** Doolittle. **29** 1996. **30** Western.

Quiz 85 Geography: On the Map

Answers - see Quiz 86, page 96

1 Which language other than English is an official language of the Channel Islands?
2 Which Tsar changed Russia's capital from Moscow to St Petersburg?
3 You would find Delphi on a map of which country?
4 What is farther north, Clacton or Brighton?
5 Which continent has an Ivory Coast?
6 On which island would you find the Giant's Causeway?
7 If you were on a French autoroute what type of road would you be on?
8 Which Gulf lies between Saudi Arabia and Iran?
9 Lake Superior is on the border of the USA and which other country?
10 Which tiny European landlocked state is a Grand Duchy?
11 Macedonia was formerly a part of which communist republic?
12 Which Himalayan kingdom has been called the world's highest rubbish dump because of waste left behind by climbers?
13 Which Australasian capital shares its name with a Duke and a boot?
14 Which river which flows through Germany is Europe's dirtiest?
15 Where would you be if you saw Nippon on the map?
16 Whose address is often referred to as Number Ten?
17 Which motorway goes past Stoke On Trent?
18 On which continent is the Basque country?
19 The Home Counties surround which city?
20 Malta is to the south of which island to the south of Italy?
21 The Ural Mountains mark the eastern frontier to which continent?
22 How is the London Orbital Motorway better known?
23 Is Moldova in Europe or Africa?
24 Which island republic lies to the north west of the UK?
25 Miami is a port in which US state?
26 Kew Gardens are next to which London river?
27 Which country has Lakes Garda, Maggiore and Como?
28 Is Madagascar an island or is it an African peninsula?
29 In which city is Red Square?
30 Which country's official languages are Hebrew and Arabic?

Answers

Pot Luck 42 (see Quiz 86, page 96)
1 Gaz. **2** Rosary. **3** Sewing Machine. **4** University. **5** Herod. **6** Duffy. **7** Celine Dion. **8** Cat. **9** M. **10** Salmon. **11** Petrol. **12** Finland. **13** Badminton. **14** Walking distance. **15** 12. **16** Gas. **17** 100. **18** Tim Henman. **19** Huit. **20** Notting Hill. **21** Blue. **22** Squirrel. **23** Five. **24** Germany. **25** Golf. **26** Deadly nightshade. **27** Cilla Black. **28** Mars. **29** Supper. **30** Blue.

Quiz 86 Pot Luck 42

Answers - see Quiz 85, page 95

1 Actor Robert Carlyle led The Full Monty as which character?
2 What does a Catholic call the string of beads used when praying?
3 In 1851, what was invented by Isaac Singer?
4 In what type of educational establishment was Educating Rita set?
5 In The Bible, which King tried to get the baby Jesus put to death?
6 Which nurse returned to Casualty in the autumn 1998 series?
7 Who had a hit with the Titanic theme song My Heart Will Go On?
8 In cartoons, what type of animal is Sylvester?
9 Which letter represents 007's boss?
10 Which fish leap up river to get to their spawning grounds?
11 What do Americans usually mean by gas?
12 In which country did saunas originate?
13 A shuttlecock is used in which game?
14 What is measured by a pedometer?
15 How many creatures give their names to Chinese years?
16 Which domestic fuel has its charges calculated in therms?
17 How many decades are there in a millennium?
18 Who was disqualified from Wimbledon in 1995 after accidentally hitting a ball-girl?
19 What is the French word for the number eight?
20 In which part of London is there an annual famous carnival?
21 If put in an alkaline solution, what colour does litmus paper become?
22 Which animal lives in a drey?
23 If Dec 1st is a Tuesday, how many Wednesdays are in the month?
24 Did Beethoven come from Austria, Germany or Holland?
25 For which sport is Sam Torrance famous?
26 Belladonna is also known by which Deadly name?
27 Who hosts the TV entertainment programme The Moment of Truth?
28 The month March is named after which Roman god?
29 Leonardo da Vinci's religious painting featured The Last... what?
30 What colour is connected to neutral in modern three core electric cable?

Answers

Geography: On the Map (see Quiz 85, page 95)
1 French. **2** Peter the Great. **3** Greece. **4** Clacton. **5** Africa. **6** Ireland. **7** Motorway. **8** Persian Gulf. **9** Canada. **10** Luxembourg. **11** Yugoslavia. **12** Nepal. **13** Wellington. **14** Rhine. **15** Japan. **16** Prime Minister. **17** M6. **18** Europe. **19** London. **20** Sicily. **21** Europe. **22** M25. **23** Europe. **24** Iceland. **25** Florida. **26** Thames. **27** Italy. **28** Island. **29** Moscow. **30** Israel.

Quiz 87 Hobbies & Leisure 3

Answers - see Quiz 88, page 98

1 What is normally the first Bank Holiday after Christmas Day?
2 Which sport would you watch at Aintree?
3 Are there more chairs at the start or end of a game of musical chairs?
4 What links a novice's ski slope and a garden centre?
5 What name is given to the promotional scheme to save points for cheaper plane travel?
6 Are boys or girls cubs?
7 What colour would a Sloane Ranger's wellies be?
8 The initials RSVP come from a request in which language?
9 What colour are most road signs on UK motorways?
10 In which UK county might you holiday on the Broads?
11 Are Open University courses usually followed by mature students or school leavers?
12 In which city is the exhibition centre Olympia?
13 What would you hire at Moss Bros?
14 Butlin's was the first type of what?
15 What is the flower shaped ribbon awarded at gymkhanas called?
16 What is a less formal name for a turf accountant?
17 Which magazine's title is the French word for 'she'?
18 On which summer bank holiday is the Notting Hill Carnival held?
19 Which public track can be used for horses but not traffic?
20 On which date in May was May Day traditionally?
21 Does a busker entertain indoors or out of doors?
22 In which month would you celebrate Hogmanay?
23 In golf, what is usually meant by the nineteenth hole?
24 What is a horse chestnut called when it's used in a children's game?
25 Which Scottish city hosts an annual arts festival?
26 What colour uniform do Guides wear?
27 Are seats in the circle of a theatre on the ground or first floor?
28 Where would a shopper be if they went to M&S?
29 If you wore jodhpurs you'd probably be about to do what?
30 On which ground in north west England do you watch Test cricket?

Answers

Pot Luck 43 (see Quiz 88, page 98)
1 Queen Elizabeth II. **2** Wales. **3** The species. **4** England. **5** Skinner. **6** Hair. **7** Cleo Laine. **8** The Teletubbies. **9** Shaken but not stirred. **10** Hadlee. **11** (West) Germany. **12** Raspberry. **13** Oskar. **14** Brazil. **15** Sunday. **16** Scarlet. **17** Isle of Wight. **18** Pet Shop Boys. **19** Dean. **20** Cat. **21** McGrath. **22** Andre Agassi. **23** Skier. **24** Jackson. **25** Salt. **26** Medieval. **27** John Major's son James. **28** Barbie. **29** Dorset. **30** Rugby Union.

Quiz 88 Pot Luck 43

Answers - see Quiz 87, page 97

1. Who described 1992 as an 'annus horribilis'?
2. In which country would you see the Great and Little Orme?
3. According to Rudyard Kipling the female of what is deadlier than the male?
4. Which country hosted soccer's 1966 World Cup?
5. In EastEnders which Ethel had a dog called Willie?
6. What falls out if you have alopecia?
7. Which singer is Mrs Johnny Dankworth?
8. Who lives at Home Hill?
9. How does James Bond like his Martini served?
10. Which Richard was the first knighted New Zealand cricketer?
11. Europe's first motorway was built in which country?
12. What rude noise is the English equivalent of a Bronx Cheer?
13. What was Schindler's first name in the film Schindler's List?
14. In which South American country was Ayrton Senna born?
15. If January 1st was on a Thursday what day would February 1st be?
16. What colour was The Pimpernel created by Baroness Orczy?
17. Shanklin and Sandown are on which Isle?
18. Which Boys had a No.1 in the 1980s with Always On My Mind?
19. Who was the male half of the Torvill and Dean partnership?
20. What kind of animal was Korky from the Dandy comic?
21. Which Rory appeared with Gary Lineker in They Think It's All Over?
22. Which US tennis player married Brooke Shields?
23. Is Alberto Tomba a skier, a track athlete or an ice hockey player?
24. Which singer Michael had a No 1 with Earth Song?
25. Sodium chloride is better known as which condiment?
26. Was Brother Cadfael a fictional medieval or Victorian detective?
27. Which Prime Minister's son did Emma Noble become engaged to?
28. Which doll has a boyfriend called Ken?
29. According to The Comic Strip, in which county did Five Go Mad?
30. If Lions are playing Wallabies what sport are you watching?

Answers

Hobbies & Leisure 3 (see Quiz 87, page 97)

1 Boxing Day. **2** Horse racing. **3** Beginning. **4** Nursery. **5** Air miles. **6** Boys. **7** Green. **8** French. **9** Blue. **10** Norfolk. **11** Mature students. **12** London. **13** Formal dress. **14** Holiday camp. **15** Rosette. **16** Bookie. **17** Elle. **18** August Bank Holiday. **19** Bridleway. **20** First. **21** Out of doors. **22** December. **23** The club-house bar. **24** Conker. **25** Edinburgh. **26** Blue. **27** First floor. **28** Marks & Spencer. **29** Horse riding. **30** Old Trafford.

Quiz 89 TV Times 3

Answers - see Quiz 90, page 100

1 Which day follows TFI on Chris Evans' show?
2 Who was the host of the variety show Lenny Goes To Town?
3 Which medical drama takes place in Holby's A & E department?
4 The Jerry Springer Show comes from which country?
5 At what time of day is Richard & Judy's magazine programme?
6 What is presented to the 'victim' at the end of This Is Your Life?
7 In ER, what is ER?
8 Which comedian John does LibDem Party Political Broadcasts?
9 How many rooms are changed in Changing Rooms?
10 Newsround is aimed at which group of viewers?
11 In which series set in Ireland did barmaid Assumpta meet a sad end?
12 Which near silent walking disaster was created by Rowan Atkinson?
13 Who is Mel Smith's TV comedy partner?
14 Which Geoff gardened at Barnsdale?
15 Which series was dubbed 'Barewatch' and 'Boobwatch'?
16 Which charity campaign has Pudsey Bear as its mascot?
17 Which Michael's 70s chat show was revived in 1998?
18 In which Practice have doctors Kerruish, Glover and Attwood worked?
19 Which was broadcast later, Newsnight or News at Ten?
20 Who is the host of GMTV's Lorraine Live?
21 Which phone number is the name of a series with Michael Buerk?
22 What follows Police, Camera..., in the show about awful drivers?
23 In which city is The Cosby Show set?
24 Which drama series where Robson and Jerome found fame is about army life?
25 On which day of the week does the so called God slot take place?
26 Which talent show features, 'Tonight Matthew I'm going to be....'?
27 Which Cilla Black series made dreams come true?
28 Which motor magazine now with Jeremy Clarkson began in 1978?
29 What is the hair link between Chris Evans and Nicholas Witchell?
30 Which Files feature Mulder and Scully?

Answers

Pot Luck 44 (see Quiz 90, page 100)
1 Eagle. **2** Wales. **3** Stairway To Heaven. **4** Faraday. **5** Paint. **6** Lyon. **7** Nicey. **8** Bell shaped. **9** Cycling. **10** Hood. **11** Water. **12** Les Battersby. **13** Metronome. **14** Before. **15** South Africa. **16** A3. **17** Slade. **18** Atmosphere. **19** Belgium. **20** Mars. **21** Carter. **22** Ear. **23** Medusa. **24** Cricket. **25** Dick. **26** 1940s. **27** Normandy. **28** George Michael. **29** Zimbabwe. **30** Sally.

Quiz 90 Pot Luck 44

Answers - see Quiz 89, page 99

1 Which comic did Dan Dare first appear in?
2 Golfer Ian Woosnam comes from which country?
3 Which song links Rolf Harris and Led Zeppelin?
4 Which inventor Michael is on a £20 note?
5 Gouache is a type of what?
6 The notorious Klaus Barbie was the Butcher of where in France?
7 Who is the mate of spoof DJ Smashy?
8 What shape is something if it is campanulate?
9 Boardman and Obree could clash in which sport?
10 Which Robin was the spoof film Men In Tights about?
11 Which word can go in front of BISCUIT, CLOSET and COLOUR?
12 As which character was Coronation Street actor Bruce Jones the neighbour from hell?
13 Which ticking instrument keeps perfect time for a musician?
14 Was the Automobile Association founded before or after World War I?
15 Which nation came back to international rugby in 1993?
16 Which is bigger A3 or A4 paper?
17 Which band featured Noddy Holder and Dave Hill?
18 The mesosphere and the stratosphere are layers of what?
19 With which country are Walloons associated?
20 What links a chocolate bar, a planet and a god of war?
21 Which Kevin was in the title of a hit for the Manic Street Preachers?
22 In which part of the body are the smallest bones?
23 In Greek legend, who had a bad hair day with snakes on her head?
24 Gubby Allen was linked with which sport?
25 What was the first name of Wacky Racer Mr Dastardly?
26 Was Chris Tarrant born in the 1940s or the 1960s?
27 Operation Overlord was the codename for the 1944 Allied invasion of where?
28 Who took a Careless Whisper to No. 1 in the 1980s?
29 Which country do golfers Nick Price and Mark McNulty come from?
30 What name is shared by actress Whittaker and the Webster she played in Corrie?

Answers

TV Times 3 (see Quiz 89, page 99)

1 Friday. **2** Lenny Henry. **3** Casualty. **4** USA. **5** Morning. **6** Book. **7** Emergency Room. **8** Cleese. **9** Two. **10** Children. **11** Ballykissangel. **12** Mr Bean. **13** Griff Rhys Jones. **14** Hamilton. **15** Baywatch. **16** Children in Need. **17** Parkinson. **18** Peak Practice. **19** Newsnight. **20** Lorraine Kelly. **21** 999. **22** Action. **23** New York. **24** Soldier Soldier. **25** Sunday. **26** Stars In Their Eyes. **27** Surprise Surprise. **28** Top Gear. **29** Red hair. **30** The X Files.

Quiz 91 Leisure: Performing Arts

Answers - see Quiz 92, page 102

1 Who sang a Barcelona duet with Freddy Mercury?
2 Which composer wrote the Four Seasons?
3 Which branch of performing is Michael Flatley famous for?
4 In which country was the Halle Orchestra founded?
5 Which dancer Wayne toured in 1998 to mark his 50th birthday?
6 Which instrument did Stephane Grapelli play?
7 Which writers of comic opera are referred to as G&S?
8 Which playwright was known as the Bard of Avon?
9 Billy Smart was associated with what type of entertainment?
10 In which country is an eisteddfod held?
11 Which Circle is a professional association of conjurors?
12 Which charity gala with many different performers is held in November and attended by the Royal Family?
13 Which Lord Andrew wrote the musical Whistle Down the Wind?
14 In Rodgers and Hammerstein who wrote the music?
15 In which country was the Bolshoi Ballet founded?
16 Which Vanessa is a famous young violinist?
17 Which London theatre shares its name with a half human, half fish mythical creature?
18 At what time of year would you go and watch a nativity play?
19 When faced with an orchestra, what does Sir Simon Rattle do?
20 The Last Night of the Proms takes place in which month?
21 A person playing a pantomime dame is usually which sex?
22 What type of singing made Maria Callas famous?
23 What was the surname of US musical composers George and Ira?
24 What is the final concert at the Promenade Concerts called?
25 Two out of the Three Tenors are which nationality?
26 Which Sir Noel wrote and starred in his plays and musicals?
27 What is the first name of Scarborough-based playwright Ayckbourn?
28 Opera singer Lesley Garrett is from which county?
29 Do you stand or sit for the Hallelujah Chorus from The Messiah?
30 In panto how do you respond to ' Oh yes it is!'?

Answers

Pot Luck 45 (see Quiz 92, page 102)

1 Fawlty Towers. **2** Middlesbrough. **3** Bill Wyman. **4** H.G. **5** Felicity. **6** The Young Ones. **7** Pottery. **8** Long haired. **9** James Bond. **10** Scarlett. **11** Wok. **12** The Archers. **13** Beef. **14** Horse. **15** Spoons. **16** Hello. **17** Nigel. **18** King Edward. **19** Crawford. **20** Arkansas. **21** Canada. **22** Etna. **23** Smoking. **24** Deer. **25** Outside. **26** Two (South Australia & New South Wales). **27** Moonlight Serenade. **28** New Testament. **29** Jeroboam. **30** Bronx.

Quiz 92 Pot Luck 45

Answers - see Quiz 91, page 101

1 Where did Polly work for Basil and Sybil?
2 Which English soccer side did Gazza make his debut for in a Wembley final?
3 Who is older Bill Wyman or the Prince of Wales?
4 What are the two initials of early 20th Century sci fi writer Wells?
5 Which Kendall starred in the sitcom Solo?
6 On which anarchic TV series did Neil, Mike, Rik and Vyvyan appear?
7 What did Clarice Cliff make?
8 Is an Afghan hound short haired or long haired?
9 Which secret agent was created by Ian Fleming?
10 Which Captain fought against the Mysterons?
11 What is a round bottomed Chinese cooking pan called?
12 In which radio series is there a pub called The Bull?
13 What sort of meat is usually in a hamburger?
14 What type of animal is a palomino?
15 What is Uri Geller famous for bending?
16 Would you say Bonjour to a French person when you say hello or goodbye?
17 Violinist Kennedy chose to drop which first name professionally?
18 Which monarch gave his name to a type of potato?
19 Which Michael created the Phantom in Lloyd Webber's musical?
20 Is Bill Clinton's home state Arkansas or Arizona?
21 In which country is Hudson Bay?
22 Which Sicilian mountain is Europe's highest volcano?
23 ASH is a pressure group against what?
24 Which animal might be fallow or red?
25 Would you find a gazebo inside or outside your home?
26 How many Australian states have South in their names?
27 Was Glenn Miller's theme tune Moonlight Sonata or Moonlight Serenade?
28 Is the book of Jude in the Old or New Testament?
29 Which is larger a magnum of champagne or a Jeroboam?
30 Which tough area of New York gives its name to a gin, vermouth and orange cocktail?

Answers

Leisure: Performing Arts (see Quiz 91, page 101)
1 Monserrat Caballe. **2** Vivaldi. **3** Dance. **4** UK. **5** Sleep. **6** Violin. **7** Gilbert & Sullivan. **8** William Shakespeare. **9** Circus. **10** Wales. **11** Magic Circle. **12** Royal Variety Show. **13** Lloyd Webber. **14** Rodgers. **15** Russia. **16** Mae. **17** Mermaid. **18** Christmas. **19** Conduct. **20** September. **21** Male. **22** Opera. **23** Gershwin. **24** Last Night of the Proms. **25** Spanish. **26** Coward. **27** Alan. **28** Yorkshire. **29** Stand. **30** "Oh no it isn't!"

Quiz 93 Sport: World Cup Fever

Answers - see Quiz 94, page 104

1 How often is the World Cup held?
2 Did Jimmy Greaves ever play in a World Cup Final?
3 Who won the last World Cup of the 20th century?
4 What colour shirts were England wearing when they won in 1966?
5 Who became known sarcastically as The Hand of God?
6 Who was sent off in France 98 and fled to Posh Spice in New York?
7 Which side from Great Britain did not make France 98?
8 Which 1966 World Cup veteran resigned as Eire manager in 1995?
9 Which British side did Brazil play in the first match of France 98?
10 Which European country did Berti Vogts manage?
11 Which TV pundit Jimmy spoke about every World Cup from 1966?
12 Who were beaten finalists in the last World Cup of the 20th century?
13 In France 98 which Caribbean side were called the Reggae Boys?
14 Who was axed from the England side in 98 after reports of kebab binges?
15 Was Sainsbury's or Tesco the official World Cup supermarket?
16 Is it true or false that Norway beat Germany in the 1995 World Cup?
17 In France 98 who did Suker play for?
18 Who was the only Englishman to lift the World Cup before 2000?
19 Which central American country was the first to host the World Cup twice, in 1986?
20 Which ex World Cup manager's autobiography is An Englishman Abroad?
21 What colour are Brazil's shirts?
22 Who were the only non Europeans to win the World Cup in the 90s?
23 Who was England's youngest player in France 98?
24 What colour coded hair was seen on the Nigerian team in France 98?
25 Which Gary was top scorer in the 1986 World Cup?
26 In which month did France 98 finish?
27 Which Scandinavian side was third in the 1994 US tournament?
28 Which South American side knocked England out of France 98?
29 In which city did France 98 begin and end?
30 On Top of the World was which country's World Cup anthem?

Answers

Pot Luck 16 (see Quiz 94, page 104)
1 Lancashire. **2** L.B.. **3** Kent. **4** Rum. **5** Locum. **6** Argentina. **7** Dog. **8** Northamptonshire. **9** D H Lawrence. **10** Apple. **11** Germany. **12** Italy. **13** Mel B (Scary Spice). **14** Gunnell. **15** London. **16** China. **17** Harrison. **18** Potter. **19** Holly. **20** Surrey. **21** Cuckoo. **22** Tenor. **23** Bit. **24** Addams. **25** Chris de Burgh. **26** Tennis. **27** Alice (in Wonderland). **28** Sleeve. **29** Celine Dion. **30** Perambulator.

Quiz 94 Pot Luck 46

Answers - see Quiz 93, page 103

1 Mike Atherton plays for which county cricket club?
2 Which were the initials of US President Johnson?
3 In which county is Ashford International station?
4 Does a Pina Colada contain rum or gin?
5 Which word for a duty doctor is a Latin name for place holder?
6 Which country's Rugby Union side are the Pumas?
7 Is a Dandie Dinmont, a dog, a cat or a horse?
8 In which county is the stately home of Althorp?
9 Which controversial author used the initials for his first names David Herbert?
10 What sort of fruit flavour does Calvados have?
11 In which country were BMW's first made?
12 St Francis of Assisi is patron saint of which country?
13 Who was the first Spice Girl to marry?
14 Which Sally was British women's team captain in the 1996 Olympics?
15 In which city is MP Diane Abbott's constituency?
16 Which country was once called Cathay?
17 Which Mr Ford starred in the 1990 movie Presumed Innocent?
18 Which Dennis created The Singing Detective?
19 Which Buddy did Alvin Stardust sing about?
20 Alec Stewart plays cricket for which English county?
21 Which bird lays its eggs in the nests of other birds?
22 Was the singer Mario Lanza a bass, baritone or tenor?
23 What name is given to the part of the bridle in a horse's mouth?
24 Wednesday and Pugsley are part of which family?
25 Christopher Davidson found fame as a singer as which Chris?
26 Maria Bueno was famous for which sport?
27 In fiction, which girl swam in a pool of her own tears?
28 A raglan forms which part of a garment?
29 Who had a huge 1995 hit with Think Twice?
30 Pram is an abbreviation of which word?

Answers

Sport: World Cup Fever (see Quiz 93, page 103)
1 Every four years. **2** No. **3** France. **4** Red. **5** Diego Maradonna. **6** David Beckham. **7** Wales. **8** Jack Charlton. **9** Scotland. **10** Germany. **11** Hill. **12** Brazil. **13** Jamaica. **14** Paul Gascoigne. **15** Sainsbury's. **16** True – Women's World Cup. **17** Croatia. **18** Bobby Moore. **19** Mexico. **20** Bobby Robson. **21** Yellow. **22** Brazil. **23** Michael Owen. **24** Green. **25** Lineker. **26** July. **27** Sweden. **28** Argentina. **29** Paris. **30** England's.

Quiz 95 Past Times: The 60s

Answers - see Quiz 96, page 106

1 Which Yasser founded the PLO?
2 Which Kennedy announced he was running for President in 1960?
3 Nikita Krushchev was head of state of which Union?
4 In which Italian city were the 1960 summer Olympics held?
5 Whose Lover was the subject of a court case in book form?
6 The USSR sent its first man where in April 1960?
7 Which Russian dancer Rudolph defected to the West?
8 Across which former European capital was a Wall built?
9 Which drug taken by pregnant mothers caused abnormalities in babies?
10 Which Harold became Labour leader in 1963?
11 Of where did Neil Armstrong say, "The surface is like fine powder"?
12 What were mailbags containing over £1 million stolen from?
13 Caroline was the name of Britain's first off shore pirate what?
14 Which British WWII leader died in 1965?
15 What sort of champion was Arkle?
16 Which communist country had its famous Red Guards?
17 Which knighted soccer star retired aged 50?
18 Who launched the Queen Elizabeth II - QE2 - on Clydebank?
19 Which model Jean was called The Shrimp?
20 Which homeless charity was set up after TV's Cathy Come Home?
21 What product was banned from TV advertising on health grounds?
22 Which Rolling Stone singer was best man at David Bailey's wedding?
23 Which notorious East End gangland twins were jailed for murder?
24 Which rock star married Patricia Beaulieu?
25 Which capital was said to Swing in the 60s?
26 Which Martin famously gave his 'I have a dream' speech?
27 If Mods rode scooters, who rode motorbikes?
28 LBJ was President of which country?
29 How were Ian Brady and Myra Hindley known?
30 Which actress Marilyn was found dead in her bungalow near Hollywood?

Answers

Pot Luck 17 (see Quiz 96, page 106)
1 Thaw. **2** Florin. **3** Smokie. **4** Chris Evans. **5** 1980. **6** Bluto. **7** Yes. **8** Liverpool. **9** Portuguese. **10** Culkin. **11** Mile. **12** Harman. **13** Cyrus. **14** 26. **15** The Kinks. **16** Greek gods. **17** Tony. **18** Borzoi. **19** Nissan. **20** Tompkinson. **21** Fox. **22** Cyrillic. **23** British Prime Ministers. **24** Champion. **25** Mick Hucknall. **26** Penicillin. **27** Bishop. **28** Golf. **29** Duck. **30** McCartney.

Quiz 96 Pot Luck 47

Answers - see Quiz 95, page 105

1 Which John married actress Sheila Hancock?
2 Which pre decimal coin had the value of two shillings?
3 Which group revived a previous hit in the 90s with the help of Roy 'Chubby' Brown?
4 Which TV presenter's shows have had Toothbrush and Breakfast in their titles?
5 Were the Olympic Games last held in Russia in 1960, 1980 or 1988?
6 Who is Popeye's rival?
7 Was Sir Walter Scott Scottish?
8 Which English soccer side was managed by the late Bob Paisley?
9 What is the main language in Brazil?
10 Which Macaulay starred in the cartoon and live action film The Pagemaster?
11 Which is greater in distance a mile or a kilometre?
12 Which MP Harriet was axed in Tony Blair's first Cabinet reshuffle?
13 Which Billy Ray's Achy Breaky Heart helped establish line dancing?
14 How many red cards are there in a standard pack of cards?
15 Ray Davies was writer and singer with which band?
16 Adonis, Apollo and Poseidon were all what?
17 Who shares a flat with Gary in Men Behaving Badly?
18 Which dog is larger a borzoi or a corgi?
19 The Micra was made by which car company?
20 Which Stephen has been the TV partner of Dervla Kirwan?
21 A vixen is the female of which animal?
22 Which alphabet is used by Muscovites?
23 What links the names Chamberlain, Heath and Wilson?
24 Which jockey Bob fought back from cancer to win the Grand National?
25 Who is Simply Red's lead singer?
26 Which was the first antibiotic to be discovered?
27 Ian Smith played which Harold in Neighbours?
28 For which sport is Sunningdale famous?
29 A Muscovy is what type of bird?
30 Which musical Paul got involved with frogs and Rupert Bear?

Answers

Past Times: The 60s (see Quiz 95, page 105)

1 Arafat. **2** John. **3** Soviet. **4** Rome. **5** Lady Chatterley's. **6** Space. **7** Nureyev. **8** Berlin. **9** Thalidomide. **10** Wilson. **11** The Moon. **12** Train. **13** Radio station. **14** Churchill. **15** Horse. **16** China. **17** Sir Stanley Matthews. **18** Queen Elizabeth II. **19** Jean Shrimpton. **20** Shelter. **21** Cigarettes. **22** Mick Jagger. **23** Kray twins. **24** Elvis Presley. **25** London. **26** Luther King. **27** Rockers. **28** USA. **29** Moors murderers. **30** Monroe.

Quiz 97 The Movies: Tough Guys

Answers - see Quiz 98, page 108

1 Which actor was nicknamed 'Bogey'?
2 Which actor Marlon was paid $18 million for nine minutes in Superman in 1978?
3 Which western star John first acted as Duke Morrison?
4 Which Samuel starred as a gangster in Pulp Fiction?
5 Which Bruce starred in The Jackal?
6 Which soccer side does Evita actor Jimmy Nail support?
7 Tough guy Robert de Niro sang about New York in which film?
8 Which lager did Crocodile Dundee star Paul Hogan advertise?
9 Which Vietnam veteran Oliver directed Platoon?
10 Which star of The Godfather bought an island called Tetiaroa?
11 Which Martin was assigned to assassinate Brando in Apocalypse Now?
12 What did George C. Scott refuse to do about his Oscar for Patton?
13 Gene Hackman played cop Popeye Doyle in which classic thriller?
14 Which tough English actor Sean is the son of a former Dr. Who?
15 Which famous US family did Arnold Schwarzenegger marry into?
16 Was Charles Bronson one of ten or fifteen children?
17 Is Bruce Willis a cop or a soldier in the Die Hard movies?
18 Which hell raiser Oliver released a single Lonely For a Girl in 1965?
19 Lee Marvin headed a Dirty cast of how many in the 1967 movie?
20 Which singer who died in 1998 was the tough guy captain in Von Ryan's Express?
21 How many gunfighters were hired in The Magnificent film of 1960?
22 On what vehicle did Steve McQueen try to flee in The Great Escape?
23 Which Sylvester starred in Judge Dredd?
24 What is the first name of Reservoir Dogs director Tarantino?
25 Which tough guy Arnold has appeared on a postage stamp of Mali?
26 Which Mel starred in the Lethal Weapon series of films?
27 Which bare-headed actor was in The Magnificent Seven and The King and I?
28 Which Clint got the part in Dirty Harry when Sinatra pulled out?
29 Which James Bond has an actor son called Jason?
30 Was The Untouchables with Kevin Costner set in the 20s, 40s or 60s?

Answers

Pot Luck 48 (see Quiz 98, page 108)
1 Tennis. **2** Heart. **3** Chris Tarrant. **4** Australia. **5** Frog. **6** Bertie Bassett.
7 Rot away. **8** Five. **9** Ten. **10** Aberdeen. **11** Boyzone. **12** Belgium.
13 Black Bess. **14** Purdy. **15** Eric Clapton. **16** Marylebone Cricket Club.
17 Bahamas. **18** The Taming of the Shrew. **19** Margaret Thatcher. **20** Henry.
21 Violin. **22** Cornwall. **23** George Cole. **24** British Prime Minister. **25** 26 miles.
26 Vingt. **27** Aircraft. **28** Wizzard. **29** Blue. **30** France.

Quiz 98 Pot Luck 48

Answers - see Quiz 97, page 107

LEVEL 1

1 For which sport is Billie-Jean King famous?
2 According to the proverb, absence makes which organ grow fonder?
3 Who hosted ITVs Who Wants to be a Millionaire?
4 In which country is Ayer's Rock?
5 Which species of creature includes the most poisonous animal in the world?
6 Which figure advertised Bassetts Liquorice Allsorts?
7 If something is biodegradable, what will it do?
8 How many noughts are in the written number two hundred thousand?
9 Every how many years is a National Census taken in Britain?
10 Where are you if you visit the Granite City?
11 Which group had a No. 1 album in 1998 with Where We Belong?
12 In which country is the town of Spa?
13 What was the name of Dick Turpin's horse?
14 In the New Avengers, which character was played by Joanna Lumley?
15 Which guitarist is nicknamed 'Slowhand'?
16 In cricket, what does the initial M stand for in MCC?
17 Nassau is the capital of which group of islands?
18 In which Shakespeare play does Kate marry Petruchio?
19 Who was Tory leader immediately before John Major?
20 Which Lenny was the first genuinely black member of the Black and White Minstrel Show?
21 Which musical instrument does Tasmin Little play?
22 Which English county boasts the longest coastline?
23 In the TV series Minder, who played Arthur Daly?
24 Eden, Heath and Macdonald have all held which important position?
25 To the nearest mile, how long is the London Marathon?
26 What is the French word for the number twenty?
27 What are DC-10s and 747s?
28 See My Baby Jive was a 70s No 1 for which magic-sounding group?
29 What colour is azure in heraldry?
30 Which country is immediately south of Belgium?

Answers

The Movies: Tough Guys (see Quiz 97, page 107)
1 Humphrey Bogart. **2** Brando. **3** John Wayne. **4** Jackson. **5** Willis. **6** Newcastle Utd. **7** New York, New York. **8** Fosters. **9** Stone. **10** Marlon Brando. **11** Sheen. **12** Accept it. **13** French Connection. **14** Pertwee. **15** Kennedy. **16** Fifteen. **17** Cop. **18** Reed. **19** Dozen. **20** Frank Sinatra. **21** Seven. **22** Motorcycle. **23** Stallone. **24** Quentin. **25** Schwarzenegger. **26** Gibson. **27** Yul Brynner. **28** Eastwood. **29** Sean Connery. **30** 20s.

Quiz 99 Past Times: The 70s

Answers - see Quiz 100, page 110

1 In which country did black activist Steve Biko die in 1977?
2 Which US President was brought down by the Watergate scandal?
3 What did a policeman use to hide a streaker's embarrassment in a famous incident at Twickenham in 1974?
4 Which London born comic Charlie was knighted?
5 Which tree population was decimated by a Dutch disease?
6 Did Skytrain provide cut price tickets by air or rail?
7 Who succeeded John Paul I as Pope?
8 The New English version of which Book was published in 1970?
9 Which Czech tennis star Martina defected to the West?
10 In which country did Pol Pot conduct a reign of terror?
11 Which Sebastian was a record breaking middle distance runner?
12 Which father of twins was the husband of the British PM?
13 Which princess was sportswoman of the year in 1971?
14 The Queen celebrated how many years on the throne in her Jubilee?
15 Which Lord disappeared after his nanny was murdered?
16 Who beat four male candidates to become Tory leader in 1975?
17 Which war ended with the fall of Saigon in 1975?
18 Which country's athletes were murdered at the 1972 Olympics?
19 John Curry won Olympic gold on what surface?
20 In which county did a Ripper carry out horrific murders?
21 Which Lord and Royal uncle was murdered off Ireland?
22 Which Mother won a Nobel Peace Prize?
23 Charles de Gaulle died after being president of which country?
24 Were Sunderland in the first or second division when they won the FA Cup in 1973?
25 Where was the monarchy restored after the death of Franco?
26 In 1971 the first British soldier was killed in which British province?
27 Evonne Goolagong from which country won Wimbledon in 1971?
28 Which Chris was Jimmy Connors' fiancee when he first won Wimbledon?
29 Which James succeeded Harold Wilson as Prime Minister?
30 David Steel became leader of which political party in 1976?

Answers

Pot Luck 49 (see Quiz 100, page 110)
1 Orange. **2** Jennifer Saunders. **3** Madonna. **4** London & Birmingham. **5** Lancashire. **6** Wren. **7** 18. **8** Martin. **9** Cricket. **10** 1940s. **11** Enya. **12** Red Indian tribes. **13** Take That. **14** White. **15** Four. **16** Matchstick Men. **17** Alfred Hitchcock. **18** Five. **19** Charles Dickens. **20** Hutch. **21** Soprano. **22** Northumberland. **23** MW. **24** Green. **25** A king. **26** Yorkshire. **27** Food. **28** Angostura Bitters. **29** Garland. **30** Queensland.

Quiz 100 Pot Luck 49

Answers - see Quiz 99, page 109

1 In international soccer, what is the main colour of Holland's shirts?
2 Who is older – Ruby Wax or Jennifer Saunders?
3 Into The Groove gave a first UK No. 1 for which singer?
4 Which two cities were linked by the M1 when it first opened?
5 Which ex-Corrie actress Sarah shares her surname with an English county?
6 What is Britain's smallest bird?
7 How many sides are there in a pair of nonagons?
8 Which George was the main producer of The Beatles' hits?
9 E W Swanton wrote about which sport?
10 Was Joanna Lumley born in the 1940s, 50s or 60s?
11 How is Eithne Ni Bhraonain better known in the music world?
12 Mohawk, Seminole and Sioux are all names of what?
13 Which star group was Jason Orange a member of?
14 Is Riesling a red or white wine?
15 How many Teletubbies are there?
16 What type of men gave Status Quo their first hit?
17 Who links the films Rebecca, Psycho and Vertigo?
18 What's the most number of Sundays that could occur in December?
19 Which author created the reclusive character Miss Havisham?
20 On TV, did David Soul play Starsky or Hutch?
21 What type of voice does opera star Lesley Garrett have?
22 What is England's most north easterly county?
23 Is Radio 5 Live broadcast on MW or FM?
24 What colour is verdigris which appears on copper or brass?
25 Who is killed if regicide is committed?
26 Ridings used to divide which county?
27 Is Robert Carrier linked with food, theatre or sport?
28 Pink gin is gin flavoured with what?
29 Which Judy starred in Meet Me In St Louis?
30 Brisbane is the capital of which Australian state?

Answers

Past Times: The 70s (see Quiz 99, page 109)
1 South Africa. **2** Nixon. **3** His helmet. **4** Chaplin. **5** Elm. **6** Air. **7** John Paul II. **8** Bible. **9** Navratilova. **10** Cambodia. **11** Coe. **12** Denis Thatcher. **13** Anne. **14** 25. **15** Lucan. **16** Margaret Thatcher. **17** Vietnam. **18** Israel. **19** Ice. **20** Yorkshire. **21** Mountbatten. **22** Teresa. **23** France. **24** Second. **25** Spain. **26** Northern Ireland. **27** Australia. **28** Evert. **29** Callaghan. **30** Liberal.

Quiz 101 Science: Technology

Answers - see Quiz 102, page 112

1 What type of energy is generated by PowerGen?
2 What type of company can be found in Silicon Glen in Scotland?
3 In a car, what might be disc or drum?
4 Was the first modern cassette made in the 40s, 60s or 70s?
5 Which type of transport has rubber skirts?
6 A rotor propels what type of aircraft?
7 Did early TV have 405 or 625 lines?
8 The Manhattan Project in the early 40s was developing what?
9 Which substance, recently found to be dangerous, is called 'woolly rock'?
10 What is the lowest number on the Beaufort Scale?
11 Apples and Apricots were what in the technological world?
12 Is coal obtained from decayed animal or plant matter?
13 What produces bubbles in the making of champagne?
14 Is the empennage of a plane at the front or the tail?
15 William Morris, Lord Nuffield was the first UK manufacturer of mass produced what?
16 What does 'P' stand for in DTP?
17 Entrepreneur Ted Turner is a big name in which industry?
18 What ill-fated personal transport was invented by Sir Clive Sinclair?
19 Which letter is farthest left on a computer keyboard?
20 Which country is the world's largest exporter of grain?
21 Which metal is used thermometers?
22 Which colour identifies an ordinary diesel pump at a service station?
23 Nylon took its name from which two cities?
24 Which underground weapon did Whitehead develop in 1866?
25 Which boom is produced by breaking the sound barrier?
26 C-Curity was the first type of which fastener?
27 What does 'C' stand for in ASCII?
28 What sort of factory did Joseph Rowntree found?
29 What does a pluviometer measure?
30 Bournville was established for the workers of which company?

Answers

Pot Luck 50 (see Quiz 102, page 112)

1 Austria. **2** Simon & Garfunkel. **3** Claustrophobia. **4** Palm Sunday. **5** Sunday. **6** September. **7** Fossils. **8** Bambi. **9** David. **10** Harry Houdini. **11** York. **12** Esther Rantzen. **13** Iron. **14** Pratchett. **15** Warwickshire. **16** American football. **17** Budgie. **18** Scotland. **19** Red Dwarf. **20** Eyre. **21** Dvorak. **22** Terry Wogan. **23** London. **24** Ireland. **25** Filbert. **26** The Archies. **27** Party. **28** Drew. **29** Independent. **30** Computer.

Quiz 102 Pot Luck 50

Answers - see Quiz 101, page 111

1 Racing driver Niki Lauda was born in which country?
2 Which duo had hits with Mrs Robinson and America?
3 What is the fear of enclosed spaces called?
4 Which Sunday comes before Easter Day?
5 On TV, which night featured a show from the London Palladium?
6 Alphabetically, which is the last of the calendar months?
7 What would a palaeontologist study?
8 Which Disney creature nickname was given to Tony Blair?
9 What is the first name of New Baywatch star Hasselhoff?
10 When Eric Weiss escaped from his name he was known as who?
11 Which race course hosts the Ebor Handicap?
12 Which female presenter fronted the long running That's Life?
13 Which metal has the chemical symbol Fe?
14 Which Terry writes the best selling sci fi Discworld novels?
15 Which English county did Brian Lara first play for?
16 What's the sport if the Chicago Bears take on the Miami Dolphins?
17 What is the name of Sarah Ferguson's little helicopter?
18 In which country did golf originate?
19 Holly the computer appeared on which TV sci fi comedy?
20 Which is Australia's largest lake?
21 Who composed the New World Symphony?
22 Who presents Auntie's Sporting Bloomers on TV?
23 In which city does The Last Night of the Proms take place?
24 Vocalist Enya hails from which country?
25 Which Street is home for Leicester City?
26 Sugar Sugar was a one off number 1 for which group?
27 Which word can go in after BIRTHDAY, HEN, LABOUR and STAG?
28 Which Barrymore was in E.T. and Batman Forever?
29 What does the I stand for in ITV?
30 What would you be using if you needed a mouse mat?

Answers

Science: Technology (see Quiz 101, page 111)
1 Electricity. **2** Computer firms. **3** Brakes. **4** 60s. **5** Hovercraft. **6** Helicopter. **7** 405. **8** Atomic bomb. **9** Asbestos. **10** 0. **11** Computers. **12** Plant. **13** Carbon dioxide. **14** Tail. **15** Cars. **16** Publishing. **17** Broadcasting. **18** C5. **19** Q. **20** USA. **21** Mercury. **22** Black. **23** New York, London. **24** Torpedo. **25** Sonic boom. **26** Zip. **27** Code. **28** Cocoa. **29** Rainfall. **30** Cadbury's.

Quiz 103 TV Gold

Answers - see Quiz 104, page 114

1 Who was head of the family in Till Death Us Do Part?
2 Which house was Revisited in the classic 80s drama?
3 Where was the BBC's 1992 ill fated soap set?
4 On which weekend evening was Jim'll Fix It broadcast?
5 In Tenko the women were imprisoned by whom?
6 What was Lovejoy's occupation?
7 Which series was about a Mobile Army Surgical Hospital in Korea?
8 Which Michael played the hapless Frank Spencer?
9 What was unusual about Hopkirk in the Randall and Hopkirk agency?
10 What institution was Please Sir set in?
11 What was the rank of Phil Silvers' Bilko?
12 Who were the US TV equivalent of the Beatles?
13 Which Leonard Rossiter sitcom sounds like a problem with old houses?
14 How was Arthur Fonzerelli known in Happy Days?
15 Which animals did Barbara Woodhouse work with?
16 Who was June in Terry and June?
17 What sort of animal was Grizzly Adams?
18 What was Torquay's most famous hotel run by Basil and Sybil?
19 Jewel in the Crown was set in wartime where?
20 In which county was All Creatures Great and Small set?
21 What sort of performers were in Spitting Image?
22 Which father of Paula Yates presented Stars on Sunday?
23 What was the profession of Albert Steptoe and son Harold?
24 Which hero was "Riding through the glen, With his band of Men"?
25 Which classic sci fi series began in the 23rd century?
26 In which country was Van der Valk set?
27 What sort of statesman was Alan B'Stard?
28 Which Eric played Hattie Jacques' brother?
29 Was it Mork or Mindy who came from the planet Ork?
30 What sort of Men were Bill and Ben?

Answers

Past Times: The 80s (see Quiz 104, page 114)
1 Margaret Thatcher. **2** London. **3** Eggs. **4** Johnson. **5** North Sea. **6** King's Cross. **7** Neil Kinnock. **8** Duchess of Windsor. **9** Zeebrugge. **10** Philippines. **11** South Africa. **12** Prince Andrew. **13** Runner. **14** Wembley. **15** Morecambe. **16** Parkinson. **17** Bradford. **18** Liberal Democrats. **19** In space. **20** Greenham. **21** Harrods. **22** Bjorn Borg. **23** Car accident. **24** Dallas. **25** Falklands. **26** Tyson. **27** Champion. **28** Reagan. **29** New York. **30** Kindergarten.

Quiz 104 Past Times: The 80s

Answers - see Quiz 103, page 113

1 Which serving British PM survived an assassination attempt?
2 In which city did the SAS storm the Iranian embassy?
3 Edwina Currie resigned over what type of farm food?
4 Which Ben was disqualified from the Seoul Olympics for drug taking?
5 In which Sea did the oil rig Piper Alpha catch fire?
6 Which north London Tube station was gutted by fire in 1987?
7 Who was Labour leader when Thatcher had her third election victory?
8 Which late Duchess's jewels were auctioned for over £30 million?
9 The Herald of Free Enterprise sank off which Belgian port?
10 President Marcos was ousted in a rebellion in which island country?
11 Desmond Tutu became an Archbishop in which country?
12 Who was the second of the Queen's sons to marry in the 80s?
13 Was Zola Budd a swimmer, a runner or a gymnast?
14 At which UK stadium was the Live Aid concert held?
15 Which Eric, half of a classic comedy duo died in 1984?
16 Which Tory minister Cecil resigned in a scandal in 1983?
17 In which Yorkshire city's football ground was there a fatal fire in '85?
18 What is the full name of the Lib Dems, formed in 1989?
19 Sally Ride became the USA's first woman where?
20 At which Common was there a camp against cruise missiles?
21 Outside which London store did a bomb explode in December 1983?
22 Which Swedish tennis star retired age 26?
23 In what type of accident was Princess Grace of Monaco killed?
24 Which soap asked the audience asked 'Who shot JR?'
25 Which war in the south Atlantic was Britain involved in?
26 Which Mike became the youngest heavyweight boxing champion?
27 Which Bob rode Aldaniti to a Grand National win in 1981?
28 Which US president was the victim of an assassination attempt?
29 In which city was Beatle John Lennon murdered?
30 Where was Lady Diana Spencer working when photographed in a seemingly see through skirt?

Answers

TV Gold (see Quiz 103, page 113)
1 Alf Garnett. **2** Brideshead. **3** Spain. **4** Saturday. **5** Japanese. **6** Antiques dealer. **7** M*A*S*H. **8** Crawford. **9** He was a ghost. **10** School. **11** Sergeant. **12** The Monkees. **13** Rising Damp. **14** The Fonz/Fonzie. **15** Dogs. **16** June Whitfield. **17** Human. **18** Fawlty Towers. **19** India. **20** Yorkshire. **21** Puppets. **22** Jess Yates. **23** Rag & bone merchants. **24** Robin Hood. **25** Star Trek. **26** Holland. **27** New Statesman. **28** Sykes. **29** Mork. **30** Flowerpot men.

Quiz 105 Pop: Charts

Answers - see Quiz 106, page 116

1 Whose album True Blue was No 1 in 28 countries?
2 What was The Spice Girls' first No 1?
3 Whose charity hit included Something About the Way You Look Tonight?
4 Which of Madonna's two hits from Evita got highest in the charts?
5 Which Frank Sinatra hit has spent most weeks in the UK charts?
6 In which decade did the UK singles charts begin?
7 Who as well as The Troggs charted with Love Is All Around?
8 Which wartime song charted with Robson & Jerome's Unchained Melody?
9 Which father and daughter had a No 1 with Somethin' Stupid?
10 How was Roberto Milani known when he had Europe's '96 top seller?
11 Which soccer side charted with Come On You Reds?
12 Whose Release Me spent a record number of weeks in the charts?
13 Was Celine Dion's Power of Love the same as Jennifer Rush's or Frankie Goes to Hollywood's?
14 Who was the first all female band to have three consecutive No 1's?
15 How many weeks did Elvis spend in the charts duetting?
16 Who spent most weeks in the UK charts, the Stones or Status Quo?
17 Which musical did Boyzone's No 1 No Matter What come from?
18 Who is the most successful Australian female to have been in the UK singles charts?
19 Billboard is a list of best selling records where?
20 Which band were in the chart most weeks in 1995 and again in 1996?
21 Which family were at No 1 with Do the Bartman?
22 Which Scandinavian country do chart toppers Aqua come from?
23 Who accompanied Vic Reeves on his No 1 hit Dizzy?
24 Whose 96 No 1s were Firestarter and Breathe?
25 Which Boys' first No 1 was West End Girls?
26 Whose Cigarettes and Alcohol was their highest chart hit at the time?
27 Which solo Briton Cliff has spent most weeks in the UK singles charts?
28 Which female solo star has spent most weeks in the British charts?
29 Love Me For a Reason charted for The Osmonds and which band?
30 Who wrote the series Crocodile Shoes and its chart songs?

Answers

Who Was Who? (see Quiz 106, page 116)
1 Bill Clinton. **2** Salvation Army. **3** Louis Pasteur. **4** Nobel. **5** Henry VIII. **6** Guy Fawkes. **7** Henry Ford. **8** Second World War. **9** India. **10** Oil. **11** Glenys Kinnock. **12** Charles. **13** Che Guevara. **14** Queen Victoria. **15** Pankhurst. **16** Saddam Hussein. **17** One. **18** American. **19** W.G.Grace. **20** 56. **21** Buster Keaton. **22** Mandela. **23** Mao Tse Tung. **24** Groucho. **25** Mary. **26** Miller. **27** Mussolini. **28** Italian. **29** Tony Blair. **30** John F Kennedy.

Quiz 106 Who Was Who?

Answers - see Quiz 105, page 115

1 Who became US President in 1992 when Governor of Arkansas?
2 Which religious Army was founded by Catherine and William Booth?
3 Which scientist gave his name to the process of pasteurisation?
4 Who left $9 million to give prizes in five different fields?
5 Which King of England provided his children with most stepmothers?
6 Who lit the fuse for the 1605 Gunpowder Plot?
7 Was it John Ford or Henry Ford who manufactured cars?
8 During which war did Anne Frank write her diary?
9 Indira Gandhi was Prime Minister of which country?
10 John Paul Getty made his millions from which commodity?
11 Who was Labour leader Neil Kinnock's wife who became an MEP?
12 Who was the first 20th century Prince of Wales to be divorced?
13 How was Argentinean Ernesto Guevara de la Serna better known?
14 William Gladstone was Prime Minister under which monarch?
15 What was suffragette leader Emmeline Goulden's married name?
16 Who became President of Iraq in 1979?
17 How many English kings have been called Stephen?
18 What was the nationality of the Duchess of Windsor?
19 Which legendary cricketer had the first names William Gilbert?
20 How old was Hitler when he died, 46, 56 or 66?
21 By which name was silent movie star Joseph Keaton better known?
22 Which Nelson was the first black President of South Africa?
23 How was Mao Zedong also known?
24 Which Marx brother had a moustache, cigar and funny walk?
25 According to The Bible who was the mother of Jesus?
26 Which trombonist Glenn became a famous bandleader?
27 Who was Italian dictator between 1926 and 1943?
28 What was the nationality of inventor Marconi?
29 Which of Queen Elizabeth II's Prime Ministers was not even born when she came to the throne?
30 Who was the youngest US President to die in office?

Answers

Pop: Charts (see Quiz 105, page 115)
1 Madonna. **2** Wannabe. **3** Elton John. **4** Don't Cry For Me Argentina. **5** My Way. **6** 50s. **7** Wet Wet Wet. **8** The White Cliffs of Dover. **9** Frank & Nancy Sinatra. **10** Robert Miles. **11** Manchester United. **12** Englebert Humperdinck. **13** Jennifer Rush's. **14** Spice Girls. **15** None. **16** Status Quo. **17** Whistle Down the Wind. **18** Kylie Minogue. **19** USA. **20** Oasis. **21** The Simpsons. **22** Denmark. **23** The Wonder Stuff. **24** Prodigy. **25** Pet Shop. **26** Oasis. **27** Richard. **28** Madonna. **29** Boyzone. **30** Jimmy Nail.

Quiz 107 Pop: Superstars

Answers - see Quiz 108, page 118

1 Sir Paul McCartney was awarded the freedom of which city?
2 Which legendary band released The Wall?
3 Which soul star Ray has the nickname The Genius?
4 Which Shirley was dubbed the Tigress from Tiger Bay?
5 Supermodel Rachel Hunter married which superstar Rod?
6 Which ex Police singer founded the Rainforest Foundation in 1988?
7 Who does not use her surname Ciccone?
8 Which brother completes the Gibb trio with Maurice and Robin?
9 Which Billy toured with Elton John in 1998?
10 Which rock superstar was Lisa Marie Presley second husband?
11 Diana Ross is billed as who on her recording of I Will Survive?
12 Montserrat Caballe recorded Barcelona with which rock legend?
13 Which drummer's solo album No Jacket Required was a best seller?
14 Which Rolling Stone did not normally play an instrument on stage?
15 Which group was heard on the soundtrack of Saturday Night Fever?
16 Whose hits range from The Laughing Gnome to Space Oddity?
17 Who sang You Don't Bring Me Flowers with Barbra Streisand?
18 Which Queen of Soul sang the best version of Nessun Dorma according to Pavarotti?
19 Which band would you find The Edge and Bono in?
20 Who lived in a mansion called Graceland?
21 Which boys liked Califrnia Girls?
22 Whose Streets of Philadelphia was his highest hit at the time in 1994?
23 Which Stevie dropped the tag Little and had hits well into adulthood?
24 Which Tina recorded Bond theme Goldeneye?
25 Which superstar founded the Rocket record label?
26 All Lionel Richie's early hits were on which record label?
27 Which Scottish football fan has the first names Roderick David?
28 Which Roy charted with Crying with kd lang four years after his death?
29 Which Barbra did actor James Brolin marry in 1998?
30 Which Barry's song Copacabana became a musical?

Answers

Leisure: The Media (see Quiz 108, page 118)
1 World Service. **2** Magazine. **3** Horse racing. **4** Radio Times. **5** Classic FM. **6** Radio 4. **7** London. **8** Sunday Sport. **9** Five. **10** Manchester. **11** Gossip column. **12** Musical. **13** Men. **14** Saturday. **15** Top shelf. **16** Financial Times. **17** Mail on Sunday. **18** Sunday. **19** BBC. **20** Hello! **21** Murdoch. **22** Three. **23** Independent. **24** Private Eye. **25** Tabloid. **26** England & Scotland. **27** Doctor. **28** Weekly. **29** Edwina Currie. **30** Frost.

Quiz 108 Leisure: The Media

Answers - see Quiz 107, page 117

1 Which BBC radio and TV service broadcasts abroad?
2 Is The Spectator a programme to watch or a magazine to read?
3 The Sporting Life devotes itself to which sport?
4 Which radio and TV listings magazine is published by the BBC?
5 Which independent radio station specialises in classical music?
6 Is The Archers on Radio 1 or Radio 4?
7 Where does Capital Radio broadcast to?
8 What is the Sunday version of Daily Sport called?
9 Which BBC Radio station has Live after its number?
10 In which north of England city is Granada TV based?
11 What sort of Column tells of stories and rumours about celebrities?
12 What does M stand for in the pop paper NME?
13 Is GQ for men or women?
14 On which day is Grandstand always broadcast on BBC1?
15 On which shelf would someone buy an 'adult' magazine?
16 What does FT stand for in the name of the financial daily newspaper?
17 What is the Daily Mail's Sunday paper called?
18 On which day of the week is the News of the World published?
19 Which corporation is known as Auntie?
20 Which magazine about celebs is based on the Spanish mag Hola!?
21 Which Rupert founded Sky Television?
22 Which page in a newspaper is famous for its nude photos?
23 What does I stand for in ITV?
24 Which satirical magazine shares its name with the nickname for a detective?
25 Which newspaper is larger, a tabloid or a broadsheet?
26 Border TV serves the borders of which two countries?
27 What professional person would read The Lancet?
28 How often does the magazine Take A Break appear?
29 Which ex MP presented Late Night Currie on Radio 5 Live?
30 Which Sir David co founded LWT and TV-am?

Answers

Pop: Superstars (see Quiz 107, page 117)
1 Liverpool. **2** Pink Floyd. **3** Charles. **4** Bassey. **5** Stewart. **6** Sting. **7** Madonna. **8** Barry. **9** Joel. **10** Michael Jackson. **11** Diana. **12** Freddy Mercury. **13** Phil Collins. **14** Mick Jagger. **15** Bee Gees. **16** David Bowie. **17** Neil Diamond. **18** Aretha Franklin. **19** U2. **20** Elvis Presley. **21** Beach Boys. **22** Bruce Springsteen. **23** Wonder. **24** Turner. **25** Elton John. **26** Motown. **27** Rod Stewart. **28** Orbison. **29** Streisand. **30** Manilow.

Quiz 109 Pop: Who's Who?

Answers - see Quiz 110, page 120

1 Who is Julian Lennon's stepmother?
2 Which pop wife has Liam and a shamrock tattooed on her ankle?
3 Which George did not make a record for five years because of a dispute with Sony?
4 In which Irish city was Sinead O'Connor born?
5 Which Elaine changed her surname from Bickerstaff and went on to star in many West End musicals?
6 Which Stevie led the campaign to commemorate Martin Luther King's birthday in the US?
7 How is Katherine Dawn Lang better known?
8 Bernie Taupin collaborated with which performer for over 20 years?
9 Which Boys were famous for their surfing sound?
10 Whose real name is Charles Edward Anderson Berry?
11 In what type of tragic accident did John Denver meet his death?
12 Which composer of Boyzone's No Matter What appeared with them on Top of the Pops?
13 Andrew Ridgeley was the less famous half of which group?
14 Which band always comes last alphabetically?
15 Which ex Jackson 5 member was 40 in 1998?
16 The Spice Girls recorded their early hits on which label?
17 PJ and Duncan were also known as who?
18 Which soul star did Bryan Ferry name his son Otis after?
19 What are the first names of the Everly Brothers?
20 Was Bryan Adams born in Canada or the USA?
21 Who was left handed, Lennon or McCartney?
22 Which ex husband of Cher died in a skiing accident ?
23 Bjork hails from which country?
24 Who made the album Let's Talk About Love?
25 Which Olivia won a Hayley Mills look alike contest?
26 Who made the album 12 Deadly Cyns?
27 Which Mark co founded Dire Straits?
28 What name links Ant and Faith?
29 Which hit by D:Ream was used in the 97 Labour election campaign?
30 Who changed his name to a symbol?

Answers

Celebs: The Royals (see Quiz 110, page 120)
1 Stark. **2** Brother in law. **3** Some of her dresses. **4** Anne. **5** Edward. **6** Princess Michael of Kent. **7** Margaret. **8** Panorama. **9** Eton. **10** Bulimia. **11** Sarah, Duchess of York. **12** Harry. **13** Andrew. **14** The Queen. **15** Britannia. **16** Miss. **17** Balmoral. **18** Hip. **19** Christmas. **20** Candle in the Wind. **21** Grace Kelly. **22** Grandmother. **23** Westminster. **24** Weight Watchers. **25** Photographer. **26** Paris. **27** Windsor. **28** Queen Victoria. **29** Navy. **30** Anne.

Quiz 110 Celebs: The Royals

Answers - see Quiz 109, page 119

1 Which famous actress Koo was romantically linked to Prince Andrew?
2 What relation is Prince Philip to Princess Margaret?
3 What did the Princess of Wales sell at auction in 1997?
4 What is the Princess Royal's real first name?
5 Which Prince's name was linked with PR girl Sophie Rhys-Jones?
6 What is the title of the wife of Prince Michael of Kent?
7 Which Princess was prevented from marrying divorced Peter Townsend in the 50s?
8 On which programme did Princess Diana say her marriage had been "a bit crowded"?
9 Prince Harry followed Prince William to which school in 1998?
10 Which dietary illness did Princess Diana allegedly suffer from?
11 Who is the mother of Princesses Beatrice and Eugenie?
12 Which son of Prince Charles has red hair?
13 Who is older, Prince Andrew or Prince Edward?
14 Which Royal is always referred to as Her Majesty?
15 Which Royal yacht was decommissioned in 1997?
16 Is Princess Anne's daughter a Princess, or a Miss?
17 Where is the Queen's holiday home north of the border?
18 What did the Queen Mother have replaced after a fall in 1997?
19 At which time of year does the Queen always make a TV broadcast?
20 What did Elton John sing at Princess Diana's funeral?
21 Which wife of Prince Rainier of Monaco was an Oscar winner?
22 What relation is the Queen Mother to Prince Charles?
23 In which Abbey did Prince Andrew and Sarah Ferguson marry?
24 Which 'Watchers' organisation did Fergie advertise?
25 Which profession is shared by Lords Snowdon and Lichfield?
26 In which city was Princess Diana tragically killed?
27 Which castle was reopened in 1998 after being damaged by fire?
28 Who was the last British monarch of the 19th century?
29 Before his marriage was Prince Philip in the army or the navy?
30 Which Princess was married to Captain Mark Phillips?

Answers

Pop: Who's Who? (see Quiz 109, page 119)
1 Yoko Ono. **2** Patsy Kensit. **3** Michael. **4** Dublin. **5** Paige. **6** Wonder. **7** k d lang. **8** Elton John. **9** Beach Boys. **10** Chuck Berry. **11** Plane crash. **12** Andrew Lloyd Webber. **13** Wham! **14** ZZ Top. **15** Michael. **16** Virgin. **17** Ant & Dec. **18** Otis Redding. **19** Don & Phil. **20** Canada. **21** McCartney. **22** Sonny. **23** Iceland. **24** Celine Dion. **25** Newton-John. **26** Cyndi Lauper. **27** Knopfler. **28** Adam. **29** Things Can Only Get Better. **30** Prince.

Quiz 111 Geography: World Tour

Answers - see Quiz 112, page 122

1 Which long river has White and Blue tributaries?
2 Which religious leader is head of state of the Vatican?
3 Is Perth on the west or east coast of Australia?
4 In which country is Calgary?
5 Does Bombay or Tokyo have the higher population?
6 What sort of Snowman is another name for the Himalayan yeti?
7 What is the world's smallest, flattest and driest continent?
8 Is Argentina in the northern or southern half of South America?
9 Pakistan and Bangladesh both border which country?
10 Which country's name is an anagram of PURE?
11 The West Indies lie in which Sea?
12 Zambia is a neighbour of which country which also begins with Z?
13 Which Egyptian canal links the Red Sea and the Mediterranean?
14 Is Ghana on the African coast or wholly inland?
15 Which ocean is the world's deepest?
16 In which country is the homeland of KwaZulu?
17 Who is commemorated at Washington's Lincoln Memorial?
18 Which US state has the zipcode (postcode) AZ?
19 New South Wales is in which country?
20 Which African desert is the world's largest?
21 Is Swaziland a monarchy or a republic?
22 Mount Kilimanjaro is the highest point of which continent?
23 Which US island state has the world's highest annual rainfall?
24 Which ocean lies to the east of South America?
25 Which Islamic Republic used to be called Persia?
26 Two thirds of Greenland lies in which Circle?
27 Is Namibia in northern or southern Africa?
28 Which country's head of state is Saddam Hussein al-Tikriti?
29 Which People's Republic has the world's largest population?
30 Alberta is a province of which country?

Answers

20th C Who's Who? (see Quiz 112, page 122)

1 Andy Warhol. **2** Saddam Hussein. **3** Jonathan Aitken. **4** Brian Epstein. **5** Gorbachev. **6** Margaret Thatcher. **7** Princess Diana. **8** Victoria. **9** Jean Shrimpton. **10** Juan Carlos. **11** Shaw. **12** Tutankhamun. **13** Jimmy Carter. **14** Gordon Brown. **15** Mother Theresa. **16** Livingstone. **17** Jim Henson. **18** Ruud Gullit. **19** Sutch. **20** Paul McCartney. **21** Martin Luther King. **22** Agnetha. **23** Dior. **24** India. **25** Albert Einstein.

Quiz 112 20th C Who's Who?

Answers - see Quiz 111, page 121

1 Who thought that everyone would be famous for 15 minutes?
2 Who led Iraq into the 90s Gulf War?
3 Which former cabinet minister was jailed for 18 months in 1999?
4 Who was manager of The Beatles?
5 Which Russian introduced policies of glasnost?
6 Who became the first woman to lead a British political party?
7 Whose dresses raised £2 million for charity in a June 97 auction?
8 Which British monarch died in 1901?
9 Which 60s model was known as 'The Shrimp'?
10 Who became king of Spain in the 70s following General Franco's death?
11 Which G B wrote the play Pygmalion that was adapted into My Fair Lady?
12 Whose ancient tomb was discovered in Egypt in 1922?
13 Who was the ex peanut farmer who became US President?
14 Who delivered Labour's first budget of the 90s?
15 Who was awarded a Nobel Peace Prize for her work with the poor in India?
16 Which Ken was leader of the GLC?
17 Who was the man who created The Muppets?
18 Who promised he would bring 'really sexy football' to Newcastle?
19 Which Screaming Lord stood unsuccessfully in many parliamentary elections?
20 Which pop star married Linda Eastman in the 60s?
21 Who declared he had 'a dream' where all Americans would live as equals?
22 Who teamed up with Benny, Bjorn and Anni-Frid to form Abba?
23 Which Christian unveiled the New Look of the late 40s?
24 Mahatma Gandhi led the non-violent struggle for which country to break free from Britain?
25 Who formulated the theory of relativity early in the century?

Answers

Geography: World Tour (see Quiz 111, page 121)
1 Nile. **2** Pope. **3** West. **4** Canada. **5** Bombay. **6** Abominable. **7** Australia. **8** Southern. **9** India. **10** Peru. **11** Caribbean. **12** Zimbabwe. **13** Suez. **14** Coast. **15** Pacific. **16** South Africa. **17** Abraham Lincoln. **18** Arizona. **19** Australia. **20** Sahara. **21** Monarchy. **22** Africa. **23** Hawaii. **24** Atlantic. **25** Iran. **26** Arctic Circle. **27** Southern. **28** Iraq. **29** China. **30** Canada.

Quiz 113 Pot Luck 51

Answers - see Quiz 114, page 124

1 Who was the first Spice Girl to leave the group?
2 What or who was Mitch, the bringer of destruction to Honduras?
3 Which Richard scripted Notting Hill?
4 What name do William Hague and Bill Clinton share?
5 Which John was dropped from a series of Sainsbury's ads?
6 What was the occupation of Beirut hostage John McCarthy?
7 What does the letter D stand for in the initials DTP?
8 Which country does soccer star Davor Suker play for?
9 Eric Clapp found fame under which name?
10 Which TV gardener established the garden at Barnsdale?
11 The board game Monopoly produced limited special edition sets linked to which 1998 event?
12 Eva Peron was the subject of which film and musical?
13 On TV, to which Matthew do wannabe stars say, "Tonight, Matthew, I'm going to be...."?
14 Which paper ran the Sophie Topless story about Sophie Rhys-Jones?
15 Where in London was the 80s Live Aid Concert staged?
16 Whose Line Is It Anyway? transferred from radio to which TV channel?
17 Robin Smith represented England at which sport?
18 Which Jack was Agriculture Minister when sale of beef on the bone was banned?
19 What type of music was Ronnie Scott associated with?
20 Which Caroline presented The Mrs Merton Show?
21 In the 90s, Formula 1 racing was controversially exempted from a ban stopping the advertising of what?
22 What two colours are the stripes on the United States of America flag?
23 Whigfield sang about which night of the week?
24 Which country won cricket's 1999 World Cup?
25 Tom Cruise was born in which decade of the century?

Answers

Celebs (see Quiz 114, page 124)
1 Kensit. **2** Texas. **3** Australia. **4** Elizabeth Hurley. **5** Ulrika. **6** Gary Rhodes. **7** 60s. **8** Cakes. **9** Burton. **10** Sophia Loren. **11** The Spice Girls. **12** Will. **13** John Major's. **14** Mel B. **15** Elvis Presley. **16** Mick Jagger. **17** Campbell. **18** Geldof. **19** Fashion design. **20** Versace. **21** Rhys-Jones. **22** Rod Stewart. **23** Ivana Trump. **24** Paris. **25** Ronald Reagan.

Quiz 114 Celebs

Answers - see Quiz 113, page 123

1 Which Patsy married Liam Gallagher?
2 Jerry Hall hails from which oil state?
3 Where does Dame Edna Everage hail from?
4 Who accompanied Hugh Grant to the premiere of Four Weddings and a Funeral in a dress held together with safety pins?
5 Which blonde Ms Jonsson advertised crisps with Gary Lineker?
6 Which celebrity chef had a TV series called Rhodes Around Britain?
7 Twiggy was the most famous model of which decade?
8 Jane Asher is also famous for baking and selling what?
9 Which Richard did Elizabeth Taylor marry twice?
10 Which Italian actress launched her own perfume Sophia?
11 Which quintet switched on the Oxford Street Christmas lights in 1996?
12 Who was Julia Carling's first husband?
13 Which Prime Minister's son did Emma Noble marry in 1999?
14 Which Spice Girl was the first to marry?
15 Michael Jackson's first wife was the daughter of which 'King'?
16 Which Rolling Stone did Jerry Hall marry?
17 Which supermodel Naomi wrote a novel called Swan?
18 Which Bob who founded Band Aid received an honorary knighthood in 1986?
19 Giorgio Armani is famous in which field?
20 Fashion designer Donatella, sister of the murdered Gianni has which surname?
21 What does the R-J part of the PR agency R-JH stand for?
22 Model Rachel Hunter was married to which veteran rock star?
23 Ivanka Trump has a similar name to her mother; who is she?
24 Brigitte Bardot was awarded the freedom of her capital city; what is it?
25 Which 1980s US president survived an assassination attempt?

Answers

Pot Luck 51 (see Quiz 113, page 123)
1 Ginger Spice - Geri Halliwell. **2** Hurricane. **3** Curtis. **4** Jefferson. **5** Cleese. **6** Journalist. **7** Desk. **8** Croatia. **9** Eric Clapton. **10** Geoff Hamilton. **11** The World Cup. **12** Evita. **13** Kelly. **14** The Sun. **15** Wembley Stadium. **16** Channel 4. **17** Cricket. **18** Cunningham. **19** Jazz. **20** Aherne. **21** Tobacco. **22** Red and white. **23** Saturday. **24** Australia. **25** 60s.

Quiz 115 Pot Luck 52

Answers - see Quiz 116, page 126

1 What is Cherie Booth's married name?
2 Which animal name was given to the terrorist Carlos who was tried in 1997?
3 In what month did Prince Edward get married?
4 Which MP Mrs Currie landed in hot water about eggs?
5 Who is Griff Rhys Jones' comic TV partner?
6 With which sport is Charles Barkley associated?
7 Which Ford first mass produced the car?
8 Which annual sporting event was hit by sit downs and go slows in 1998?
9 Which song took Rolf Harris back to the charts in the 90s?
10 Which Michael revived his TV chat show of the 70s in the late 90s?
11 In ASCII what does the letter C stand for ?
12 Guides wear what colour of uniform?
13 Who was the first of the Queen's children to marry?
14 Truro is the administrative centre of which English county?
15 Clare Short has represented which party in parliament?
16 What kind of Girls featured in Anna Friel's film set in the Second World War?
17 In banking what does T stand for in TSB?
18 Which comedy show, broadcast around the time of the evening news, launched the career of Rowan Atkinson?
19 Django Reinhardt was associated with which musical instrument?
20 Whose first European ad campaign was for Max Factor in 1999?
21 What did Ceylon change its name to it 1970?
22 Chris Woods represented England at which sport?
23 In which country was comedian Dave Allen born?
24 What colour did the Redcoats adopt at Butlins after a 90s revamp?
25 The deepwater port of Malmo was developed in which country?

Answers

TV – On the Box (see Quiz 116, page 126)
1 Emergency. **2** Cheers. **3** Ireland. **4** How. **5** Dexter. **6** Fox. **7** The Three Musketeers. **8** Baywatch. **9** Last of the Summer Wine. **10** Blake's 7. **11** Casualty. **12** East Anglia. **13** Morton. **14** Gary. **15** Noel Edmonds. **16** Railways. **17** Cricket. **18** Peak Practice. **19** Glasgow. **20** Hospital. **21** Simpson. **22** Soldier Soldier. **23** Colorado. **24** Son. **25** This Life.

Quiz 116 TV - On the Box

Answers - see Quiz 115, page 125

1 What does E stand for in the medical drama ER?
2 In which series did Dr Frasier Crane first appear?
3 In which country was Ballykissangel set?
4 Which children's show was introduced with, and named after a native North American greeting?
5 Which Colin created Inspector Morse and appeared as an extra in every episode of the series?
6 What type of animal was Basil Brush?
7 Dogtanian and the Three Muskehounds was based on which classic book?
8 In which US TV series did Pamela Anderson shoot to fame?
9 Which long running comedy series about three OAPs was filmed in Holmfirth?
10 Which Sci-Fi freedom fighters were led by a man called Roj Blake?
11 In which show might you see Charlie and Duffy in A & E?
12 In which part of Eastern Britain was Lovejoy set?
13 Which Andrew wrote the book on which the Sky mini series Diana: Her True Story was based?
14 Who was Tony's flatmate in Men Behaving Badly?
15 On whose show were Gotcha Oscar's presented?
16 Oh Doctor Beeching was a sitcom about the closure of what?
17 Which sport was the subject of the sitcom Outside Edge?
18 Which drama series told of a Practice called The Beeches in Derbyshire?
19 Rab C. Nesbitt was a native of which Scottish city?
20 80s drama St Elsewhere was set in what type of institution?
21 What was the surname of cartoon characters Homer, Marge and Bart?
22 In which army series did Robson and Jerome find fame?
23 South Park is situated in which US state famous for its ski resorts?
24 What relation was Harold to Albert Steptoe?
25 Which series about twentysomething lawyers starred Daniela Nardini and Jack Davenport?

Answers

Pot Luck 52 (see Quiz 115, page 125)
1 Blair. **2** The Jackal. **3** June. **4** Edwina. **5** Mel Smith. **6** Basketball. **7** Henry. **8** Tour de France. **9** Stairway To Heaven. **10** Parkinson. **11** Code. **12** Blue. **13** Anne. **14** Cornwall. **15** Labour. **16** Land. **17** Trustee. **18** Not the Nine O'Clock News. **19** Guitar. **20** Madonna. **21** Sri Lanka. **22** Soccer. **23** Ireland. **24** Red. **25** Sweden.

Quiz 117 Pot Luck 53

Answers - see Quiz 118, page 128

1 What was the name given to the first cloned sheep?
2 Which bear became the mascot of the Children In Need appeals?
3 The Millennium Dome is in which part of London?
4 Doris Kapelhoff found fame by adopting which time related name?
5 Tessa Sanderson is associated with which athletic event?
6 The Cosby Show was set in which American city?
7 In an Evita song what word follows, "Don't cry for me..."?
8 Which Greg was BBC Sports Personality of the Year in 1997?
9 Which Tom married Nicole Kidman?
10 Prince Edward was made Earl of where?
11 Which soccer team does Jarvis Cocker support?
12 Jamie Lee Curtis was born in which decade of the century?
13 Country House was a hit for which band?
14 On a computer keyboard what letter is far left on the top row of letters?
15 Mussolini was dictator in which country?
16 Antonio Carluccio writes about which country's food?
17 Which country does golfer Greg Norman come from?
18 Which Irish presenter introduced the sporting gaffe programme Oddballs?
19 Which RAF pilot Andy broke the sound barrier travelling on land?
20 Which sporting personality was born Shirley Crabtree?
21 In which country were Fiat cars first produced?
22 Which director Mr Berkeley included elaborate choreography in his films?
23 Former athlete Seb Coe became an MP for which party?
24 In which city was Gianni Versace shot?
25 In children's TV how were Anthony McPartlin and Declan Donnelly first known?

Answers

Soccer (see Quiz 118, page 128)
1 Aberdeen. **2** David Batty. **3** The Divine Ponytail. **4** Italy. **5** Bolton. **6** Solskjaer. **7** Kenny Dalglish. **8** Nottm Forest. **9** Aston Villa. **10** Tony Adams. **11** Brazil. **12** Leeds. **13** Dennis Bergkamp. **14** Holland. **15** Southampton. **16** Eagle. **17** Roker Park. **18** Arsenal. **19** Blackburn. **20** Terry Venables. **21** Gordon Banks. **22** Watford. **23** Dave Beasant. **24** Chelsea. **25** Aston Villa.

Quiz 118 Soccer

Answers - see Quiz 117, page 127

1 Alex Ferguson joined Man Utd after managing which club?
2 Who had the last kick in England's 1998 World Cup campaign?
3 What nickname was Italian superstar Roberto Baggio given?
4 Which country does world record transfer man Christian Vieri play for?
5 Which soccer team moved to the Reebok Stadium in the 90s?
6 Who hit Man Utd's winner in the 1999 European Champions' Cup Final?
7 Who was Blackburn's manager when they won the Premier League?
8 In 1999 Ron Atkinson announced his retirement as a soccer boss while with which club?
9 John Gregory took over from Brian Little as boss of which club?
10 Which Arsenal player was sent to jail for a drink-driving offence in 1990?
11 Carlos Alberto was a World Cup winning skipper of which country?
12 Jonathan Woodgate was with which club when he first played for England?
13 Which 90s star is known as 'The Iceman'?
14 Ronald Coeman was a star international with which country?
15 Alan Shearer and Matt Le Tissier have both been at which club?
16 Manager Jim Smith is known as the Bald what?
17 Which soccer ground did Sunderland leave in 1997?
18 At which soccer club did David O' Leary establish an appearance record?
19 England players Shearer, Sherwood, Sutton have all played for which soccer club?
20 Which British manager put Barcelona back on winning ways in the 1980s?
21 Which English keeper made the "save of the century" against Brazil in a 1970 World Cup game?
22 With which club did John Barnes begin his league soccer career?
23 Which keeper of the 80s and 90s glories in the nickname 'Lurch'?
24 At which British soccer club did an Italian take over from a Dutchman?
25 Dwight Yorke joined Man Utd from which club?

Answers

Pot Luck 53 (see Quiz 117, page 127)
1 Dolly. **2** Pudsey. **3** Greenwich. **4** Doris Day. **5** Javelin. **6** New York. **7** Argentina. **8** Rusedski. **9** Hanks. **10** Wessex. **11** Sheff Weds. **12** 50s. **13** Oasis. **14** Q. **15** Italy. **16** Italy. **17** Australia. **18** Eamonn Holmes. **19** Green. **20** Big Daddy. **21** Italy. **22** Busby. **23** Conservative. **24** Miami. **25** Ant & Dec.

Quiz 119 Pot Luck 54

Answers - see Quiz 120, page 130

1 Who set up the Virgin group?
2 Most people know this, but what is Michael Caine's real first name?
3 Who did Ffion Jenkins marry?
4 With which sport is Oliver Bierhoff associated?
5 Which word went with Britannia to describe the supposedly vibrant late 90s?
6 According to the TV theme song what do neighbours become?
7 Which country did Greta Garbo come from?
8 Robbie Coltrane and Whoopi Goldberg have played in films where their characters disguise themselves as what?
9 Which cash-making event was cancelled after revelations about Will Carling's private life in 1998?
10 Which three letters came to describe a farm shop where the buyer gathers in the goods?
11 In which country did Ho Chi Minh come to power?
12 Entertainer Michael Parker changed his last name to what?
13 Which area of West London established a summer holiday carnival?
14 Which Man From Auntie, Ben replaced Terry Wogan temporarily on Wogan while the Irishman went on holiday?
15 The village at Bournville near Birmingham was set up for workers of which chocolate factory?
16 Which musical instrument did Pablo Casals play?
17 Which English nurse Edith was executed by the Germans in WWI?
18 Catherine and William Booth were founders of which Army?
19 Which country has A as its international vehicle registration letter?
20 Which Kate became the face of L'Oreal in 1998?
21 In 1999, which BBC 1 show was dropped after a rumpus over fake guests?
22 Which Welsh politician Aneurin oversaw the formation of the welfare state?
23 What was the first name of Laurie in A Bit of Fry & Laurie on TV?
24 Everything Changes was a 90s No 1 for which group?
25 What did the U stand for in USSR?

Answers

Blockbusters (see Quiz 120, page 130)

1 Leonardo DiCaprio. **2** Evita. **3** Costner. **4** Lightyear. **5** D Day. **6** Attenborough. **7** Whitney Houston. **8** Aladdin. **9** Bram Stoker's. **10** Sophie's Choice. **11** An Officer and a Gentleman. **12** E.T. **13** Kingsley. **14** Love Story. **15** Orange. **16** Alien. **17** Casablanca. **18** Psycho. **19** Chicago. **20** Austria. **21** King Kong. **22** Snow White and the Seven Dwarfs. **23** Sally. **24** The Lion King. **25** Gone With the Wind.

Quiz 120 Blockbusters

Answers - see Quiz 119, page 129

LEVEL 1

1 Who played Jack in Titanic?
2 Which 1996 musical had Madonna making 85 costume changes?
3 Which Kevin starred in the spectacularly money-losing Waterworld?
4 Which Buzz from Toy Story caused a Christmas buying frenzy in 1996?
5 Which Landings were the subject of Saving Private Ryan?
6 Which British actor/director Richard was Dr Hammond in Jurassic Park?
7 Who sang I Will Always Love You in her film, The Bodyguard?
8 In which Disney classic was Robin Williams first the voice of the Genie?
9 Whose name appears with Dracula in the title of the 1992 movie?
10 In which 80s film did Meryl Streep play a Polish holocaust survivor?
11 Up Where We Belong was the theme music to which 80s film with Richard Gere and Debra Winger?
12 Which 1982 Spielberg classic was about a little boy and his pet alien?
13 Which actor Ben played the title role in Gandhi, and also played Ron Jenkins in Coronation Street?
14 Which 70s film used the line "Love means never having to say you're sorry."?
15 Which fruit is named in the title of the controversial Clockwork film directed by Stanley Kubrick?
16 Which film, the first of a series with Sigourney Weaver, had the line "In Space no one can hear you scream" on the cinema poster?
17 Which wartime classic, named after a port of North Africa starred Humphrey Bogart and Ingrid Bergman?
18 In which blockbuster did Anthony Perkins first appear as Norman Bates?
19 In Some Like It Hot, which gangster city are Jack Lemmon and Tony Curtis forced to leave after witnessing the St Valentine's Day massacre?
20 In which country did The Sound of Music take place?
21 Which film about a gorilla was a massive success for RKO in 1933 and has had a cult following ever since?
22 What was the first full length colour animated film?
23 If Billy Crystal was Harry who was Meg Ryan?
24 In which 90s film did Jeremy Irons speak the voice of wicked feline Scar?
25 Which 30s film about the American Civil War is "the first blockbuster"?

Answers

Pot Luck 54 (see Quiz 119, page 129)
1 Richard Branson. **2** Maurice. **3** William Hague. **4** Soccer. **5** Cool. **6** Good friends. **7** Sweden. **8** Nuns. **9** His testimonial. **10** PYO. **11** Vietnam. **12** Barrymore. **13** Notting Hill. **14** Elton. **15** Cadbury's. **16** Cello. **17** Cavell. **18** Salvation Army. **19** Austria. **20** Moss. **21** The Vanessa Show. **22** Bevan. **23** Hugh. **24** Take That. **25** Union.

Quiz 121 Entertainment

Answers - see Quiz 122, page 132

1 Which association for magicians was founded in 1905?
2 The Lord's Taverners raise money by entertaining with what activity?
3 The Aldeburgh Festival takes place in which east of England county?
4 What type of shooting season begins on 12th August?
5 Which London theatre takes its name from the Mermaid Tavern where writers met in Shakespeare's time?
6 Which playwright Sir Alan founded a theatre in Scarborough?
7 Pinewood Studios provide material for which industry?
8 If you watched a point to point what would you be watching?
9 If a film has a PG classification whose Guidance is needed to watch it?
10 In which London Hall does the Last Night of the Proms take place?
11 Who are G & S?
12 What type of entertainer is Wayne Sleep?
13 What did the King do during the Hallelujah Chorus of Handel's Messiah which means now everyone has to do it?
14 Which playwright Noel, whose centenary was celebrated in 1999, wrote Hay Fever and Private Lives?
15 What would you be most likely to be watching if the audience shouted "He's behind you" to someone on the stage?
16 Which peer who writes musicals attended the wedding of Prince Edward and Sophie Rhys-Jones?
17 Which musical instrument does Vanessa Mae play?
18 What entertainment consists of people singing to a backing tape?
19 If you were watching the Red Arrows what type of display would you be watching?
20 What was the New Philharmonia Orchestra called after it had been established 32 years?
21 What does O stand for in NYO, the leading group of young musicians?
22 Which town in Sussex has hosted a drama festival annually since 1962?
23 What type of Derby was first held at the White City in 1927?
24 In 1990 the Sadler's Wells Ballet moved to which Midlands city?
25 The NFT is a National Theatre which shows what?

Answers

***Pot Luck* 55** (see Quiz 122, page 132)
1 Mick Jagger. **2** Individual. **3** Swimming. **4** Three Lions. **5** Avon. **6** Violin. **7** Jack Straw. **8** Bugs Bunny. **9** Essex. **10** Agatha Christie. **11** Wales. **12** Chamberlain. **13** Dr Finlay. **14** Frank Sinatra. **15** Brand. **16** Lawyer. **17** Amis. **18** Meatloaf. **19** Edmund. **20** Pakistan. **21** Red Nose. **22** Liverpool. **23** Keith. **24** 60s. **25** New Mexico.

Quiz 122 Pot Luck 55

Answers - see Quiz 121, page 131

1 In 1990 who got married to Jerry Hall?
2 What does the I stand for in the savings accounts known as ISAS?
3 In which sport did Adrian Moorhouse set world records?
4 Which football song took Baddiel and Skinner to No 1?
5 Bristol is the administrative centre of which English county?
6 Nigel Kennedy is associated with which instrument?
7 In the 90s which Home Secretary had his son named in a drugs case?
8 Which cartoon character says "What's up, Doc?"?
9 Stansted airport was built in which county?
10 In fiction, who was the creator of Jane Marple?
11 Where was comedian Max Boyce born?
12 Which Neville was British Prime Minister at the outbreak of World War II?
13 A J Cronin provided the books - or casebook - that became which TV doctor?
14 Who had a worldwide hit with Strangers In The Night?
15 Which Jo had a TV series called Through The Cakehole?
16 Bill Clinton trained to do which day job?
17 Which Kingsley wrote the novel Lucky Jim?
18 Under what name did Marvin Addy become famous?
19 What was Blackadder's first name as played by Rowan Atkinson?
20 Both father and daughter of the Bhutto family have been Prime Minister of which country?
21 What is the symbol for Comic Relief?
22 In which city was Carla Lane's TV sitcom Bread set?
23 What is the first name of flamboyant chef Floyd?
24 Johnny Depp was born in which decade of the century?
25 Which US state, which joined the Union in 1912, has New and the name of a country in its name?

Answers

Entertainment (see Quiz 121, page 131)
1 Magic Circle. **2** Cricket. **3** Suffolk. **4** Grouse. **5** Mermaid. **6** Ayckbourn. **7** Film. **8** Horse race. **9** Parental. **10** Albert Hall. **11** Gilbert & Sullivan. **12** Dancer. **13** Stand up. **14** Coward. **15** Pantomime. **16** Andrew Lloyd Webber. **17** Violin. **18** Karaoke. **19** Air Display. **20** The Philharmonia Orchestra. **21** Orchestra. **22** Chichester. **23** Greyhound. **24** Birmingham. **25** Films.

Quiz 123 Around The UK

Answers - see Quiz 124, page 134

1 The A2 ends up at which Channel port?
2 What colour are road signs which lead to heritage sites and places of interest?
3 What type of Show is held regularly at Farnborough?
4 In 1988 which Norfolk waterways were designated a national park?
5 Aston University was founded in 1966 in which city?
6 What is Britain's second largest airport after Heathrow?
7 On which Devon Moor is there a famous prison?
8 London's Carnaby Street shot to fame in the 60s for what type of shops?
9 In which London Lane is the Dorchester Hotel?
10 In which Scottish city is an annual festival of music and drama held?
11 What sort of thoroughfare is the Grand Union?
12 The Fastnet Race is over what type of surface?
13 In which Yorkshire city is the National Railway Museum?
14 Aintree racecourse is near which UK city?
15 Which industry famously moved to Wapping from Central London in the 1980s?
16 Which leisure park is near Stoke on Trent in Staffordshire?
17 Where in Wales is the Driver and Vehicle Licensing Centre?
18 Which cultural centre, the London base of the RSC, was opened in 1982?
19 In which area of London is the All England Tennis Club?
20 The first Borstal opened in which SE England county in 1902?
21 What type of products does Fortnum & Mason sell?
22 Glamis Castle near Dundee was the home of which royal before her marriage?
23 If you caught the train called The Clansman you would travel from London to which part of the UK?
24 Which Birmingham shopping centre was opened in 1960 on the site of a former cattle market?
25 Holyhead is on which island off Wales?

Answers

Pot Luck 56 (see Quiz 124, page 134)

1 N Ireland. **2** Dwight. **3** Muir. **4** 90s. **5** Women. **6** Dermot Morgan. **7** George Bush. **8** Everett. **9** 60s. **10** Rose. **11** Rory Bremner. **12** Diaries. **13** Cruelty. **14** Cher. **15** Pinter. **16** Leisure centre. **17** Curie. **18** Boxing. **19** Paris. **20** Conservative. **21** Laurel & Hardy. **22** South Africa. **23** Langtry. **24** House painter. **25** Rugby League.

Quiz 124 Pot Luck 56

Answers - see Quiz 123, page 133

1 The 90s Good Friday agreement sought peace in which country?
2 Elton John was born with which surname?
3 Which Frank formed a comedy writing team with Denis Norden?
4 In which decade did Channel 5 begin broadcasting?
5 Until 1998 what had been banned for 200 years by the MCC?
6 Which actor starred in the TV comedy Father Ted?
7 Who was the outgoing president when Bill Clinton took office?
8 Maurice Cole found fame as which Kenny?
9 The first modern cassette was produced in which decade?
10 Which Justin set the 98 Open alight as an amateur?
11 Which impressionist had a TV series called Who Else?
12 What did politician Richard Crossman leave behind that was published in the 70s after his death?
13 What does the letter C stand for in RSPCA?
14 Who had a 90s hit with The Shoop Shoop Song?
15 Which Harold wrote the play The Caretaker?
16 What was the setting for the TV sitcom The Brittas Empire?
17 Which chemist Marie became the first woman to win a Nobel prize?
18 With which sport is Herbie Hide associated?
19 In which city was Charles de Gaulle airport built?
20 Norman Fowler has represented which party in parliament?
21 In 1930 which comic duo made the film Another Fine Mess?
22 PW Botha was Prime Minister of which country?
23 Which Lily was the mistress of Edward VII?
24 What was the occupation of Jacko in TV's Brush Strokes?
25 Andy Gregory represented England at which sport?

Answers

Around the UK (see Quiz 123, page 133)
1 Dover. **2** Brown. **3** Air. **4** Broads. **5** Birmingham. **6** Gatwick. **7** Dartmoor. **8** Boutiques. **9** Park Lane. **10** Edinburgh. **11** Canal. **12** Water. **13** York. **14** Liverpool. **15** Newspaper. **16** Alton Towers. **17** Swansea. **18** Barbican. **19** Wimbledon. **20** Kent. **21** Food. **22** The Queen Mother. **23** Scotland. **24** Bull Ring. **25** Anglesey.

Quiz 125 Karaoke

Answers - see Quiz 126, page 136

1 Which song starts, 'It's a little bit funny, This feeling inside'?
2 Which Shania Twain song includes, "Okay, so you're Brad Pitt"?
3 What is the first word of She?
4 In Gina G's Eurovision song what follows "Ooh ahh just a little..."?
5 Which Cliff Richard hit starts, "Used to think that life was sweet, Used to think we were so complete"?
6 Which Dire Straits song starts, "These mist covered mountains..."?
7 Which Swedish Eurovision winner's song said "Take me to your heaven.."?
8 Which chilly Madonna song begins "You only see what your eyes want to see"?
9 Which organ of the body is mentioned in the theme song to Titanic?
10 Judy Garland sang about going somewhere over the what?
11 Who Get Going When The Going Gets Tough?
12 Which Queen classic starts, "Is this the real life..."?
13 In Candle in the Wind 1997 what did Elton John sing instead of Goodbye Norma Jean?
14 In 1996 which band sang "It's only words and words are all I have....." as The Bee Gees had done in 1968?
15 What number was Perfect according to The Beautiful South in 1998?
16 In the Bowie song who was Ground Control trying to make contact with?
17 How many times did the Spice Girls sing "really" in the first two lines of Wannabe?
18 What's the response to, "See you later, alligator"?
19 Which song starts, "Sometimes it's hard to be a woman"?
20 Which group thought, "It's fun to stay at the YMCA"?
21 Which Elton John song has the colour yellow in the title?
22 Which words of encouragement did S Club 7 sing after "Don't stop.." in Bring It All Back?
23 Who was "the fastest milkman in the West"?
24 Who made Little Richard sing Good Golly?
25 Which song begins "I feel it in my fingers"?

Answers

Pot Luck 57 (see Quiz 126, page 136)

1 Men's lavatory. **2** John Cleese. **3** Atherton. **4** Pig. **5** London. **6** John Smith. **7** Drat. **8** Windsor. **9** Three. **10** Ford. **11** Rowing. **12** Egypt. **13** Wimbledon. **14** 60s. **15** Marti Caine. **16** 40s. **17** South Africa. **18** Citizen Smith. **19** Sutcliffe. **20** Major. **21** Mastermind. **22** Birmingham. **23** Simply Red. **24** Hoover. **25** John Peel.

Quiz 126 Pot Luck 57

Answers - see Quiz 125, page 135

1 In what type of public building was George Michael arrested and charged with committing a "lewd act"?
2 Which comedian was born as John Cheese?
3 Which Michael led England's cricket team for over 50 games in the 90s?
4 What type of animal was Babe in the film of the same name?
5 In which city was the Barbican Centre built?
6 Who did Tony Blair replace as leader of the Labour Party?
7 Cartoon racer Dick Dastardly exclaims, "Drat and double" what?
8 Which British royal residence was badly damaged by fire in the early 90s?
9 How many colours are there on the Belgian flag?
10 Which car manufacturer introduced the Granada?
11 Steve Redgrave won Olympic gold in which sport?
12 In which country was the ancient tomb of Tutankhamun discovered?
13 Which soccer team does June Whitfield support?
14 Matt Dillon was born in which decade of the century?
15 Which comedienne first introduced herself as a gawky Sheffield housewife when she appeared on New Faces in 1975?
16 Bob Dylan was born in which decade of the 20th century?
17 Which country does cricketer Daryll Cullinan play for?
18 In which sitcom did Wolfie Smith appear?
19 Which Peter was the Yorkshire Ripper?
20 Which John was MP for Huntingdon in the 90s?
21 Which long running TV quiz show had started and finally finished in 1997?
22 Where is comedian Jasper Carrott's home town?
23 Which group recorded the best selling album Stars?
24 Which word connects the FBI and a vacuum cleaner?
25 John Ravenscroft became better known as which DJ?

Answers

Karaoke (see Quiz 125, page 135)
1 Your Song. **2** That Don't Impress Me Much. **3** She. **4** Bit.
5 We Don't Talk Anymore. **6** Brothers In Arms. **7** Charlotte Nilsson. **8** Frozen. **9** Heart.
10 Rainbow. **11** The Tough. **12** Bohemian Rhapsody. **13** England's rose. **14** Boyzone.
15 10. **16** Major Tom. **17** 4. **18** In a while, crocodile. **19** Stand By Your Man.
20 Village People. **21** Goodbye Yellow Brick Road. **22** Never give up. **23** Ernie.
24 Miss Molly. **25** Love Is All Around.

Quiz 127 60s Newsround

Answers - see Quiz 128, page 138

1 Which Harold became leader of a British political party in the 60s?
2 Who managed England to World Cup triumph?
3 Which Basil was involved in the cancelling of an English tour to South Africa?
4 Mrs Gandhi became Prime Minister in which country?
5 Donald Campbell was killed trying to break which speed record?
6 Which literary Lady had a Lover that resulted in an Old Bailey obscenity trial?
7 Dubcek's reforms were crushed by Soviet tanks in which country?
8 Maria Bueno was a 60s champion in which sport?
9 Which city became Brazil's new capital in 1960?
10 The World Wildlife Fund was set up with which animal as its logo?
11 The LSE, the scene of student unrest, was the London School of what?
12 Which Italian city hosted the 1960 Olympics?
13 Where in America was the world's biggest rock festival staged?
14 Pierre Trudeau became Prime Minister of which country?
15 Who was the only British winner of the British Open in the 60s?
16 Mia Farrow's controversial film concerned whose baby?
17 What type of vehicle was involved in the fatal accident at Chappaquiddick?
18 Which pop star married a Cynthia and later a Yoko?
19 What was Vidal Sassoon creating?
20 What was the name of call girl Miss Keeler involved in a ministerial sex scandal?
21 Which road was linked with the murder trial involving James Hanratty?
22 What type of creature was headline making Goldie who escaped in London?
23 Who was 'the Louisville Lip'?
24 Who was Lee Harvey Oswald charged with murdering?
25 Which Francis completed his solo round the world yacht journey?

Answers

Pot Luck 58 (see Quiz 128, page 138)

1 Faith healer. **2** Magnus Magnusson. **3** Rubik. **4** Michael Jackson's. **5** Germany. **6** Wannabe. **7** David Blunkett. **8** Wales. **9** Sophia Loren. **10** I Believe. **11** Clary. **12** Birds. **13** Cheshire. **14** Sean Connery. **15** W Indies. **16** His wife. **17** Comic Relief. **18** Archbishop of Canterbury. **19** Daphne. **20** Liberation Army. **21** Black. **22** Frank Butcher. **23** Do The Bartman. **24** Boxing. **25** India.

Quiz 128 Pot Luck 58

Answers - see Quiz 127, page 137

1 What was Eileen Drewery's role in England's 1998 World Cup preparations?
2 Which quizmaster said, "I've started so I'll finish"?
3 Who created the three-dimensional cube in the 70s and 80s craze?
4 Whose son was called Prince Michael Jr?
5 Which European country was divided into East and West in 1949?
6 Which Spice Girls hit starts, "I'll tell you what I want"?
7 Which government minister took his dog to work?
8 Which country does Ray Reardon come from?
9 Sophia Scicoloni became famous as which actress?
10 What are the first two words of the much recorded song I Believe?
11 Which Julian once called himself The Joan Collins Fan Club?
12 What does the letter B stand for in RSPB?
13 Chester is the administrative centre of which English county?
14 Who played James Bond in Doctor No?
15 The legendary cricketer Learie Constantine played for which country?
16 Who did Doctor Crippen poison?
17 What name is given to the charity which was set up by comedians to raise money for those in need?
18 Which high office has been held by Dr George Carey?
19 What was the first name of Rebecca writer du Maurier?
20 If the K stands for Kosovo what do L and A stand for in the KLA?
21 What colour is Mickey Mouse's nose?
22 Which EastEnders landlord found fame as himself on The Comedians?
23 What was The Simpsons 90s No 1 hit?
24 With which sport is Thomas Hearns associated?
25 Madhur Jaffrey chiefly writes about cookery from which country of the world?

Answers

60s Newsround (see Quiz 127, page 137)
1 Wilson. **2** Alf Ramsey. **3** D'Oliveira. **4** India. **5** Water. **6** Lady Chatterley. **7** Czechoslovakia. **8** Tennis. **9** Brasilia. **10** Panda. **11** Economics. **12** Rome. **13** Woodstock. **14** Canada. **15** Tony Jacklin. **16** Rosemary's. **17** Car. **18** John Lennon. **19** Hairstyles. **20** Christine. **21** A6. **22** Eagle. **23** Cassius Clay. **24** President Kennedy. **25** Chichester.

Quiz 129 Famous Names

Answers - see Quiz 130, page 140

1 What is novelist Lord Archer's first name?
2 By which first name is Jeremy John Durham Ashdown best known ?
3 What is Zoe Ball's dad called?
4 What is the name of Margaret Thatcher's husband?
5 Which part of him did Ken Dodd insure for £4 million?
6 Betty Boothroyd became the first female Speaker where?
7 How was Elaine Bickerstaff better known on the West End stage?
8 Which chain of environmentally friendly shops did Anita Roddick found?
9 What did Nigel Kennedy change his name to, professionally in the late 90s?
10 Which Gordon was Tony Blair's first Chancellor of the Exchequer?
11 Which musical instrument is Dudley Moore famous for playing?
12 How is Paul O'Grady better known in high heels, blonde wig and Liverpool accent?
13 Martina Navratilova changed nationality from Czech to what?
14 Why would you consult Nicky Clarke professionally?
15 Which two initials is crime novelist Baroness James known by?
16 Henry Cecil is a famous name in which sport?
17 Which Nigel found fame as a writer of a newspaper Diary about celebs?
18 In 1999 Sean Connery campaigned on behalf of which political party?
19 Eddie George became Governor of what in 1993?
20 What is Ffion Jenkins married surname?
21 Michael Flatley was dubbed Lord of the what?
22 Which Spice nickname did Geri Halliwell have?
23 Which actor Stephen walked out of the West End play Cell Mates in 1995?
24 Michael Heseltine's nickname was that of which film hero?
25 Opera star Lesley Garrett hails from which county?

Answers

Pot Luck 59 (see Quiz 130, page 140)

1 Deirdre Rachid. **2** 40s. **3** Viagra. **4** R2D2. **5** Joan Rivers. **6** Kubrick. **7** North. **8** Clarice. **9** Information. **10** Lillee. **11** Conley. **12** Judy Garland. **13** America. **14** Parkinson. **15** Ireland. **16** The Menace. **17** Soccer. **18** Jean Harlow. **19** Six. **20** Duke. **21** 1984. **22** Quark. **23** Malta. **24** Labour. **25** 70s.

Quiz 130 Pot Luck 59

Answers - see Quiz 129, page 139

1 Who was the 'Weatherfield One'?
2 In which decade was the atomic bomb dropped on Hiroshima?
3 Which anti-impotence treatment became the 90s fastest selling prescription drug?
4 Who was C-3PO's robot companion in the original Star Wars movies?
5 Under what name did sharp-tongued Joan Molinsky become famous?
6 Which director Stanley made 2001 A Space Odyssey?
7 Which US Colonel featured in the 'Irangate' court trials?
8 In fiction and film what is the first name of female FBI agent Starling?
9 What does the I stand for in the initials IT?
10 William Hague gave which Peter the push as Tory deputy leader?
11 Which Brian presented the National Lottery Show, promising "it could change your life forever!"?
12 How did Frances Gumm become known on stage?
13 A company from which country featured in the 1999 take over of ASDA?
14 A famous appearance on whose chat show established Billy Connolly's popularity outside his homeland?
15 Charles Haughey was Prime Minister of which country?
16 Which Dennis has a dog called Gnasher?
17 Kenny Sansom represented England at which sport?
18 Who was Hollywood's first 'Blonde Bombshell'?
19 At the end of the 20th C how many UK monarchs had been called George?
20 What was the name of those hazardous good old boys Bo and Luke?
21 Which year is used as the title of a George Orwell book?
22 In computer software what goes before XPress?
23 The deepwater port of Valletta was developed on which island?
24 In the 80s Roy Jenkins left which political party to launch the SDP?
25 In which decade was the centenary of the Wimbledon championships?

Answers

Famous Names (see Quiz 129, page 139)
1 Jeffrey. **2** Paddy. **3** Johnny. **4** Denis. **5** Teeth. **6** House of Commons.
7 Elaine Paige. **8** Body Shop. **9** Kennedy. **10** Brown. **11** Piano. **12** Lily Savage.
13 American. **14** To do your hair. **15** P D. **16** Horse racing. **17** Dempster.
18 Scots Nationalist. **19** Bank of England. **20** Hague. **21** Dance. **22** Ginger.
23 Fry. **24** Tarzan. **25** Yorkshire.

Quiz 131 TV Classics

Answers - see Quiz 132, page 142

1 Which drama series was based on the books of vet James Herriot?
2 Going Straight was the follow up to which classic prison sitcom?
3 In 70s/80s TV how was The Hulk described?
4 Which Croft & Perry sitcom was set in holiday camp?
5 Auf Wiedersehen Pet was chiefly set on a building site where?
6 Which classic game show with a crossbow was called Der Goldener Schuss in Germany?
7 Which show spawned the catchphrase "Here's one I made earlier"?
8 How were Terry Collier and Bob Ferris known collectively?
9 Which children's TV classic asked "Who was that masked man?"?
10 Which satirical series lampooned politicians through latex puppets?
11 Which Citizen's catchphrase was "Power to the People"?
12 What was Dr Who's Time Machine called?
13 Elizabeth R , with Glenda Jackson, was based on the life of whom?
14 The Fall and Rise of which Reginald starred Leonard Rossiter?
15 What was the female follow up to The Man from U.N.C.L.E called?
16 Which green vegetable was the booby prize on Crackerjack?
17 In which comedy classic did John Cleese announce "And now for something completely different."?
18 In Morecambe & Wise shows, Eric's comment "you can't see the join" referred to what?
19 In The Muppet Show what sort of creature was Kermit?
20 Which character's catchphrase was "I don't believe it"?
21 What were Cassandra and Raquel's surnames after they married Del and Rodney?
22 Open All Hours was set in what type of establishment?
23 Which children's character had a famous black and white cat?
24 What was Frank Spencer's wife called in Some Mothers Do 'Ave 'Em?
25 Which silent puppet had friends called Sweep and Soo?

Answers

Pot Luck 60 (see Quiz 132, page 142)
1 Croft. **2** 60s. **3** Keeler. **4** Aaron. **5** Malta. **6** Everything I do.
7 Astaire & Rogers. **8** Paris. **9** Elizabeth. **10** Dustin Hoffman. **11** Corporation.
12 Vic Reeves. **13** Horse racing. **14** Bush. **15** Vanilla Ice. **16** Miners.
17 Humberside. **18** Prevention. **19** Coogan. **20** Smith. **21** In the world.
22 Boxing. **23** Antiques. **24** Dad's Army. **25** Z.

Quiz 132 Pot Luck 60

Answers - see Quiz 131, page 141

1 Which Lara featured in computer game Tomb Raider II?
2 In what decade did The Sun newspaper launch in Britain?
3 Which Christine featured in a 60s sex scandal involving a cabinet minister?
4 What was Elvis Presley's middle name?
5 Which country has M as its international vehicle registration letter?
6 In Bryan Adams' mega hit which three words come before, "I do it for you"?
7 What were the last names of movie duo Fred and Ginger?
8 In which city was the Three Tenors 1998 World Cup concert?
9 What is the first name of The Queen Mother?
10 Which actor appeared in drag in the movie Tootsie?
11 What does the C stand for in BBC?
12 Jim Moir is better known as which comedian?
13 With which sport is Walter Swinburn associated?
14 Bill Clinton took over from which US President?
15 Who had a 90s No 1 with Ice Ice Baby?
16 Which group of workers staged a year long strike in the 80s over closures?
17 Hull is the administrative centre of which English county?
18 What does P stand for in NSPCC?
19 Which comedian Steve created Portuguese superstar Tony Ferrino?
20 Which Bessie was known as Empress of the Blues?
21 Carlsberg was advertised as "probably the best lager" where?
22 Jim Watt was a world champion in which sport?
23 On TV, what type of goods did Lovejoy deal in?
24 Which classic sitcom was set at Walmington on Sea?
25 On a computer keyboard what letter is far left on the lowest row of letters?

Answers

TV Classics (see Quiz 131, page 141)
1 All Creatures Great and Small. **2** Porridge. **3** Incredible. **4** Hi-De-Hi!. **5** Germany. **6** The Golden Shot. **7** Blue Peter. **8** The Likely Lads. **9** The Lone Ranger. **10** Spitting Image. **11** Smith. **12** Tardis. **13** Elizabeth I. **14** Perrin. **15** The Girl from U.N.C.L.E.. **16** Cabbage. **17** Monty Python's Flying Circus. **18** Ernie's wig. **19** Frog. **20** Victor Meldrew. **21** Trotter. **22** Shop. **23** Postman Pat. **24** Betty. **25** Sooty.

Quiz 133 Sport: 90s Action Replay

Answers - see Quiz 134, page 144

1 How many goals were scored in the 1998 World Cup Final?
2 Rugby's man mountain Jonah Lomu plays for which country?
3 Which country hosted the 1998 Winter Olympics?
4 Who did Man Utd defeat in the 1999 European Champions' Cup Final?
5 In 1998 England won a Test series against which country?
6 Which racing team dropped Damon Hill the season he became world champion?
7 Albertville and Lillehammer were the two 90s venues for which event?
8 Which was the first team not called United to win the Premiership?
9 Which best-on-the-planet trophy did Francois Pienaar collect in 1995?
10 Which team inflicted W Indies' first home Test series defeat in over 20 years?
11 Which team were FA Cup beaten finalists in two consecutive seasons?
12 Where do the Super Bowl winning Cowboys come from?
13 Which England skipper resigned after allegations about taking cocaine?
14 Which man managed victory in all the tennis Grand Slam titles?
15 Teddy Sheringham joined Man Utd from which club?
16 Who does Michael Schumacher drive for?
17 Who advertised Adidas and Brylcreem?
18 What did Miguel Indurain win each year from 1991 to 1995?
19 Which Liverpool star was charged with match fixing?
20 Jonathan Edwards was a world champion in 1995 in which athletic event?
21 Ganguly and Tendulkar have played cricket for which country?
22 Which team bought out the Stewart motor racing team?
23 Defeat by which country prompted the Graham Taylor turnip jibes?
24 Which Rugby League team became known as Rhinos?
25 Which England cricketer was accused of ball tampering in a Test?

Answers

Pot Luck 61 (see Quiz 134, page 144)
1 Spurs. **2** David Copperfield. **3** Cat. **4** Japan. **5** Tony Curtis. **6** Cricket. **7** The Comets. **8** Bobby Robson. **9** Circus. **10** David Mellor. **11** Frankfurt. **12** Paul Gascoigne. **13** Dawson. **14** USA. **15** London. **16** Sarah Ferguson. **17** Rugby Union. **18** 75. **19** Piano. **20** Labour. **21** Greta Garbo. **22** Hound Of The Baskervilles. **23** 70s. **24** American football. **25** Kent .

Quiz 134 Pot Luck 61

Answers - see Quiz 133, page 143

1 Which British soccer club was managed by Christian Gross?
2 Magician David Kotkin managed to change his name to what?
3 What type of animal was 90s Downing Street resident Humphrey?
4 The US declared war on which country after the bombing of Pearl Harbour?
5 Which actor is the dad of Jamie Lee Curtis?
6 With which sport is Chris Cairns associated?
7 Which group backed Bill Haley in the 50s?
8 Who was the last soccer manager to take England to the World Cup semis?
9 Billy Smart produced what type of family entertainment?
10 Which Tory in the 90s became known as the 'Minister For Fun'?
11 What is the main airport in Germany?
12 Which soccer player was married for a time to Sheryl Failes?
13 Which Les performed the famous Cissie and Ada sketch with Roy Barraclough in his TV series?
14 In which country did the McCarthy witch hunts take place?
15 The Last Night of the Proms concert originated in which city?
16 Who wrote about a little helicopter named Budgie?
17 Mike Teague represented England at which sport?
18 Which two numbers go with the Rover car launched in 99?
19 Singer Nat King Cole was also very talented on which musical instrument?
20 Barbara Castle has represented which party in parliament?
21 How did Greta Gustaffson become better known as an actress?
22 Which spectral hound of the moors first appeared in a classic 1902 detective story?
23 Drew Barrymore was born in which decade of the century?
24 Which sport do the Chicago Bears play?
25 The Darling Buds of May was set in which English county?

Answers

Sport: 90s Action Replay (see Quiz 133, page 143)
1 Three. **2** New Zealand. **3** Japan. **4** Bayern Munich. **5** South Africa. **6** Williams. **7** Winter Olympics. **8** Blackburn Rovers. **9** Rugby World Cup. **10** Australia. **11** Newcastle. **12** Dallas. **13** Lawrence Dallaglio. **14** Andre Agassi. **15** Spurs. **16** Ferrari. **17** David Beckham. **18** Tour de France. **19** Bruce Grobbelaar. **20** Triple Jump. **21** India. **22** Ford. **23** Sweden. **24** Leeds. **25** Mike Atherton.

Quiz 135 Movies - Who's Who?

Answers - see Quiz 136, page 146

1 Where was Leonardo DiCaprio born?
2 In which 1998 film did Anderson & Duchovny reprise their TV roles of Mulder & Scully?
3 Who or what is Gromit?
4 Who replaced Timothy Dalton as James Bond?
5 Which star of Home Alone was the highest paid child movie star of the 20th century?
6 Which star of Grease had a career revival with Pulp Fiction?
7 Which Tom married Nicole Kidman?
8 Who met husband Richard Burton on the set of Cleopatra?
9 Which drummer/singer Phil played the title role in Buster?
10 Who went to No 1 with Night Fever after writing the music for Saturday Night Fever?
11 Which film director was involved in a long running custody battle for his children with Mia Farrow?
12 Which ex Funny Girl starred with Nick Nolte in The Prince of Tides?
13 Who was the Pretty Woman in the 1990 film with Richard Gere?
14 Which director of Schindler's List and E.T. was the most commercially successful cinema director of the century?
15 By which first name is Andrew Blyth Barrymore known in E.T.?
16 What relation is Jeff to Beau Bridges?
17 Which star of Rocky said "I built my body to carry my brain around"?
18 Which ex Brookside actress played Nick Leeson's wife in the film Rogue Trader about the fall of Barings Bank?
19 Which talk show hostess appeared in The Color Purple?
20 Which controversial 80s/90s singer/actress married Sean Penn in 1985?
21 In which country was Arnold Schwarzenegger born?
22 Which pop star's first film was Purple Rain?
23 Which Scottish comedian played John Brown in Mrs Brown?
24 Cate Blanchett won a BAFTA playing which Queen?
25 Which girl band announced they would make their screen debut in Honest?

Answers

Pot Luck 62 (see Quiz 136, page 146)
1 Jackie. **2** Basketball. **3** Hurricane. **4** Hughes. **5** Mike Tyson. **6** Elvis Presley. **7** Popeye. **8** Liverpool. **9** Snoopy Doggy Dogg. **10** Rugby Union. **11** North. **12** Dee. **13** Brooke. **14** Sandringham. **15** Photographic. **16** Prodigy. **17** Horse racing. **18** Nancy. **19** Des O'Connor. **20** Guitar. **21** Glasgow. **22** Knowsley. **23** Margaret Thatcher. **24** Skiffle. **25** Dodd.

Quiz 136 Pot Luck 62

Answers - see Quiz 135, page 145

1 In the 60s what was the name of US President Kennedy's wife?
2 With which sport is Michael Jordan associated?
3 What was Georges that left a trail of destruction in Florida in 1998?
4 Which Ted was a 90s Poet Laureate?
5 Which world heavyweight boxing champion was jailed in the 90s?
6 Way Down was a hit for which singer after his death?
7 Which spinach-eating sailor has Robin Williams played on film?
8 In which city were the Shankly Gates built?
9 Under what canine name does rapper Calvin Broadus operate?
10 Sean Fitzpatrick represented New Zealand at which sport?
11 What does the N stand for in NATO?
12 Who was comedian Jack in Jack & Jeremy's Real Lives?
13 Which poet Rupert died on his way to action in World War I?
14 Which royal residence does the Queen use in Norfolk?
15 George Eastman invented what type of equipment?
16 Firestarter was a 90s No 1 for which group?
17 Dick Francis novels revolve around which sport?
18 What's the first name of Frank Sinatra's elder daughter?
19 Which comedian/singer/TV presenter was always the butt of Morecambe & Wise's jokes?
20 Chet Atkins is associated with which musical instrument?
21 Which British city was the Cultural Capital of Europe in 1990?
22 Which Safari Park was set up near to Liverpool?
23 Geoffrey Howe was deputy to which Prime Minister?
24 Which 50s music craze featured a washboard?
25 Which Ken is famous for his vocabulary which includes 'plumpshiousness' and 'tattifilarious'?

Answers

Movies – Who's Who? (see Quiz 135, page 145)
1 Hollywood. **2** The X Files. **3** Dog. **4** Pierce Brosnan. **5** Macaulay Culkin. **6** John Travolta. **7** Cruise. **8** Elizabeth Taylor. **9** Collins. **10** The Bee Gees. **11** Woody Allen. **12** Barbra Streisand. **13** Julia Roberts. **14** Steven Spielberg. **15** Drew. **16** Brother. **17** Sylvester Stallone. **18** Anna Friel. **19** Oprah Winfrey. **20** Madonna. **21** Austria. **22** Prince. **23** Billy Connolly. **24** Elizabeth. **25** All Saints.

Quiz 137 Euro Tour

Answers - see Quiz 138, page 148

1 Which southern French town holds an annual international Film Festival?
2 How was Eurotunnel known before its name change in 1998?
3 La Scala is the world's most famous what?
4 Andorra is at the foot of which mountains?
5 Which Arctic country's Finnish name is Lapin Li?
6 Which country is known locally as Osterreich?
7 The Left Bank generally refers to the Left Bank of the Seine in which city?
8 Which Mediterranean island's capital is Valletta?
9 Which country was divided into East and West between the 1940s and 1990s?
10 The Strait of Gibraltar connects the Atlantic Ocean with which Sea?
11 The airline Danair is based where?
12 Which mountainous European country is divided into cantons?
13 Flemish is an official language of which kingdom?
14 Which English location would the French call Douvres?
15 In Greenland a native of the country might be called Inuit or what?
16 Which country is also called the Hellenic Republic?
17 In Norway, a fjord is made up largely of what?
18 Majorca is part of which group of islands?
19 Which German city is known locally as Koln?
20 Tuscany is part of which country?
21 What is Europe's most mountainous country?
22 The province of Calabria is at the southernmost tip of which country?
23 The island of Rhodes belongs to which Mediterranean country?
24 Alsace is a province of which country?
25 What is the currency of Spain?

Answers

***Pot Luck* 63** (see Quiz 138, page 148)
1 Paul McCartney. **2** United States. **3** A bank. **4** Telecommunications. **5** Fox. **6** Dad's Army. **7** .uk. **8** Barbra Streisand. **9** 90s. **10** Soccer. **11** Maureen Lipman. **12** Waite. **13** Man Utd. **14** 30s. **15** Ellen. **16** Dali. **17** USA. **18** Kenny Everett. **19** Roald Dahl. **20** Duke. **21** Tibet. **22** Movies. **23** Sunday. **24** Little. **25** The Fall & Rise of Reginald Perrin.

Quiz 138 Pot Luck 63

Answers - see Quiz 137, page 147

1 Which of the Beatles was first to be widowed?
2 In which country were the 1996 Olympic Games held?
3 In Mask Jim Carrey starred as someone working where?
4 The independent body Oftel regulates which service?
5 In the X Files what is Mulder's first name?
6 Which much repeated comedy series featured ARP Warden Hodges?
7 A UK internet user would use what punctuation mark and letters?
8 In 1998 actor James Brolin married which singer/actress?
9 In which decade did Buckingham Palace first open to the public?
10 Johnny Haynes captained England in which sport?
11 Who played Beattie in a series of telephone ads?
12 Which Terry became a high profile hostage in Lebanon?
13 Which soccer team does Mick Hucknall follow?
14 Woody Allen was born in which decade of last century?
15 Which series with Ellen DeGeneres was originally called These Friends of Mine?
16 Which Spanish Salvador was a surrealist artist?
17 Which country does golfer Ben Crenshaw come from?
18 Which outrageous radio DJ was born Maurice Cole in Liverpool in 1944?
19 Who wrote Charlie and The Chocolate Factory?
20 Bandleader Edward Ellington was known by what nickname?
21 The Dalai Lama fled which country in the 50s?
22 What did Cecil B de Mille make?
23 Which day of the week in Ireland was named Bloody after the shootings of 1972?
24 What was added to Stevie Wonder's name when he was a youngster?
25 Which sitcom with Leonard Rossiter was called Reggie when it was transferred to the USA?

Answers

Euro Tour (see Quiz 137, page 147)

1 Cannes. **2** Le Shuttle. **3** Opera House. **4** Pyrenees. **5** Lapland. **6** Austria. **7** Paris. **8** Malta. **9** Germany. **10** Mediterranean. **11** Denmark. **12** Switzerland. **13** Belgium. **14** Dover. **15** Eskimo. **16** Greece. **17** Water. **18** Balearics. **19** Cologne. **20** Italy. **21** Switzerland. **22** Italy. **23** Greece. **24** France. **25** Peseta.

Quiz 139 Pop Charts

Answers - see Quiz 140, page 150

1 What was Billie's first No 1?
2 Which port provided a hit for The Beautiful South?
3 What's the only battle to have been the one-word title of a No 1?
4 What colour was UB40's Wine?
5 Which Bob Dylan song was used as the song for Dunblane?
6 Which magazine shares its name with a Madonna No 1?
7 What went with Tonic for Spacedust?
8 Who had her first No 1 as Mrs Sonny Bono?
9 Which seabird took Fleetwood Mac to No 1?
10 Which chart smashing group featured Adams, Brown and Chisholm?
11 50+ Deborah Harry returned to the 99 charts with which group?
12 Which Dad's Army actor had a surprise No 1 with Grandad?
13 Which country does Britney Spears come from?
14 Who did Faith Evans team up with for I'll Be Missing You?
15 Which Starsky and Hutch actor topped the charts?
16 Bitter Sweet Symphony was the first top ten hit for which band?
17 Who is the only Bryan to have had a record at No 1 for 16 weeks?
18 Which Lou wrote A Perfect Day?
19 Who had her first No 1 with Wuthering Heights?
20 Suzanne Vega was in who's Diner?
21 Which song was a No 1 for Nilsson and Mariah Carey?
22 Which film provided a best selling album for Whitney Houston?
23 Who recorded Riders On The Storm?
24 Who did Chrissie Hynde guest with for I Got You Babe?
25 Gazza sang with Lindisfarne about the fog on which river?

Answers

Pot Luck 64 (see Quiz 140, page 150)
1 Comet. **2** Oxford. **3** Alcohol. **4** Argentina. **5** Margaret Thatcher. **6** Violin. **7** Watergate. **8** Soccer. **9** Elton John. **10** Second decade. **11** Questions. **12** Fleming. **13** Dogs. **14** Marylebone. **15** Linda McCartney. **16** Basil Brush. **17** Nuremberg. **18** Cary Grant. **19** Judge. **20** Wall Street. **21** Jeeves. **22** Marlon Brando. **23** David Soul. **24** Republic of Ireland. **25** Father Ted.

Quiz 140 Pot Luck 64

Answers - see Quiz 139, page 149

1 A 1997 phenomena, Hale-Bop was a type of what?
2 The charity Oxfam began in which city?
3 The sale of what was prohibited in America during prohibition?
4 Michael Owen scored a wonder World Cup goal against which country?
5 Which former British Prime Minister leader called for clemency for General Pinochet?
6 Which instrument was associated with Stephane Grapelli?
7 What was the name of the scandal that brought down US President Richard Nixon?
8 With which sport is Thierry Henry associated?
9 Who duetted with Kiki Dee on True Love?
10 In which decade of the 20th Century was the battle of the Somme?
11 Former MP Neil Hamilton was involved in the cash for what scandal?
12 Which Ian created the character James Bond?
13 In movies, who or what were Lady and The Tramp?
14 What does the M stand for in MCC?
15 Which friend of Carla Lane and fellow campaigning vegetarian appeared in an episode of her sitcom Bread in 1988?
16 Which TV fox went "Boom boom!"?
17 Which trials of 1946 dealt with Nazi war criminals?
18 Archibald Leach became known as which Hollywood actor?
19 The controversial James Pickles hit the headlines while serving as a what?
20 The New York Stock Exchange was established on which street?
21 In fiction, what was the name of Bertie Wooster's manservant?
22 Which American actor refused his Oscar awarded for The Godfather?
23 David Solberg became a famous actor/singer under which name?
24 Which country did Ray Houghton play soccer for?
25 Which series about a group of anarchic priests was set on Craggy Island?

Answers

Pop Charts (see Quiz 139, page 149)

1 Because We Want To. **2** Rotterdam. **3** Waterloo. **4** Red. **5** Knockin' On Heaven's Door. **6** Vogue. **7** Gym. **8** Cher. **9** Albatross. **10** Spice Girls. **11** Blondie. **12** Clive Dunn. **13** US. **14** Puff Daddy. **15** David Soul. **16** Verve. **17** Adams. **18** Reed. **19** Kate Bush. **20** Tom's. **21** Without You. **22** The Bodyguard. **23** The Doors. **24** UB40. **25** Tyne.

Quiz 141 70s Newsround

Answers - see Quiz 142, page 152

1 What did Ceylon change its name to?
2 What was the name of the mansion where Elvis Presley died?
3 Which English soccer team did the only 70s FA Cup and League double?
4 Who had a Christmas special watched by an amazing 28 million people?
5 Who did Captain Mark Phillips marry at Westminster Abbey?
6 Which Brit won the ladies singles at Wimbledon?
7 Queen had their first No 1 with which record?
8 What was introduced in the 70s version of D-Day?
9 What was the nickname of Lord Lucan who vanished in the 70s?
10 Which Spare magazine was founded as part of the feminist movement?
11 Who was Satchmo who passed away in 1971?
12 The monarchy was restored to power in which European country?
13 Who or what was Chia Chia?
14 What type of Fields were linked with Cambodia?
15 The Aswan High Dam was opened in which country?
16 In 1976 which jockey won the Derby for a record seventh time?
17 In 1979 the Shah was forced to flee from which country?
18 Bobby Robson managed which soccer side to their first FA Cup triumph?
19 Sir Anthony Blunt was revealed to have led a secret life as what?
20 Which Czechoslovakian born sportswoman Martina defected to America?
21 What were the sea borne refugees fleeing Vietnam known as?
22 Who won the Eurovision Song Contest for Sweden?
23 In which country was a 2000 year old lifesize terracotta army discovered?
24 Johan Cruyff played in a World Cup Final for which country?
25 What was the name of the fashionable short pants worn by women?

Answers

Pot Luck 65 (see Quiz 142, page 152)
1 Barings. **2** Peace. **3** Athletics. **4** Hom. **5** Lost World. **6** Demi. **7** Conservative. **8** Glasgow. **9** Piper. **10** Red and white. **11** 50s. **12** Brookside. **13** Japan. **14** Paul Scholes. **15** Polly. **16** Hawaii. **17** West Germany. **18** Nottm Forest. **19** Golf. **20** Crane. **21** Attlee. **22** Poetry. **23** Russia. **24** Calls. **25** Birmingham.

Quiz 142 **Pot Luck 65**

Answers - see Quiz 141, page 151

1 Nick Leeson was involved with the collapse of which bank?
2 In 1998 David Trimble and John Hulme shared The Nobel Prize for what?
3 In which sport did David Moorcroft set world records?
4 Which Ken fronted a TV series about his Hot Wok?
5 What was the film sequel to Jurassic Park?
6 Patrick Swayze teamed up with which Moore in the movie Ghost?
7 Norman Lamont has represented which party in parliament?
8 Kenny Dalglish was born in which city?
9 In pop music what is the surname of teenage chart topper Billie?
10 Which two colours form the background of the Austrian flag?
11 Kevin Costner was born in which decade of the 20th century?
12 Which soap featured the character Beth Jordache?
13 In the 40s Hirohito was Emperor of which country?
14 Who was the first Englishman sent off in a Wembley soccer international?
15 What was the name of the chambermaid in Fawlty Towers?
16 Which was the 50th state to become part of the United States of America?
17 In the Cold War in which country was Checkpoint Charlie?
18 Roy Keane joined Man Utd from which club?
19 Popular entertainer Bing Crosby died after completing a game of what?
20 What is Frasier's surname in the sitcom of the same name?
21 Which Clement was Prime Minister in the 40s?
22 What type of works did W H Auden write?
23 Early in the century which country had a parliament called the Duma?
24 In the title of a J B Priestley play what does An Inspector do?
25 Which soccer club has Jasper Carrot among its supporters?

Answers

70s Newsround (see Quiz 141, page 151)
1 Sri Lanka. **2** Graceland. **3** Arsenal. **4** Morecambe & Wise. **5** Princess Anne. **6** Virginia Wade. **7** Bohemian Rhapsody. **8** Decimal coins. **9** Lucky. **10** Spare Rib. **11** Louis Armstrong. **12** Spain. **13** Giant Panda. **14** Killing. **15** Egypt. **16** Lester Piggott. **17** Iran. **18** Ipswich. **19** Spy. **20** Navratilova. **21** Boat People. **22** Abba. **23** China. **24** Netherlands. **25** Hot pants.

Quiz 143 **Headline Makers**

Answers - see Quiz 144, page 154

1. Which MP David, was exposed as having an affair in 1992?
2. Which rock legend Mick was David Bailey's best man?
3. Allan Lamb changed nationality from South African to what?
4. Which former actor and US President received an honorary knighthood?
5. Which Foreign Secretary did Gaynor Regan marry in 1998?
6. Which nanny Louise was tried on TV in the US over the death of a baby in her care?
7. What was the first name of Miss Lewinsky whose White House activities almost brought down Bill Clinton?
8. Who stormed off court at the end of the 1999 French Open and had to have her mother coax her back?
9. Who was South Africa's first black president?
10. In 1995 astronaut Michael Foale was the first Briton to walk where?
11. Which US President born in 1946 was called The Comeback Kid?
12. Which leader Boris succeeded Mikhail Gorbachev?
13. Which eastern European country did Pope John Paul II come from?
14. What was the name of Nelson Mandela's wife when he was released from prison?
15. Which Prime Minister was known as The Iron Lady?
16. Which tennis player famously yelled "You cannot be serious!" at an umpire?
17. Lord Lloyd Webber, Jim Davidson and Bob Monkhouse have all famously supported which political party?
18. Which Arthur was the miners' leader in the 1980s?
19. Which soccer star Paul recorded a rap song called Geordie Boys?
20. Which PM's wife of the latter half of the 20th century was made a High Court judge?
21. What is the first name of Dr Mowlam, who was Tony Blair's first Northern Ireland Secretary?
22. Which Julia was the first to present the news on BBC and ITV?
23. What colour suit is Independent MP and former news journalist Martin Bell famous for wearing?
24. British nurses Lucille McLauchlan and Deborah Parry were accused of murdering an Australian colleague in which country?
25. Matthew Simmons hit the headlines after he was kicked by which then Man Utd French footballer?

Answers

Pot Luck 66 (see Quiz 144, page 154)

1 My Way. **2** Tony Blair. **3** Bunk. **4** Kevin Costner. **5** Australia. **6** MPs. **7** Minogue. **8** South Africa. **9** Travolta. **10** Blue. **11** Australia. **12** Queen. **13** Crystal. **14** John F Kennedy. **15** Tank. **16** M8. **17** Kim. **18** Golf. **19** Lawson. **20** Ella. **21** Novelist. **22** Australia. **23** Berlin. **24** Jennifer Aniston. **25** Austria.

Quiz 144 Pot Luck 66

Answers - see Quiz 143, page 153

1. Which Sinatra song manages to rhyme a line with "shy way"?
2. Which politician was nicknamed 'Bambi'?
3. Henry Ford claimed that, 'History is...' what?
4. In the cost-a-lot to make movie Waterworld who played Mariner?
5. Rupert Murdoch comes from which country?
6. In 1996, which group of people voted themselves a 26% pay rise?
7. What name is shared by pop star sisters Dannii and Kylie?
8. Black activist Steve Biko died in which country in the 70s?
9. Which John was the star of the film Grease?
10. What colour are the Smurfs?
11. Mark Taylor played cricket for which country?
12. Which group had a 90s hit with These Are The Days of Our Lives?
13. What does the C stand for in LCD?
14. In 1963 who famously said "Ich bin ein Berliner"?
15. Churchill, Sherman and Panzer were all developed as types of what?
16. Which motorway forms the Edinburgh to Glasgow route?
17. Who sang in the pop duo with Mel Appleby?
18. With which sport is Fred Couples associated?
19. Which Nigel was an 80s Chancellor?
20. What was the first name of jazz giant Ms Fitzgerald?
21. What is the occupation of Beryl Bainbridge?
22. Robert Menzies was Prime Minister of which country?
23. Which Irving penned the song White Christmas?
24. Who played Rachel Green in Friends?
25. Which country was racing's Niki Lauda born in?

Answers

Headline Makers (see Quiz 143, page 153)

1 Mellor. **2** Jagger. **3** British. **4** Ronald Reagan. **5** Robin Cook. **6** Woodward. **7** Monica. **8** Martina Hingis. **9** Nelson Mandela. **10** Space. **11** Bill Clinton. **12** Yeltsin. **13** Poland. **14** Winnie. **15** Margaret Thatcher. **16** John McEnroe. **17** Tory. **18** Scargill. **19** Gascoigne. **20** Cherie Booth. **21** Mo. **22** Somerville. **23** White. **24** Saudi Arabia. **25** Eric Cantona.

Quiz 145 TV Comedy

Answers - see Quiz 146, page 156

1 Absolutely Fabulous started life as a sketch on which comedy duo's show?
2 What was 'dropped' in the comedy about the Globelink newsroom?
3 How was David Jason's Sidney Charles Larkin known in The Darling Buds of May?
4 Which US actress Ellen was the star of Ellen?
5 Which sitcom was based in a French cafe in occupied France?
6 Who hosted Fantasy Football League with David Baddiel?
7 Which laconic comedian Dave first found fame on the Val Doonican show?
8 Which clerical sitcom was set on Craggy Island?
9 Which US series was about a lawyer called Ally?
10 Which Towers provided a comedy series for Torquay?
11 Who completed the trio with Filthy and Rich in the Young Ones styled comedy?
12 Who was Butt-Head's comedy partner?
13 Which female duo first found fame on The Comic Strip Presents?
14 How many friends were there in Friends?
15 Which Ruby was the American in Girls On Top?
16 Which Benny created Fred Scuttle and Professor Marvel in his saucy seaside postcard style show?
17 Goodnight Sweetheart was based in the 90s and which other decade?
18 Which 90s sitcom was about two sisters in Chigwell with a man mad neighbour?
19 Which Tony lived at 23 Railway Cuttings, East Cheam?
20 Who accompanied Hale in the sketches of The Two Rons?
21 Which Mr Atkinson played Blackadder?
22 Which sitcom was based on writer Jimmy Perry's experiences in the Home Guard?
23 Which Harry created Wayne and Waynetta Slob?
24 In which city was Bread set?
25 Which 60s singer Adam played the title role in Budgie?

Answers

Pot Luck 67 (see Quiz 146, page 156)
1 Pizza. **2** Hockey. **3** Ankle. **4** Scargill. **5** Ronald Reagan. **6** Wonderwoman. **7** Berlin. **8** Robin Hood. **9** Video. **10** Hillman. **11** Ruby Wax. **12** Postman Pat. **13** Spain. **14** Photographer. **15** Comedies. **16** Three. **17** India. **18** Bergerac. **19** Piano. **20** John Major. **21** Cats. **22** Tiger. **23** Spain. **24** Nicholas Lyndhurst. **25** 40s.

Quiz 146 Pot Luck 67

Answers - see Quiz 145, page 155

1 What was the favourite food of the Teenage Mutant Ninja Turtles?
2 Janet Sixsmith has played over a hundred times for England in which sport?
3 Where does Patsy Kensit have a shamrock and the word 'Liam' tattooed?
4 Which Arthur led the miners in the 80s strikes?
5 Who was the first ex-movie actor to become President of the United States?
6 Who was Diana Prince able to change into?
7 Which European city was divided by a wall in the 60s?
8 Who was the Prince of Thieves in a 90s blockbuster movie title?
9 Betamax was a type of what?
10 Which car manufacturer introduced the Hunter, Imp and Minx?
11 Who played Shelley - the only American - in Girls on Top?
12 Who drives a vehicle with the registration PAT 1?
13 The deepwater port of Alicante was built in which country?
14 David Bailey became famous as a what?
15 What type of films were associated with Ealing in the 40s and 50s?
16 How many lions appear on England's soccer badge?
17 Which country does cricketer Anil Kumble play for?
18 Which detective series was set in Jersey?
19 Thelonious Monk was associated with which musical instrument?
20 In the 90s which political leader said, "Well, who'd have thought it?"?
21 Which stage musical does the song Memory come from?
22 In advertising which animal is linked with Esso?
23 In which country is Barajas airport?
24 Which star of Only Fools and Horses and Goodnight Sweetheart played Ronnie Barker's son in Going Straight?
25 Harrison Ford was born in which decade of the 20th century?

Answers

TV Comedy (see Quiz 145, page 155)
1 French & Saunders. **2** The Dead Donkey. **3** Pop. **4** Ellen DeGeneres. **5** Allo Allo. **6** Frank Skinner. **7** Allen. **8** Father Ted. **9** Ally McBeal. **10** Fawlty Towers. **11** Catflap. **12** Beavis. **13** French & Saunders. **14** Six. **15** Wax. **16** Hill. **17** 1940s. **18** Birds of a Feather. **19** Hancock. **20** Pace. **21** Rowan. **22** Dad's Army. **23** Enfield. **24** Liverpool. **25** Faith.

Quiz 147 Sporting Who's Who?

Answers - see Quiz 148, page 158

1 Who was the youngest Wimbledon women's champion of the 20th century?
2 In which country was Greg Rusedski born?
3 Which manager was in charge of Nottm Forest for over 18 years?
4 Which boxer took to wearing a monocle?
5 Who was the first member of the Royal family to be BBC Sports Personality Of The Year?
6 Who was Man Utd's captain in the 1999 European Champions' Cup Final?
7 Who was the first rugby union player to reach 50 international tries?
8 Who was England's captain in cricket's 1999 World Cup?
9 Boxer Naseem Hamed was brought up in which English city?
10 Who didn't make England's World Cup squad for France after much publicised kebab consuming sessions?
11 What nickname was given to basketball's Wilt Chamberlain?
12 Who was Edson Arantes do Nascimento?
13 Who is France's most successful motor racing driver of all time?
14 Who resigned as Welsh manager in 1999?
15 Which British runner became the oldest ever Olympic 100m winner?
16 Who was the first person to run a mile in under four minutes?
17 What was Dean's first name in the Torvill & Dean skating partnership?
18 Who was known as 'The Golden Bear'?
19 Who was the Joe who first defeated Muhammad Ali?
20 In the 90s who advertised Umbro, McDonalds and Lucozade?
21 In the 90s who was known as 'Bumble'?
22 Who was the first manager to have taken charge of both Australia and England?
23 In the 96 Olympics which Michael won both 200 and 400m?
24 What name was shared by motor racing's brothers Emerson and Wilson?
25 Which tennis player had a father named Peter who was jailed for tax irregularities?

Answers

Pot Luck 68 (see Quiz 148, page 158)

1 Drowned. **2** Dover. **3** Crinkley. **4** Chelsea. **5** Britannia. **6** The Bee Gees. **7** Starr. **8** United States. **9** Sri Lanka. **10** Anthea Turner. **11** White. **12** Chess. **13** Lancashire. **14** McKenzie. **15** Office. **16** Sparrow. **17** Johannesburg. **18** Cricket. **19** Franklin. **20** Larkins. **21** 90s. **22** Two. **23** London. **24** Denmark. **25** Oliver.

Quiz 148 Pot Luck 68

Answers - see Quiz 147, page 157

1 How was tycoon Robert Maxwell said to have died?
2 In the 90s what was Britain's busiest ferry passenger port?
3 What sort of Bottom did Noel Edmonds introduce to TV?
4 Which soccer side does former PM John Major support?
5 Which royal ship was decommissioned in 1997?
6 Under what name have Barry, Maurice and Robin been operating for over 30 years?
7 Which Kenneth was the independent prosecutor in the Bill Clinton affair?
8 In which country did Marilyn Monroe die?
9 Which team won the 1996 cricket World Cup?
10 Who was the first female presenter of the National Lottery?
11 What colour did guests wear for Mel B's wedding?
12 Nigel Short represented England at which indoor sport?
13 Preston is the administrative centre of which English county?
14 Which Kelvin used to edit The Sun?
15 What does the O stand for in HMSO?
16 What was Gary's surname in Goodnight Sweetheart?
17 In which city was Jan Smuts airport built?
18 With which sport is Vivian Richards associated?
19 Which Aretha has been dubbed the Queen Of Soul?
20 Which family feature in The Darling Buds Of May?
21 In which decade did Sir Cliff Richard receive his knighthood?
22 How many couples made up the main cast of The Good Life?
23 Fictional Grange Hill Comprehensive is set in which real city?
24 Peter Schmeichel played soccer for which country?
25 Which musical features the song As Long As He Needs Me?

Answers

Sporting Who's Who? (see Quiz 147, page 157)
1 Martina Hingis. **2** Canada. **3** Brian Clough. **4** Chris Eubank. **5** Princess Anne. **6** Schmeichel. **7** David Campese. **8** Alec Stewart. **9** Sheffield. **10** Paul Gascoigne. **11** The Stilt. **12** Pele. **13** Alain Prost. **14** Bobby Gould. **15** Linford Christie. **16** Roger Bannister. **17** Christopher. **18** Jack Nicklaus. **19** Frazier. **20** Alan Shearer. **21** David Lloyd. **22** Terry Venables. **23** Johnson. **24** Fittipaldi. **25** Steffi Graf.

Quiz 149 Action Movies

Answers - see Quiz 150, page 160

1 Which Steven directed Saving Private Ryan?
2 Air Force One deals with the holding to ransom of whom?
3 Which Tom played spy Ethan Hunt in Mission: Impossible?
4 Which 90s James Bond starred in Dante's Peak?
5 Which unlucky Apollo Mission was filmed in 1995 with Tom Hanks?
6 Which Judge from 2000 AD comic appeared on film in 1995?
7 Which Australian actor starred in and directed Braveheart?
8 Which Antarctic creature gives its name to the villain played by Danny De Vito in Batman Returns?
9 What type of creatures were Donatello, Raphael, Michaelangelo and Leonardo?
10 What is the profession of Harrison Ford in the Indiana Jones movies?
11 In which city does the action of Batman take place?
12 Which month is part of the title of the film where Tom Cruise plays war veteran Ron Kovic?
13 Which actor Daniel starred as Hawkeye in The Last of the Mohicans?
14 In which series of films were Danny Glover and Mel Gibson teamed in 1987, 1989, 1992 and 1998?
15 Top Gun is about which of the armed services?
16 The action of The Killing Fields takes place in which country?
17 What was the first Bond movie with Sean Connery?
18 Which actor, famous for spaghetti westerns, got the role in Dirty Harry after Frank Sinatra dropped out?
19 Which Gene played Popeye Doyle in The French Connection?
20 The Poseidon Adventure is about a disaster on what type of transport?
21 Enter the Dragon was the first US kung fu film of which Mr Lee?
22 In which city does Robert de Niro operate as a sinister Taxi Driver?
23 The Shootist was the last film to star which John, famous for his western roles?
24 Which creature was a threat to holidaymakers in Jaws?
25 In which 1999 film did Sean Connery star with Catherine Zeta Jones?

Answers

Pot Luck 69 (see Quiz 150, page 160)
1 The Queen. **2** Sue Barker. **3** France. **4** Kenneth. **5** Tweety Pie. **6** United States. **7** Alex Ferguson. **8** Eton. **9** Dublin. **10** Walters. **11** Great Britain. **12** Billy Connolly. **13** Burgess. **14** Kuwait. **15** Elvis Presley. **16** 50s. **17** Cricket. **18** Bardot. **19** 1945. **20** Rabbit. **21** Labour. **22** Braine. **23** Eight. **24** Harris. **25** Canada.

Quiz 150 Pot Luck 69

Answers - see Quiz 149, page 159

1 Who described 1992 as an "Annus horribilis"?
2 Which lady replaced David Coleman on TV's A Question Of Sport?
3 Which country kept saying no as Britain tried to join the European Union?
4 Which entertainer Williams wrote the autobiography Just Williams?
5 What's the name of the bird that cartoon cat Sylvester chases in vain?
6 Which country had a president known as LBJ?
7 Which Scottish soccer boss was the first to win the English double twice?
8 Which school did Prince Harry go to when he was 13?
9 Sinead O'Connor comes from which city?
10 Which Julie starred in the film Educating Rita?
11 In athletics, which country topped the medal table at the 1998 European Championship?
12 Which comedian is known as The Big Yin?
13 Which Guy the spy fled to Russia along with Donald Maclean?
14 Iraq invaded which neighbouring state to start the 90s Gulf War?
15 Which American has had most solo No 1 hits in the UK?
16 Stephen Fry was born in which decade of the 20th century?
17 Fred Titmus represented England at which sport?
18 Which actress Brigitte became the leading sex symbol of the 50s?
19 In which year did the Second World War end?
20 What kind of creature was Dylan in the Magic Roundabout?
21 Margaret Beckett has represented which party in parliament?
22 Which John wrote the novel Room at The Top?
23 At the end of the 20th C how many UK monarchs had been called Edward?
24 Which Thomas wrote The Silence Of The Lambs?
25 Which country does motor racing's Jacques Villeneuve come from?

Answers

Action Movies (see Quiz 149, page 159)
1 Spielberg. **2** US President. **3** Cruise. **4** Pierce Brosnan. **5** 13. **6** Dredd. **7** Mel Gibson. **8** Penguin. **9** Turtles. **10** Archaeologist. **11** Gotham. **12** July. **13** Day-Lewis. **14** Lethal Weapon. **15** Air Force. **16** Cambodia. **17** Dr No. **18** Clint Eastwood. **19** Hackman. **20** Ship. **21** Bruce. **22** New York. **23** Wayne. **24** Shark. **25** Entrapment.

Quiz 151 On the Road

Answers - see Quiz 152, page 162

1 Which city is the southernmost point of the A1?
2 What colour are the lines in a box junction?
3 How frequently must a three year old car have an MOT in Great Britain?
4 What colour Cross Code gives advice on crossing the road?
5 What does a red and amber traffic light mean?
6 On the road, what shape are most warning signs?
7 Which name for a very large truck gets its name from an Indian god?
8 Which London road race is held annually for professionals and those raising money for charity?
9 Which registration letter was the first to be introduced in a month other than August?
10 Which 24 Hour Race in France uses normal roads as part of the race track?
11 What is the minimum number of L plates a learner driver must have?
12 What is the type of driving licence a learner driver must have called?
13 Which government publication for all road users was first published in 1931?
14 Which Garages near Oxford originally produced the MG sports car?
15 The Milk Race is an annual race around Britain's roads on what form of transport?
16 How is the London Orbital Motorway also known?
17 An orange badge displayed in a car's windscreen means the driver is what?
18 Which Way begins West of Sheffield and stretches to Southern Scotland?
19 A memorial to which Queen stands in front of Buckingham Palace?
20 Which motoring association has an actual club in London, as its name implies?
21 Which national BBC Radio news and sport station broadcasts travel updates, usually every 15 minutes?
22 What colour card allows a motorist to travel abroad?
23 The letter H on a road sign means what?
24 What does G stand for in HGV?
25 What colour is the background of motorway signs?

Answers

Pot Luck 70 (see Quiz 152, page 162)
1 Dunblane. **2** Geri Halliwell - Ginger Spice. **3** Shark. **4** Green. **5** Wales. **6** Car. **7** The Wombles. **8** Rolls Royce. **9** Fish. **10** Cabaret. **11** 90s. **12** Coronation Street. **13** Tennis. **14** Belgium. **15** Sitcom. **16** Secondary. **17** Derbyshire. **18** Three. **19** Victoria. **20** Baez. **21** Syndrome. **22** Are You Being Served? **23** Piano. **24** Sweden. **25** Red.

Quiz 152 Pot Luck 70

Answers - see Quiz 151, page 161

1 In which Scottish town did Thomas Hamilton carry out a shooting atrocity?
2 Which Spice Girl wore a Union Jack dress?
3 What type of creature was the star of the film Jaws?
4 What colour goes with white and red on the Bulgarian flag?
5 Soccer's Peter Nicholas won 73 international caps for which country?
6 Princess Grace of Monaco died after an accident in which form of transport?
7 In books and pop music, who tidied up on Wimbledon Common?
8 Who produced the car known as The Silver Ghost ?
9 Which TV Michael is linked with underestimating the 1987 hurricanes?
10 Which musical does Cabaret come from?
11 The driving test introduced a written section in which decade?
12 Derek Wilton appeared in which TV soap?
13 With which sport is Helena Sukova associated?
14 Which country has B as its international vehicle registration letter?
15 The description situation comedy is usually shortened to what?
16 What does the S stand for in GCSE?
17 Matlock is the administrative centre of which English county?
18 How many Goodies were there?
19 Who was the British monarch at the start of the 20th century?
20 Which folksinger Joan featured in the civil rights and anti-Vietnam movements?
21 What does the letter S stand for in AIDS?
22 Grace and Favour was the sequel to which sitcom about Grace Brothers?
23 What instrument did 50s and 60s star Russ Conway play?
24 Which country did Bjorn Borg come from?
25 On TV, what colour was Inspector Morse's jag?

Answers

On the Road (see Quiz 151, page 161)
1 London. **2** Yellow. **3** Once a year. **4** Green. **5** Stop. **6** Triangular. **7** Juggernaut. **8** Marathon. **9** T. **10** Le Mans. **11** Two. **12** Provisional. **13** Highway Code. **14** Morris. **15** Cycles. **16** M25. **17** Disabled. **18** Pennine Way. **19** Victoria. **20** RAC - Royal Automobile Club. **21** Radio 5 Live. **22** Green. **23** Hospital. **24** Goods. **25** Blue.

Quiz 153 Music - Who's Who?

Answers - see Quiz 154, page 164

1 Who wrote the lyrics for the 90s Candle In The Wind?
2 Who is the Sid of Nancy and Sid notoriety?
3 Who is Blur's lead singer?
4 Who led the Blonde Ambition world tour of 1990?
5 Who wrote, sang and played the guitar on The Streets of London?
6 Which group's music featured in the frock horror film Priscilla Queen Of The Desert ?
7 Who had his first No 1 in the 70s with Maggie May?
8 Who first hit the top ten with Cornflake Girl?
9 Who said Go West in 1993?
10 Who was the Gary who sang with the Union Gap?
11 Who created the character Ziggy Stardust?
12 Who was 'The Boss'?
13 Under what name had the late Mary O'Brien been famous?
14 Who did Louise Nurding leave in 1995?
15 Who charted by saying Eh-Oh!?
16 Who had a singer Roger Daltrey and a drummer Keith Moon?
17 Which country does Bjork come from?
18 Who has been both Bad and Dangerous?
19 Who linked up with Aitken and Waterman?
20 Who was backed by Blockheads?
21 Who first charted back in the 70s with Seven Seas Of Rhye?
22 Who was Addicted to Love in the 80s?
23 Who had a hit with Orinoco Flow?
24 Who was backed by the Wailers?
25 Who was the big O?

Answers

Pot Luck 71 (see Quiz 154, page 164)
1 Belgrade. **2** Wallace. **3** 70s. **4** Stephenson. **5** Che Guevara. **6** Larry Grayson. **7** Welles. **8** Italy. **9** Pink Floyd. **10** Dialling. **11** 40s. **12** Hale & Pace. **13** Greene. **14** Canada. **15** Records. **16** BMW. **17** Tony Hancock. **18** London. **19** One. **20** W. **21** Tennis. **22** Florida. **23** Knowing Me, Knowing You. **24** Sunset Boulevard. **25** Millwall.

Quiz 154 Pot Luck 71

Answers - see Quiz 153, page 163

1 Which city became the capital of Serbia?
2 Who is Gromit's partner?
3 In which decade did Great Britain go into Europe?
4 Which Pamela married Billy Connolly?
5 Which revolutionary's face appeared on countless 60s posters with the words Viva Che?
6 Which comedian's catchphrases included "Shut That Door"?
7 Which Orson directed the film classic Citizen Kane?
8 Which country does soccer star Christian Vieri play for?
9 Who recorded the album Dark Side Of The Moon?
10 In telecommunications, what does the second D stand for in IDD?
11 Goldie Hawn was born in which decade of the 20th century?
12 Which comic duo has the first names Gareth & Norman?
13 Which Graham wrote the novel Brighton Rock?
14 Which country does Wayne Gretzky come from?
15 Berry Gordy became famous as a producer of what?
16 Which company took over Rover in 1994?
17 Which late great comedian created the character whose first names were Anthony Aloysius St John?
18 Which was the most heavily blitzed UK city in World War II?
19 At the end of the 20th C how many UK monarchs had been called Anne?
20 On a computer keyboard what letter is between Q and E?
21 Angela Mortimer represented Britain at which sport?
22 Disney World is situated in which US State?
23 Which Alan Partridge show has the name of an Abba hit?
24 The character Norma Desmond appears in which musical?
25 Which soccer team does Danny Baker follow?

Answers

Music – Who's Who? (see Quiz 153, page 163)
1 Bernie Taupin. **2** Sid Vicious. **3** Damon Albarn. **4** Madonna. **5** Ralph McTell. **6** Abba. **7** Rod Stewart. **8** Tori Amos. **9** Pet Shop Boys. **10** Puckett. **11** David Bowie. **12** Bruce Springsteen. **13** Dusty Springfield. **14** Eternal. **15** Teletubbies. **16** The Who. **17** Iceland. **18** Michael Jackson. **19** Stock. **20** Ian Dury. **21** Queen. **22** Robert Palmer. **23** Enya. **24** Bob Marley. **25** Roy Orbison.

Quiz 155 80s Newsround

Answers - see Quiz 156, page 166

1 Which Scottish border town was the scene of a jumbo jet disaster?
2 Who or what was Mary Rose, making an appearance after 500 years?
3 Which soap had Britain asking, "Who shot JR?"?
4 Which US President was linked with the 'Star Wars' policy?
5 An IRA car bomb was detonated outside which major London store?
6 Which Neil was elected leader of the Labour Party?
7 Who won the ladies singles most times at Wimbledon in the 80s?
8 Which John portrayed The Elephant Man on film?
9 Solidarity was the mass movement of the people in which country?
10 Sarah Ferguson became Duchess of where?
11 What kind of disaster claimed some 100,000 lives in Armenia in 1988?
12 Which golfer Sandy triumphed at the US Masters?
13 In 1980 the SAS spectacularly freed hostages in which embassy in London?
14 Don't Die Of Ignorance was the message put out to combat which disease?
15 Which tennis ace completed his fifth successive Wimbledon singles triumph?
16 What did the L stand for in GLC?
17 Who became the world's youngest ever boxing heavyweight champion?
18 Which Jeffrey resigned as deputy chairman of the Tory party?
19 Which city was devastated by an earthquake in 1985 and then hosted the World Cup in 1986?
20 What was the so-called Black day for the City in the late 80s?
21 There was fighting around Port Stanley on which Islands?
22 Tiananmen Square was a scene of conflict in which country?
23 In which English city were Liverpool supporters crushed by crowds at an FA Cup semi final?
24 Which organisation had their ship the Rainbow Warrior sunk?
25 What type of disaster happened at Bradford City's stadium?

Answers

Pot Luck 72 (see Quiz 156, page 166)
1 William Hague. **2** Basketball. **3** Mini. **4** Books. **5** Dogs. **6** Germany. **7** Grievous. **8** Harding. **9** The Lone Ranger. **10** Exchange. **11** M6. **12** Isaac. **13** Marvin. **14** Martina Hingis. **15** Oasis. **16** Eunuch. **17** Labour. **18** Russia. **19** Trumpet. **20** Tennis. **21** Bomb. **22** Slob. **23** Le Bon. **24** Chandler. **25** The BBC.

Quiz 156 Pot Luck 72

Answers - see Quiz 155, page 165

1 Which 90s British political leader gave his marriage vows in Welsh?
2 With which sport is Shaquille O'Neal associated?
3 What type of skirt was the main fashion style of the 60s?
4 In Notting Hill what does the Hugh Grant character deal in?
5 In the 90s certain Newcastle Utd directors described the women of the area as being like which creatures?
6 Chancellor Helmut Kohl led which country in the 80s and 90s?
7 What does the G mean in GBH?
8 Which comedian Mike called himself The Rochdale Cowboy?
9 The William Tell Overture provided the title music to which TV western?
10 In finance what does the E in ERM stand for?
11 Which motorway links Carlisle to the Midlands?
12 What is the first name of sci-fi writer Asimov?
13 Which Hank played lead guitar with The Shadows?
14 Who did Jelena Dokic beat in the first round of Wimbledon 1999?
15 Who had a 90s No 1 with Don't Look Back In Anger?
16 In 1970 Germaine Greer produced the feminist book The Female what?
17 Keir Hardie was the first leader of which 20th C political party?
18 In which country is Archangel airport?
19 Quincy Jones was associated with which brass instrument?
20 Buster Mottram represented Britain at which sport?
21 What type of tragedy blighted Omagh in 1998?
22 What was the surname of Harry Enfield's creations Wayne and Waynetta?
23 Which Simon sang with Duran Duran?
24 Which Raymond wrote the detective novel Farewell My Lovely?
25 Relating to the TV show Auntie's Bloomers, who is Auntie?

Answers

80s Newsround (see Quiz 155, page 165)
1 Lockerbie. **2** Ship. **3** Dallas. **4** Reagan. **5** Harrods. **6** Kinnock. **7** Martina Navratilova. **8** Hurt. **9** Poland. **10** York. **11** Earthquake. **12** Lyle. **13** Iranian. **14** AIDS. **15** Bjorn Borg. **16** London. **17** Mike Tyson. **18** Archer. **19** Mexico. **20** Monday. **21** Falkland Islands. **22** China. **23** Sheffield. **24** Greenpeace. **25** Fire.

Quiz 157 Heroes & Villains

Answers - see Quiz 158, page 168

1 In which US city was Al Capone crime king during the Prohibition?
2 Which US President George was the US's youngest ever pilot in WWII?
3 Which American leader did Lee Harvey Oswald assassinate?
4 What was the first name of Mr Waite held hostage in Beirut in the 1980s?
5 In 1987 Lester Piggott was jailed for not paying what?
6 In 1995 O.J. Simpson was cleared of murdering which of his relatives?
7 Pol Pot led the Khmer Rouge on which continent?
8 Archbishop Desmond Tutu fought for civil rights in which country?
9 Which ex Minister Aitken was jailed in 1999 over a failed libel case?
10 Simon Weston became famous for his courage following horrific injuries in which war?
11 What nationality was Brian Keenan, held hostage with John McCarthy?
12 Which nickname was given to Boston murderer Albert de Salvo?
13 Which Lord vanished after his children's nanny was found murdered?
14 Which media magnate mysteriously disappeared off his yacht in 1991?
15 John Glenn became the oldest man to travel where when he boarded the Discovery in 1998?
16 Richard Bacon resigned from which TV show after drug allegations?
17 Which part of Evander Holyfield did Mike Tyson bite off during a fight?
18 Prosecutor Kenneth Starr was involved in impeachment proceedings against which US President?
19 Which French footballer David was chosen to publicise the dangers of landmines after the death of Diana Princess of Wales?
20 Which controversial politician Ann became Shadow Home Secretary in William Hague's 1999 Shadow Cabinet reshuffle?
21 Which colour precedes the name of Mr Adair, the firefighter who fought the Piper Alpha blaze in the 1980s?
22 What was the occupation of Nick Leeson when he brought down Barings?
23 Which disgraced Duchess had a satellite TV show called Surviving Life?
24 What was the nationality of the driver of the car in which Princess Diana died?
25 Who left his job on Radio 1 because he didn't want to work on Fridays?

Answers

Pot Luck 73 (see Quiz 158, page 168)

1 Albright. **2** Terry Venables. **3** Turnip. **4** Plays. **5** Blood. **6** A scarecrow. **7** Rice. **8** Oil. **9** Blair. **10** Soccer. **11** Lenny Henry. **12** Omelette. **13** Eden. **14** Noble. **15** Greg Rusedski. **16** Paddington. **17** South Africa. **18** Jim Davidson. **19** Australia. **20** Labour. **21** 40s. **22** Ireland. **23** Architects. **24** Cyprus. **25** Hudd.

Quiz 158 Pot Luck 73

Answers - see Quiz 157, page 167

1 Which Madeline became the first US Secretary of State?
2 Which former England soccer coach was banned from holding company directorships?
3 On TV, Baldrick was attracted to what type of vegetable?
4 Sir Alan Ayckbourn became famous for writing what?
5 Politician Enoch Powell graphically spoke of rivers of what?
6 On TV, what was Worzel Gummidge?
7 Which Tim co-wrote the musical Chess?
8 What type of cargo was carried by the stricken vessel the Torrey Canyon?
9 In 1983 which Tony became MP for Sedgefield?
10 Francis Lee represented England at which sport?
11 Which member of TV's Tiswas team impersonated Trevor McDonald as Trevor McDoughnut?
12 Writer Arnold Bennett gave his name to what type of food dish?
13 Which British Prime Minister resigned over the Suez Crisis?
14 Which Kara acted ignobly by flogging a saucy shot of Sophie Rhys-Jones?
15 Which tennis player had an acrimonious split with coach Tony Pickard in 1998?
16 In fiction, which bear was found at a London station?
17 Which country does golfer Ernie Els come from?
18 Which host of The Generation Game starred in the sitcom Home James?
19 In which country did The Flying Doctor usually do his rounds?
20 Diane Abbott has represented which party in parliament?
21 David Bowie was born in which decade of the 20th century?
22 Dramatist Brendan Behan came from which country?
23 Who or what were Gropius and Le Corbusier?
24 Archbishop Makarios was president of which Mediterranean island?
25 Which Roy's comedy radio series about items in the news began in 1975?

Answers

Heroes & Villains (see Quiz 157, page 167)
1 Chicago. **2** Bush. **3** John F Kennedy. **4** Terry. **5** Taxes. **6** His wife. **7** Asia. **8** South Africa. **9** Jonathan. **10** Falklands. **11** Irish. **12** Strangler. **13** Lucan. **14** Robert Maxwell. **15** Space. **16** Blue Peter. **17** Ear. **18** Clinton. **19** Ginola. **20** Widdecombe. **21** Red. **22** Banker. **23** York. **24** French. **25** Chris Evans.

Quiz 159 TV Cops & Robbers

Answers - see Quiz 160, page 170

1 Which US cop show was set in Hill Street Station?
2 PC Rowan upheld law and order in Aidensfield in which series?
3 Which Inspector was famous for his red Jag, crosswords and Wagner?
4 Which 80s hit was set on the island of Jersey?
5 Which John starred as Kavanagh QC?
6 Which crime series with Telly Savalas was known as The Lion Without a Mane in Germany?
7 Which 90s series was dubbed Between the Sheets because of its main character's personal affairs?
8 What was the profession of medieval sleuth Cadfael?
9 Where was the Vice tackled by Sonny Crockett and Ricardo Tubbs?
10 Which 80s/90s show once held a 30 minute slot three times a week?
11 Which unmarried female detective was created by Agatha Christie?
12 Which Lynda La Plante series featured DCI Jane Tennison?
13 In which country was Prisoner: Cell Block H set?
14 Which show featured private eye Jim Rockford?
15 Which Geordie actor Jimmy starred as Spender?
16 How was Ken Hutchinson known in the 70s series with David Soul and Paul Michael Glaser?
17 In which series did Robbie Coltrane play Fitz?
18 Which Hamish operated in Lochdubh?
19 On which channel was LA Law first broadcast in the UK?
20 Who was Dalziel's detective partner, from the novels by Reginald Hill?
21 Which series with Dennis Waterman and John Thaw got its name for the rhyming slang for Flying Squad?
22 What sort of Line was a police sitcom with Rowan Atkinson?
23 In which Dutch city did Van der Valk take place?
24 Which Cars provided police transport in the classic crime series of the 60s and 70s?
25 Which thriller series had a team of crime fighters with lots of electronic devices to help with their investigations?

Answers

Pot Luck 74 (see Quiz 160, page 170)
1 Geoff Boycott. **2** Uma Thurman. **3** Railway. **4** Rod Stewart. **5** Edna Everage. **6** Edward VIII. **7** Elizabeth Taylor. **8** 1980s. **9** Soccer. **10** Glasgow. **11** Supermac. **12** Operator. **13** Arthur Hailey. **14** Tina Turner. **15** Norden. **16** France. **17** Yuri Gagarin. **18** Diary. **19** Wales. **20** Weather. **21** Al Gore. **22** Not. **23** Tarzan. **24** Springsteen. **25** Allie.

Quiz 160 Pot Luck 74

Answers - see Quiz 159, page 169

1 Which ex Yorkshire cricketer was involved in a French assault case?
2 Who played Emma Peel in the 90s film version of The Avengers?
3 The Beeching report led to drastic reductions in which service?
4 Which veteran pop singer has the first names Roderick David?
5 Which TV 'Dame' has a friend called Madge Allsop?
6 After ruling as a monarch who became The Duke of Windsor?
7 Who liked Richard Burton so much that she married him twice?
8 In which decade did people last get the chance to see Haley's Comet?
9 With which sport is Colin Hendry associated?
10 Taggart was set in which city?
11 Which heroic nickname was given to statesman Harold Macmillan?
12 Dialling 100 on a BT telephone will put you through to which service?
13 The novel Airport was a best seller for which author?
14 Which female sang the Bond theme to Goldeneye?
15 Which Denis presents ITV's show of outtakes It'll be Alright On the Night?
16 The D Day landings took place in which country?
17 Who was the first man to fly in space?
18 What did teenager Anne Frank leave behind that was published after her death?
19 Which country did soccer keeper Jack Kelsey play for?
20 In her first TV appearances Ulrika Jonsson presented information about what?
21 Who was Bill Clinton's first vice president?
22 What does N stand for in NIMBY?
23 Which character is the most famous creation of Edgar Rice Burroughs?
24 Which Bruce declared he was Born In The USA?
25 Who was Kate's friend in the 80s sitcom with Susan Saint James and Jane Curtin?

Answers

TV Cops & Robbers (see Quiz 159, page 169)
1 Hill Street Blues. **2** Heartbeat. **3** Morse. **4** Bergerac. **5** Thaw. **6** Kojak. **7** Between the Lines. **8** Monk. **9** Miami. **10** The Bill. **11** Miss Marple. **12** Prime Suspect. **13** Australia. **14** The Rockford Files. **15** Nail. **16** Hutch. **17** Cracker. **18** Macbeth. **19** ITV. **20** Pascoe. **21** The Sweeney. **22** Thin Blue. **23** Amsterdam. **24** Z Cars. **25** Bugs.

Quiz 161 Summer Sports

Answers - see Quiz 162, page 172

1 How is British sportsman Francis Thompson more usually known?
2 Which county did Brian Lara first play for in England?
3 Which 30 plus player won his first golf Major at the 1998 US Masters?
4 Which country does tennis player Pat Rafter come from?
5 Which team play cricket at home at Grace Road?
6 Which golfer was Europe's leading moneywinner of 1998?
7 Who started his breakaway cricket 'Circus' in the 70s?
8 How many times did Ivan Lendl win Wimbledon singles?
9 Which cricketing County added Lightning to their name?
10 What is Denise Lewis's main athletic event?
11 Which British golfer regained the US Masters in 1996?
12 Who won Wimbledon in 1998 after twice losing in the final?
13 How many teams reached the second round of cricket's 1999 World Cup?
14 Which country does Goran Ivanisevic come from?
15 In which month is The Derby run?
16 What sport is the winner of the Harry Vardon trophy playing?
17 What is the specialist fielding position of India's Moin Khan?
18 Which Mark was captain of the European 1999 Ryder Cup team?
19 Which British Fred was a Wimbledon singles winner in the 1930s?
20 Athlete Zola Budd was born in which country?
21 Who captained the West Indies in the 1999 World Cup?
22 What sport is staged at the Roland Garros?
23 Which golfer split from his coach David Leadbetter in 1998?
24 How many Brits were in the top ten seeds for Wimbledon 1999?
25 Which phone company has sponsored the Derby?

Answers

***Pot Luck* 75** (see Quiz 162, page 172)
1 INXS. **2** Books. **3** Dick Tracy. **4** Darts. **5** Alan Freeman. **6** Batman. **7** Buckinghamshire. **8** O J Simpson. **9** Kray. **10** Bryan. **11** Geoff Boycott. **12** Willis. **13** 20s. **14** Pakistan. **15** Tatum O'Neal. **16** Eighties. **17** Goodman. **18** Barrie. **19** Sean Penn. **20** Hockey. **21** Guts. **22** The Widow. **23** Federal. **24** Jill Dando. **25** Soccer.

Quiz 162 Pot Luck 75

Answers - see Quiz 161, page 171

LEVEL 1 

1. Michael Hutchence was leader singer with which group?
2. Foyle's in London sells what product?
3. In which film did Madonna play Breathless Mahoney?
4. In which sport did Phil Taylor become a world champion?
5. Which DJ became known as 'Fluff'?
6. Which caped crusader operated in Gotham City?
7. Aylesbury is the administrative centre of which English county?
8. Which controversial American sportsman had the first names Orenthal James?
9. Which Twins were involved in an incident in East End's Blind Beggar pub?
10. Which Ferry helped launch Roxy Music?
11. Which Yorkshire batsman played cricket for England from 1964 to 1981?
12. Demi Moore married which Bruce?
13. Marlon Brando was born in which decade of the 20th century?
14. Ms Bhutto became Prime Minister in which state?
15. Which actress did John McEnroe marry?
16. Which decade received A Kick Up it in the form of a TV comedy sketch show?
17. Which bandleader Benny was 'The King of Swing'?
18. Which author JM wrote Peter Pan?
19. In 1987 Madonna filed for divorce from which husband?
20. Sean Kerley represented Britain at which sport?
21. General George Patton was known as Old Blood and what?
22. Who was Kit's comedy partner in the 90s TV show?
23. What does the F stand for in FBI?
24. Who was Sue Cook's replacement on Crimewatch UK?
25. What type of sport is played at Gay Meadow?

Answers

Summer Sports (see Quiz 161, page 171)
1 Daley Thompson. **2** Warwickshire. **3** Mark O'Meara. **4** Australia. **5** Leicestershire. **6** Colin Montgomerie. **7** Kerry Packer. **8** Never. **9** Lancashire. **10** Heptathlon. **11** Nick Faldo. **12** Jana Novotna. **13** Six. **14** Croatia. **15** June. **16** Golf. **17** Wicket keeper. **18** James. **19** Perry. **20** South Africa. **21** Brian Lara. **22** Tennis. **23** Nick Faldo. **24** Two. **25** Vodafone.

Quiz 163 90s Movies

Answers - see Quiz 164, page 174

1 Where are the Sliding Doors in the movie with Gwyneth Paltrow?
2 The action of Saving Private Ryan takes place during which war?
3 In which movie is Truman Burbank a popular character?
4 Which ex 007 played the Scottish villain in The Avengers?
5 In Doctor Dolittle Eddie Murphy has the ability to talk to whom?
6 Which Zorro film was released in 1998?
7 Which giant lizard was the star of the 1998 movie with Matthew Broderick?
8 Which star of ER played Batman in the 1997 Batman & Robin?
9 What was the first Spice Girls' film called?
10 Which part does Matt Damon play in Good Will Hunting?
11 Which 1996 remake replaced animated dogs with real ones and starred Glenn Close?
12 Which Fiennes starred in The English Patient?
13 Which 90s film of a Shakespeare play starred Leonardo DiCaprio and Claire Daines?
14 In which country of the UK was Trainspotting set?
15 In Batman Forever which villain was played by Jim Carrey?
16 What sort of animal was Babe?
17 Which Disney movie was based on the life of a native North American?
18 What was the occupation of Susan Sarandon in Dead Man Walking?
19 Which Story was the first ever completely computer animated movie?
20 Which knighted British pop star wrote the music for The Lion King?
21 Philadelphia became the first mainstream Hollywood film to tackle which disease?
22 Which blonde famously crossed her legs in Basic Instinct?
23 Who shared the title with Thelma in the 1991 film directed by Ridley Scott?
24 What sort of shop does Hugh Grant own in Notting Hill?
25 Val Kilmer played Jim Morrison in the 1991 movie about which rock band?

Answers

Pot Luck 76 (see Quiz 164, page 174)
1 Prescott. **2** Delia Smith. **3** Otis Redding. **4** Jackson. **5** Vietnam. **6** Ike. **7** Red. **8** Skiing. **9** Last of the Summer Wine. **10** Tennis. **11** Do. **12** Australia. **13** Bragg. **14** Spain. **15** Yorkshire. **16** Two. **17** AUS. **18** Golf. **19** Red. **20** Horse. **21** Harpo. **22** Lettuce. **23** Conservative. **24** Lennox Lewis. **25** Piano.

Quiz 164 Pot Luck 76

Answers - see Quiz 163, page 173

1 Which MP John got a soaking at the Brit Awards?
2 Which cookery writer produced a Summer and a Winter Collection which rocketed to the top of the bestseller list?
3 Dock Of The Bay was a hit for which singer after his death?
4 Which Welshman Colin became a world record holder in hurdling?
5 The movie Platoon was about war in which country?
6 What was the nickname of US President Dwight Eisenhower?
7 White and what other colour feature on the Canadian flag?
8 An accident in which sporting activity claimed Sonny Bono's life?
9 Which sitcom has had elderly characters called Foggy Dewhurst, Seymour Utterthwaite and Wally Batty?
10 In which sport did John Lloyd represented Britain?
11 What does the D stand for in a DIY store?
12 In the 90s Paul Keating was Prime Minister of which country?
13 Which Melvyn is a TV arts presenter and a novelist?
14 The deepwater port of Alicante was built in which country?
15 Darren Gough plays cricket for which county?
16 How many Likely Lads were there?
17 What are the international vehicle registration letters of Australia?
18 With which sport is Corey Pavin associated?
19 First World War flying ace Manfred von Richtofen was what coloured Baron?
20 Quick Draw McGraw was what kind of cartoon creature?
21 Which of the Marx Brothers never spoke on film?
22 Tom Thumb and Little Gem were developed as types of what?
23 Virginia Bottomley has represented which party in parliament?
24 Which British boxer successfully defended his WBC heavyweight title in 1997?
25 Ray Charles was associated with which musical instrument?

Answers

90s Movies (see Quiz 163, page 173)
1 Tube Train. **2** WWII. **3** The Truman Show. **4** Sean Connery. **5** Animals.
6 The Mask of Zorro. **7** Godzilla. **8** George Clooney. **9** Spiceworld: The Movie.
10 Will Hunting **11** 101 Dalmatians. **12** Ralph. **13** Romeo & Juliet. **14** Scotland.
15 The Riddler. **16** Pig . **17** Pocahontas. **18** Nun. **19** Toy Story. **20** Elton John.
21 AIDS. **22** Sharon Stone. **23** Louise. **24** Bookshop. **25** The Doors.

Quiz 165 World Tour

Answers - see Quiz 166, page 176

1 Which city is called Kapstad in Afrikaans?
2 Which language apart from English is an official language of Canada?
3 Okinawa is a volcano in which country?
4 In which country is an Afghani a unit of currency?
5 Lesotho is a southern African kingdom surrounded by which country?
6 Madagascar is off which coast of Africa?
7 Antigua and Barbuda lie in which Sea?
8 Ottawa is which country's capital?
9 The Chinese city of Beijing was previously known as what?
10 Argentina's east coast lies on which ocean?
11 Which South American Canal joins the Atlantic to the Pacific oceans?
12 What is the largest country in South America?
13 Which two letters follow the name of the US capital Washington?
14 What is the Great Barrier Reef made from?
15 Which Chinese landmark was viewed from space?
16 For most of the 20th Century St Petersburg has been named after which Soviet hero?
17 Which US holiday state has the Everglades National Park?
18 How was the Cote d'Ivoire previously known?
19 Which northerly US state, one of four beginning with A, joined the Union in 1959?
20 In the USA what is a zip code?
21 The Victoria Falls are shared between Zimbabwe and which other country beginning with the same letter?
22 Which US state is famous for Disneyland and the film industry?
23 Manhattan is a part of which US city?
24 What are the Islas Canarias in English?
25 Which Australian province has New at the beginning of its name?

Answers

Pot Luck 77 (see Quiz 166, page 176)
1 Prescott. **2** Kenneth Grahame. **3** Belgium. **4** James Garner. **5** Red. **6** Disarmament. **7** 60s. **8** Sherlock Holmes. **9** Ireland. **10** Lotus. **11** Plane. **12** Man Utd. **13** Monday. **14** Little & Large. **15** 70s. **16** Winston Churchill. **17** Australia. **18** Germany. **19** Fred Astaire. **20** X. **21** Liver Birds. **22** M3. **23** Soccer. **24** China. **25** Ballet.

Quiz 166 Pot Luck 77

Answers - see Quiz 165, page 175

1 Which John was MP for Kingston upon Hull in the 90s?
2 Who wrote the children's classic The Wind In The Willows?
3 Scene of an 80s soccer crowd disaster, Heysel Stadium is in which country?
4 James Baumgarner changed his name slightly to become which actor?
5 The majority of London buses are what colour?
6 What does the D stand for in CND?
7 Nicholas Cage was born in which decade of the century?
8 Which TV sleuth was played by Jeremy Brett?
9 Eamon de Valera was Prime Minister of which country?
10 Which car manufacturer introduced the Eclat, Elan and Elite models?
11 A crash in what type of vehicle claimed John Denver's life?
12 Which soccer team does Zoe Ball follow?
13 In the 90s most Bank Holidays fall on which day?
14 How were contrasting comedy duo Syd and Eddie better known?
15 In which decade did Star Wars hit the movie screens?
16 Which British leader famously said, "This was their finest hour"?
17 Which country does cricketer Stuart MacGill play for?
18 In which country was Karl Marx born?
19 Who was the male lead in the 30s song and dance film Top Hat?
20 Malcolm Little replaced his surname with which letter of the alphabet?
21 Which Birds were Beryl and Sandra on TV?
22 Which motorway links London to Winchester?
23 Danny McGrain represented Scotland at which sport?
24 In the 60s, in which Asian country did a Cultural Revolution take place?
25 In which branch of the arts did Dame Alicia Markova find fame?

Answers

World Tour (see Quiz 165, page 175)
1 Cape Town. **2** French. **3** Japan. **4** Afghanistan. **5** South Africa. **6** East. **7** Caribbean. **8** Canada. **9** Peking. **10** Atlantic. **11** Panama. **12** Brazil. **13** DC. **14** Coral. **15** Great Wall of China. **16** Lenin. **17** Florida. **18** Ivory Coast. **19** Alaska. **20** Post code. **21** Zambia. **22** California. **23** New York. **24** Canary Islands. **25** South Wales.

Quiz 167 Bands

Answers - see Quiz 168, page 178

1 Which band included Phil Collins and Peter Gabriel?
2 Which band recorded the album The Joshua Tree?
3 Marti Pellow was the lead singer with which group?
4 In the 70s who put A Message In A Bottle?
5 Who fronted the Boomtown Rats?
6 Which boy band had No 1s with Babe and Sure?
7 Dave Gilmore and Roger Waters were in which long lasting group?
8 Which group became the first to have the word Pumpkins in their name?
9 Which group flew into the Hotel California?
10 Which Paul was in Style Council and Jam?
11 Who did Vic Reeves sing with?
12 Which US Boys band featured three members of the Wilson family?
13 Which band recorded the album Parallel Lines?
14 How many members were there in the Eurythmics?
15 Which movement did The Sex Pistols begin?
16 What word was replaced by the letter T in T. Rex?
17 How many brothers were in the original Jackson family line up?
18 How many boys were there in the Pet Shop Boys?
19 What was Adam backed by?
20 Which band actually had Noddy as lead singer?
21 What did the letter O stand for in ELO?
22 Pictures of Matchstick Men was the first hit for which veteran rockers?
23 Teeny boppers The Bay City Rollers were from which country?
24 Which band featured Paul McGuigan on bass?
25 Which all time great band featured Harrison and Starkey?

Answers

Pot Luck 78 (see Quiz 168, page 178)
1 Newcastle. **2** Spock. **3** Maid Marian. **4** Two. **5** 80s. **6** Message. **7** School. **8** Republic of Ireland. **9** Paris. **10** Chariots of Fire. **11** New York. **12** England. **13** Mary Whitehouse. **14** Norfolk. **15** Producer. **16** Peach. **17** Betty Boothroyd. **18** Golf. **19** Venice. **20** Bruce Forsyth. **21** Chandler. **22** USSR. **23** Six. **24** Barbera. **25** Vet.

Quiz 168 Pot Luck 78

Answers - see Quiz 167, page 177

1 In 1998 Freddie Shepherd resigned as club chairman of which soccer club?
2 Which parenting guru Doctor wrote Baby and Child Care?
3 Who was in charge of the Merry Men in the role reversal children's sitcom about Robin Hood?
4 At the end of the 20th C how many UK monarchs had been called Charles?
5 In which decade did Eric Morecambe die?
6 In pop music, what did the Police find In A Bottle?
7 In book and film what was St Trinian's?
8 Paul McGrath played soccer for which international team?
9 Dutch born spy Mata Hari was a dancer in which European city?
10 Which film was about the Olympic Games of 1924?
11 President Kennedy international airport is in which US city?
12 Which country does opera diva Lesley Garrett come from?
13 Whose name was part of a TV Experience where she would have certainly disapproved of the show's content?
14 Norwich is the administrative centre of which English county?
15 Louis B Mayer had which job in the film industry?
16 Australian singer Nellie Melba had a dish named after her containing which fruit?
17 Who was Speaker of the House of Commons for the greater part of the 90s?
18 With which sport is Nick Price associated?
19 In which city was the Marco Polo airport built?
20 Which entertainer said, "Nice to see you, to see you - nice"?
21 Which Raymond wrote the novel The Big Sleep?
22 In 1990 Lithuania declared its independence from what?
23 At the end of the 20th C how many UK monarchs had been called George?
24 Who teamed up with Hanna to form a studio producing cartoon films?
25 What is the last word of the James Herriot book It Shouldn't Happen To A ______?

Answers

Bands (see Quiz 167, page 177)
1 Genesis. **2** U2. **3** Wet Wet Wet. **4** Police. **5** Bob Geldof. **6** Take That. **7** Pink Floyd. **8** Smashing Pumpkins. **9** The Eagles. **10** Weller. **11** The Wonder Stuff. **12** The Beach Boys. **13** Blondie. **14** Two. **15** Punk. **16** Tyrannnosaurus. **17** Five. **18** Two. **19** The Ants. **20** Slade. **21** Orchestra. **22** Status Quo. **23** Scotland. **24** Oasis. **25** The Beatles.

Quiz 169 Leaders

Answers - see Quiz 170, page 180

1 Bob Hawke and Paul Keating were Prime Ministers of which country?
2 In which country did Gadaffi seize power in the 60s?
3 Who was British Prime Minister at the time of the Gulf War?
4 What was the last name of Ferdinand and Imelda, leaders of the Philippines?
5 Who was Prime Minister of the UK throughout the 80s?
6 Who seized power in Cuba in the late 50s?
7 Which words did Winston Churchill use to describe the East and West divide in Europe?
8 Diana, Princess of Wales led the campaign against the use of which explosive devices?
9 Haile Selassie ruled in which country?
10 How many general elections did Mrs Thatcher win?
11 Which 90s leader said, "I did not have sexual relations with that woman"?
12 Who was the leader of the brutal Khmer Rouge government?
13 In which decade was Nelson Mandela sent to prison in South Africa?
14 What did the letter A stand for in Mandela's ANC?
15 Who became Britain's youngest Prime Minister of the century?
16 The death of which General led to the restoration of the monarchy in Spain?
17 In the 90s Silvio Berlusconi won the general election in which country?
18 David Ben-Gurion was the first Prime Minister of which new state?
19 In which country did Lech Walesa lead the conflict against the communist government?
20 Which Chris was the last British governor of Hong Kong?
21 Who was known as Il Duce ?
22 Ayatollah Khomeini ordered a death threat on which UK based writer?
23 Which US President had a daughter named Chelsea?
24 Nicholas II was the last person to hold which title in Russia?
25 Idi Amin became president of which country?

Answers

Pot Luck 79 (see Quiz 170, page 180)
1 Quad bike. **2** 40s. **3** Gary Rhodes. **4** Aberdeen. **5** Hitler. **6** Oil. **7** Indianapolis. **8** M*A*S*H. **9** Salman Rushdie. **10** Winnie-The-Pooh. **11** Cricket. **12** Cecil. **13** Exhibition. **14** 30s. **15** Acid rain. **16** Marilyn Monroe. **17** Plane. **18** Spike Milligan. **19** Poems. **20** Lib/Dem. **21** A6. **22** Prince Andrew. **23** Cello. **24** December. **25** Italy.

Quiz 170 Pot Luck 79

Answers - see Quiz 169, page 179

1 Rik Mayall suffered a serious accident in the 90s involving what type of vehicle?
2 In which decade was Prince Charles born?
3 Which chef has a restaurant called City Rhodes?
4 In which British city was Dyce airport built?
5 Who set out his political views in Mein Kampf?
6 In the 70s Arab countries reduced exports of what to the West?
7 Which American city is the site of an annual 500 mile motor race?
8 Which sitcom about an army hospital in Korea was transmitted in the UK without the canned laughter of the US version ?
9 Who wrote the controversial book The Satanic Verses?
10 Which fictional bear thought he had "very little brain"?
11 Phil DeFreitas played for England at which sport?
12 Which Tory minister Parkinson resigned in an 80s scandal?
13 What does the E stand for in the NEC established at Birmingham?
14 Michael Caine was born in which decade of the 20th century?
15 In the 80s what type of environmentally damaging rain was causing concern?
16 Playwright Arthur Miller was married to which famous blonde actress?
17 US bandleader Glenn Miller disappeared after setting off on a journey in what type of transport?
18 Which member of The Goons wrote Adolf Hitler, My Part in his Downfall?
19 John Betjeman was famous for writing what type of works?
20 In the 90s Alan Beith has represented which party in parliament?
21 Which A road in Britain used to be known as the Great North Road?
22 Which famous father had daughters called Beatrice and Eugenie?
23 Jacqueline Du Pre was associated with which musical instrument?
24 In the sitcom if Zoe Angell was May what month was Alec Callender?
25 Which country does motor racing's Jarno Trulli come from?

Answers

Leaders (see Quiz 169, page 179)
1 Australia. **2** Libya. **3** John Major. **4** Marcos. **5** Margaret Thatcher. **6** Castro. **7** Iron Curtain. **8** Land mines. **9** Ethiopia. **10** Three. **11** Bill Clinton. **12** Pol Pot. **13** 60s. **14** African. **15** Tony Blair. **16** Franco. **17** Italy. **18** Israel. **19** Poland. **20** Patten. **21** Mussolini. **22** Salman Rushdie. **23** Clinton. **24** Tsar. **25** Uganda.

Quiz 171 Personalities

Answers - see Quiz 172, page 182

1 What is David Bailey famous for?
2 What colour is Barbara Cartland's most seen in?
3 Which Max is famous as a PR man?
4 Dr Stefan Buczacki is an expert in what?
5 Which large opera star launched a perfume for men named after him?
6 What is the name of Joan Collins novelist sister?
7 Which part of his body did goalkeeper David Seaman insure for £1 million?
8 Which actor Kenneth was Emma Thompson's first husband?
9 Who is Gloria Hunniford's TV presenter daughter?
10 Brooklyn Beckham is the son of which Spice Girl ?
11 What is Hillary Clinton's daughter called?
12 What type of dance was Rudolf Nureyev famous for?
13 How did US Ambassador Shirley Temple Black earn fame as a child?
14 Which singer Cleo is married to Johnny Dankworth?
15 What is the name of Wendy Turner's older TV presenter sister?
16 What is the name of the MEP who is Neil Kinnock's wife?
17 Unlike his name suggests, who is the oldest daily presenter on BBC Radio 2?
18 Which Yorkshire cricketer Geoffrey was born the same day as Manfred Mann?
19 What is the birthday of Mario Andretti, who only has a real birthday every four years?
20 Which musical was based on Wild West star Annie Oakley?
21 Whose has a catchphrase "You'll like this - not a lot!"?
22 Which comedy duo were 'the one with the glasses and the one with the short fat hairy legs'?
23 Which cricket commentator was known as Johnners?
24 Which Prime Minister's wife became a Dame in the 1999 Queen's birthday honours?
25 Eileen Drewery was a spiritual healer who helped which England football manager?

Answers

Pot Luck 80 (see Quiz 172, page 182)
1 Israel. **2** India. **3** Dollar. **4** Life. **5** Italy. **6** Mary Poppins. **7** An oil rig. **8** Red. **9** August. **10** Wales. **11** Kylie Minogue. **12** The Phantom Of The Opera. **13** Tennis. **14** Cumbria. **15** The Few. **16** Robert. **17** Yacht. **18** Paintings. **19** Ireland. **20** Labour. **21** Aeroplanes. **22** 70s. **23** Cricket. **24** Poland. **25** Monkhouse.

Quiz 172 Pot Luck 80

Answers - see Quiz 171, page 181

1 Dana International won the Eurovision Song Contest for which country?
2 The disastrous poison gas leak at Bhopal took place in which country?
3 In the US what became known as a 'greenback'?
4 In advertising PAL was said to prolong active what?
5 In which country is Ciampino airport?
6 In Julie Andrews first film she played which nanny?
7 Who or what was Piper Alpha?
8 What is the main colour on the Chinese flag?
9 The UK's Summer Bank Holiday falls in which month?
10 Sir Anthony Hopkins was born in which part of the UK?
11 The TV special Men Behaving Very Badly Indeed concentrated on the lads' fixation with which Australian singer/actress?
12 Which stage musical was set in the Paris Opera House?
13 With which sport is Cedric Pioline associated?
14 Carlisle is the administrative centre of which English county?
15 Which two words did Churchill use to dub the Battle of Britain pilots?
16 What is the first name of Zimbabwean statesman Mugabe?
17 On what type of vehicle did Rupert Murdoch remarry in 1999?
18 Claude Oscar Monet was famous for what ?
19 Lord Mountbatten was murdered off the coast of which country?
20 In the 80s Shirley Williams left which political party to launch the SDP?
21 Freddie Laker set up low cost travel in what type of transport?
22 In which decade did Elvis Presley die?
23 Mike Denness captained England in which sport?
24 The deepwater port of Gdansk was developed in which country?
25 Which veteran stand up comic Bob had his own show On the Spot in the mid 90s?

Answers

Personalities (see Quiz 171, page 181)
1 Photography. **2** Pink. **3** Clifford. **4** Gardening. **5** Luciano Pavarotti. **6** Jackie. **7** Hands. **8** Branagh. **9** Caron Keating. **10** Victoria. **11** Chelsea. **12** Ballet. **13** Film star. **14** Laine. **15** Anthea. **16** Glenys. **17** Jimmy Young. **18** Boycott. **19** 29th February. **20** Annie Get Your Gun. **21** Paul Daniels. **22** Morecambe & Wise. **23** Bryan Johnston. **24** Norma Major. **25** Glenn Hoddle.

Quiz 173 TV Famous Faces

Answers - see Quiz 174, page 184

1 Which comedian Paul shares his surname with campaigner Mary?
2 Which Royal read one of his own stories on Jackanory in 1983?
3 Which Kenny's shows were "in the best possible taste"?
4 Which June was married to Terry in a series of classic sitcoms?
5 Which Alan was a character created by Steve Coogan?
6 Which New Faces winner created the characters PC Ganga and Theophilus P Wildebeeste?
7 Which female Radio DJ succeeded Emma Forbes on Live & Kicking?
8 Which actress Alex played Moll Flanders then moved to the US for ER?
9 Which former tennis player and sports presenter hosted the BBC coverage of the last Royal Wedding of the 20th century?
10 Which Pamela was the female comedian on Not the Nine O'Clock News?
11 Which Sean starred as Sharpe in the series about the Napoleonic Wars?
12 Which pop drummer narrated Thomas the Tank Engine on TV?
13 Dawn French played the Vicar of which English village in the sitcom of the same name?
14 Which comedienne and writer Victoria had a series As Seen on TV?
15 In which Files would Mulder and Scully appear?
16 Which knighted Cabinet Secretary was played by Nigel Hawthorne in Yes Minister?
17 Colin Firth played Darcy in which classic Jane Austen adaptation in 1995?
18 Which four brothers, Joe, Mark, Paul and Stephen, starred in the drama set in Ireland, The Hanging Gale?
19 Which Attenborough brother presented The Private Life of Plants?
20 What was the occupation of Jemma Redgrave in the Victorian drama Bramwell?
21 Which Paula featured on Cue Paula on The Big Breakfast?
22 Which Jonathan replaced Barry Norman on BBC's Film programme in 1999?
23 Which newsreader Trevor received a knighthood in the last Queen's Birthday Honours of the 20th century?
24 Which Nick was the first presenter of Crimewatch UK?
25 Which Charlton advertised Shredded Wheat on TV?

Answers

Pot Luck 81 (see Quiz 174, page 184)
1 The Guardian. **2** Tosh Lines. **3** 60s. **4** Monty Python. **5** Israel. **6** Department. **7** Tom Hanks. **8** Denmark. **9** Adams. **10** Corgi. **11** Bear. **12** 20s. **13** D H Lawrence. **14** Football. **15** Ballet. **16** Sid and Nancy. **17** Germany. **18** Novelist. **19** Gary Barlow. **20** Rugby Union. **21** Greece. **22** Anton. **23** Morecambe & Wise. **24** Oil. **25** A.

Quiz 174 **Pot Luck 81**

Answers - see Quiz 173, page 183

1 Which newspaper was involved in the Jonathan Aitken perjury affair?
2 Who did Kevin Lloyd play in The Bill?
3 Robert Carlyle was born in which decade of the 20th century?
4 Which cult comedy team first performed the Dead Parrot Sketch?
5 Shimon Peres was Prime Minister of which country?
6 In police matters what does the D stand for in CID?
7 Which actor played Forrest Gump?
8 Which country does soccer star Tore Andre Flo play for?
9 Which Douglas wrote The Hitch Hiker's Guide To The Galaxy?
10 What is the Queen's favourite breed of dog?
11 What kind of creature is Muppet Fozzie?
12 In which decade was the General Strike in Britain?
13 Who wrote the novels Sons And Lovers and Women In Love?
14 Pavarotti singing Nessun Dorma was used in 1990 alongside broadcasts of which sport?
15 Anna Pavlova found fame in what field?
16 In which film did Gary Oldman get to act Vicious?
17 Which country has D as its international vehicle registration letter?
18 What is the occupation of Maeve Binchy?
19 Who had a 90s No 1 with Forever Love?
20 Wade Dooley represented England at which sport?
21 In which country was Prince Philip born?
22 What is the first name of the chef who opened Mosimann's in London in 1988?
23 Glenda Jackson, Andre Previn and Shirley Bassey were famous guests on which comedy duo's famous shows?
24 What did John Paul Getty make his fortune from?
25 On a computer keyboard what letter is far left on the second row of letters?

Answers

TV Famous Faces (see Quiz 173, page 183)

1 Whitehouse. **2** Prince Charles. **3** Everett. **4** Whitfield. **5** Partridge. **6** Lenny Henry. **7** Zoe Ball. **8** Kingston. **9** Sue Barker. **10** Stephenson. **11** Bean. **12** Ringo Starr. **13** Dibley. **14** Wood. **15** The X Files. **16** Sir Humphrey. **17** Pride & Prejudice. **18** McGann. **19** David. **20** Doctor. **21** Yates. **22** Ross. **23** McDonald. **24** Ross. **25** Jack.

Quiz 175 Darts & Snooker

Answers - see Quiz 176, page 186

1 Who was snooker's world champion most times in the 80s?
2 What does the letter O stand for in BDO?
3 Cliff Thorburn - 'The Grinder' - came from which country?
4 Which ball is worth one point less than a black?
5 Which John scored the first nine-dart 501 in a major tournament?
6 Moving anti clockwise on a dartboard which number is after 1?
7 Which snooker player was nicknamed 'Whirlwind'?
8 Which Sunday paper ran a darts competition from the 40s to the early 90s?
9 In which decade was snooker's World Championship first staged at The Crucible?
10 Which Leighton became darts' first World Professional Championship?
11 Who took over No 1 ranking from Stephen Hendry?
12 Which English darts player was awarded an MBE in 1989?
13 Which London soccer team is Barry Hearne connected with?
14 Dennis Priestley plays for which country?
15 Which snooker player was known as 'Hurricane'?
16 On a dartboard which number is directly opposite the 6?
17 Which 'veteran' sensationally beat Stephen Hendry in the first round of the 1998 World Championship?
18 What's the smallest three-dart score made with three trebles all in different even numbers?
19 Which player broke up Hendry's World Championship monopoly of the early 90s?
20 What does the B stand for in the WPBSA?
21 Which darts player is known as 'Barney Rubble'?
22 Who is Gary Lineker's big mate in the snooker world?
23 Can you raise a glass and name the sponsor of the WDC Darts Championship?
24 Which ball is worth one point more than a blue?
25 Who is the first Ken to win snooker's World Championship?

Answers

Pot Luck 82 (see Quiz 176, page 186)
1 United States. **2** Motor car. **3** Gorbachev. **4** Orton. **5** South Africa. **6** Williams. **7** Eye. **8** Doctor. **9** Horticultural. **10** Cycling. **11** Wedges. **12** Glenys. **13** Monk. **14** Ireland. **15** Sugar. **16** Rose. **17** Labour. **18** Princess Margaret. **19** Brother. **20** Las Vegas. **21** 30s. **22** Basketball. **23** Coronation Street. **24** Canada. **25** Joseph Conrad.

Quiz 176 Pot Luck 82

Answers - see Quiz 175, page 185

1 The Louise Woodward affair was tried in which country?
2 In its early days what was offered for sale "in any colour as long as it's black"?
3 Which Russian leader had a pronounced birthmark on his forehead?
4 Which Joe wrote the play Entertaining Mr Sloane?
5 Which country was readmitted into international rugby fixtures in 1993?
6 Which future superstar Robin played Mork in Mork and Mindy?
7 Which Private magazine led the 60s satire boom?
8 David Owen, now Lord Owen, was trained in what profession before becoming a politician?
9 In the world of plants and gardening what type of Royal Society is the RHS?
10 Tony Doyle represented Britain at which sport?
11 What do players try to collect in the board game Trivial Pursuit?
12 What is the name of Neil Kinnock's wife?
13 The influential Russian figure Rasputin followed which profession?
14 Mary Robinson became the first president of which country in 1990?
15 Which nickname did fighter Ray Robinson have?
16 Geoff Boycott has had which kind of plant named after him?
17 Paul Boateng has represented which party in parliament?
18 Which royal married Lord Snowdon?
19 In the cookery world, what relation is Albert to Michel Roux?
20 Mrs Merton took her chat show - and her pensioner audience - to which US entertainment venue for a series of her shows?
21 Warren Beatty was born in which decade of the 20th century?
22 With which sport is Grant Hill associated?
23 Maud Grimes is a character from which soap?
24 Brian Mulrooney was Prime Minister of which country in the 80s and 90s?
25 Who wrote the novels Lord Jim and Heart of Darkness?

Answers

Darts & Snooker (see Quiz 175, page 185)
1 Steve Davis. **2** Organisation. **3** Canada. **4** Pink. **5** Lowe. **6** 20. **7** Jimmy White. **8** News Of The World. **9** 70s. **10** Rees. **11** John Higgins. **12** Eric Bristow. **13** Leyton Orient. **14** England. **15** Alex Higgins. **16** 1. **17** Jimmy White. **18** 36. **19** John Parrott. **20** Billiards. **21** Raymond Van Barneveld. **22** Willie Thorne. **23** Skol. **24** Pink. **25** Docherty.

Quiz 177 Actresses

Answers - see Quiz 178, page 188

1 Who cried during her Oscar winning speech for Shakespeare in Love?
2 Who starred in Mermaids and went to No 1 with The Shoop Shoop Song?
3 Which pop star Lisa made her movie debut in Swing?
4 Sigourney Weaver in Alien II and Demi Moore in G.I. Jane shaved what?
5 Who won an Oscar for her first film role in Mary Poppins?
6 Which actress and fitness guru Jane married CNN mogul Ted Turner?
7 Which actress appeared on the cinema poster for Titanic?
8 In The Seven Year Itch whose white skirt is billowing around because of hot air blowing up from a grating?
9 Which superstar was nicknamed 'The Swedish Sphinx'?
10 What is Goldie Hawn's real name?
11 How is Mary Elizabeth Spacek known in the film world?
12 Who was cast as Princess Leia in Star Wars after her film debut in Shampoo with Warren Beatty?
13 Melanie Griffith married which star of Evita and The Mask of Zorro?
14 Which Oscar winning black actress played the medium Oda Mae Brown in Ghost?
15 For which role did Michelle Pfeiffer wear 63 catsuits in Batman returns?
16 Which plant was Uma Thurman named after in Batman & Robin?
17 Which actress has children called Scout and Rumer from her marriage to Bruce Willis?
18 In which 1979 film with Bo Derek was the title simply a number?
19 Which actress who starred in Fatal Attraction won a Tony for her role in Sunset Boulevard on Broadway?
20 Which star of Sliding Doors split with fiance Brad Pitt in 1997?
21 Which wife of Paul Newman played Tom Hanks mother in Philadelphia?
22 Which Ms Smith played the Mother Superior opposite Whoopi Goldberg in Sister Act?
23 Which Redgrave was Oscar nominated for Gods and Monsters?
24 Janet Leigh played one of the most horrific scenes where in a motel?
25 Which French sex symbol became an animal rights campaigner later in her life?

Answers

Pot Luck 83 (see Quiz 178, page 188)
1 Ginola. **2** Ralph Fiennes. **3** USSR. **4** Arts. **5** San Francisco. **6** Rabbits. **7** Racehorses. **8** Novelist. **9** Sony. **10** Athletics. **11** Len Fairclough. **12** Aeroplanes. **13** Eleanor. **14** L. **15** Ivory trading. **16** 60s. **17** South Africa. **18** Dawn French. **19** M1. **20** India. **21** Jockey. **22** New Zealand. **23** West Ham. **24** MP. **25** George Michael.

Quiz 178 Pot Luck 83

Answers - see Quiz 177, page 187

1 Which soccer player David became part of the campaign against landmines?
2 Who played Steed in the 90s film version of The Avengers?
3 In the 80s Afghanistan was occupied by troops from which country?
4 What does the second A stand for in BAFTA?
5 In the 60s in which American city were you supposed to wear flowers in your hair?
6 The song Bright Eyes is about what kind of animals?
7 The Aga Khan is renowned as a breeder of which animals?
8 What is the trade of Martin Amis?
9 Which company launched the first personal stereo system?
10 Peter Elliott represented Britain at which sport?
11 Which character did Peter Adamson play in Coronation Street?
12 Dennis Bergkamp has a fear of travelling in what?
13 What was the first name of Franklin D Roosevelt's wife and US First Lady?
14 What letter does a car driver display until gaining a full licence?
15 A worldwide ban on what was introduced in 1990 to try and save the elephant population?
16 Helena Bonham-Carter was born in which decade of the 20th century?
17 Which country does cricketer Jacques Kallis play for?
18 Which comedy actress and wife of Lenny Henry played the sinister lead roles in Murder Most Horrid?
19 Which motorway links London and Leeds?
20 Sitar player Ravi Shankar came from which country?
21 What was the profession of sportsman Sir Gordon Richards?
22 Where was Dame Kiri Te Kanawa born?
23 Which soccer club did Alf Garnett support?
24 In the 80s sitcom what was the occupation of Alan B'Stard as played by Rik Mayall?
25 Jesus To A Child was a 90s No 1 for which solo singer?

Answers

Actresses (see Quiz 177, page 187)
1 Gwyneth Paltrow. **2** Cher. **3** Stansfield. **4** Heads. **5** Julie Andrews. **6** Fonda. **7** Kate Winslet. **8** Marilyn Monroe. **9** Greta Garbo. **10** Goldie Hawn. **11** Sissy. **12** Carrie Fisher. **13** Antonio Banderas. **14** Whoopi Goldberg. **15** Catwoman. **16** Ivy. **17** Demi Moore. **18** 10. **19** Glenn Close. **20** Gwyneth Paltrow. **21** Joanne Woodward. **22** Maggie. **23** Lynn. **24** Shower. **25** Brigitte Bardot.

Quiz 179 Books

Answers - see Quiz 180, page 190

1 Which Book of Records was first published in 1955?
2 Which book by Peter Benchley made into a film by Spielberg, was originally called The Summer of the Shark?
3 Which tennis player Martina wrote a novel called Total Zone?
4 Which MP Tony wrote lengthy diaries of his years in office?
5 James Alfred Wright was better known as James who when writing about his experiences as a Yorkshire vet?
6 In Peter Pan what sort of animal was Nana?
7 What was Thomas Harris's sequel to Silence of the Lambs called?
8 Cornish restaurateur Rick Stein's books are about what type of food?
9 Which novelist Barbara was Princess Diana's step grandmother?
10 Which King's novels such as Carrie and The Shining have been made into successful films?
11 Who is Dalziel's detective partner as created by Reginald Hill?
12 Which offbeat fictional detective was created by R.D. Wingfield and was played on TV by David Jason?
13 Which crime writing Dame is the best selling fiction author in the world?
14 What was the name of Martin Amis's famous author father?
15 What is the name of Joan Collins novelist sister?
16 Novelist Jeffrey Archer was once Chairman of which political party?
17 Which Jaguar driving, crossword fanatic detective was created by Colin Dexter?
18 Whose autobiography, written with the help of Andrew Morton was written about the Clinton White House Scandal?
19 Jamie Oliver wrote a book about his work called The Naked what?
20 Which tycoon and entrepreneur in the fields of music, airlines and cola wrote Losing My Virginity?
21 Which Bill wrote Notes From a Small Island?
22 Pongo was one of 101 what in the novel by Dodie Smith?
23 The novel The Sheep Pig was turned into a movie called what?
24 Which Cooper followed Polo and Riders with Score!?
25 One of the Famous Five was what type of pet animal?

Answers

Pot Luck 84 (see Quiz 180, page 190)
1 Bentley. **2** Evans. **3** Make it. **4** Red. **5** Olympic Games. **6** Stamped.
7 Dudley Moore. **8** Michael Heseltine. **9** Japan. **10** Cricket. **11** Ireland.
12 Frederick Forsyth. **13** Soccer. **14** Roux. **15** 20s. **16** USA.
17 Not the Nine O'Clock News. **18** Iraq. **19** Hot-air balloon. **20** Joseph.
21 Turin. **22** Sobers. **23** Plane. **24** Wigan. **25** November.

Quiz 180 Pot Luck 84

Answers - see Quiz 179, page 189

1 Which Derek was finally cleared of murder 45 years after he was hanged?
2 Which Godfrey was an England wicket keeper?
3 In a Spice Girls hit what follows "swing it, shake it, move it..."?
4 What is the main colour featured on the flag of Denmark?
5 What did Britain stage in 1908 and 1948?
6 What does the letter S stand for in SAE?
7 Who appeared with Peter Cook in Not Only... But Also?
8 Which Tory became Deputy Prime Minister in 1995?
9 The world's longest tunnel the Seikan tunnel was built in which country?
10 Rachel Heyhoe Flint played for England at which sport?
11 Garrett Fitzgerald was Prime Minister of which country?
12 Who wrote the thriller novel The Day Of The Jackal?
13 With which sport is Marcelo Salas associated?
14 Albert and Michael are which brothers in the world of food?
15 Magician Paul Daniels was born in which decade?
16 Michael Dukakis missed out in his attempts to become President of where?
17 The American Not Necessarily the News was based on which UK show with Pamela Stephenson, Mel Smith and others?
18 In the 80s which country was responsible for ethnic attacks on the Kurds?
19 Despite owning an airline and a railway, Richard Branson makes headlines travelling by what means?
20 What was Stalin's first name?
21 Which Shroud was declared a fake in the 80s?
22 Which West Indian cricketer had the first names Garfield St Auburn?
23 What was the Sopwith Camel?
24 Which Rugby League side became Warriors in the late 90s?
25 Remembrance Day is in which month?

Answers

Books (see Quiz 179, page 189)
1 Guinness. **2** Jaws. **3** Navratilova. **4** Benn. **5** Herriot. **6** Dog. **7** Hannibal. **8** Fish. **9** Cartland. **10** Stephen. **11** Pascoe. **12** Frost. **13** Agatha Christie. **14** Kingsley. **15** Jackie. **16** Tory. **17** Morse. **18** Monica Lewinsky. **19** Chef. **20** Richard Branson. **21** Bryson. **22** Dalmatians. **23** Babe. **24** Jilly. **25** Dog.

Quiz 181 Musical Superstars

Answers - see Quiz 182, page 192

1 Who recorded the Immaculate Collection?
2 What was certainly the debut album by Oasis?
3 Which Lionel sang with The Commodores?
4 In which US state was Elvis Presley's mansion?
5 What was the title of the first album from The Spice Girls?
6 I Will Always Love You was an early 90s hit for which superstar?
7 Alan, Jay and Donny were part of which 70s group?
8 Who first charted as a solo performer with Careless Whisper?
9 Which group is made up of Gibbs?
10 What instrument does Charlie Watts play in the Rolling Stones?
11 Who was the first to leave Take That?
12 Who teamed up with Barbra Streisand for Tell Him?
13 Who was the original lead singer with The Supremes?
14 How many people were in the original Queen?
15 Who became the most famous group formed in Colchester?
16 In which decade was Elton John's original Candle In The Wind a hit?
17 Baker, Bruce and Clapton formed which 60s supergroup?
18 In 1996 Robert Hoskins was convicted of stalking which star?
19 Which supergroup contains The Edge?
20 Who has recorded with Elton John, Queen, Lisa Stansfield and Toby Bourke?
21 Which band produced the mega selling album Rumours?
22 What was the first All Saints record to sell a million?
23 Visions Of Love was the first British top ten hit for which female superstar?
24 Which Hotel gave Elvis his first British chart hit?
25 Which group wrote the songs for the movie Saturday Night Fever?

Answers

Pot Luck 85 (see Quiz 182, page 192)

1 Glenn. **2** Tarrant. **3** Bowls. **4** Gordon. **5** Deputy Dawg. **6** Kent. **7** Pierce Brosnan. **8** Corporation. **9** 60s. **10** Ireland. **11** Dutch. **12** 1471. **13** Tom Finney. **14** O 'Connor. **15** Simply Red. **16** Baldwin. **17** Music. **18** Austria. **19** Boris Karloff. **20** Tennis. **21** Bears. **22** The Crickets. **23** Andrew. **24** A40. **25** Meldrew.

Quiz 182 Pot Luck 85

Answers - see Quiz 181, page 191

1 Which John travelled in space over 35 years after his first flight?
2 Which Chris appeared in a beach snap with Sophie Rhys-Jones?
3 In which sport was Willie Wood a world champion?
4 What is the first name of Mr Sumner aka Sting?
5 Which cartoon character says "Dagnabit"?
6 Maidstone is the administrative centre of which English county?
7 Who played James Bond in Tomorrow Never Dies?
8 What does the C stand for in BBC?
9 Brad Pitt was born in which decade of the 20th century?
10 Which country does Enya come from?
11 What type of elm disease swept through Britain in the 70s?
12 On a BT phone what number is dialled to find the number of your last caller?
13 Which soccer star was known as the 'Preston Plumber'?
14 Which surname is shared by comics Des and Tom, one from London the other from Liverpool?
15 Who had a 90s No 1 with Fairground?
16 Which Stanley was a British Prime Minister in the 20s and 30s?
17 In which branch of the arts was John Barbirolli connected?
18 In which European country is Klagenfurt airport?
19 Which horror movie actor was quite literally a Pratt from birth?
20 Suzanne Lenglen was a champion in which sport?
21 Margarete Steiff made what kind of toy creature?
22 Which group backed Buddy Holly?
23 Which Prince was a helicopter pilot during the Falklands War?
24 Which A road links Oxford and London?
25 Patrick and Pippa lived next door to which Margaret and Victor?

Answers

Musical Superstars (see Quiz 181, page 191)
1 Madonna. **2** Definitely Maybe. **3** Richie. **4** Tennessee. **5** Spice. **6** Whitney Houston. **7** The Osmonds. **8** George Michael. **9** The Bee Gees. **10** Drums. **11** Robbie Williams. **12** Celine Dion. **13** Diana Ross. **14** Four. **15** Blur. **16** 70s. **17** Cream. **18** Madonna. **19** U2. **20** George Michael. **21** Fleetwood Mac. **22** Never Ever. **23** Mariah Carey. **24** Heartbreak. **25** The Bee Gees.

Quiz 183 Rich & Famous

Answers - see Quiz 184, page 194

1 Which Knightsbridge store did Mohammed Al-Fayed buy by outwitting rival Tiny Rowland?
2 Who was the first Beatle to be knighted?
3 Habitat was founded by which Terence?
4 What was the profession of Margaret Thatcher's father?
5 Which Princess was the youngest daughter of Mrs Frances Shand Kydd?
6 Which Rupert launched the satellite TV station which became Sky?
7 To the nearest five years, how old would Marilyn Monroe have been in 2000?
8 Which Swedish tennis player was John McEnroe's best man?
9 How many Beatles were not known by their real names?
10 Which opera singer gave her name to a kind of peach dessert?
11 Which tennis player was nicknamed Pistol Pete?
12 The ship Queen Elizabeth was named after who?
13 Which MP was immortalised in Madame Tussaud's in 1995 shortly after becoming leader of his party?
14 Dame Shirley Porter is heiress to which major supermarket chain?
15 Which Spice Girl sang Happy Birthday to Prince Charles at his 50th birthday party?
16 Whose head was due to be lost on banknotes when Britain joined the single European currency?
17 Who was enganged to Michael Hutchence of INXS when he died?
18 What was Camilla Shand's surname after her first marriage?
19 In which country did Princess Anne marry for the second time?
20 Which skinny Sixties model married actor Leigh Lawson?
21 Carol Vorderman agreed a multi million pound contract to do sums on which TV show?
22 William Henry Gates III amassed his fortune from which source?
23 Which British PM's father was a trapeze artist?
24 Which Duchess had a weeping Jana Novotna on her shoulder after the Czech player lost her Wimbledon final?
25 Which 90s Wimbledon champion married actress Brooke Shields?

Answers

Pot Luck 86 (see Quiz 184, page 194)
1 George. **2** Dark blue. **3** Gas mask. **4** Dickens. **5** John Lennon. **6** The Trotters. **7** Africa. **8** Health. **9** School. **10** Cricket. **11** Russia. **12** Helen. **13** E. **14** Blues. **15** Steam train. **16** George Orwell. **17** Portugal. **18** Golf. **19** The Pretenders. **20** Open All Hours. **21** Reliant. **22** Oscar Wilde. **23** Sri Lanka. **24** 60s. **25** Paris.

Quiz 184 Pot Luck 86

Answers - see Quiz 183, page 193

1 Which Eddie was a 90s governor of the Bank of England?
2 In the game Monopoly what colour are both Mayfair and Park Lane?
3 What type of mask was issued to all people in Britain in 1939?
4 Which Charles appears on the back of a £10 note?
5 Imagine was a hit for which singer after his death?
6 Whose business vehicle has New York, Paris, Peckham written on the side?
7 Albert Schweitzer is best remembered for his work on which continent?
8 What does the H stand for in the world organization WHO?
9 Where was the action of Please Sir! set?
10 Keith Fletcher captained England at which sport?
11 In which country did the Bolsheviks seize power?
12 Which actress Mirren was the star of TV's Prime Suspect?
13 What letter is used for numbers relating to food additives?
14 John Lee Hooker is associated with which type of music?
15 Who or what was the Flying Scotsman?
16 Who wrote Animal Farm?
17 The deepwater port of Faro was developed in which country?
18 With which sport is Ronan Rafferty associated?
19 Chrissie Hynde first had a No 1 as lead singer with which group?
20 How was Arkwright's shop described in the title of the sitcom with Ronnie Barker and David Jason?
21 Which car manufacturer introduced the Robin?
22 Who wrote the play The Importance of Being Earnest?
23 The Tamil Tigers were fighting for a separate state within which country?
24 In which decade was Radio 1 launched?
25 The Pompidou centre was built in which European city?

Answers

Rich & Famous (see Quiz 183, page 193)
1 Harrods. **2** Paul McCartney. **3** Conran. **4** Grocer. **5** Diana. **6** Murdoch. **7** 74. **8** Bjorn Borg. **9** One. **10** Melba. **11** Pete Sampras. **12** Queen Mother. **13** Tony Blair. **14** Tesco. **15** Geri. **16** The Queen. **17** Paula Yates. **18** Parker-Bowles. **19** Scotland. **20** Twiggy. **21** Countdown. **22** Computer software. **23** John Major. **24** Kent. **25** Andre Agassi.

Quiz 185 TV Quiz & Game Shows

Answers - see Quiz 186, page 196

1 Wolf, Amazon and Saracen competed in which show?
2 Which satirical show hosted by Angus Deayton was derived from Radio 4's The News Quiz?
3 Which knockabout game show spawned a version with The Duke & Duchess of York, Princess Anne and Prince Edward as contestants?
4 Which show first hosted by Terry Wogan gave losers a model of a cheque book and pen?
5 Which show named after Superman's home planet tried to find the 'Super being of Great Britain'?
6 Which show introduced the phrase "I've started so I'll finish."?
7 Which Cilla Black show was called The Dating Game in the USA?
8 What is reduced from fifteen to one in Fifteen to One?
9 On Blockbusters who was often asked "Can I Have a P please Bob"?
10 Who presented the first series of The Generation Game on UK TV?
11 Which Marti hosted New Faces?
12 Which Stars programme featured the catchphrase 'Ulrika-ka-ka-ka-ka'?
13 How was Michael Barrymore's show Strike It Lucky renamed?
14 Which afternoon programme was based on the French show Les Chiffres et les Lettres - Numbers and Letters?
15 Which Ms Rice led contestants in Treasure Hunt?
16 Which student quiz had a starter for ten?
17 In which show did one contestant throw darts and one answer questions?
18 Which Ian has edited Private Eye and was a regular on Have I Got News For You?
19 What was the name of the National Lottery show which included a quiz?
20 Who first hosted Who Wants to be A Millionaire?
21 In which show hosted by Roy Walker did contestants try to guess well known phrases from computerised images?
22 Which group of people make up the audience of Man O Man?
23 What is Masterchef for young contestants called?
24 In the title of the cookery challenge show what follows Can't Cook?
25 Which Sue was the first regular female presenter of A Question of Sport?

Answers

Pot Luck 87 (see Quiz 186, page 196)
1 Davies. **2** Association. **3** Russia. **4** Michael Jackson. **5** German airforce. **6** 90s. **7** Elizabeth II. **8** Midland. **9** Sebastian. **10** White. **11** Stormin' Norman. **12** Barnsley. **13** Blue. **14** Home. **15** Mean. **16** Wimbledon. **17** West Indies. **18** Conservative. **19** Sega. **20** France. **21** 50s. **22** Porridge. **23** Wall. **24** Snooker. **25** EastEnders.

Quiz 186 Pot Luck 87

Answers - see Quiz 185, page 195

1 Which Ron resigned from the government after a "moment of madness" on Clapham Common?
2 In medicine, what does the A stand for in BMA?
3 Viktor Chernomyrdin was Prime Minister of which country?
4 Who had a 90s solo No 1 with Earth Song?
5 What was the Luftwaffe in World War II?
6 In which decade did The Big Issue go on sale in London?
7 Which monarch launched HMS Sheffield and HMS Invincible?
8 In advertising which bank was described as the listening bank?
9 Which Coe was a world record breaking middle distance runner?
10 The game Scrabble uses tiles of what colour?
11 What was Gulf War general Norman Schwarzkopf's nickname?
12 Which soccer team does Michael Parkinson support?
13 Which colour follows Porterhouse in the comedy series with David Jason?
14 In the movie title, where was Macauley Culkin left Alone?
15 What does the M mean in GMT?
16 At which sporting arena did Cliff Richard lead a sing-a-long when rain stopped play in 1996?
17 Which country does cricketer Carl Hooper play for?
18 Gillian Shepherd has represented which party in parliament?
19 Which company developed Sonic the Hedgehog?
20 Which country developed the TGV high speed train?
21 Madonna was born in which decade of the 20th century?
22 Which comedy series about life behind bars was called On the Rocks in the USA?
23 The 20s crash on which Street triggered America's 'Great Depression'?
24 Allison Fisher was a world champion in which sport?
25 The character Lofty Holloway appeared in which TV soap?

Answers

TV Quiz & Game Shows (see Quiz 185, page 195)
1 Gladiators. **2** Have I Got News For You. **3** It's A Knockout. **4** Blankety Blank. **5** The Krypton Factor. **6** Mastermind. **7** Blind Date. **8** Number of contestants. **9** Bob Holness. **10** Bruce Forsyth. **11** Caine. **12** Shooting Stars. **13** Strike It Rich. **14** Countdown. **15** Anneka. **16** University Challenge. **17** Bullseye. **18** Hislop. **19** Winning Lines. **20** Chris Tarrant. **21** Catchphrase. **22** Women. **23** Junior Masterchef. **24** Won't Cook. **25** Barker.

Quiz 187 Sporting Chance 4

Answers - see Quiz 188, page 198

1 Wentworth Golf Club is in which English county?
2 Susan Brown was the first woman to take part in which race?
3 Which country was captained by Dunga?
4 Which sporting ground has a Nursery End and a Pavilion End?
5 In which sport does the Fastnet Race take place?
6 What is the colour of the stage leader's jersey in the Tour de France?
7 Who did England have to beat to stay in cricket's 1999 World Cup - and didn't?
8 In what year was soccer's World Cup last held in the 80s?
9 Rugby is played at Ellis Park in which city?
10 Mark Spitz landed how many golds in the 1972 Olympics?
11 Yapping Deng was a world champion in which sport?
12 Who captained South Africa in cricket's 1999 World Cup?
13 In which sport were Lonsdale Belts awarded?
14 Who was England's first Italian Footballer Of The Year?
15 Andy Caddick played for England at which sport?
16 In which decade did Man Utd players die in the Munich Air Disaster?
17 Which baseball team are Giants?
18 In a nickname, what rank of the peerage was given to Ted Dexter?
19 The Australian Dawn Fraser was famous for which sport?
20 Which soccer team used to play at Ayresome Park?
21 Who or what became known as The Crafty Cockney?
22 The final of which tennis Grand Slam tournament is played in a Meadow?
23 At which circuit does the San Marino Grand Prix take place?
24 The Fosbury Flop was developed in which sport?
25 In which country in mainland Europe did Ian Rush play club soccer?

Answers

Pot Luck 88 (see Quiz 188, page 198)
1 Geri Halliwell. **2** White. **3** Speak. **4** Ashdown. **5** Piano. **6** 80s. **7** Vic. **8** Congress. **9** Blue. **10** Nuclear missiles. **11** Prince. **12** Nelson Mandela. **13** Greenhouse. **14** Paris. **15** 1995. **16** Pacino. **17** Rugby League. **18** Suffolk. **19** C. **20** One. **21** Edna Everage. **22** Wright. **23** Tina Turner. **24** Horse racing. **25** 50s.

Quiz 188 **Pot Luck 88**

Answers - see Quiz 187, page 197

LEVEL 1 

1 Who sang Happy Birthday to Prince Charles on his 50th bash?
2 What colour are the stars on the United States of America flag?
3 What did mime artist Marcel Marceau do in the film Silent Movie for the first and only time in his career as an entertainer?
4 Which politician Paddy was a former Marine?
5 Which musical instrument is associated with Vladimir Ashkenazy?
6 In which decade was Britain's worst storm of the 20th century?
7 Which Mr Reeves' real name is Jim Moir?
8 What does the C stand for in TUC?
9 What colour were Frank Sinatra's eyes?
10 In 1987 the Russians and the Americans signed the Washington summit agreement to limit what?
11 In 1993 which pop artist changed his name to a symbol?
12 Who did F W de Klerk share the Nobel Peace prize with?
13 Identified in the 80s, global warming is known as what 'Effect'?
14 Euro Disney is on the outskirts of which city?
15 In what year was the 50th anniversary of VE Day?
16 Which Al had a starring role in the epic movie The Godfather?
17 Neil Fox represented Great Britain at which sport?
18 Ipswich is the administrative centre of which English county?
19 What was Rab Nesbitt's middle initial?
20 At the end of the 20th C how many UK monarchs had been called Victoria?
21 Which entertainment industry Dame sang the praise of the gladiola?
22 What was the name of flight pioneers Orville and Wilbur?
23 What's Love Got To Do With It? was a film about which female singer?
24 With which sport is Steve Cauthen associated?
25 John Travolta was born in which decade of the 20th century?

Answers

Sporting Chance 4 (see Quiz 187, page 197)
1 Surrey. **2** The Boat Race. **3** Brazil. **4** Lord's. **5** Yachting. **6** Yellow. **7** India. **8** 1986. **9** Johannesburg. **10** Seven. **11** Table tennis. **12** Hanse Cronje. **13** Boxing. **14** Gianfranco Zola. **15** Cricket. **16** 50s. **17** San Francisco. **18** Lord. **19** Swimming. **20** Middlesbrough. **21** Eric Bristow. **22** US Open. **23** Imola. **24** High jump. **25** Italy.

Quiz 189 Comedies

Answers - see Quiz 190, page 200

1 Which Jim played Truman in The Truman Show?
2 Who was the near silent subject of The Ultimate Disaster Movie in 1997?
3 Which 90s movie told of a group of stripping Sheffield steel workers?
4 In the 1994 movie what did Jim Carrey find that turned him from a bank clerk into a comic book character, in the film of the same name?
5 Which Blackadder star played the vicar in Four Weddings and a Funeral?
6 Which 1994 movie was based on a TV cartoon and was set in Bedrock?
7 In Forrest Gump, his mum says Life is like a box of what?
8 What was A Fish called in the movie with Michael Palin and John Cleese?
9 Which blonde country star had a cameo role in The Beverly Hillbillies?
10 What is the name of the nanny Robin Williams becomes to look after his estranged children in the 1993 film?
11 Where did Deloris, played by Whoopi Goldberg, find refuge in Sister Act?
12 Whose World was a 1992 film with Mike Myers and Dana Carvey?
13 Which Carry On film was released in the 500th anniversary year of Columbus' arrival in the Americas?
14 Postcards From the Edge was based on the life of which actress Carrie?
15 In which movie did Macaulay Culkin first play abandoned child Kevin McCallister?
16 Which Bruce is the voice of Mikey in Look Who's Talking?
17 Why was Mick Dundee nicknamed Crocodile?
18 Which Michael played teenager Marty in Back to the Future?
19 In which 80s comedy did Dustin Hoffman play an actor who pretends to be a woman to get a part in a soap?
20 Which member of Arthur's staff was played by John Gielgud in the 80s film with Dudley Moore?
21 There's Something About whom in the politically incorrect comedy with Cameron Diaz?
22 Which crawling insects are the major stars of A Bug's Life?
23 Which spinach eating cartoon character was played by Robin Williams?
24 Which silent movie star created the comic character The Little Tramp?
25 Which brothers starred in Monkey Business and A Night at the Opera?

Answers

Pot Luck 89 (see Quiz 190, page 200)
1 Israel. **2** Pakistan. **3** 60s. **4** Ripping. **5** Poppy. **6** Actress. **7** Bombs. **8** Previn. **9** Italy. **10** Golf. **11** Fugees. **12** Ferry. **13** Edinburgh. **14** Potato. **15** Iraq. **16** Doncaster. **17** Rudyard. **18** Antarctic. **19** Films. **20** M62. **21** Guitar. **22** Temple. **23** Landlord. **24** Carpenter. **25** United Kingdom.

Quiz 190 Pot Luck 89

Answers - see Quiz 189, page 199

1 Assassinated Prime Minister Rabin led which country?
2 Who were beaten finalists in cricket's 1999 World Cup?
3 Julia Roberts was born in which decade of the 20th century?
4 Which Yarns were a series of comedy films with stars such as Michael Palin?
5 Remembrance Sunday is linked with which flower?
6 Dame Peggy Ashcroft became famous as what?
7 The Wellington aircraft was built to carry what?
8 Mia Farrow was once married to which Andre?
9 Which country has I as its international vehicle registration letter?
10 Bernard Gallagher played for Scotland at which sport?
11 Killing Me Softly was a 90s No 1 for which group?
12 Meeting disaster in the 80s, what was the Herald of Free Enterprise?
13 In which British city was Turnhouse airport built?
14 Desiree and Pentland Javelin have been developed as varieties of what?
15 Iran was at war with which neighbour for most of the 80s?
16 Which Rugby League team added Dragons to their name in the 90s?
17 Which Mr Kipling wrote The Jungle Book and the Just So Stories?
18 Naturalist Sir Peter Scott's father perished exploring which continent?
19 In which area of the entertainment industry did Mack Sennett find fame?
20 Which motorway links Liverpool and Humberside?
21 Muddy Waters was associated with which musical instrument?
22 Which former child movie star Shirley became a US ambassador?
23 In Rising Damp what was the occupation of Rigsby?
24 What was the surname of brother and sister pop duo Richard and Karen?
25 Which country does motor racing's Eddie Irvine come from?

Answers

Comedies (see Quiz 189, page 199)
1 Carrey. **2** Bean. **3** The Full Monty. **4** The Mask. **5** Rowan Atkinson. **6** The Flintstones. **7** Chocolates. **8** Wanda. **9** Dolly Parton. **10** Mrs Doubtfire. **11** Convent. **12** Wayne's. **13** Carry on Columbus. **14** Fisher. **15** Home Alone. **16** Willis. **17** He survived a crocodile attack. **18** J Fox. **19** Tootsie. **20** Valet. **21** Mary. **22** Ants. **23** Popeye. **24** Charlie Chaplin. **25** Marx Brothers.

Quiz 191 Media

Answers - see Quiz 192, page 202

1 In which city is Anglia TV based?
2 In 1991 which BBC World Service was added to the radio service?
3 Which flagship BBC TV programme for children began in 1958?
4 GMTV broadcasts on which TV channel?
5 Which major independent radio station opened in 1973 to broadcast to London?
6 Which classical radio station has its own magazine?
7 Granada TV is based in which city?
8 Grandstand is chiefly broadcast on which day of the week?
9 Which city name did The Guardian have in its name until 1961?
10 Which magazine is an English version of the Spanish celebrity mag Hola!?
11 Which sister paper to the Independent is not published Monday to Friday?
12 What did J stand for in the music station JFM?
13 What did W stand for in LWT?
14 Which UK soccer club was the first to have its own TV station?
15 In spring 1999 which late evening news programme disappeared from our TV screens?
16 What does E stand for in the music paper NME?
17 In which newspaper were 'Page 3' girls first seen?
18 What name is given to papers like The Sun and The Mirror as opposed to broadsheets?
19 What is the subject of The Nigel Dempster pages in The Daily Mail?
20 Which major TV listings magazine does not have TV or television in its title?
21 Which radio programme comes from Borsetshire?
22 What does the second B stand for in BSkyB?
23 Where is Channel TV based?
24 Border TV is based on the borders of which two countries?
25 In which decade of the 20th century was GQ magazine founded?

Answers

Pot Luck 90 (see Quiz 192, page 202)
1 Margaret Thatcher. **2** Demi Moore. **3** Katrina. **4** Divorce. **5** Seal. **6** Paddy Ashdown. **7** Industry. **8** 50s. **9** United States. **10** Soccer. **11** Essex. **12** Nuclear power. **13** Snooker. **14** Hampshire. **15** Labour. **16** Miniskirt. **17** Scotland. **18** 1980s. **19** Boyzone. **20** Brighton. **21** Tennis. **22** Kim. **23** Spain. **24** 50s. **25** Laugh In.

Quiz 192 Pot Luck 90

Answers - see Quiz 191, page 201

1 Who declared, "The lady's not for turning"?
2 In the 90s film, who played G I Jane?
3 Who won the Eurovision Song Contest along with the Waves?
4 In February 1996 the Princess of Wales agreed to Prince Charles' request for what?
5 Who won a Grammy for Kiss From A Rose?
6 Who stepped down as Lib Dem leader in 1999?
7 What does the I stand for in CBI?
8 Rowan Atkinson was born in which decade of the 20th century?
9 In which country was John Lennon murdered?
10 Johnny Giles represented the Republic of Ireland at which sport?
11 Which singer David starred in The River in the 80s sitcom?
12 Chernobyl witnessed a disaster at what type of power station?
13 With which sport is Peter Ebdon associated?
14 Winchester is the administrative centre of which English county?
15 Dennis Skinner has represented which party in parliament?
16 Which item of clothing introduced by Mary Quant symbolised the Swinging Sixties ?
17 Robert Carlyle was born in which part of the UK?
18 In which decade did the sitcom Roseanne begin?
19 Who had a 90s No 1 with A Different Beat?
20 At which seaside town was an 80s Tory party conference victim of an IRA bomb?
21 Which sport did Fred Perry take up after becoming world champion at table tennis?
22 Double agent Harold Philby was known by which first name?
23 In which country was Pablo Picasso born?
24 In which decade of the 20th century did Elvis Presley shoot to fame?
25 What followed the names of Rowan and Martin in the classic 60s comedy series?

Answers

Media (see Quiz 191, page 201)
1 Norwich. **2** TV. **3** Blue Peter. **4** ITV. **5** Capital Radio. **6** Classic FM. **7** Manchester. **8** Saturday. **9** Manchester. **10** Hello. **11** Independent on Sunday. **12** Jazz. **13** Weekend. **14** Manchester Utd. **15** News At Ten. **16** Express. **17** The Sun. **18** Tabloids. **19** Celebrity gossip. **20** Radio Times. **21** The Archers. **22** Broadcasting. **23** Channel Islands. **24** England & Scotland. **25** 80s.

Quiz 193 80s Pop

Answers - see Quiz 194, page 204

1 Duran Duran were part of which New movement?
2 What Purple thing topped the US album charts for 20 weeks?
3 What was the second name of the group starting Spandau?
4 Which pop singer starred in the movie The Jazz Singer?
5 Who was Shaky?
6 Who had the best selling album Diva?
7 What number featured in the name of the Fun Boy band?
8 Which Belinda sang that Heaven Is A Place On Earth?
9 Who sang - in Australian - Je Ne Sais Pas Pourquoi?
10 Which King was back in the charts with the re-issued When I Fall In Love?
11 What colour of Box recorded Ride On Time?
12 Who teamed up with Barbara Dickson for I Know Him So Well?
13 Which Bunny had a string of dance successes?
14 What was Diana Ross' only 80s No 1?
15 Who duetted with David Bowie on the No 1 hit Dancing In The Street?
16 Which female solo singer had most chart weeks in 1985,1986 and 1987?
17 How many hits did Rolf Harris have in the 80s?
18 According to Michael Ball, Love Changes what?
19 Who charted with the old Supremes hit You Can't Hurry Love?
20 Who duetted with Kylie Minogue for a No 1?
21 Which Jennifer sang about The Power of Love?
22 Which charity song was a hit for Band Aid?
23 Every Loser Wins was a winner for which soap actor?
24 Which Sledge had a hit with Frankie?
25 Who was Saving All My Love For You?

Answers

Pot Luck 91 (see Quiz 194, page 204)
1 Jeep. **2** Rosie. **3** Dr No. **4** Belgium. **5** Lee. **6** I'm free. **7** Bypass. **8** Holland. **9** Oxo cubes. **10** Patsy Kensit. **11** T. **12** Dad's. **13** Manchester. **14** 50s. **15** James. **16** Beef. **17** Harry Secombe. **18** Robin Williams. **19** Guitar. **20** Badminton. **21** Wimbledon. **22** Newcastle. **23** His heart. **24** Lily. **25** WBA.

Quiz 194 Pot Luck 91

Answers - see Quiz 193, page 203

1 Which machine's name comes from some letters in the words 'general purpose'?
2 Who did writer Laurie Lee take Cider with?
3 Ursula Andrews was the Bond girl in which movie?
4 In the 90s which European country had a King Albert?
5 In the 70s who formed a singing duo with Peters?
6 In Are You Being Served, what was John Inman's catchphrase?
7 In the mid 90s what were the Newbury protesters protesting about?
8 Which country does soccer star Pierre Van Hooijdonk play for?
9 Lynda Bellingham who appeared in Second Thoughts was famous for advertising which cooking ingredient?
10 Who did Liam Gallagher marry in April 1997?
11 On a computer keyboard what letter is immediately to the right of the R?
12 The Home Guard was popularly known as whose Army?
13 Piccadilly Radio broadcasts to which major city?
14 In what decade was the FA Cup game known as the Matthews' Final?
15 Which thriller writer uses the initials PD?
16 The BSE crisis related to what type of meat?
17 Which Goon was Welsh?
18 Who played the movie role of Mrs Doubtfire?
19 Mark Knopfler is associated with which musical instrument?
20 Gillian Gilks played for England at which sport?
21 On which Common could you discover The Wombles?
22 Andy Cole joined Man Utd from which club?
23 What did Tony Bennett leave in San Francisco?
24 On TV what is the name of Jason and Bunty Savage's mum?
25 Which Midlands soccer team does Frank Skinner follow?

Answers

80s Pop (see Quiz 193, page 203)
1 Romantics. **2** Rain. **3** Ballet. **4** Neil Diamond. **5** Shakin' Stevens. **6** Annie Lennox. **7** Three. **8** Carlisle. **9** Kylie Minogue. **10** Nat King Cole. **11** Black. **12** Elaine Paige. **13** Jive Bunny. **14** Chain Reaction. **15** Mick Jagger. **16** Madonna. **17** None. **18** Everything. **19** Phil Collins. **20** Jason Donovan. **21** Rush. **22** Do They Know It's Christmas?. **23** Nick Berry. **24** Sister Sledge. **25** Whitney Houston.

Quiz 195 Famous Firsts

Answers - see Quiz 196, page 206

1 Which type of transport was designed by Christopher Cockerell in the 50s?
2 C-Curity was the name of the first type of what?
3 Who was the first man to set foot on the moon?
4 Ruud Gullit became the Premiership's first black manager at which club?
5 Golda Meir was the first female Prime Minister of which country?
6 In which country did the Grunge movement first begin?
7 Helen Sharman was the first British woman to go where?
8 The Bates Motel first appeared in which film?
9 Christiaan Barnard carried out which medical first?
10 Who was the first Spanish golfer to win the British Open?
11 In which decade did the first wheel clamps arrive in Britain?
12 Which Charles first flew non-stop across the Atlantic?
13 Who was the first of Tony Blair's MPs to have won a film Oscar?
14 In 1975, which Arthur became the first black champion in the Men's Singles at Wimbledon?
15 Who starred in the first talkie movie?
16 The first successful cloning of an adult took place with what type of animal?
17 Which major sporting contest first took place in 1930?
18 Which Alexander discovered the first antibiotic?
19 Who was the leader of the first successful expedition to the South Pole?
20 Who were the first group seen on Channel 5?
21 In Jan 1974 professional football in Britain was played for the first time on which day?
22 Which brothers made the first powered plane flight?
23 Which famous first is claimed by Hillary and Tenzing?
24 Who was the first British monarch to abdicate in this century?
25 Which country was the first to send a woman into space?

Answers

Pot Luck 92 (see Quiz 196, page 206)

1 British Gas. **2** Barbie. **3** Quotient. **4** Yeltsin. **5** Fred Astaire. **6** Red. **7** Jerry. **8** David. **9** Apricot. **10** The Simpson. **11** Labour. **12** Soccer. **13** Uruguay. **14** Take That. **15** Schools. **16** Liverpool. **17** Noel Coward. **18** London. **19** 90s. **20** Enid Blyton. **21** Swimming. **22** WWI. **23** Dylan Thomas. **24** Calf. **25** Finland.

Quiz 196 Pot Luck 92

Answers - see Quiz 195, page 205

LEVEL 1

1 Don't Tell Sid was used in adverts to promote sales of shares in what?
2 In a toy store, who became Ken's girlfriend?
3 If I stands for Intelligence what does Q stand for in IQ?
4 In 1991, which Boris became president of the Russian Federation?
5 Frederick Austerlitz became better known as which entertainer?
6 What colour is the background of the Turkish flag?
7 What is Seinfeld's first name?
8 Which Attenborough made the Life On Earth TV series?
9 Which fruit along with an apple gave its name to a computer range?
10 Which cartoon family who first appeared in the US in the 80s were created by Matt Groening?
11 In the 80s David Owen left which political party to launch the SDP?
12 With which sport is Gabriel Batistu associated?
13 The deepwater port of Fray Bentos was built in which country?
14 Who had a 90s No 1 with Never Forget?
15 Implementation of the National Curriculum concerns which establishments?
16 English soccer clubs were banned from Europe in the mid 80s after a final involving which English club?
17 Who wrote the play Blithe Spirit?
18 In which city was teenager Stephen Lawrence stabbed to death?
19 In which decade did Croatia appoint their first president?
20 Who created Noddy?
21 Duncan Goodhew represented Britain at which sport?
22 Francois Mitterand was born during which 20th century war?
23 Who wrote the poetic study of Welsh life Under Milk Wood?
24 What was the surname of Steve Coogan's brother and sister creations Paul & Paula?
25 Which country does motor racing's Mika Hakkinen come from?

Answers

Famous Firsts (see Quiz 195, page 205)
1 Hovercraft. **2** Zip fastener. **3** Neil Armstrong. **4** Chelsea. **5** Israel. **6** United States. **7** Space. **8** Psycho. **9** Heart transplant. **10** Severiano Ballesteros. **11** 80s. **12** Lindbergh. **13** Glenda Jackson. **14** Ashe. **15** Al Jolson. **16** Sheep. **17** Soccer World Cup. **18** Fleming. **19** Roald Amundsen. **20** Spice Girls. **21** Sunday. **22** Wright. **23** Climbing Everest. **24** Edward VIII. **25** USSR.

Quiz 197 The Royals

Answers - see Quiz 198, page 208

1 John Bryan was reputedly what type of adviser to the Duchess of York?
2 Which prince is the Queen's youngest son?
3 What is Prince Harry's real first name?
4 How is Prince Michael of Kent's wife known?
5 Which princess has a holiday villa on Mustique?
6 What is Prince Charles' Gloucestershire home called?
7 Who was Princess Diana referring to when she said her marriage was 'a bit crowded'?
8 Which Prince was born on the Greek island of Corfu?
9 Which Scottish school did Princes Charles, Andrew and Edward all attend?
10 Which Princess is the mother of Peter Phillips?
11 How many daughters does the Queen Mother have?
12 In which cathedral did Prince Charles marry Lady Diana Spencer?
13 Which Royal was once the BBC Sports Personality of the Year?
14 Anthony Armstrong Jones took an Earldom named after which mountain after his marriage to Princess Margaret?
15 Which hair colour is shared by Earl Spencer and his nephew Prince Harry?
16 What is the name of the Spencer ancestral home in Northamptonshire?
17 With which royal's name was Koo Stark's linked in the early 80s?
18 Which name of a castle does Prince Edward use as a professional surname when working in the media?
19 At which English university did Prince Charles study?
20 Which school did Princess William and Harry attend in the late 90s?
21 In which 80s war did Prince Andrew serve?
22 Major Ronald Ferguson is the father of which Duchess?
23 Which Royal wrote The Old Man of Lochnagar?
24 Which branch of the construction industry is Viscount Linley involved in?
25 Which Royal has had a collection of his paintings exhibited?

Answers

***Pot Luck* 93** (see Quiz 198, page 208)
1 Taggart. **2** Vauxhall. **3** Manchester. **4** Twist. **5** Heseltine. **6** London. **7** Tina Turner. **8** Victory. **9** 70s. **10** Soccer. **11** Chocolate. **12** New York. **13** Michael Crawford. **14** John McEnroe. **15** Yugoslavia. **16** Wham. **17** Australia. **18** Acquired. **19** East 17. **20** Scotland. **21** Conservative. **22** Newman. **23** Valentino. **24** Laurence. **25** Mel & Griff.

Quiz 198 Pot Luck 93

Answers - see Quiz 197, page 207

1. Which TV tech was played by Mark McManus?
2. Which car manufacturer introduced the Ventura, Victor and Viscount?
3. In 1990 there was serious rioting in Strangeways prison in which city?
4. Chubby Checker was linked with which dance craze?
5. In 80s politics which Michael resigned over the Westland affair?
6. In which city did Prince Andrew marry Fergie?
7. Singer Anne Mae Bullock found fame under which name?
8. In World War II people were urged to Dig For what?
9. Winona Ryder was born in which decade of the 20th century?
10. Ronnie Clayton played for England at which sport?
11. In fiction, what kind of factory was Roald Dahl's Charlie connected with?
12. Nylon gets its name from London and which other city?
13. Who played Frank Spencer before achieving huge success as The Phantom of the Opera?
14. Which volatile tennis player asked Steffi Graf to partner him in Wimbledon's 1999 Mixed Doubles?
15. In the 90s Macedonia has declared its independence from which country?
16. Andrew Ridgeley was the less famous half of which 80s pop duo?
17. Which country does cricketer Paul Reiffel play for?
18. What does the letter A stand for in AIDS?
19. Stay Another Day was a 90s No 1 which group?
20. Trainspotting was set in which country?
21. John McGregor has represented which party in parliament?
22. Which film star Paul promotes his own salad dressing?
23. Which Italian film star with the same first name as himself did Rudolf Nureyev play in a film in 1977?
24. What was the first name of Baron Olivier of Brighton?
25. What are the first names of Smith & Jones?

Answers

The Royals (see Quiz 197, page 207)

1 Financial. **2** Edward. **3** Henry. **4** Princess Michael of Kent. **5** Margaret. **6** Highgrove. **7** Camilla Parker Bowles. **8** Philip. **9** Gordonstoun. **10** Anne. **11** Two. **12** St Paul's. **13** Princess Anne. **14** Snowdon. **15** Red. **16** Althorp. **17** Prince Andrew. **18** Windsor. **19** Cambridge. **20** Eton. **21** Falklands. **22** York. **23** Prince Charles. **24** Carpentry. **25** Prince Charles.

Quiz 199 Americans

Answers - see Quiz 200, page 210

1 Which was the field event among Jesse Owens' four Olympic golds in 1936?
2 What was Walt Disney's first feature length cartoon film?
3 The life of press baron William Randolph Hearst was used as the basis of which Orson Welles film?
4 Which aunt of George Clooney starred opposite Bing Crosby in White Christmas?
5 Where in France was Glenn Miller flying to when his airplane went missing?
6 Which Thomas announced the invention of the electric battery in 1902?
7 Who became the world's first oil billionaire in 1916?
8 Dwight D Eisenhower was Allied Supreme Commander in which region in 1944?
9 Which future US President did Jacqueline Bouvier marry in September 1953?
10 Which film star did Prince Rainier of Monaco marry in April 1956?
11 In which state beginning with I was Buddy Holly killed?
12 Edward White was the first American to walk where?
13 Which Kennedy was killed by Sirhan Sirhan?
14 At which European Olympics did Mark Spitz win his record seven gold medals?
15 Who was President of the USA immediately before Bill Clinton?
16 Which American athlete Mary fell over during the final of the 3000 metres at the LA Olympics?
17 Which President did John Hinckley try to assassinate in 1981?
18 Which famous Chicago gangster offered a reward of $10,000 when the Lindbergh baby was kidnapped?
19 Which playwright Arthur was Marilyn Monroe's last husband?
20 Which Arthur was the first black tennis player to win the US Open?
21 Which future Vice President and defeated Presidential candidate was elected Senator for Tennessee in 1985?
22 Which Louis led a jazz band called The All Stars?
23 Which President of the USA called the Soviet Union the 'evil empire'?
24 What sort of Bomber was boxer Joe Louis according to his nickname?
25 Who died first, Laurel or Hardy?

Answers

Pot Luck 94 (see Quiz 200, page 210)
1 Zimbabwe. **2** Culture. **3** Rudolf Hess. **4** Lecter. **5** Frederick . **6** Woody Allen. **7** Buddy Holly. **8** Essex. **9** Paxman. **10** Atomic Bomb. **11** Mike Baldwin. **12** The Beatles. **13** Disease. **14** Spitting Image. **15** Golding. **16** The Thin Blue Line. **17** Take That. **18** Steptoe. **19** Terry. **20** USA. **21** Ernie Wise. **22** M11. **23** James Bond. **24** Diving. **25** Starr.

Quiz 200 Pot Luck 94

Answers - see Quiz 199, page 209

1 Robert Mugabe was the first Prime Minister of which country?
2 Boy George fronted which Club?
3 Which Nazi died in jail after being imprisoned for 46 years?
4 In fiction what is the last name of Dr Hannibal - the Cannibal?
5 Who sang Little Donkey with Nina?
6 How did Allen Stewart Konigsberg become better known?
7 Brown-Eyed Handsome Man was a hit for which singer after his death?
8 Chelmsford is the administrative centre of which English county?
9 Which Jeremy was a 90s University Challenge presenter?
10 What was developed in the 40s Manhattan Project?
11 Which character did Johnny Briggs play in Coronation Street?
12 Which group sacked drummer Pete Best before they hit the big time?
13 In medicine, what does the D stand for in CJD?
14 Fluck & Law were famous for their puppets on which show?
15 Which William wrote the novel Lord Of The Flies?
16 Which sitcom with Rowan Atkinson was set in Gasforth Police station?
17 Who had a 90s No 1 with Back For Good?
18 What was the surname of the father and son rag and bone men who lived at Mews Cottage, Oil Drum Lane?
19 What is the first name of best selling sci fi writer Pratchett?
20 Cookery writer and TV presenter Loyd Grossman hails from which country?
21 Which late comedian had "short, fat, hairy legs"?
22 Which motorway links London to Cambridge?
23 Timothy Dalton and Pierce Brosnan have both played which character?
24 Which sport in the Olympics includes pikes, tucks and twists?
25 Which Freddie, born Freddie Fowell, earned a reputation as one of Britain's most outrageous comedians?

Answers

Americans (see Quiz 199, page 209)
1 Long jump. **2** Snow White & the Seven Dwarfs. **3** Citizen Kane. **4** Rosemary Clooney. **5** Paris. **6** Thomas Edison. **7** John D Rockefeller. **8** Europe. **9** John F Kennedy. **10** Grace Kelly. **11** Iowa. **12** In space. **13** Bobby Kennedy. **14** Munich. **15** George Bush. **16** Mary Decker. **17** Ronald Reagan. **18** Al Capone. **19** Arthur Miller. **20** Arthur Ashe. **21** Al Gore. **22** Louis Armstrong. **23** Ronald Reagan. **24** The Brown Bomber . **25** Hardy.

Quiz 201 TV Soaps

Answers - see Quiz 202, page 212

1 Which Grove was a popular teen soap?
2 In which soap was Blake married to Alexis then Krystle?
3 Which member of the Mitchell family was killed on New Year's Eve 1998?
4 Which soap community has the postcode E20?
5 In which soap was the body of a wife beater famously buried under the patio?
6 Which day of the week is the EastEnders omnibus edition?
7 Which chocolate makers first sponsored Coronation Street in 1996?
8 Which doomed BBC soap was set in Spain?
9 The Colbys was a spin off from which US soap?
10 What was Emmerdale called when it was first screened in the afternoon?
11 Knots Landing was a spin off from which oil based soap?
12 As opposed to oil, Falcon Crest was about which commodity California is famous for?
13 Which Ken is the only original member of the Coronation Street cast?
14 In which Ward was the Emergency in TV's first medical soap?
15 In 1993 Emmerdale suffered an air disaster similar to which real life tragedy?
16 Which late comedian Larry was Meg Richardson's wedding chauffeur in Crossroads?
17 Which soap launched the pop careers of Kylie Minogue and Jason Donovan?
18 Which soap ran the classic cliff hanger 'Who shot J.R.?'?
19 How did Take The High Road change its name from 1995 onwards?
20 Which blonde replaced Vera behind the bar at the Rovers Return?
21 In Coronation Street what does Mike Baldwin's factory make?
22 In EastEnders, who did Peggy marry in 1999?
23 In which Cheshire location was Hollyoaks set?
24 Which soap from Down Under was created to rival Neighbours?
25 Which soap for children was set in a London comprehensive?

Answers

Pot Luck 95 (see Quiz 202, page 212)
1 Spencer. **2** Stevie Wonder. **3** S. **4** Drew. **5** Newton and Ridley. **6** Cricket. **7** Monster. **8** John Wayne. **9** Stephen King. **10** Breathing. **11** Wednesday. **12** Cardiff. **13** Japan. **14** Promise. **15** Crystal Palace. **16** Goebbels. **17** Isle of Man. **18** Golf. **19** 50s. **20** Chile. **21** Evander Holyfield. **22** Tarbuck. **23** Guitar. **24** India. **25** St George's.

Quiz 202 Pot Luck 95

Answers - see Quiz 201, page 211

1 Which Earl was the brother of Diana, Princess of Wales?
2 In music who "just called to say I love you"?
3 A Swedish car displays which international vehicle registration mark?
4 Which of the Barrymore family featured in the film Batman Forever?
5 What type of beer is served in Coronation Street's Rovers' Return?
6 Derek Underwood played which sport for England?
7 The MRLP is what kind of Raving Loony Party?
8 Marion Morrison become famous under which name?
9 Who wrote the novel The Shining?
10 What does the B stand for in SCUBA diving?
11 On which day was the midweek Lottery first drawn?
12 Which Welsh city had a millennium sports stadium built?
13 The deepwater port of Kagoshima was built in which country?
14 In advertising, Fry's Turkish Delight was described as being "Full of Eastern" what?
15 Which soccer team does Jo Brand follow?
16 Which Joseph was Hitler's minister of propaganda?
17 On which Isle was Ronaldsway airport built?
18 With which sport is Curtis Strange associated?
19 Cheery entertainer Jim Davidson was born is which decade?
20 General Pinochet was a former ruler of which country?
21 Who lost part of his ear to the teeth of Mike Tyson in 1997?
22 Which Liverpool comedian Jimmy went to the same school as John Lennon?
23 BB King is associated with which musical instrument?
24 Lord Mountbatten was the last viceroy of which country?
25 In which chapel did Edward and Sophie Rhys-Jones get married?

Answers

TV Soaps (see Quiz 201, page 211)
1 Byker. **2** Dynasty. **3** Tiffany. **4** Walford. **5** Brookside. **6** Sunday. **7** Cadbury's. **8** El Dorado. **9** Dynasty. **10** Emmerdale Farm. **11** Dallas. **12** Wine. **13** Barlow. **14** 10. **15** Lockerbie. **16** Grayson. **17** Neighbours. **18** Dallas. **19** High Road. **20** Natalie. **21** Underwear. **22** Frank. **23** Chester. **24** Home & Away. **25** Grange Hill.

Quiz 203 Horse Racing

Answers - see Quiz 204, page 214

1 Who returned to racing in 1990 when he was over 50?
2 Which horse was first to win the Grand National three times?
3 Where is the William Hill Lincoln Handicap held?
4 Trainers Lynda and John Ramsden won a libel case against which paper?
5 In which country was Shergar captured?
6 In which month is the Melbourne Cup held?
7 Who was National Hunt champion jockey from 1986 to 1992?
8 Which horse Benny won the 1997 Derby?
9 Which English classic is held at Doncaster?
10 What is a £500 bet known as?
11 Which horse race was abandoned in 1997 after a bomb scare?
12 The Prix du Jockey-Club is held at which race course?
13 Which horse had the nickname Corky?
14 Which Gordon a trainer of over 2000 winners died in September 1998?
15 Which country hosts the Belmont and Preakness Stakes?
16 Who chartered a train from Victoria to Epsom to watch the 1997 Derby at a cost of over £11,000?
17 Which race meeting is described as Glorious?
18 The 12th Earl of where gave his name to a famous race?
19 Which horsewoman was the first Mrs Mark Phillips?
20 After a Saturday bomb threat in 1997 on which day was the National run?
21 The Curragh is in which Irish County?
22 Which horse was the first to win Horse of the Year four times?
23 Where did Frankie Dettori have his record breaking seven wins?
24 Which horse won the Derby by a record distance in 1981?
25 In which country is Flemington Park race course?

Answers

The Oscars (see Quiz 204, page 214)
1 Hepburn. **2** Titanic. **3** Thompson. **4** Tom Hanks. **5** Elizabeth I. **6** Kevin Costner. **7** Dustin Hoffman. **8** The Godfather. **9** Titanic. **10** Pianist. **11** Braveheart. **12** Park. **13** Tim Rice. **14** The Silence of the Lambs. **15** John Wayne. **16** The English Patient. **17** Tandy. **18** George. **19** The Full Monty. **20** Vietnam. **21** Christie. **22** Shirley Valentine. **23** Anthony Hopkins. **24** West Side Story. **25** Butch Cassidy & The Sundance Kid.

Quiz 204 The Oscars

Answers - see Quiz 203, page 213

LEVEL 1 

1 Which veteran actress Katharine was the first actress to win four Oscars?
2 Which 1997 movie equalled Ben Hur's record 11 Oscars?
3 Which Emma won an Oscar for her screenplay of Sense and Sensibility?
4 Who won his second Oscar in successive years for Forrest Gump?
5 Judi Dench won an Oscar as which Queen in Shakespeare in Love?
6 Who won Best Actor and Best Director Oscar for Dances With Wolves?
7 Who won his second Oscar for the autistic Raymond in Rain Man?
8 In the 70s which gangster film won an Oscar as did its sequel?
9 In 1997 James Cameron won an Oscar for which blockbuster?
10 Geoffrey Rush won an Oscar for Shine, as what type of musician?
11 For which film about a Scottish hero did Mel Gibson win his first Oscars for Best Picture and Best Director?
12 Which Nick won an Oscar for The Wrong Trousers?
13 Which lyricist who has worked with Elton John and Andrew Lloyd Webber won an award for A Whole New World from Aladdin?
14 In which film did Jodie Foster play FBI agent Clarice Starling?
15 Who won an Oscar wearing an eye patch in True Grit?
16 Which film with Ralph Fiennes won Anthony Minghella an Oscar?
17 Which Jessica was the then oldest Oscar winner for Driving Miss Daisy?
18 Nigel Hawthorne was Oscar nominated for The Madness of which King?
19 Which Oscar nominated film had You Sexy Thing as its theme song?
20 The multi Oscar winning The Deer Hunter was about steelworkers who went to fight where?
21 Which Julie won an Oscar for Darling in 1965 and was Oscar nominated in 1998 for Afterglow?
22 For which 80s film was Pauline Collins nominated for playing a bored Liverpool housewife?
23 Which Oscar winner from The Silence of the Lambs campaigned to save Snowdonia in 1998?
24 Which musical based on Romeo & Juliet was a 60s Oscar winner?
25 Raindrops Keep Falling On My Head was an Oscar winner from which movie with Robert Redford & Paul Newman?

Answers

Horse Racing (see Quiz 203, page 213)

1 Lester Piggott. **2** Red Rum. **3** Doncaster. **4** The Sporting Life. **5** Ireland. **6** November. **7** Peter Scudamore. **8** The Dip. **9** St Leger. **10** Monkey. **11** National. **12** Chantilly. **13** Corbiere. **14** Richards. **15** United States. **16** The Queen. **17** Goodwood. **18** Derby. **19** Princess Anne. **20** Monday. **21** Kildare. **22** Desert Orchid. **23** Ascot. **24** Shergar. **25** Australia.

Quiz 205 On Line

Answers - see Quiz 206, page 216

1 What does the first W stand for in WWW?
2 If you surf the Internet what do you do?
3 Which page of a Web site is called a Home Page?
4 In addition to the computer what else must a modem be plugged into?
5 What does Q mean in FAQ?
6 What does S mean in ISP?
7 In which country did the Internet start?
8 A small a in a circle (@) is pronounced how?
9 What name is given to the software program needed to access the Web?
10 What goes after Netscape in the name of a popular Internet browser?
11 If you have an active Internet connection you are said to be on what?
12 What is the opposite of downloading?
13 What is freeware?
14 If you log off what do you do?
15 What is netiquette?
16 What is the minimum number of computers which can be networked?
17 What letter appears on the computer screen when you are using Microsoft Internet Explorer?
18 Which name of something used by avid readers is the Netscape Navigator name for Favorites?
19 Where does bounced e mail return to?
20 Which 'space' refers to the Internet and all that goes with it?
21 What does offline mean?
22 A newbie is a new what?
23 In an e mail address how is a symbol like a full stop said out loud?
24 What name is given to a program designed to cause damage by attaching itself to other programs?
25 What is Microsoft's browser software called?

Answers

Pop 90s (see Quiz 206, page 216)
1 Finally. **2** Nirvana. **3** Spice Girls. **4** Robson & Jerome. **5** Barbie. **6** Snoop Doggy Dog. **7** All Saints. **8** B*Witched. **9** Piper. **10** The Full Monty. **11** He shot himself. **12** Man City,. **13** Wannabe. **14** Man Utd. **15** The Corrs. **16** Fatboy Slim. **17** Oasis. **18** Manic Street Preachers. **19** Erasure. **20** Paula Yates. **21** Prodigy. **22** Small. **23** Mr Blobby. **24** Sinead O'Connor. **25** Guinness.

Quiz 206 Pop 90s

Answers - see Quiz 205, page 215

1 What was finally a top ten hit for Ce Ce Peniston on its 1992 re-release?
2 Who recorded the album Nevermind?
3 Who had a Christmas No 1 in 1996, 1997 and 1998?
4 Who had a hit with the old song I Believe?
5 What kind of Doll did Aqua sing about?
6 Whose debut album was called Doggystyle?
7 Which girl group led the 1995 Party In The Park for the Prince's Trust?
8 Edele and Keavy Lynch were together in which group?
9 What is Billie's surname?
10 Which film revived the 70s song You Sexy Thing?
11 How did Kurt Kobain end his life?
12 Which team do the Gallagher brothers support?
13 What was the first single of The Spice Girls?
14 Which soccer team sang Come On You Reds?
15 Whose debut album was Talk On Corners?
16 Norman Cook is better known as which club DJ?
17 Which group's first No 1 was Some Might Say?
18 Richie Edwards vanished in 1995 leaving behind which group?
19 Who had success with Abba-esque?
20 Who was Mrs Bob Geldof when the 90s started?
21 Which alternative dance group first charted with Charly?
22 Which Heather sang with M People?
23 Which chart topper was pink, tall, spotted and very destructive?
24 Whose Nothing Compares 2 U made No 1 in both the UK and the US?
25 An advert for which drink led to Perez Prado back in the charts?

Answers

On Line (see Quiz 205, page 215)
1 World. **2** Look around. **3** First. **4** Phone. **5** Question. **6** Service. **7** USA. **8** At. **9** Browser. **10** Navigator. **11** Line. **12** Uploading. **13** Free software. **14** Disconnect. **15** Good behaviour on the net. **16** Two. **17** E. **18** Bookmarks. **19** Sender. **20** Cyberspace. **21** Not connected. **22** Internet user. **23** Dot. **24** Virus. **25** Internet Explorer.

Quiz 207 Technology

Answers - see Quiz 208, page 218

1 What does the G stand for in WYSIWYG?
2 In which decade was the Sony Walkman stereo launched?
3 Oftel regulates which industry?
4 Which phone company adopted a colour name before going into the red?
5 Which UK motor company produced the Prefect?
6 What kind of codes did American supermarkets introduce in the mid 70s?
7 What does the B stand for in IBM?
8 The Three Mile Island nuclear leak in the 70s was in which country?
9 What did pirate radio stations broadcast?
10 Which Bill formed Microsoft?
11 Which 'unsinkable' craft sank in 1912?
12 Which Clarence pioneered quick freezing in the food industry?
13 The tallest tower of the 70s, the Sears Tower, was built in which country?
14 Foods will not brown in what type of oven?
15 What used to go round at thirty three and a third r.p.m.?
16 In which decade was the Channel Tunnel first opened?
17 What did Lazlo Biro invent in the 30s?
18 The wide-bodied passenger carrying Boeing 747 became known as what type of jet?
19 Which popular small car was introduced by Austin Morris at the end of the 50s?
20 Which country combined with Britain in building Concorde?
21 What touches the surface of a CD when playing?
22 What does the F stand for in FM?
23 The Sony company originated in which country?
24 Modulator-Demodulator is usually shortened to what?
25 What was the middle name of TV pioneer John Baird?

Answers

Screen Greats (see Quiz 211, page 221)
1 Frankenstein. **2** Tony. **3** John F Kennedy. **4** Dynasty. **5** Bette Davis. **6** Harrison. **7** San Francisco. **8** Buddhism. **9** Humphrey Bogart. **10** Germany. **11** Michael Caine. **12** Frank Sinatra. **13** England. **14** Marlon Brando. **15** Fred Astaire/Ginger Rogers. **16** Gene Kelly. **17** James Dean. **18** Monaco. **19** Star Wars. **20** Bob Hope. **21** Kirk. **22** Crawford. **23** Nicholson. **24** Zhivago. **25** Dustin Hoffman.

Quiz 208 Unforgettables

Answers - see Quiz 211, page 221

1 Which member of T Rex died exactly the same day as Maria Callas?
2 Which part of the brilliant Albert Einstein was preserved after his death?
3 Which Princess and former film star died in a car crash near Monte Carlo in 1982?
4 How many times did Greta (I want to be alone) Garbo marry?
5 Linda McCartney launched a range of what type of food?
6 Which opera singer's real name was Maria Kalogeropoulos?
7 Yitzhak Rabin was Prime Minister of which country when he was assassinated in 1995?
8 Which Yuri made the first human journey into space?
9 Which fuel made millions for J. Paul Getty?
10 How was Argentinian revolutionary Ernesto Guevara de la Serna better known?
11 Charles de Gaulle was President of which European country?
12 Who was the youngest US President to die in office?
13 T.E.Lawrence's name is mostly associated with which country?
14 Yehudi Menuhin was famous for playing which musical instrument?
15 Glenn Miller's plane disappeared during which war?
16 Which blonde icon made her name in Gentlemen Prefer Blondes?
17 Fans visit Graceland in the USA to pay tribute to which rock legend?
18 In which country did Mother Theresa found her mission to help the destitute?
19 Who was the first Queen of England in the 20th century?
20 What was the name of the musical about rock legend Buddy Holly?
21 Who killed Cleopatra?
22 To the nearest five years, how old would John Lennon have been in 2000?
23 Which knighted Man Utd manager switched on the Blackpool illuminations in 1968?
24 John Wayne had an airport named after him in his home country. Where is it?
25 Which British born veteran American comedian Bob received a knighthood in 1998?

Answers

Technology (see Quiz 207, page 217)
1 Get. **2** 70s. **3** Telecommunications. **4** Orange. **5** Ford. **6** Bar codes. **7** Business. **8** United States. **9** Pop music. **10** Gates. **11** Titanic. **12** Birdseye. **13** United States. **14** Microwave. **15** Long playing records. **16** 90s. **17** Ballpoint pen. **18** Jumbo. **19** Mini. **20** France. **21** Nothing. **22** Frequency. **23** Japan. **24** Modem. **25** Logie.

Quiz 209 TV Times

Answers - see Quiz 210, page 220

LEVEL 1 

1 In which country was Due South set?
2 Which George played Doug Ross in ER?
3 Which show was set in a Boston bar "Where everybody know your name"?
4 In which decade was the first Eurovision Song Contest?
5 In which Yorkshire location was Band of Gold set?
6 Which ex Bond Girl Jane played Dr Quinn: Medicine Woman?
7 Which animated series was originally to have been called The Flagstones?
8 Which other Kelly presented the first series of Game For A Laugh with Henry?
9 Henry Winkler's Arthur Fonzarelli was better known as what?
10 How many sisters established The House of Elliot?
11 Which Jim might have fixed it for you?
12 What was the first name of arch snob Mrs Bucket - pronounced Bouquet?
13 The Larry Sanders Show was a spoof of what type of show?
14 In Last of the Summer Wine what wrinkled part of Nora Batty was a source of fascination for Compo?
15 Which action drama centred on Blue Watch B25, Blackwall?
16 The Mary Whitehouse Experience came to TV from which radio station?
17 I Could Be So Good for You was a Dennis Waterman hit from which show he starred in with George Cole?
18 Caroline Aherne was the alter ego of which pensioner chat show hostess?
19 Which cult sci fi series was originally to have been called Wagon Train to the Stars?
20 Which show featured Noo Noo the vacuum cleaner?
21 Which so called yuppie drama series was set in Philadelphia and was first shown in the UK on Channel 4?
22 Which East London football team did Alf Garnett support?
23 In the 70s series what followed Tinker, Tailor, Soldier in the title?
24 Which line followed "It's goodnight from me..." on The Two Ronnies?
25 What was the job of Hudson in Upstairs Downstairs?

Answers

Sports Bag (see Quiz 210, page 220)
1 Earvin. **2** Two. **3** Barcelona. **4** Leeds. **5** American Football. **6** Argentina. **7** Long jump. **8** Channel. **9** Marathon. **10** January. **11** Scotland. **12** Football. **13** Soccer - Fulham. **14** Sri Lanka. **15** Polo. **16** Baltimore. **17** Flo-Jo. **18** Dusty. **19** Amateur. **20** Celtic. **21** Baseball. **22** Mansell. **23** Paris. **24** N Ireland. **25** S Africa.

Quiz 210 Sports Bag

Answers - see Quiz 209, page 219

1 What is 'Magic' Johnson's first name?
2 How many attempts at the target does a player get in curling?
3 In which Spanish city were the 1992 Olympics held?
4 Eric Cantona joined Man Utd from which club?
5 The Vince Lombardi trophy is awarded in which sport?
6 Gabriela Sabatini comes from which country?
7 In which event did Bob Beaman hold an Olympic record for over 20 years?
8 Graeme Le Saux was born in which group of islands?
9 What did Dionico Ceron win three years in a row in England's capital city?
10 In which month of the year is the Super Bowl held?
11 In 1999 Ian McGeechan became coach of which international rugby team?
12 What word can follow American, Association or Gaelic to name a sport?
13 Which sport has a team that plays at a Cottage?
14 Which country won cricket's 1996 World Cup?
15 In which sport is the Cowdray Park Cup awarded?
16 In American Football where do the Colts come from?
17 What was athlete Florence Griffith-Joyner usually known as?
18 Rugby's William Henry Hare was better known by what nickname?
19 In athletics, what does the first A stand for in the initials IAAF?
20 Which team did Jock Stein lead to European Cup success?
21 Micky Mantle played which sport?
22 Which Nigel was BBC Sports Personality in 1992?
23 In which city does the Tour de France finish?
24 Norman Whiteside became the youngest soccer player of the 20th century for which international side?
25 Who played Australia in cricket's drawn 1999 World Cup semi-final?

Answers

TV Times (see Quiz 209, page 219)
1 Canada. **2** Clooney. **3** Cheers. **4** 50s. **5** Bradford. **6** Seymour. **7** The Flintstones. **8** Matthew. **9** The Fonz. **10** Two. **11** Saville. **12** Hyacinth. **13** Chat show. **14** Stockings. **15** London's Burning. **16** Radio 1. **17** Minder. **18** Mrs Merton. **19** Star Trek. **20** Teletubbies. **21** Thirtysomething. **22** West Ham. **23** Spy. **24** And it's goodnight from him. **25** Butler.

Quiz 211 Screen Greats

Answers - see Quiz 207, page 217

1 Boris Karloff starred as which monster in one of the first horror movies?
2 Which actor is the father of actress Jamie Lee Curtis?
3 Arnold Schwarzenegger married the niece of which US president?
4 Which TV soap was Rock Hudson a star of shortly before his death?
5 Which actress born Ruth Elizabeth Davis was the first female president of the Academy of Motion Picture Arts & Sciences?
6 Which Ford of Star Wars was voted Film Star of the century by a panel of critics in 1994?
7 In which city did Steve McQueen take part in the car chase in Bullitt?
8 Richard Gere is a follower of which eastern religion?
9 Which screen great was Lauren Bacall married to at the time of his death?
10 In which country was Marlene Dietrich born?
11 Who found fame as Alfie?
12 Which Oscar winner for From Here To Eternity, more famous as Ol' Blue Eyes the singer, died in 1998?
13 In which country was Cary Grant born as Archie Leach?
14 Which star of The Godfather in the 70s played opposite Vivien Leigh in A Streetcar Named Desire in the 50s?
15 Which dancing duo's first film together was called Flying Down to Rio?
16 Which dancer, the star of Singing in the Rain, never won an Oscar?
17 Rebel Without A Cause made a star of which actor whose life was cut short in a car accident?
18 Grace Kelly became Princess of which principality where her film To Catch a Thief was set?
19 In which movie did Alec Guinness first appear as Ben Obi Wan Kenobi?
20 Which comedian starred with Bing Crosby in the Road films?
21 What was the name of Michael Douglas's father?
22 Which star Joan was the subject of the movie Mommie Dearest?
23 Which Jack won an Oscar for One Flew Over the Cuckoo's Nest?
24 Which Russian Doctor was played in the 60s by Omar Sharif?
25 Who found fame trying to resist the charms of Mrs Robinson in The Graduate?

Answers

Unforgettables (see Quiz 208, page 218)
1 Marc Bolan. **2** Brain. **3** Grace. **4** Never. **5** Vegetarian. **6** Maria Callas. **7** Israel. **8** Gagarin. **9** Oil. **10** Che Guevara. **11** France. **12** Kennedy. **13** Arabia. **14** Violin. **15** World War II. **16** Marilyn Monroe. **17** Elvis Presley. **18** India. **19** Victoria. **20** Buddy. **21** Cleopatra. **22** 60. **23** Matt Busby. **24** USA. **25** Hope.

Medium Questions

Here are the medium questions. Now these are your common or garden, average, straight down the middle questions. They wouldn't dare be so easy that everyone in the pub is blurting out the answers without even pausing to think, nor would they deign be so hard as to confound your punters utterly, and so lend the pub an eerily confused state.

No. No these are as nice and reliable as a set of questions could be, similar to your honest pub dog. The kind of faithful canine who quietly laps up the icy cold water provided by the barman on a hot summer's eve. That's as opposed to the sort of dog who wilfully attacks tradespeople and well-meaning visitors.

As long as your teams are made up of fairly regular people then these questions should be the ones that form the largest part of your quiz. And even if this isn't the case, everyone ought to have a mid-point within their intelligence to cope with these questions. Somewhere between, say, an impressive ability to quote something apt from the Bard, to an embarrassing and somewhat unnecessary tendancy to memorize the names, dates of birth and favourite colours of all of the members of the newest boy band.

Quiz 1 Pot Luck 1

Answers - see Quiz 2, page 224

1 Stamp duty is normally paid on the sale of what?
2 Where is the Ceremony of the Keys held every evening?
3 What does a BACS system transfer?
4 Who wears a chasuble?
5 Who or what is your doppelganger?
6 Emphysema affects which part of the body?
7 Which term for school or university is from the Latin meaning 'bounteous mother'?
8 Which salts are hydrated magnesium sulphate?
9 What is the UK equivalent of the US Bureau of Consumer Protection?
10 What did Plaid Cymru add to its name in 1998?
11 Which punctuation mark would an American call a period?
12 At what age does a student now usually take a GCE exam?
13 Where were the Elgin marbles from originally?
14 Which song starts, "Friday night and the lights are low"?
15 According to legend, what will happen to Gibraltar's ape population if the British leave?
16 Is BST before or behind GMT?
17 What is notable about the staff and patients of the Elizabeth Garrett Anderson Hospital?
18 How many valves does a bugle have?
19 What name is given to the compulsive eating disorder?
20 What is a Blenheim Orange?
21 Which childhood disease is also called varicella?
22 What do citronella candles smell of?
23 Which part of the anatomy shares its name with a punctuation mark?
24 Which tax did council tax immediately replace?
25 Which English archbishop signs his name Ebor?
26 Which saint was born in Lourdes?
27 Which proposal for a single currency shares its name with a bird?
28 Where is the auditory canal?
29 Where is a fresco painted?
30 How long must a person have had to be dead to qualify for a blue plaque?

Answers

Sport: Cricket (see Quiz 2, page 224)
1 Geoffrey Boycott. **2** Richie Benaud. **3** Tony Lewis. **4** Trevor McDonald. **5** Terrence. **6** Kapil Dev. **7** Somerset. **8** Denis Compton. **9** Shakoor Rana. **10** Dennis Lillee. **11** Michael Atherton. **12** The Oval. **13** Graham Alan Gooch. **14** Wasim Akram. **15** Headingley. **16** Muthiah Muralitharan. **17** William Gilbert. **18** David Gower. **19** Leicestershire. **20** Lancashire. **21** Sunglasses. **22** Sunil Gavaskar. **23** Hansie Cronje. **24** Don Bradman. **25** Graeme Hick. **26** Imran Khan. **27** Antigua. **28** The Times. **29** Sri Lanka. **30** Left.

Quiz 2 Sport: Cricket

Answers - see Quiz 1, page 223

1 Who did David Gower overtake as England's most prolific run scorer in 1992?
2 Which Australian commentates on TV each summer?
3 Which former test cricketer became President of the MCC in 1998?
4 Which newsreader has written biographies of Viv Richards and Clive Lloyd?
5 What is Ian Botham's middle name?
6 Which Indian was the second bowler to reach 400 Test wickets?
7 Which English county did Viv Richards play for?
8 Which cricketer was the first British sportsman to appear in a major advertising campaign?
9 Which umpire did Gatting publicly argue with in Faisalabad?
10 Which Australian was the first man to take 300 wickets in Test cricket?
11 Who stood in the most tests as England captain?
12 Which is the most southerly of the six regular English Test grounds?
13 Which cricketer's initials are GAG?
14 Who left Lancashire in 1998 to return to Pakistan to clear his name?
15 At which ground did England beat South Africa to clinch the 1998 series?
16 David Lloyd was reprimanded for criticising which Sri Lankan bowler in 1998?
17 What were W.G. Grace's first two names?
18 Whose record did Graham Gooch pass when he became England's leading run scorer?
19 Which county has won two championships in the last three years of the 20th Century?
20 Who won the 1998 Nat West Trophy?
21 In 1996 Darren Gough became the first England bowler to bowl wearing what?
22 Which Indian cricketer scored 10,122 runs in 125 matches between 1971 and 1987?
23 Who captained the South Africans on their 1998 England tour?
24 Which cricketer's bat was auctioned for £23,000 in 1997?
25 Which Rhodesian became Zimbabwe's youngest professional at the age of 17 in 1985?
26 Who captained Pakistan in the 1992 World Cup victory?
27 On which island did Brian Lara make his record breaking 375?
28 In which newspaper was it announced that English cricket had died, leading to competition for the Ashes?
29 In which country is Khettarama Stadium?
30 Which hand does David Gower write with?

Answers

Pot Luck 1 (see Quiz 1, page 223)
1 House. **2** Tower of London **3** Money. **4** Priest. **5** Double. **6** Lungs. **7** Alma Mater. **8** Epsom salts. **9** Office of Fair Trading. **10** The Party of Wales. **11** Full stop. **12** 18. **13** Greece. **14** Dancing Queen. **15** It will die out. **16** Before. **17** Women. **18** None. **19** Bulimia. **20** Apple. **21** Chicken pox. **22** Lemons. **23** Colon. **24** Community Charge or Poll Tax. **25** York. **26** Bernadette. **27** EMU. **28** In the ear. **29** On a wall. **30** 20 years.

Quiz 3 Pot Luck 2

Answers - see Quiz 4, page 226

1 Which Dunfermline East MP has been in the Cabinet in the 90s?
2 Why does a glow worm glow?
3 Who wrote the Kirsty MacColl hit A New England?
4 Princess Margaret was advised against marrying Peter Townsend for what reason?
5 Cambodian leader Saloth Sar was better known by what name?
6 How many holes are most major golf tournaments played over?
7 In the song, what colour rose is linked with Texas?
8 Tokai wine comes from which country?
9 In which month did Samuel Pepys begin his famous diary?
10 Who was Lord Lucan said to have murdered?
11 Mont Blanc stands in France as well as which other country?
12 William Wilkins designed which London gallery?
13 Which city has an American football team called the Cowboys?
14 Which is the world's oldest surviving republic?
15 Which Latin words did H M the Queen use to describe the year 1992?
16 Which cave is the most famous on the Scottish Isle of Staffa?
17 Cars with the international vehicle registration SF come from where?
18 Number 22 in bingo is represented by a pair of little what?
19 What is the core of an ear of maize called?
20 What was the title of the Eurovision winner for Bucks Fizz?
21 In Porterhouse Blue which actor played Skullion?
22 Which country's stamps show the word "Hellas"?
23 Who were the subject of the Cat and Mouse Act of 1913?
24 How many points are scored for a motor racing Grand Prix win?
25 What is the largest structure ever made by living creatures?
26 Papworth Hospital is in which county?
27 Who said, "Float like a butterfly, sting like a bee"?
28 Which magazine was first published in the 1840s and last in the 1990s?
29 Which road is crossed by the horses during the Grand National?
30 Which religious ceremony comes from the Greek word for 'to dip'?

Answers

The Movies: All Action (see Quiz 4, page 226)
1 Goldeneye. **2** Platoon. **3** Jeremy Irons. **4** The Hunt for Red October. **5** Charles Bronson. **6** Jim Carrey. **7** Best Director. **8** Wesley Snipes. **9** Live and Let Die. **10** Faye Dunaway. **11** Donald Pleasence. **12** Die Hard with a Vengeance. **13** Harrison Ford. **14** Marseilles . **15** Apollo 13. **16** Bruce Willis. **17** Popeye Doyle. **18** James Caan. **19** Irish. **20** Brad Pitt. **21** Lost in Space. **22** Phil Collins. **23** Cabbie. **24** Paul & Linda McCartney. **25** JFK. **26** Sean Bean. **27** The China Syndrome. **28** Arnold Schwarzenegger. **29** New York. **30** Leonardo DiCaprio.

Quiz 4 The Movies: All Action

Answers - see Quiz 3, page 225

1 Which Bond film shares its name with Ian Fleming's Jamaican home?
2 What was the third of Oliver Stone's films about Vietnam?
3 Which English Oscar winner was the villain in Die Hard III?
4 Patriot Games was the sequel to which film with Alec Baldwin?
5 Who played Bernardo in The Magnificent Seven and Danny Velinski in The Great Escape?
6 Who was The Riddler in Batman Forever?
7 Which Oscar did Kevin Costner win for Dances With Wolves?
8 Who played the defrosted super-villain in Demolition Man?
9 What was Roger Moore's first Bond film in 1973?
10 Who had her first major starring role in Bonnie & Clyde?
11 Who plays the President in Escape From New York?
12 Which was the third Die Hard film?
13 Who played Indiana Jones?
14 Where was French Connection II set?
15 Astronaut Jim Lovell was portrayed by Tom Hanks in which film?
16 Who heads the crew which saves the world in Armageddon?
17 Who did Gene Hackman play in The French Connection?
18 Who played Sonny Corleone in The Godfather and its sequel?
19 What nationality cop did Sean Connery play in The Untouchables?
20 Who co starred with Morgan Freeman in Seven?
21 Which 1998 film of a 60s cult TV series starred Gary Oldman and William Hurt?
22 Who played the train robber of the title role in Buster?
23 What was Mel Gibson's job in the 1997 thriller Conspiracy Theory?
24 Which husband and wife were Oscar nominated for the song from Live And Let Die?
25 Which Oliver Stone movie with Kevin Costner was about events prior to Kennedy's assassination?
26 Which Yorkshireman played the IRA terrorist in Patriot Games?
27 In which '79 movie with Jack Lemmon was Jane Fonda urged to keep quiet about a nuclear accident?
28 Who was the construction worker who had flashbacks in Total Recall?
29 Where does the action of Godzilla take place?
30 Who played two roles in the 90s version of The Man in the Iron Mask?

Answers

Pot Luck 2 (see Quiz 3, page 225)

1 Gordon Brown. **2** To attract mates. **3** Billy Bragg. **4** He was a divorcee. **5** Pol Pot. **6** 72. **7** Yellow. **8** Hungary. **9** January. **10** Sandra Rivett. **11** Italy. **12** The National Gallery. **13** Dallas. **14** San Marino. **15** Annus horribilis. **16** Fingal's cave. **17** Finland. **18** Two little ducks. **19** A corncob. **20** Making Your Mind Up. **21** David Jason. **22** Greece. **23** Suffragettes. **24** 10. **25.** The Great Barrier Reef. **26** Cambridgeshire. **27** Muhammad Ali. **28** Punch. **29** Melling Road. **30** Baptism.

Quiz 5 Pot Luck 3

Answers - see Quiz 6, page 228

1 Which U2 member was once the All-Ireland Junior Chess Champion?
2 Who won 100m gold at the 1988 Olympics and was then disqualified?
3 Spy-writer David J. Cornwell writes under which name?
4 What is the unit of measurement for the brightness of stars?
5 Which "-ology" is the study of birds' eggs?
6 Which Dire Straits album included Money for Nothing?
7 Who were Janet, Pam, Barbara, Jack, Peter, George and Colin?
8 In which country would you be to visit Agadir?
9 What name is given to a bell tower not attached to a church?
10 Van Pelt is the surname of which Peanuts character?
11 What is the best hand in a game of poker?
12 The Virgin record label was launched by which instrumental album?
13 Which crab lives in a whelk or winkle shell?
14 In the official conker rules, how many strikes per turn are allowed?
15 Which country celebrated its bicentenary in 1988?
16 What word commonly describes a spasm of the diaphragm?
17 Daniel Carroll found theatrical fame under which name?
18 In pop music, who looked into his father's eyes?
19 Who lit the funeral pyre of Mrs Indira Gandhi?
20 Which country has Jones as its most common name but no J in its alphabet?
21 What name was given to the first antibiotic?
22 According to the advert, which city is home to "probably the best lager in the world"?
23 Switzerland's Mont Cervin is better known by what name?
24 Who wrote the novel Where Eagles Dare?
25 Which England cricket captain had the middle name Dylan?
26 What do the initials CND stand for?
27 What is the collective name for a group of frogs?
28 Who was the first act to have seven consecutive US No 1 singles?
29 Eton school is in which county?
30 Which country was first to host Summer and Winter Olympics in the same year?

Answers

Leisure: Food & Drink 1 (see Quiz 6, page 228)

1 Fish. **2** Kirschwasser. **3** Gin. **4** Sugar. **5** November. **6** Curry powder. **7** Greece. **8** Halal. **9** 20. **10** Kiwi fruit. **11** Gelatine. **12** Marty Wilde. **13** Mrs Beeton. **14** Nut. **15** Coca Cola. **16** Elizabeth David. **17** Clarified butter. **18** Carrot. **19** Bloody Mary. **20** Manchester United. **21** Nouvelle cuisine. **22** Aluminium. **23** Jennifer Paterson. **24** Rhodes to Home. **25** Black. **26** Fred Trueman. **27** Poisonous raw. **28** Mushroom. **29** Cherry. **30** Milk.

Quiz 6 Leisure: Food & Drink 1

Answers - see Quiz 5, page 227

1 What type of food is gravadlax?
2 Which type of brandy is made from cherries?
3 Which spirit is Pimm's No 1 based on?
4 Aspartame is an alternative to what when added to food?
5 In which month does Beaujolais Nouveau arrive?
6 Which powder includes turmeric, fenugreek, chillies and cumin?
7 Which country produces more than 70% of the world's olive oil?
8 What name is given to food prepared according to Muslim law?
9 How many standard wine bottles make up a Nebuchadnezzar?
10 Which fruit is also called the Chinese gooseberry?
11 Agar agar is a vegetarian alternative to what?
12 Which 50s pop star's name is cockney rhyming slang for mild?
13 How is cook Isabella Mary Mayson better known?
14 What sort of food is a macadamia?
15 Atlanta is the headquarters of which drinks company?
16 Which pioneering cookery writer wrote Mediterranean Food and French Country Cooking in the 50s?
17 What is ghee?
18 Caraway is related to which family of vegetables?
19 Which queen's nickname is the name of a cocktail?
20 Which football team does Gary Rhodes support?
21 Which term coined in the 70s describes food which does not have rich sauces?
22 What are most beer and soft drinks cans made from?
23 Which of the Two Fat Ladies rode the motorbike?
24 What was Gary Rhodes' range of convenience foods called?
25 What colour are fully ripened olives?
26 The Fiery Fred pub was named after whom?
27 Why do cashew nuts have to be roasted to be eaten?
28 What is a morel?
29 What is a morello?
30 Which drink did Bob Geldof advertise?

Answers

Pot Luck 3 (see Quiz 5, page 227)
1 Bono. **2** Ben Johnson. **3** John Le Carre. **4** Magnitude. **5** Oology. **6** Brothers In Arms. **7** The Secret Seven. **8** Morocco. **9** A campanile. **10** Lucy. **11** Royal flush. **12** Tubular Bells. **13** Hermit crab. **14** Three. **15** Australia. **16** Hiccough. **17** Danny La Rue. **18** Eric Clapton. **19** Rajiv Gandhi. **20** Wales. **21** Penicillin. **22** Copenhagen. **23** The Matterhorn. **24** Alistair MacLean. **25** Bob Willis. **26** Campaign for Nuclear Disarmament. **27** An army (or colony). **28** Whitney Houston. **29** Berkshire. **30** France.

Quiz 7 Pot Luck 4

Answers - see Quiz 8, page 230

1 The illness pertussis is more commonly called what?
2 Why do woodpeckers peck at trees?
3 Which rock is the largest monolith in the world?
4 Which Spanish team were the first winners of the European Cup?
5 What type of animal can be Texel and Romney Marsh?
6 Where would you hurt if you were kicked on the tarsus?
7 The Bee Gees were born on which island?
8 What action does a dromophobic fear?
9 In which country is the world's second highest mountain, K2?
10 What nationality is Salman Rushdie?
11 Which Test cricketer played in an FA Cup Final for Arsenal?
12 Which tanker went down on the Seven Stones reef off Land's End?
13 Which large forest is the nearest to London's Liverpool Street Station?
14 Which hit by Judy Collins entered the UK charts on eight occasions?
15 In 1978 how many different Popes were there?
16 In which decade did Constantinople become Istanbul?
17 How many bridesmaids attended Princess Diana?
18 Which poet gave his name to a Cape to the south of Brisbane?
19 Which Russian town produced deformed sheep after a 80s disaster?
20 What is Paul McCartney's first name?
21 Which drug took its name from the Greek god of dreams?
22 Which is the largest borough in the city of New York?
23 Which doll's name gave Aqua a No 1 hit?
24 Which other brook is there on the Grand National course with Becher's?
25 What is examined using an otoscope?
26 What is measured on the Mercalli Scale?
27 Along with Doric and Ionic, what is the third Greek order of architecture?
28 What is lowered by a Beta Blocker?
29 How many pieces does each backgammon player use?
30 A Blue Orpington is a type of what?

Answers

Nature: Animal World (see Quiz 8, page 230)
1 Suffocation. **2** Sett. **3** Velvet. **4** Black. **5** Dachshund. **6** It cannot bark. **7** Afrikaans. **8** Mauritius. **9** Antelope. **10** Snow leopard. **11** Fight. **12** Squirrel. **13** One. **14** Cattle. **15** Hearing. **16** 32. **17** Fawn. **18** Hooves. **19** Blood of birds and mammals. **20** Sheep. **21** Pink. **22** White. **23** Japan. **24** Caribou. **25** Lemurs. **26** White / cream. **27** V shape. **28** Elk. **29** Sand. **30** Border collie.

Quiz 8 Nature: Animal World

Answers - see Quiz 7, page 229

LEVEL 2

1. How do the anaconda's victims die?
2. What is the badger's system of burrows called?
3. What is the skin on a deer's antlers called?
4. What colour face does a Suffolk sheep have?
5. Which small breed of dog has a German name meaning badger dog?
6. What is unusual about the sound of the dingo?
7. Aardvark means 'earth pig' in which African language?
8. On which island was the dodo formerly found?
9. What is an impala?
10. What type of leopard is another name for the ounce?
11. Pit bull terriers were bred to do what?
12. To which family does the prairie dog belong?
13. Does the Indian rhinoceros have one or two horns?
14. Bovine Spongiform Encephalitis is a fatal disease of which animals?
15. Tinnitus affects which of the senses?
16. How many teeth do human adults have?
17. What is the most common colour of a Great Dane?
18. What does an ungulate animal have?
19. What do vampire bats feed on?
20. Lanolin is a by product of which domestic animal?
21. If a mammal has albinism what colour are its eyes?
22. What colour are dalmatians when they are born?
23. The tosa is a dog native to which country?
24. What is the reindeer of North America called?
25. Which group of primates are found only on Madagascar?
26. What colour is the coat of a samoyed?
27. What shaped mark does an adder have on its head?
28. What is another name for the wapiti?
29. What do alligators lay their eggs in?
30. Which dog do shepherds now most commonly use for herding sheep?

Answers

Pot Luck 4 (see Quiz 7, page 229)
1 Whooping cough. **2** To catch insects. **3** Ayers Rock. **4** Real Madrid. **5** Sheep. **6** Ankle. **7** Isle of Man. **8** Crossing the road. **9** Pakistan. **10** British. **11** Denis Compton. **12** Torrey Canyon. **13** Epping Forest. **14** Amazing Grace. **15** Three. **16** 1930s. **17** Five. **18** Byron. **19** Chernobyl. **20** James. **21** Morphine. **22** Queens. **23** Barbie. **24** Valentine's. **25** Ear. **26** Earthquakes. **27** Corinthian. **28** Blood pressure. **29** 15. **30** Chicken.

Quiz 9 Pot Luck 5

Answers - see Quiz 10, page 232

1 In which US state is Death Valley?
2 Which Sea does the River Jordan flow into?
3 Who was Speaker of the House after Bernard Weatherill?
4 Who had Top Ten hits with All Night Long and I Surrender?
5 Which BBC magazine was launched in 1929?
6 What did Captain Cook call the Islands of Tonga?
7 Which celebrity was murdered in 1980 outside New York's Dakota Building?
8 Who played Lennie Godber in the TV series Porridge?
9 Which naval base is situated in Hampshire?
10 Which TV actress links EastEnders with The Hello Girls?
11 What is Marc Bolan's son's Christian name?
12 Which war is the first for which there are photographic records?
13 Writer Mary Westmacott is better known by what name?
14 Who or what was a ducat?
15 Which day is the last quarter day in a calendar year in England?
16 Which actor links The Charmer with Dangerfield?
17 In The Bible, who was Jacob's youngest son?
18 What was suffragette Mrs Pankhurst's Christian name?
19 In which sport is the Plunkett Shield competed for?
20 Which animal has breeds called Roscommon, Kerry Hill, Ryedale?
21 Which two countries was the Cod War of the 70s between?
22 What colour are Rupert Bear's trousers?
23 Who is Gary Lineker's sidekick on They Think It's All Over?
24 Which animal can be red, arctic, bat-eared and fennec?
25 Newman Noggs appears in which Charles Dickens novel?
26 What name is given to the base of your spine?
27 Who did Sandy Powell ask "Can You Hear Me, ..?"
28 Which actress links the films Ghostbusters and Alien?
29 Who had hits with Do You Feel My Love and Electric Avenue?
30 Which word describes both a blunt sword and a very thin sheet of metal?

Answers

Geography: The UK (see Quiz 10, page 232)
1 Brighton. **2** Melinda Messenger. **3** South Kensington. **4** Stoke Mandeville. **5** Suffolk. **6** Severn Tunnel. **7** Newgate. **8** Canary Wharf (Isle of Dogs). **9** Salopian. **10** Army exercises. **11** Essex & Suffolk. **12** Bristol. **13** M6. **14** Glastonbury. **15** Big Ben. **16** Fruit, vegetables & flowers. **17** Windscale. **18** Horses. **19** Clyde. **20** Nottingham. **21** Wiltshire. **22** Edinburgh. **23** Petticoat Lane. **24** Papworth. **25** Hyde Park. **26** Aberdeen. **27** Bath. **28** Straits of Dover. **29** Swansea. **30** Bristol.

Quiz 10 Geography: The UK

Answers - see Quiz 9, page 231

1 Which seaside resort has Lanes and a nudist beach?
2 Which Page Three blonde is Swindon's most famous export?
3 In which part of London is the Natural History Museum?
4 Where is the National Spinal Injuries Unit?
5 In which county is Sizewell nuclear power station?
6 What is Britain's longest tunnel?
7 The Old Bailey is on the site of which former prison?
8 Where in London would a Canary sit on Dogs?
9 What is a native of Shropshire called?
10 What is Salisbury Plain primarily used for?
11 In which two counties is Constable Country?
12 Where is the Clifton Suspension Bridge?
13 Spaghetti Junction is on which road?
14 Which Somerset town is said to be the burial place of King Arthur?
15 Which bell was named after Benjamin Hall?
16 What is sold at Spitalfields market?
17 What was the former name of Sellafield?
18 Which animals are kept in the Royal Mews near Buckingham Palace?
19 Holy Loch is an inlet of which river?
20 Which city has an annual Goose Fair?
21 In which English county is Europe's largest stone circle?
22 Which castle is at the west end of the Royal Mile?
23 How is the Sunday market in London's Middlesex Street better known?
24 Which Cambridgeshire hospital is famous for its transplant surgery?
25 Speaker's Corner is on the corner of what?
26 Where is the administrative headquarters of the Grampian region?
27 Which city has a famous Royal Crescent?
28 The Goodwin Sands are at the entrance to which straits?
29 Where is the DVLC?
30 Where is Temple Meads railway station?

Answers

Pot Luck 5 (see Quiz 9, page 231)
1 California. **2** Dead Sea. **3** Betty Boothroyd. **4** Rainbow. **5** The Listener. **6** The Friendly Islands. **7** John Lennon. **8** Richard Beckinsale. **9** Gosport. **10** Letitia Dean. **11** Roland. **12** Crimean. **13** Agatha Christie. **14** A coin. **15** Christmas Day. **16** Nigel Havers. **17** Benjamin. **18** Emmeline. **19** Cricket. **20** Sheep. **21** Iceland and Britain. **22** Yellow. **23** Rory McGrath. **24** Fox. **25** Nicholas Nickleby. **26** Coccyx. **27** Mother. **28** Sigourney Weaver. **29** Eddy Grant. **30** Foil.

Quiz 11 TV: Adverts

Answers - see Quiz 12, page 234

1 Carol Vorderman was sacked from Tomorrow's World for advertising what?
2 Which credit card did Rowan Atkinson publicise by not having one?
3 Which opera singer has sung on Kenco Coffee and Renault car ads?
4 Who played the jilted lover in the 80s VW commercial?
5 Which 'pensioner' advertised British Gas with her 'son' Malcolm?
6 For which supermarket did Wood & Walters push their trolleys round country lanes?
7 Which Blankety Blank presenter did Polly Peck hire to advertise their tights?
8 Which soap powder did Shane Richie promote in his doorstep raids?
9 Who advertised Cinzano with Leonard Rossiter?
10 Which juice did Fergie advertise in the US?
11 Lynda Bellingham first found fame advertising what?
12 Which supermarket did John Cleese promote in a loud checked suit?
13 Which company had the slogan 'It's good to talk'?
14 Which cat put its paw in the tin of cat food?
15 Which soap star appeared in a BT ad digging his allotment?
16 Which star of Brushstrokes can be found cleaning bathrooms and kitchens in TV ads?
17 In the Renault ad did Nicole marry Reeves or Mortimer?
18 What type of coffee did Gareth Hunt and Diane Keen enjoy?
19 Which star of Friends uses L'Oreal "Because I'm worth it!"?
20 Which song accompanies Ian McCaskill's BT ad?
21 Emma Forbes' mother advertised which washing up liquid?
22 Which margarine did 'Victor Meldrew' encourage us to eat?
23 Who cried when his Walkers Crisps were taken from him?
24 Ironically Julie Peasgood advertised which product?
25 Which fast food chain did soccer stars Waddle, Pearce and Southgate promote?
26 Which breakfast cereal was Jackie Charlton seen eating with his grandson?
27 Messrs Venables, Robson and Taylor collectively promoted which book?
28 Geoffrey Palmer from As Time Goes By advised to "slam in" what ?
29 Bruce Forsyth dresses up as a judge to advertise what product?
30 Which supermarket did Michael Barrymore advertise in the autumn of 1998?

Answers

Pot Luck 6 (see Quiz 12, page 234)
1 Yellowstone National Park. **2** International Monetary Fund. **3** Volcanic gases. **4** Lentils. **5** Sheffield. **6** Kate Bush. **7** Cashew nut. **8** Hattie Jacques. **9** A will. **10** Thanksgiving. **11** Black. **12** The Wailers. **13** International Velvet. **14** National Exhibition Centre. **15** Boy George. **16** 21. **17** Versailles. **18** Iraq. **19** Scotland. **20** Belshazzar. **21** White rum. **22** Thunder & lightning. **23** Mick Hucknall. **24** The Andes. **25** The Derby. **26** An unborn baby. **27** Prunella Scales. **28** The peacock. **29** The Baltic. **30** Frogmore.

Quiz 12 Pot Luck 6

Answers - see Quiz 11, page 233

1 In which US National Park is the Old Faithful geyser?
2 What do the initials IMF stand for?
3 What is emitted from a fumarole?
4 What is the main ingredient in dhal, the Indian dish?
5 In which city is Bramall Lane?
6 Which female had a UK top-three LP in 1982 called The Dreaming?
7 Mozambique is the world's largest producer of which nut?
8 How is Josephina Jacques known in Carry On films?
9 To what would a codicil be added?
10 Which American annual celebration was first marked during 1789?
11 The first Girl Guides had to wear what colour stockings?
12 Which band claimed fifty per cent of Bob Marley's estate?
13 Which film was the follow-up to National Velvet?
14 What does NEC stand for around Birmingham?
15 Who left Bow Wow Wow to form Culture Club?
16 What is the maximum score in blackjack?
17 Which building in France has a famous Hall of Mirrors?
18 What is the modern name of the country where the Hanging Gardens of Babylon were?
19 Which country did Arsenal keeper Bob Wilson play for?
20 In The Bible, which character saw the first writing on the wall?
21 A Daiquiri is made from fruit juice and which alcoholic drink?
22 Astraphobia is the fear of which meteorological event?
23 Which male pop superstar once played with the Frantic Elevators?
24 Machu Picchu is in which mountain range?
25 What is the English equivalent of the Melbourne Cup?
26 What is surrounded by amniotic fluid?
27 Who links Fawlty Towers and After Henry?
28 Which bird is India's national symbol?
29 Which sea is the least salty in the world?
30 Where was The Duke of Windsor buried in 1972?

Answers

TV: Adverts (see Quiz 11, page 233)

1 Ariel. **2** Barclaycard. **3** Lesley Garrett. **4** Paula Hamilton. **5** Mrs Merton. **6** Asda. **7** Lily Savage. **8** Daz. **9** Joan Collins. **10** Cranberry. **11** Oxo. **12** Sainsbury's. **13** BT. **14** Arthur. **15** Arthur Fowler. **16** Karl Howman. **17** Mortimer. **18** Nescafe. **19** Jennifer Aniston. **20** Bring Me Sunshine. **21** Fairy. **22** Flora. **23** Paul Gascoigne. **24** Frozen peas. **25** Pizza Hut. **26** Shredded Wheat. **27** Yellow Pages. **28** The lamb. **29** Furniture. **30** Kwik Save.

Quiz 13 Pop Music: The 60s

Answers - see Quiz 14, page 236

1 Which No 1 hit for the Archies was in the charts for twenty six weeks?
2 Which Park was a hit for the Small Faces in 1967?
3 Who was singing about Sheila in 1962 and Dizzy in 1969?
4 Which 60s hit for Kitty Lester was an 80s hit for Alison Moyet?
5 When did the Shirelles want to know Will You Still Love Me...?
6 Which crime busting organisation gave the Shadows a 1961 hit?
7 What was Petula Clark's first No 1 UK hit in 1961?
8 Which three numbers gave Len Barry his No 3 hit in 1965?
9 Who had consecutive hits with Daydream and Summer In The City?
10 What was over for the Seekers in their 1965 UK No 1 hit?
11 Which 1965 Shirley Ellis hit was a 1982 hit for the Belle Stars?
12 What were Emile Ford and the Checkmates Counting in 1960?
13 What was the Searchers first No 1 ?
14 What was on the other side of Shirley Bassey's Reach for the Stars?
15 Whose first Top Ten hit was 5-4-3-2-1 in 1964?
16 Which country was in the title of a '63 hit by Matt Monro?
17 Who recorded the original of the song used in Four Weddings and a Funeral?
18 What Girl was Neil Sedaka singing about in 1961?
19 The song Starry Eyed was a No 1 on 1st January 1960 for which Michael?
20 Which words of exclamation were a 1960 No 4 hit for Peter Sellers?
21 Which Opportunity Knocks star had a hit with Those Were The Days?
22 What did The Move say they could hear grow in a 1967 hit title?
23 Which 60s hit for Kenny Lynch was a No 1 for Robson and Jerome in 1995?
24 Who were Glad All Over in their No 1 hit from 1963?
25 What was 'skipped' in the lyrics of Whiter Shade Of Pale?
26 What type of Feelings did Tom Jones have in his 1967 hit?
27 Which Group had consecutive No 1s with Keep On Running and Somebody Help Me?
28 To which religious building were the Dixie Cups going in 1964?
29 Which weather sounding group had hits with Robot and Globetrotter?
30 Which 1960s star appeared with Zoe Wanamaker in Love Hurts?

Answers

Pot Luck 7 (see Quiz 14, page 236)
1 1950s. **2** The Undertones. **3** The Hobbit. **4** Jeanette MacDonald. **5** Excalibur. **6** Woody Allen. **7** Colchester. **8** Uncle Mac. **9** You walk. **10** McAliskey. **11** Roy Wood. **12** Brookside. **13** Arthur Lucan. **14** Eric Idle. **15** Hairy. **16** Ernie Els. **17** George III. **18** A dog. **19** Chariots of Fire. **20** Red Square, Moscow. **21** Private Fraser. **22** Ultravox. **23** Sheep & goats. **24** Mumps. **25** Shirley Williams. **26** A bolt or quarrel. **27** Amsterdam. **28** Shirley Temple. **29** Pig. **30** George VI.

Quiz 14 Pot Luck 7

Answers - see Quiz 13, page 235

1 In which decade did Lester Piggott first win the Derby?
2 Who had hits with My Perfect Cousin and Jimmy Jimmy?
3 Which folklore fantasy tale is subtitled There and Back Again?
4 Who was Nelson Eddy's singing partner in many musical films?
5 Which famous sword is sometimes called Caliburn?
6 Which famous film director has a son called Satchel?
7 Which is further north, Chelmsford or Colchester?
8 Children's broadcaster Derek McCulloch was known on the radio as whom?
9 What is your mode of transport if you go by Walker's Bus?
10 What is former MP Bernadette Devlin's married name?
11 Which Wizzard star formed ELO in 1971?
12 In which TV soap was Trevor Jordache buried under the patio?
13 Who played Old Mother Riley in films and on stage?
14 Which member of the Monty Python team was born on the same day as John Major?
15 What does the word piliferous mean?
16 Who won the Toyota world matchplay championship at his first attempt in 1994?
17 Which King George bought Buckingham Palace?
18 What kind of animal is a Schnauzer?
19 Which Oscar winning film gave Vangelis a No 12 hit in 1981?
20 In which famous Square is St Basil's cathedral?
21 In the series Dad's Army which soldier's daytime job was an undertaker?
22 Who had hits with All Stood Still and Visions in Blue?
23 Which animals are attacked by a disease called Scrapie?
24 Which childhood disease affects the parotid salivary gland?
25 Which female MP was one of the founder members of the SDP?
26 What can be fired by a crossbow?
27 In which city was Anne Frank when she wrote her diary?
28 Which actress played lead in the films Dimples and Curly Top?
29 Lard is mainly produced from which animal?
30 Which king was the last Emperor of India?

Answers

Pop Music: 60s (see Quiz 13, page 235)

1 Sugar Sugar. **2** Itchycoo Park. **3** Tommy Roe. **4** Love Letters. **5** Tomorrow. **6** FBI. **7** Sailor. **8** 1-2-3. **9** Lovin' Spoonful. **10** The Carnival Is Over. **11** The Clapping Song. **12** Teardrops. **13** Sweets For My Sweet. **14** Climb Ev'ry Mountain. **15** Manfred Mann. **16** Russia. **17** Troggs. **18** Calendar Girl. **19** Holliday. **20** Goodness Gracious Me. **21** Mary Hopkin. **22** The Grass. **23** Up On The Roof. **24** Dave Clark Five. **25** The Light Fandango. **26** Funny Familiar Forgotten. **27** Spencer Davis. **28** Chapel of Love. **29** Tornadoes. **30** Adam Faith.

Quiz 15 Sport: Football UK

Answers - see Quiz 16, page 238

1 Who succeeded Ossie Ardiles as Spurs manager?
2 Which football team was involved in an aircrash in March 1998?
3 Which English international played for three Italian clubs before moving to Arsenal?
4 Who was fined £20,000 for making a video on how to foul players?
5 Whose 1996 penalty miss prompted Des Lynam to say "You can come out from behind your sofas now."?
6 Who was PFA Young Player of the year in '95 and '96?
7 Who left Tottenham immediately before George Graham took over?
8 Which football manager is singer Louise's father in law?
9 Which club side was Alan Ball playing for during the 1966 World Cup?
10 What is Glenn Hoddle in the cockney rhyming slang dictionary?
11 Which was the first Lancashire side Kenny Dalglish managed?
12 How is Mrs Paul Peschilsolido better known?
13 Which striker has been player of the year at Everton and at Spurs?
14 Who was Man Utd manager immediately prior to Alex Ferguson?
15 Ian McShane's father was on the books of which football club?
16 Who was the first UK manager to walk out on a contract and work abroad?
17 Who has managed Internazionale of Milan and Blackburn Rovers?
18 Which 80s FA Cup winners came nearest the start of the alphabet?
19 Who was Gullit's first signing when he took over at Newcastle?
20 How does the resolving of the 1999 FA CUP Final differ from those 127 years before?
21 Who did Bruce Rioch replace at Norwich for the start of the 1998-99 season?
22 Who was made Northern Ireland manager in February 1998?
23 Which England player was seen on the town wearing a sarong prior to France 98?
24 Who should Scotland have been playing when they arrived for a World Cup qualifier with no opposition?
25 Which ex international managed Burnley in the 1997-98 season?
26 Who did Jack Charlton play all his League football with?
27 George Graham was accused of taking a 'bung' in the transfer of which player?
28 Who sponsored the Scottish Premier Division in the 1995-96 season?
29 What did Man Utd have advertised on their shirts in the 1998 Charity Shield game?
30 Which Yorkshire side does actor Sean Bean support?

Answers

Pot Luck 8 (see Quiz 16, page 238)
1 Docklands. **2** Casanova. **3** David Bowie. **4** Everglades. **5** A waterhole. **6** 21. **7** Asia Minor. **8** Will Carling. **9** Loose rocks. **10** Cardiff. **11** Dysentery. **12** Trilby. **13** Corinth Canal. **14** London. **15** Elizabeth Bennet. **16** Football match. **17** Bhopal. **18** Hudson Bay. **19** 155. **20** Stevie Wonder. **21** Italy. **22** Agnes Baden-Powell. **23** 1990. **24** Band Aid. **25** Dodecanese. **26** Clay. **27** Vogue. **28** September 15th. **29** 1972. **30** The Queen was pregnant.

Quiz 16 Pot Luck 8

Answers - see Quiz 15, page 237

1 Canary Wharf is in which London development?
2 Who wrote twelve volumes on Casanova?
3 Which superstar was a former member of the group the King Bees?
4 Which Florida national park has a highway called Alligator Alley?
5 What do Australians mean when they talk about a billabong?
6 How old was Billy The Kid when he died?
7 What was the former name of Turkey?
8 Julia Smith became the wife of which famous sportsman?
9 What on a mountainside is scree?
10 Which city is James Callaghan the Baron of?
11 What killed Sir Francis Drake?
12 What type of hat took its name from a novel by George DuMaurier?
13 The Aegean Sea is linked to the Ionian Sea by which canal?
14 Florence Nightingale was given the Freedom of which city in 1908?
15 Who is the heroine in Jane Austen's Pride and Prejudice?
16 What game started the 1969 war between El Salvador and Honduras?
17 In the 80s two thousand people were killed by a gas leak in which Indian town?
18 Which Bay is the largest in the world?
19 What is the highest break in snooker with the advantage of a free black ball?
20 Which blind music star ran for Mayor of Detroit in 1989?
21 In which country was Ted Dexter born?
22 Who was responsible for setting up the Girl Guides movement?
23 In what year was Nelson Mandela released from prison?
24 Which charity was in business from 1984-89 and raised £90 million?
25 Rhodes is the largest of which group of islands?
26 What is a sumo wrestling ring made from?
27 The film Dick Tracy was promoted by which Madonna single?
28 The Battle of Britain is remembered on which date?
29 Which year did John Lennon perform his final live concert?
30 The 1959 Royal Variety Performance was cancelled for what reason?

Answers

Sport: Football UK (see Quiz 15, page 237)

1 Gerry Francis. **2** Leeds Utd. **3** David Platt. **4** Vinnie Jones. **5** Gareth Southgate. **6** Robbie Fowler. **7** Christian Gross. **8** Harry Redknapp. **9** Blackpool. **10** Doddle. **11** Blackburn Rovers. **12** Karren Brady. **13** Gary Lineker. **14** Ron Atkinson. **15** Manchester United. **16** Graeme Souness. **17** Roy Hodgson. **18** Coventry. **19** Rui Costa. **20** No replay. **21** Mike Walker. **22** Lawrie McMenemy. **23** David Beckham. **24** Estonia. **25** Chris Waddle. **26** Leeds Utd. **27** John Jensen. **28** Bell's. **29** SHARP. **30** Sheffield United.

Quiz 17 Movies: Animation

Answers - see Quiz 18, page 240

1 Which Ponchielli piece features in Fantasia?
2 Which US born Australian was the voice of John Smith in Pocahontas?
3 In which movie does a cub called Simba first appear?
4 What was the sequel to Aladdin called?
5 What colour are Mickey Mouse's gloves?
6 Perdita and Pongo are what type of animals?
7 How many Oscars in total, was Disney given for Snow White and the Seven Dwarfs?
8 Which 1991 animated film was later a musical in London and the US?
9 Who is the best known rabbit in Bambi?
10 Which king is 'the King of the Swingers' in Jungle Book?
11 Which of the Gabor sisters was a voice in The Aristocats?
12 Who created Tom and Jerry at MGM in the 40s?
13 What did Dumbo do immediately before his ears grew so big?
14 Which film of a fairy tale features the song Bibbidy Bobbidy Boo?
15 Which part did Kathleen Turner voice in Who Framed Roger Rabbit??
16 Which Disney film was the first with a synchronised soundtrack?
17 Colours of the Wind was a hit song from which movie?
18 Which film with an animated sequence featured Angela Lansbury using her magic powers against the Nazis?
19 Who sings 'he's a tramp' in Lady and the Tramp?
20 Where did Kim Basinger star as a sexy animated doodle, Holly, brought over to the real world?
21 Who sang in Aladdin after making her name in Miss Saigon?
22 Which 1990 film was about pizza loving, sewer dwelling reptiles?
23 Which was the first film to feature, appropriately enough, computer-animated sequences?
24 What type of orphaned creature featured in The Land Before Time?
25 Which was the first animated film in the 90s which Tim Rice won an Oscar for?
26 Which dancer commissioned Hanna and Barbera to do an animation sequence in Anchors Aweigh in 1945?
27 Which Tchaikovsky ballet piece features in Fantasia?
28 In which film does Shere Khan appear?
29 Which characters made their debut in Puss Gets the Boot in 1940?
30 Which animals feature in Oliver and Company?

Answers

Pot Luck 9 (see Quiz 18, page 240)
1 Cuba. **2** California. **3** Blueberry. **4** Vodka and orange juice. **5** Canada. **6** Skin. **7** Spain. **8** 1940s. **9** Willow. **10** Cricket. **11** Australia. **12** Julian Clary. **13** Scotland and England. **14** Sesame seeds. **15** A. **16** Hampshire. **17** King Lear. **18** Government Issue. **19** Samantha Janus. **20** Acetylene. **21** Redcurrants. **22** A river bed. **23** USA. **24** Carbon. **25** Oxford. **26** The bark. **27** Mega. **28** Gumbo. **29** Mark Knopfler. **30** Charlie Drake.

Quiz 18 Pot Luck 9

Answers - see Quiz 17, page 239

1 Cars with the international vehicle registration C come from where?
2 The Paul Getty Museum is in which American state?
3 What is the American equivalent of an English bilberry?
4 What is added to Galliano to make a Harvey Wallbanger?
5 Which country is nearest to where the Titanic was found?
6 An average man has twenty square feet of what about his person?
7 In which country were the last summer Olympics of the 20th century in Europe?
8 In which decade was Cassius Clay - later Muhammad Ali - born?
9 From which tree family is the basket making osier a member?
10 Which sport other than rugby is played for the Currie Cup?
11 In which country is the Great Sandy Desert?
12 Who had Sticky Moments On Tour?
13 The Cheviot hills run along the boundary between which countries?
14 Which seeds are in the sweet, Halva?
15 What note does an orchestra tune to?
16 In which county is Damon Hill's mansion called Hydon End?
17 Which Shakespeare play was banned during George III's time of madness?
18 Before being used as a name for US soldiers, what did 'GI' stand for?
19 Who played Pauli in the TV series Liverpool One?
20 Which gas is produced by adding water to calcium carbide?
21 Which berries are used in a Cumberland sauce?
22 What is a wadi?
23 In which country is the Potomac River?
24 Which element has the highest melting point?
25 Which University did Jeffrey Archer attend?
26 Which part of a tree gives Angostura Bitters its taste?
27 What is the metric word for a million?
28 What is the southern American stew of rice and okra called?
29 Which famous pop guitarist performed with the Notting Hillbillies?
30 Whose catchphrase was "Hello my darlings"?

Answers

Movies: Animation (see Quiz 17, page 239)

1 Dance of the Hours. **2** Mel Gibson. **3** The Lion King. **4** The Return of Jafar. **5** White. **6** Dalmatians. **7** Eight. **8** Beauty and the Beast. **9** Thumper. **10** Louie. **11** Eva. **12** Hanna & Barbera. **13** He sneezed. **14** Cinderella. **15** Jessica Rabbit. **16** Steamboat Willie. **17** Pocahontas. **18** Bedknobs & Broomsticks. **19** Peggy Lee. **20** Cool World. **21** Lea Salonga. **22** Teenage Mutant Ninja Turtles. **23** Tron. **24** Dinosaur. **25** Aladdin. **26** Gene Kelly. **27** Nutcracker Suite. **28** Jungle Book. **29** Tom & Jerry. **30** Cats and dogs.

Quiz 19 Leisure: Books 1

Answers - see Quiz 20, page 242

1 Where according to The Bible is the site of the final battle between nations which will end the world?
2 In which Dickens novel did Uriah Heep appear?
3 Old Possum's Book of Practical Cats is composed of what?
4 To £5,000 how much do you receive for winning the Booker Prize?
5 In which book did John Braine introduce Joe Lampton?
6 What type of book is the OED?
7 What is the subject of Desmond Morris's The Naked Ape?
8 What type of books did Patricia Highsmith write?
9 Which detective first appeared in A Study in Scarlet in 1887?
10 In which Holy Book other than The Bible is there the Garden of Eden?
11 Which Gothic horror story has the alternative title The Modern Prometheus?
12 For what type of book is Samuel Pepys famous for?
13 Who wrote The Female Eunuch in 1970?
14 In which county were Jane Austen and Charles Dickens born?
15 Which former politician narrated the diaries of his dog Buster?
16 In Charlie and the Chocolate Factory, what is Charlie's surname?
17 Which ex jockey wrote a book of short stories called Field of Thirteen?
18 Whose horror stories include Carrie and The Shining?
19 According to the 1998 Guiness Book of Records, who is the most mentioned man on the Internet?
20 Who wrote Das Kapital?
21 How many lines are there in a limerick?
22 Which writer and politician bought poet Rupert Brooke's house?
23 Which fictional barrister was created by John Mortimer?
24 Whose first novel, A Woman of Substance became a best seller?
25 Which nonagenarian had written 700 romantic novels by the end of the 20th century?
26 The Day of the Jackal is about an assassination plot on whom?
27 For which Salman Rushdie book did the Ayatollah impose a fatwa?
28 Who wrote It's All Over Now after her brief marriage to Bill Wyman?
29 To five years, how old was Mary Wesley when her first bestseller was published?
30 Award winning novelist Ben Okri hails from which country?

Answers

Pot Luck 10 (see Quiz 20, page 242)
1 Cross Fell, Cumbria. **2** McLaren. **3** 27. **4** Henry Cooper. **5** Their Mum. **6** Hyde Park. **7** Frank Bruno. **8** Phone cards. **9** Steve Davis. **10** Graeme Hick. **11** Sullivan. **12** Tottenham Hotspur. **13** 20th. **14** Nevada. **15** Five. **16** Pavlova. **17** Volga. **18** Asparagus. **19** Clint Eastwood. **20** Mack Sennett. **21** Michael Henchard. **22** The alphabet. **23** Queen Mother's 90th birthday. **24** Montreux. **25** Rhodes. **26** Pickwick Papers. **27** Ferrari. **28** Lily. **29** Tea. **30** 1960s.

Quiz 20 Pot Luck 10

Answers - see Quiz 19, page 241

1 What is the highest point of the Pennines?
2 What F1 team was James Hunt in when he won the World Championship?
3 How many years was Nelson Mandela held in prison?
4 Which British boxer was the first to win three Lonsdale belts outright?
5 Who, according to a NOP survey in 1998, do young men call most on their mobile phones?
6 In which London park is Rotten Row?
7 Who said, "Scared of Tyson? I'm more scared of your hair-do"?
8 What will a green phone kiosk only take for payment?
9 Which snooker star was nicknamed 'Interesting' by Spitting Image?
10 In 1988 who scored 405 not out at Taunton?
11 Who died first Gilbert or Sullivan?
12 Which was the first London football club to win a European title?
13 In which century did Joan of Arc become a saint?
14 Which American state is called the 'Gambling State'?
15 Did John Glenn's first spaceflight last five, ten or 24 hours?
16 Which dessert is named after a famous ballerina?
17 Which river flows from northern Moscow to the Caspian Sea?
18 A Bruxelloise sauce is flavoured with which vegetable?
19 Who was the leading actor in Play Misty for Me with Jessica Walker?
20 Who created the Keystone Kops?
21 Who was the Mayor of Casterbridge in the Thomas Hardy novel?
22 What does an alphabetarian study?
23 What occasioned the replacement of the Royal Variety Performance in 1990 with a concert?
24 In which Swiss resort are the Golden Rose TV accolades awarded?
25 Which island is the largest of the Dodecanese group?
26 In which Papers would you find Count Smorltork?
27 Which F1 team scored a 1-2 at Monza during the 1998 Italian GP?
28 To which flower family does garlic belong?
29 Which drink can be green, black and oolong?
30 In which decade was the first American Superbowl?

Answers

Leisure: Books 1 (see Quiz 19, page 241)
1 Armageddon. **2** David Copperfield. **3** Poems. **4** £20,000. **5** Room at the Top.
6 Dictionary. **7** Man. **8** Crime fiction. **9** Sherlock Holmes. **10** Koran.
11 Frankenstein. **12** Diary. **13** Germaine Greer. **14** Hampshire. **15** Roy Hattersley.
16 Buckett. **17** Dick Francis. **18** Stephen King. **19** Bill Clinton. **20** Karl Marx.
21 Five. **22** Jeffrey Archer. **23** Rumpole. **24** Barbara Taylor Bradford.
25 Barbara Cartland. **26** Charles de Gaulle. **27** The Satanic Verses.
28 Mandy Smith. **29** 70. **30** Nigeria.

Quiz 21 Food & Drink

Answers - see Quiz 22, page 244

1 What colour is the flesh of a cantaloupe melon?
2 Simnel cake was traditionally eaten on which Sunday?
3 What is the fishy ingredient in Scotch woodcock?
4 What is a champignon?
5 Which spirit is Russia famous for producing?
6 Which drink did Paul Hogan advertise?
7 What is added to pasta to make it green?
8 Which drink is grown in the Douro basin and exported from Oporto?
9 Which cooking pot cooks food at a higher temperature than boiling point?
10 What is another name for dietary fibre?
11 Which sauce/salad shares its name with Latin big band music?
12 Where did satsumas originate?
13 What are cornichons?
14 Puerto Rico and Jamaica are the main producers of which spirit?
15 What colour is cayenne pepper?
16 What type of pastry is used to make a steak and kidney pudding?
17 Which drink is served in a schooner?
18 What is a Laxton's Superb?
19 Which seafood, usually fried in breadcrumbs, is the Italian name for shrimps?
20 Tofu and TVP come from which bean?
21 Tartrazine colours food which colour?
22 What is added to whisky to make a whisky mac?
23 Where would you buy a pint of Shires?
24 What colour is Double Gloucester cheese?
25 Which Mexican drink is distilled from the agave plant?
26 Which black, gourmet fungus is a native of France's Perigord region?
27 Which expensive vinegar is aged in wooden barrels?
28 Which grain is whisky made from?
29 What is red wine made with that white wine is not?
30 Vermouth is wine flavoured with what?

Answers

TV: Children's TV (see Quiz 22, page 244)

1 Sesame Street. **2** Keith Chegwin. **3** Play School. **4** Jamie Theakston. **5** Lulu. **6** Doctor. **7** Live & Kicking. **8** Johnny Ball (Zoe). **9** Grange Hill. **10** Janet Street-Porter. **11** Dr Who. **12** The Top Ten of Everything. **13** Blue & white stripes. **14** Basil Brush. **15** Richard Briers . **16** Flag. **17** Home Hill. **18** Ed Stewart. **19** Fred Flintstone. **20** Neil Buchanan. **21** Tony Hart. **22** Fred Dineage. **23** Playdays. **24** He-Man. **25** Blue. **26** Poddington Peas. **27** Greendale. **28** Snake. **29** Rainbow. **30** David Jason.

Quiz 22 TV: Children's TV

Answers - see Quiz 21, page 243

1 On which show did The Muppets first regularly appear?
2 Which star of Swop Shop and Saturday Superstore went to the same university as Bill Clinton?
3 In which show was Humpty a regular feature?
4 Who presented Live and Kicking with Zoe Ball?
5 What was the name of elephant who disgraced herself on Blue Peter?
6 What is the profession of Newsround's David Bull?
7 Rugrats appears within which other programme?
8 Which former Play School presenter has a famous DJ daughter?
9 Tucker's Luck was a spin off from which drama series?
10 Who was executive director of 'yoof TV's' Def II?
11 Which sci fi series hit the screens at teatime the day after Kennedy was assassinated?
12 Which best selling book by Russell Ash was turned into a TV show?
13 What colour was Andy Pandy's suit?
14 Which puppet fox had the catchphrase "Boom boom"?
15 Which Good Life star narrated Roobarb and Custard?
16 Other than a TV show what is a Blue Peter?
17 Where do The Teletubbies live?
18 Which ex Crackerjack presenter went on to present a daily show on Radio 2?
19 Whose catchphrase is "Yabba dabba doo!"?
20 Which Neil has presented Art Attack?
21 Which TV artist designed the Blue Peter logo?
22 Who has presented How and How 2?
23 Which show has a Poppy Stop?
24 Which hero did Prince Adam turn into with the aid of power from Greyskull castle?
25 What colour are Smurfs?
26 In which show would you see Zip-Pea?
27 Where is the Rev Timms' parish in Postman Pat?
28 What sort of creature is Sooty's friend Ramsbottom?
29 Rod, Jane and Freddy was a spin off from which children's series?
30 Who was the voice of Dangermouse?

Answers

Food & Drink (see Quiz 21, page 243)

1 Orange. **2** Mothering Sunday. **3** Anchovies. **4** Mushroom. **5** Vodka. **6** Foster's lager. **7** Spinach. **8** Port. **9** Pressure cooker. **10** Roughage. **11** Salsa. **12** Japan. **13** Gherkins (pickled cucumbers). **14** Rum. **15** Red. **16** Suet pastry. **17** Sherry. **18** Apple. **19** Scampi. **20** Soya . **21** Yellow. **22** Ginger wine. **23** Ambridge. **24** Orange-red. **25** Tequila. **26** Truffle. **27** Balsamic. **28** Malted barley. **29** Skins of the grape. **30** Bitter herbs.

Quiz 23 Pot Luck 11

Answers - see Quiz 24, page 246

1 Who supposedly brought about the downfall of Barings Bank?
2 Which country was the first to legalise abortion?
3 Which Eurovision winning group formed the Polar Music Company?
4 In 1954, which Chris won the first BBC Sports Personality of the Year?
5 Mount Elbert is the highest peak in which American mountain range?
6 Adam and Eve were the main characters in which work by John Milton?
7 In 1992, London and which other English city were home to over a million people?
8 Whose murder conviction was overturned after 45 years in 1998?
9 Which famous riding school is in Austria?
10 What colour traditionally is an Indian wedding sari?
11 Which county first won the Benson and Hedges Cricket Cup twice?
12 Which Copenhagen statue is a memorial to Hans Christian Andersen?
13 Which Derbyshire town is famous for the church with a crooked spire?
14 The Parthenon in Athens was built as a temple to whom?
15 Martin Fry and Mark White were members of which 1980s band?
16 Which glands produce white blood cells?
17 What sort of creature is a guillemot?
18 What was the first film Bogart and Bacall starred in together?
19 Which Norfolk model advertises L'Oreal Elvive hair products?
20 Which girl's name gave the Damned their only top ten hit?
21 Which chess piece can only move diagonally?
22 Which gentle water creature gives its name to a Florida river?
23 William 'Fatty' Foulkes played which sport?
24 Which oil company was founded by John D Rockefeller?
25 At which Southwark inn did Chaucer's Canterbury Pilgrims meet?
26 Joseph Marie Jacquard is most remembered for which invention?
27 Before Winston Churchill went bald, what colour was his hair?
28 The word micro is what fraction in the metric system?
29 Which county included W. G. Grace as a team member?
30 Which musical instrument was first developed by Bartolomeo Cristofori?

Answers

Law & Order (see Quiz 24, page 246)
1 Haiti. **2** Bluebeard. **3** 20th (1941). **4** Ruth Ellis. **5** Dr Crippen. **6** Philip Lawrence. **7** Official Secrets Act. **8** Lester Piggott. **9** Slavery. **10** Director of Public Prosecutions. **11** Cape Town. **12** St Valentine's Day. **13** Nick Leeson. **14** Michael Howard. **15** Iceland. **16** Back To Basics. **17** Treason. **18** Colditz. **19** Ethiopia didn't have electricity. **20** Cromwell Street. **21** Richard I. **22** Jack Straw. **23** Louise Woodward. **24** Road rage attack. **25** Robert Maxwell. **26** Peter Sutcliffe. **27** The Butcher of Lyon. **28** The Ritz. **29** Saudi Arabia. **30** The Clintons.

Quiz 24 Law & Order

Answers - see Quiz 23, page 245

LEVEL 2 

1 Which country had the private security force the Tontons Macoutes?
2 What was the nickname of mass murderer Gilles de Rais who killed six of his seven wives?
3 In which century was the last execution at the Tower of London?
4 Which woman was hanged in 1955 for murdering David Blakely?
5 Cora was the wife of which doctor who murdered her?
6 In the 90s which London head teacher was killed outside his school?
7 Which Act bans the disclosure of confidential items from government sources by its employees?
8 Which world famous jockey was jailed in 1987 for tax evasion?
9 What did abolitionism seek to abolish?
10 What is the DPP, a post created in 1985?
11 Robben Island was a prison near which city?
12 Which Day saw seven of Bugs Moran's gang murdered by members of Al Capone's, disguised as policemen?
13 Whose crime was recounted in the film Rogue Trader?
14 Which ex Home Secretary spent a night behind bars in October '98?
15 The Althing is the parliament of which country?
16 Which phrase used by John Major in 1993 was used as a slogan to return to traditional British values?
17 In 1965 capital punishment was abolished except for which crime?
18 How was the prison camp Oflag IVC near Leipzig better known?
19 In what way was Ethiopian Emperor Menelik III thwarted in bringing the electric chair to his country?
20 What was the Gloucester street where Rose & Frederick West lived?
21 Robin Hood is said to have lived in Sherwood Forest during the reign of which king?
22 Which Home Secretary took his son to the police after allegations of drug selling?
23 Which British nanny's US trial was televised after a baby died in her care?
24 Why was the death of Stephen Cameron in 1996 a tragic first?
25 Who fell from the Lady Ghislaine leaving debts behind him?
26 What is the real name of the criminal dubbed The Yorkshire Ripper?
27 What was the nickname of Nazi war criminal Klaus Barbie?
28 Jonathan Aitken's court case centred on a stay in which Paris hotel?
29 Where had Deborah Parry been imprisoned before her return in '98?
30 In the US whose involvement in the Whitewater affair had lengthy repercussions?

Answers

Pot Luck 11 (see Quiz 23, page 245)
1 Nick Leeson. **2** Iceland. **3** Abba. **4** Chris Chataway. **5** The Rockies. **6** Paradise Lost. **7** Birmingham. **8** Derek Bentley. **9** The Spanish Riding School. **10** Scarlet. **11** Leicestershire. **12** The Little Mermaid. **13** Chesterfield. **14** Athena. **15** ABC. **16** Lymph glands. **17** Bird. **18** To Have and Have Not. **19** Kate Moss. **20** Eloise. **21** The Bishop. **22** The Manatee. **23** Football. **24** Standard Oil. **25** The Tabard Inn. **26** The Jacquard loom. **27** Red. **28** A millionth. **29** Gloucestershire. **30** The piano.

Quiz 25 Pot Luck 12

Answers - see Quiz 26, page 248

1 What nationality was the spy Mata Hari?
2 The Dickens' work Edwin Drood is different for what reason?
3 Which Australian soap star had the biggest selling UK single in 1988?
4 What were the Boston Tea Party protesters against?
5 What is a Wessex Saddleback?
6 Which former Olympian advertised Ribena?
7 Lyncanthropy involves men changing into what?
8 Which city's American football team is known as the Vikings?
9 Queen Wilhelmina who died in 1962 was Queen of which country?
10 The pop band America were formed in which country?
11 In curling how many shots at the target is each player allowed?
12 What was Janet Street-Porter's beastly last name before marriage?
13 Which Band Aid No 1 hit was written by Midge Ure and Bob Geldof?
14 What was the capital of West Germany?
15 Which American symbol was famously painted by Jasper Johns?
16 In fencing how many hits must a male fencer score for a win?
17 In gin rummy how many cards are dealt per player?
18 What nationality was the inventor of the Geiger counter?
19 Before it moved to Wales on which London hill was the Royal Mint?
20 In which century was the first circumnavigation of the earth?
21 Which is further south, Cardiff or Oxford?
22 Which river rises in the Black Forest?
23 Which road vehicle takes its name from the Hindu God Jagganath?
24 In which South American country is the condor sacred?
25 The first modern Olympics were held in which city?
26 Which East Anglian Cathedral spire is second highest in the country?
27 What have you on your mouth if you suffer from herpes labialis?
28 Prince Edward resigned from which part of the military in 1987?
29 Mike Burden is the sidekick to which TV detective?
30 What was Fred Wedlock according to the title of his one off hit?

Answers

Communications (see Quiz 26, page 248)

1 Stansted. **2** Leeds. **3** Philips. **4** Decibel. **5** British Airways. **6** Telephone handset. **7** Trans Siberian. **8** Paris. **9** 999 service. **10** Nothing. **11** £500. **12** Acoustics. **13** The Speaking Clock. **14** Swiftair. **15** Video Cassette Recorder. **16** USA. **17** FBI's. **18** Derbyshire. **19** A12. **20** ADA. **21** Dundee. **22** Grand Canal. **23** Alaska. **24** A. **25** M62. **26** Some insects. **27** 8. **28** Moscow. **29** Madam Mayor. **30** Channel Tunnel.

Quiz 26 Communications

Answers - see Quiz 25, page 247

1 What is Britain's third largest airport?
2 Which northern city has the dialling code 0113?
3 Which company launched the CD-i in 1992?
4 dB is the symbol for what?
5 Which major company owns the budget airline Go?
6 An acoustic coupler allows computer data to be transmitted through what?
7 Which railway links European Russia with the Pacific?
8 Which city linked up with London by phone in 1891?
9 Which vital communications linked began in July 1937?
10 How much is the maximum charge for postage in Andorra?
11 What is the maximum compensation offered by Royal Mail on their Registered service?
12 What is the science of sound and its transmission called?
13 What is another name for Timeline?
14 What is the Royal Mail's express airmail service called?
15 What is a VCR?
16 Which country has the most telephone subscribers?
17 On whose website did Leslie Ibsen Rogge appear, leading to his arrest?
18 In which county is East Midlands airport?
19 Which A road links London with East Anglia?
20 Which computer language was named after Ada Augusta Byron?
21 Which is the nearest city to the Tay road bridge?
22 Which waterway does Venice's Rialto bridge span?
23 Which state is the northern terminus of the Pan American highway?
24 In France all motorways begin with which letter?
25 Which motorway links Hull and Leeds?
26 Which living creatures can you send through the post?
27 How many bits are there in a byte?
28 In which city is the TASS news agency based?
29 How would you verbally address a Mayor who is a woman?
30 Which tunnel goes from Cheriton to Sargette?

Answers

Pot Luck 12 (see Quiz 25, page 247)
1 Dutch. **2** It is not finished. **3** Kylie Minogue. **4** Tea taxes. **5** Pig.
6 Sharron Davies. **7** Wolves. **8** Minnesota. **9** Holland. **10** England. **11** 2.
12 Bull. **13** Do They Know it's Christmas? **14** Bonn. **15** The stars & stripes.
16 Five. **17** 10. **18** German. **19** Tower Hill. **20** 16th. **21** Cardiff. **22** Danube.
23 Juggernaut. **24** Peru. **25** Athens. **26** Norwich. **27** Cold Sores. **28** The Marines.
29 Reg Wexford. **30** The Oldest Swinger in Town.

Quiz 27 Pot Luck 13

Answers - see Quiz 28, page 250

1 Who had a No 1 UK hit with The Reflex?
2 In English what is the only anagram of the word ENGLISH?
3 Which rules are American football played to?
4 In which South African city was the 1995 Rugby Union World Cup Final?
5 Which musical was based on the play Pygmalion?
6 If you suffer from bulimia, what do you have a compulsive urge to do?
7 Who is Boo-Boo's best friend?
8 Which triangular shaped Indian pastry contains meat or vegetables?
9 Which part of Spain is named after its many castles?
10 The range of the pH scale is zero to what?
11 Which everyday objects can be decorated with the King's Pattern?
12 Stage performer Boy Bruce the Mighty Atom became known as who?
13 Which Russian word means "speaking aloud"?
14 Which Top Ten "ride" was taken by the group Roxette?
15 What is the name of the world's largest Gulf?
16 Which actor played Selwyn Froggatt on TV?
17 Ouzo is what flavour?
18 What does a trishaw driver do with his legs?
19 Which hospital did TV Doctor Kildare work at?
20 Which is the slowest swimming stroke?
21 What is the best selling single of all time?
22 What does E stand for in "E-numbers"?
23 In Peter Pan which part of Peter was kept in a drawer?
24 What word links an ice cream holder and a brass instrument?
25 The thistle is the heraldic emblem of which country?
26 What is the middle name of Princess Margaret?
27 What is the epicarp of an orange?
28 Which character was played by Ken Kercheval in Dallas?
29 Which three Time Travel films were directed by Robert Zemeckis?
30 Which European country has the only active volcanoes in Europe?

Answers

Pop Music: The 70s (see Quiz 28, page 250)
1 Love Me For A Reason. **2** Pigeon. **3** Cher . **4** Eddie Holman. **5** Dawn. **6** The Pina Colada Song. **7** Heart. **8** Squeeze. **9** January. **10** The Kinks. **11** 10538. **12** Matthews Southern Comfort. **13** Girls. **14** On My Radio. **15** The Floral Dance. **16** Minnie Riperton. **17** Sweet Sensation. **18** Paul Simon. **19** Nathan Jones. **20** B A Robertson. **21** Rainbow. **22** New York. **23** Samantha. **24** Summer Nights. **25** The Commodores. **26** Rivers of Babylon. **27** Midnight. **28** In The Summertime. **29** Donna Summer. **30** Eye Level.

Quiz 28 Pop Music: The 70s

Answers - see Quiz 27, page 249

1 Which 70s hit by the Osmonds gave Boyzone a hit in '94?
2 Which Lieutenant's only UK No 1 hit was Mouldy Old Dough ?
3 Who sang that she was 'born in the wagon of a travelling show'?
4 (Hey There) Lonely Girl was the only UK hit for which vocalist?
5 Tony Orlando sang in which group that had a girl's name?
6 Rupert Holmes' 1980 No 23 hit Escape is also known as what?
7 Which part of the body was mentioned in the title of a Blondie hit?
8 Who were Up The Junction in 1979?
9 Which month links Pilot and part of a song title for Barbara Dickson?
10 Whose hits from 1970 include Victoria and Apeman?
11 What was the number of ELO's Overture in their first hit?
12 The No 1 UK hit Woodstock was a one hit wonder for which group?
13 What Talk gave Dave Edmunds his 1979 No 4 UK hit?
14 What in 1979 was the only Top Ten hit by the group Selector?
15 What links Terry Wogan and the Brighouse and Rastrick Brass Band?
16 Loving You was a high pitched No 2 UK hit for which female singer?
17 Which group had a No 1 UK hit with Sad Sweet Dreamer?
18 Who wanted to be taken to the Mardi Gras?
19 Which 1971 Supremes hit was later a hit for Bananarama?
20 Who had hits with Bang Bang and Knocked It Off in 1979?
21 The 1979 No 6 hit Since You've Been Gone was a hit for who?
22 Which US city was named twice in a Gerard Kenny hit from 1978?
23 Who did Cliff Richard say Hello to when he said Goodbye to Sam?
24 In which song do the chorus beg, "Tell me more, tell me more!"?
25 Which group had hits in the 70s with Easy, Still and Sail On?
26 What was on the other side of Boney M's Brown Girl In The Ring?
27 What time was Gladys Knight's train leaving for Georgia?
28 Which Mungo Jerry hit was used in an anti drink-drive campaign?
29 Which disco style singer had the word Love in the title of four of her first five Top Ten hits?
30 Which No 1 from 1972 was the theme for the Van Der Valk series?

Answers

Pot Luck 13 (see Quiz 27 page 249)
1 Duran Duran. **2** Shingle. **3** The Harvard rules. **4** Johannesburg. **5** My Fair Lady. **6** Eat. **7** Yogi Bear. **8** Samosa. **9** Castile. **10** Fourteen. **11** Cutlery. **12** Bruce Forsyth. **13** Glasnost. **14** Joyride. **15** Gulf of Mexico. **16** Bill Maynard. **17** Aniseed. **18** Pedal. **19** Blair Hospital. **20** Breast stroke. **21** Candle In the Wind (1997). **22** European. **23** His shadow. **24** Cornet. **25** Scotland. **26** Rose. **27** The peel. **28** Cliff Barnes. **29** Back to the Future. **30** Italy.

Quiz 29 Pot Luck 14

Answers - see Quiz 30, page 252

1 If a bridge player has a Yarborough, what is the top scoring card?
2 In the film Batman Forever, which actor played Batman?
3 In the Grand National, how many times did Red Rum run?
4 Which was the first railway terminus in London?
5 Which term is used when a mortgage is more than the value of a house?
6 Whose hits include Slave to Love and This is Tomorrow?
7 What is a Clouded Yellow?
8 How was Agatha Miller better known?
9 El Paso is in which American state?
10 Which road leads from Westminster to Blackfriars along the north bank of the Thames?
11 The first player to score 100 Premier League goals played for which club?
12 In which board game is FIDE the governing body?
13 Which colour links an imperial butterfly and a medal?
14 In which year did TV soap EastEnders first appear?
15 What is the Mirror of Diana, located in Northern Italy?
16 Beta Vulgaris is the Latin name for which crop?
17 Which film featured the Joe Cocker hit Up Where We Belong?
18 Who wrote the opera from which Here Comes the Bride is taken?
19 Lime Street Station is in which English city?
20 Cars with the international vehicle registration IS come from where?
21 Which magazine, established in 1922, claims to be the most widely read in the world?
22 What happened to Ken Barlow's second wife in Coronation Street?
23 What type of fruit is a Laxton Superb?
24 Which airport is near to the English city of Carlisle?
25 A sericulturist breeds which creatures?
26 Who played the young Emma Harte in A Woman of Substance?
27 What term describes the fineness of yarns?
28 Where do mice live who are proverbially poor?
29 Joseph Grimaldi achieved everlasting fame as what?
30 Who made history in 1982 by going to an Anglican service in Canterbury Cathedral?

Answers

World Football (see Quiz 30, page 252)
1 Japan. **2** Lazio. **3** Ruud Gullit. **4** Gary Lineker. **5** Australia. **6** Croatia. **7** Barcelona. **8** Prague. **9** Tenerife. **10** Mario Zagallo. **11** Benfica. **12** Germany. **13** Davor Suker. **14** Argentina. **15** Roger Milla. **16** Uruguay. **17** Gerard Houllier. **18** Edson Arrentes do Nascimento. **19** Italy. **20** Brazil. **21** Emmanuel Petit. **22** Ronaldo's. **23** Raddy Antic. **24** Dennis Bergkamp. **25** Matthias Sammer. **26** St Denis. **27** Dunga. **28** Stanley Matthews. **29** FC Copenhagen. **30** Alexi Lalas.

Quiz 30 World Football

Answers - see Quiz 29, page 251

1 In which country is the club Grampus Eight?
2 Which Italian team did Gazza play for?
3 Who was Dutch captain when they won the European Championship in 1988?
4 Who was leading scorer in the 1986 World Cup finals?
5 Which international side did Venables manage after England?
6 Who won the third place final in the 1998 World Cup?
7 Which side did Cruyff move to from Ajax in 1973?
8 Dukla and Sparta are from which European city?
9 Where did Emerson go when he left Middlesbrough?
10 Which Brazilian football coach was sacked after France '98?
11 Which Portuguese side did Graeme Souness manage?
12 Which country ran a full page 'thank you' ad in The Times after Euro 96?
13 Who won the Golden Boot in the 1998 World Cup?
14 Cesar Menotti managed which victorious World Cup side?
15 Who is the oldest player ever to score in the World Cup finals?
16 Penarol is a club side in which country?
17 Which Frenchman moved to Liverpool when Ronnie Moran retired?
18 What is Pele's full name?
19 Who, with England and Holland, was eliminated from France 98 on penalties?
20 In which country is the world's largest football stadium?
21 Who scored the last goal in France 98?
22 Whose much seen girlfriend in France 98 was Suzana Werner?
23 Which Yugoslavian international midfielder played for Luton Town?
24 Which overseas star won most Premiership player of the month awards in 1997-98?
25 Which German won European Player of the Year in 1996?
26 In which stadium was the opening match of France 98?
27 Who captained Brazil in the 98 World Cup Finals?
28 Who was the first European Footballer of the Year?
29 Which club did Brian Laudrup transfer to in November 1998?
30 Which US star of the 94 World Cup became the first American player to take part in Italy's Serie A?

Answers

Pot Luck 14 (see Quiz 29, page 251)

1 Nine. **2** Val Kilmer. **3** Five. **4** Euston Station. **5** Negative equity. **6** Bryan Ferry's. **7** A Butterfly. **8** Agatha Christie. **9** Texas. **10** The Embankment. **11** Blackburn (Alan Shearer). **12** Chess. **13** Purple. **14** 1985. **15** A lake. **16** Sugar beet. **17** An Officer and a Gentleman. **18** Wagner. **19** Liverpool. **20** Iceland. **21** Reader's Digest. **22** She committed suicide. **23** An apple. **24** Crosby. **25** Silkworms. **26** Jenny Seagrove. **27** Denier. **28** Church. **29** A clown. **30** The Pope.

Quiz 31 Pot Luck 15

Answers - see Quiz 32, page 254

1 In which UK city was the de Lorean sports car factory set up in '78?
2 The TV show It'll Be Alright on the Night is presented by whom?
3 Which group had a No 1 UK hit in 1992 with Ebenezer Goode?
4 In which sport were Jack Broughton and James Figg champions?
5 Which Aldous Huxley novel is set in the seventh century AF?
6 Which instrument was Jose Feliciano famous for playing?
7 Which Queen was played in films by Jean Simmons and Bette Davis?
8 Which actor links Chancer, Chariots of Fire and The Whistle Blower?
9 Which musical instruments represent Peter in Peter and the Wolf?
10 Which WPC was shot and murdered at the Libyan Embassy?
11 A glaive was what kind of weapon?
12 In which century was the first Indianapolis 500 first held?
13 In which country do soldiers wear skirts called fustanella?
14 What can be done if an object is scissile?
15 Which film studios were founded by Harry, Sam, Albert and Jack?
16 Which word can describe a listening device, an illness and an insect?
17 Which famous actress starred in Courage of Lassie and Lassie Come Home?
18 Who was older when they died, Benny Hill or Richard Burton?
19 Who did Mark Hughes join when he left Man Utd for a second time?
20 What type of fruit is a jargonelle?
21 Which part of the head is studied by a phrenologist?
22 Whose ancestral home is Woburn Abbey?
23 Who wrote the poem Four Quartets?
24 Which children's game is played on the fingers with looped string?
25 Jane Harris and Nel Mangel appeared in which soap?
26 Brassica Rapa is the Latin name for which vegetable?
27 Which band's hits include Infinite Dreams and Holy Smoke?
28 Which Generation Game assistant was born on the same day as Julian Lloyd Webber?
29 Excess bile pigment in the bloodstream causes which illness?
30 Who was Dennis Bergkamp named after?

Answers

Movie Blockbusters (see Quiz 32, page 254)

1 Five. **2** Chocolate. **3** The Robe **4** Francis Ford Coppola. **5** Normandy. **6** M*A*S*H. **7** Hearst. **8** Crocodile Dundee. **9** Gary Oldman. **10** Midnight Cowboy. **11** Dan Aykroyd. **12** The English Patient. **13** Vito Corleone. **14** Pierce Brosnan. **15** Ron Kovic. **16** Gone With the Wind. **17** Wall Street. **18** Braveheart. **19** Dune. **20** John Huston. **21** Terminator II. **22** Austrian. **23** All About Eve. **24** 1930s. **25** Goldblum. **26** Jim Carrey. **27** Carrie Fisher. **28** Celine Dion. **29** Judi Dench. **30** Cop.

Quiz 32 Movie Blockbusters

Answers - see Quiz 31, page 253

LEVEL 2

1. How many crew members were there in the Nostromo in Alien?
2. What type of sauce was used in the shower scene in Psycho?
3. Which 1953 film was the first made in Cinemascope?
4. Who directed The Godfather and all its sequels?
5. Saving Private Ryan dealt with events in which part of France?
6. Which antiwar comedy did Robert Altman direct?
7. Which newspaper magnate was said to be the model for Orson Welles' Citizen Kane?
8. Which 80s film was the most profitable in Australian history?
9. Who played The Count in Bram Stoker's Dracula?
10. What was John Schlesinger's first US film, made in 1969 with Dustin Hoffman and Jon Voight?
11. Who starred in, and co wrote Ghostbusters?
12. Which 1990s film starred Juliette Binoche and Kristin Scott Thomas?
13. What was the name of Marlon Brando's character in The Godfather?
14. Which James Bond actor starred in Dante's Peak?
15. What was the name of Tom Cruise's character in Born on the Fourth of July?
16. In which classic did Olivia de Havilland play Melanie Wilkes?
17. In which film did Michael Douglas say "Greed is good"?
18. What was Mel Gibson's first film as actor, director and producer?
19. Which David Lynch space epic was based on the work of Frank Herbert?
20. Who was directing The African Queen when his daughter Anjelica was born?
21. Which sequel had the subtitle Judgement Day?
22. What is Schindler's nationality in Schindler's List?
23. What was the last film before Titanic to win 14 Oscar nominations?
24. In which decade was Gone With the Wind made?
25. Which Jeff was the mathematician in Jurassic Park?
26. Who became a human cartoon in The Mask?
27. Who played Princess Leia in the Star Wars Trilogy?
28. Who sang the theme song for Titanic?
29. Who was M in Tomorrow Never Dies?
30. What was Michael Douglas' profession in Basic Instinct?

Answers

Pot Luck 15 (see Quiz 31, page 253)

1 Belfast. **2** Denis Norden. **3** The Shamen. **4** Boxing. **5** Brave New World. **6** Guitar. **7** Elizabeth I. **8** Nigel Havers. **9** Violins. **10** Yvonne Fletcher. **11** A sword. **12** 20th. **13** Greece. **14** It can be cut. **15** Warner Brothers. **16** A bug. **17** Elizabeth Taylor. **18** Richard Burton. **19** Chelsea. **20** A pear. **21** The skull. **22** Dukes of Bedford. **23** T.S. Eliot. **24** Cat's Cradle. **25** Neighbours. **26** Turnip. **27** Iron Maiden. **28** Anthea Redfern. **29** Jaundice. **30** Denis Law.

Quiz 33 TV: Cops & Robbers

Answers - see Quiz 34, page 256

1 Which TV cop was christened Ilynea Lydia Mironoff?
2 In the title of the program, what shows Life on the Streets?
3 Which show features DCI Michael Jardine?
4 What was Paul Nicholls' first major series after leaving EastEnders?
5 Who was Don Johnson's character in Miami Vice?
6 What was the name of law enforcer Michael Knight's computer buddy?
7 Which show consists of films of dangerous driving shot by traffic police?
8 Which series featured the Wentworth Detention Centre?
9 Who played the TV Avengers role played by Uma Thurman on the big screen?
10 Which member of the Ruth Rendell Mysteries cast also scripted some of the shows?
11 In which series did the character Charlie Barlow first find fame?
12 Which Blue Peter presenter played Dangerfield's son in the police surgeon series?
13 In which 90s series did Neil Pearson star as Det Sup Tony Clark?
14 In which police station was Frank Farillo the chief?
15 What was Fitz's full name in Cracker?
16 Peter Falk played which offbeat TV cop?
17 Which real crime series was based on the German File XY Unsolved?
18 In which series did Rowan Atkinson appear as a police officer?
19 Who was the British half of Dempsey and Makepeace?
20 Which long-running show increased the length of episodes in 1998 to one hour in a bid to improve ratings?
21 Stacey Keach played which detective from Mickey Spillane's novels?
22 The Body in the Library was the first in an 80s series about which sleuth?
23 Which series began with an Armchair Theatre production Regan?
24 Loretta Swit from M*A*S*H was replaced by Sharon Gless in which US series?
25 Who played barrister Kavanagh in the TV series?
26 Which detective was based at Denton police station?
27 How long did the Morse episodes usually last?
28 In which series did Samantha Janus star as Isobel de Pauli?
29 In which series did Charlie Hungerford appear?
30 Which series was based on the Constable novels by Nicholas Rea?

Answers

Pot Luck 16 (see Quiz 34, page 256)
1 Hamlet. **2** Liverpool. **3** Take That. **4** Surrey. **5** Elizabeth I. **6** Argentinean. **7** Tutti Frutti. **8** A boat. **9** Rockall. **10** Portillo. **11** Fox. **12** Rudyard Kipling. **13** Van Gogh. **14** Trams. **15** George I. **16** Johnny Dankworth. **17** Chaka Khan. **18** Martyn Lewis. **19** Stirling Moss. **20** Michel Platini. **21** Scurvy. **22** Household linen. **23** Glucose. **24** Sheridan. **25** Cinzano. **26** Best Supporting Actress. **27** July, August. **28** Fairy tales. **29** Epiglottis. **30** Much.

Quiz 34 Pot Luck 16

Answers - see Quiz 33, page 255

1 In which Shakespeare play does a ghost walk on the battlements?
2 Which city did comedian Tommy Handley come from?
3 Which group had No 1 hits with Babe and Pray in 1993?
4 Charterhouse Public School is found in which county?
5 Miranda Richardson played who in the second Blackadder series?
6 What nationality is Javier Frana, the tennis player?
7 Which 1987 TV series featured the ageing rock band The Majestics?
8 What is a gallivat?
9 Which British island is 230 miles west of the Hebrides in the Atlantic?
10 Which Michael lost his Enfield seat in the 1997 general election?
11 A skulk is the collective name for a group of which animal?
12 Who wrote How the Leopard Got His Spots?
13 Who painted the picture called Irises?
14 On which forms of transport would you find knifeboards?
15 Handel's Water Music was composed for which English King?
16 Who is Cleo Laine's bandleader husband?
17 Who had UK hits with Ain't Nobody and I'm Every Woman?
18 Which BBC newsreader advertised Cow & Gate baby food as a child?
19 Which racing driver appeared in the film Casino Royale?
20 From 1983-85 which Frenchman was European Footballer of the Year?
21 What disease are you suffering if you are scorbutic?
22 If you bought something in a white sale, what would you be buying?
23 What is the other name for grape-sugar?
24 Who wrote the play The School for Scandal?
25 Which drink was advertised by Joan Collins and Leonard Rossiter?
26 The film The Piano received Oscars for Best Actress and Best what?
27 In a single calendar year which two consecutive months total most days?
28 What did Charles Perrault collect?
29 Which flap of cartilage prevents food from entering your windpipe?
30 Which member of Robin Hood's gang was the son of a miller?

Answers

TV: Cops & Robbers (see Quiz 33, page 255)
1 Helen Mirren. **2** Homicide. **3** Taggart. **4** City Central. **5** Sonny Crockett. **6** KITT. **7** Police, Camera, Action!. **8** Prisoner Cell Block H. **9** Diana Rigg. **10** George Baker. **11** Z Cars. **12** Tim Vincent. **13** Between the Lines. **14** Hill St. **15** Eddie Fitzgerald. **16** Columbo. **17** Crimewatch UK. **18** The Thin Blue Line. **19** Makepeace. **20** The Bill. **21** Mike Hammer. **22** Miss Marple. **23** The Sweeney. **24** Cagney & Lacey. **25** John Thaw. **26** Jack Frost. **27** Two hours. **28** Liverpool One. **29** Bergerac. **30** Heartbeat.

Quiz 35 Euro Tour

Answers - see Quiz 36, page 258

1 What are the three Baltic states?
2 In which country does the Douro reach the Atlantic?
3 What is the capital of Catalonia?
4 What is Northern Ireland's chief non edible agricultural product?
5 What do the Germans call Bavaria?
6 Which European capital stands on the river Liffey?
7 What is the Eiffel Tower made from?
8 How is the Danish region of Jylland known in English?
9 In which forest does the Danube rise?
10 Which was the first country to legalise voluntary euthanasia?
11 What covers most of Finland?
12 In which country is the world's highest dam?
13 What is the capital of the Ukraine?
14 What is a remarkable feature of the caves at Lascaux in SW France?
15 What is Europe's highest capital city?
16 Where is France's Tomb of the Unknown Soldier?
17 Which area of the Rhone delta is famous for its nature reserve?
18 In which country would you find Kerkyra?
19 What are the two official European languages of Luxembourg?
20 The Magyars are the largest ethnic group of which country?
21 Where is Castilian an official language?
22 Abruzzi is a mountainous region of which country?
23 Which is the largest of the Balearic Islands?
24 On which island was the Mafia founded?
25 What is the UK's chief Atlantic port?
26 Tallinn is the capital of which Baltic state?
27 What is the main religion of Albania?
28 In which country would you meet Walloons?
29 What is the official residence of the French President?
30 Where in Britain is Europe's second tallest building?

Answers

Pot Luck 17 (see Quiz 36, page 258)
1 Matt Frewer. **2** Culture Club. **3** Keith. **4** High Chapparal. **5** Midsummer Day. **6** Ronnie Biggs. **7** Elvis Presley. **8** Mary Quant. **9** Ice skating. **10** Henry Crabbe. **11** Hedges and shrubs. **12** Michael Caine. **13** Saint Swithin. **14** C & F. **15** A vaulting horse. **16** Cricket. **17** A fox. **18** A tub of lard. **19** Isle of Man. **20** Correct English. **21** 1,440. **22** Dr Hook. **23** A duck. **24** Hurdles. **25** Idaho. **26** The Winchester. **27** Brunel. **28** Griffith. **29** Spiders. **30** Paul Young.

Quiz 36 Pot Luck 17

Answers - see Quiz 35, page 257

1 Which actor played the TV android Max Headroom?
2 Whose hits include Victims and Church of the Poison Mind?
3 What is Rupert Murdoch's first name?
4 Which ranch was owned by John Cannon?
5 In a calendar year what is the second quarter day in England?
6 Which robber on the run was in the film The Great Rock and Roll Swindle?
7 Who was older when they died John Lennon or Elvis Presley?
8 Which fashion designer opened a shop in 1957 called Bazaar?
9 In which sport would you find a movement called a Salchow?
10 What is the name of the detective in Pie In The Sky?
11 What material does a topiarist work with?
12 Which actor was Rita's tutor in the film Educating Rita?
13 Which Saint has 15th July as his Feast Day?
14 Which two musical notes do not have flats on black keys?
15 In The Wooden Horse what was used to disguise the digging of an escape tunnel?
16 Sabina Park is most famous for which sport?
17 Which animal can be described as vulpine?
18 In Have I Got News for You what stood in for Roy Hattersley ?
19 Where are Union Mills and Onchan Head in the British Isles?
20 Author H.W. Fowler produced a book in 1926 as a guide to what?
21 How many minutes are there in a day?
22 Who had a hit on the telephone in 1972 with Sylvia's Mother?
23 What was Howard in the film Howard - A New Kind of Hero?
24 What can be 84cm, 91cm or 106cm in height in sport ?
25 The towns of Anaconda and Moscow are in which US State?
26 In the TV series Minder which club was owned by Dave?
27 The university sited in Uxbridge is named after which engineer?
28 Which Melanie has been the partner of Antonio Banderas?
29 Which creatures mainly belong to the arachnidae family?
30 Who had hits with Senza Una Donna and Come Back and Stay?

Answers

Euro Tour (see Quiz 35, page 257)
1 Estonia, Latvia and Lithuania. **2** Portugal. **3** Barcelona. **4** Flax. **5** Bayern. **6** Dublin. **7** Iron. **8** Jutland. **9** Black Forest. **10** Netherlands. **11** Trees. **12** Switzerland. **13** Kiev. **14** Cave paintings. **15** Madrid. **16** Under L'Arc de Triomphe. **17** Camargue. **18** Greece. **19** French & German. **20** Hungary. **21** Spain. **22** Italy. **23** Majorca. **24** Sicily. **25** Liverpool. **26** Estonia. **27** Muslim. **28** Belgium. **29** Elysee Palace. **30** Canary Wharf.

Quiz 37 Hobbies & Leisure 1

Answers - see Quiz 38, page 260

1 The Sealed Knot Society re-enacts what?
2 Which racecourse has a famous Royal Enclosure?
3 What is the Quorn in Leicestershire?
4 What colour are hotels in Monopoly?
5 Where is the National Motor Museum?
6 What is the maximum number of pieces on a chessboard at any one time?
7 What was the yachting trophy the America's Cup named after?
8 In which month do the French celebrate Bastille Day?
9 If you played outdoor hockey in the US what would it be called?
10 In which musical is the song Summertime?
11 Where in London did Laura Ashley open her first shop?
12 What is the world's biggest selling copyrighted game?
13 Which organisation is the largest private landowner in Britain?
14 How high is a netball post?
15 If you have a credit card what is an APR?
16 Where did karaoke singing originate?
17 Who opened a bistro called Le Petit Blanc in 1984?
18 Who replaced Melvyn Bragg on Radio 4's Start the Week?
19 Where was the first Virgin record shop?
20 During which months was the museum to Diana, Princess of Wales open at Althorp in 1998?
21 What might a numismatist collect along with coins?
22 Which day at Royal Ascot is Ladies' Day?
23 Who founded a theme park called Dollywood?
24 Bronco busting and steer wrestling take place at what type of event?
25 Which form of tennis is played on a smaller court usually by children?
26 In which US state did skateboarding begin as an alternative to surfing?
27 How many pins must be knocked down in skittles?
28 Which game is played at Hurlingham?
29 In slalom skiing what must you turn between?
30 What would be your hobby if you used slip?

Answers

Pot Luck 18 (see Quiz 38, page 260)
1 A bear. **2** Graham Hill. **3** The Booker Prize. **4** Reet Petite. **5** A fish. **6** Kelsey Grammer. **7** Spring. **8** Roots Hall. **9** Both beheaded. **10** Rattlesnakes. **11** Larry Grayson. **12** The Comet. **13** Saxophone. **14** Iron Maiden. **15** Eliza Doolittle. **16** Land. **17** A farrow. **18** Abel Magwitch. **19** Michael Crichton. **20** 32. **21** Regent's Park. **22** Turn at different speeds. **23** Gross Domestic Product. **24** Africa. **25** Friday. **26** Manitoba. **27** A bat. **28** Stevie Wonder. **29** Antwerp. **30** Lady Day.

Quiz 38 Pot Luck 18

Answers - see Quiz 37, page 259

1 Which animal can be described as ursine?
2 Who was older when they died Graham Hill or James Hunt?
3 Which prize for fiction was instigated in 1969?
4 Which Jackie Wilson hit was No 1 nearly thirty years after it was made?
5 A tarpon is a type of what?
6 Who played Frasier Crane in Frasier and Cheers?
7 If something is vernal, what is it connected with?
8 Where do Southend United football club play their home games?
9 How did both James I's mother and son die?
10 The sidewinder belongs to which group of snakes?
11 Who in 1987 presented the TV show Sweethearts?
12 Which was the first commercial jet aircraft in the world?
13 Jazz musician John Coltrane played which instrument?
14 Who had UK hits with Run to the Hills and The Evil That Men Do?
15 Which part was played by Audrey Hepburn in the film My Fair Lady?
16 Wapentakes, hundreds and hides were all areas of what?
17 What is the collective name for a litter of piglets?
18 Who gave Pip his wealth in Great Expectations?
19 Who wrote the novel Jurassic Park?
20 How many squares have pieces on them at the start of a chess game?
21 In which London park are The Holme, The Broad Walk and Winfield House?
22 What does the differential on a car allow the driving wheels to do?
23 The abbreviation GDP stands for what?
24 The Gulf of Sidra is located off the coast of which continent?
25 Which day of the week is named after the Norse Goddess Freya?
26 Winnipeg is the capital of which Canadian province?
27 What type of creature is a flying fox?
28 Whose hits include I Wish, Lately and Do I Do?
29 Where in Belgium were the 1920 Olympics held?
30 In a calendar year what is the first quarter day in England?

Answers

Hobbies & Leisure 1 (see Quiz 37, page 259)
1 Battles of the English Civil War. **2** Ascot. **3** Hunt. **4** Red. **5** Beaulieu. **6** 32. **7** Schooner America. **8** July. **9** Field hockey. **10** Porgy & Bess. **11** Kensington. **12** Monopoly. **13** National Trust. **14** 10 feet (3.05m). **15** Annual Percentage Rate. **16** Japan. **17** Raymond Blanc. **18** Jeremy Paxman. **19** Oxford Street. **20** July and August. **21** Medals. **22** Second day. **23** Dolly Parton. **24** Rodeo. **25** Short tennis. **26** California. **27** Nine. **28** Polo. **29** Flags. **30** Pottery.

Quiz 39 People & Places

Answers - see Quiz 40, page 262

1 Which US President's father was a former Ambassador in the UK?
2 Edith Cresson was which country's PM from 1991-1992?
3 The Downing Street Declaration in 1993 involved the Prime Ministers of which two countries?
4 Which family died at Ekaterinburg in 1918?
5 Which school provided the UK with 19 Prime Ministers before 2000?
6 In which war did British soldiers first wear balaclava helmets?
7 Which mountaineer was the first person since Scott to reach the South Pole overland, in 1958?
8 The 'Bomb Plot' of 1944 failed to assassinate whom?
9 What was the minimum age for joining the UK Home Guard in WWII?
10 Which former US President was a distant relative of Princess Diana?
11 Who was the first woman President of Ireland?
12 In which US state did Martin Luther King lead the 1955 bus boycott?
13 Who lost power in Germany in 1998 after 16 years?
14 Who became Secretary General of the UN in 1997?
15 Who was Bonnie Prince Charlie disguised as when he escaped to France with Flora MacDonald?
16 Who defected to the USSR with Guy Burgess in 1951?
17 Carlos Menem became President of which country in 1989?
18 Who was the first Governor General of India, until 1948?
19 What was the alliance between the Germans and the Italians in World War II called?
20 Where in the East End of London did Jack the Ripper operate?
21 As a double agent, Mata Hari was executed by whom?
22 Mrs Meir was the first woman PM in which country?
23 Who was the USA's first Roman Catholic President?
24 Aung San Suu Kyi is an opposition leader in which country?
25 Which Panamanian leader was nicknamed Pineapple Face?
26 Which Pass did Hannibal use to cross the Alps?
27 Who became President of Ireland in 1997?
28 In which Vietnamese village were 109 civilians massacred by US troops in 1968?
29 Who was the first woman US Secretary of State?
30 Where did Tung Chee-Hwa become chief executive in July 1997?

Answers

Pot Luck 19 (see Quiz 40, page 262)
1 One square mile. **2** Slaves. **3** Stocks & share prices. **4** Fleet Air Arm. **5** Father of the House. **6** 70. **7** Park Lane. **8** Moses. **9** Cunard. **10** Corgi. **11** Kent and Sussex. **12** Red. **13** RAF. **14** Director of Public Prosecutions. **15** 48. **16** Ageism. **17** Antarctica. **18** Railway carriage. **19** High blood pressure. **20** Wheel clamp. **21** Vice Squad. **22** When ill. **23** The soul. **24** Smith Square. **25** A cough. **26** Westminster Cathedral. **27** Orange. **28** Siouxsie and the Banshees. **29** Single parent families. **30** A Stateless Person.

Quiz 40 Pot Luck 19

Answers - see Quiz 39, page 261

1 What is the area of the City of London?
2 What is the last word of Rule Britannia?
3 What does the Footsie show?
4 Which branch of the Royal Navy is concerned with aviation?
5 What name is given to the MP who has served in the House of Commons the longest?
6 A driving licence is issued until the driver reaches what age?
7 In which Lane is London's Dorchester Hotel?
8 In The Old Testament Aaron was the elder brother of which prophet?
9 Which shipping company operated the Queen Mary and the Queen Elizabeth?
10 Which dog's name comes from the Welsh for dwarf dog?
11 In which two English counties are the Cinque Ports?
12 What colour coats do Chelsea Pensioners wear in the summer?
13 Cranwell trains cadets for which of the armed forces?
14 Who is the DPP?
15 How many kilometres per hour is 30 miles an hour?
16 What is discrimination against the elderly called?
17 In 1991 a 50 year mining ban was agreed for which area of the world?
18 In what type of vehicle was the 1918 World War armistice signed?
19 What is another name for hypertension?
20 What is another name for a Denver boot?
21 Which police department deals with illegal gambling and pornography?
22 When might an employee receive SSP?
23 In religious terms what does absolution purify?
24 In which London square is the HQ of the Tory party?
25 Which condition will an antitussive help alleviate?
26 What is the principal Roman Catholic church in England?
27 What colour is a disabled driver's badge?
28 Who had hits with Dear Prudence and Hong Kong Gardens?
29 Which families does Gingerbread help?
30 In law, what is a citizen of no particular nation called?

Answers

People & Places (see Quiz 39, page 261)
1 Kennedy. **2** France. **3** UK & Ireland. **4** The Romanovs. **5** Eton. **6** Crimean War. **7** Edmund Hillary. **8** Hitler. **9** 17. **10** Ronald Reagan. **11** Mary Robinson. **12** Alabama. **13** Helmut Kohl. **14** Kofi Annan. **15** Flora's maid. **16** Donald Maclean. **17** Argentina. **18** Lord Mountbatten. **19** Axis. **20** Whitechapel. **21** The French. **22** Israel. **23** John F Kennedy. **24** Myanmar. **25** Noriega. **26** Little St Bernard. **27** Mary McAleese. **28** My Lai. **29** Madeleine Albright. **30** Hong Kong.

Quiz 41 Pop Music: The 80s

Answers - see Quiz 42, page 264

1 Which hit was No 2 for Rick Astley and No 4 for Nat King Cole in '87?
2 What was the first Top Ten hit for Tanita Tikaram?
3 What were 'shattered' in the 1987 No 5 hit for Johnny Hates Jazz?
4 Who joined Kenny Rogers on We've Got Tonight?
5 Which Jimmy Nail hit was a cover of a Rose Royce hit?
6 New Edition got to No 1 in '83 with which Girl?
7 Who were spun around by their No 1 You Spin Me Round (like a record)?
8 Which group had top ten hits with Breakout and Surrender?
9 Whose first UK No 1 hit West End Girls?
10 What was KC and the Sunshine Band's only UK No 1 in the 80s?
11 Which twins had hits with Love On Your Side and Doctor Doctor?
12 Which town got The Specials to No 1 in 1981?
13 What followed Ooh La La La in the 1982 hit for Kool and the Gang?
14 The name of which Asian country gave Kim Wilde an 80s hit?
15 What followed the title of Soul II Soul's first UK No 1 Back To Life?
16 Where did Lipps Inc. take us to in their No 2 from 1980?
17 Which antipodean title was a No 1 for Men at Work in 1983?
18 The song Intuition was the only UK Top Ten single for which duo?
19 Mental As Anything had a No 3 with Live It Up from which film?
20 Who joined Julio Inglesias on his No 5 success My Love ?
21 Which animal was sleeping on the No 1 hit by Tight Fit?
22 Which '87 Billy Idol hit was a cover of an earlier Tommy James hit?
23 What was Simply Red's first Top Ten UK hit?
24 Which Del Shannon hit became an 80s hit for Icehouse?
25 Which Dutch female group had hits with History and Body and Soul?
26 What in 1986 was Spandau Ballet's last UK Top Ten hit?
27 Who joined Fun Boy Three on It Ain't What You Do in 1982?
28 Which day links a No 2 by the Bangles with a No 3 by New Order?
29 Who gave Karel Fialka his only Top Ten success in 1987?
30 Whose first Top Ten hit was Harvest For The World in 1988?

Answers

Pot Luck 20 (see Quiz 42, page 264)
1 Whiskey. **2** Hull. **3** The Pope. **4** Tuberculosis. **5** On the bridge. **6** Alexander Pope. **7** The Man From UNCLE. **8** Fennel. **9** Deep Purple. **10** Monkey bread. **11** A prison. **12** Kate Moss. **13** Carmichael. **14** Harold Wilson. **15** Lassie. **16** French. **17** Trees. **18** The Sex Pistols. **19** Gardner. **20** In water. **21** A dog. **22** Harry. **23** Denmark and Norway. **24** Grace Kelly. **25** Animals. **26** Edinburgh. **27** Ecuador. **28** George Gershwin. **29** Conciliation. **30** Que Sera Sera.

Quiz 42 Pot Luck 20

Answers - see Quiz 41, page 263

1 Which drink did American Indians call Firewater in the Wild West ?
2 In which city are the Ferens Art Gallery and Town Docks Museum?
3 Who sends encyclical letters?
4 The White Death was a name for which former common disease?
5 According to the song, where does everyone dance in Avignon?
6 Who wrote, "To err is human, to forgive, divine"?
7 In which TV series were the agents given orders by Mr Waverly?
8 Which leaves taste of aniseed?
9 Which group had a top ten hit with Black Knight?
10 What is the fruit of a baobab tree called?
11 What was a bridewell?
12 Which model's childhood nickname was 'Mosschops'?
13 Which actor Ian played the leading role in the film Private's Progress?
14 "A week is a long time in politics," was said by which politician?
15 Which animal movie star was nicknamed Greer Garson in furs?
16 What is the official language of the Ivory Coast?
17 What are pruned in coppicing?
18 Which group featured in The Great Rock 'n Roll Swindle?
19 Which Ava was one of Frank Sinatra's wives?
20 If a plant is a hydrophyte where does it live?
21 A papillon is a type of what?
22 What was Bing Crosby's first name?
23 Which two countries are separated by the Skagerrak?
24 Which royal film star appeared in Dial M for Murder?
25 What does the Blue Cross Charity, founded in 1897, provide aid to?
26 In which Scottish city are Salisbury Crags?
27 Which South American country has the sucre as the unit of currency?
28 Who composed the music for the musical Strike Up The Band?
29 What does the C stand for in ACAS?
30 Which song was sung in three different films by Doris Day?

Answers

Pop Music: The 80s (see Quiz 41, page 263)
1 When I Fall In Love. **2** Good Tradition. **3** Dreams. **4** Sheena Easton. **5** Love Don't Live Here Anymore. **6** Candy Girl. **7** Dead Or Alive. **8** Swing Out Sister. **9** Pet Shop Boys. **10** Give It Up. **11** Thompson Twins. **12** Ghost Town. **13** Let's Go Dancin'. **14** Cambodia. **15** However Do You Want Me. **16** Funky Town. **17** Down Under. **18** Linx. **19** Crocodile Dundee. **20** Stevie Wonder. **21** Lion. **22** Mony Mony. **23** Holding Back the Years. **24** Hey Little Girl. **25** Mai Tai. **26** Through the Barricades. **27** Bananarama. **28** Monday. **29** Matthew. **30** Christians.

Quiz 43 Sport: Horse Racing

Answers - see Quiz 44, page 266

1 Which American was UK champion jockey in 1984, 1985 and 1987?
2 In which month does the Cheltenham Festival take place?
3 Which two races make up the autumn double?
4 How long is the Derby?
5 How many times did Willie Carson win the Derby?
6 Which Cabinet Minister has been the Glasgow Herald's racing tipster?
7 Who had nine Derby wins and was champion jockey 11 times?
8 Which British racehorse owner sold Vernons Pools in 1988?
9 Who was Champion Jockey a record 26 times between 1925 and 1953?
10 Which John and Peter were joint Champion Jockeys in 1982?
11 Which Classic was the first to be run on a Sunday in England?
12 In 1995 which horse won the Derby, the King George VI and the Prix de l'Arc de Triomphe?
13 Alex Greaves was the first female jockey in which race?
14 Where is Valentine's Brook?
15 At which racecourse is the Steward's Cup competed for annually?
16 Who was riding Devon Loch when it so nearly won the National?
17 What is Frankie Dettori's real first name?
18 Which Monkee was an apprentice jockey?
19 Which horse won the Cheltenham Gold Cup in 1964, '65 and '66?
20 Who was the UK's first overseas champion jockey after Steve Cauthen?
21 Where is Tattenham Corner?
22 What is the highest jump in the Grand National?
23 Where did Walter Swinburn sustain severe injuries in February 1997?
24 Who won the Grand National in 1993?
25 Which auctioneers were founded in London in 1766 but now have annual sales in Newmarket?
26 Which racecourse is near Bognor Regis?
27 What was unusual about the status of Mr Frisk's winning rider in the 1990 National?
28 How old are horses who run in nursery stakes?
29 In which month is Royal Ascot?
30 Whose total of 1,374 winners was a world record after the 1990-91 season?

Answers

TV: Sitcoms (see Quiz 44, page 266)
1 Dermot. **2** Gareth Blackstock. **3** Only Fools and Horses. **4** Drop The Dead Donkey. **5** Richard Wilson. **6** Jean Alexander. **7** Seinfeld. **8** Phoebe. **9** Till Death Us Do Part. **10** Fawlty Towers. **11** Porridge. **12** Annie. **13** Cockerel. **14** Thelma. **15** Napoleon. **16** Bubble. **17** After Henry. **18** Are You Being Served?. **19** Gary Sparrow. **20** As Time Goes By. **21** Barker. **22** Arnold Rimmer. **23** They were witches. **24** Baldrick. **25** Allo Allo. **26** Green. **27** Christopher Biggins. **28** Geraldine Grainger. **29** Bottom. **30** Gordon.

Quiz 44 TV: Sitcoms

Answers - see Quiz 43, page 265

1 What was the name of Harry Enfield's character in Men Behaving Badly?
2 What was the name of the Chef in Chef!?
3 What was the most successful sitcom of the 80s?
4 Which series took place at the Globelink News Office?
5 Which sit com star worked in a hospital laboratory before becoming an actor?
6 Which former soap star plays Auntie Wainwright in Last of the Summer Wine?
7 Which US sitcom, which had 180 episodes, finished in May 1998?
8 Who was the 40s publican's daughter in Goodnight Sweetheart?
9 All in the Family was a US spin off from which UK sitcom?
10 Where would you find guests Major Gowen, Miss Tibbs and Miss Gatsby?
11 Going Straight was the sequel to what?
12 What was the name of Jim Hacker's wife in Yes Minister?
13 In The Good Life, who or what was Lenin?
14 In The Likely Lads, who did Bob marry?
15 In Dad's Army what did the air raid warden always call Mainwaring?
16 Who was Edina's PA in Absolutely Fabulous?
17 Which series with Prunella Scales as Sarah France had three years on radio before transferring to TV?
18 Grace and Favour was a sequel to which sitcom?
19 What is the name of the time traveller in Goodnight Sweetheart?
20 Which show's theme song begins, "You must remember this..."?
21 Which Ronnie's famous roles have included Arkwright and Fletcher?
22 Which obnoxious character did Chris Barrie play in Red Dwarf?
23 What was strange about Samantha Stephens and her mother Endora?
24 Who was Blackadder's servant?
25 Which sitcom was a send up of Secret Army?
26 What was Dorien's surname in Birds of a Feather?
27 Who was the effeminate Lukewarm in Porridge?
28 What was the Vicar of Dibley's name?
29 In which series did Richie and Eddie first appear?
30 What was Brittas's first name in The Brittas Empire?

Answers

Sport: Horse Racing (see Quiz 43, page 265)
1 Steve Cauthen. **2** March. **3** Cesarewitch and the Cambridgeshire. **4** A mile and a half. **5** Four. **6** Robin Cook. **7** Lester Piggott. **8** Robert Sangster. **9** Gordon Richards. **10** Scudamore & Francome. **11** 1,000 Guineas. **12** Lammtarra. **13** The Derby. **14** Aintree. **15** Goodwood. **16** Dick Francis. **17** Lanfranco. **18** Davy Jones. **19** Arkle. **20** Frankie Dettori. **21** Epsom. **22** The Chair. **23** Hong Kong. **24** No one, it was abandoned. **25** Tattersall's. **26** Fontwell Park. **27** Amateur. **28** Two. **29** June. **30** Peter Scudamore.

Quiz 45 Pot Luck 21

Answers - see Quiz 46, page 268

1 If you nictitate at someone, what do you do?
2 Who offered Demi Moore a million dollars in Indecent Proposal?
3 Monument Valley is in which American state?
4 Which island off the north Devon coast is named after the Norse for puffin?
5 Who had a Top Ten hit in the 80s with Sledgehammer?
6 On 14th April 1912, what occurred off Newfoundland?
7 Who was Des Lynam's co-presenter on the first series of How Do They Do That?
8 Which instrument was played by David in The Bible?
9 Who is taller Madonna or Dawn French?
10 Which organisation was founded in 1953 by Reverend Chad Varah?
11 In corned beef what are the corns?
12 Which people used knotted cords called quipu for calculation?
13 Which character was played by Maggie Smith in Sister Act?
14 Who wrote the novel Journey to the Centre of the Earth?
15 At which school was Thomas Arnold a famous headmaster?
16 What was a Mae West to an airman?
17 How many squadrons make up a wing in the Royal Air Force?
18 Who followed U Thant as Secretary General of the United Nations?
19 Which high street chain was founded in 1961 by Selim Zilkha?
20 What does the book Glass's Guide contain?
21 Who had a big hit with Sowing the Seeds of Love?
22 Actor Bruce Willis played which character in Moonlighting?
23 What is an aspen?
24 The Battle of Pinkie of 1547 was fought in which country?
25 What nationality was Amy Johnson?
26 Which animal has the longest pregnancy?
27 Anything above scale 12 on the Beaufort Scale would describe what?
28 Which group were made up of Cass, Michelle, John and Denny?
29 Cars with the international vehicle registration PA come from where?
30 Who did Shylock want to take his pound of flesh from?

Answers

Musical Movies (see Quiz 46, page 268)
1 Abba: The Movie. **2** Ursula Andress. **3** Cyd Charisse. **4** Maurice Chevalier. **5** The Philadelphia Story. **6** Martin Scorsese. **7** The Blackboard Jungle. **8** Whitney Houston. **9** Richard E Grant. **10** Master of ceremonies. **11** Antonio Banderas. **12** The Nightmate Before Christmas. **13** Rex Harrison. **14** Paris. **15** Marlon Brando. **16** Yul Brynner. **17** Baron Georg Von Trapp. **18** Freddie Eynsford-Hill. **19** Saturday Night Fever. **20** Autry. **21** 1950s. **22** Albert Finney. **23** South Pacific. **24** Chim Chim Cheree. **25** Help! **26** Fiddler on the Roof. **27** Jonathan Pryce. **28** Sammy Davis Jr. **29** Cabaret. **30** Monroe.

Quiz 46 Musical Movies

Answers - see Quiz 45, page 267

1 What was the name of the smash movie about 70s superband Abba?
2 Which Bond girl starred with Elvis Presley in Fun in Acapulco?
3 Who danced with Gene Kelly in the Broadway Ballet section of Singin' In the Rain?
4 Who sang Thank Heaven for Little Girls in Gigi?
5 High Society was a musical version of which classic?
6 Which controversial figure directed the musical New York, New York?
7 In which film did Bill Haley sing Rock Around the Clock?
8 Who sang most of the soundtrack of The Bodyguard?
9 Who had a managerial role in Spiceworld?
10 Joel Grey won an Oscar for which role in the 70s classic Cabaret?
11 Who played Che in the film version of Evita?
12 Which Tim Burton film featured a hostile takeover of present delivery at Christmas?
13 Who played the Doctor in the musical film version of Doctor Doolittle?
14 Where is Gigi set?
15 Which tough guy actor played Sky Masterson in Guys and Dolls?
16 Which star of The King and I was born in Russia?
17 Who does Julie Andrews marry in The Sound of Music?
18 Which character sings On the Street Where You Live in My Fair Lady?
19 Which 70s film became a stage musical in London in 1998?
20 Which Gene was the singing cowboy?
21 In which decade does the action of Grease take place?
22 Which English actor played the millionaire benefactor in Annie?
23 In which musical does Nurse Nellie Forbush appear?
24 Which of the many songs in Mary Poppins won the Oscar?
25 What was The Beatles' second film?
26 Which musical is the tale of a Jewish milkman in pre revolutionary Russia?
27 Who played Eva's husband in Evita?
28 Who led 'The Rhythm of Life' sequence in Sweet Charity?
29 Which 70s musical film was set in pre war Berlin?
30 Which Marilyn sang Diamonds are a Girl's Best Friend?

Answers

Pot Luck 21 (see Quiz 45, page 267)
1 Wink. **2** Robert Redford. **3** Arizona. **4** Lundy. **5** Peter Gabriel. **6** The Titanic sank. **7** Jennie Hull. **8** Harp. **9** Madonna. **10** Samaritans. **11** Salt. **12** The Incas. **13** Mother Superior. **14** Jules Verne. **15** Rugby School. **16** Lifejacket. **17** Three. **18** Kurt Waldheim. **19** Mothercare. **20** Vehicle prices. **21** Tears for Fears. **22** David Addison. **23** A tree. **24** Scotland. **25** British. **26** Elephant. **27** Hurricane. **28** The Mamas and Papas. **29** Panama. **30** Antonio.

Quiz 47 Pot Luck 22

Answers - see Quiz 48, page 270

1 What is a pickled gherkin made from?
2 Which cricketer is a team captain on TV's They Think It's All Over?
3 Who had hits with Ben and Take That Look Off Your Face?
4 Pooh Bah appears in which Gilbert and Sullivan operetta?
5 Which Classic race is run over the longest distance?
6 Who was the brother of Flopsy, Mopsy and Cottontail?
7 What form did the head of the Sphinx take?
8 Which voice in singing is pitched between a tenor and a soprano?
9 Which birds collect in a covey?
10 Who wrote The Phoenix and the Carpet?
11 Titian is what colour?
12 What part did Madonna play in the film Shanghai Surprise?
13 Which former England manager was born on the same day as Yoko Ono?
14 Which almost eradicated disease was called Phthisis?
15 The Moonstone by Wilkie Collins is about a jewel from which country?
16 In which country is Lake Bala the largest natural lake?
17 In which town were the Marsh Farm riots in July 1995?
18 The US state of Maryland was named after the wife of which King?
19 Who had hits with Be Bop A Lula and Pistol Packin' Mama?
20 Which tennis star was sued by Judy Nelson for palimony?
21 Who played Mark Antony opposite Liz Taylor in the film Cleopatra?
22 Who was Gloria Hunniford named after?
23 Which football manager once played in a band called Revelation Time?
24 What is the first name of P.D. James' detective Dalgleish?
25 Which part did Dustin Hoffman play in the film Hook?
26 What was the title of the 1994 East 17 Christmas No 1 UK hit?
27 Who was British PM directly before Edward Heath?
28 Which Open win was Nick Faldo's first?
29 What can be solo boxing, a lush mineral or a round timber?
30 Which part did Gene Hackman play in the Superman films?

Answers

Living World (see Quiz 48, page 270)

1 Tidal wave. **2** On the skin. **3** CJD. **4** Worm. **5** Haematology. **6** Hermaphrodite. **7** Falcon. **8** Ear. **9** Marine snail. **10** Knee. **11** Pigeons. **12** Anaemia. **13** Orange. **14** Fungus. **15** Skin. **16** Abdomen. **17** Shoulder blade. **18** Fish. **19** Short sighted. **20** 12. **21** Lungs. **22** Acne. **23** The kiss of life. **24** Tuberculosis. **25** Base of the brain. **26** Achilles tendon. **27** Liver. **28** Green. **29** Kidney. **30** Herring.

Quiz 48 Living World

Answers - see Quiz 47, page 269

1 Tsunami is another name for what type of wave?
2 Where would a melanoma appear?
3 Which disease in humans has been linked to the cattle disease BSE?
4 What sort of creature is a fluke?
5 Which branch of medicine is concerned with disorders of the blood?
6 What name is given to an organism which is both male and female?
7 What sort of bird is a Merlin?
8 Which part of the body might suffer from labyrinthitis?
9 What sort of creature is an abalone?
10 Where is a bird's patella?
11 Which racing creatures live in lofts?
12 What condition is caused by a shortage of haemoglobin?
13 What colour are the spots on a plaice?
14 What is a puffball?
15 Which part of the body does scabies affect?
16 Which digestive organ lies below the thorax in invertebrates?
17 Where is a human's scapula?
18 What do most sharks live on?
19 If a person has myopia what problem does he or she have?
20 How many pairs of ribs does a human have?
21 Pulmonary refers to which part of the body?
22 Which skin disorder is caused by inflammation of the sebaceous glands?
23 What is the popular name for mouth to mouth recussitation?
24 A BCG is a vaccination against which disease?
25 Where is the pituitary gland?
26 Which tendon pins the calf muscle to the heel bone?
27 Hepatic refers to which organ of the body?
28 What colour head does a male mallard usually have?
29 The adrenal gland is above which organ?
30 The pilchard is a member of which fish family?

Answers

Pot Luck 22 (see Quiz 47, page 269)

1 A cucumber. **2** David Gower. **3** Marti Webb. **4** The Mikado. **5** St Leger. **6** Peter (Rabbit). **7** A Human. **8** An Alto. **9** Partridges. **10** E. Nesbit. **11** Red. **12** A missionary. **13** Bobby Robson. **14** Tuberculosis. **15** India. **16** Wales. **17** Luton. **18** Charles I. **19** Gene Vincent. **20** Martina Navratilova. **21** Richard Burton. **22** Gloria Swanson. **23** Ruud Gullit. **24** Adam. **25** Captain Hook. **26** Stay Another Day. **27** Harold Wilson. **28** British. **29** Spar. **30** Lex Luthor.

Quiz 49 Pot Luck 23

Answers - see Quiz 50, page 272

1 Which Diane has been Sean Connery's wife?
2 The city of Philadelphia was founded by which religious group?
3 Where would you normally play shovel-board?
4 Which is further north Blackburn or Blackpool?
5 Whose hits include Gangsters and Too Much Too Young?
6 Which motor racing team is named after the sacred flower in India?
7 Donald McGill was particularly associated with what seaside art form?
8 Who wrote Willie Wonka and the Chocolate Factory?
9 Who narrates Treasure Island other than Jim Hawkins?
10 What is the New Zealand National Day called?
11 Paul Merson made his league debut with which club?
12 Which ship sent the first S.O.S?
13 What did the craft in the film Fantastic Voyage enter into?
14 In the Bond movie Goldeneye which Dame played M?
15 Which flower is on the badge of the Boy Scouts?
16 Which former Lebanese hostage wrote a book with Jill Morrell?
17 Maddy Magellan is the partner of which fictional detective?
18 Which Marlon Brando film is based on Conrad's Heart of Darkness?
19 In which group of islands is Panay?
20 HMS Ark Royal featured in which TV series?
21 The Sierra Nevada mountains are in which American state?
22 Who played Edward in TV's Edward and Mrs Simpson?
23 STASHING is an anagram of which famous battle?
24 Which pop star Linda took the lead in the film of Pirates of Penzance?
25 Whose hits include Kayleigh and Lavender?
26 Was the Sopwith Camel designed by Sopwith or Camel?
27 Which county did Godfrey Evans play cricket for?
28 Who wrote The Singing Detective?
29 Which word links a pastime, a small horse and a small falcon?
30 Which daily food includes the protein casein?

Answers

Famous Celebs (see Quiz 50, page 272)
1 Mohammed Al-Fayed. **2** Longleat. **3** Sarah. **4** Pamela Anderson. **5** Alan Clark. **6** Antonia de Sancha. **7** Edwina Currie. **8** Countess Spencer. **9** Holloway Prison. **10** Credit card fraud. **11** Texas. **12** Michael Heseltine. **13** Everton. **14** Jemima Khan. **15** Max Clifford. **16** Loos. **17** Sir Cameron Mackintosh. **18** Julia Carling. **19** David Bailey. **20** Elizabeth Hurley . **21** Diana, Princess of Wales. **22** Lord Snowdon. **23** Spencer. **24** Peter Stringfellow. **25** French. **26** Vivienne Westwood. **27** Chef. **28** Prince Andrew. **29** Tesco. **30** Rod Stewart.

Quiz 50 Famous Celebs

Answers - see Quiz 49, page 271

1 Who owns The Ritz in Paris?
2 Which stately home and safari park belongs to the Marquis of Bath?
3 What were two out of Andrew Lloyd-Webber's three wives called?
4 Who has Tommy Lee's name tattooed on her wedding finger?
5 Which Tory MP philanderer said "Only domestic servants apologise" after his Diaries were published?
6 The story of whose affair with David Mellor broke in 1992?
7 Which outspoken ex MP shares her birthday with Margaret Thatcher?
8 What was the previous title of Raine, Comtesse de Chambrun?
9 Where did Geri Halliwell have a meeting behind closed doors to launch 1998 Breast Cancer Awareness Week?
10 For what offence was Stephen Fry jailed, aged 17?
11 Jerry Hall is from which US state?
12 Whose heart attack in Venice prevented him from pursuing the Tory leadership?
13 Theatre impresario Bill Kenwright is a director of which soccer club?
14 Which late billionaire's daughter has a son called Sulaiman?
15 Which PR man acted for Mandy Allwood and Bienvenida Buck?
16 Lady Lucinda Lambton is an expert on which convenient necessity?
17 Which knighted impresario had a record six West End musicals running in 1996?
18 Which estranged wife made a spoof film clip of Diana watching open heart surgery?
19 Which photographer discovered Jean Shrimpton in the Sixties?
20 Who became the face of Estee Lauder in the mid 90s?
21 Who was Mrs Frances Shand Kydd's youngest daughter?
22 How was Anthony Armstrong-Jones known after his royal marriage?
23 Which future Earl did model Victoria Lockwood marry in 1990?
24 Which Sheffield born nightclub owner's most famous club is named after him?
25 What is the nationality of designer Catherine Walker?
26 Which outrageous designer was once the partner of Sex Pistols' manager Malcolm McLaren?
27 In which profession did Marco Pierre White find fame?
28 Whose name was linked with researcher Henrietta Peace's in '97?
29 Dame Shirley Porter is heiress to which supermarket chain?
30 Model Rachel Hunter married which rock star in 1990?

Answers

Pot Luck 23 (see Quiz 49, page 271)

1 Cilento. **2** The Quakers. **3** On a ship's deck. **4** Blackpool. **5** The Specials. **6** Lotus. **7** Postcards. **8** Roald Dahl. **9** Dr Livesey. **10** Waitangi Day. **11** Arsenal. **12** Titanic. **13** A Man's body. **14** Judi Dench. **15** Fleur de Lis. **16** John McCarthy. **17** Jonathan Creek. **18** Apocalypse Now. **19** Philippines. **20** Sailing. **21** California. **22** Edward Fox. **23** Hastings. **24** Ronstadt. **25** Marillion. **26** Sopwith. **27** Kent. **28** Dennis Potter. **29** A hobby. **30** Milk.

Quiz 51 Pot Luck 24

Answers - see Quiz 52, page 274

1 Which England player was likened to Mary Poppins by a director of his own club?
2 What would you do with a saxhorn?
3 Who was singer Lorna Luft's famous actress mother?
4 Who had hits with Living on the Ceiling and Blind Vision?
5 Who built the second block of nine cells at Wormwood Scrubs?
6 In Moonlighting which actress played Maddie Hayes?
7 Which is the largest and oldest Australian city?
8 Which sport says "Go out there and win one for the Gipper"?
9 How is the wife of a Knight addressed?
10 Light, Home and Third used to be what?
11 What name is given to a person who eats no food of animal origin?
12 Who wrote the song Moon River?
13 Who led the Scottish troops at Bannockburn?
14 Which Palace is the official home of the French president?
15 What is a water moccasin?
16 In which group of islands are St Martin's, St Mary's and Tresco?
17 Which people made an idol in the form of a Golden Calf in The Bible?
18 Which actor starred in the film North By Northwest?
19 Which city is called the City of Brotherly Love?
20 In which sport were John Louis and Barry Briggs associated?
21 Whose biography was called Neither Shaken Nor Stirred?
22 Which famous Falls are on the Zambezi river?
23 What kind of flower can be a goldilocks?
24 Which state was TV's Knots Landing set in?
25 If you are member of the Q Guild, what is your profession?
26 Which creature's name can go in front of crab, plant, wasp and monkey?
27 How many cards are in a tarot pack?
28 In Trading Places who traded places with Dan Aykroyd?
29 Diluted acetic acid is the correct name for which foodstuff?
30 Whose hits include The Bitch is Back and Kiss the Bride?

Answers

Leisure 2 (see Quiz 52, page 274)

1 Role Playing. **2** Boules. **3** May. **4** Scotland. **5** 22. **6** Sumo wrestling. **7** Lawn tennis. **8** Their hands. **9** Yin and Yang. **10** York. **11** Weightlifting. **12** Bonsai. **13** Plastic shuttlecocks. **14** Scotland. **15** Windsurfing. **16** Lego. **17** Horse racing, cards. **18** Michael Caine. **19** Phillip Schofield. **20** Three hours. **21** Fibreglass. **22** One. **23** AA. **24** China. **25** MCC. **26** Hamley's Regent Street, London. **27** In its ear. **28** Ever After. **29** Swimming. **30** Four.

Quiz 52 Leisure

Answers - see Quiz 51, page 273

1 What imaginative type of Game is known by the initials RPG?
2 Which French game's name is the French word for balls?
3 In which month is Spring Bank Holiday?
4 In World Cup Monopoly which team was the equivalent of Old Kent Road?
5 How many balls are needed to play a game of snooker?
6 What is the national sport of Japan?
7 What is lawn tennis called when played on shale or clay?
8 In volleyball what do players hit the ball with?
9 What is the Chinese for 'dark' and 'light' believed to maintain equilibrium?
10 Where is the Jorvik Viking Museum?
11 In which sport would you snatch and jerk?
12 The name of which type of tree cultivation comes from the Japanese for 'bowl cultivation'?
13 Which major change was introduced in badminton in 1949?
14 In which country is the oldest angling club in the world?
15 What is another name for boardsailing?
16 Which toy was invented by Danes Ole and Godtfred Christiansen?
17 If you were at or playing Newmarket which leisure pursuits would you be following?
18 Which cockney actor was a part owner of Langan's Brasserie?
19 Who played Dr Doolittle when it first appeared on the London stage?
20 Approximately how long does the journey from London to Paris take via Eurostar?
21 What are canoes made from?
22 If you received cotton, how many wedding anniversaries would you be celebrating?
23 Which UK motoring association describes itself as the fourth emergency service?
24 Which is the largest country where membership of the Scouts is not allowed?
25 Which club founded in 1787 voted to allow women members in 1998?
26 Where is the world's oldest toyshop?
27 Where does a Steiff teddy bear have its tag of authenticity?
28 What was the 1998 movie based on Cinderella, and starring Drew Barrymore called?
29 If you joined the Wasps in Wigan what sport would you compete in?
30 How many tournaments make up the Grand Slam in golf?

Answers

Pot Luck 24 (see Quiz 51, page 273)
1 Alan Shearer. **2** Play it. **3** Judy Garland. **4** Blancmange. **5** The convicts. **6** Cybill Shepherd. **7** Sydney. **8** American Football. **9** Lady. **10** Radio channels. **11** A vegan. **12** Henry Mancini. **13** Robert the Bruce. **14** Elysee. **15** Snake. **16** Scilly Isles. **17** The Israelites. **18** Cary Grant. **19** Philadelphia. **20** Speedway. **21** Sean Connery. **22** Victoria Falls. **23** A buttercup. **24** California. **25** A Butcher. **26** Spider. **27** 78. **28** Eddie Murphy. **29** Vinegar. **30** Elton John.

Quiz 53 Pot Luck 25

Answers - see Quiz 54, page 276

LEVEL 2 

1 Dame Anna Neagle played which part in the 1950 film Odette?
2 Dove Cottage was home of which poet?
3 Which Pole was first reached in 1909?
4 Which Day replaced Empire Day in 1958?
5 Alfred the Great ruled which Kingdom?
6 Estoril is a resort north east of which major city?
7 The Duke of Windsor was Governor of which island group in 1939?
8 Who was the founder lead singer with Led Zeppelin in 1968?
9 Freddie Powell found fame as which crazy comic?
10 Which British surgeon was a pioneer in improving surgery hygiene?
11 Who was the female lead in Singing in the Rain?
12 Which common garden flower has the name Dianthus barbatus?
13 Where were the Spode pottery works established in the 1760s?
14 Cars with the international vehicle registration BG come from where?
15 Which Club included Mr Winkle and Mr Tupman as members?
16 Never Say Die was the first Derby winner for which famous jockey?
17 Which steam locomotive record is held by The Mallard?
18 Which castle is the largest in Britain?
19 Edwin Hubble was concerned with which branch of science?
20 Which part did Albert Finney play in the 1974 film Murder on the Orient Express?
21 Sir Alfred Munnings is famous for painting which animals?
22 Comic character Dan Dare was known as the pilot of what?
23 Colonel Thomas Blood tried to steal what in 1671?
24 Which country is the major exporter of teak in the world?
25 What sort of creature was a brawn?
26 If you suffered a myocardial infraction, what would have happened?
27 Who partnered Annie Lennox in the Eurythmics?
28 The Peace River is in which country?
29 In 1957, in which US state were there race riots at Little Rock?
30 Which racing driver once played in a band called Sex Hitler and the Hormones?

Answers

Pop Music: The 90s (see Quiz 54, page 276)
1 I Believe. **2** Clannad. **3** Sting & Bryan Adams. **4** Saturday. **5** Gabrielle. **6** Boombastic. **7** Colchester. **8** Dunblane. **9** Without You. **10** Would I Lie To You. **11** Gina G. **12** The Bodyguard. **13** Shanice. **14** Fairground. **15** Boyz II Men. **16** Looking Up. **17** I Wonder Why. **18** Spice Girls. **19** Cecilia. **20** Peter Andre. **21** Too Young to Die. **22** Ebeneezer Goode. **23** The Simpsons. **24** Kylie Minogue. **25** Think Twice. **26** Shiny Happy People. **27** Doop. **28** Beverley Craven. **29** The Real Thing. **30** Lady Marmalade.

Quiz 54 Pop Music: The 90s

Answers - see Quiz 53, page 275

1 What was the other side of Robson and Jerome's Up On The Roof?
2 Which Irish band did a TV concert as a tribute to Brian Keenan in '91?
3 Which two singers joined Rod Stewart on the 1994 hit All For Love?
4 What night links Whigfield, Alexander O'Neal and Omar?
5 Who featured on East 17's No. 2 If You Ever in 1996?
6 Which 1995 hit gave Shaggy his second No 1?
7 Blur were formed in which East Anglian town?
8 Knockin' On Heaven's Door was covered following which tragedy?
9 Which song title links No 1s for Mariah Carey and Nilsson?
10 Which title links the Eurythmics to a 1992 No 1 for Charles and Eddy?
11 Which female sang the British Eurovision entry the year before Katrina and the Waves?
12 Which film featured the song that was Whitney Houston's fourth UK No 1?
13 I Love Your Smile was a hit in '92 for which US female artist?
14 What was Simply Red's first UK No 1 in 1995?
15 Who partnered Mariah Carey on One Sweet Day?
16 What was EastEnders' Michelle Gayle's first hit?
17 What was Curtis Stigers' first UK Top Ten success?
18 Which group held the Christmas single and album top spots in 1996?
19 Which female name was a No. 4 hit for Suggs in 1996?
20 Whose first two UK No 1s were Flava and I Feel You?
21 What was Jamiroquai's first UK Top Ten hit?
22 Which song title gave The Shamen their only No 1 in 1992?
23 Who were No.1 in 1991 with Do the Bartman?
24 Better the Devil You Know was a hit for Sonia and which soap star?
25 What was the first UK No 1 for Celine Dion?
26 What kind of people did R.E.M. take to No 6 in 1991?
27 What was the one hit wonder of the Dutch duo Doop?
28 Whose highest chart position was No 3 in 1991 with Promise Me?
29 Which Tony Di Bart No 1 hit from 1994 is the name of a group?
30 Which All Saints No 1 was a cover of a 70s hit for Labelle?

Answers

Pot Luck 25 (see Quiz 53, page 275)

1 Odette. **2** William Wordsworth. **3** North. **4** Commonwealth Day. **5** Wessex. **6** Lisbon. **7** Bahamas. **8** Robert Plant. **9** Freddie Starr. **10** Joseph Lister. **11** Debbie Reynolds. **12** Sweet William. **13** Stoke. **14** Bulgaria. **15** Pickwick Club. **16** Lester Piggott. **17** Speed record. **18** Windsor. **19** Astronomy. **20** Hercule Poirot. **21** Horses. **22** The Future. **23** Crown Jewels. **24** Myanmar (Burma). **25** A wild pig. **26** A heart attack. **27** Dave Stewart. **28** Canada. **29** Arkansas. **30** Damon Hill.

Quiz 55 TV: Soaps

Answers - see Quiz 56, page 278

1 Who in EastEnders had an affair with his mother in law?
2 What was Coronation Street originally going to be called?
3 What was the name of Joan Collins' character in Dynasty?
4 The Hart family appeared in which daily soap?
5 Which ex husband of Joan Collins appeared on EastEnders?
6 Who played mechanic Chris in Coronation Street and left to pursue a pop career?
7 Which Corrie star produced a fitness video called Rapid Results?
8 In Coronation Street, what is Spider's real name?
9 In which soap were Shane and Angel an item?
10 How did Kathy Glover's husband die in Emmerdale?
11 In Coronation Street what was Fiona's baby called?
12 Where did Kathy Mitchell go when she left Albert Square?
13 What form of transport did Cindy use to leave for France in EastEnders?
14 Who did Dannii Minogue play in Home & Away?
15 Which Kemp joined Ross Kemp on the EastEnders cast?
16 In Corrie which of the Battersby girls is Janice's daughter?
17 Which Kim disappeared from Emmerdale and was thought to have been murdered?
18 Which soap did Silent Witness star Amanda Burton appear in?
19 Which TV company first produced Emmerdale Farm?
20 Which role did Norman Bowler play in Emmerdale?
21 Who left Albert Square for America but returned as a director of the soap?
22 Which member of Emmerdale's Dingle family went on to present You've Been Framed?
23 Who was buried under the patio in Brookside?
24 Which TV comedian's daughter is in the radio soap The Archers?
25 Whose son in Corrie was once played by his real son Linus?
26 Where did Mavis go when she left The Street?
27 Which country group is made up of members of the Emmerdale cast?
28 Damon & Debbie was a short lived spin off from which soap?
29 Which star of The Good Sex Guide shared a cell with Deirdre in Coronation Street?
30 Which soap had a bar called the Waterhole?

Answers

Pot Luck 26 (see Quiz 56, page 278)
1 Quantum Leap. **2** Lucille. **3** Fencing. **4** John Fowles. **5** John Major. **6** Sam the piano player. **7** Noel Coward. **8** Tony Blair. **9** Simple Minds. **10** Dr Who. **11** Beatrix Potter. **12** 10,800. **13** Timmy. **14** Bricklaying. **15** I'm Into Something Good. **16** India. **17** Begging. **18** Agatha Christie. **19** Aberdeen. **20** Whitechapel. **21** Hitler. **22** Middlemarch. **23** Peak District. **24** Table Tennis. **25** Dog licence. **26** Vulture. **27** Australia. **28** Beverley Craven. **29** Ben Kingsley. **30** Ray Reardon.

Quiz 56 Pot Luck 26

Answers - see Quiz 55, page 277

1 In which TV series did Scott Bakula leap in time?
2 Which Kenny Rogers' hit starts, "On a bar in Toledo..."
3 In which sport is there a piste other than skiing?
4 Who wrote The French Lieutenant's Woman?
5 Which Chancellor of the Exchequer introduced TESSA?
6 Which character was played by Dooley Wilson in Casablanca?
7 Who wrote the play Private Lives?
8 Which politician once played in a band called Ugly Rumours?
9 Whose hits include Waterfront and Alive and Kicking?
10 Voords, Krotons and Autons have all appeared on which TV series?
11 Which children's writer's real name was Mrs Heelis?
12 How many seconds are there in three hours?
13 What was the dog called in the Famous Five books?
14 If you were using Dutch or Diaper Bonds what would you be doing?
15 What was Herman's Hermits only No 1 UK hit?
16 In which country was Salman Rushdie born?
17 What are you doing if you are mendicanting?
18 Who wrote the novel Murder in Mesopotamia in 1936?
19 Which team from outside Glasgow won the Scottish FA Cup three times from 1982-84?
20 In Monopoly, what is the next property after the Old Kent Road?
21 Whose mountain retreat was at Berchtesgaden?
22 Dorothea Brooke is the central character in which novel?
23 Which was the first British National Park?
24 Fred Perry was World Champion in 1929 in which sport?
25 Which licence was abolished in 1988 after 192 years?
26 The condor belongs to which family of birds?
27 In which country is Arnhem Land?
28 Whose hits include Promise Me and Woman to Woman?
29 Which actor was Gandhi in the 1982 film?
30 Who was first to win four World Snooker Championships in a row?

Answers

TV: Soaps (see Quiz 55, page 277)
1 Grant Mitchell. **2** Florizel Street. **3** Alexis Carrington. **4** Family Affairs. **5** Anthony Newley. **6** Matthew Marsden. **7** Beverley Callard. **8** Geoffrey. **9** Home and Away. **10** In a fire. **11** Morgan. **12** South Africa. **13** Eurostar. **14** Emma. **15** Martin. **16** Toyah. **17** Tate. **18** Brookside. **19** Yorkshire TV. **20** Frank Tate. **21** Susan Tully (Michelle Fowler). **22** Mandy. **23** Trevor Jordache. **24** Jasper Carrott. **25** William Roache's. **26** Lake District. **27** The Woolpackers. **28** Brookside. **29** Margi Clarke. **30** Neighbours.

Quiz 57 Sport: Hot Wheels

Answers - see Quiz 58, page 280

1 What does TT stand for in the Isle of Man races?
2 Who first had a record breaking car and a boat called Bluebird?
3 Which is the nearest motor racing track to Towcester?
4 Which team did Jim Clark spend all his racing career with?
5 How many people are in the car in drag racing?
6 Which Belgian cyclist was known as 'The Cannibal'?
7 How many times did Stirling Moss win the world championship?
8 In which country was the first organised car race?
9 Which Labour Party supporter is the head of Formula 1?
10 By 1993 which French driver had won 51 Grand Prix from 199 starts?
11 Which ex world champion was killed at the San Marino Grand Prix in 1993?
12 Which motor racing Park is east of Chester?
13 What type of racing is known in the US as Demolition Derbies?
14 How frequently does the Tour de France take place?
15 Who was the first man to be world champion on two and four wheels?
16 What relation was Emerson to Christian Fittipaldi?
17 Which Japanese team won its first F1 Grand prix in 1967?
18 Who was the first man to win a Grand Prix in a car he designed?
19 Who was Williams' highest placed driver in 1995?
20 In 1994 who was the first Austrian to win the German Grand Prix since Niki Lauda?
21 Which Briton was the first world driver's champion to win Le Mans, in 1972?
22 In which country did the first mountain bike world championship take place?
23 Which Briton did Alain Prost overtake for a record number of Grand Prix wins?
24 Which was the first manufacturer to have over 100 Grand Prix wins?
25 Which famous British car won the Monte Carlo rally in 1967?
26 Who was the first Briton to wear the Tour de France yellow jersey after Tommy Simpson?
27 Who was the first British F1 Champion after James Hunt?
28 Who was the first driver to be sacked by Benetton twice?
29 Who was the first Frenchman to win the World Grand Prix title in '85?
30 Where is the home of the French Grand Prix?

Answers

Pot Luck 27 (see Quiz 58, page 280)
1 Fred Perry. **2** Wizzard. **3** Karl Marx. **4** An insect. **5** Skull. **6** Woody Guthrie. **7** Winston Graham. **8** A clock. **9** Russia. **10** Belfast. **11** Bruce Lee. **12** Joy Adamson. **13** Flies. **14** First signatory. **15** Michaelmas Day. **16** A dress. **17** Volcanic eruption. **18** Oak. **19** Goldfinger. **20** Desert-dweller. **21** Remington. **22** Augustus. **23** Rod. **24** Bob Hoskins. **25** The haggis. **26** Jim Reeves. **27** Messengers. **28** Una Stubbs. **29** Tomato. **30** Neneh Cherry.

Quiz 58 Pot Luck 27

Answers - see Quiz 57, page 279

1 Which tennis player died on the same day as Donald Pleasence?
2 Whose hits include Ball Park Incident and Rock'n Roll Winter?
3 Who produced the Communist Manifesto with Friedrich Engels?
4 What is a firebrat?
5 Where are your fontanelles?
6 Which American protest singer is linked to the 'dustbowl ballads'?
7 Who wrote the stories subsequently televised as Poldark?
8 In which time device would you find an escapement?
9 The port of Archangel is in which country?
10 The Titanic was launched in which city?
11 Film star Lee Yuen Kam achieved fame as which kung fu expert?
12 Which famous woman who worked with African wildlife was murdered in 1985?
13 Which dirty insects are members of the Diptera family?
14 John Hancock was first to do what at the American Declaration of Independence?
15 In a calendar year what is the third quarter day in England?
16 What is a dirndl?
17 What, in 1902, destroyed the Martinique village of St Pierre?
18 Cork is produced mainly from which species of tree?
19 In which Bond film does the character 'Oddjob' appear?
20 What does the word 'Bedouin' mean?
21 Which family made typewriters and invented the breech-loading rifle?
22 Who was the first Roman Emperor?
23 Which word can be a unit of measure, a stick or a fishing implement?
24 Which actor played a black prostitute's minder in the film Mona Lisa?
25 What did Robert Burns call "great chieftain o' the puddin' race"?
26 Welcome To My World was the first Top Ten hit for whom?
27 Is St Gabriel the patron saint of messengers, millers or musicians?
28 Which actress played the daughter of Alf Garnett?
29 A love apple is an archaic term for what?
30 Whose hits include Manchild and Buffalo Stance?

Answers

Sport: Hot Wheels (see Quiz 57, page 279)

1 Tourist Trophy. **2** Malcolm Campbell. **3** Silverstone. **4** Lotus. **5** One. **6** Eddie Merckx. **7** Never. **8** France. **9** Bernie Ecclestone. **10** Alain Prost. **11** Ayrton Senna. **12** Oulton Park. **13** Stock car racing. **14** Annually. **15** John Surtees. **16** Uncle. **17** Honda. **18** Jack Brabham. **19** Damon Hill. **20** Gerhard Berger. **21** Graham Hill. **22** France. **23** Jackie Stewart. **24** Ferrari. **25** Mini. **26** Chris Boardman. **27** Nigel Mansell. **28** Johnny Herbert. **29** Alain Prost. **30** Magny Cours.

Quiz 59 Movie Superstars

Answers - see Quiz 60, page 282

1 Which actor/director started the trend for spaghetti westerns?
2 What was the nationality of Meryl Streep's character in A Cry in the Dark?
3 Who was shunned by Hollywood in the 40s when she left her husband for Roberto Rossellini?
4 Which poet's name was the middle name of James Dean?
5 Who was Hollywood's first black superstar?
6 Which famous dancer played a straight role in On the Beach?
7 Which Burt appeared in Bean-The Ultimate Disaster Movie?
8 On the set of which film did the Richard Burton/Elizabeth Taylor affair begin?
9 Who, famous as a gangster roles, was a founder of the Screen Actors Guild?
10 Who received her first Oscar nomination for Silkwood?
11 Whose roles vary from Cruella de Vil on film to Norma Desmond on stage?
12 How old was Macaulay Culkin when he was first married?
13 Which married superstars starred in The Big Sleep in 1946?
14 Which comedian co founded United Artists in 1919?
15 Dietrich appeared in the German The Blue Angel, who appeared in the US version?
16 Which actor's last film was The Misfits in 1960?
17 Who was voted No 1 pin up by US soldiers in WWII?
18 How many parts did Alec Guinness play in Kind Hearts and Coronets?
19 What is the profession of Nicole Kidman's father?
20 In which country did Charlie Chaplin spend the final years of his life?
21 Who was Truman in The Truman Show?
22 Which superstar did Tony Curtis parody in Some Like It Hot?
23 Who played the title role in the 1990 Cyrano de Bergerac?
24 Who is the physician in the 90s remake of Doctor Doolittle?
25 How many Road films did Crosby, Hope and Lamour make?
26 Who was the psychotic cabbie in Scorsese's Taxi Driver?
27 Who announced her retirement when she married Ted Turner in '91?
28 Who was Jodie Foster's character in The Silence of the Lambs?
29 Who directed The Horse Whisperer?
30 Who played Margo Channing in All About Eve?

Answers

Pot Luck 28 (see Quiz 60, page 282)
1 Three. **2** A Helicopter. **3** Maria Callas. **4** M People. **5** Labrador. **6** Gabrielle. **7** The Old Curiosity Shop. **8** Greece. **9** On the seabed. **10** Kent. **11** Shoes. **12** Melvyn Hayes. **13** Sistine. **14** Sonny Bono. **15** Bismarck. **16** Le Mans. **17** Sap. **18** Peru. **19** The World War. **20** Pregnant. **21** Jackie Rae. **22** Aphrodite. **23** Bits and pieces. **24** Guildford. **25** Isle of Wight. **26** The Lion King. **27** Nkima. **28** Whitesnake. **29** Commissioner Dreyfus. **30** A supermarket.

Quiz 60 Pot Luck 28

Answers - see Quiz 59, page 281

1 How many times did Joe Frasier fight Muhammad Ali?
2 What was designed and made in a viable form by Sikorsky in 1941?
3 Which opera singer died on the same day as Marc Bolan?
4 Who had hits with One Night in Heaven and Moving On Up?
5 Which 'dog like' peninsula formed Canada's tenth province in 1949?
6 What was Coco Chanel's Christian name?
7 Quilp appears in a book about what kind of Shop?
8 In which European country are the Pindus Mountains?
9 If a creature is demersal, where does it live?
10 In which county was the first Youth Custody Centre set up in 1908?
11 Espadrilles are a type of what?
12 Who played the part of 'Gloria' in It Ain't Half Hot, Mum?
13 Michaelangelo painted the ceiling of which famous Chapel?
14 Which rock musician died on the same day as cricketer David Bairstow?
15 Who was called the 'Iron Chancellor'?
16 Where is motor racing's Grand Prix d'Endurance staged?
17 If a creature is succivorous what does it feed on?
18 The source of the Amazon is in which South American country?
19 Al Capone said he was accused of every death except the casualty list of what?
20 If something or someone is gravid what does it mean?
21 Who was the first presenter of the TV series The Golden Shot?
22 In Greek mythology, who was the mother of Eros?
23 What does 'Chop Suey' literally mean?
24 In which city is the University of Surrey?
25 Carisbrooke Castle is on which Isle?
26 In which Disney film is a young lion called Simba?
27 What was the name of Tarzan's monkey friend in the Tarzan stories?
28 Which heavy band's hits include Here I Go Again and Is This Love?
29 Which part was played by Herbert Lom in the Pink Panther films?
30 The 1984 TV series Tripper's Day was set in what type of shop?

Answers

Movie Superstars (see Quiz 59, page 281)
1 Clint Eastwood. **2** Australian. **3** Ingrid Bergman. **4** Byron. **5** Sidney Poitier. **6** Fred Astaire. **7** Reynolds. **8** Cleopatra. **9** James Cagney. **10** Cher. **11** Glenn Close. **12** 17. **13** Lauren Bacall and Humphrey Bogart. **14** Charlie Chaplin. **15** Dietrich. **16** Clark Gable. **17** Betty Grable. **18** Eight. **19** Psychologist. **20** Switzerland. **21** Jim Carrey. **22** Cary Grant. **23** Gerard Depardieu. **24** Eddie Murphy. **25** Seven. **26** Robert de Niro. **27** Jane Fonda. **28** Clarice Starling. **29** Robert Redford. **30** Bette Davis.

Quiz 61 On the Map

Answers - see Quiz 62, page 284

1 Which South American city has a famous Copacabana beach?
2 The Bass Strait divides which two islands?
3 Which Middle East capital is known locally as El Qahira?
4 Where is the official country home of US Presidents?
5 Whose Vineyard is an island off Cape Cod?
6 Where was Checkpoint Charlie?
7 Which US state has a 'pan handle' separating the Atlantic from the Gulf of Mexico?
8 In which two countries is the Dead Sea?
9 The site of ancient Babylon is now in which country?
10 On which river is the Aswan Dam?
11 Which continent produces almost 50% of the world's cars?
12 The Fens were formerly a bay of which Sea?
13 What is Japan's highest peak?
14 To which country do the Galapagos Islands belong?
15 Aconcagua is an extinct volcano in which mountain range?
16 Where in California is the lowest point of the western hemisphere?
17 In which London Square is the US Embassy?
18 Ellis Island is in which harbour?
19 Which city is known to Afrikaaners as Kaapstad?
20 On which Sea is the Gaza Strip?
21 What are the three divisions of Glamorgan?
22 Which river cuts through the Grand Canyon?
23 In which Ethiopian city is the HQ of the Organisation of African Unity?
24 Which continents are separated by the Dardanelles?
25 Which US state capital means 'sheltered bay' in Hawaiian?
26 Hampstead is part of which London borough?
27 Which country owns the southernmost part of South America?
28 Where is the seat of the UN International Court of Justice?
29 The Golan Heights are on the border of which two countries?
30 Which is the saltiest of the main oceans?

Answers

Pot Luck 29 (see Quiz 62, page 284)

1 West Side Story. **2** Tom and Jerry. **3** Love. **4** John Hunt. **5** Solomon. **6** The Real Thing. **7** Rugby League. **8** Potato famine. **9** Language sounds. **10** Joe Louis. **11** Tom Cruise. **12** Robert Mugabe. **13** Calcium. **14** 40. **15** Honeysuckle. **16** Basil Brush. **17** Mike McGear. **18** Nine. **19** Rock Hudson. **20** Fred Astaire. **21** Trampolining. **22** Niagara Falls. **23** Bournemouth. **24** Pele. **25** Mariah Carey. **26** A Nelson. **27** Britain. **28** Freddie Laker. **29** Holland. **30** 15th.

Quiz 62 Pot Luck 29

Answers - see Quiz 61, page 283

LEVEL 2 

1 The song America comes from which musical?
2 Which cartoon duo starred in the Oscar winning film Quiet Please?
3 Kate Bush had an album called The Hounds Of ...what?
4 In 1953 who was leader of the British expedition which conquered Everest?
5 In The Bible who did the Queen of Sheba visit according to Kings I?
6 Who had a UK Top Ten hit with Can You Feel the Force?
7 Which sport was founded in Britain on 28th August 1895?
8 Black Forty Seven in Ireland in the 19th century related to what?
9 What is phonetics the study of?
10 Who was World Heavyweight boxing champion in WWII?
11 Which actor links Risky Business, Cocktail and Top Gun?
12 Who was the first president of Zimbabwe?
13 Which element is found in shells, bones and teeth?
14 How old are you if you are a quadragenarian?
15 Which flower is also called the Woodbine?
16 Which children's TV puppet was operated by Ivan Owen?
17 Paul McCartney's brother Mike is known as whom?
18 What is the most times a day of the week can occur in two months?
19 Who was older when they died Humphrey Bogart or Rock Hudson?
20 Who starred opposite Judy Garland in the film Easter Parade?
21 In which sport are there moves called Triffus, Rudolf and Miller?
22 The Horseshoe and American combine to form which famous falls?
23 Which is further west, Bognor or Bournemouth?
24 Which Brazilian footballer appeared in a film called Hotshot?
25 Who has had hits with Hero and Anytime You Need A Friend?
26 What name is given to a score of 111 in cricket?
27 In Orwell's 1984 what is called Airstrip One?
28 Whose cheap transatlantic air service in 1977 was called 'Skytrain'?
29 Which team did Argentina beat in the 1978 Football World Cup Final?
30 In which century was the Battle of Agincourt?

Answers

On the Map (see Quiz 61, page 283)
1 Rio de Janeiro. **2** Australia & Tasmania. **3** Cairo. **4** Camp David. **5** Martha's Vineyard. **6** Between East and West Berlin. **7** Florida. **8** Israel & Jordan. **9** Iraq. **10** Nile. **11** Europe. **12** North Sea. **13** Mount Fujiyama. **14** Ecuador. **15** Andes. **16** Death Valley. **17** Grosvenor. **18** New York. **19** Cape Town. **20** Mediterranean. **21** Mid, South, West. **22** Colorado. **23** Addis Ababa. **24** Europe & Asia. **25** Honolulu. **26** Camden. **27** Chile. **28** The Hague. **29** Israel & Syria. **30** Atlantic.

Quiz 63 Nature: Plant World

Answers - see Quiz 64, page 286

1 Which cereal can survive in the widest range of climatic conditions?
2 The hellebore is known as what type of rose?
3 What colour are edelweiss flowers?
4 Which plant is St Patrick said to have used to illustrate the Holy Trinity?
5 Succulents live in areas lacking in what?
6 How many points does a sycamore leaf have?
7 What is the ornamental shaping of trees and shrubs called?
8 What is an alternative name for the narcotic and analgesic aconite?
9 What colour are laburnum flowers?
10 What is another name for a yam?
11 What shape are flowers which include the name campanula?
12 What is a frond on a plant?
13 Which climbing plant is also called hedera helix?
14 Agronomy is the study of what?
15 What is a Sturmer?
16 Which fruit is called 'earth berry' in German from where the plant grows?
17 What is another name for belladonna?
18 What is the effect on the nervous system of taking hemlock?
19 Are the male, female or either hop plants used to make beer?
20 What is the most common plant grown in Assam in India?
21 Aspen is what type of tree?
22 Which ingredient in tonic water is found in cinchona bark?
23 The ground powder form turmeric dyes food which colour?
24 The pineapple plant is native to which continent?
25 What is the purpose of a plant's petals?
26 Which type of pesticide is used to kill weeds?
27 What colour are the leaves of a poinsettia?
28 What name is given to the wild yellow iris?
29 Which plant is famous for having a 'clock'?
30 What colour are borage flowers?

Answers

Pot Luck 30 (see Quiz 64, page 286)
1 Nancy Reagan. **2** Kool & The Gang. **3** The sun (Bright area). **4** Australia. **5** Sierra Leone. **6** Devon. **7** Sherry. **8** Lotus. **9** Statue of Zeus. **10** 15th. **11** Cacao. **12** G B Shaw. **13** An elephant. **14** Firm when bitten. **15** Oliver Cromwell. **16** Emporio Label. **17** Bob Geldof. **18** A weaver. **19** The lion. **20** Tom Kite. **21** London. **22** Thanksgiving Day. **23** Jemma Redgrave. **24** Van Gogh. **25** A cob. **26** I'm Still Waiting. **27** Offspring. **28** Genesis. **29** Richard O'Brien. **30** A juke box.

Quiz 64 Pot Luck 30

Answers - see Quiz 63, page 285

1 Which former First Lady was nicknamed 'The Smiling Mamba'?
2 Who had hits with Joanna and Celebration?
3 Where would you see a facula?
4 DJ Alan Freeman was born in which country?
5 Which country has a unit of currency called the Leone?
6 The seaside town of Westward Ho is in which county?
7 Oloroso is a type of which drink?
8 Which car manufacturer designed the winning bike for Chris Boardman?
9 Which Wonder of the World statue was at Olympia?
10 In which century did William Caxton establish the first English printing press?
11 Cocoa is prepared from the seeds of which tree?
12 Who wrote Androcles and the Lion?
13 What is driven by a mahout?
14 What does the cooking expression al dente mean?
15 Which Oliver was Lord Protector of Britain?
16 Which label is distinguished as fashion designed by Armani?
17 Which celeb's childhood nickname was Liver Lips?
18 Who would use a jacquard?
19 In The Wizard of Oz, which animal was seeking courage?
20 Who captained the US Ryder Cup team in 1997?
21 In which city is the HQ of Amnesty International?
22 Pumpkin Pie is the traditional dessert on which special American day?
23 Who played Eleanor Bramwell in the TV series of the same name?
24 Who painted The Starry Night?
25 Which word can be a swan, a horse, a bread roll and a basket?
26 What was Diana Ross's first solo Number 1 in the UK?
27 What are progeny?
28 Who had hits with I Can't Dance and Invisible Touch?
29 Who preceded Ed Tudor-Pole as host of the Crystal Maze?
30 If you heard a John Gabel Entertainer, what would be playing?

Answers

Nature: Plant World (see Quiz 63, page 285)
1 Barley. **2** Christmas rose. **3** White. **4** Shamrock. **5** Water. **6** Five. **7** Topiary. **8** Monkshood. **9** Yellow. **10** Sweet potato. **11** Bell shaped. **12** Leaf. **13** Ivy. **14** Crops and soils. **15** Apple. **16** Strawberry. **17** Deadly nightshade. **18** Paralysis. **19** Female. **20** Tea. **21** Poplar. **22** Quinine. **23** Yellow. **24** South America. **25** Attract pollinators. **26** Herbicide. **27** Red. **28** Flag. **29** Dandelion. **30** Blue.

Quiz 65 Past Times: The 70s

Answers - see Quiz 66, page 288

1 Germany's Red Army Faction was popularly called what after its two founders?
2 The Equal Opportunities Commission was set up to implement which act?
3 Who became US Vice President after Spiro Agnew resigned?
4 Where did the Gang of Four seize power in 1976?
5 Which natural disaster did Guatemala city suffer in 1976?
6 In the Vietnam War who or what was Agent Orange?
7 Who was Nixon's White House Chief of Staff at the height of the Watergate scandal?
8 On which Pennsylvania Island was there a nuclear leak in 1979?
9 In 1978 Mujaheddin resistance began in which country?
10 Who made a precocious speech aged 16 at the 1977 Tory Party conference?
11 Who opened her first Body Shop in 1976?
12 Where was Obote replaced by Amin in 1971?
13 The Pahlavi Dynasty was overthrown by the Islamic revolution in which country?
14 Which Argentine leader died in 1974 and was succeeded by his third wife?
15 Which woman MP did Jack Straw replace as MP for Blackburn?
16 How were Patrick Armstrong, Gerard Conlon, Paul Hill and Carole Richardson known collectively?
17 Which dictator was deposed in Cambodia in 1979?
18 Which 'King' died in 1977 aged 42?
19 What was Harare called until the end of the 1970s?
20 What was inside US incendiary bombs during the Vietnam War?
21 Which title did Quintin Hogg take when made Lord Chancellor in '70?
22 SALT negotiations took place between which two countries?
23 Which future Labour leader became Trade & Industry Secretary in '78?
24 Mario Soares was exiled from which country in 1970?
25 In which country was a monarchy restored in 1975?
26 The Sandinistas overthrew which government in 1979?
27 Who succeeded Heath as Tory leader?
28 Sapporo was the centre of the 1972 winter Olympics in which country?
29 Which country did the USSR invade in 1979?
30 In which department was Thatcher a Minister before leading the Party?

Answers

TV: TV Times 1 (see Quiz 66, page 288)
1 The Teletones. **2** Nephew. **3** Warrior. **4** Miss America. **5** New Faces. **6** Helicopters. **7** Liverpool. **8** Eddie Izzard. **9** Elton John. **10** Ulrika Jonsson. **11** Assumpta. **12** Carla Lane. **13** Shoplifting. **14** David Coleman. **15** Pink. **16** Trevor McDonald. **17** Bingo. **18** Jennifer Paterson. **19** Tony Slattery. **20** Torvill & Dean. **21** Delia Smith. **22** Televangelism. **23** Anthony Andrews. **24** Sian Lloyd. **25** Sam Malone. **26** The Bee Gees. **27** Wimbledon. **28** Ricki Lake. **29** John Virgo. **30** On a bed.

Quiz 66 TV: TV Times 1

Answers - see Quiz 65, page 287

1 What is the name of the singing group in The Hello Girls?
2 What relation is ER's George Clooney to US singer Rosemary?
3 Which Gladiator was jailed in 1998 for corruption?
4 Superwoman Lynda Carter held which beauty queen title?
5 On which TV show was Jim Davidson 'discovered'?
6 Outside TV what type of transport business does Noel Edmonds run?
7 Where was This Morning first broadcast from?
8 Which They Think It's All Over panellist wears most make up?
9 The TV profile Tantrums and Tiaras was about which pop superstar?
10 Which TV presenter's relationship with Stan Collymore ended violently in Paris during the 1998 World Cup?
11 Who was the first landlady of Fitzgerald's in Ballykissangel?
12 Which TV playwright founded Animal Line with Linda McCartney?
13 What was Richard Madeley arrested for in 1990?
14 Which veteran sports commentator won the Manchester Mile in 1949?
15 What colour does TV critic Nina Myskow usually wear?
16 Which News At Ten presenter had the first British TV interview with Nelson Mandela after his release?
17 Which game was Bob's Full House based on?
18 Which late TV cook wore a diamond studded crash helmet?
19 Who presented the C5 medical quiz show Tibs and Fibs?
20 Who were the first couple to be BBC Sports Personality of the Year?
21 Which cook founded Sainsbury's The Magazine with her husband?
22 In the US Jim Bakker and Jimmy Swaggart are famous for what type of show?
23 Which star of Brideshead Revisited shares a birthday with sports commentator Brendan Foster?
24 Which weather girl went to the same university as Glenys Kinnock?
25 Which character did Ted Danson play in Cheers?
26 Which pop group walked out on Clive Anderson on his All Talk show?
27 Which London soccer side does June Whitfield support?
28 Which talk show hostess appeared in the film Hairspray with Divine?
29 Who is the resident snooker player on Big Break?
30 Where did Paula Yates conduct her Big Breakfast interviews?

Answers

Past Times: The 70s (see Quiz 65, page 287)

1 Baader-Meinhof Gang. **2** Sex Discrimination Act. **3** Gerald Ford. **4** China. **5** Earthquake. **6** Weedkiller. **7** Alexander Haig. **8** Three Mile Island. **9** Afghanistan. **10** William Hague. **11** Anita Roddick. **12** Uganda. **13** Iran. **14** Peron. **15** Barbara Castle. **16** The Guildford Four. **17** Pol Pot. **18** Elvis Presley. **19** Salisbury. **20** Napalm. **21** Lord Hailsham. **22** USA & USSR. **23** John Smith. **24** Portugal. **25** Spain. **26** Nicaragua. **27** Thatcher. **28** Japan. **29** Afghanistan. **30** Education.

Quiz 67 Pot Luck 31

Answers - see Quiz 68, page 290

1 What was Annie Oakley's first name?
2 Which famous survey started in 1086?
3 What was Roger's wife called in the film Who Framed Roger Rabbit?
4 Ronald Reagan was in which political party?
5 Who is taller – Claire Rayner or Pauline Quirke?
6 In The Bible, what was the prophet Elijah carried up to heaven in?
7 What nationality was Casanova?
8 What was Al Jolson's most famous line?
9 If a substance is oleaginous what does it mainly contain?
10 Which General led the junta in the 1982 seizure of the Falklands?
11 Which famous Castle is on the River Dee?
12 What did the Owl and the Pussycat dine on?
13 Vera Welch sang under what name?
14 Which Christopher was a policeman before he became a champion skater?
15 Which outlandish musician's real name was Simon Ritchie?
16 Which handicapped physicist has appeared in adverts for 'BT'?
17 Who is buried at the Arc de Triomphe?
18 During exercise which acid builds up in the muscles?
19 Who is spiritual leader to the Ismaili sect of Muslims?
20 Which singer had a backing group called the Checkmates?
21 What is added to egg yolks and vanilla to make advocaat?
22 Who played 'Blanco' in the TV series Porridge?
23 What nationality was Rachmaninov the composer?
24 What is xerography?
25 Which 1956 hit links The Platters with a 1987 Freddie Mercury hit?
26 Which Dutch town is particularly famous for its blue pottery?
27 Where would you find an apse?
28 What was abolished on 18th December 1969 in Britain?
29 Which tycoon started the newspaper called Today?
30 Who was the first golfer to lose play-offs in all four majors?

Answers

Pop Music: Albums (see Quiz 68, page 290)
1 Chris Rea. **2** Chicago XIII. **3** Eternal. **4** George Michael. **5** News of the World. **6** The Revolution. **7** Pet Shop Boys. **8** Frank Sinatra. **9** Wet Wet Wet. **10** Sting. **11** No Parlez. **12** River Deep - Mountain High. **13** Wannabe. **14** Definitely/Maybe. **15** Pulp. **16** Just Good Friends. **17** Emmerdance. **8** Blue. **19** Physical. **20** Slippery When Wet. **21** The Rolling Stones. **22** Sex. **23** Nigel Kennedy. **24** Gasoline Alley. **25** Goat. **26** The Wall. **27** Enya. **28** Waterloo. **29** Ten. **30** Diva.

Quiz 68 Pop Music: Albums

Answers - see Quiz 67, page 289

1. Who released the album Auberge?
2. What was the thirteenth album released by Chicago?
3. Which group's debut album, Always & Forever, shadowed their name?
4. Whose debut solo album was called Faith?
5. Which Queen album shares its name with a newspaper?
6. On the 80s album Purple Rain who backed Prince?
7. Which duo released albums called Introspective and Very?
8. Which US superstar has had over 70 chart albums in his career?
9. High On the Happy Side was a No 1 album for which band in '92?
10. Who guested with Dire Straits on the Money For Nothing track?
11. Which phrase with a French flavour was the title of Paul Young's debut album?
12. What was the title of Ike and Tina Turner's only album?
13. What is the first track on Spice?
14. A picture of Burt Bacharach appeared on the cover of which best selling 90s album?
15. Whose debut album was called Different Class?
16. Which Paul Nicholas album was named after a sitcom in which he starred?
17. What was the title of the album by the Woolpackers?
18. On the Beautiful South's 1996 album what is the Colour?
19. Which Olivia Newton-John '81 album could describe some exercise?
20. Which Bon Jovi album was best kept dry?
21. What was the title of the first album released by The Rolling Stones?
22. What were Madonna's book and 1992 album called?
23. Which musician took Vivaldi's The Four Seasons into the charts?
24. Rod Stewart's first album was called after which alley?
25. What animal is on the cover of the Beach Boy's album Pet Sounds?
26. Which construction has given its name to a Pink Floyd album?
27. Which Irish singer got to No 1 with Shepherd Moons?
28. Which battle was the title of the first Abba album?
29. How many Good Reasons had Jason Donovan on his first No 1?
30. Which Annie Lennox album topped the charts in 1993?

Answers

Pot Luck 31 (see Quiz 67, page 289)
1 Phoebe. **2** Domesday Book. **3** Jessica. **4** Republican Party. **5** Claire Rayner. **6** A fiery chariot. **7** Italian. **8** You ain't heard nothing yet. **9** Oil. **10** Galtieri. **11** Balmoral. **12** Mince and slices of quince. **13** Vera Lynn . **14** Dean. **15** Sid Vicious. **16** Stephen Hawking. **17** The Unknown Soldier. **18** Lactic Acid. **19** The Aga Khan. **20** Emile Ford. **21** Brandy. **22** David Jason. **23** Russian. **24** Photocopying. **25** The Great Pretender. **26** Delft. **27** A church. **28** Death Penalty. **29** Eddie Shah. **30** Greg Norman.

Quiz 69 Pot Luck 32

Answers - see Quiz 70, page 292

1 Who formed the famous dance troupe the Bluebell Girls?
2 Whose CDs include Seven Year Itch and Stickin' to my Guns?
3 What would you do with a futon?
4 Which play is performed every ten years at Oberammagau?
5 Which wood was mainly used by Thomas Chippendale?
6 In which London area is The Royal Hospital?
7 Which Lynne is Duggie Brown's sister?
8 Bruce Willis destroyed a plane with his cigarette lighter in which film?
9 What does a blue flag at a beach mean?
10 Which carbohydrate causes jam to gel?
11 If a dog is suffering from 'hard pad' what form of disease has it got?
12 What is a hawser?
13 What was Roy Schneider's profession in the film Jaws?
14 Theophobia is a fear of what?
15 In which French town was Joan of Arc burnt at the stake?
16 What was the name of cowboy Tom Mix's horse ?
17 The quail is the smallest member of which bird species?
18 What is the singular of axes in mathematics?
19 Which actress's real name was Maria Magdalena von Losch?
20 Which port is the most easterly in Britain?
21 What is the common weather in a pluvial region?
22 Which Polynesian word means prohibited or forbidden?
23 What colour is the egg of a kingfisher?
24 The Dodecanese Islands are in which sea?
25 What nationality was Secretary General of the UN Boutros Boutros Ghali?
26 What part was played by Irene Handl in For the Love of Ada?
27 Whose hits include Sunny Afternoon and Tired of Waiting For You?
28 What is on top of the Mona Lisa's left hand?
29 What do Americans call Perspex?
30 In fishing what is another name for a pike-perch?

Answers

Leisure 3 (see Quiz 70, page 292)
1 Deep sea diving. **2** Stamps. **3** Green. **4** Circular. **5** Yoga. **6** Cribbage.
7 Admiral's Cup. **8** Lacrosse. **9** Gare Du Nord. **10** RSPB. **11** Pottery.
12 Star Wars. **13** 13 tricks by one team. **14** Harrods. **15** Synchronised swimming.
16 Cadbury, Fry, Rowntree. **17** The Netherlands. **18** Tennis. **19** Pizza Express.
20 Golf Club. **21** Women's Institute. **22** World Wildlife Fund. **23** Whipsnade.
24 Tintin. **25** Dark green. **26** Hammer. **27** Wrestling. **28** Isle of Wight.
29 York. **30** Leicester.

Quiz 70 Leisure 3

Answers - see Quiz 69, page 291

1 After what sort of activity might you suffer from the bends?
2 What would you buy from Stanley Gibbons?
3 What colour are houses in Monopoly?
4 What shape is a sumo wrestling ring?
5 Which Hindu system of philosophy is used as a means of exercise and meditation in the west?
6 In which game do you score 'one for his knob'?
7 The Fastnet race is part of the contest for which Cup?
8 Which game's name comes from a piece of its equipment looking like a bishop's crosier?
9 At which station do you arrive in Paris if you have travelled from the UK by Eurostar?
10 The YOC is the junior branch of which organisation?
11 If you were a collector of Clarice Cliff what would you collect?
12 A Monopoly game based on which Sci-fi film was released in 1997?
13 What is a grand slam in Bridge?
14 House of Fraser owns which major London store?
15 What sort of swimming takes place with musical accompaniment?
16 Which three Quaker families made most of Britain's chocolate?
17 In which country is De Efteling Theme Park?
18 Which sport is played at London's Queen's Club?
19 Which pizza restaurant was the first of a chain founded in London?
20 What sort of club is the Royal and Ancient?
21 Which organisation's anthem is Jerusalem?
22 What was the Worldwide Fund for Nature formerly called?
23 Which open air zoo is near Dunstable in Bedfordshire?
24 Which boy reporter was created by Belgian artist Herge?
25 What colour carrier bag do you get when you shop at Laura Ashley?
26 In athletics, what is attached to a chain and a handle and thrown?
27 Which sport has Greco-Roman and Freestyle, as two distinct styles?
28 The annual Round the Isle race goes round which Isle?
29 Where is the National Railway Museum?
30 Where were Walker's Crisps first made?

Answers

Pot Luck 32 (see Quiz 69, page 291)
1 Margaret Kelly. **2** Etta James. **3** Sleep on it. **4** The Passion Play. **5** Mahogany. **6** Chelsea. **7** Lynne Perrie. **8** Die Hard 2. **9** Clean & pollution free. **10** Pectin. **11** Distemper. **12** A rope. **13** Police Chief. **14** God. **15** Rouen. **16** Tony. **17** Partridge. **18** Axis. **19** Marlene Dietrich. **20** Lowestoft. **21** Rain. **22** Taboo. **23** White. **24** Aegean Sea. **25** Egyptian. **26** Ada. **27** The Kinks. **28** Her right hand. **29** Plexiglass. **30** Zander.

Quiz 71 Pot Luck 33

Answers - see Quiz 72, page 294

1 What describes descending a sheer face by sliding down a rope?
2 Donna Reed replaced Barbara Bel Geddes in which TV series?
3 Who is Princess Alexandra's son?
4 Which animal is feared by a hippophobe?
5 Whose hits include Wide Boy and Wouldn't It Be Good?
6 The novel Shirley was written by which of the Bronte sisters?
7 In which London building does the Lutine Bell hang?
8 Which is further south, Folkestone or Southampton?
9 Which American sportsman was said to be earning more than the US president in 1925?
10 Which famous bear came from Peru?
11 What did the S stand for in Charlie Chaplin's middle name?
12 Who was Shirley MacLaine named after?
13 What is a passepied?
14 Which species can be Fairy, Black-footed and Crested?
15 Which game uses flattened iron rings thrown at a hob?
16 What was the title of Captain Sensible's No 1 UK hit in 1982?
17 Which European Commissioner once played in a band called The Rebels?
18 Which country won the 1992 World Cup cricket final?
19 What is tansy?
20 Which island is in the Bay of Naples?
21 Whose hits include Something About You and Lessons In Love?
22 Cyril Mead became known as which comic?
23 In the order of accession to the British throne who is the first female?
24 In which London Square is the American Embassy?
25 What is a taipan?
26 Is Coventry north or south of Leicester?
27 Which English King was the last to die in battle?
28 Who was older when they died Peter Sellers or Tony Hancock?
29 What is the smallest administrative unit in the Church of England?
30 In Pride and Prejudice who does Elizabeth Bennet finally marry?

Answers

Record Breakers (see Quiz 72, page 294)

1 Donald Budge. **2** Kapil Dev. **3** Stefan Edberg. **4** Chris Evert. **5** Nick Faldo. **6** Sally Gunnell. **7** Billie Jean King. **8** Skiing. **9** Gabriela Sabatini. **10** Brian Lara. **11** Seven. **12** Ian Woosnam. **13** Steve Ovett's. **14** Karen Pickering. **15** Steve Davis. **16** Frankie Fredericks. **17** Sandy Lyle. **18** Sugar Ray Leonard. **19** Monica Seles. **20** James Wattana. **21** Freestyle & butterfly. **22** Ian Rush. **23** Mike Powell. **24** Seve Ballesteros. **25** Johnny Haynes. **26** Ed Moses. **27** Geoff Capes. **28** McColgan. **29** Ipswich. **30** Graham Hill.

Quiz 72 Record Breakers

Answers - see Quiz 71, page 293

LEVEL 2 

1. Which American was the first to win the Men's Singles Grand Slam?
2. Who in 1979 became the youngest player to complete the double of 1,000 runs and 100 wickets?
3. Which Swede, in 1987 was the first man for 40 years to win a match at Wimbledon without losing a game?
4. Who was the first woman tennis player to win $1 million?
5. Who was the first Briton after 1950 to win the British Open golf three years in succession?
6. Who was the first woman athlete to win the athletics Grand Slam?
7. Which woman won 20 Wimbledon titles between 1961 and 1979?
8. Franz Klammer was a record breaker in which sport?
9. Which woman became the youngest Wimbledon semi finalist for 99 years in 1986?
10. Who broke the world record for an individual innings of 501 in 1994?
11. How many world records did Mark Spitz break when he won his seven gold medals?
12. Who, in 1987, was the first British golfer to win the World Match-Play Championship?
13. Whose 1500m world record did Steve Cram break in 1985?
14. Who was the first British woman swimmer to win a world title?
15. Who made the first televised 147 break in snooker in 1982?
16. Which Namibian was the first to break the indoor 20 second barrier?
17. Who was the first British winner of the US Masters in 1988?
18. In 1988 who became the first boxer to win world titles at five official weights?
19. Who in 1991 was the youngest woman ever to have the No 1 tennis ranking?
20. Who was the first Thai snooker player to win a major tournament?
21. In 1972 Mark Spitz broke Olympic records doing which two strokes?
22. Who holds the record for most goals scored in FA Cup Finals?
23. Who broke Bob Beaman's long jump record set at the 1968 Olympics?
24. Who was the then youngest ever winner of the US Masters in 1980?
25. Who was the first British soccer player to earn £100 per week?
26. Which US hurdler was undefeated in 122 races?
27. Which British shot putter was world No 1 in 1975?
28. Which Liz won the fastest ever debut marathon when she won in New York in 1991?
29. Which Town did Man Utd beat by a record nine goals in 1995?
30. Who in 1968 became the oldest Briton to win a Grand Prix?

Answers

Pot Luck 33 (see Quiz 71, page 293)

1 Abseiling. **2** Dallas. **3** James Ogilvy. **4** Horses. **5** Nik Kershaw. **6** Charlotte. **7** Lloyds of London. **8** Southampton. **9** Babe Ruth. **10** Paddington. **11** Spencer. **12** Shirley Temple. **13** A dance. **14** Penguins. **15** Quoits. **16** Happy Talk. **17** Neil Kinnock. **18** Pakistan. **19** A herb. **20** Capri. **21** Level 42. **22** Syd Little. **23** Princess Beatrice. **24** Grosvenor Square. **25** A snake. **26** South. **27** Richard III. **28** Peter Sellers. **29** A Parish. **30** Mr Darcy.

Quiz 73 Pot Luck 34

Answers - see Quiz 74, page 296

1. Where is fibrin found in your body?
2. Which two countries are on the Iberian peninsula?
3. Which group had hits including Homely Girl and Kingston Town?
4. The word 'ketchup' comes which language?
5. Who played the priest in the TV series The Paradise Club?
6. Which species of bird does the wapacat belong to?
7. Which Marx brother died on the same day as Joyce Grenfell?
8. Woburn Abbey is the home of which family?
9. What is a durian?
10. Which film starred John Cleese as an under pressure headmaster?
11. The composer Bela Bartok came from which country?
12. What can be an animal enclosure or a unit of weight?
13. What does the abbreviation BHP stand for?
14. Which poetic names lend themselves to an expression for a devoted, elderly couple?
15. How does a judge hear a case when it is heard In Camera?
16. From 1968 to 1970 which actor was Mr Universe?
17. What does the word 'biscuit' literally mean?
18. The Lent Lily is sometimes used as another name for which flower?
19. What is a Tree Ear?
20. What was Little Lord Fauntleroy's name?
21. Toad of Toad Hall was a dramatised version of which Kenneth Grahame tale?
22. Which sport is Clare Francis famous for?
23. In the film Look Who's Talking whose voice was the baby's thoughts?
24. Which tree usually provides the wood for the Highland Games caber?
25. Whose hits include Wishing Well and All Right Now?
26. What colour is the tongue of a giraffe?
27. Which actor played the title role in Judge Dredd?
28. Californian, Yellow Horned and Opium are all types of which flower?
29. Where is the Sea of Vapours?
30. What is the wading bird the bittern's cry called?

Answers

The Oscars (see Quiz 74, page 296)
1 Cher. **2** Casablanca. **3** The Deer Hunter. **4** Christy Brown. **5** Henry Fonda. **6** As Good As It Gets. **7** Philadelphia. **8** Marlee Matlin. **9** James Cameron. **10** Philadelphia, Forrest Gump. **11** Gary Cooper. **12** Butler. **13** 1930s. **14** Woody Allen. **15** The Godfather. **16** Dustin Hoffman. **17** Frank Sinatra. **18** Schindler's List. **19** She never spoke. **20** Walter & John Huston. **21** Meryl Streep. **22** Bette Davis. **23** Jessica Tandy. **24** Eight (all of them). **25** Kathy Bates. **26** Oscar. **27** Vivien Leigh. **28** Anthony Minghella. **29** Tatum O'Neal. **30** Helena Bonham-Carter.

Quiz 74 The Oscars

Answers - see Quiz 73, page 295

1 Which singing Oscar winner said, "women get all excited about nothing - then marry him"?
2 Which World War II film would have been called Dar el-Beida had it been titled in the local language?
3 Which Michael Cimino film about Vietnam won five Oscars in the 70s?
4 Who did Daniel-Day Lewis portray in My Left Foot?
5 Which veteran won an Oscar in 1981 two years after his daughter?
6 For which movie did Helen Hunt win in 1997?
7 For which film did Tom Hanks win playing a lawyer dying from AIDS?
8 Who overcame deafness to win for Children of a Lesser God?
9 Who won the Best Director award for Titanic?
10 For which films did Tom Hanks win in successive years?
11 Who won the Best Actor Oscar for High Noon?
12 What type of worker did John Gielgud play when he won his Oscar for Arthur?
13 In which decade did Katharine Hepburn win her first Oscar?
14 Who won three Oscars for Annie Hall?
15 For which film did Brando win his second Oscar?
16 Who won his first best actor Oscar for Kramer vs. Kramer?
17 Which singer won an Oscar for From Here to Eternity?
18 For which film did Steven Spielberg win his first award?
19 What was unusual about Holly Hunter's performance in The Piano?
20 Which father and son actor and director won for The Treasure of the Sierra Madre?
21 In the year Gandhi won almost everything who was Best Actress for Sophie's Choice?
22 Who won Oscars for Dangerous, Jezebel and All About Eve?
23 Who won as Dan Aykroyd's mother in Driving Miss Daisy?
24 How many times between 1990 and 1997 did Best Picture and Best Director Oscars go to the same film?
25 Who played the psychotic nurse in Misery and won Best Actress?
26 What did Anthony Hopkins win first, a knighthood or an Oscar?
27 Who won for her role as Blanche in A Streetcar Named Desire?
28 Who won Best Director for The English Patient?
29 Who won for her first film Paper Moon?
30 Which actress was nominated for The Wings of the Dove?

Answers

Pot Luck 34 (see Quiz 73, page 295)
1 In the blood. **2** Spain and Portugal. **3** UB40. **4** Chinese. **5** Don Henderson. **6** An owl. **7** Zeppo. **8** Dukes of Bedford. **9** A fruit. **10** Clockwise. **11** Hungary . **12** Pound. **13** Brake horse-power. **14** Darby and Joan. **15** In private. **16** Arnold Schwarzenegger. **17** 'Twice-cooked'. **18** Daffodil. **19** A mushroom. **20** Cedric Errol. **21** The Wind In The Willows. **22** Sailing. **23** Bruce Willis. **24** Larch. **25** Free. **26** Blue. **27** Sylvester Stallone. **28** Poppy. **29** The Moon. **30** A Boom.

Quiz 75 Pot Luck 35

Answers - see Quiz 76, page 298

1 What are Spode, Bow and Chelsea all types of?
2 A covey is the collective name for a group of which birds?
3 Which Italian area produces Chianti?
4 Which scale measures the level of alkalinity and acidity?
5 Who did Jackie Kennedy marry in 1968?
6 Where will you return to if you throw a coin into the Trevi Fountain?
7 What in your body are affected by phlebitis?
8 In which Open did Ballesteros win his first pro tournament, in 1974?
9 Whose hits include Again and That's the Way Love Goes ?
10 Which TV character lived on Scatterbrook Farm?
11 Which High Street travel agent's devised the holiday package tour?
12 In finance what is a PEP?
13 Which store chain claims they are "never knowingly undersold"?
14 What does the Greek odeon mean?
15 If you were using a tambour, what needlecraft would you be doing?
16 What is the currency of Greece?
17 Which TV detective was played by George Peppard?
18 In which century was cockfighting banned?
19 Which supermarket chain paid for the new National Gallery wing opened in 1991?
20 Cars with the international vehicle registration ET come from where?
21 Who started the Habitat chain of shops in 1964?
22 Who is smaller Janet Street Porter or Naomi Campbell?
23 Edmonton is the capital of which Canadian province?
24 Who played Shirley Valentine in the film?
25 What is the white of an egg called as an alternative to albumen?
26 Which 007 actor was also TV's Remington Steele?
27 The Ashanti tribe live in which African country?
28 Whose hits include Finally and We Got a Love Thing?
29 What is held annually in London in Ranelagh Gardens?
30 Where was tennis star Monica Seles playing when she was stabbed?

Answers

Famous Names (see Quiz 76, page 298)
1 Gianni Versace. **2** Pierre Cardin. **3** Queen Mother. **4** Ffion. **5** Getty. **6** Madonna. **7** Elizabeth. **8** Pakistan. **9** Mao Zedong. **10** Monica Lewinsky. **11** Bryan Ferry. **12** Vivienne Westwood. **13** Pamela Anderson. **14** Emma Forbes. **15** Both vicars. **16** Tony Blair. **17** Jack Rosenthal. **18** Brian Jones. **19** The Duchess of York. **20** Carol. **21** Football. **22** Egyptian. **23** Jane. **24** Gloria Hunniford. **25** Imelda Marcos. **26** Step daughter. **27** Michael. **28** Lord of the Dance. **29** Magic Johnson. **30** A fashion label.

Quiz 76 Famous Names

Answers - see Quiz 75, page 297

1 Whose funeral in Milan in 1997 was attended by Elton John and Naomi Campbell?
2 Which Frenchman was the first to launch menswear and ready to wear collections?
3 How is the former Lady Elizabeth Bowes-Lyon better known?
4 What is the first name of Mrs William Hague?
5 Which oil billionaire founded the world's highest funded art gallery?
6 Which famous American enrolled her baby daughter for Cheltenham Ladies College in September 1998?
7 What is John and Norma Major's daughter called?
8 Where did Diana make a fund raising trip to with Jemima Khan?
9 Chiang Ching was the third wife of which political leader?
10 Linda Tripp was the confidante of which famous name?
11 Which singer has a son called Otis after Otis Redding?
12 Which fashion designer launched a perfume called Boudoir?
13 According to the Guiness Book of Records who is the most mentioned woman on the Internet?
14 Who is Nanette Newman's famous TV presenter daughter?
15 What did David Frost's and Virginia Wade's father have in common?
16 Whose first names are Anthony Charles Lynton?
17 Which playwright is Maureen Lipman's husband?
18 Which Rolling Stone bought, and died at A.A. Milne's house?
19 Who was described in Blackwell's Worst Dressed list as 'the bare toed terror of London town'?
20 What is Margaret Thatcher's journalist daughter called?
21 At which sport did Pope John Paul II excel in his youth?
22 What is the nationality of ex UN secretary Boutros Boutros-Ghali?
23 Which name is shared by the Duchess of York's sister and one of Princess Diana's sisters?
24 Who married millionaire hairdresser Stephen Way in 1998?
25 Who was the wife of Ferdinand Marcos at the time of his death?
26 What relation was Cherie Blair to Pat Phoenix, who played Elsie Tanner in Coronation Street?
27 What was the first name of Marks of Marks & Spencer?
28 What links Nataraja in Hinduism and performer Michael Flatley?
29 Who was the first basketball player to declare he was HIV positive?
30 What is Red or Dead?

Answers

Pot Luck 35 (see Quiz 75, page 297)
1 Porcelain. **2** Partridges. **3** Tuscany. **4** pH scale. **5** Aristotle Onassis. **6** Rome. **7** Veins. **8** Dutch. **9** Janet Jackson. **10** Worzel Gummidge. **11** Thomas Cook. **12** Personal Equity Plan. **13** John Lewis Partnership. **14** Theatre. **15** Embroidery. **16** Drachma. **17** Banacek. **18** 19th century. **19** Sainsbury's. **20** Egypt. **21** Terence Conran. **22** Naomi Campbell. **23** Alberta. **24** Pauline Collins. **25** Glair. **26** Pierce Brosnan. **27** Ghana. **28** Ce Ce Peniston. **29** Chelsea Flower Show. **30** Hamburg.

Quiz 77 TV: TV Times 2

Answers - see Quiz 78, page 300

1 Which show provided BBC sales with a third of their 1997 profits?
2 Which woman writer created the character Jane Tennison?
3 Which ex Home Secretary was born the same day as ex Goodie Bill Oddie?
4 What is Dr Ross's first name in ER?
5 In which decade was Parliament first televised?
6 Which daughter of a famous footballer presented On The Ball with Barry Venison?
7 Which rugby player joined Ulrika Jonsson as a Gladiators presenter?
8 Who played Owen Springer in Reckless?
9 Which priest replaced Father Peter in Ballykissangel?
10 Who presents the rural life show Countryfile?
11 On GMTV where did Mark Freden regularly report from?
12 Which superstar did Matthew Corbett abandon finally in 1998?
13 Which role did Denise Robertson have on This Morning?
14 Who is the male wine expert on Food and Drink?
15 Who was the blonde captain on Shooting Stars?
16 How is TV presenter Leslie Heseltine better known?
17 How many letters make up the conundrum in Countdown?
18 What is Channel 5's daily quiz for older contestants called?
19 Who contracted amoebic dysentery while making a Holiday show with her daughter?
20 Frasier was a spin off from which series?
21 Who plays Ally McBeal?
22 How many points do you get for a starter in University Challenge?
23 To whom did The Duchess of York dedicate the first of her Sky chat shows in October 1998?
24 On which show did Tommy Walsh and Charlie Dimmock find fame?
25 For which sport did Frank Bough win an Oxbridge blue?
26 Who did David Dimbleby replace on Question Time?
27 Who wrote the acclaimed series of monologues Talking Heads?
28 Who played Darcy in Pride and Prejudice?
29 Which fivesome helped launch Channel 5?
30 Jimmy Savile received an honorary doctorate from which university?

Answers

Pot Luck 36 (see Quiz 78, page 300)

1 Michael Praed. **2** Leprosy. **3** Sugar Candy. **4** Mustard. **5** Tam O'Shanter. **6** On the Moon. **7** Peach & plum. **8** Chromium. **9** The bones. **10** An oak tree. **11** Aspirin. **12** Your Eminence. **13** 1983. **14** Vicky MacDonald. **15** Blackcurrant. **16** Belisha Beacon. **17** Arizona. **18** Daphne du Maurier. **19** Leo Sayer. **20** The Netherlands. **21** 1/10th. **22** Aestivation. **23** 88. **24** Niamh Kavanagh. **25** A flower. **26** Oxo. **27** The brain. **28** Cannon. **29** Bathsheba. **30** J. B. Priestley.

Quiz 78 Pot Luck 36

Answers - see Quiz 77, page 299

1 Which actor played both Prince of Moldavia and Robin Hood on TV?
2 What did Robert the Bruce die of?
3 What type of kisses did Mac and Katie Kissoon sing about?
4 Dijon is famous for which condiment?
5 Which Robbie Burns hero gave his name to a flat cap?
6 Where is the Bay of Rainbows?
7 A nectarine is a cross between which two fruits?
8 What makes stainless steel stainless?
9 What is affected by osteomyelitis?
10 What is Charles II said to have hidden in after the Battle of Worcester?
11 What is the common name for the medication acetylsalicylic acid?
12 How is a Cardinal addressed?
13 When was the wearing of seat belts in the front of a car made compulsory?
14 In Coronation Street who was Alec Gilroy's grand daughter?
15 Which fruit is in creme de cassis?
16 Which beacon was named after a 1930s Minister of Transport?
17 The Painted Desert is in which American state?
18 Who wrote My Cousin Rachel and Frenchman's Creek?
19 Whose hits include Moonlighting and More Than I Can Say?
20 Queen Juliana abdicated from which country's throne in 1980?
21 What fraction is a cable of a nautical mile?
22 What is the opposite of hibernation?
23 How many keys does a normal piano have?
24 Which female Irish singer won the Eurovision Song Contest with In Your Eyes?
25 What is a corn-cockle?
26 What did Mary Holland advertise on TV for eighteen years?
27 Which part of the body uses forty per cent of the oxygen in blood?
28 Which corpulent TV detective was played by William Conrad?
29 Who was the mother of King Solomon?
30 Who wrote The Good Companions?

Answers

TV: TV Times 2 (see Quiz 77, page 299)

1 The Teletubbies. **2** Lynda La Plante. **3** Michael Howard. **4** Doug. **5** 1980s. **6** Gabby Yorath. **7** Jeremy Guscott. **8** Robson Green. **9** Father Aidan. **10** John Craven. **11** Hollywood. **12** Sooty. **13** Agony aunt. **14** Oz Clarke. **15** Ulrika Jonsson. **16** Les Dennis. **17** Nine. **18** 100 Per Cent Gold. **19** Esther Rantzen. **20** Cheers. **21** Calista Flockhart. **22** 10. **23** Her late mother. **24** Ground Force. **25** Soccer. **26** Peter Sissons. **27** Alan Bennett. **28** Colin Firth. **29** The Spice Girls. **30** Leeds.

Quiz 79 Science: Space

Answers - see Quiz 80, page 302

1 Where are the headquarters of the European Space Agency?
2 Which word describes a body in free fall in space?
3 Which planet has the satellite Europa?
4 Which space station is named after the Russian word for 'peace'?
5 Ranger and Surveyor probes preceded exploration of where?
6 What name is given to a site for watching astronomical phenomena?
7 In which decade was Sputnik 1 launched?
8 Saturn rockets were developed for which moon programme?
9 Who was Soyuz TM-12's British passenger in 1991?
10 The first non-stop transatlantic flight was between which two countries?
11 What does a space shuttle land on when it returns to Earth?
12 What is the Oort cloud made out of?
13 Which Space Agency built Ariane?
14 Which communications satellite was the first to relay live TV transmissions?
15 Which rockets shared their name with the giant children of Uranus and Gaia in Greek myth?
16 Which part of the moon did Armstrong first walk on?
17 Which of our planets is nearest the end of the alphabet?
18 Claudie Andre-Deshays was the first woman in space from which country?
19 Whose spacecraft was Vostok 1?
20 After retiring as an astronaut John Glenn followed a career in what?
21 Which clouds are formed highest above the ground?
22 How was Michael Collins a pioneer of lunar flight?
23 What is the largest planet in the solar system?
24 Phobos is a moon of which planet?
25 What was Skylab?
26 Which pioneering spacecraft was first launched in April 1981?
27 What is Jupiter's red spot made from?
28 Which country launched the first space probe in 1959?
29 Which constellation is known as The Hunter?
30 Which is larger, Mars or Earth?

Answers

Pot Luck 37 (see Quiz 80, page 302)
1 Make-up artist. **2** George V. **3** A Will. **4** Nixon. **5** Daphne du Maurier. **6** Rioja. **7** Clot. **8** 1959. **9** Tampa. **10** Steven Spielberg. **11** 17th. **12** Shallot. **13** The Grampians. **14** Optician's. **15** Blind. **16** Grounds called The Stadium Of Light. **17** St. Mark. **18** The Great Pyramids of Giza. **19** Sausage. **20** Joseph Priestley. **21** Geoffrey Boycott. **22** B2. **23** British Prime Ministers. **24** Zacharias. **25** Eat. **26** W.H. Smiths. **27** Sinn Fein. **28** Legs. **29** Danube. **30** Yoghurt.

Quiz 80 Pot Luck 37

Answers - see Quiz 79, page 301

1 In what capacity did Boy George work for the RSC?
2 Which king unveiled the Victoria memorial?
3 What is made by a testator?
4 Who telephoned Neil Armstrong during his first moon walk?
5 Which novelist had three novels adapted by Alfred Hitchcock to films?
6 Which wine growing region is divided into Baja, Alta and Alavesa?
7 What does fibrin cause to happen to blood?
8 Did Buddy Holly die in 1956, 1959 or 1961?
9 Which Florida city was the setting for Burt Reynolds' Bandits?
10 Which director appeared in The Blues Brothers?
11 In which century was the Taj Mahal constructed?
12 A Bordelaise sauce is flavoured by which vegetable?
13 Ben Nevis is in which mountain range?
14 Where would you probably be looking at a Snellen Chart?
15 In Bingo, what are numbers ending in zero called?
16 What do Sunderland and Benfica soccer clubs share?
17 Who is the Patron Saint of Venice?
18 What are Mycerinus and Cheprun the second two greatest of?
19 What would you be eating if you ate a Spanish chorizo?
20 Which scientist first discovered the composition of air?
21 Which ex Yorkshire cricketer was born on the same day as Manfred Mann?
22 Which letter and number represent the vitamin riboflavin?
23 Derby, Pelham and Russell have all been what?
24 Who was John the Baptist's father?
25 In 1909 what were imprisoned suffragettes forced to do?
26 Euston became Britain's first railway station to have what in 1848?
27 In 1921 which political party burnt down Dublin's Custom House?
28 Which part of your body is protected by puttees?
29 Which river flows through six different European countries?
30 What is the main ingredient in an Indian raita?

Answers

Science: Space (see Quiz 79, page 301)
1 Paris. **2** Weightless. **3** Jupiter. **4** Mir. **5** The Moon. **6** Observatory. **7** 50s. **8** Apollo. **9** Helen Sharman. **10** Canada & Ireland. **11** Runway. **12** Comets. **13** European. **14** Telstar. **15** Titan. **16** Sea of Tranquillity. **17** Venus. **18** France. **19** Yuri Gagarin. **20** Politics. **21** Cirrus. **22** He didn't walk on the moon on the first lunar flight. **23** Jupiter. **24** Mars. **25** Space station. **26** Space shuttle. **27** Gases. **28** USSR. **29** Orion. **30** Earth.

Quiz 81 Performing Arts

Answers - see Quiz 82, page 304

1 Which opera venue is near Lewes?
2 Sir John Barbirolli was conductor of which orchestra at the time of his death?
3 If a sonata is for instruments what is a cantata written for?
4 Which London theatre was the home of Gilbert & Sullivan operas?
5 Sadler's Wells theatre is famous for which performing arts?
6 Equity in the USA deals only with performers where?
7 Wayne Sleep was principal dancer with which ballet company?
8 What do you press with the right hand on an accordion?
9 Which of the Three Tenors played the title role in the film version of Otello in 1986?
10 How many strings are there on a double bass?
11 Richard Eyre replaced Peter Hall as artistic director at which London theatre?
12 What were all Joseph Grimaldi's clowns called?
13 What shape is the sound box on a balalaika?
14 Which male voice is between bass and tenor?
15 Where is an annual Fringe Festival held?
16 In which US city was the Actors Studio founded?
17 What is the official name of London's Drury Lane theatre?
18 Miles Davis is famous for playing which musical instrument?
19 Which king did Handel write The Water Music for?
20 Whose 1986 recording of Vivaldi's The Four Seasons sold over a million copies?
21 What was Paul McCartney's first classical oratorio?
22 An anthem is usually accompanied by which musical instrument?
23 Which mime artist created the clown-harlequin Bip?
24 Who is The Violinist?
25 Which theatre near Blackfriars was London's first new theatre in 300 years when opened in 1959?
26 What was the slogan of London's Windmill Theatre?
27 Which musical instruments did Leo Fender create?
28 What was the first black-owned record company in the USA?
29 Who has written more plays, Shakespeare or Ayckbourn?
30 Alan Bleasdale hails from which city?

Answers

Pot Luck 38 (see Quiz 82, page 304)
1 Hertfordshire. **2** A miller. **3** Frank Morgan. **4** Tax Exempt Special Savings Account. **5** Rome. **6** Canada. **7** Michael Bentine. **8** Nijinsky. **9** Grass. **10** Ten Pole Tudor. **11** Star fish. **12** Quaver. **13** Vicarage. **14** Glenn Miller. **15** Trollope. **16** Borneo. **17** The Trunk. **18** Maggie Smith. **19** Lactose. **20** Fluke. **21** Vera Lynn. **22** Little Women. **23** Mick Jagger. **24** Dachshunds. **25** Judaea. **26** Prince Edward. **27** Maud Grimes. **28** Tavares. **29** A barrister. **30** Shell-shaped.

Quiz 82 Pot Luck 38

Answers - see Quiz 81, page 303

1 Hemel Hempstead and St Albans are in which county?
2 Who would use a quern?
3 Who played the title role in the film The Wizard of Oz?
4 What does the acronym TESSA stand for?
5 The Spanish Steps are in which European city?
6 Cars with the international vehicle registration CDN come from where?
7 Which zany comedian devised the TV show It's A Square World?
8 Which Russian sounding horse won the 2000 Guineas, St Leger and the Derby in 1970?
9 What kind of a plant is fescue?
10 Who had hits with Swords of a Thousand Men and Who Killed Bambi?
11 What type of sea creature is a brittle star?
12 Musically which note is half the value of a crotchet?
13 Murder At The... where was Miss Marple's first appearance?
14 Who was Glenn Hoddle named after?
15 Which writer Anthony created the county of Barsetshire?
16 What is the largest island in Asia?
17 Which part of an elephant has 40,000 muscles?
18 Who played the lead role in the film The Prime Of Miss Jean Brodie?
19 Which type of sugar is found in milk?
20 What word can describe a lucky chance and the hook of an anchor?
21 Which female vocalist was known as 'The Forces Sweetheart'?
22 Which novel preceded Good Wives?
23 Which pop star married Bianca de Macias in May 1971?
24 Which breed of dog was originally bred to hunt badgers?
25 Herod the Great ruled which kingdom?
26 Which Prince's childhood nickname was JAWS?
27 In Coronation Street who was Reg Holdsworth's mother-in-law?
28 Who had hits with Whodunnit and More Than A Woman?
29 What is the English equivalent of a Scottish Advocate?
30 What shape is a dish called a coquille?

Answers

Performing Arts (see Quiz 81, page 303)
1 Glyndebourne. **2** Halle. **3** Voices. **4** Savoy. **5** Opera and ballet. **6** Theatre. **7** Royal Ballet. **8** Piano-style keyboard. **9** Placido Domingo. **10** Four. **11** National. **12** Joey. **13** Triangular. **14** Baritone. **15** Edinburgh. **16** New York. **17** Theatre Royal. **18** Trumpet. **19** George I. **20** Nigel Kennedy. **21** Liverpool Oratorio. **22** Organ. **23** Marcel Marceau. **24** Vanessa Mae. **25** Mermaid. **26** We never closed. **27** Electric guitars. **28** Tamla Motown. **29** Ayckbourn. **30** Liverpool.

Quiz 83 Country & Western

Answers - see Quiz 84, page 306

1 Who had a hit in 1972 with A Thing Called Love?
2 Which hit in letters followed Stand by Your Man for Tammy Wynette?
3 Which group had a No 1 hit in 1976 with Mississippi?
4 Which famous country singer was kidnapped in 1979?
5 Whose song was a No. 1 for John Denver in 1974?
6 Which Patsy Cline hit was covered by Julio Iglesias in 1994?
7 In which year was Achey Breaky Heart a hit for Billy Ray Cyrus?
8 Who had a No 11 UK hit with Talking In Your Sleep in 1978?
9 Hiram Williams is the real name of which singer?
10 Which opera singer joined John Denver to record Perhaps Love?
11 What surname links 70s star Daniel and 50s star Pat?
12 Which Kris wrote Help Me Make It Through the Night?
13 Who had a hit in the summer of 1998 with How Do I?
14 Who wrote the autobiography Coal Miner's Daughter?
15 Who joined Kenny Rogers on the No 7 hit Islands In The Stream?
16 What is Reba McEntire's real name?
17 Which specialist type of singing links Frank Ifield and Slim Whitman?
18 Who duetted with Mark Knopfler on the album Neck and Neck?
19 In the No 1, which drums were heard by Jim Reeves?
20 Who sang All I Have To Do Is Dream with Bobbie Gentry in 1969?
21 Who had a backing band called the Waylors?
22 What is the name of the theme park owned by Dolly Parton?
23 George Jones' 1975 hit The Battle told of the split from his wife. Who was she?
24 Which Banks were a hit in 1971 for Olivia Newton-John?
25 Which song was a No 2 UK hit for Tammy Wynette and KLF in 1991?
26 Who wrote the classic song Crazy?
27 Who formed the Trio with Dolly Parton and Linda Ronstadt?
28 Who took Cotton Eye Joe to No 1 in 1994?
29 Which No 9 for Elvis was a No 10 for Carl Perkins in 1956?
30 Which 'modern girl' joined Kenny Rogers on We've Got Tonight?

Answers

Pot Luck 39 (see Quiz 84, page 306)

1 Rose. **2** Cousins. **3** Cuba. **4** Seaweed. **5** Sweet. **6** Victoria. **7** Oil tanker. **8** Theatre Royal. **9** Blood poisoning. **10** Leopards. **11** Anthony Eden. **12** Macduff. **13** Automatic pilot. **14** Suffolk. **15** Soles of your feet. **16** Bolero. **17** Racehorses. **18** Passepartout. **19** Pierre Trudeau. **20** Cary Grant. **21** 1970s. **22** The Lion, The Witch and the Wardrobe. **23** Nose. **24** British Grand Prix. **25** Iraq. **26** Supergrass. **27** William Beveridge. **28** I Just Called to say I Love You. **29** A horse. **30** Thumb.

Quiz 84 Pot Luck 39

Answers - see Quiz 83, page 305

1 What was the name of Kate Winslet's character in Titanic?
2 What is the relationship between Prince Edward and Lord Lindley?
3 Which Caribbean country won the 1992 Olympic Gold Medal for baseball?
4 What is kelp?
5 Who had hits with Fox On The Run and Wig-Wam Bam?
6 What name is an African lake, a station and a former Queen?
7 What type of vessel was the Torrey Canyon?
8 What is the name of the most famous theatre in London's Drury Lane?
9 What is the more common name for toxaemia?
10 Which members of the big cat family collect in a leap?
11 Who preceded Harold Macmillan as Prime Minister?
12 In the Shakespeare play who killed Macbeth?
13 The Christian name George lends itself to which part of a plane?
14 Newmarket and Ipswich are both in which county?
15 Reflexology treats your body through what?
16 What can be a short jacket and a dance?
17 What are auctioned at Tattersalls?
18 Who was Phileas Fogg's companion in Around the World in 80 Days?
19 Which French-Canadian became Canadian Prime Minister in 1968?
20 Archibald Leach born in Bristol became which Hollywood star?
21 In which decade did John Wayne die?
22 Which is the second novel set in the magical kingdom of Narnia?
23 Which part of your body would interest a rhinologist?
24 In 1926 what was held for the first time at Brooklands?
25 Mesopotamia was the ancient name for which modern day country?
26 Who had hits with Alright and Going Out in '95 and '96?
27 Whose report in the 1940s was vital in setting up the welfare state?
28 Which Stevie Wonder No 1 was in the film The Woman In Red?
29 What type of animal is a Lippizaner?
30 Which digit is your pollex?

Answers

Country & Western (see Quiz 83, page 305)
1 Johnny Cash. **2** D.I.V.O.R.C.E. **3** Pussycat. **4** Tammy Wynette. **5** Annie's Song. **6** Crazy. **7** 1992. **8** Crystal Gayle. **9** Hank Williams. **10** Placido Domingo. **11** Boone. **12** Kristofferson. **13** Leanne Rimes. **14** Loretta Lynn. **15** Dolly Parton. **16** Reba McEntire. **17** Yodelling. **18** Chet Atkins. **19** Distant Drums. **20** Glen Campbell. **21** Waylon Jennings. **22** Dollywood. **23** Tammy Wynette. **24** The Ohio. **25** Justified and Ancient. **26** Willie Nelson. **27** Emmylou Harris. **28** Rednex. **29** Blue Suede Shoes. **30** Sheena Easton.

Quiz 85 Sport: Rugby

Answers - see Quiz 86, page 308

1. Which Australian was the first to score 60 tries in international rugby?
2. Who played the opening match at the new Millennium Stadium for the 1999 World Cup?
3. Who was the first English player to play in 50 internationals?
4. Which country in 1995 asked to increase the number of teams in the Five Nations Cup?
5. Which colours do Bath play in?
6. Which Welsh Union player was a regular captain on A Question of Sport?
7. In which part of London did the London Bronco's start out?
8. Which TV channel sponsored a Floodlit Rugby League Trophy?
9. For which side did Brian Bevan score 740 tries in 620 matches?
10. What were Bradford before they were Bulls?
11. Who retired as Scottish captain after the 1995 World Cup?
12. Who was Wigan's leading try scorer in the 1994/5 season?
13. Where would you watch Rhinos playing rugby?
14. Which Harlequins hooker was nicknamed 'Pitbull'?
15. Which international side has the shortest name?
16. Who are the two sides in the Varsity Match?
17. Which rugby team plays its home games at Welford Road?
18. Who was leading try scorer in the 1995 rugby union World Cup?
19. In 1998 what colour cards were substituted for yellow ones?
20. Who joined Leeds in 1991 after playing on the other side of the Pennines since 1984?
21. What did Bath Football Club change its name to in the mid 90s?
22. Who was the first non-white Springbok, before the end of apartheid?
23. Which rugby side added Warriors to its name?
24. In which decade was Rugby Union last played in the Olympics?
25. How old was Will Carling when he was first made England Captain?
26. Who played a record breaking 69 times at fly half for England between 1985 and 1995?
27. In 1980 who led England to their first Grand Slam in 23 years?
28. Where is the annual Varsity match played?
29. How many years had Wigan's unbeaten run in the FA Challenge Cup lasted when it ended in 1996?
30. Who did Martin Offiah play for in his first years as a League player?

Answers

Pot Luck 40 (see Quiz 86, page 308)
1 Shoulder blade. **2** Stour. **3** Sex Pistols. **4** Falmouth and Cambourne. **5** India. **6** Judo. **7** Henry I. **8** The wind. **9** Maastricht. **10** Oscar Blaketon. **11** British Honduras. **12** Don Johnson. **13** Jenkins. **14** River Soar. **15** Francis. **16** My Son, My Son. **17** Individual Savings Account. **18** Duke of Marlborough. **19** Peter. **20** A knot. **21** Zirconium. **22** London. **23** A ship. **24** Colorado. **25** Racey. **26** The Castle of Mey. **27** London's Burning. **28** The Merry Monarch. **29** Norfolk. **30** Patrick Duffy.

Quiz 86 Pot Luck 40

Answers - see Quiz 85, page 307

1 Where in your body is your scapula?
2 Canterbury stands on which river?
3 Who had hits with God Save The Queen and C'Mon Everybody?
4 Sebastian Coe became MP for which constituency in 1992?
5 Which former colony was called the jewel in Queen Victoria's crown?
6 What was the sport of Karen Briggs and Nicola Fairbrother?
7 Which Henry became King of England in 1100?
8 In the film Mary Poppins, Mary said she would stay until what changed?
9 Which Treaty on European Union was signed in December 1991?
10 Which character is played by Derek Fowlds in Heartbeat?
11 What was the former name of Belize?
12 Which actor married Melanie Griffith twice?
13 What was Ffion Hague's maiden name?
14 Which River does Leicester stand on?
15 What is decathlon champion Daley Thompson's first name?
16 Which Vera Lynn song was a No 1 UK hit in 1954?
17 In finance what is an ISA?
18 Who was given Blenheim Palace as a reward for his military service?
19 In The Bible, who denied Jesus three times before the cock crowed twice?
20 A Turk's Head is a type of what?
21 Alphabetically which chemical element is the last?
22 Which European capital was considered cleanest in a 1995 survey?
23 What is a frigatoon?
24 'The Garden of the Gods' is in which American state?
25 Who had hits with Lay Your Love On Me and Some Girls?
26 Which castle was bought by the Queen Mother in 1952?
27 Which TV series has characters called Gracie, Sicknote and George?
28 What was King Charles II's nickname?
29 Kings Lynn and Norwich are both in which county?
30 Which actor links Bobby Ewing to The Man From Atlantis?

Answers

Sport: Rugby (see Quiz 85, page 307)
1 David Campese. **2** Wales & Argentina. **3** Rory Underwood. **4** Italy. **5** Blue, black and white. **6** Gareth Edwards. **7** Fulham. **8** BBC2. **9** Warrington. **10** Northern. **11** Gavin Hastings. **12** Martin Offiah. **13** Leeds. **14** Brian Moore. **15** Fiji. **16** Oxford University and Cambridge University. **17** Leicester. **18** Jonah Lomu. **19** White. **20** Ellery Hanley. **21** Bath Rugby Club. **22** Errol Tobias. **23** Wigan. **24** 1920s. **25** 22. **26** Rob Andrew. **27** Bill Beaumont. **28** Twickenham. **29** Eight. **30** Widnes.

Quiz 87 Movies: Westerns

Answers - see Quiz 88, page 310

1 What was the first film in which Clint Eastwood starred as 'The man with no name'?
2 Who played the sadistic sheriff in Eastwood's Unforgiven?
3 Which actor's films include Big Jim McLain, McLintock and McQ?
4 Which star of Maverick played Brett Maverick in the TV series?
5 Which Oscar did Kevin Costner win for Dances With Wolves?
6 What is the name of the original tale that the Magificent Seven is based on?
7 What weather feature was in the title of the song from Butch Cassidy won an Oscar?
8 Who was the star of Jeremiah Johnson?
9 Which comedy actor starred in the comedy western The Paleface?
10 Who starred with brother Charlie Sheen in Young Guns?
11 Who was the title character in the surreal western The Seven Faces of Dr. Lao?
12 Who played the woman poker player in Maverick?
13 Which actor was The Bad?
14 Which Back to the Future film returns to the Wild West?
15 In which musical western does the song Wandrin' Star appear?
16 Which Hollywood legend was the narrator in How The West Was Won?
17 Which film was originally called Per un Pugno di Dollari?
18 Which country singer was in True Grit?
19 Which son of a M*A*S*H star appeared in Young Guns II?
20 Who did John Wayne play in The Alamo?
21 Clint Eastwood became mayor of which town?
22 Which 1985 film was a revised remake of the classic Shane?
23 Where is the village where the action of The Magnificent Seven centres?
24 Where was The Good, the Bad and the Ugly made?
25 What was the name of Mel Brooks' spoof western?
26 Which English comic appeared in Desperado?
27 Which 80s teenage western starred actors known as the Brat Pack?
28 What was Tonto's horse called?
29 Who was Gene Autry's most famous horse?
30 Traditionally, what colour is the western hero's hat?

Answers

TV: TV Times 3 (see Quiz 88, page 310)

1 Andrew. **2** William G Stewart. **3** Watchdog. **4** Coronation Street. **5** Helen Baxendale. **6** Anna. **7** Holiday Heaven. **8** Blue Peter. **9** Geoff Hamilton. **10** Liverpool. **11** Mel Smith & Griff Rhys-Jones. **12** Los Angeles. **13** Sandi Toksvig. **14** BBC Breakfast News . **15** BBC2. **16** John Stapleton. **17** Murray Walker. **18** Blockbusters. **19** Spencer Tracy. **20** Shauna Lowry. **21** Kevin. **22** Gymnastics. **23** All Creatures Great and Small. **24** Hugh Scully. **25** Michael Palin. **26** Monica Lewinsky. **27** Blackburn Rovers. **28** Selfridges. **29** £5. **30** Cook.

Quiz 88 TV: TV Times 3

Answers - see Quiz 87, page 309

1 Men Behaving Badly's Leslie Ash was born the same day as which Prince?
2 Who presents Channel 4's Fifteen To One?
3 Alice Beer first found fame on which show?
4 Which show was first broadcast on Friday 9th December 1960?
5 Which Cardiac Arrest star also starred in Friends?
6 What was the lawyer played by Daniela Nardini in This Life called?
7 Which series featured celebs returning to a previous vacation destination?
8 Which children's show has the theme music Barnacle Bill?
9 Whose last series was Paradise Gardens?
10 In which city did the docu soap Hotel take place?
11 Which comedy duo are famous for their head-to-head discussions?
12 In which city did lifeguard Mitch Buchanan work?
13 Who was the female team captain in the 90s Call My Bluff?
14 What did the BBC's Breakfast Time change its name to?
15 Fully Booked was first on which channel?
16 Who moved to GMTV after his The Time The Place was axed?
17 Which voice of motor racing moved to ITV to cover the sport?
18 In which show might a contestant ask "Could I have a P please, Bob?"
19 Who is Robbie Coltrane's son Spencer named after?
20 Which redhead assisted Rolf Harris at the Animal Hospital?
21 What was the name of the spotty teenager played by Harry Enfield?
22 Presenter Suzanne Dando represented Great Britain at which sport?
23 Which series centred on Skeldale House?
24 Who hosted Antiques Roadshow through most of the 90s?
25 Who tried to emulate Phileas Fogg in a 1989 documentary?
26 Who did Roseanne offer a million dollars to appear on her talk show in October 1998?
27 Which Lancashire soccer side does Jim Bowen support?
28 Which store was the subject of The Shop?
29 How much are the ingredients worth on Ready Steady Cook?
30 What did Susan Brookes do on This Morning?

Answers

Movies: Westerns (see Quiz 87, page 309)
1 A Fistful of Dollars. **2** Gene Hackman. **3** John Wayne. **4** James Garner. **5** Best Director. **6** The Seven Samurai. **7** Raindrops. **8** Robert Redford. **9** Bob Hope. **10** Emilio Estevez. **11** Tony Randall. **12** Jodie Foster. **13** Lee van Cleef. **14** No. III. **15** Paint Your Wagon. **16** Spencer Tracy. **17** A Fistful of Dollars. **18** Glen Campbell. **19** Kiefer Sutherland. **20** Davy Crockett. **21** Carmel. **22** Pale Rider. **23** Mexico. **24** Italy. **25** Blazing Saddles. **26** John Cleese. **27** Young Guns. **28** Scout. **29** Champion. **30** White.

Quiz 89 Pot Luck 41

Answers - see Quiz 90, page 312

1 Which Queen wrote the Casket Letters?
2 Which former Take That star had Child at No 3 in 1996?
3 What can be metric royal, metric demy and metric crown?
4 In which TV series was the character 'Boss Hogg'?
5 Which film star married Prince Aly Khan?
6 Which almond cake is traditionally made for Mothering Sunday?
7 Who had hits with We Are Glass and Cars ?
8 What would an Australian call trousers?
9 Which actress had lead roles in the films Out of Africa and Silkwood?
10 Which two European languages are spoken in Madagascar?
11 Which country has the shortest coastline in the world?
12 What were the giant insects in the science fiction film Them?
13 Which famous TV cook took his show Around Britain?
14 During which war does Norman Mailer's The Naked and the Dead take place?
15 Aylesbury and Milton Keynes are both in which county?
16 Which actress is Jack Davenport's mother?
17 Which animal was used by Jenner to develop the vaccine against smallpox?
18 What is a davenport?
19 Which singer starred alongside Kyle McLachlan in Dune?
20 Who composed the music for The Good, the Bad and the Ugly?
21 Who had hits with Blue Monday and World In Motion?
22 What kind of musical instrument was a kit?
23 Which former tennis player bought Hull FC?
24 Which John Carpenter film set in the antarctic starred Kurt Russell?
25 Name the first yacht to win the America's Cup?
26 Which singing sisters were called Patti, Laverne and Maxine?
27 In which country are the guerrilla group the Tamil Tigers?
28 What name is given to the principal female singer in an opera?
29 The dish Eggs Florentine contains which vegetable?
30 Which town was Barbara Castle's parliamentary constituency?

Answers

World Tour (see Quiz 90, page 312)
1 Atlantic. **2** Las Vegas. **3** Broadway. **4** Inuit (Eskimos). **5** Cape of Good Hope. **6** Wind. **7** Honshu. **8** Australia. **9** Washington. **10** K2. **11** Okovango. **12** Indian. **13** Hawaii. **14** China. **15** Namibia. **16** Gobi. **17** Dow Jones. **18** Eskimo. **19** Michigan. **20** Zambia and Zimbabwe. **21** Trinidad. **22** French. **23** Canaries. **24** North coast of Africa. **25** Manhattan. **26** Tip of South America. **27** Greenland. **28** Kilimanjaro. **29** Israel. **30** Pakistan & Afghanistan.

Quiz 90 World Tour

Answers - see Quiz 89, page 311

1 The Sargasso Sea is part of which ocean?
2 Which US city's name means 'The Fields'?
3 How is New York's 'Great White Way' also known?
4 Which Canadians speak Inuktitut?
5 Which Cape was originally called the Cape of Storms?
6 In America what type of natural phenomenon is a Chinook?
7 What is the principal island of Japan?
8 Where is the town of Kurri Kurri?
9 Where is the HQ of the International Monetary Fund?
10 By which abbreviation is the mountain Chogori known?
11 What is the only permanent river in the Kalahari desert?
12 Which Ocean's deepest point is the Java Trench?
13 Where would you be if someone put a lei round your neck?
14 Where is the world's longest canal?
15 Afrikaans is the official language of which country in addition to South Africa?
16 In which desert is the Bactrian camel found?
17 What is the name of the index on the New York Stock Exchange?
18 Which group of people have a name meaning 'eater of raw meat'?
19 Which is the only Great Lake wholly in the USA?
20 The Kariba Dam is on the border of which two countries?
21 Calypso is the traditional song form of which Caribbean island?
22 Which European language is spoken in Chad?
23 Las Palmas is in which island group?
24 Approximately where was Carthage to be found?
25 Wall Street and Broadway lie on which island?
26 Where is the Magellan Strait?
27 What is the largest island between the North Atlantic and the Arctic?
28 What is Africa's highest volcano?
29 Where is there a Parliament called the Knesset?
30 Which two countries does the Khyber Pass separate?

Answers

Pot Luck 41 (see Quiz 89, page 311)
1 Mary, Queen of Scots. **2** Mark Owen. **3** Sizes of paper. **4** The Dukes of Hazzard. **5** Rita Hayworth. **6** Simnel Cake. **7** Gary Numan. **8** Strides. **9** Meryl Streep. **10** French & English. **11** Monaco. **12** Ants. **13** Gary Rhodes. **14** WWII. **15** Buckinghamshire. **16** Maria Aitken. **17** Cow. **18** A sofa or desk. **19** Sting. **20** Ennio Morricone. **21** New Order. **22** A small violin. **23** David Lloyd. **24** The Thing. **25** America. **26** The Andrews Sisters. **27** Sri Lanka. **28** Prima Donna. **29** Spinach. **30** Blackburn.

Quiz 91 Pot Luck 42

Answers - see Quiz 92, page 314

1 What is saxifrage?
2 Family wise what do Henry Cooper and Carol Thatcher have in common?
3 Who hoisted himself onto Sinbad the Sailor's shoulders?
4 How much are you paid if you hold an honorary post?
5 Which actor played the leading role in the film Brothers In Law?
6 What can be a five card game, a smooth, woolly surface or a sleep?
7 Which club did Will Carling play for?
8 Which sport is Britain's Yvonne MacGregor associated with?
9 Whose music albums have included An Innocent Man?
10 'Englander' is an anagram of which country?
11 Which actress played Michael Douglas's wife in Fatal Attraction?
12 What is a melodeon?
13 Which animal family are impala, eland and dik-dik all from?
14 Who would have been granted a Ticket of Leave?
15 In TV's Upstairs Downstairs what was the name of the cook?
16 Whose hits include Dancin' On the Ceiling and Do It To Me?
17 Which stone is inscribed "Cormac McCarthy fortis me fieri fecit AD 1446"?
18 Which actor played the leading role in the TV drama Shogun?
19 What name is given to withered apples used to make rough cider?
20 Who composed the music for the musical Lady Be Good?
21 What is a grackle?
22 Which building was erected in 1851 for the Great Exhibition?
23 Which children's TV series has included Tucker Jenkins and Zammo?
24 Which Corrie character died with Gilbert and Sullivan playing in his car?
25 Which branch would you hold out to seek peace?
26 Arthur Hastings was the sidekick of which fictional sleuth?
27 Whose hits include Detroit City and Love Me Tonight?
28 The leader of an orchestra plays which instrument?
29 What was Mab's job in fairy folklore?
30 Which actress was left on a desert island in TV's Girl Friday?

Answers

Past Times: The 80s (see Quiz 92, page 314)
1 UK and Eire. **2** Chernobyl. **3** FW de Klerk. **4** Dubcek. **5** Salman Rushdie. **6** Michael Foot. **7** Mitterrand. **8** Galtieri. **9** Derek Hatton. **10** Jamaica. **11** Greenpeace. **12** Iceland. **13** Twice. **14** Shirley Williams. **15** Ken Livingstone. **16** Monday. **17** The Labour Party. **18** Grand Hotel. **19** Slobodan Milosevic. **20** Montserrat. **21** Mubarak. **22** Irangate. **23** David Blunkett. **24** Jimmy Carter. **25** Peter Mandelson. **26** Local authority. **27** Benazir Bhutto. **28** Zimbabwe. **29** South Africa. **30** Mikhail Gorbachev.

Quiz 92 Past Times: The 80s

Answers - see Quiz 91, page 313

1 The Hillsborough Agreement was between which two countries?
2 Where was there a major nuclear leak in the USSR in 1986?
3 Who was the last white President of South Africa, elected in 1989?
4 Which former liberal leader was made speaker of the national assembly of Czechoslovakia in 1989?
5 A fatwa calling for the death of which writer was made by Iran in '89?
6 Who succeeded Callaghan as Labour leader?
7 Who became France's first socialist president in 1981?
8 Who was Argentine President during the Falklands Conflict?
9 Which ex deputy leader of Liverpool Council was expelled form the Labour Party in 1987?
10 Michael Manley became leader of where in 1989?
11 Who owned Rainbow Warrior, sunk by the French in 1985?
12 Vigdis Finnbogadottir became head of state in which country?
13 How many times was Margaret Thatcher elected PM in the 80s?
14 Who was the only woman founder of the SDP?
15 Who was leader of the GLC from 1981-86?
16 What was the Black day of the week of the 1987 stockmarket crash?
17 Who moved from Transport House to Walworth Road in 1980?
18 In which hotel was the Brighton bomb in 1984?
19 Who became President of Serbia in 1986?
20 Most of which Caribbean island's buildings were destroyed by hurricane Hugo in 1989?
21 Who became Egyptian President after Sadat's assassination?
22 What was the name of the scandal over arms for hostages in which Oliver North was implicated?
23 Which Cabinet Minister was leader of Sheffield City Council for most of the 80s?
24 Who did Ronald Reagan defeat to become US President in 1980?
25 Which spin doctor did Neil Kinnock engage to run the 1987 election campaign?
26 In 1989 state schools were allowed to opt out of whose control?
27 Which woman became PM of Pakistan after the death of Zia in a plane crash?
28 Where did the parties of ZANU and ZAPU merge in 1987?
29 In 1986 the pass laws, concerning the carrying of identity documents, were repealed in which country?
30 Which Russian leader introduced the policy of perestroika?

Answers

Pot Luck 42 (see Quiz 91, page 313)

1 A small rock plant. **2** Twins. **3** The Old Man of the Sea. **4** Nothing. **5** Ian Carmichael. **6** A nap. **7** Harlequins. **8** Cycling. **9** Billy Joel. **10** Greenland. **11** Anne Archer. **12** A musical instrument. **13** Antelope. **14** A convict. **15** Mrs Bridges. **16** Lionel Richie. **17** The Blarney Stone. **18** Richard Chamberlain. **19** Scrumps. **20** George Gershwin. **21** A bird. **22** Crystal Palace. **23** Grange Hill. **24** Derek Wilton. **25** Olive. **26** Hercule Poirot. **27** Tom Jones. **28** Violin. **29** A midwife. **30** Joanna Lumley.

Quiz 93 Pot Luck 43

Answers - see Quiz 94, page 316

1 What type of animal is a Sooty Mangabey?
2 Which drink was advertised as 'drunk for a penny; dead drunk for tuppence'?
3 Who did William III defeat in 1690 at the Battle of the Boyne?
4 Rupert Bear is linked with which newspaper?
5 In Old English which word meant a field?
6 What were the eldest sons of French kings called from the 14th century?
7 Ely stands on which river?
8 Which 60s singer married the designer Jeff Banks?
9 In 1945, who became British Prime Minister?
10 Which plant has a flower called the 'poor man's weather-glass'?
11 Who had hits with The Streak and Misty in the 70s?
12 Who was President of the Philippines from 1965 to 1986?
13 Which Gate is a memorial for British Soldiers who fell at Ypres?
14 Who played Fred Kite in the film I'm Alright, Jack?
15 Which entertainer was married to his manager Cheryl St Clair?
16 Which complaint was the Jacuzzi originally developed to help?
17 What did Anna Karenina throw herself under in the Tolstoy novel?
18 Who wrote Dr Zhivago?
19 In which soap does the Cat & Fiddle rival The Bull?
20 Which comedian was Connie Booth married to?
21 What did people find in the book Lost Horizon?
22 Who preceded Edward VI as Monarch?
23 In the film The Tommy Steele Story who played Tommy Steele?
24 Who finished his radio show with "B.F.N. Bye for now"?
25 Who had hits with The Logical Song and Dreamer?
26 In which year was Lord Mountbatten murdered?
27 What is the start of Psalm 23?
28 Which shaggy horned wild cattle live in the Tibetan mountains?
29 What was a gulag in Russia?
30 In the 1953 film Houdini who played the title role?

Answers

Leisure: Books 2 (see Quiz 94, page 316)
1 Oxford. **2** Lake District. **3** Slavery. **4** Dictionary. **5** Jeeves. **6** The Greatest. **7** Lord Peter Wimsey. **8** Black Beauty. **9** Spycatcher. **10** Childcare. **11** Joan Collins. **12** Nigel Lawson. **13** Maeve Binchy. **14** Oranges. **15** Ruth Rendell. **16** Bill Bryson. **17** Agatha Christie. **18** The Godfather. **19** The English Patient. **20** John Le Carre. **21** Schindler's Ark. **22** Marie Stopes. **23** The Odessa File. **24** Edwina Currie. **25** Detective novel. **26** Jeffrey Archer. **27** Wales. **28** A Tale of Two Cities. **29** Exodus. **30** Simenon.

Quiz 94 Leisure: Books 2

Answers - see Quiz 93, page 315

1 In which university city is the Bodleian Library?
2 In which District did Beatrix Potter live?
3 Uncle Tom's Cabin was a novel which argued against what?
4 In the US what type of book is Webster famous for?
5 Who is the most famous manservant created by P.G.Wodehouse?
6 What was Muhammad Ali's autobiography called?
7 Which Dorothy L Sayers' creation was Harriet Vane's husband?
8 Which children's classic was written to encourage adults to be kinder to horses?
9 Which book by ex intelligence agent Peter Wright, did the British government try to have banned?
10 What was the subject of Benjamin Spock's most famous books?
11 Which soap star wrote Prime Time?
12 Which ex Chancellor of the Exchequer wrote a diet book?
13 Whose first successful novel was Light A Penny Candle?
14 What 'Are Not the Only Fruit' according to Jeanette Winterson?
15 Who wrote the detective novel Road Rage?
16 Who wrote A Walk in the Woods?
17 The Murder of Roger Ackroyd was an early novel by whom?
18 Which is Mario Puzo's most famous novel, first published in 1969?
19 Which Michael Ondaatje book was made into an Oscar winning film with Ralph Fiennes?
20 Who created George Smiley?
21 Which was the first Thomas Keneally book to win the Booker Prize?
22 Which birth control campaigner wrote the book Married Love?
23 What was Frederick Forsyth's follow up to The Day of the Jackal?
24 Which ex MP's first novel was A Parliamentary Affair?
25 The Woman in White is the first novel of what type in English?
26 Whose Not a Penny More, Not a Penny Less was written to clear bankruptcy debts?
27 In Colin Dexter's books where does Lewis come from?
28 Which Dickens' novel is about the French Revolution?
29 What is the second book of the Old Testament?
30 Which Georges wrote over a hundred novels featuring Jules Maigret?

Answers

Pot Luck 43 (see Quiz 93, page 315)
1 Monkey. **2** Gin. **3** James II. **4** Daily Express. **5** An acre. **6** Dauphin.
7 The Ouse. **8** Sandie Shaw. **9** Clement Attlee. **10** Scarlet Pimpernel.
11 Ray Stevens. **12** Ferdinand Marcos. **13** Menin Gate. **14** Peter Sellers.
15 Michael Barrymore. **16** Arthritis. **17** A train. **18** Boris Pasternak.
19 The Archers. **20** John Cleese. **21** Shangri-La. **22** Henry VIII.
23 Tommy Steele. **24** Jimmy Young. **25** Supertramp. **26** 1979.
27 The Lord is my shepherd. **28** Yaks. **29** A prison camp. **30** Tony Curtis.

Quiz 95 Pot Luck 44

Answers - see Quiz 96, page 318

1. What did MGM stand for?
2. What colour is puce?
3. What is the French equivalent of the Italian race Giro D'Italia?
4. Who was the first presenter of the TV series Tomorrow's World?
5. Which cartoon character was the 'fastest mouse in Mexico'?
6. Who had 90s No 1 hits with The Power and Rhythm Is A Dancer?
7. Which US state is the second smallest?
8. According to the saying, who rush in where angels fear to tread?
9. What is Blue Vinney?
10. Who wrote Five Children and It and Wet Magic?
11. Which terrier is the largest of the breed?
12. Who was the head of the German SS?
13. What is studied by a haematologist?
14. Which county is Morganwg Ganol in Welsh?
15. What type of creature is a turnstone?
16. Which country from 1867-1914 had a governor called The Khedive?
17. In the film The Great Escape which actor played the Forger?
18. Which Egyptian President was assassinated in 1981?
19. In the TV series To The Manor Born what was the name of the butler?
20. What is Paddy Ashdown's first Christian name?
21. Who had hits with Kiss from a Rose and Crazy?
22. The town of Newcastle is in which Australian state?
23. What was Marc Bolan's real name?
24. What type of food is a bullace?
25. What is a snake's cast off skin called?
26. The holiday camp Maplins featured in which TV series?
27. Which TV Arts presenter was Director General of the BBC from 1968-75?
28. What is mineral water mixed with quinine called?
29. Cars with the international vehicle registration CDN come from where?
30. What was sought by Jason and the Argonauts?

Answers

Pop Music: Groups (see Quiz 96, page 318)

1 The Blue Flames. **2** Swedish. **3** Two. **4** Summer Love. **5** The News. **6** Chairmen of the Board. **7** Our eyes. **8** In Perfect Harmony. **9** Vic Reeves. **10** Def Leppard. **11** Live Forever. **12** Good Vibrations. **13** New York. **14** Three Lions. **15** Cream. **16** Rainbow. **17** California. **18** All Day and All of the Night. **19** Computer Love/The Model. **20** To Trancentral. **21** Bread. **22** Jake. **23** The Bangles. **24** Clannad. **25** Moving On Up. **26** My Perfect Cousin. **27** Elkie Brooks. **28** Heaven 17. **29** Cosmic Girl. **30** Las Vegas.

Quiz 96 Pop Music: Groups

Answers - see Quiz 95, page 317

1 What was the name of Georgie Fame's backing group?
2 What nationality were All That She Wants group Ace of Base?
3 How many Princes were in the Spin Doctors UK No 3 hit?
4 What Sensation were the Bay City Rollers singing about in 1974?
5 Huey Lewis was vocalist for which group?
6 Which Company band had a hit with Give Me Just A Little More Time?
7 What did Go West close in their No 5 from 1985?
8 What followed in brackets on I'd Like To Teach the World to Sing?
9 Who did the Wonder Stuff serve as backing group for?
10 Which heavy band took When Love and Hate Collide to No 2?
11 What was Oasis' first UK Top Ten single?
12 What was The Beach Boys' first UK No 1?
13 In Which American city was the Pogues Fairytale?
14 Which Lightning Seeds No 1 was the official song of the England Football Team in 1996?
15 Ginger, Jack and Eric formed which trio?
16 Which British group had a No 3 hit with I Surrender in 1981?
17 Which Hotel was visited by the Eagles in 1977?
18 What part of the day took the Stranglers to No 7 in 1988?
19 In 1982, what was the name of the first UK No 1 by a German group?
20 Which Last Train did KLF catch in their No 2 UK hit in 1991?
21 Singer/ songwriter David Gates led which group?
22 Who was the brother in the title of a track by Free from 1970?
23 Which girl band had hits with Manic Monday and Walk Like An Egyptian?
24 Which Irish group had a No 5 hit with the Theme from Harry's Game?
25 What action were M People doing in their No 2 UK hit from 1993?
26 What relative was Perfect according to the hit by the Undertones?
27 Who was the female artist in Vinegar Joe?
28 Which group had hits in '83 with Temptation and Come Live With Me?
29 What sort of girl took Jamiroquai to No 6 in 1996?
30 Where was ZZ Top on the No 10 hit Viva?

Answers

Pot Luck 44 (see Quiz 95, page 317)
1 Metro Goldwyn Mayer. **2** Purple brown. **3** Tour De France. **4** Raymond Baxter. **5** Speedy Gonzales. **6** Snap. **7** Delaware. **8** Fools. **9** Cheese. **10** E. Nesbit. **11** Airedale. **12** Himmler. **13** Blood. **14** Mid Glamorgan. **15** A bird. **16** Egypt. **17** Donald Pleasence. **18** Anwar Sadat. **19** Brabinger. **20** Jeremy. **21** Seal. **22** New South Wales. **23** Mark Field. **24** A fruit (plum). **25** Slough. **26** Hi De Hi. **27** Huw Wheldon. **28** Tonic water. **29** Canada. **30** The Golden Fleece.

Quiz 97 Pot Luck 45

Answers - see Quiz 98, page 320

1 Who was the first Briton to hold a world javelin record?
2 Who performed and wrote the theme for Ghostbusters?
3 How many players are there in a Canadian football team?
4 Chester Whites, Durocs and Hampshire are all types of what animal?
5 What is killed by an analgesic?
6 The Dufourspitze is the highest mountain where?
7 When do ducks always lay their eggs?
8 Which Laura had a hit with Gloria?
9 Who preceded Corazon Aquino as President of the Philippines?
10 Which test would you be taking if you underwent a polygraph test?
11 Which American city's football team is called the Bears?
12 Which vitamin deficiency causes rickets?
13 Which suspension bridge crosses the River Avon?
14 Which volcano erupted in 1883 and lies between Java and Sumatra?
15 What is the vocal tinkling sound made by a deer called?
16 Which sea surrounds Heligoland?
17 How many inches above grass should the top of a croquet hoop be?
18 The pituitary gland controls the production of what in the body?
19 Which prefix is a tenth in the metric system?
20 How many pounds does the Olympic hammer weigh?
21 What was the name of the Boswell's daughter in Bread?
22 What was a Minster originally attached to?
23 What is the popular name for the wood-hyacinth?
24 Where is Britain's National Horseracing Museum?
25 Who did James Earl Ray assassinate?
26 Who was the only female in Edward Heath's first cabinet?
27 Which fault line is San Francisco on?
28 Who won 100m gold at the 1988 Olympics after Ben Johnson's disqualification?
29 Where was the terrorist group ETA mainly active?
30 Who was called the Father of Medicine?

Answers

Sport: Who's Who? (see Quiz 98, page 320)

1 Sonny Liston. **2** Natalie Tauziat. **3** Rocky Marciano. **4** Al Joyner. **5** Joe DiMaggio. **6** Jake La Motta. **7** Silver. **8** Ray Reardon. **9** Boris Becker. **10** Mary Decker Slaney. **11** Italy. **12** Ernie Els. **13** Nick Faldo. **14** Steve Davis. **15** Goran Ivanisevic. **16** Paul Ince. **17** Chris Evert. **18** Davis. **19** Squash. **20** Denise Lewis. **21** Damon Hill. **22** Rocket. **23** John Conteh. **24** Judo. **25** Mike Tyson. **26** Conchita Martinez. **27** Bernard Gallacher. **28** Snooker. **29** Peter Fleming. **30** Nigel Benn.

Quiz 98 Sport: Who's Who?

Answers - see Quiz 97, page 319

1 Who did Muhammad Ali beat when he first became World Champion?
2 Who was runner up to Jana Novotna in the Wimbledon final in 1998?
3 Who was the first heavyweight boxing champion to retire undefeated?
4 Who was the late Flo Jo's husband?
5 Which husband of Marilyn Monroe was elected to the Baseball Hall of Fame?
6 Whose life was recorded on film in Raging Bull?
7 What colour individual medal did Sharron Davies win at the Moscow Olympics?
8 Which snooker champion was unkindly nicknamed Dracula?
9 Which German tennis player was born on Billie Jean King's 23rd birthday?
10 Who did Zola Budd trip up at the Los Angeles Olympics in 1984?
11 British born long jumper Fiona May represents which country in international athletics?
12 Which South African golfer's real first name is Theodore?
13 Which golfer split with his coach and his girlfriend in September '98?
14 Who did Stephen Hendry replace as world No 1 in the 1989-90 season?
15 Who is Croatia's No 1 tennis player?
16 Which sometime England captain is a cousin of boxer Nigel Benn?
17 Who lost most Ladies Singles finals at Wimbledon in the 80s?
18 Which surname has been shared by three world snooker champions?
19 Peter Nicol won Commonwealth gold for Scotland in which sport?
20 Who successfully defended her heptathlon title at the 1998 Commonwealth Games?
21 Who won his first Grand Prix since 1996 in Belgium in 1998?
22 Which Gladiator competed in the heptathlon in the 1998 Commonwealth Games?
23 Which Liverpudlian won the WBC Light Heavyweight Title in 1974?
24 Sharron Davies' one time fiancé Neil Adams was an international in which sport?
25 Who replaced Leon Spinks as Heavyweight Champion in 1987?
26 Who defeated Navratilova in her last Wimbledon singles final?
27 Who captained Europe to Ryder Cup success in 1995?
28 Allison Fisher is a former world champion in which sport?
29 Who did John McEnroe win five Wimbledon Doubles titles with?
30 Which boxer is nicknamed 'The Dark Destroyer'?

Answers

Pot Luck 45 (see Quiz 97, page 319)

1 Fatima Whitbread. **2** Ray Parker, Jr. **3** Twelve. **4** Pigs. **5** Pain. **6** Switzerland. **7** In the morning. **8** Branigan. **9** President Marcos. **10** A lie detector. **11** Chicago. **12** D. **13** The Clifton. **14** Krakatoa. **15** A bell. **16** The North Sea. **17** Twelve. **18** Hormones. **19** Deci. **20** 16. **21** Aveline. **22** Monastery. **23** The bluebell. **24** Newmarket. **25** Martin Luther King. **26** Margaret Thatcher. **27** San Andreas. **28** Carl Lewis. **29** Spain. **30** Hippocrates.

Quiz 99 TV: TV Gold

Answers - see Quiz 100, page 322

1 Which Game For a Laugh presenters had the same surname?
2 Who was the subject of The Naked Civil Servant with John Hurt?
3 Which sitcom told of Tooting revolutionary Wolfie?
4 Who found fame as The Saint?
5 Who played Louie de Palma in Taxi?
6 Which spaghetti western star played in Rawhide for six years?
7 Who conducted Eric Morecambe playing Grieg's Piano Concerto?
8 Which reporter found fame during her reporting of the Iranian Embassy siege in 1980?
9 In which weekly drama slot was Cathy Come Home first shown?
10 Before WWII which was the single most watched event on TV?
11 Who was the main character on The Phil Silvers Show?
12 Who became Mrs Clayton Farlow in Dallas?
13 Which series looked back at film clips 25 years old?
14 How were Bruce Wayne and Dick Grayson better known?
15 Which Carry On regular was the star of Bless This House?
16 Who was 'lower class' on The Frost Report after John Cleese and Ronnie Barker?
17 Which soap was originally called The Midland Road?
18 Which famous singer/actor's daughter shot JR?
19 Which Corrie star joined the cast in 1961 as Miss Nugent?
20 What was the surname of Morticia and Gomez?
21 Which area of the country received TV after the area London in 1949?
22 In which sitcom did Richard Beckinsale play Alan Moore?
23 Which series told of the bizarre life of the Clampett family?
24 Which comedian played Colin in Colin's Sandwich?
25 Which show has numbered David Jacobs, Noel Edmonds and Rosemarie Ford among its presenters?
26 What was the BBC's first soap of the 60s?
27 Who was the Scottish undertaker in Dad's Army?
28 The controversial Death of a Princess caused a rift with which country in 1980?
29 Who had a long running TV show before starring in Mary Poppins?
30 Who is the only Corrie star remaining from the original cast?

Answers

Pot Luck 46 (see Quiz 100, page 322)
1 Dance. **2** Gunpowder. **3** Nebuchadnezzar. **4** Sioux. **5** Golf. **6** James I. **7** Violin. **8** In loco parentis. **9** Dublin. **10** Jersey. **11** Ealing. **12** A.E. Housman. **13** Harvard. **14** Alessandro Volta. **15** House of Representatives. **16** A race or racial group. **17** The end of the world. **18** Lion. **19** Playboy. **20** Hitchcock. **21** Four. **22** Amelia Earhart. **23** Austria. **24** Rubber. **25** Gold, platinum, silver. **26** £1.05. **27** Bay. **28** Hyde Park. **29** Hormone replacement therapy. **30** Alimentary canal.

Quiz 100 Pot Luck 46

Answers - see Quiz 99, page 321

LEVEL 2

1 In Cuba what is a habanera?
2 Which black powder is the oldest known explosive?
3 Who condemned Shadrach, Meshach and Abednego to the Fiery Furnace?
4 Which tribe did Sitting Bull belong to?
5 Sam Snead found fame in which sport?
6 Who was king at the time of the Gunpowder Plot?
7 Which musical instrument did Jack Benny play?
8 Which Latin phrase means 'in place of a parent'?
9 Dun Laoghaire is a port and suburb of where?
10 Gerald Durrell was a director of which zoo?
11 Michael Balcon was head of which influential studios?
12 Who wrote A Shropshire Lad?
13 What is the oldest university in the USA?
14 Who was the volt named after?
15 What is the lower house of the US Congress called?
16 Genocide is the destruction of what?
17 In Scandinavian myth what is Gotterdammerung?
18 Which animals' legs did the Griffin have?
19 Which magazine was famous for its nude centrefold?
20 Which director made Blackmail, Britain's first successful talkie?
21 How many tournaments make up tennis's Grand Slam?
22 With which woman aviator did Frederick Noonan perish?
23 In which country was Hitler born?
24 What is a puck made from in ice hockey?
25 On which three metals would you see a hallmark?
26 In modern currency how much is a guinea?
27 What is the Great Australian Bight?
28 Where in London was the Great Exhibition of 1851?
29 What is HRT?
30 Which canal is also called the gut?

Answers

TV: TV Gold (see Quiz 99, page 321)
1 Matthew & Henry Kelly. **2** Quentin Crisp. **3** Citizen Smith. **4** Roger Moore. **5** Danny De Vito. **6** Clint Eastwood. **7** Andre Previn. **8** Kate Adie. **9** The Wednesday Play. **10** George VI's coronation. **11** Bilko. **12** Miss Ellie. **13** All Our Yesterdays. **14** Batman and Robin. **15** Sid James. **16** Ronnie Corbett. **17** Crossroads. **18** Bing Crosby's (Mary). **19** Eileen Derbyshire. **20** Addams. **21** Midlands. **22** Rising Damp. **23** The Beverly Hillbillies. **24** Mel Smith. **25** Come Dancing. **26** Compact. **27** Private Fraser. **28** Saudi Arabia. **29** Dick Van Dyke. **30** William Roache.

Quiz 101 Movies: People

Answers - see Quiz 102, page 324

1 Which actor is the son of a Poet Laureate?
2 Which 'Chinese Western' actor's real name was Lee Yuen Kam?
3 Which singer and actress was in Dick Tracy?
4 Kenneth Branagh cast which toothy comedian as Yorick in Hamlet?
5 Who played the adult Damien in The Omen films?
6 Which pop wife appeared with Robert Redford, aged four, in The Great Gatsby?
7 Which early screen comedian's real name was Louis Cristillo?
8 Who played Cruella de Vil's sidekick Jasper in 101 Dalmatians?
9 Who beat Meryl Streep for the lead role in The Horse Whisperer?
10 Which Glaswegian played a gangster in Goldeneye?
11 Which serious actress played comedy opposite Schwarzenegger in Junior?
12 Who directed, scripted, composed and starred in Yentl?
13 Which ex child star was US Ambassador to Czechoslovakia in 1989?
14 How were producers Harry, Albert, Sam and Jack known collectively?
15 What was Groucho Marx's real first name?
16 Which Cockney actor married the former Miss Guyana in 1973?
17 Which horror writer directed the film Maximum Overdrive?
18 Who had larger feet, Marilyn Monroe or Daryl Hannah?
19 Which star of Look Who's Talking Too was a regular on TV's Cheers?
20 Which Fonda starred in the remake of Nikita?
21 Who is Joely Richardson's famous mother?
22 Which comedies was Michael Balcon responsible for?
23 Which actress wrote Postcards From the Edge?
24 Who was the first Bond girl?
25 Which conductor is Woody Allen's father in law?
26 Which surname was shared by John, Lionel, Ethel and Drew?
27 Who played Batman in Batman Forever?
28 What was Ex-python Terry Gilliam's futuristic nightmare film, surreally named for a South American country?
29 Who bought the screen rights to Dick Tracy and made a film from it?
30 Which blonde actress is Mrs Alec Baldwin?

Answers

Pot Luck 47 (see Quiz 102, page 324)
1 The Pope. **2** Estate car. **3** The deaf. **4** Relate. **5** Ofwat. **6** Tibet. **7** Tax. **8** Munich. **9** Two. **10** SAS. **11** France (de Nimes). **12** Operation Desert Storm. **13** Franz Beckenbauer. **14** Leek. **15** Kite shaped. **16** Election. **17** Teeth or bone. **18** Variety Club. **19** Thames. **20** Houses of Parliament. **21** Special Branch. **22** Hospital. **23** American Revolution. **24** Sleeping policeman. **25** Nurse. **26** Merchant Navy. **27** Third degree. **28** Young children. **29** Lutine Bell. **30** Red.

Quiz 102 Pot Luck 47

Answers - see Quiz 101, page 323

1 Who would deliver an edict called a bull?
2 What is a shooting brake?
3 Who does the RNID provide help for?
4 What is the Marriage Guidance Council now called?
5 How is the Office of Water Services also known?
6 The Dalai Lama is the spiritual leader of where?
7 In English history what was danegeld?
8 What is the capital of Bavaria?
9 How many days does a decathlon event last?
10 The US Delta Force is based on which British anti terrorist force?
11 In which country did denim originate?
12 What was the codename for the operation to eject the Iraqis from Kuwait in 1991?
13 Who was the first person to manage and captain a World Cup winning soccer side?
14 David was responsible for the adoption of what as a Welsh emblem?
15 What shape is the approved mark of the British Standards Institution?
16 At what occasion do you see a returning officer?
17 Caries is the decay and deterioration of what?
18 Which Club's President is the Chief Barker?
19 On which river does swan-upping take place?
20 Where in London is the Strangers' Gallery?
21 Which police department deals with political security in the UK?
22 What sort of institution is UCH?
23 The Battle of Bunker Hill was the first major engagement of what?
24 What name is given to a bump in the road to slow down traffic?
25 What is the profession of an RGN?
26 Whose flag is the red ensign?
27 Which degree of burns is life threatening?
28 Who does a Norland nurse work with?
29 Which bell is found in the building of Lloyd's of London?
30 What colour is the ceremonial dress of a Yeoman of the Guard?

Answers

Movies: People (see Quiz 101, page 323)
1 Daniel Day-Lewis. **2** Bruce Lee. **3** Madonna. **4** Ken Dodd. **5** Sam Neill. **6** Patsy Kensit. **7** Lou Costello. **8** Hugh Laurie. **9** Kristin Scott Thomas. **10** Robbie Coltrane. **11** Emma Thompson. **12** Barbra Streisand. **13** Shirley Temple. **14** Warner Brothers. **15** Julius. **16** Michael Caine. **17** Stephen King. **18** Daryl Hannah. **19** Kirstie Alley. **20** Bridget. **21** Vanessa Redgrave. **22** Ealing. **23** Carrie Fisher. **24** Ursula Andress. **25** Andre Previn. **26** Barrymore. **27** Val Kilmer. **28** Brazil. **29** Warren Beatty. **30** Kim Basinger.

Quiz 103 Leisure: Media

Answers - see Quiz 104, page 326

1 What is Portland Place's most famous House?
2 What does CNN stand for?
3 Which listings magazine celebrated its 75th birthday in 1998?
4 What is Britain's principal world news agency?
5 Which magazine is supposedly edited by Lord Gnome?
6 Where is Grampian TV based?
7 What does the ASA control?
8 What is the magazine of the Consumer's Association?
9 Who is the Daily Mail's most famous cartoon dog?
10 Where is The People's Daily a top selling papers?
11 Which long-running futuristic comic featured Judge Dredd and Rogue Trooper?
12 Country Life was once edited by which royal photographer?
13 Red and yellow were the colours of which comic strip Rovers?
14 What is the full official title of GQ?
15 Which organisation had a magazine called "Expression!"?
16 Which daily paper founded in 1859 is devoted to horse racing?
17 In which part of the Commonwealth might you tune in to Penguin Radio?
18 Which Times Supplement is aimed at teachers?
19 How is the New Musical Express better known?
20 How does Dennis the Menace's mother always address her husband?
21 Which US based magazine was the world's best seller until the 80s?
22 How is the journalists' trade union commonly known?
23 Which famous magazine was founded by Hugh Hefner?
24 Where is Yorkshire TV based?
25 In which part of London are Richard Murdoch's newspapers based?
26 Which was the ill-fated satellite TV company that competed with Sky?
27 Which major UK daily newspaper, still in circulation, did Robert Maxwell own?
28 Which left wing faction had a newspaper called Militant?
29 Which major Murdoch UK paper has the longest name?
30 Which women's magazine did Cherie Blair guest edit?

Answers

Pot Luck 48 (see Quiz 104, page 326)

1 New Kids on the Block. **2** Juliet Bravo. **3** Smallpox. **4** Ben Hur. **5** In space. **6** Bradford City's. **7** Pat Garrett. **8** The Queen. **9** Britain's. **10** Hot and spicy. **11** Petula Clark. **12** Richard III. **13** Anglesey. **14** Bad Manners. **15** Tenerife. **16** Barry McGuigan. **17** Columbia. **18** M4. **19** An Emirate. **20** Dresden. **21** Niki Lauda. **22** Pacific. **23** The Gridiron. **24** Poetry. **25** Cambridge. **26** Prince. **27** The seahorse. **28** Manoeuvres. **29** Leather. **30** Nikita.

Quiz 104 Pot Luck 48

Answers - see Quiz 103, page 325

1 In the music world what did NKOTB stand for?
2 Hartley was the fictional town setting for which TV police serial?
3 Variola is the proper name for which killer disease?
4 Who competed against Messala in a literary chariot race?
5 Where did Laika, the first dog in space, die?
6 Which British stadium saw the worst soccer tragedy in 1985?
7 Which sheriff killed Billy the Kid?
8 Who had a well publicised conversation with Michael Fagan in 1982?
9 In a 1991 survey which country's inhabitants used the most soap per capita?
10 Is a piri-piri sauce sweet, or hot and spicy?
11 Which Swiss resident won a Grammie for singing Downtown?
12 Which Richard died at the Battle of Bosworth Field?
13 Which is largest, the Isle of Wight or Anglesey?
14 Buster Bloodvessel was a member of which Ska-revival band?
15 Which holiday island saw the worst ever air crash with 582 deaths?
16 Which former world boxing champion has the Christian name Finbar?
17 What does the "C" stand for in the musical initials "CBS"?
18 Which motorway joins with the M25 at Heathrow Airport?
19 What is controlled by an Emir?
20 In World War II which German city suffered the most civilian deaths?
21 Which living motor racing driver had been given the last rites before becoming World Champion?
22 What name is given to the most westerly time zone in America?
23 What is an American football pitch also called?
24 Thomas Hardy wrote what type of material for the last twelve years of his life?
25 Which is further east, Cambridge or Peterborough?
26 Which male pop superstar wrote the Bangles Manic Monday hit?
27 Which is the slowest moving fish?
28 What did the "M" stand for in the name of the band OMD?
29 Cordwainers mainly worked with which material?
30 Which Elton John hit was the first name of Russian leader Kruschev?

Answers

Leisure: Media (see Quiz 103, page 325)
1 Broadcasting House. **2** Cable News Network. **3** Radio Times. **4** Reuters. **5** Private Eye. **6** Aberdeen. **7** Advertising. **8** Which? **9** Fred Basset. **10** China. **11** 2001AD. **12** Lord Snowdon. **13** Melchester. **14** Gentlemen's Quarterly. **15** American Express. **16** The Sporting Life. **17** Falkland Islands. **18** Educational. **19** NME. **20** Dad. **21** Reader's Digest. **22** NUJ. **23** Playboy. **24** Leeds. **25** Wapping. **26** BSB. **27** Daily Mirror. **28** Militant Tendency. **29** The News of the World. **30** Prima.

Quiz 105 Technology

Answers - see Quiz 106, page 328

1 What is Computer Assisted in the acronym CAD?
2 In which US state is the so called Silicon Glen?
3 Which bank does the CWS own?
4 In the oil industry what is the tower called which hoists the drill pipes?
5 What does the T stand for in DTP?
6 Which early adding device comes from the Latin meaning 'a flat surface'?
7 What does DERV stand for?
8 Exxon is the US's largest concern in which industry?
9 What does ICI stand for?
10 Which industry's members belong to Unison?
11 Who founded Habitat?
12 What is antiknock added to to reduce knocking?
13 What type of institution was BCCI?
14 Who founded Amstrad?
15 What does a Geiger counter measure?
16 What is the full name of CFCs?
17 For which industry is London's Wardour Street famous?
18 Where is Britain's largest North Sea oil terminal?
19 Which copying machine did Chester Carlson invent?
20 Who is the US's largest vehicle manufacturer?
21 What was the world's longest bridge when it was opened in 1980?
22 What is a country's GNP?
23 What does W stand for in the AWACS surveillance system?
24 What is the study of motion and impact of projectiles?
25 Which country has the world's largest electricity grid system?
26 Where is the BASF group based?
27 What is the world's largest packaged food company?
28 What is a computer's smallest unit of information?
29 Where did Lord Nuffield, aka William Morris, build up his car business?
30 What does the 'M' in IBM stand for?

Answers

Pot Luck 49 (see Quiz 106, page 328)
1 Jingles. **2** A stilt. **3** Horse fair. **4** 1st October. **5** A mountain. **6** USA. **7** Face the Music. **8** Buddy Holly. **9** Horses. **10** Lethbridge-Stewart. **11** Billy Connolly. **12** French. **13** Barnsdale. **14** Coming Home. **15** Madrid. **16** Howard's Way. **17** The Times. **18** Demi Moore. **19** Italy. **20** Order of the Garter. **21** Ronnie Corbett. **22** Christopher Robin. **23** Two. **24** Christmas Day. **25** Mulder and Scully. **26** Snakes. **27** Bones. **28** Staffordshire. **29** Javelin. **30** Caskets.

Quiz 106 Pot Luck 49

Answers - see Quiz 105, page 327

1 What are the metal discs in the rim of a tambourine called?
2 Which word can be a pole with a foot rest or a wading bird?
3 What annual event is the Cumbrian town of Appleby noted for?
4 On what date does the pheasant shooting season legally start?
5 Who or what is Cader Idris?
6 Mr Birdseye – of frozen food fame – came from which country?
7 Richard Baker was a regular panellist on which musical TV quiz?
8 Which 1950s pop star had the first names Charles Hardin?
9 Which animals can be affected by a disease called vives?
10 Which Brigadier appeared in Dr Who?
11 Who played Mr Brown in the film Mrs Brown?
12 What is the official language of Haiti?
13 What was the name of Geoff Hamilton's garden?
14 Jane Fonda won a Best Actress Oscar for her role in which 1978 film?
15 Barajas airport is in which city?
16 Jack Rolfe and Charles Frere were characters in which TV series?
17 What is the oldest daily newspaper in England?
18 Demetria Guynes is better known as which actress?
19 Which country surrounds San Marino?
20 Which Order is the highest in the Order of Chivalry in Britain?
21 Who played the leading role in the TV series Sorry?
22 What was the name of A.A. Milne's son?
23 How many hours are there in a dog watch at sea?
24 In a calendar year what is the name given to the final quarter day?
25 Fox and Dana are the first names of which pair?
26 What did Saint Patrick rid Ireland of according to legend?
27 What are osselets and ossicles?
28 Alton Towers Leisure Park is in which county?
29 Steve Backley held the world record in which sports event?
30 In The Merchant of Venice the suitors pick one of three what?

Answers

Technology (see Quiz 105, page 327)
1 Design. **2** California. **3** Co-op Bank. **4** Derrick. **5** Top. **6** Abacus.
7 Diesel Engine Road Vehicle. **8** Oil. **9** International Chemical Industries.
10 Health industry. **11** Terence Conran. **12** Petrol. **13** Bank. **14** Alan Sugar.
15 Radioactivity. **16** ChloroFluoroCarbons. **17** Film industry. **18** Sullom Voe.
19 Xerox photocopier. **20** General Motors. **21** Humber Bridge.
22 Gross National Product. **23** Warning. **24** Ballistics. **25** Britain. **26** Germany.
27 Nestle. **28** Bit. **29** Oxford. **30** Machines.

Quiz 107 The Royals

Answers - see Quiz 108, page 330

1 What was Diana's official title at the time of her death?
2 Who is the oldest in line to the throne after Prince Charles?
3 Which Prince was a guest on the Des O'Connor Show in 1998?
4 On which island was Princess Margaret when she suffered a stroke?
5 Who was older, Princess Diana's mother or her stepmother?
6 In which country did the former Edward VIII marry Mrs Simpson?
7 Albert succeeded Baudouin in which country?
8 In which country did Fergie's mother spend the latter part of her life?
9 What does the Queen's only nephew do for a living?
10 At which sport did Harry excel in his first few weeks at Eton?
11 Who is the only child of the Queen not to have been divorced?
12 Who is third in line to the throne?
13 Who survived the crash in which Princess Diana died?
14 Which cavalryman co wrote A Princess In Love with Anna Pasternak?
15 Seven kings of which country have been called Haakon?
16 Which Princess is the mother of Viscount Linley?
17 Which Princess is known by her husband's name?
18 Which former Royal residence was damaged by fire in 1986?
19 'Tiggy' Legge-Bourke was PA to which Prince for three years?
20 Which Princess is the mother of Marina Mowatt?
21 Who was Princess Diana's chauffeur on her final fatal car journey?
22 Which Royal companion is the great granddaughter of Edward VII's mistress Alice Keppel?
23 Which grand child of the Queen had her tongue pierced?
24 Which Royal in law was dubbed 'Fog' because he was thick and wet?
25 Who took the official engagement photos of Charles and Diana?
26 Who is Lady Sarah Chatto's aunt on her mother's side?
27 Which Princess married the son of a director of Walls sausages?
28 In which royal castle is St George's Chapel?
29 Which musical instrument does Princess Margaret play?
30 In 1994 Diana took an advisory role for which organisation?

Answers

Pot Luck 50 (see Quiz 108, page 330)
1 Chester. **2** Sixpence. **3** Steal. **4** Laughing gas. **5** Florence Nightingale.
6 Liverpool. **7** 1977. **8** A pack of tarot cards. **9** December 25th. **10** Arnold Palmer.
11 Loyd Grossman. **12** Lou Reed. **13** Bailey. **14** Wigan Pier. **15** You have a bite.
16 Manchester. **17** Avalon. **18** Kingston Upon Hull. **19** MCC. **20** Steve Davis.
21 Andrew. **22** Beethoven. **23** X rays. **24** Three. **25** Rudolf Nureyev.
26 Barbara Cartland. **27** Saddle. **28** Zambia. **29** 17th. **30** Four.

Quiz 108 Pot Luck 50

Answers - see Quiz 107, page 329

1 Deva was a Roman city now known as what?
2 What was the top price for goods in the first British Woolworth's?
3 What does a kleptomaniac do?
4 What is the popular name for the anaesthetic nitrous oxide?
5 Who was the first woman to be awarded the Order of Merit?
6 The doomed ship Titanic was registered in which English city?
7 In which year did Marc Bolan die?
8 What is made up of the minor arcana and the major arcana?
9 The Romanian dictator Ceausescu was executed on which day in 1989?
10 Who was the last playing Ryder Cup captain, in the 60s?
11 Which food show presenter once played in a band called Jet Bronx and the Forbidden?
12 Which Lou was vocalist with the Velvet Underground?
13 Which shipping forecast area is due north of Rockall?
14 Which pier featured in a George Orwell book title?
15 If you are an angler why are you pleased if your monkey starts to climb?
16 In which city was painter LS Lowry born?
17 Where was King Arthur taken after his last battle?
18 What is Hull's full name?
19 Which all male bastion allowed women members for the first time in September 1998?
20 Who made the first televised 147 in snooker, in 1982?
21 Which Prince's childhood nickname was 'The Sniggerer'?
22 Who wrote the Emperor Concerto?
23 For which medical breakthrough did Roentgen win the Nobel Prize in 1901?
24 How many Inns of Court are there in London?
25 Which ballet dancer died on the same day as Dizzy Gillespie?
26 Whose codename was 'Pink' before she was surprised on This Is Your Life?
27 What is a pommel a part of?
28 Cars with the international vehicle registration Z come from where?
29 In which century was the Battle of Naseby?
30 How many pecks are there in a bushel?

Answers

The Royals (see Quiz 107, page 329)
1 Diana, Princess of Wales. **2** Prince Andrew. **3** Edward. **4** Mustique. **5** Stepmother. **6** France. **7** Belgium. **8** Argentina. **9** Make furniture. **10** Football. **11** Prince Edward. **12** Prince Harry. **13** Trevor Reece Jones. **14** James Hewitt. **15** Norway. **16** Margaret. **17** Michael of Kent. **18** Hampton Court. **19** Charles. **20** Alexandra. **21** Henri Paul. **22** Camilla Parker Bowles. **23** Zara Phillips. **24** Mark Phillips. **25** Lord Snowdon. **26** The Queen. **27** Anne. **28** Windsor. **29** Piano. **30** International Red Cross.

Quiz 109 Who Was Who?

Answers - see Quiz 110, page 332

1 Who was Chancellor, Foreign Secretary and PM between 1964 and 1979?
2 Which nation introduced chocolate to Europe?
3 Which American was known as Ike?
4 Which future President organised the Free French Forces in WWII?
5 What was Indira Gandhi's maiden name?
6 Who became US Vice President in 1993?
7 Which title did Hitler take as Nazi leader?
8 Who was the last Tsarina of Russia?
9 Who was Soviet Foreign Minister from 1957 to 1985?
10 Whose resignation on 1st November 1990 began Thatcher's downfall?
11 Whose 1963 Report led to the closure of many railway stations?
12 Who was famous for his pictures of Campbell's Soup cans?
13 Who was British Prime Minister during the abdication crisis?
14 For how long were Hitler and Eva Braun married?
15 In 1996 who had served longer continuously as a Minister, John Major or Kenneth Clarke?
16 Which athlete became MP for Falmouth and Cambourne in 1992?
17 Which world leader celebrated his 80th birthday in July 1998?
18 Who was the first Archbishop of Canterbury?
19 Which US President publicly pardoned ex President Nixon?
20 Who had the title Il Duce?
21 Which US evangelist asked his flock to make a "decision for Christ"?
22 In 1990 which ex PM went to Iraq to try to secure the release of British hostages?
23 Who was the youngest queen of Henry VIII to be beheaded?
24 Which Prime Minister introduced the Citizen's Charter?
25 Who became Defence Secretary in May 1997?
26 What was the name of Horatio Nelson's daughter by Emma Hamilton?
27 Who said her boss Michael Howard had "something of the night about him"?
28 What was the religion of a French Huguenot?
29 Whose Report formed the basis for the British welfare state?
30 In which category did Einstein win his Nobel prize in 1921?

Answers

Pop Who's Who? (see Quiz 110, page 332)
1 Bay City Rollers. **2** Barbra Streisand. **3** Bill Tarmey. **4** Shakin' Stevens
5 Kate Bush. **6** Chris De Burgh. **7** Two. **8** The Spice Girls. **9** Bono.
10 Richard Clayderman. **11** George Michael. **12** Emerson, Lake & Palmer.
13 Judith Durham. **14** Meatloaf. **15** Celine Dion. **16** Michael Caine.
17 Bill Medley. **18** Ken Hutchinson - Hutch. **19** Right Said Fred. **20** David Bowie.
21 Lily the Pink. **22** George Michael. **23** Rod Stewart. **24** Shirley Bassey. **25** Morgen.
26 Coco Hernandez. **27** Jarvis Cocker. **28** The Kemp Brothers. **29** Victoria 'Posh'.
30 Nick Berry.

Quiz 110 Pop Who's Who?

Answers - see Quiz 109, page 331

LEVEL 2

1 The Longmuir brothers were in which 70s teeny bop group?
2 Who partnered Don Johnson on the Goya theme Till I Loved You?
3 Which Coronation Street star had a hit in '94 with Wind Beneath My Wings?
4 Which UK male vocalist's real name is Michael Barratt?
5 Who duetted with Peter Gabriel on Don't Give Up?
6 Christopher John Davidson is the real name of which Irish vocalist?
7 How many members are there in D:Ream?
8 Who launched the British Legion Poppy Appeal with Dame Vera Lynn in 1997?
9 Who featured on the 1986 Clannad hit In a Lifetime?
10 Which pianist and instrumentalist's real name is Philippe Pages?
11 Who was the younger of the two Wham! members?
12 Keith, Greg and Carl were the Christian names of which 70s trio?
13 Who was lead female singer with 60s group The Seekers?
14 Marvin Lee Aday is better known as which dead ringer vocalist?
15 Who had a No 5 UK hit with the theme song Because You Loved Me?
16 Which actor shares his name with a 1984 hit by Madness?
17 Who sang the theme tune to Dirty Dancing with Jennifer Warnes?
18 Which TV detective had a No 1 hit with Don't Give Up On Us in 1976?
19 Which group share their name with a Bernard Cribbins 1962 hit?
20 Who joined with Queen in the 1981 No 1 hit Under Pressure?
21 Who invented Medicinal Compound according to the 1968 No 1?
22 Which superstar has an autobiography called Bare?
23 Which pop legend said, "I really wanted to be a soccer star"?
24 Who partnered Chris Rea on the 1996 hit 'Disco' La Passione?
25 Complete the A-ha trio - Pal, Mags and ....?
26 Which character was played by Irene Cara in Fame?
27 Who interrupted Michael Jackson's Earth Song at the 1996 Brit Awards?
28 Which brothers were members of Spandau Ballet?
29 Who was the first Spice Girl to get engaged?
30 Who links the '86 hit Every Loser Wins and the '92 hit Heartbeat?

Answers

Who Was Who? (see Quiz 109, page 331)
1 James Callaghan. **2** Spain. **3** President Eisenhower. **4** De Gaulle. **5** Nehru. **6** Al Gore. **7** Fuhrer. **8** Alexandra. **9** Andrei Gromyko. **10** Sir Geoffrey Howe. **11** Beeching. **12** Andy Warhol. **13** Baldwin. **14** One day. **15** Kenneth Clarke. **16** Sebastian Coe. **17** Nelson Mandela. **18** St Augustine. **19** Gerald Ford. **20** Mussolini. **21** Billy Graham. **22** Edward Heath. **23** Catherine Howard. **24** John Major. **25** George Robertson. **26** Horatia. **27** Ann Widdecombe. **28** Protestant. **29** Beveridge. **30** Physics.

Quiz 111 TV Who's Who?

Answers - see Quiz 112, page 334

LEVEL 2

1 Which comedian wrote Blackadder with Richard Curtis?
2 Who hosted the talent spotting show My Kind of People?
3 Who replaced Anneka Rice on Carlton TV's Capital Woman?
4 David Dimbleby's first wife wrote what type of books?
5 Which comedian created the character Stavros?
6 Who has the car number plate COM 1C?
7 Which star of The Grand is President of the Dyslexia Institute?
8 Which first name is shared by subsequent stars of Dangerfield?
9 Who told Noel Edmonds live that co presenter Anthea Turner's interviews sent him to sleep?
10 Which radio name replaced Richard Baker presenting The Proms?
11 Which blonde first presented Big Breakfast with Chris Evans?
12 Julie Walters hails from which city?
13 Who replaced Carol Drinkwater as Helen in All Creatures Great and Small?
14 Which Doctor is a regular on Newsnight?
15 In which docu soap did Jeremy Spake find fame?
16 Who is actor Michael Williams' wife?
17 How is Derrick Evans better known?
18 Who became Jim Davidson's regular assistant on The Generation Game?
19 Which ex Radio 2 presenter moved to Open House on Channel 5?
20 Who could you regularly have Breakfast With... on Sunday mornings?
21 Who replaced Vanessa on ITV's morning talk show?
22 What did Trude Mostue train to be on TV?
23 Who first presented Changing Rooms?
24 In which drama series did the character Dr Beth Glover appear?
25 Who was the first woman tennis player to be BBC Sports Personality of the Year?
26 Who was the interviewer on C4's The Last Resort?
27 Who presented the National Lottery's fourth birthday show in 1998?
28 Who did Fergie play in Friends?
29 Who was the woman driver from hell in BBC's docu soap?
30 Who moved from Newsnight to Tomorrow's World?

Answers

Pot Luck 51 (see Quiz 112, page 334)

1 Spain. **2** Margaret Thatcher. **3** 60s. **4** Tony Adams. **5** 4th July. **6** Boris Gardiner. **7** Kent. **8** A restaurant. **9** Hats. **10** Tutankhamen's tomb. **11** Bland. **12** First decade. **13** Tracy Vincenzo. **14** Oscar Wilde. **15** Judo. **16** C. **17** Noel Coward. **18** 1973. **19** Four. **20** Paul Ince. **21** 50s. **22** C S Lewis. **23** Texas. **24** Piltdown Man. **25** Both known as Gentleman Jim.

Quiz 112 Pot Luck 51

Answers - see Quiz 111, page 333

1. Most of The Three Tenors come from which country?
2. Who remarked that, "every Prime Minister needs a Willie"?
3. In which decade was the World Wildlife Fund set up?
4. Which soccer player's 1998 book was titled Addicted?
5. On which date was the movie Independence Day screened in America?
6. Who had an 80s No 1 with I Want To Wake Up With You?
7. In cricket which English team became Sptifires in the 90s?
8. What was 'Pie in the Sky' in the name of the series with Richard Griffiths?
9. What were ladies asked not to wear at Prince Edward and Sophie's wedding?
10. What did Dr Howard Carter discover?
11. Which Sir Christopher was a 90s chairman of the BBC?
12. In which decade of this century was the Cullinan diamond discovered?
13. Which Bond girl was played by Diana Rigg?
14. Whose last words were reputedly, "Either this wallpaper goes or I do"?
15. At which sport did Neil Adams win international success?
16. Post WWII tanks all begin with which letter of the alphabet?
17. Who wrote the song Mad Dogs And Englishmen?
18. In which year did the UK join the European Union?
19. How many years does it take to paint the Forth Railway Bridge from end to end?
20. Which England soccer player has the middle names Emerson Carlyle?
21. In which decade was Kim Basinger born?
22. Who wrote the children's classic The Lion, The Witch And The Wardrobe?
23. Amarillo airport was built in which US state?
24. Bones of which Man were supposedly discovered in Sussex in 1912?
25. What's the link between boxing champion James Corbett and country singer Jim Reeves?

Answers

TV Who's Who? (see Quiz 111, page 333)

1 Ben Elton. **2** Michael Barrymore. **3** Julia Carling. **4** Cookery books. **5** Harry Enfield. **6** Jimmy Tarbuck. **7** Susan Hampshire. **8** Nigel. **9** Eamonn Holmes. **10** James Naughtie. **11** Gaby Roslin. **12** Birmingham. **13** Lynda Bellingham. **14** Mark Porter. **15** Airport. **16** Judi Dench. **17** Mr Motivator. **18** Melanie Stace. **19** Gloria Hunniford. **20** Frost. **21** Trisha Goddard. **22** Vet. **23** Carol Smillie. **24** Peak Practice. **25** Ann Jones. **26** Jonathan Ross. **27** Dale Winton. **28** Herself. **29** Maureen Reece. **30** Peter Snow.

Quiz 113 20th C Who's Who?

Answers - see Quiz 114, page 336

1 Who did Pope John Paul II succeed as Pope?
2 What did the letter F stand for in the name of President J F Kennedy?
3 Gitta Sereny courted controversy for writing a book about which convicted killer?
4 Who became the first woman prime minister of an Islamic nation?
5 Who said, "The Trent is lovely too. I've walked on it for 18 years"?
6 Tom Whittaker was the first man to climb Everest in what circumstances?
7 Who was posthumously pardoned in 1998 after being hanged for the murder of a policeman in 1953?
8 Who replaced Mary Robinson as president of Ireland in 1997?
9 Which American president had the middle name Baines?
10 Which Russian dictator imposed a reign of terror throughout the 30s and 40s?
11 On TV who originally asked contestants to Take Their Pick?
12 Who was the only female MP in The Gang of Four?
13 Who made the official speech opening the Scottish Parliament?
14 Who once described his paintings as "hand-painted dream photographs"?
15 Donald Woods escaped which country in 1979, a story later made into a film Cry Freedom?
16 What was the name of the Chinese leader whose widow was arrested for trying to overthrow the government in the 1970s?
17 Where was Ronnie Biggs arrested in 1974 after over eight years on the run?
18 Which manager signed the first Catholic player for Glasgow Rangers?
19 In 1968 The Oscars were postponed for 48 hours because of whose death?
20 Who succeeded Lal Bahadur Shastri as Prime Minister of India?
21 In the 1960s the Queen dedicated an acre of ground in the UK to the memory of whom?
22 Who created Fantasyland, Adventureland and Frontierland?
23 Who led so called witch hunts against communists in the USA after WWII?
24 Which kidnap victim was involved in a bank raid, brandishing a gun, even after a ransom had been paid?
25 Who was Master of the Rolls from 1962 to 1982?

Answers

Pot Luck 52 (see Quiz 114, page 336)
1 Lindsay Davenport. **2** The Detectives. **3** Minister of Foreign Affairs. **4** Ben Elton. **5** With A Little Help From My Friends. **6** Atlanta. **7** My Fair Lady. **8** 70s. **9** England. **10** Virginia Wade. **11** Clunk, click. **12** Winston Churchill. **13** Letitia Dean. **14** Fugees. **15** The Netherlands. **16** Spurs. **17** Sleep. **18** Switzerland. **19** Richard Nixon. **20** Rugby Union. **21** Buffalo Bill. **22** Joseph Conrad. **23** Conciliation. **24** Legs. **25** 60s.

Quiz 114 Pot Luck 52

Answers - see Quiz 113, page 335

1 After a tennis match with Amelia Mauresmo who said "...I thought I was playing a guy"?
2 Which spoof crime series was a spin off from Canned Carrott?
3 What post did Edward Shevardnadze hold in the USSR from 1985 to 1990?
4 Who wrote the 90s novel Gridlock?
5 What was Wet Wet Wet's first No 1?
6 In baseball where do the Braves come from?
7 Which musical featured the song Wouldn't It Be Luvverly?
8 In which decade of the 20th century was HMS Ark Royal withdrawn from service?
9 Which country did the composer Frederick Delius come from?
10 Which lady was the BBC Sports Personality of 1977?
11 In 70s car seat belt ads, what should you do every trip?
12 Who did Clement Attlee replace as Prime Minister?
13 Who left EastEnders and starred in a series set in a Derby telephone exchange?
14 Who made No 1 with Ready Or Not?
15 De Efteling Theme Park is in which country?
16 Erik Thorstvedt won the FA Cup as a keeper at which club?
17 According to the Monty Python team what does a lumberjack do all night?
18 Agno international airport is in which country?
19 Who said, "There will be no whitewash in the White House"?
20 At which sport did Paul Ackford represent England?
21 How did William Cody become better known?
22 Early in the century who wrote the novel Nostromo?
23 What did the letter C stand for in ACAS?
24 What part of Betty Grable was insured for over a million dollars?
25 In which decade was Top Of The Pops first broadcast?

Answers

20th C Who's Who? (see Quiz 113, page 335)
1 John Paul I. **2** Fitzgerald. **3** Mary Bell. **4** Benazir Bhutto. **5** Brian Clough. **6** He only has one leg. **7** Derek Bentley. **8** Mary McAleese. **9** Lyndon Johnson. **10** Stalin. **11** Michael Miles. **12** Shirley Williams. **13** The Queen. **14** Salvador Dali. **15** South Africa. **16** Mao Tse Tung. **17** Brazil. **18** Graeme Souness. **19** Martin Luther King. **20** Indira Gandhi. **21** President Kennedy. **22** Walt Disney. **23** McCarthy. **24** Patty Hearst. **25** Lord Denning.

Quiz 115 Diana, Princess of Wales

Answers - see Quiz 116, page 338

1 Who designed Diana's wedding dress?
2 Who coined the phrase The People's Princess about Diana?
3 What was the name of the kindergarten where Diana worked before her marriage?
4 What colour suit did Diana wear in her engagement photograph?
5 Which film star did Diana famously dance with at The White House?
6 Diana became an ambassador for which charity's campaign to ban land mines?
7 Which auctioneers auctioned Diana's dresses in 1997?
8 Which Palace was Diana's home in the last year of her life?
9 Who interviewed Diana during her famous Panorama interview?
10 With which ballet dancer did Diana dance to Uptown Girl at a charity gala in 1985?
11 In 1996 Diana visited the Shaukat Kanum cancer hospital in Pakistan which was built in the memory of whose mother?
12 What was the name of Diana's mother at the time of Diana's marriage?
13 In which hospital was Diana photographed watching a heart operation?
14 Which official title did Diana have after her divorce?
15 To the nearest £3 million what was Diana's divorce settlement?
16 In which city did the auction of Diana's dresses take place?
17 What was the name of the driver of the car in which Diana met her death?
18 Who wrote the 1992 biography, written with Diana's knowledge, which revealed personal details of Charles and Diana's married life?
19 In early July 1997 Diana and her sons were on holiday on whose yacht?
20 What are Diana's two sister called?
21 In 1987 what special ward, the first in Britain, was opened by Diana?
22 At which theme park was Diana photographed, soaking wet, with William and Harry in 1994?
23 On which Royal estate was Diana born?
24 In what capacity was Paul Burrel employed by Diana?
25 Whose book in 1998 criticised Diana and was itself disapproved of by Prince Charles and Camilla Parker-Bowles?

Answers

***Pot Luck* 53** (see Quiz 116, page 338)
1 John Lennon. **2** Korean. **3** Andy Goram. **4** Baroness Orczy. **5** Mastermind. **6** Sister Sledge. **7** Stephen Hendry. **8** Heartbeat. **9** Scarf - it was caught in a moving car wheel. **10** Belgium. **11** Switzerland. **12** Summerhill. **13** Len Deighton. **14** Don't Make Me Wait. **15** Rugby Union. **16** M3. **17** Bras. **18** 50s. **19** Between The Lines. **20** Barcelona. **21** On Her Majesty's Secret Service. **22** Pottery. **23** 7 million. **24** Warriors. **25** Leeds.

Quiz 116 Pot Luck 53

Answers - see Quiz 115, page 337

1 Opened in June 1999, the Matthew Street Gallery in Liverpool was dedicated to the works of who?
2 Neil Armstrong was a pilot in which war?
3 Which international soccer keeper of the 90s also played cricket for Scotland?
4 Who wrote the Scarlet Pimpernel?
5 In 1997 which long running TV quiz had started so it finished?
6 Who had an 80s No 1 with Frankie?
7 Which snooker star has a son called Blain?
8 Which series was based on the 'Constable' novels by Nicholas Rhea?
9 Which item of clothing cost Isadora Duncan her life?
10 Which soccer country beat the Republic of Ireland in the play off for France 98?
11 In which country was Ursula Andress born?
12 Zoe Redhead was headmistress of which school in the news in the 90s?
13 Who had the novels Spy Hook and Spy Line published in the 80s?
14 What was the first UK Top Ten hit for 911?
15 At which sport did Gary Armstrong represent Scotland?
16 Which motorway goes from London to Winchester?
17 In the summer of 1999 Anna Kournikova signed a lucrative contract to model what?
18 In which decade did Belgium join the European Union?
19 In which series did Neil Pearson play Tony Clark?
20 In which city did Man Utd win the 1999 European Champions' Cup Final?
21 Louis Armstrong sang the title song for which Bond film?
22 What did Clarice Cliff create?
23 To the nearest million what is the population of London?
24 In Rugby League what did Wigan add to their name in the 90s?
25 Which city is the home of Yorkshire TV?

Answers

Diana, Princess of Wales (see Quiz 115, page 337)
1 The Emanuels. **2** Tony Blair. **3** Young England. **4** Blue. **5** John Travolta.
6 Red Cross. **7** Christie's. **8** Kensington. **9** Martin Bashir. **10** Wayne Sleep.
11 Imran Khan. **12** Frances Shand Kydd. **13** Harefield. **14** Diana, Princess of Wales.
15 £15 Million. **16** New York. **17** Henri Paul. **18** Andrew Morton.
19 Mohammed Al Fayed's. **20** Sarah & Jane. **21** Aids. **22** Thorpe Park.
23 Sandringham. **24** Butler. **25** Penny Junor.

Quiz 117 20th C TV Soaps

Answers - see Quiz 118, page 340

1 Which character did Paul Nicholls play in EastEnders?
2 Lorraine Brownlow was what relation to Natalie in Coronation Street?
3 What was the name of Deirdre's blonde cellmate played by Margi Clarke?
4 Which future EastEnders actor played runaway Graham Lodsworth in Emmerdale?
5 Which Queen Vic landlady won The Rear of the Year award in 1987?
6 Which country did Kathy go to when she left Albert Square?
7 By the beginning of 1999 how many wives had Ken Barlow had?
8 Onslow from Keeping Up Appearances was a regular in which soap for eight years?
9 Which Jacob was buried in the very first episode of Emmerdale?
10 Which soap had a supermarket called Bettabuys?
11 What is Betty Williams' speciality in the Rovers Return?
12 Which ex Vic landlady was in a pop group called Milan?
13 What was the name of Alec Gilroy's granddaughter who married Steve McDonald?
14 Which Neighbours' star's sister appeared in rival soap Home & Away?
15 Who wrote the theme to Crossroads and Neighbours?
16 The video Naked Truths is about which soap family?
17 Who was the hairdresser Ms Middleton played by Angela Griffin in Coronation Street?
18 Civvy Street was a one hour special spin off from which soap?
19 How many times a week was Coronation Street broadcast when it began?
20 At which Farm did Kim and Frank Tate live in Emmerdale?
21 Which soap was the first to have an Afro Caribbean character as a regular cast member?
22 In which decade did the magazine soap Compact begin?
23 Which soap was headed in its early days by the Lockhead family?
24 What was the name of Anna Friel's character when she was in Brookside?
25 In Coronation Street what was Deirdre's first married name?

Answers

Pot Luck 54 (see Quiz 118, page 340)
1 88888. **2** Heart transplant. **3** The King And I. **4** Phoenix. **5** USA. **6** Mel C. **7** Airport. **8** Zimbabwe. **9** Breakfast Time. **10** Sebastian Coe. **11** Wystan Hugh. **12** Leonard Rossiter. **13** Deep Blue Something. **14** Basketball. **15** Hare. **16** Tony. **17** The Derby. **18** Aldous Huxley. **19** Spain. **20** 50s. **21** France. **22** Quarterly. **23** Bangladesh. **24** Ava Gardner. **25** Petra.

Quiz 118 Pot Luck 54

Answers - see Quiz 117, page 339

1 Nick Leeson hid his debts in a secret account with which number?
2 Louis Washkansky was the first recipient of what?
3 Which musical featured the song Hello Young Lovers?
4 In cricket what did Yorkshire add to their name in the 90s?
5 In which country was Mel Gibson born?
6 Which Spice Girl teamed with Bryan Adams on When You're Gone?
7 Where is the Glasgow terminus of the M8?
8 Canaan Banana was the first president of which country?
9 What was Britain's first breakfast TV programme called?
10 Which athlete was the BBC Sports Personality the year after Steve Ovett won the award?
11 What did the W H stand for in the name of the poet W H Auden?
12 In TV ads, who shared a glass of Cinzano with Joan Collins?
13 Who made No 1 with Breakfast At Tiffany's?
14 In which sport could the Trailblazers take on the Warriors?
15 1999 is the Chinese year of which creature?
16 What was the name of Natalie's drug dealer son in Coronation Street?
17 Which sporting event was featured in the first outside TV broadcast?
18 Who wrote the novel Brave New World?
19 Asturias international airport is in which country?
20 In which decade was Jenny Agutter born?
21 Goalkeeper Bernard Lama has played for which country?
22 What did the Q originally stand for in the magazine GQ?
23 East Pakistan has become known as what?
24 Who married Mickey Rooney, Artie Shaw and Frank Sinatra?
25 Which dog clocked up an amazing 550 plus hours of air time on BBC TV?

Answers

20th C TV Soaps (see Quiz 117, page 339)
1 Joe Wicks. **2** Niece. **3** Jackie. **4** Ross Kemp. **5** Angie. **6** South Africa. **7** Three. **8** Coronation Street. **9** Sugden. **10** Coronation Street. **11** Hotpot. **12** Tiffany. **13** Vicky. **14** Kylie Minogue's - Dannii. **15** Tony Hatch. **16** The Mitchells. **17** Fiona. **18** EastEnders. **19** Twice. **20** Home Farm. **21** Crossroads. **22** 60s. **23** Eldorado. **24** Beth Jordache. **25** Langton.

Quiz 119 Soccer

Answers - see Quiz 120, page 342

1 Peter Schmeichel joined Man Utd from which club?
2 Which side finished fourth in the 1998 World Cup?
3 In 1999's European Champions' Cup Final which player scored the first goal?
4 Which soccer club began the century known as Newton Heath?
5 What was the half-time Argentina v England score in the 1998 World Cup?
6 Pierluigi Casiraghi joined Chelsea in 1998 from which club?
7 At which club did Ron Atkinson replace Dr Josef Venglos as manager?
8 Which club became Britains first to have an all-seater stadium?
9 Who was the first England manager to be born in Worksop?
10 In the 60s and 70s Ron Harris set an appearance record at which soccer club?
11 Who scored Scotland's only goal from outfield play in France 98?
12 Darren Anderton first played league soccer with which club?
13 Which British club in the 1980s became the first to install an artificial pitch?
14 Who was the first 50 plus player to turn out in a top flight league game in England?
15 Who became the first Croatian international to play for an English club?
16 Which German team were first to win the European Cup?
17 Who was the first World Cup winning skipper to play in the Premiership?
18 Which manager took Peter Beardsley to Newcastle?
19 With 96 caps Jan Ceulemans set an appearance record for which country?
20 In the 90s, which British manager won successive titles with PSV Eindhoven?
21 Which Scottish international played for Barcelona in the 80s?
22 Who were England's first opponents in the 1998 World Cup in France?
23 Who was the first keeper to captain an FA Cup winning team at Wembley?
24 Who followed Bob Shankly as Liverpool manager?
25 Coventry first won the FA Cup in which decade?

Answers

Pot Luck 55 (see Quiz 120, page 342)
1 Carlton. **2** Aviator. **3** Poland. **4** Cycling. **5** Den Watts. **6** T'Pau. **7** Karl Benz. **8** Irving Berlin. **9** Asher. **10** Sale Of The Century. **11** Jack Cunningham. **12** BG. **13** Bruce Willis. **14** Peter Jay. **15** Thomas. **16** Nile. **17** National Geographic. **18** Leeds. **19** Washington. **20** Congress. **21** N Ireland. **22** John Thaw. **23** Scunthorpe. **24** Morocco. **25** J R R Tolkein.

Quiz 120 Pot Luck 55

Answers - see Quiz 119, page 341

1 Which company replaced Thames TV in the early 1990s?
2 How did Jean Batten achieve fame?
3 In which country was Menachem Begin, a Prime Minister of Israel born?
4 With which sport is Bernard Hinault associated?
5 Which character from Albert Square played DI Mick Raynor in a 90s crime series?
6 Who had an 80s No 1 with China In Your Hand?
7 Who did Gottlieb Daimler team up with to form a motor company?
8 Who penned Alexander's Ragtime Band?
9 Which Jane married Gerald Scarfe?
10 What was the first UK Top Ten hit for Sleeper?
11 Copeland has been the 90s seat of which prominent Labour politician?
12 What are the international registration letters of a vehicle from Bulgaria?
13 Who released the single Secret Agent Man - James Bond Is Back in '87?
14 Which co founder of TV am was once married to Tony Blair's Leader of the House of Lords?
15 What was the first name of Dr Barnardo founder of Barnardo's Homes?
16 On which river was the Aswan High Dam built?
17 Which famous magazine was started by Alexander Graham Bell?
18 In which city was Jimmy's set?
19 In American Football where do the Redskins come from?
20 In African politics, what does the letter C stand for in ANC?
21 In which country was Kenneth Branagh born?
22 Who played the tough cop character Jack Regan?
23 Which soccer team did Ian Botham play for?
24 In which country is the deepwater port of Agadir?
25 Which writer created Bilbo Baggins?

Answers

Soccer (see Quiz 119, page 341)
1 Brondby. **2** Holland. **3** Basler. **4** Man Utd. **5** 2-2. **6** Lazio. **7** Aston Villa. **8** Aberdeen. **9** Graham Taylor. **10** Chelsea. **11** Craig Burley. **12** Portsmouth. **13** QPR. **14** Stanley Matthews. **15** Igor Stimac. **16** Bayern Munich. **17** Deschamps. **18** Kevin Keegan. **19** Belgium. **20** Bobby Robson. **21** Steve Archibald. **22** Tunisia. **23** Dave Beasant. **24** Bob Paisley. **25** 80s.

Quiz 121 Movies: Blockbusters

Answers - see Quiz 122, page 344

1 What was Anna Chancellor's nickname in Four Weddings and a Funeral?
2 Which member of the Corleone family did Al Pacino play in The Godfather?
3 In which film did Michael Douglas and Glenn Close play Dan Gallagher and Alex Forrest?
4 Who played Amon Goeth in Schindler's List?
5 Which of his characters did Robin Williams say was a cross between Bill Forsyth, Alastair Sim and the Queen Mother?
6 The Third Man was set in which European city?
7 The action of which 70s movie revolves around the Kit Kat Club in Berlin?
8 In which part of New York did Shaft take place?
9 Which trilogy of films with Michael J Fox featured a De Lorean sports car?
10 Who played the role on film in Shadowlands which Nigel Hawthorne had made his own on the stage?
11 What was the first name of Private Ryan?
12 Which Orson Welles movie was voted top US movie of all time by the US Film Institute in 1998?
13 The action of Trainspotting takes place in Edinburgh, but where was the movie filmed?
14 Which Scottish hero was released on video to coincide with the opening of the 90s Scottish Parliament?
15 Who played the villainous Sir August de Wynter in The Avengers?
16 What was the sequel to Jurassic Park called?
17 Which actor was the narrator in Evita?
18 Dante's Peak featured which type of natural disaster?
19 In which country does the action in The Piano take place?
20 In which blockbusting 60s musical did the Sharks meet the Jets?
21 How many tunnels were built in The Great Escape?
22 Who was Julius Caesar in Cleopatra with Elizabeth Taylor in the title role?
23 What was the second Bond movie with Sean Connery?
24 Who played the architect of the skyscraper in The Towering Inferno?
25 Who played Dr Zhivago's wife in Dr Zhivago?

Answers

Pot Luck 56 (see Quiz 122, page 344)

1 Greta Garbo. **2** Boston. **3** Wake Me Up Before You Go Go. **4** 1972. **5** White. **6** Liverpool. **7** America. **8** Perry Mason. **9** Vic Reeves. **10** Harold Wilson. **11** Fiddler on the Roof. **12** Tesco. **13** Michael Buerk. **14** Outhere Brothers. **15** Croquet. **16** Carousel. **17** Susan Tully. **18** John Galsworthy. **19** Egypt. **20** 10. **21** Paul Gascoigne. **22** Consumers. **23** Arnold Ridley. **24** QPR. **25** Champion.

Quiz 122 Pot Luck 56

Answers - see Quiz 121, page 343

1. Who lived under the pseudonym of Harriet Brown in New York from the 40s to the 90s?
2. In baseball where do the Red Sox come from?
3. What was Wham's first No 1?
4. In which year was Bloody Sunday in Londonderry?
5. What was the main colour of a Stormtrooper in Star Wars?
6. Which club did Stan Collymore join when he left Nottm Forest?
7. Which country did Albert Einstein move to as the Nazis rose to power?
8. Which lawyer made Raymond Burr famous?
9. Who joined The Wonder Stuff on the UK No 1 Dizzy?
10. Who was Prime Minister when England won the World Cup?
11. If I Were A Rich Man was a big hit from which stage show?
12. Sir Leslie Porter is a former chairman of which supermarket chain?
13. Which TV reporter's stories of the famine in 1984 inspired Bob Geldof to set up Band Aid?
14. Who made No 1 with Boom Boom Boom?
15. At which sport did Nigel Aspinall win international success?
16. Which musical featured the song You'll Never Walk Alone?
17. Which EastEnders actress directed Barbara Windsor in her harrowing cancer scare scenes in the soap?
18. Who wrote the novels on which BBC's classic series The Forsythe Saga was based?
19. Luxor international airport is in which country?
20. In the 90s how many points have been awarded for finishing first in a Grand Prix?
21. Which footballer was the BBC Sports Personality of 1990?
22. Which? is the magazine of which Association?
23. Who played Private Godfrey in Dad's Army?
24. David Seaman first played for England when he was with which club?
25. What was the name of Gene Autry's horse?

Answers

Movies: Blockbusters (see Quiz 121, page 343)

1 Duckface. **2** Michael. **3** Fatal Attraction. **4** Ralph Fiennes. **5** Mrs Doubtfire. **6** Vienna. **7** Cabaret. **8** Harlem. **9** Back To The Future. **10** Anthony Hopkins. **11** James. **12** Citizen Kane. **13** Glasgow. **14** Braveheart. **15** Sean Connery. **16** The Lost World: Jurassic Park. **17** Antonio Banderas. **18** Volcano. **19** New Zealand. **20** West Side Story. **21** Three. **22** Rex Harrison. **23** From Russia With Love. **24** Paul Newman. **25** Geraldine Chaplin.

Quiz 123 Around The UK

Answers - see Quiz 124, page 346

LEVEL 2

1. The research laboratories at Porton Down ar near which cathedral town?
2. To the nearest 100ft how tall is the Canary Wharf Tower?
3. Where did the Royal Mint move to from Tower Hill London in 1968?
4. According to a University of East Anglia report which year of the 90s was the hottest ever recorded in the UK?
5. Where did the National Horseracing Museum open in 1983?
6. Where was the site of the Millennium Exhibition and the Millennium Dome chosen to be?
7. Which Cheshire village was the home of nanny Louise Woodward?
8. Which castle was restored by the end of 1997 at a cost of £37 million?
9. Which English county has the place with the longest name - Sutton-Under-Whitestonecliffe ?
10. Where is the annual music festival founded by Benjamin Britten held?
11. The first of a chain of which holiday centres opened in Skegness in 1936?
12. Which branch of the armed services is trained at Cranwell in Lincolnshire?
13. Where is the Government Communications Headquarters?
14. In the 1990s which theatre was rebuilt on the site of an Elizabethan theatre?
15. Which military museum was founded in London in 1917?
16. Which airport in the English capital was built in 1987?
17. Which social organisation's name is the Latin word for table?
18. Metrolink operates a train service around which city?
19. Which city has a railway station called Temple Meades?
20. Beaulieu in Hampshire has a famous museum of what?
21. In 1991 the Sainsbury Wing was built as an extension to which Gallery?
22. The Burrell Gallery is in which Scottish city?
23. In which inner city was the first National Garden Festival held in 1984?
24. Which company merged with Stena to face the cross Channel competition for services through the Channel Tunnel?
25. Where is the Open University based?

Answers

***Pot Luck* 57** (see Quiz 124, page 346)

1 20s. **2** Escher. **3** Chicago. **4** Helen Baxendale. **5** Dwight Eisenhower. **6** Wham! **7** Boris Becker. **8** Christian Science Church. **9** 50s. **10** Jewelled eggs. **11** Sydney. **12** 50p. **13** Leeds. **14** Phantom Of The Opera. **15** Nagasaki. **16** Mandy Rice Davies. **17** Simba. **18** Margot Fonteyn. **19** Splash it all over. **20** Live And Let Die. **21** Queen Elizabeth II. **22** Walk This Way. **23** Margaret Mitchell. **24** 80s. **25** William Hartnell.

Quiz 124 Pot Luck 57

Answers - see Quiz 123, page 345

1 In which decade did Alexander Fleming discover penicillin?
2 Which Dutch graphic artist - initials M C - was a creator of optical illusions?
3 In which city is O'Hare International airport?
4 Who played Claire Maitland in Cardiac Arrest?
5 Which US President was backed by the "I like Ike" campaign?
6 Who had an 80s No 1 with Freedom?
7 Which Wimbledon champion once had soccer trials with Bayern Munich?
8 Which movement was founded by Mary Baker Eddy?
9 In which decade was Dennis Potter's Lipstick on Your Collar set?
10 What was the speciality of jewellery maker Peter Faberge?
11 Which city with 3 million inhabitants is Australia's largest by population?
12 In decimal currency how much did the first TV licence cost?
13 Which Rugby League team became Rhinos in the 90s?
14 Which musical featured the song All I Ask Of You?
15 Which was the second city to be hit by an atomic bomb in World War II?
16 Who famously said, "Well he would say that, wouldn't he?"?
17 In the movie of the same name, what is The Lion King's name?
18 Under what name did Peggy Hookham entertain audiences?
19 In TV ads what should you do with Brut according to Henry Cooper?
20 Paul McCartney and Wings provided the title song for which Bond film?
21 As a child who called herself 'Lilibet'?
22 What was the first UK Top Ten hit for the Run-DMC?
23 Who wrote the novel Gone With The Wind?
24 In which decade did Greece join the European Union?
25 Who played the first TV Doctor Who?

Answers

Around the UK (see Quiz 123, page 345)
1 Salisbury. **2** 800ft. **3** Cardiff. **4** 1995. **5** Newmarket. **6** Greenwich. **7** Elton. **8** Windsor. **9** North Yorkshire. **10** Aldeburgh. **11** Butlin's. **12** RAF. **13** Cheltenham. **14** Globe. **15** Imperial War Museum. **16** London City Airport. **17** Mensa. **18** Manchester. **19** Bristol. **20** Cars. **21** National Gallery. **22** Glasgow. **23** Liverpool. **24** P & O. **25** Milton Keynes.

Quiz 125 Music - Girl Power

Answers - see Quiz 126, page 348

LEVEL 2

1 How many of The Corrs are female?
2 In which decade was vocalist Karen Carpenter born?
3 Whose real name is Gaynor Hopkins?
4 Which soap star had a 1990 hit with Just This Side of Love?
5 Shout was the first hit for which solo female star?
6 Which comedienne featured on the B side of the Comic Relief hit The Stonk?
7 In 1995 the album Daydream topped the charts for which female vocalist?
8 How many girls were in the group Ace of Base?
9 In which decade was vocalist Lisa Stansfield born?
10 Who released an album called Jagged Little Pill?
11 Who asked Unbreak My Heart in 1997?
12 Which Spice Girls hit was No 1 at the beginning of 1997?
13 In 1995 which soapstar was Happy Just to Be with You?
14 Who was a Professional Widow according to her 1997 hit?
15 What was Madonna's third UK No 1?
16 In which country was Neneh Cherry born?
17 What was Whitney Houston's first UK top ten hit?
18 Who released a UK No 1 album in 1992 called Shepherd Moons?
19 Which country was represented by Celine Dion at the Eurovision Song Contest?
20 Which female vocalist said All I Want for Christmas is You in 1994?
21 Who duetted with Peter Gabriel on Don't Give Up?
22 Who got to No 1 in 1994 in her first-ever week in the UK charts?
23 Who released the top selling album Guilty in 1980?
24 Which female artist had huge success with the album The Kick Inside?
25 Who won a US Song of the Year Award in 1995 for Breathe Again ?

Answers

***Pot Luck* 58** (see Quiz 126, page 348)

1 Haiti. **2** Chris Kelly. **3** Worcestershire. **4** Tonight Tonight. **5** Canberra. **6** Barbuda. **7** Gigi. **8** Basset hound. **9** Dallas. **10** Belize. **11** Perfect Day. **12** Mail. **13** 18 million. **14** Right Said Fred. **15** J B Priestley. **16** Harold Macmillan. **17** Michael. **18** Hong Kong. **19** Aspidistra. **20** Jacques Delors. **21** Italy. **22** A J. **23** Wilson. **24** Tiger. **25** Austria.

Quiz 126 Pot Luck 58

Answers - see Quiz 125, page 347

1 In which country did the notorious security force the Tontons Macoutes operate?
2 Which producer of Kavanagh QC has been a regular on Food & Drink?
3 In cricket which English team became Royals in the 90s?
4 What was the first UK Top Ten hit for the Smashing Pumpkins?
5 What became the capital of Australia during the 20th century?
6 On which Caribbean island did Princess Diana spend her first Christmas after her divorce was announced?
7 Which musical featured the song Thank Heaven For Little Girls?
8 What breed of dog did Columbo own?
9 In basketball where do the Mavericks come from?
10 British Honduras has become known as what?
11 Which song was released to raise funds for Children in Need in 1997?
12 For many years Fred Basset has been a regular of which Daily paper?
13 To the nearest million what is the population of Australia?
14 Who made No 1 with Deeply Dippy?
15 Who wrote The Good Companions?
16 Which Prime Minister replaced Anthony Eden?
17 Who did Liz leave Coronation Street with?
18 The Queen Elizabeth liner was destroyed by fire in the 70s in which harbour?
19 Gracie Fields sang about the Biggest what In The World?
20 Who took over as President of the European Commission in January 1985?
21 Malpensa international airport is in which country?
22 Which were the initials of Doctor Finlay creator Cronin?
23 Who was Cohen's fullback partner in England's World Cup winning team?
24 1998 was the Chinese year of which creature?
25 Which country does musician Alfred Brendel come from?

Answers

Music - Girl Power (see Quiz 125, page 347)
1 Three. **2** 1950s. **3** Bonnie Tyler. **4** Malandra Burrows. **5** Lulu. **6** Victoria Wood. **7** Mariah Carey. **8** Two. **9** 60s. **10** Alanis Morisette. **11** Toni Braxton. **12** 2 Become 1. **13** Michelle Gayle. **14** Tori Amos. **15** La Isla Bonita. **16** Sweden. **17** Saving All My Love For You. **18** Enya. **19** Switzerland. **20** Mariah Carey. **21** Kate Bush. **22** Whigfield. **23** Barbra Streisand. **24** Kate Bush. **25** Toni Braxton.

Quiz 127 War Zones

Answers - see Quiz 128, page 350

1 Which US General along with Schwarzkopf was leader in the Gulf War?
2 The Taliban were a guerrilla group in which country?
3 How long did the Arab Israeli War of 1967 last?
4 Who, during the Vietnam war was known as Hanoi Jane?
5 Which breakaway Russian republic had Grozny as its capital?
6 Which country's 'Spring' was halted by the arrival of Soviet tanks in 1968?
7 Where was the Bay of Pigs whose invasion sparked a world crisis in the 60s?
8 Which country pulled out of Vietnam in the 1950s?
9 Where did the Enola Gay drop a devastating bomb in WWII?
10 In which country is Passchendaele, scene of battle in WWI?
11 Whose forces were defeated at the Battle of Midway in 1942?
12 Who were defeated along with the Germans at El Alamein?
13 During World War 1 what kind of gas was used in the trenches?
14 What Operation was the codename for the D Day landings?
15 Which major weapon of war was used for the first time in 1916?
16 The Tamil Tigers were fighting for a separate state on which island?
17 Muhammad Ali refused to fight in which war?
18 War broke out in Biafra in the 60s when it broke away from which country?
19 Where did Nazi leader Rudolf Hess crashland in 1941?
20 Which 'Lord' was executed for treason in 1946 for broadcasting Nazi propaganda?
21 During which war was OXFAM set up?
22 In WWII who was in charge of the Afrika Korps?
23 The EOKA were a terrorist group operating on which island?
24 What was the number of the British Armoured Division known as The Desert Rats?
25 Which city was besieged by German troops for over 900 days in WWII?

Answers

Pot Luck 59 (see Quiz 128, page 350)
1 1940s. **2** Radium. **3** Pomeroy's. **4** Fergal Sharkey. **5** Lightning. **6** Wimbledon. **7** S. **8** Half A Sixpence. **9** Nikkei. **10** Whatever Happened To The Likely Lads. **11** George Robertson. **12** TR. **13** James Naughtie. **14** Henry James. **15** Hockey. **16** Slade. **17** Haematology. **18** Brown. **19** 1979. **20** Nigel Kennedy. **21** Crown Court. **22** Nitrous oxide. **23** Newspaper cartoonists. **24** 50s. **25** Minnesota.

Quiz 128 Pot Luck 59

Answers - see Quiz 127, page 349

1 In which decade was the last execution at the Tower of London?
2 Which element along with polonium did the Curies discover?
3 Which Wine Bar did Rumpole frequent?
4 Who had an 80s No 1 with A Good Heart?
5 What does Blitz mean?
6 Nigel Winterburn joined Arsenal from which soccer club?
7 On a computer keyboard which letter is between A and D?
8 Which musical featured the song Flash Bang, Wallop?
9 What is the Japanese share index called?
10 In which TV series sequel did Bob marry Thelma?
11 Hamilton was the 90s seat of which prominent Labour politician?
12 What are the international registration letters of a vehicle from Turkey?
13 Who hosted the Proms on TV when Richard Baker retired?
14 Who wrote the Turn of The Screw in the 19th C and The Ambassadors in the 20th?
15 At which sport did Phil Barber win international success?
16 Who were the first act to have three singles enter at the UK No. 1?
17 Which branch of medicine is concerned with disorders of the blood?
18 What is the surname of William in Richal Crompton's William books?
19 In which year did Muhammad Ali announce his retirement?
20 Whose 80s recording of Vivaldi's Four Seasons sold a million?
21 What was the 60s equivalent of the 90s series The Verdict called?
22 What is the correct name of laughing gas?
23 Jak and Trog were examples of what?
24 In which decade was Kirstie Alley born?
25 In American Football where do the Vikings come from?

Answers

War Zones (see Quiz 127, page 349)
1 Powell. **2** Afghanistan. **3** Six Days. **4** Jane Fonda. **5** Chechenia. **6** Czechoslovakia. **7** Cuba. **8** France. **9** Hiroshima. **10** Belgium. **11** Japan. **12** Italians. **13** Mustard gas. **14** Overlord. **15** Tank. **16** Sri Lanka. **17** Vietnam. **18** Nigeria. **19** Scotland. **20** Lord Haw-Haw. **21** WWII. **22** Rommel. **23** Cyprus. **24** 7th. **25** Leningrad.

Quiz 129 20th C Famous Names

Answers - see Quiz 130, page 352

1 Which British Dame became the first woman to win two Olivier awards for best actress in the same year - in 1996?
2 Israel Moses Sieff was head of which British chain of stores?
3 Who was Deep Blue, Gary Kasparov's famous chess opponent?
4 Which comic became the BBC's youngest scriptwriter in 1980, aged 21?
5 Which chef opened a restaurant called Woz?
6 Which MP announced in 1996 that she had been reunited with the son she gave up for adoption 31 years before?
7 What relation was the Queen's Private Secretary Robert Fellowes to the late Diana Princess of Wales?
8 Who is the great grand daughter of Prime Minister Herbert Asquith?
9 What is the name of gourmet Egon Ronay's designer daughter?
10 In 1991 who was voted 'the most successful Australian to get to the top with least ability' by students in Adelaide?
11 What was the first name of the baby in the Louise Woodward case?
12 Which Rugby player did Julia Smith marry in 1994?
13 What is Tony Blair's daughter called?
14 Which musical instrument does astronomer Patrick Moore play?
15 Gerald Scarfe is famous as what?
16 What was the name of Mrs Neil Hamilton who forcefully defended her husband over sleaze allegations?
17 Ulrich Salchow was the first Olympic medallist in his sport and gave his name to one of its jumps; what sport is it?
18 Which veteran DJ's autobiography was called As It Happens?
19 Which photographer have Catherine Deneuve and Marie Helvin married?
20 Which cartoon strip was Charles Schulz most famous creation?
21 Who was the sole survivor of the car crash in which Princess Diana died?
22 Who sold the story of David Mellor & Antonia de Sancha to the papers?
23 In which area of London did Ronnie Scott open his jazz club in 1959?
24 Which singer and comedian published a volume of autobiography in 1989 called Arias and Raspberries?
25 David Sheppard, the Bishop of Liverpool, was famous for what sport?

Answers

Pot Luck 60 (see Quiz 130, page 352)

1 Open. **2** Green. **3** Bob Dylan. **4** Lord's. **5** Caroline. **6** Chicago. **7** Lakesiders. **8** Encore Une Fois. **9** Sandown. **10** Cat. **11** Hall. **12** Australia. **13** George V. **14** Tasmin Archer. **15** DNA. **16** Leslie Ash. **17** 20s. **18** Ruth Rendell. **19** Israel. **20** One Day In Your Life. **21** India. **22** Rudyard Kipling. **23** Florida. **24** Radio Times. **25** Emlyn.

Quiz 130 Pot Luck 60

Answers - see Quiz 129, page 351

LEVEL 2 

1 Which university is at Milton Keynes?
2 In Cluedo what is the colour of the vicar?
3 Which singer "ain't gonna work on Maggie's farm no more"?
4 Middlesex play most of their home cricket fixtures at which ground?
5 Which Princess's husband was killed in 1990 when his powerboat went out of control?
6 In baseball where do the White Sox come from?
7 On which docu soap did Emma Boundy find fame?
8 What was the first UK Top Ten hit for Sash!?
9 Which race course is at Esher?
10 Which creature is seen when Coronation Street starts?
11 Which Peter was artistic director of London's National Theatre?
12 Where is the wine growing Barossa Valley?
13 Which monarch reigned in Britain at the start of the First World War?
14 Who made No 1 with Sleeping Satellite?
15 Crick, Watson and Wilkins determined the structure of what?
16 Which star of Men Behaving Badly once presented The Tube?
17 In which decade did writer Thomas Hardy die?
18 Who wrote the novels A Judgement In Stone and The Killing Doll?
19 In which country is the deepwater port of Ashdod?
20 What was Michael Jackson's first solo No 1 in the UK?
21 In which country was Julie Christie born?
22 Who wrote that "the female of the species is deadlier than the male"?
23 Key West airport was built in which US state?
24 Which BBC periodical first came out in 1929?
25 Lots of Hughes's have played soccer for Wales, but who is England's most capped Hughes?

Answers

20th C Famous Names (see Quiz 129, page 351)
1 Judi Dench. **2** Marks & Spencer. **3** Computer. **4** Ben Elton. **5** Anthony Worrall-Thompson. **6** Claire Short. **7** Brother in Law. **8** Helena Bonham Carter. **9** Edina. **10** Kylie Minogue. **11** Matthew. **12** Will Carling. **13** Kathryn. **14** Xylophone. **15** Cartoonist. **16** Christine. **17** Skating. **18** Jimmy Savile. **19** David Bailey. **20** Peanuts. **21** Trevor Rees-Jones. **22** Max Clifford. **23** Soho. **24** Harry Secombe. **25** Cricketer.

Quiz 131 TV: Famous Faces

Answers - see Quiz 132, page 354

1 Scott Chisholm found fame promoting what type of TV programmes?
2 Who left News At Ten to help launch the BBC's Breakfast Time?
3 Who was the antiques expert on the 1999 series of Going For a Song?
4 Trude Mostue found fame in a docu soap about which profession?
5 Which Dingle from Emmerdale presented You've Been Framed?
6 Which They Think It's All Over regular had a beard?
7 Which extrovert TV chef was a member of the Calypso Twins?
8 How is Meg Lake better known?
9 On which show did Jane McDonald shoot to fame?
10 Who was the Six O'Clock News anchorman when the programme was revamped in 1999?
11 Who was The Naked Chef?
12 Who replaced Peter Sissons as host of Question Time?
13 Who presented the BBC's daytime Wimbledon coverage during most of the late 1990s?
14 My Kind of People was LWT talent spotting show fronted by whom?
15 Who played gamekeeper Mellors opposite Joely Richardson in the D H Lawrence TV adaptation?
16 In 1997 who played Max de Winter in a TV adaptation of Daphne DuMaurier's Rebecca?
17 Who moved from Whose Line Is It Anyway to Call My Bluff?
18 Who was the sole regular male team member in Victoria Wood - As Seen on TV?
19 Which ex Blue Peter presenter introduced Mad About Pets?
20 Who was the team captain opposing Jack Dee in the first series of It's Only TV but I Like It?
21 Which character had a hit single with a song of the theme music from EastEnders?
22 Who presented the very first edition of Top of the Pops?
23 David Jason's first long running serious TV role was as which character?
24 Who was behind the yoof series DEF II?
25 Who became Gardener's World's regular presenter after the death of Geoff Hamilton?

Answers

Pot Luck 61 (see Quiz 132, page 354)
1 50s. **2** Miss Marple. **3** HIV. **4** Scorpions. **5** Georgia. **6** Mel and Kim. **7** Dave. **8** South Korea. **9** The Rolling Stones. **10** Nigel Mansell. **11** J K Chesterton. **12** Paisley. **13** Octopussy. **14** The Blue Mountains. **15** Forget Me Nots. **16** Shauna Lowry. **17** 90s. **18** Briggs. **19** Richard Nixon. **20** Burning. **21** China. **22** Zambia. **23** Percentage. **24** 20s . **25** Shredded Wheat.

Quiz 132 Pot Luck 61

Answers - see Quiz 131, page 353

1 In which decade was the last hanging of a woman in the UK?
2 Inspector Slack was always on the case with which amateur sleuth?
3 Robert Gallo was one of the pioneers in the identification of which virus?
4 In cricket what did Derbyshire add to their name in the 90s?
5 What is the home state of ex US President Jimmy Carter?
6 Who had an 80s No 1 with Respectable?
7 In Only Fools and Horses what does Trigger call Del Boy?
8 Where is the HQ of the multinational Samsung?
9 Until his death in 1969, Brian Jones was in which pop band?
10 Which speed star was the BBC Sports Personality of the Year in 1986 and 1992?
11 Who wrote the Father Brown novels?
12 Where in the UK was Tom Conti born?
13 Which Bond girl was played by Maud Adams?
14 Which mountain range to the west of Sydney, was badly damaged by bush fires in 1993?
15 Which flowers gave the title to a No 8 UK hit in 1982 for Patrice Rushen?
16 Which Irish presenter worked on Animal Hospital?
17 In which decade did Austria join the European Union?
18 Which Raymond created The Snowman?
19 Which US President was inaugurated in 1969?
20 In the patriotic World War I song what should we Keep the Home Fires doing?
21 Translated as The People's Daily, in which country is this a major seller?
22 Vehicles from which country use the international registration letter Z?
23 In finance what does the letter P stand for in APR?
24 In which decade was comic actor Frank Thornton born?
25 In TV ads which breakfast cereal did Jackie Charlton and his grandson tuck into?

Answers

TV: Famous Faces (see Quiz 131, page 353)
1 Children's. **2** Selina Scott. **3** Eric Knowles. **4** Vets. **5** Mandy. **6** Rory McGrath. **7** Ainsley Harriott. **8** Mystic Meg. **9** The Cruise. **10** Huw Edwards. **11** Jamie Oliver. **12** David Dimbleby. **13** Desmond Lynam. **14** Michael Barrymore. **15** Sean Bean. **16** Charles Dance. **17** Sandi Toksvig. **18** Duncan Preston. **19** John Noakes. **20** Julian Clary. **21** Angie. **22** Jimmy Savile. **23** Jack Frost. **24** Janet Street Porter. **25** Alan Titchmarsh.

Quiz 133 Sport - 90s Action Replay

Answers - see Quiz 134, page 356

1 Which English bowler took a 90s hat trick against the West Indies?
2 In which US state were the last summer Olympics of the century held?
3 Who were the opponents in Schmeichel's last league game for Man Utd?
4 Who beat Tim Henman in his first Wimbledon singles semi-final?
5 Who missed England's last penalty in the Euro 96 shoot out v Germany?
6 In 1995, which England captain was sacked and then reinstated within a few days?
7 Who inflicted Nigel Benn's first defeat as a professional?
8 Who was the last team to be relegated from the Premiership in the 20th century?
9 Which team won cricket's county championship in 1990 and 1991?
10 Yuan Yuan was caught carrying drugs for which Chinese team?
11 Which Grand Slam did Pete Sampras not win in the century?
12 Man Utd bought Gary Pallister from and sold him back to which club?
13 In baseball who set a record with 70 home runs?
14 In 1998 Tegla Loroupe set a new world record in the women's section of which event?
15 Which soccer team moved to Pride Park in the 90s?
16 How long was swimmer Michelle de Bruin banned for attempting to manipulate a drugs test?
17 Who did Mike Atherton replace as England's cricket captain?
18 In which sport did Andy Thomson become a world champion?
19 Which legendary American golfer played his last British Open in 1995?
20 The scorer of Romania's last minute winner v England in the 98 World Cup played with which English club?
21 Which cricketing county won a sideboard full of trophies with Dermot Reeve as skipper?
22 Which jockey rode over 200 winners in both 1997 and 1998?
23 Who won a record ninth Wimbledon singles title in 1991?
24 In 1995 Man Utd set a record Premier score by beating which team 9-0 ?
25 Which English wicket keeper set a new record of 11 dismissals in a test in 1995?

Answers

Pot Luck 62 (see Quiz 134, page 356)
1 Star Wars. **2** Teacher. **3** Cricket. **4** The music. **5** Joy. **6** Pussycat. **7** Seventy Six. **8** Skiing. **9** Old Possum. **10** Ox. **11** UK Living. **12** Prosecution. **13** Jancis. **14** Snap. **15** Rugby Union. **16** Private Eye. **17** That's Life. **18** Osborne House. **19** Spain. **20** Basketball. **21** Sheena Easton. **22** Dashiell Hammett. **23** 20s. **24** Graham Taylor. **25** Wilson.

Quiz 134 Pot Luck 62

Answers - see Quiz 133, page 355

1 In 1999 Pepsi-Cola launched a series of collectable cans linked with what?
2 What was the profession of Philip Lawrence who was tragically killed in the 90s?
3 Which sport did aristocratic sleuth Lord Peter Wimsey play?
4 When The Sound of Music was first shown in Korea what was not included?
5 What kind of ride was taken by Roxette in a No 4 UK hit from 1991?
6 What was Kojak's pet name for people?
7 How many trombones featured in a title of a song from The Music Man?
8 With which sport is Marc Giradelli associated?
9 Whose name features in the title of the Book Of Practical Cats?
10 1997 was the Chinese year of which creature?
11 Which satellite channel used the slogan 'You can't help getting involved'?
12 The DPP is the director of public what?
13 What is wine writer Ms Robinson's first name?
14 Who made No 1 with The Power?
15 At which sport did Stuart Barnes win international success?
16 Publishing magnate Lord Gnome is connected with which publication?
17 Which consumer programme was a follow up to Braden's Week?
18 In which royal residence did Queen Victoria die?
19 Pamplona international airport is in which country?
20 In which sport could the Jazz take on the Grizzlies?
21 Who sang the title song for the Bond film For Your Eyes Only?
22 Who wrote the detective novel The Maltese Falcon?
23 In which decade was comedian Benny Hill born?
24 Gary Lineker played his last ever England game under which manager?
25 Which Francis was the first regular weatherman on BBC's Breakfast Time?

Answers

Sport - 90s Action Replay (see Quiz 133, page 355)
1 Dominic Cork. **2** Georgia. **3** Spurs. **4** Pete Sampras. **5** Gareth Southgate. **6** Will Carling. **7** Chris Eubank. **8** Charlton Athletic. **9** Essex. **10** Swimming. **11** French. **12** Nottm Forest. **13** Mark McGwire. **14** Marathon. **15** Derby. **16** 4 years. **17** Graham Gooch. **18** Bowls. **19** Arnold Palmer. **20** Chelsea - it was Dan Petrescu. **21** Warwickshire. **22** Kieren Fallon. **23** Martina Navratilova. **24** Ipswich. **25** Jack Russell.

Quiz 135 Movies Who's Who?

Answers - see Quiz 136, page 358

1 Who has the nickname Sly?
2 Which Richard found fame in Withnail and I?
3 Who won best actress at the 1997 Cannes Film festival for her role in Nil By Mouth?
4 Which activist did Denzel Washington play in Cry Freedom?
5 Which actress's official title is Lady Haden-Guest?
6 Which actor shot to fame in 1980 with American Gigolo?
7 Who briefly changed his name to Lenny Williams but returned to his Italian sounding name?
8 Who could not accept the offer to play 007 first time round as he was committed to playing Remington Steele?
9 What is the name of John Travolta's son - so called because of the actor's passion for aeroplanes?
10 How was Joanne Whalley known after her marriage to a fellow actor?
11 Actress Glenda Jackson became MP for which constituency?
12 Who dubbed Kenneth Branagh's voice for the French version of Henry V?
13 Who reputedly was in discussion with Diana, Princess of Wales about making a sequel to The Bodyguard shortly before her death?
14 How did Christopher Reeve suffer the appalling injuries which brought about his paralysis in 1995?
15 Which Oscar winning actor was the voice of John Smith in Pocahontas?
16 Who is Jason Gould's mum who starred with him in Prince of Tides?
17 Which James Bond appeared in Spiceworld: The Movie?
18 Who did Antonio Banderas marry after they met on the set of Two Much?
19 Who wrote the novel on which Trainspotting was based?
20 Which actress won an Oscar for her screenplay adaptation of Jane Austen's Sense & Sensibility?
21 In which city was Hugh Grant arrested with Divine Brown?
22 Which English actor was the voice of Scar in The Lion King?
23 Which child star appeared in Richie Rich?
24 Who or what was Clyde with Clint Eastwood in Any Which Way You Can?
25 Who played the doctor who cared for John Merrick in The Elephant Man?

Answers

Pot Luck 63 (see Quiz 136, page 358)
1 John Higgins. **2** Mary Quant . **3** Crockett. **4** Public Employees. **5** Mines. **6** Madonna. **7** Korea. **8** Barnes. **9** Tiffany's. **10** Ethiopia. **11** Dean Martin. **12** IND. **13** Cape Canaveral. **14** 500 miles. **15** Donna Summer. **16** Columbia. **17** Wendy Richard. **18** Emirates. **19** 70s. **20** Cherry. **21** Vikings. **22** P. **23** 7 million. **24** Double Diamond. **25** New Orleans.

Quiz 136 Pot Luck 63

Answers - see Quiz 135, page 357

1. Who moved up to No 1 ranking for snooker's 1998-99 season?
2. Whose clothes shop Bazaar was a trendsetter in the 60s?
3. Which detective lived on a boat called St Vitus Dance?
4. NUPE was the National Union of what?
5. In WWII where did the Bevin Boys work?
6. Who had an 80s No 1 with Like A Prayer?
7. In which eastern country were the Moonies founded in 1954?
8. In Coronation Street what was the surname of Colin and the late Des?
9. Truman Capote wrote about Breakfast at which place?
10. Abyssinia has become known as what?
11. Which US singer said, "You're not drunk if you can lie on the floor without holding on"?
12. What are the international registration letters of a vehicle from India?
13. What is the name of the USA's main space exploration centre in Florida?
14. How long is Indianapolis's most famous motor race?
15. Who was the first female to have three consecutive US No 1 albums?
16. On which river was the Grand Coulee built?
17. Which star of Are You Being Served? became a regular panellist on radio's Just A Minute?
18. In the Arab world what does the letter E stand for in UAE?
19. In which decade was Ewan McGregor born?
20. What kind of orchard did Chekhov write a play about?
21. In Rugby League what did Widnes add to their name in the 90s?
22. On a computer keyboard which letter on the same line is immediately right of the O?
23. To the nearest million what is the population of New York?
24. In TV advertising which beer was said to "work wonders"?
25. In American Football where do the Saints come from?

Answers

Movies Who's Who (see Quiz 135, page 357)

1 Sylvester Stallone. **2** E. Grant. **3** Kathy Burke. **4** Steve Biko. **5** Jamie Lee Curtis. **6** Richard Gere. **7** Leonardo DiCaprio. **8** Pierce Brosnan. **9** Jett. **10** Joanne Whalley Kilmer. **11** Hampstead & Highgate. **12** Gerard Depardieu. **13** Kevin Costner. **14** Fell from a horse. **15** Mel Gibson. **16** Barbra Streisand. **17** Roger Moore. **18** Melanie Griffith. **19** Irvine Welsh. **20** Emma Thompson. **21** Los Angeles. **22** Jeremy Irons. **23** Macaulay Culkin. **24** Orang Utan. **25** Anthony Hopkins.

Quiz 137 Euro Tour

Answers - see Quiz 138, page 360

1 What colour did Air France repaint some Concorde jets to advertise Pepsi?
2 How was Eurotunnel known before its name change in 1998?
3 Where is the French terminus for the Hoverspeed service?
4 Which European town gave its name to a Treaty which symbolises closer economic links between European countries?
5 In which European country did Victoria Adams marry David Beckham?
6 What is the oldest university in Northern Ireland called - founded in 1908?
7 Sullom Voe is famous for exporting which commodity?
8 How are Belgian World Airlines also known?
9 Which country lies to the north of Austria and to the south of Poland?
10 How many independent 'Baltic states' are there?
11 On which date in 1999 did Duty Free Shopping dramatically change?
12 Where is the Belgian terminus for Eurostar trains?
13 When did Euro Disney - now Disneyland Paris - open?
14 In 1998 a new breed of mosquito was discovered on which underground system?
15 Where is the Donana National Park?
16 In which country was the Angel of the North erected in 1998?
17 Which home of champagne in France was also where the German High Command surrendered in WWII?
18 What name is given to the popular holiday area between Marseille and La Spezia?
19 Which British architect was responsible with Renzo Piano for the famous Pompidou Centre in Paris?
20 In which European city is The Atomium?
21 Which tourist islands include the lesser known Cabrera and Formentera?
22 Which winter sports venue, home of the Cresta Run, has hosted two Olympic Games in the 20th century?
23 What is Ireland's longest river and greatest source of electric power?
24 The Simplon Tunnel links Italy with which country?
25 On which Sea does Croatia stand?

Answers

Pot Luck 64 (see Quiz 138, page 360)

1 BMW. **2** Jack Dempsey. **3** Van Clomp. **4** Think Twice. **5** Eleven. **6** Billy Connolly. **7** White. **8** Kismet. **9** Seattle. **10** Alan Sillitoe. **11** Jimi Hendrix. **12** Lego. **13** Ukraine. **14** Stiltskin. **15** California. **16** 21. **17** Ariel. **18** Japan. **19** Lazy. **20** Bobby Moore. **21** New Orleans. **22** Roger Moore. **23** Paper handkerchiefs. **24** Ipswich. **25** Buckett.

Quiz 138 Pot Luck 64

Answers - see Quiz 137, page 359

1. Which company took over Rover in 1994?
2. "Honey, I just forgot to duck" were the words of which sportsman?
3. On TV which character painted The Fallen Madonna with the Big Boobies?
4. What was Celine Dion's first UK No 1?
5. How many individual bets make up a Yankee?
6. Which comedian said, "Marriage is a wonderful invention - but so is the bicycle repair kit"?
7. Which colour appears with blue on the U N flag?
8. Which musical featured the song Too Darn Hot?
9. In basketball where do the Supersonics come from?
10. Who wrote The Loneliness Of The Long Distance Runner?
11. Which late rock star said, "When you're dead you're made for life"?
12. Which toy was the brainchild of Ole Kirk Christiansen of Denmark?
13. In which country is Chernobyl, scene of a nuclear leak when it was still part of the USSR?
14. Who made No 1 with Inside?
15. In which US state was the J Paul Getty Museum founded?
16. In 1928 what became the minimum age at which a woman could vote?
17. Advertising which product caused Carol Vorderman to be dropped from hosting Tomorrow's World?
18. Osaka international airport is in which country?
19. What were Suede in their No 9 UK hit from 1997?
20. Which soccer player was the BBC Sports Personality of 1966?
21. Which US town became known as the home of jazz?
22. Which James Bond appeared in The Persuaders?
23. What were marketed as Celluwipes when they were first developed?
24. Roger Osborne's goal sealed the first FA Cup Final triumph for which club?
25. In fiction, what was the name of Charlie the Chocolate Factory owner?

Answers

Euro Tour (see Quiz 137, page 359)
1 Blue. **2** Le Shuttle. **3** Boulogne. **4** Maastricht. **5** Ireland. **6** Queen's University. **7** Oil. **8** SABENA. **9** Czech Republic. **10** Three. **11** 30th June. **12** Brussels Midi. **13** 1992. **14** London. **15** Spain. **16** England. **17** Reims. **18** Riviera. **19** Richard Rogers. **20** Brussels. **21** Balearics. **22** St Moritz. **23** Shannon. **24** Switzerland. **25** Adriatic.

Quiz 139 Pop Music: Charts

Answers - see Quiz 140, page 362

1 Which all boy group's first No 1 in 1989 was You Got It (The Right Stuff)?
2 Denis was the first UK hit for which group?
3 Who had an album in the 90s called Said and Done?
4 Which film featured the No 1 UK hit Take My Breath Away?
5 What was the Osmonds' only UK No 1 hit?
6 Who had an 80s hit with Good Tradition?
7 Which decade saw the introduction of the Grammy award?
8 Which group's first hit was Labour of Love?
9 What was Simply Red's first top ten single?
10 How many centimetres did an LP measure across?
11 In which decade did Imagine by John Lennon reach No 1 in the UK?
12 Who wrote the UK chart topper I Will Always Love You?
13 Which artist has had the most chart album hits in the US?
14 Who spent most weeks in the UK singles charts in 1996?
15 Who topped the album charts in 1990 with But Seriously?
16 Which American's first Top Ten album was 52nd Street?
17 Which game was in the title of a Pet Shop Boys hit from 1988?
18 During which decade did CDs officially go on sale in Europe?
19 Which group topped the album charts with Turtle Power?
20 Whose first hit in the 90s was End of the Road?
21 Who released an album in 1996 called Travelling Without Meaning?
22 Which country singer from the 80s sang Thank God I'm a Country Boy?
23 Who had an album called Take Two released in 1996?
24 Roxy Music had their first UK hit in which decade?
25 Which group topped the album charts in 1995 with Nobody Else?

Answers

Pot Luck 65 (see Quiz 140, page 362)
1 Peter Phillips. **2** Ian Wright. **3** China. **4** American. **5** Nurse. **6** Pet Shop Boys. **7** Leicestershire. **8** Two. **9** Billy. **10** Robin Cook. **11** Red. **12** August. **13** Roses. **14** Michael. **15** Squash. **16** Ant and Dec. **17** Film director. **18** 50s. **19** Rowan Atkinson. **20** Brazil. **21** Code. **22** Alexander Solzhenitzyn. **23** Spain. **24** Toronto. **25** USA.

Quiz 140 Pot Luck 65

Answers - see Quiz 139, page 361

1 Who is the Queen's eldest grandson?
2 Which soccer star hosted a Friday Night TV chat show?
3 In which country was power seized in the 70s by the Gang Of Four?
4 What was the nationality of composer Aaron Copland?
5 What was the occupation of Edith Cavell who was shot by the Germans in WWI?
6 Who had an 80s No 1 with West End Girls?
7 In cricket which English team became Foxes in the 90s?
8 How many Nobel prizes did Marie Curie win?
9 In EastEnders who was the youngest of the Jackson family when they left Albert Square for their own protection?
10 Livingstone has been the 90s seat of which prominent politician?
11 The Suez Canal connects the Mediterranean Sea to which other Sea?
12 Which summer month is the title of an album by Eric Clapton?
13 What are Ena Sharples and Elizabeth of Glamis?
14 What is Terry Wogan's first name?
15 At which sport did Jonah Barrington win international success?
16 How are PJ and Duncan also known?
17 How did Satyajit Ray achieve fame?
18 In which decade did France join the European Union?
19 In TV advertising who promoted Barclaycard by the fact that he didn't possess one?
20 In which country is the deepwater port of Belem?
21 In computer language what does the letter C stand for in ASCII?
22 Which Russian writer wrote Cancer Ward?
23 Vehicles from which country use the international registration letter E?
24 In baseball where do the Blue Jays come from?
25 In which country was Danny De Vito born?

Answers

Pop Music: Charts (see Quiz 139, page 361)
1 New Kids On The Block. **2** Blondie. **3** Boyzone. **4** Top Gun. **5** Love Me For A Reason. **6** Tanita Tikaram. **7** 50s. **8** Hue and Cry. **9** Holding Back The Years. **10** 30. **11** 80s. **12** Dolly Parton. **13** Elvis Presley. **14** Oasis. **15** Phil Collins. **16** Billy Joel. **17** Dominoes. **18** 80s. **19** Partners In Kryme. **20** Boyz II Men. **21** Jamiroquai. **22** John Denver. **23** Robson and Jerome. **24** 1970s. **25** Take That.

Quiz 141 80s Newsround

Answers - see Quiz 142, page 364

1 The world was first aware of the Chernobyl disaster after detectors were triggered at a nuclear plant in which country?
2 Christa McAuliffe died in an accident in what type of vehicle in 1986?
3 Where was John Paul II when an attempt was made on his life in 1981?
4 Which form of death penalty was abolished by Francois Mitterand?
5 Who succeeded Brezhnev as Soviet premier?
6 Which drink did the Coca Cola Company launch in 1982?
7 Which film actor became mayor of Carmel, California in 1986?
8 How did James F Fixx, promoter of jogging for good health, die in 1984?
9 Where did teenager Mathias Rust land his plane in 1987 much to the surprise of the country's authorities?
10 What colour wedding gown, veil and train did Paula Yates wear for her wedding to Bob Geldof?
11 Where did Torvill and Dean win Olympic gold with their Bolero routine?
12 Where did the US side of the Band Aid concert tale place?
13 Natan Sharansky was released from prison in the USSR to begin a new life where?
14 Which country was the first to make catalytic convertors compulsory?
15 Which organ was transplanted with heart and lungs in the first triple transplant operation in the UK?
16 How were the balls at Wimbledon different in 1986 from previous years?
17 In which country was the first permanent bungee jumping site situated?
18 Which capital city was the scene of a major summit between Reagan and Gorbachev in 1986?
19 Proceedings in which House were first on TV in January 1985?
20 Who co-wrote the Band Aid song with Bob Geldof?
21 Virgin Atlantic flights first went to New York from which UK airport?
22 Which keeper was beaten by Maradona's "hand of God" 1986 World Cup goal?
23 Which oil tanker disastrously ran aground off Brittany in 1987?
24 In which year did the £1 note cease to be legal tender in England?
25 Which country celebrated its bicentenary in 1988?

Answers

Pot Luck 66 (see Quiz 142, page 364)

1 Soup. **2** Pam Shriver. **3** Gerald Ford. **4** Cancer. **5** Eastman. **6** Nescafe. **7** Felt tips. **8** Rainbow. **9** Lynda La Plante. **10** Boxing. **11** Amelia Earhart. **12** Bodyline. **13** St Bernard dog. **14** Shamen. **15** Sony. **16** Italy. **17** Switzerland. **18** Les Sealey. **19** Rat. **20** 6. **21** Octopussy. **22** Russ Abbot. **23** 30s. **24** Evelyn Waugh. **25** France.

Quiz 142 Pot Luck 66

Answers - see Quiz 141, page 363

LEVEL 2 

1 Andy Warhol's 60s exhibition featured cans of which product?
2 Which doubles partner of Martina Navratilova commentated for the BBC at Wimbledon during the 1990s?
3 Who became US vice president when Spiro Agnew resigned?
4 What claimed the life of the singer Kathleen Ferrier?
5 Which George invented the Kodak roll-film camera?
6 In TV ads which coffee did Gareth Hunt and Diane Keen drink?
7 What type of pens did Pentel create?
8 Which children's show had a pink hippo called George?
9 Which writer created the series Prime Suspect which starred Helen Mirren?
10 Ezzard Charles was a world champion in which sport?
11 Who was the first woman to make a solo flight across the Atlantic?
12 Harold Larwood's bowling for England v Australia ensured the series was known as what?
13 Who or what was Schnorbitz?
14 Who made No 1 with Ebeneezer Goode?
15 Who along with Philips developed the CD in the late 70s?
16 San Giusto international airport is in which country?
17 Where is the multinational Nestlé based?
18 Who was in goal for Man Utd in the 1990 FA Cup Final replay but not in the original Final?
19 1996 was the Chinese year of which creature?
20 In the 90s how many points have been awarded for finishing second in a Grand Prix?
21 Rita Coolidge sang the title song for which Bond film?
22 Who hosted a TV Madhouse and played Fagin on stage in the 1990s?
23 In which decade of the century was Sir John Hall born?
24 Who wrote the novel Brideshead Revisited?
25 Which country became the first in the world to issue the dreaded parking ticket?

Answers

80s Newsround (see Quiz 141, page 363)
1 Sweden. **2** Space Shuttle. **3** Rome. **4** Guillotine. **5** Andropov. **6** Diet Coke. **7** Clint Eastwood. **8** Heart attack while jogging. **9** Red Square. **10** Scarlet. **11** Yugoslavia. **12** Philadelphia. **13** Israel. **14** Switzerland. **15** Liver. **16** Yellow. **17** New Zealand. **18** Reykjavik. **19** House of Lords. **20** Midge Ure. **21** Gatwick. **22** Peter Shilton. **23** Amoco Cadiz. **24** 1988. **25** Australia.

Quiz 143 20th C Celebs

Answers - see Quiz 144, page 366

LEVEL 2

1 Who did Myte Garcia marry in 1996 by pointing to his symbol?
2 What did Bob Geldof and Paula Yates agree to swap as part of their divorce settlement?
3 In 1992 whose name was linked with then Tory minister David Mellor?
4 What is the name of Prince Edward's TV production company?
5 Who in 1994 put an ad in The Times with Richard Gere to say their marriage was still strong?
6 Which perfume house did Madonna advertise in the late 1990s?
7 Who accused Bill Clinton of sexual harassment after an incident in a hotel in 1991?
8 Model Ms Bourret is usually known by her first name alone; what is it?
9 Which royal spouse designed the Aviary at London Zoo?
10 Sir Richard Attenborough was a director of which London soccer side from 1969-1982?
11 Who did Anthea Turner say she was leaving husband Pete Powell for in 1998?
12 Which film producer is the father in law of Loyd Grossman?
13 Which gourmet and wit described Margaret Thatcher as Attila the Hen?
14 In 1998 Cristina Sanchez became the first woman to become what?
15 Which celebrity restaurants do Stallone, Willis and Schwarzenegger own?
16 Derrick Evans is better known as which Mr?
17 How many brothers and sisters does Dale Winton have?
18 Who protested about Michael Jackson during the Brit Awards in 1996?
19 Which British redhead did Paris Match sign as a regular writer in 1996?
20 Who has Patsy tattooed on his arm?
21 Which racing driver has a wife called Georgie?
22 Sir Magdi Yacoub became famous in which medical field?
23 In 1997 who did Kelly Fisher claim she was engaged to when photos of him with someone else appeared in the papers?
24 Where in London was the house Peter Mandelson bought with the help of a loan from Geoffrey Robinson?
25 Where was Nick Leeson released from jail in July 1999?

Answers

Pot Luck 67 (see Quiz 144, page 366)

1 It's All Over Now. **2** Rome. **3** Birds of a Feather. **4** Peter Wright. **5** Swimming. **6** Kylie Minogue. **7** Y. **8** 1990. **9** The Nag's Head. **10** Keighley. **11** Choreography. **12** H. **13** Mel Smith. **14** Farming. **15** Seattle. **16** Laurence Olivier. **17** Mike Yarwood. **18** Foreign. **19** Fay Weldon. **20** Yorkshire. **21** 60s. **22** Dennis Potter. **23** Krypton. **24** Frosties. **25** William.

Quiz 144 Pot Luck 67

Answers - see Quiz 143, page 365

1 Which Stones' song title did Mandy Smith use for her book following her marriage to Bill Wyman?
2 The treaty signed to establish the EEC was the Treaty Of where?
3 Mrs Stubbs and Mrs Theodopolopoudos were the stars of which TV series?
4 Who wrote Spycatcher in 1987?
5 With which sport is Matt Biondi associated?
6 Who had an 80s No 1 with Hand On Your Heart?
7 On a computer keyboard which letter is between T and U?
8 In which year was Germany unified towards the end of the 20th century?
9 What is Del Boy's local in Only Fools and Horses?
10 Which Rugby League team became Cougars in the 90s?
11 For what was Frederick Ashton famous?
12 What is the international registration letter of a vehicle from Hungary?
13 Which comedian was Rockin' Around the Christmas Tree in a 1987 hit?
14 At the end of his life Indian chief Geronimo had taken to what kind of work?
15 In American Football where do the Seahawks come from?
16 Who was the first director of the National Theatre Company in Great Britain?
17 Who was famous for his impersonations of Harold Wilson and Edward Heath?
18 In language teaching what does the letter F stand for in TEFL?
19 Who wrote The Life And Loves Of A She Devil?
20 Arnold Sidebottom a Man Utd player of the 70s played first class cricket for which county?
21 In which decade was Demi Moore born?
22 Which TV playwright wrote the controversial Casanova?
23 Which gas shares its name with Superman's home?
24 "They're grrrreat!" describes which product in advertising?
25 In horse racing what is Dick Hern's real first name?

Answers

20th C Celebs (see Quiz 143, page 365)
1 Prince. **2** Houses. **3** Antonia de Sancha. **4** Ardent. **5** Cindy Crawford. **6** Max Factor. **7** Paula Jones. **8** Caprice. **9** Lord Snowdon. **10** Chelsea. **11** Grant Bovey. **12** David Puttnam. **13** Clement Freud. **14** Matador. **15** Planet Hollywood. **16** Motivator. **17** None. **18** Jarvis Cocker. **19** The Duchess of York. **20** Liam Gallagher. **21** Damon Hill. **22** Heart transplants. **23** Dodi Fayed. **24** Notting Hill. **25** Singapore.

Quiz 145 TV Presenters

Answers - see Quiz 146, page 368

1 Who first presented The Good Sex Guide?
2 Who interviewed Tony Blair at the launch of 5 News on Channel 5?
3 Who went on from being a researcher on Kilroy to co presenting Watchdog with Anne Robinson?
4 Who replaced Gaby Roslin on The Big Breakfast?
5 Carol Vorderman was dropped from the BBC's Tomorrow's World for advertising what commodity?
6 Which GMTV presenter is the wife of reporter Martin Frizell?
7 Which duo, who were successful on TV am, provided BBC opposition to Richard & Judy on the morning sofa?
8 Which sport is Chris Tarrant's main hobby?
9 Who presented Blue Peter and The Money Programme?
10 Which news presenter went to school with Paul McCartney?
11 Which regular stand in for Wogan had her own - unsuccessful - show Saturday Matters?
12 Which 90s news presenter bemoaned the fact that there was too little good news on TV?
13 Who was the first regular presenter of Nine O'Clock Live on GMTV?
14 Paradise Gardens was the last series made by which TV favourite?
15 Who was the first presenter of Don't Forget Your Toothbrush?
16 Who was dubbed TV's Mr Sex?
17 Whose third wife is a former Puerto Rican beauty queen Wilnelia Merced?
18 Who was the presenter of The Cook Report?
19 Who moved on from Newsround to The Travel Show?
20 Which lady presented Sunday Sunday for LWT for eight years in the 80s?
21 On Breakfast Time what feature did The Green Goddess always present?
22 Who presented LWT's long time Saturday night celebrity show from 1984-1993?
23 Which knight presents Through the Keyhole?
24 Which former Blue Peter presenter took over from Sean Maguire as Marty in Dangerfield?
25 Which TV and radio journalist wrote and broadcast the Letter to Daniel?

Answers

Pot Luck 68 (see Quiz 146, page 368)
1 Nick Park. **2** Fifth Avenue. **3** Stone Roses. **4** Lions. **5** Sample name on a recruitment form. **6** Princess of Wales. **7** Exporting. **8** Lord Longford. **9** Greenland. **10** John Curry. **11** Fred Perry. **12** Children. **13** 30 million. **14** George. **15** Athletics. **16** Bruce Springsteen. **17** Brabinger. **18** Basketball. **19** Ghana. **20** Maria McKee. **21** United. **22** Nottm Forest. **23** Muriel Spark. **24** Switzerland. **25** Cry.

Quiz 146 Pot Luck 68

Answers - see Quiz 145, page 367

1 Who won an Oscar in 1994 for best animation for The Wrong Trousers?
2 Which New York thoroughfare is famous for its fashionable stores?
3 Who had a 90s hit with Elephant Stone?
4 In cricket what did Surrey add to their name in the 90s?
5 Why were British soldiers in WWI called Tommies (short for Tommy Atkins)?
6 Before his resignation in 1996 which Royal did Patrick Jephson work for?
7 What does E stand for in OPEC?
8 Who was the father of Lady Antonia Fraser?
9 In addition to Denmark and the Faeroe Islands where is the Danish krone a unit of currency?
10 Which John was the BBC Sports Personality of the Year in 1976?
11 Who was the last Briton of the 20th century to win the men's singles at Wimbledon?
12 UNICEF is responsible for which specific group of people?
13 To the nearest million what is the population of Canada?
14 What was the first name of Le Carre's spy Smiley?
15 With which sport was David Bedford associated?
16 Who did a cover of the Carpenters' Santa Claus is Comin' To Town in 1985?
17 In To The Manor Born what was the butler called?
18 In which sport could the Lakers play the Clippers in a derby game?
19 The Gold Coast has become known as what?
20 Who made No 1 with Show Me Heaven?
21 Which soap back in the 60s was about a soccer club?
22 Gazza injured himself in an FA Cup Final for Spurs against which team?
23 Who wrote The Prime Of Miss Jean Brodie?
24 Agno international airport is in which country?
25 What notable thing did tough guy Humphrey Bogart do throughout his wedding to Lauren Bacall?

Answers

TV Presenters (see Quiz 145, page 367)

1 Margi Clarke. **2** Kirsty Young. **3** Alice Beer. **4** Zoe Ball. **5** Soap powder. **6** Fiona Phillips. **7** Anne & Nick. **8** Fishing. **9** Valerie Singleton. **10** Peter Sissons. **11** Sue Lawley. **12** Martyn Lewis. **13** Lorraine Kelly. **14** Geoff Hamilton. **15** Chris Evans. **16** Angus Deayton. **17** Bruce Forsyth. **18** Roger Cook. **19** Juliet Morris. **20** Gloria Hunniford. **21** Keep fit. **22** Michael Aspel. **23** David Frost. **24** Tim Vincent. **25** Fergal Keane.

Quiz 147 Sporting Legends

Answers - see Quiz 148, page 370

1 Which jockey was born on Bonfire Night?
2 Michael Jordan was a super scorer for which team?
3 Who was the Louisville Lip?
4 Cricket's Alfred Freeman was known by which nickname?
5 In which decade was Daley Thompson born?
6 Who won swimming gold in the 100m freestyle at the 56, 60 and 64 Olympics?
7 Sergey Bubka has broken the world record on over 30 occasions in which event?
8 Ian Botham made his England debut while playing for which county?
9 How old was Nadia Comaneci when she won Olympic Gold as a gymnast?
10 Joe diMaggio was known as what kind of Joe?
11 Apart from sprinting in which event did Carl Lewis twice take Olympic gold?
12 Who was the first Brit to be British and US Open champion at the same time?
13 Gary Sobers hit six sixes in an over against which county?
14 Walter Swinburne won his first Derby on which legendary horse?
15 Who was the first British soccer player to be transferred to a foreign club?
16 Racing's Juan Manuel Fangio came from which country?
17 What did the G stand for in W G Grace's name?
18 Who was the first Scottish soccer player to gain 100 caps?
19 What position did Bill Beaumont play?
20 Who is Pakistan's all time leading Test wicket taker?
21 Which England soccer World Cup winner was knighted in 1998?
22 Which country did long distance runner Emil Zatopek come from?
23 Who was the first batsman to hit over 500 in a first class cricket game?
24 Who did Pete Sampras beat in the final to take his sixth Wimbledon singles title?
25 Who has been champion jockey on the flat most times in the 20th century?

Answers

Pot Luck 69 (see Quiz 148, page 370)
1 Lovejoy. **2** Andrei Sakharov. **3** Farce. **4** Lumiere Brothers. **5** Agreement. **6** Falco. **7** Joe Louis. **8** John Craven. **9** Carousel. **10** Daz. **11** William Claude. **12** Alamein. **13** Nick Berry. **14** George V. **15** Edinburgh. **16** Wall Street. **17** Norway. **18** Arthur Conan Doyle. **19** Michael Parkinson. **20** Barry. **21** Firemen. **22** 70s. **23** Ash - it was Goldfinger. **24** Atlanta. **25** Swedish.

Quiz 148 Pot Luck 69

Answers - see Quiz 147, page 369

1. Who had sidekicks called Eric and Tinker?
2. Which physicist was involved in the development of nuclear weapons in the USSR but became a dissident under Communist rule?
3. What type of plays did Georges Feydeau specialise in writing?
4. Which French brothers invented the first films?
5. What does A stand for in GATT?
6. Who had an 80s No 1 with Rock Me Amadeus?
7. Who was boxing's heavyweight champion throughout the 40s?
8. Who presented News Swap on Multi Coloured Swap Shop?
9. Which musical featured the song When I Marry Mr Snow?
10. In TV ads Shane Richie knocked at doors holding a packet of what?
11. What did the W C stand for in W C Fields' names?
12. Field Marshal Montgomery became Viscount Montgomery of where?
13. Who first sang the theme music to Heartbeat?
14. Who was Queen Elizabeth II's paternal grandfather?
15. In which city was Sean Connery born?
16. Where would you see the Dow Jones index?
17. Vehicles from which country use the international registration letter N?
18. Early in the century who wrote the novel The Lost World?
19. Who was the first person to interview George Michael about his arrest?
20. Which member of the Gibb family made a cameo appearance on Only Fools and Horses?
21. What does the letter F stand for in ASLEF?
22. In which decade did Denmark join the European Union?
23. Which group used a Bond film title for a 1996 top ten hit?
24. In American Football where do the Falcons come from?
25. Which language does the word ombudsman derive from?

Answers

Sporting Legends (see Quiz 147, page 369)
1 Lester Piggott. **2** Chicago Bulls. **3** Muhammad Ali - born as Cassius Clay. **4** Titch. **5** 50s. **6** Dawn Fraser. **7** Pole vault. **8** Somerset. **9** 14. **10** Joltin'. **11** Long jump. **12** Tony Jacklin. **13** Glamorgan. **14** Shergar. **15** John Charles. **16** Argentina. **17** Gilbert. **18** Kenny Dalglish. **19** Lock. **20** Wasim Akram. **21** Geoff Hurst. **22** Czechoslovakia. **23** Brian Lara. **24** Andre Agassi. **25** Gordon Richards.

Quiz 149 Sci Fi & Fantasy Movies

Answers - see Quiz 150, page 372

1 Who played Dr Who in the 90s movie made for TV?
2 Who starred in the lead role in the The Fly opposite Geena Davis?
3 What was the fourth Alien film called?
4 Who received $3 million to recreate her five year TV role on film with her male partner?
5 Who tries to save the world from virtual reality in The Matrix?
6 Which spin off from a 60s sitcom was a 1999 movie with Jeff Daniels and Christopher Lloyd?
7 Who played Batman immediately before George Clooney?
8 In which 1998 film did Bruce Willis lead a team to confront a deadly threat from outer space?
9 Which tough guy played Mr Freeze in Batman & Robin?
10 Which 1996 film has its climax on 4th July?
11 In which sci fi classic did the space ship Nostromo first appear?
12 Which important US building has its roof ripped off in Superman II?
13 What was the first sequel to Star Wars?
14 What was the name of Drew Barrymore's character in E.T.?
15 Who played Rick Deckard in Blade Runner?
16 What number Star Trek movie was called The Wrath of Khan?
17 Which UK pop singer and environmental campaigner appeared in Dune?
18 Which decade does Michael J Fox go back to in Back to the Future?
19 Which Star Trek star directed Three Men and a Baby?
20 Who played the young Obi-Wan Kenobi in the Star Wars prequel?
21 Which 1968 sci fi classic was based on The Sentinel by Arthur C Clarke?
22 What was the subtitle of Terminator 2?
23 In which city does the action of the 1998 movie Godzilla take place?
24 What is the name of the Darth Vader to be in Episode 1 _ The Phantom Menace?
25 Who did Jane Fonda play in the 60s movie of the same name where she constantly lost her clothes?

Answers

Pot Luck 70 (see Quiz 150, page 372)

1 50s. **2** Colditz. **3** Wilson. **4** Chariots of Fire. **5** John Betjeman. **6** Gareth Southgate. **7** Harry Connick Jnr. **8** Leslie Crowther. **9** Rudolf Hess. **10** Bowls. **11** Nancy Sinatra. **12** Kakadu National Park. **13** Neville Chamberlain. **14** Carole King. **15** Durham. **16** Italy. **17** Holby City Hospital. **18** Women's Institute - it's Jerusalem. **19** Atlanta. **20** Egypt. **21** Oscar Wilde. **22** Orient. **23** Washington. **24** Gabby Yorath. **25** Nash.

Quiz 150 Pot Luck 70

Answers - see Quiz 149, page 371

1 In which decade this century did Ronnie Scott's Soho jazz club open?
2 How was Oflag IVC prison camp better known?
3 Which Dad's Army character was married in real life to Hattie Jacques?
4 Which film theme did the BBC use for the 1984 Olympics?
5 Who wrote the line, "Come friendly bombs fall on Slough"?
6 Who advertised Pizza Hut along with Stuart Pearce and Chris Waddle?
7 Who recorded the When Harry Met Sally soundtrack?
8 Who presented The Price is Right in the UK before Bruce Forsyth?
9 Who was the last inmate of Spandau jail in Berlin?
10 Del Ballard Jnr was a world champion in which sport?
11 Who sang the title song for the Bond film You Only Live Twice?
12 Which national park, famous for aboriginal rock paintings is near Darwin?
13 Who was British Prime Minister when World War II broke out?
14 To whom did the Bee Gees pay tribute in Tapestry Revisited?
15 Which cricket county decided they had become Dynamos in the 90s?
16 In which country is the deepwater port of Brindisi?
17 Where did Dr Baz Samuels work?
18 Which group starts a meeting by singing the words, "And did those feet....."?
19 In basketball where do the Hawks come from?
20 In which country was Omar Sharif born?
21 Who wrote The Picture Of Dorian Gray?
22 Peter Shilton completed his 1000th league game with which London club?
23 Spokane airport was built in which US state?
24 Who presented On The Ball in 1999 with Barry Venison?
25 Who sang with Crosby, Stills and Young?

Answers

Sci Fi & Fantasy Movies (see Quiz 149, page 371)
1 Paul McGann. **2** Jeff Goldblum. **3** Alien Resurrection.
4 Gillian Anderson - in The X Files. **5** Keanu Reeves. **6** My Favourite Martian.
7 Val Kilmer. **8** Armageddon. **9** Arnold Schwarzenegger. **10** Independence Day.
11 Alien. **12** The White House. **13** The Empire Strikes Back. **14** Gertie.
15 Harrison Ford. **16** II. **17** Sting. **18** 50s. **19** Leonard Nimoy. **20** Ewan McGregor.
21 2001: A Space Odyssey. **22** Judgment Day. **23** New York. **24** Anakin Skywalker.
25 Barbarella.

Quiz 151 On the Road

Answers - see Quiz 152, page 374

1 Which rules of the road for children was first published in 1971?
2 GT after a car's name means what?
3 Which margarine company sponsored the 1997 London Marathon?
4 How is a pedestrian light controlled crossing more commonly known?
5 How many National Parks does the Pennine Way pass through?
6 Which illegal act is committed most frequently in cars?
7 What is London's Middlesex Street called on Sundays?
8 In 1974 roads in Rutland became roads in which county?
9 How was Sellafield known before 1981?
10 Which motorway crosses the estuary of the river Severn?
11 Which county saw the protests about the building of the Newbury bypass in the mid 90s?
12 What was the car toll for the new Severn Bridge when it opened in 1996?
13 What name is given to low bumps in the road which slow down traffic?
14 In which Road is the headquarters of the Labour Party?
15 How is a Denver boot also known?
16 How many yellow lines show that you can never park or unload in that location?
17 What letter or letters make up the sign for a Tourist Information office?
18 The Scilly Isles come under the authority of which English county?
19 What is the maximum speed limit in kilometres on a motorway?
20 What name is given to a short narrow road which links an A road to a motorway?
21 Which two counties do the North Downs run through?
22 What is the maximum custodial penalty for causing death by dangerous driving?
23 30 inside a blue circle with no red border means what when on the road?
24 What is the administrative centre of Cornwall?
25 What colour is a sign indicating an English Heritage site?

Answers

Pot Luck 71 (see Quiz 152, page 374)
1 Purple. **2** John Ford. **3** Antarctica. **4** Robin Beck. **5** Evacuation of Dunkirk. **6** Montreal. **7** X-rays. **8** Oklahoma. **9** Keith Richard. **10** GBZ. **11** Which? **12** Squash. **13** Holly Goodhead. **14** VAT. **15** Judo. **16** Renault. **17** Tahiti. **18** Leicester. **19** Essex. **20** Related. **21** Edwina Currie. **22** Oxford Street. **23** Ronan Keating. **24** 6. **25** He was pregnant.

Quiz 152 Pot Luck 71

Answers - see Quiz 151, page 373

1 Which colour were David Beckham and Posh's going away outfits?
2 Sean O'Feeney worked under what name as a movie director?
3 The hole in the ozone layer formed over which continent?
4 Who had an 80s No 1 with First Time?
5 In WWII what was called Operation Dynamo?
6 In baseball where do the Expos come from?
7 What was Wilhelm Rontgen's most important discovery?
8 Which US state gave its name to a musical by Rodgers & Hammerstein?
9 Who said, "I never had any problems with drugs only with policemen"?
10 What are the international registration letters of a vehicle from Gibraltar?
11 What is the magazine of the Consumer's Association called?
12 Susan Devoy has been a 90s world champion in which sport?
13 Which Bond girl was played by Lois Chiles?
14 What replaced purchase tax in 1973?
15 At which sport did Diane Bell win international success?
16 People loved the ads, but which make of car did Papa promote?
17 Which tropical island was a UK top ten hit for David Essex in 1983?
18 In which English city were Walkers crisps first manufactured?
19 Who won the 1998 Benson & Hedges cricket final by 192 runs?
20 What does the letter R stand for in SERPS?
21 Which ex MP wrote the novel A Parliamentary Affair?
22 In which London Street was the first Virgin record shop?
23 Which singer compered the 1998 Miss World contest for TV in the UK?
24 What was Tim Henman seeded at for Wimbledon 1999?
25 In the movie Junior what was different about the Schwarzenegger character?

Answers

On the Road (see Quiz 151, page 373)
1 Green Cross Code. **2** Gran turismo. **3** Flora. **4** Pelican crossing. **5** Three. **6** Speeding. **7** Petticoat Lane. **8** Leicestershire. **9** Windscale. **10** M4. **11** Berkshire. **12** £3.80. **13** Sleeping policeman. **14** Walworth. **15** Wheel clamp. **16** Two. **17** I. **18** Cornwall. **19** 113. **20** Slip road. **21** Kent & Surrey. **22** 10 years. **23** Minimum speed 30. **24** Truro. **25** Brown.

Quiz 153 Pop: Who's Who?

Answers - see Quiz 154, page 376

1 Which female vocalist was a member of the Eurythmics?
2 Which vocalist's real name is Michael Barratt?
3 Paul Weller was the lead singer of which group in the early 80s?
4 Which Gibb brother is the eldest?
5 Who played Aidan Brosnan in Eastenders?
6 Who duetted with Peabo Bryson on Beauty and the Beast?
7 What is Paul McCartney's real first name?
8 Who sang on If You Ever with East 17 in 1996?
9 Which country does Eddy Grant originate from?
10 Sting's Englishman in New York was used to advertise which make of car?
11 The Kemp brother were in which 80s group?
12 Who was the lead singer of Yazoo?
13 William Broad became better known under which name?
14 Morten Harket was part of which 80s group?
15 Who accompanied Boyz II Men on the hit One Sweet Day?
16 Which liquid refreshment was advertised by Bob Geldof in 1987?
17 Who duetted on the '93 hit I've Got You Under My Skin with Frank Sinatra?
18 Who said drug taking was as normal as having a cup of tea in 1997?
19 Who Lost her Heart to a Starship Trooper?
20 Which popular singer duetted with Elton John on Slow Rivers?
21 Vincent Furnier became better known as whom?
22 Who sang with Phil Collins on the 1985 hit Separate Lives?
23 In which decade was female vocalist Annie Lennox born?
24 Who sang with Kenny Rogers on We've Got Tonight?
25 Whose debut single in 1996 was called Anything?

Answers

***Pot Luck* 72** (see Quiz 154, page 376)
1 Birkdale. **2** Thailand. **3** Stranglers. **4** St. Mary Mead. **5** £5. **6** Law. **7** Essex. **8** Mary Rose. **9** Fiddler On The Roof. **10** Fencing. **11** Pray. **12** Basketball. **13** Bob Wilson. **14** Arthur. **15** 50s. **16** Moscow. **17** Joan Collins. **18** Spain. **19** Muhammad Ali. **20** Humphrey Lyttleton. **21** Colorado. **22** Food Hamper. **23** Bear. **24** Paul Gascoigne. **25** Glasgow to London.

Quiz 154 Pot Luck 72

Answers - see Quiz 153, page 375

1 Mark O'Meara first won the British Open at which course?
2 Which country designated Chachoengsao as its new capital?
3 Who had an 80s hit with Golden Brown?
4 Which village is the home of Agatha Christie sleuth Miss Marple?
5 The Duke of Wellington appeared on the back of which British banknote?
6 What was Mahatma Gandhi's profession outside politics?
7 In cricket which English team turned into Eagles in the 90s?
8 What rose from the Solent in 1982?
9 Which musical featured the song Sunrise Sunset?
10 Sergey Golubitsky has been a world champion in which sport?
11 What was Take That's first UK No 1?
12 In which sport could the Bucks take on the Raptors?
13 Who presented Football Focus before moving to ITV in the mid 90s?
14 What is the second of Prince William's four names?
15 In which decade did Germany join the European Union?
16 In which city was Michael Jackson a Stranger in 1996?
17 Which actress wrote the novel Prime Time in the 1980s?
18 Vigo international airport is in which country?
19 Who said, "When you are as great as I am, it's hard to be humble"?
20 Which jazz trumpeter hosted radio's I'm Sorry I Haven't A Clue?
21 On which river was the Hoover dam built?
22 If you lose on Ready Steady Cook what do you receive?
23 1995 was the Chinese year of which creature?
24 Shearer and who else scored when England beat Scotland in Euro 96?
25 The train in the Great Train Robbery was making which journey?

Answers

Pop: Who's Who? (see Quiz 151, page 375)
1 Annie Lennox. **2** Shakin' Stevens. **3** The Jam. **4** Barry. **5** Sean Maguire. **6** Celine Dion. **7** James. **8** Gabrielle. **9** Guyana. **10** Rover. **11** Spandau Ballet. **12** Alison Moyet. **13** Billy Idol. **14** A-ha. **15** Mariah Carey. **16** Milk. **17** Bono. **18** Noel Gallagher. **19** Sarah Brightman. **20** Cliff Richard. **21** Alice Cooper. **22** Marilyn Martin. **23** 50s. **24** Sheena Easton. **25** 3T.

Quiz 155 90s Newsround

Answers - see Quiz 156, page 378

1 Which hotel had Princess Diana and Dodi Fayed just left when they were involved in their fatal car crash?
2 Who ran against Bill Clinton in the 1996 US election?
3 Ian Botham and Allan Lamb lost a libel case against which other cricketer?
4 Who in 1997 met an old school friend in The Big Issue office?
5 13 year old Sarah Cook hit the headlines after marrying a waiter while on holiday where?
6 Sandra Gregory was given a 25 year sentence for drug smuggling where?
7 In 1999 what sort of savings plan replaced Tessa?
8 In which city was Mother Teresa buried?
9 Which English city was blasted by an IRA bomb in June 1996?
10 Which Club finally voted in 1998 to admit women members?
11 In which city did Louise Woodward's US trial take place?
12 Which toy was the panic buy of Christmas 1997 due to a shortage in supply?
13 Who recorded Monica Lewinsky's conversations about her affair with Bill Clinton?
14 In '98 the US Embassy was bombed in which country with many fatalities?
15 Legal proceedings began against Scotsman Jim Sutherland for flouting a ban on what?
16 The Duchess of York's mother was killed near her home in which country?
17 How was eco warrior Daniel Hooper better known?
18 Which American was the first US pop star to perform in a sanction free South Africa?
19 What was the name of the low fat burger launched by McDonalds?
20 Neil & Jamie Acourt were involved in the court case about which victim?
21 Which politician said her boss, "had something of the night about him"?
22 Which Building Society was floated in 1997 with members each receiving a windfall?
23 Which former MP did William Hague make Party Chairman in 1997?
24 In which town was Gianni Versace shot?
25 In 1991 which country mourned the loss of King Olaf?

Answers

Pot Luck 73 (see Quiz 156, page 378)
1 The Social Democratic Party. **2** Christina Onassis. **3** New Zealand. **4** Pankhurst. **5** Detroit. **6** Wham!. **7** The Rat Pack. **8** Brazil. **9** Gillette. **10** Agatha Christie. **11** James. **12** 1997. **13** Boyz II Men. **14** Wolves. **15** National Motor. **16** X. **17** Pepsi. **18** Kirsty Young. **19** Manchester. **20** Houston. **21** Douglas Adams. **22** Luxembourg. **23** Bovine. **24** 8 million. **25** Eva Herzigova.

Quiz 156 Pot Luck 73

Answers - see Quiz 155, page 377

1 Bill Rodgers and Roy Jenkins were founder members of which party?
2 Athina Roussel is the daughter of which multi millionairess?
3 Who won the first Rugby Union World Cup, held in 1987?
4 What was the name of the family that led the suffragette movement?
5 Which Michigan town is well known as a manufacturer of motor vehicles?
6 Who had an 80s No 1 with The Edge Of Heaven?
7 What nickname was given to the group of performers which included Sammy Davis Jr and Frank Sinatra?
8 Which country has the greatest number of Roman Catholics?
9 Who first sponsored the cricket trophy now known as the NatWest Trophy?
10 Which writer was married to archaeologist Sir Max Mallowan?
11 What is Paul McCartney's first Christian name?
12 In which year did Britain's lease on Hong Kong officially expire?
13 Who made No 1 with End Of The Road?
14 In Rugby League what did Warrington add to their name in the 90s?
15 Which museum has been established at Beaulieu?
16 On a computer keyboard which letter is immediately right of the Z?
17 What was advertised by Rod Stewart and Tina Turner's version of It Takes Two?
18 Who won Celebrity Stars in their Eyes as Peggy Lee?
19 Where was the soap Albion Market set?
20 In American Football where do the Oilers come from?
21 Who wrote Dirk Gently's Holistic Detective Agency?
22 Vehicles from which country use the international registration letter L?
23 What did the letter B stand for in BSE?
24 To the nearest million what is the population of Tokyo?
25 In advertising who said, "Hello boys"?

Answers

90s Newsround (see Quiz 155, page 377)
1 Ritz. **2** Bob Dole. **3** Imran Khan. **4** Prince Charles. **5** Turkey. **6** Thailand. **7** Isa. **8** Calcutta. **9** Manchester. **10** MCC. **11** Boston. **12** Teletubbies. **13** Linda Tripp. **14** Kenya. **15** Selling beef on the bone. **16** Argentina. **17** Swampy. **18** Paul Simon. **19** McLean. **20** Stephen Lawrence. **21** Ann Widdecombe. **22** Halifax. **23** Lord Parkinson. **24** Miami. **25** Norway.

Quiz 157 20th C Brat Pack

Answers - see Quiz 158, page 380

LEVEL 2

1 Nigel Short was the youngest champion in which game in 1984?
2 What did Woody Allen call his son as a tribute to Louis 'Satchmo' Armstrong?
3 Which comedian is the father of Lucy Davis who plays Hayley in The Archers?
4 Linus Roache's father plays which character in a TV soap?
5 Which 80s Wimbledon Men's Singles champion is the father of twins?
6 Which soul singer is Whitney Houston's godmother?
7 Who was the most famous Head Girl at Kesteven and Grantham Girls' School?
8 What did Mel B call her baby with Jimmy Gulzar?
9 Where did Princess Anne's daughter Zara famously sport a stud in 1998?
10 What type of car did Prince William receive for his 17th birthday?
11 What is the name of Paul and Linda McCartney's only son?
12 Which son of Camilla Parker Bowles was exposed in a drugs scandal in the summer of 1999?
13 Which pop star has a son called Prince Michael?
14 Which politician was writer Vera Brittain's daughter?
15 What relation is Joely Richardson to Vanessa Redgrave?
16 What are the surnames of the Sawalha sisters of AbFab and EastEnders fame?
17 Melanie Molitor is the mum of which former tennis world No 1?
18 How is John Major's celebrity brother known?
19 Finty Williams is the daughter of which film and theatre Dame?
20 Which Biblical name does Boris Becker's older son have?
21 Princess Anne's son Peter Phillips was Head Boy at which famous school?
22 Who is Julian Lennon's step mother?
23 Which university did Tony Blair and Bill Clinton both attend in their younger days?
24 How many sisters and half sisters combined does Cherie Booth have?
25 Which footballer had his baby's name printed on his football socks?

Answers

Pot Luck 74 (see Quiz 158, page 380)
1 Gardening. **2** Exxon Valdiz. **3** Saudi Arabia. **4** Charles Lindbergh. **5** 80s.
6 Minnesota. **7** Oil. **8** Home. **9** The Bay City Rollers. **10** Burma. **11** Polo.
12 Noel Coward. **13** Ford. **14** The Man With The Golden Gun. **15** Horse racing.
16 Suez. **17** Oxo. **18** Saul Bellow. **19** Kevin Keegan. **20** Indonesia. **21** Windmill.
22 Frisbees. **23** Enigma. **24** Chile. **25** Pat Eddery.

Quiz 158 Pot Luck 74

Answers - see Quiz 157, page 379

1 In July 1999 it was announced Kim Wilde would host a TV show about what?
2 Which tanker was the cause of a massive oil spill in Alaska in 1989?
3 Released in 1998, in which country had Deborah Parry been imprisoned?
4 Who flew in The Spirit Of St Louis?
5 In which decade did Levi's first use a classic hit to advertise?
6 In baseball where do the Twins come from?
7 What made John D Rockefeller seriously rich?
8 What does H stand for in the video system VHS as launched by JVC in 1976?
9 Which 70s group's members were Les, Eric, Woody, Alan and Derek?
10 Which country took the name Myanmar officially in 1989?
11 Which sport takes place at Hurlingham?
12 Who wrote Bitter Sweet and Private Lives?
13 Who succeeded Nixon as President of the USA in 1974?
14 Lulu sang the title song for which Bond film?
15 Terry Biddlecombe was connected with which sport?
16 Which canal was the work of Ferdinand de Lesseps?
17 Which product used the advertising slogan, "Gives a meal man appeal"?
18 Who wrote the novels Humboldt's Gift and Herzog?
19 Which English international soccer player was nicknamed 'Mighty Mouse'?
20 The Dutch East Indies have become known as what?
21 Which London theatre used to claim that, "we never closed"?
22 US students used aluminium flan cases to 'invent' what?
23 Who made No 1 with Sadness Part 1?
24 Punto Arenas International airport is in which country?
25 Who rode a hat-trick of Prix de l'Arc de Triomphe victories in the mid 80s?

Answers

20th C Brat Pack (see Quiz 157, page 379)
1 Chess. **2** Satchel. **3** Jasper Carrott. **4** Ken Barlow. **5** Pat Cash. **6** Aretha Franklin. **7** Margaret Thatcher. **8** Phoenix Chi. **9** Tongue. **10** Golf. **11** James. **12** Tom. **13** Michael Jackson. **14** Shirley Williams. **15** Daughter. **16** Julia & Nadia. **17** Martina Hingis. **18** Terry Major-Ball. **19** Judi Dench. **20** Noah. **21** Gordonstoun. **22** Yoko Ono. **23** Oxford. **24** Six. **25** David Beckham.

Quiz 159 TV Classics

Answers - see Quiz 160, page 382

1 Who was News At Ten's first woman presenter?
2 What was Kojak's first name?
3 In which English county was Lovejoy filmed?
4 Which Olympic Games were the first to be televised?
5 Who was Edina's PA in AbFab?
6 Who was the astrologer on the BBC's Breakfast Time?
7 How much were the 'cheapest' questions worth in the first series of Sale of the century?
8 What was the name of the 70s comedy series based on the Carry On films?
9 Which game was Celebrity Squares based on?
10 Which ship featured in Sailor?
11 When the Boat Comes In was set in which part of the UK?
12 Which classic 80s drama series shot Anthony Andrews and Jeremy Irons to fame?
13 Which actor was The Bounder?
14 What was the name of the David Attenborough series set in the south Atlantic?
15 Which character in The X Files is the name of a mystery person implicated in the Watergate affair?
16 Which cult series asked, "Who killed Laura Palmer?"?
17 Which classic British sitcom spawned the catchphrase "you dirty old man!"?
18 Which show was blamed by a British police chief for making police officers "drive like maniacs"?
19 Who plays the nurse in Hancock's classic The Blood Donor?
20 In the early 80s if David McCallum was Steel who was Sapphire?
21 What was Rumpole's first name?
22 Which drama series featured a ship called The Charlotte Rhodes?
23 Which actress played the scatty mum in Not In Front of the Children?
24 Which future husband of Demi Moore found fame in the TV series Moonlighting?
25 How many Monkees were there?

Answers

***Pot Luck* 75** (see Quiz 160, page 382)
1 August. **2** Tiggy Legge Bourke. **3** Jam. **4** Dragons. **5** Alligator.
6 She became a professional. **7** Butcher Of Lyons. **8** Alan Freeman. **9** Ngaio Marsh.
10 Melbourne. **11** Jane Seymour. **12** PE. **13** Sally Magnusson. **14** Athletics.
15 Glasgow. **16** Boots. **17** 80s. **18** Belgium. **19** Malcolm Bradbury. **20** Jeremy Beadle.
21 Stamps. **22** Australia. **23** Cincinnati. **24** 50s. **25** Doodlebug.

Quiz 160 Pot Luck 75

Answers - see Quiz 159, page 381

1 Which month in 1914 did WWI begin?
2 Who was Princes William and Harry's nanny after their parents separation?
3 Who had an 80s No 1 with Beat Surrender?
4 In cricket what did Glamorgan add to their name in the 90s?
5 What was Crockett's pet in Miami Vice?
6 What stopped Suzanne Lenglen playing at Wimbledon after 1926?
7 What was the nickname of Klaus Barbie the Nazi war criminal?
8 Which veteran DJ used to advertise Brentford Nylons?
9 Who wrote The Inspector Alleyn Mysteries?
10 Which Australian city hosted its final Formula 1 race in 1995?
11 Which actress gave birth to twins at the age of 44 in 1995?
12 What are the international registration letters of a vehicle from Peru?
13 On TV who interviewed Earl Spencer at length several months after Princess Diana's death?
14 With which sport is Said Aouita associated?
15 In which city was Robbie Coltrane born?
16 Which company used the Hollies hit I'm Alive to advertise in 1997?
17 In which decade did Portugal join the European Union?
18 In which country was Jean Claude van Damme born?
19 Who wrote the novel Eating People Is Wrong?
20 Who presented You've Been Framed before Lisa Riley?
21 The name Stanley Gibbons has become associated with what?
22 In which country is the deepwater port of Dampier?
23 Which city has a team of Reds and a team of Bengals?
24 In which decade was Andie MacDowell born?
25 How did the German V-1 flying bomb become known?

Answers

TV Classics (see Quiz 159, page 381)
1 Anna Ford. **2** Theo. **3** Suffolk. **4** 1948. **5** Bubbles. **6** Russell Grant. **7** £1. **8** Carry on Laughing. **9** Noughts & Crosses. **10** Ark Royal. **11** North East England. **12** Brideshead Revisited. **13** Peter Bowles. **14** Life in the Freezer. **15** Deep Throat. **16** Twin Peaks. **17** Steptoe and Son. **18** Starsky & Hutch. **19** June Whitfield. **20** Joanna Lumley. **21** Horace. **22** The Onedin Line. **23** Wendy Craig. **24** Bruce Willis. **25** Four.

Quiz 161 Cricket

Answers - see Quiz 162, page 384

1 Who followed Viv Richards as West Indian captain?
2 Who along with Mark Waugh accepted money from an Indian bookmaker for "weather forecasts"?
3 Who was the last man out in the Australia v S Africa semi final tie in 1999?
4 Who were England playing in the Atherton 'ball tampering' incident?
5 What was the nickname of England pace bowler David Lawrence?
6 Who were the opponents in Mike Atherton's last series as England skipper?
7 Who was man of the match in the 1999 World Cup final?
8 Administrator Lord MacLaurin was a former chairman of which supermarket group?
9 Who was the first bowler since Laker to take all ten wickets in the same Test innings?
10 Which country were the last to be admitted to the County circuit in the century?
11 Which team won the 1992 World Cup?
12 Which visiting bowler took nine wickets in a Test in England in the 90s?
13 At which ground did Atherton and Donald have their famous 'battle' of 1998?
14 Who preceded Ray Illingworth as chairman of the Test selectors?
15 England batsman Aftab Habib managed only one first class game for which county?
16 Who was England's leading wicket taker on the 97-98 W Indies tour?
17 What was Clive Lloyd's middle name?
18 Where are the Eden Gardens?
19 In what year did Graham Gooch first play for England?
20 Which Minor County did England keeper Chris Read play for?
21 Steve James was playing for which county when first capped for England?
22 Which team have won the county championship most in the 20th century?
23 What colour were the Australian trousers in the 1999 World Cup final?
24 Who was the first player to score 100 and take eight wickets in an innings in the same Test?
25 Which English keeper had the middle names Philip Eric?

Answers

***Pot Luck* 76** (see Quiz 162, page 384)
1 Her father. **2** Careless Whisper. **3** Capt W E Johns. **4** Manhattan. **5** 60s. **6** Mia Farrow. **7** Nothing. **8** Guys And Dolls. **9** Washington. **10** Anne Robinson. **11** Michael Foot. **12** Five Go Mad in Dorset. **13** Afghanistan. **14** Culture Beat. **15** 3. **16** Hailsham. **17** F Scott Fitzgerald. **18** Turkey. **19** Live And Let Die. **20** Eintracht Frankfurt. **21** Budd - Billy Budd. **22** Sarah Brightman. **23** Air. **24** Asda. **25** A butterfly.

Quiz 162 Pot Luck 76

Answers - see Quiz 161, page 383

1 The Queen's first corgi was bought for her by whom?
2 What was George Michael's first solo No 1?
3 Who created the flying ace Biggles?
4 Which part of New York borough is most famous for its skyline of high rise buildings?
5 In which decade of the century did Yorkshire last win cricket's County Championship?
6 Which one time wife of Frank Sinatra starred in Peyton Place?
7 What did the 'S' stand for in Harry S Truman's name?
8 Which musical featured the song Sit Down You're Rockin' The Boat?
9 In basketball where do the Wizards come from?
10 Who was the first regular female presenter of TV's Points of View?
11 Who did Neil Kinnock succeed as Labour Party leader?
12 Which Enid Blyton spoof was made by the Comic Strip?
13 Which country did USSR invade in 1979?
14 Who made No 1 with Mr Vain?
15 In the 90s how many points have been awarded for finishing fourth in a Grand Prix?
16 Quintin Hogg became which Lord?
17 Who wrote The Great Gatsby?
18 Adona international airport is in which country?
19 In which Bond film did Jane Seymour appear?
20 Who did Real Madrid beat in the famous 7-3 European Cup Final?
21 Which William was in the title of an opera by Benjamin Britten?
22 Which singer led the dance troupe Hot Gossip on The Kenny Everett Video Show?
23 What did the letter A stand for in SAS?
24 Wood and Walters trolleyed into the country to advertise which supermarket?
25 What was Muhammad Ali said to float like?

Answers

Cricket (see Quiz 161, page 383)
1 Richie Richardson. **2** Shane Warne. **3** Allan Donald. **4** South Africa. **5** Syd. **6** W Indies. **7** Shane Warne. **8** Tesco. **9** Anil Kumble. **10** Durham. **11** Pakistan. **12** Muttiah Muralitharan. **13** Trent Bridge. **14** Ted Dexter. **15** Middlesex. **16** Angus Fraser. **17** Hubert. **18** Calcutta. **19** 1975. **20** Devon. **21** Glamorgan. **22** Yorkshire. **23** Yellow. **24** Ian Botham. **25** Alan Knott.

Quiz 163 90s Movies

Answers - see Quiz 164, page 386

1 Which ER star played opposite Jenny Seagrove in Don't Go Breaking My Heart?
2 Beloved in 1999 was whose first movie since The Color Purple in 1985?
3 In Stepmom who played Susan Sarandon's daughter?
4 Who played the colliery band leader in Brassed Off?
5 In which 90s movie did Al Pacino play retired Colonel Frank Slade?
6 Which sitcom star appeared on the big screen in The Object of My Affection?
7 Who played Drew Barrymore's stepmother in Ever After?
8 Which US president did Anthony Hopkins play in a film whose title was simply his name?
9 Which Schwarzenegger movie about a man who gets pregnant was originally titled Oh Baby?
10 In which movie did Jane Horrocks play a girl who can sing like the great musical stars?
11 Which star of Cheers co starred with Whoopi Goldberg in Made in America?
12 Which The Bridges of Madison County star became a father again aged 65?
13 Who was the star of the dark thriller 8mm?
14 Where was the 1990s version of Dickens Great Expectations set?
15 Which King did Leonardo DiCaprio play in The Man in the Iron Mask?
16 Which regular member of the Friends cast starred in Lost in Space?
17 Which role did Rupert Everett play in The Madness of King George?
18 Which animation film was originally a 50s musical set in Siam?
19 What is the name of Kate Winslet's character in Titanic?
20 Who played the title role in Emma?
21 Which character did Julia Roberts play in Steven Spielberg's Hook?
22 Which movie was a biopic about the life of David Helfgott?
23 Which Apollo mission was filmed in 1995 with Tom Hanks?
24 In which film did Susan Sarandon play Sister Helen Prejean?
25 What was Pierce Brosnan's first outing as 007?

Answers

Pot Luck 77 (see Quiz 164, page 386)

1 Lady Ghislaine. **2** Steelbacks. **3** Peter Davison. **4** Meridian. **5** France had won the World Cup. **6** Kenny Rogers. **7** Mae West. **8** Priscilla Presley. **9** Baader-Meinhof Gang. **10** Halifax. **11** Pop. **12** Bobby Robson. **13** Vita Sackville-West. **14** Guildford Four. **15** Swimming. **16** Peggy Lee. **17** Alf Garnett. **18** Boxing. **19** Helicopter. **20** San Diego. **21** Graham Greene. **22** Vatican City. **23** Jamie Theakston. **24** Richard Hadlee. **25** Pussy Galore.

Quiz 164 Pot Luck 77

Answers - see Quiz 163, page 385

1. What was the name of the boat on which Robert Maxwell was last seen alive?
2. In 90s cricket what did Northamptonshire add to their name?
3. Private detective Albert Campion was played by which ex Dr Who?
4. Who took over the ITV franchise from TVS in 1991?
5. Why were people partying in Paris the evening before Bastille Day in 1998?
6. Who had an 80s No 1 with Coward Of The County?
7. Who said, "To err is human but it feels divine"?
8. Which widow of a rock star appeared in Dallas?
9. The German terrorist group The Red Army Faction were more usually as which Gang?
10. Which Rugby League team made a fashion statement and became Blue Sox in the 90s?
11. Birds Eye Peas were advertised as being, "Fresh as the moment when the pod went..." what?
12. Which soccer manager's autobiography was An Englishman Abroad?
13. Who created a famous garden at Sissinghurst in Kent?
14. How were Armstrong, Conlon, Hill and Richardson known collectively?
15. At which sport did Ian Black win international success?
16. Who performed He's A Tramp in the Disney movie Lady And The Tramp?
17. Which character first said "bloody" 78 times in a TV comedy show?
18. Jersey Joe Walcott was a world champion in which sport?
19. Igor Sikorsky developed which means of transport?
20. In American Football where do the Chargers come from?
21. Who wrote the novel The Power and The Glory?
22. Vehicles from which place use the international registration letter V?
23. In 1998 which Top of the Pops presenter was voted Britain's best dressed man in 1998?
24. Who was the first New Zealand cricketer to be knighted?
25. Which Bond girl was Honor Blackman?

Answers

90s Movies (see Quiz 163, page 385)

1 Anthony Edwards. **2** Oprah Winfrey. **3** Julia Roberts. **4** Pete Postlethwaite. **5** Scent of a Woman. **6** Jennifer Aniston. **7** Anjelica Houston. **8** Nixon. **9** Junior. **10** Little Voice. **11** Ted Danson. **12** Clint Eastwood. **13** Nicolas Cage. **14** New York. **15** Louis XIV. **16** Matt LeBlanc. **17** The Prince of Wales. **18** The King and I. **19** Rose. **20** Gwyneth Paltrow. **21** Tinkerbell. **22** Shine. **23** 13. **24** Dead Man Walking. **25** Goldeneye.

Quiz 165 World Tour

Answers - see Quiz 166, page 388

1 In which country are the world's tallest buildings, the Petronas Towers?
2 In 1997 which airline replaced the flag on its tail fin with ethnic designs from around the world?
3 Where is there the valley of the Kings, scene of a terrorist attack in 1997?
4 In which decade of the 20th century did the first scheduled passenger air service begin?
5 What was Ethiopia called before it was called Ethiopia?
6 What is California's answer to Scotland's Silicon Glen called?
7 What name was given to the effect which warmed the waters of the Pacific, notably in the 1990s?
8 Andy Elson's world tour by balloon was thwarted in 1998 because he could not cross which country's air space?
9 What was Ho Chi Minh city before it was called Ho Chi Minh city?
10 In which continent is over half of the world's rainforests?
11 What was replaced by Brasilia as Brazil's capital in the 60s?
12 Which country is known as the Land of the Long White Cloud?
13 Which desert expanded by 251,000 sq miles between 1940 and 1990?
14 What was St Petersburg called for most of the 20th century?
15 On which island will you find Bondi Beach?
16 Which Californian resort is famous for its Golden Gate bridge?
17 In which country is the headquarters of the Save the Children Fund?
18 Which country contains the Biblical rivers of the Tigris and the Euphrates?
19 Transamazonica is a roadway across which large South American country?
20 Which German airport has am main after its name?
21 If a car's index mark is GBA, where does it come from?
22 What is the Pacific terminus of the Trans Siberian Railway?
23 In which US state did skateboards originate as an alternative to surfing?
24 Which item essential for world travel, is made in Seattle?
25 To the nearest thousand, how many islands does Indonesia have?

Answers

Pot Luck 78 (see Quiz 166, page 388)
1 Edwina Currie. **2** Jimmy Smits. **3** Blackburn. **4** Arnold Bennett. **5** Bucks Fizz. **6** Detroit. **7** Anita Roddick. **8** Dangermouse. **9** Warwickshire. **10** Simple Minds. **11** Squash. **12** CH. **13** Six. **14** Tights. **15** Dog. **16** Jack and Annie Walker. **17** The Round Table. **18** Walter Matthau. **19** Francis Chichester. **20** Bowler hat. **21** Inkatha. **22** Courage. **23** Batley. **24** Be prepared. **25** 60s.

Quiz 166 Pot Luck 78

Answers - see Quiz 165, page 387

1. Which former Tory MP lost the Derbyshire South seat in 1997?
2. In NYPD Blue who played Bobby Simone?
3. Barbara Castle was a long standing PM for which constituency?
4. Who wrote the Clayhanger series of novels?
5. Who had an 80s No 1 with Making Your Mind Up?
6. In baseball where do the Tigers come from?
7. Who founded Body Shop?
8. Whose secret agent partner was Penfold?
9. In cricket which English team became Bears in the 90s?
10. Which group had a No 1 album in 1986 titled Once Upon A Time?
11. Jonathan Power has been a world champion in which sport?
12. What are the international registration letters of a vehicle from Switzerland?
13. How much in old pence was a tanner worth in predecimal days?
14. In Germany what are strumpfhose?
15. 1994 was the Chinese year of which creature?
16. Who were the first landlords of the Rovers Return in Coronation Street?
17. "Adopt, adapt, improve" was adopted as which group's motto?
18. Which actor's real name is Walter Matasschansayasky?
19. Who sailed solo round the world in Gipsy Moth IV in 1966-67?
20. What did Tic-Tac throw in the Bond movies with deadly results?
21. In S Africa what does the I stand for in IFP?
22. In TV ads which drink claimed, "It's what your right arm's for"?
23. Which Rugby League team became Bulldogs in the 90s?
24. What is the motto of the Scout movement?
25. In which decade was Hugh Grant born?

Answers

World Tour (see Quiz 165, page 387)

1 Malaysia. **2** British Airways. **3** Egypt. **4** 2nd decade - it was 1914. **5** Abyssinia. **6** Silicon Valley. **7** El Nino. **8** China's. **9** Saigon. **10** America. **11** Rio de Janeiro. **12** New Zealand. **13** Sahara. **14** Leningrad. **15** Australia. **16** San Francisco. **17** England. **18** Iraq. **19** Brazil. **20** Frankfurt. **21** Alderney. **22** Vladivostok. **23** California. **24** Jets. **25** 13.

Quiz 167 Bands

Answers - see Quiz 168, page 390

1 The Proclaimers were King of the what in 1990?
2 Chrissie Hynde was the female member of which successful band?
3 Which band had a 90s album titled Our Town - Greatest Hits?
4 Which Irish group has a name which means family?
5 Which groups first hit was titled House of Love?
6 Who rereleased the 1984 No 8 hit Young At Heart in 1993?
7 Which group recorded the track that Welsh soccer fans changed to Bobby Gould Must Go?
8 Which group was founded by Ian Broudie?
9 Which hit making band featured Andy Summers and Stewart Copeland?
10 In which city were Pulp formed?
11 Falco's Rock Me Amadeus was sung in which language?
12 How many songs by the Bee Gees were in the film Saturday Night Fever?
13 Which Status Quo hit opened the 1985 Live Aid concert?
14 Who released an album in 1996 called A Different Beat?
15 Who told us to Keep On Running in a 60s No 1 hit?
16 Who had an insect sounding hit with The Fly in 1991?
17 Siobhan Fahey and Marcella Detroit were in which band in the 90s?
18 How many members are in the group Boyz II Men?
19 Where is the native home country of Bjorn Again?
20 Which 60s group included Pete Quaife and Mick Avory?
21 Which all girl group were first to sell more than a million copies of an album in the UK?
22 Who were Naked In The Rain in a No. 4 hit from July 1990?
23 Who formed a rock band in 1989 called Tin Machine?
24 What was 2 Unlimited's first UK No 1 from 1993?
25 Which company used Queen's I Want To Break Free in TV commercials?

Answers

UK Leaders (see Quiz 168, page 390)

1 11 years. **2** 43. **3** Margaret Thatcher. **4** Chancellor of the Exchequer. **5** William Hague. **6** Norman Tebbit. **7** Kenneth Clarke. **8** Ramsay MacDonald. **9** Michael Heseltine. **10** Conservative. **11** Transport. **12** Harold Macmillan. **13** Ken Livingstone. **14** Peter Lilley. **15** James Callaghan. **16** John Major. **17** Robert Runcie. **18** John Gummer. **19** Geoffrey Howe. **20** John Major. **21** Bernard Ingham. **22** Huntingdon. **23** Kesteven. **24** Spencer. **25** Edward Heath.

Quiz 168 UK Leaders

Answers - see Quiz 167, page 389

1 For how long did the UK's first woman Prime Minister hold this office?
2 How old was Tony Blair when he became PM?
3 Who did Paul Gascoigne describe as "nice and cuddly"?
4 What position in government did John Major hold before he became PM?
5 Who won Leon Brittan's parliamentary seat when he became an EC Commissioner?
6 Which Tory Party Chairman and MP for Chingford's wife was paralysed in the Brighton bombing of 1984?
7 Who was Education Secretary, Home Secretary and Chancellor in the 90s?
8 Who was the first Labour Prime Minister?
9 In the 1990 Tory leadership who first stood against Margaret Thatcher?
10 As Prime Minister Andrew Bonar Law represented which party?
11 Former Labour leader Neil Kinnock was a European Commissioner in charge of which department?
12 Who was the last prime minister to be created an earl?
13 Which left wing MP and former council leader wrote If Voting Changed Anything They'd Abolish It?
14 Who was sacked as Deputy Leader of the Tory Party in William Hague's first major reshuffle?
15 Baroness Margaret Jay is the daughter of which ex PM?
16 Who delivered the first Budget speech to be televised - in March 1990?
17 Who did George Carey replace as Archbishop of Canterbury?
18 Which MP shared a beefburger with his young daughter to try and prove British beef was safe to eat?
19 Whose resignation speech in 1990, with allusions to a game of cricket, precipitated the downfall of Margaret Thatcher?
20 Who was Britain's second youngest PM in the 20th century?
21 Who was Mrs Thatcher's press secretary during her last years as PM?
22 What was John Major's constituency when he was PM?
23 On leaving No 10 Margaret Thatcher became which Baroness?
24 Which middle name did Winston Churchill share with Charlie Chaplin?
25 Who was the 20th century's longest serving MP for Old Bexley and Sidcup?

Answers

Bands (see Quiz 167, page 389)
1 Road. **2** Pretenders. **3** Deacon Blue. **4** Clannad. **5** East 17. **6** Bluebells.
7 Manic Street Preachers. **8** The Lightning Seeds. **9** The Police. **10** Sheffield.
11 German. **12** 7. **13** Rockin' All Over The World. **14** Boyzone.
15 Spencer Davis Group. **16** U2. **17** Shakespear's Sister. **18** Four. **19** Australia.
20 The Kinks. **21** Eternal. **22** Blue Pearl. **23** David Bowie. **24** No Limit. **25** Shell.

Quiz 169 Pot Luck 79

Answers - see Quiz 170, page 392

1 Dunfermline East has been the 90s seat of which prominent politician?
2 Who wrote the novel Watership Down?
3 Who played Timothy Lumsden in Sorry!?
4 Which food was not rationed in World War II but was rationed after it?
5 In advertising campaign, which sign meant "happy motoring"?
6 Who had an 80s No 1 with The Tide Is High?
7 Della Street was whose secretary?
8 What is Mick Jagger's middle name?
9 In basketball where do the Suns come from?
10 In TV ads what colour was Arthur the cat?
11 Who was the first chemist to be Britain's Prime Minister?
12 Under which name did the frock wearing Daniel Carroll find fame?
13 Which country lies immediately to the south of Estonia?
14 Which show gave Barbara Dickson a hit with Another Suitcase in Another Hall?
15 Who was Prime Minister of Australia from 1983-1991?
16 On which river was the Kariba dam built?
17 Which Dennis Potter drama was shown in 1987, eleven years after it was banned from TV screens?
18 Who set fire to his guitar at the Monterey Pop Festival in 1967?
19 In which Bond film did Britt Ekland appear?
20 Vehicles from which country use the international registration letter P?
21 Which female presenter interviewed Charles and Diana before their wedding?
22 Other than the title of a movie, what is Airforce One in the USA?
23 In which decade did Spain join the European Union?
24 Which city does writer Beryl Bainbridge come from?
25 A Fistful of Dollars was filmed on location in which country?

Answers

20th C Headline Makers (see Quiz 170, page 392)
1 Fire fighter. **2** Princess Diana. **3** Eight. **4** Head teacher. **5** Jamie Shea. **6** Edwina Currie. **7** Chris Sutton. **8** Luciano Pavarotti. **9** Brighton Bomber. **10** Oklahoma. **11** Ken Livingstone. **12** Hillary Clinton. **13** Michael Portillo. **14** Hospice Movement. **15** Helen Sharman. **16** Belgium. **17** Jonathan Aitken. **18** Bramley. **19** C5. **20** Neil Kinnock. **21** Lisa Potts. **22** Murray Walker. **23** Margaret Thatcher. **24** Tracie Andrews. **25** Virginia Wade.

Quiz 170 20th C Headline Makers

Answers - see Quiz 169, page 391

1 Fleur Lombard was the first woman to die on duty in which profession?
2 Who took out an injunction against Martin Steenning after he tried to take photographs of her?
3 How many babies did Mandy Allwood expect when she sold her story?
4 What was the occupation of Philip Lawrence who was killed outside his place of work in December 1995?
5 What was the name of the NATO spokesman in the 1999 Kosovo crisis?
6 Which former Tory MP hosted a late night Radio 5 Live phone in show?
7 Which British player moved to Chelsea in July 1999 for a cool £10 million?
8 Nicoletta Mantovani hit the headlines through her relationship with which big figure in the entertainment world?
9 Released on June 22nd 1999, Patrick Magee was known as which Bomber?
10 Timothy McVeigh was convicted for which bombing?
11 Who was dubbed Red Ken?
12 Which First Lady had to give evidence over the Whitewater scandal?
13 Which outgoing MP in the 1997 General Election had the initials MDX?
14 What movement for the terminally ill was begun by Cicely Saunders?
15 Which woman space traveller published The Space Place in 1997?
16 Marc Dutroux hit the headlines over a 'house of horrors' in which country?
17 Who penned a ballad from Belmarsh Gaol?
18 What was the surname of the couple who disappeared with their foster daughters after they feared they would be taken away from them?
19 What was Clive Sinclair's personal transport vehicle called?
20 Which party leader once made a pop video with Tracey Ullman?
21 Who defended her nursery children from a machete attack in 1995?
22 Which sports commentator said, "Do my eyes deceive me or is Senna's Lotus sounding a bit rough!"?
23 About which British politician did Francois Mitterand say, "She has the mouth of Marilyn Monroe and the eyes of Caligula"?
24 Who was convicted of murdering her fiance Lee Harvey after she alleged he had been killed in a road rage attack?
25 Who was the last British Wimbledon singles champion of the 20th century?

Answers

Pot Luck 79 (see Quiz 169, page 391)
1 Gordon Brown. **2** Richard Adams. **3** Ronnie Corbett. **4** Bread. **5** Esso. **6** Blondie. **7** Perry Mason. **8** Philip. **9** Phoenix. **10** White. **11** Margaret Thatcher. **12** Danny La Rue. **13** Latvia. **14** Evita. **15** Bob Hawke. **16** Zambezi. **17** Brimstone and Treacle. **18** Jimi Hendrix. **19** The Man With The Golden Gun. **20** Portugal. **21** Angela Rippon. **22** The President's plane. **23** 80s. **24** Liverpool. **25** Italy.

Quiz 171 Pot Luck 80

Answers - see Quiz 172, page 394

1 What was the frequency of Radio Luxembourg?
2 What is the set of fans at the front of a jet engine called?
3 On TV who presented Saturday Night Armistice?
4 In cricket what did Sussex add to their name in the 90s?
5 Who had a national airline called Garuda?
6 Which British PM imposed a10.30pm TV curfew in 1973?
7 Which musical featured the song Rhythm Of Life?
8 Who was the first tennis player to be BBC Sports Personality in the 1990s?
9 In which month of the year is Battle of Britain week?
10 How is Declan McManus better known?
11 Which daughter of feminist writer Vera Brittain became a British MP?
12 Who was the first US golfer to win the US amateur title in three consecutive years?
13 Which British entertainer used the catchphrase, "She knows, you know"?
14 Who made No 1 with Boombastic?
15 In American Football where do the Chiefs come from?
16 Where in Devon is the railway station St. David's?
17 What was advertised by persuading you that your fingers should do the walking?
18 Entebbe international airport is in which country?
19 What is David Frost's middle name?
20 What does the letter C stand for in the media organisation CNN?
21 Who said, "I married beneath me. All women do"?
22 What relation is TV cook Sophie Grigson to late cookery expert Jane?
23 Which American novelist wrote For Whom the Bell Tolls?
24 Andy Linnighan scored a last minute FA Cup winner for which team?
25 Sheryl Crow sang the title song for which Bond film?

Answers

TV Sitcoms (see Quiz 172, page 394)
1 Magda. **2** Lisa Kudrow. **3** Samantha Janus. **4** Caroline Aherne. **5** Roger Lloyd Pack. **6** Leadbetter. **7** Nick Hancock. **8** Chef!. **9** India. **10** Nurse. **11** Administrative Affairs. **12** Grandad. **13** Ebenezer Blackadder. **14** Garth. **15** Emmet. **16** Pauline Quirke & Linda Robson. **17** Yes Minister. **18** Waiting For God. **19** Honor Blackman. **20** 2 Point 4 Children. **21** Shirley Temple. **22** The Thin Blue Line. **23** Rising Damp. **24** Arkwright. **25** To The Manor Born.

Quiz 172 TV Sitcoms

Answers - see Quiz 171, page 393

1 Who was Patsy's boss in Absolutely Fabulous, as played by Kathy Burke?
2 Which member of the cast of Friends has a son called Julian in real life?
3 Which star of the sitcom Babes in the Wood represented the UK in the Eurovision Song Contest in 1991?
4 Which premature pensioner played Denise in The Royle Family?
5 Which actor from Only Fools and Horses is the father of Emily Lloyd?
6 What was the surname of the couple who lived next door to the Goods in The Good Life?
7 Which They Think It's All Over regular starred in Holding the Baby?
8 Which sitcom was based in the restaurant Le Chateau Anglais?
9 Where was It Ain't Half Hot Mum set?
10 What was the occupation of Gladys Emmanuel in Open All Hours?
11 In the first series of Yes Minister what was Jim Hacker's department?
12 Which elderly relative did the Trotters live with in the first series of Only Fools and Horses?
13 What was Blackadder called in Blackadder's Christmas Carol?
14 What was Tracey's son called in Birds of a Feather?
15 Who was the brother of Hyacinth Bucket's neighbour Elizabeth?
16 Which two sitcom stars advertised Surf soap powder?
17 In which sitcom did Margaret Thatcher read a scene with its stars at an awards ceremony in 1984?
18 Which series revolved around Diana and Tom in a retirement home?
19 Which ex Bond girl played the mother in law in The Upper Hand?
20 Which sitcom centred on Bill and Ben and their family?
21 What was Alf Garnett's film star nickname for his son in law?
22 Which series with Rowan Atkinson and James Dreyfus was set in the fictitious town of Gasforth?
23 Miss Jones was the only female lodger in which sitcom with Leonard Rossiter?
24 Who was the shop owner in Open All Hours?
25 Grantleigh, in the village Cricket St Thomas was the setting for which series?

Answers

Pot Luck 80 (see Quiz 171, page 393)

1 208. **2** Compressor. **3** Armando Iannucci. **4** Sharks. **5** Indonesia. **6** Heath. **7** Sweet Charity. **8** Greg Rusedski. **9** September. **10** Elvis Costello. **11** Shirley Williams. **12** Tiger Woods. **13** Hylda Baker. **14** Shaggy. **15** Kansas City. **16** Exeter. **17** Yellow pages. **18** Uganda. **19** Paradine. **20** Cable. **21** Nancy Astor. **22** Daughter. **23** Ernest Hemingway. **24** Arsenal. **25** Tomorrow Never Dies.

Quiz 173 Pot Luck 81

Answers - see Quiz 174, page 396

1 Which US city was named after a British Prime Minister?
2 Where is the normal terminus if you travel from Bristol to London?
3 Who had an 80s No 1 with I Want To Know What Love Is?
4 If E=mc2 according to Einstein, what does m stand for?
5 Which Tory MP lost the Edinburgh Pentlands seat in 1997?
6 In baseball where do the Brewers come from?
7 Which insurance company said they wouldn't make a drama out of a crisis?
8 Under what name was Lionel Begleiter better known?
9 Rushcliffe has been the 80s and 90s seat of which prominent politician?
10 The Harry Lime theme was used in which film?
11 Geet Sethi has been a world champion in which sport?
12 What are the international registration letters of a vehicle from Iceland?
13 In early TV ads Consulate cigarettes were described as, "Cool as a.." what?
14 Where in Libya did Australian troops take a seaport occupied by the Italians in 1941?
15 At which sport did Karen Briggs win international success in the 80s and 90s?
16 Under which name did Alfonso D'Abruzzo find fime as an actor?
17 According to the inventor Thomas Edison genius is made up how many per cent of inspiration?
18 In which decade was Emily Lloyd born?
19 Which C S wrote The African Queen?
20 Who was world professional billiards champion between 1968 and 1980?
21 On a US Monopoly board, what are B & O, Reading, Short Line and Pennsylvania?
22 Which ex MP's memoirs were logged in Upwardly Mobile?
23 To the nearest million what is the population of Madrid?
24 In Rugby League what did Oldham add to their name in the 90s?
25 Who had the catchphrase, "By Jove, I needed that"?

Answers

Motor Sports (see Quiz 174, page 396)
1 Australian. **2** 70s. **3** Johnny Herbert. **4** Hockenheim. **5** Williams. **6** Le Mans 24 Hours. **7** Colin McRae. **8** Florida. **9** Belgian. **10** 20s. **11** Williams. **12** Keke Rosberg. **13** Stewart. **14** 100. **15** Canadian. **16** Michael Schumacher. **17** London. **18** Ricardo Patrese. **19** McLaren. **20** Mike Hawthorn. **21** 4. **22** Hungarian. **23** Lotus. **24** 1993. **25** Benetton.

Quiz 174 Motor Sports

Answers - see Quiz 173, page 395

1 In which 98 Grand Prix did David Coulthard move aside to let Mika Hakkinen win?
2 In which decade did Frank Williams launch his own racing team?
3 Which British driver got himself in the money stakes with deals with Sauber and Sony Playstation?
4 On which race track was Jim Clark killed?
5 Heinz-Harlad Frentzen moved to Jordan from which team?
6 Which motor race was first held on the old Sarthe circuit?
7 Who was the first Brit to claim the World Rally title?
8 In which US state is the Daytona Beach circuit?
9 Which Grand Prix provided Damon Hill's only victory in 1998?
10 In which decade was the Le Mans 24 hour race first held?
11 Which team did Nigel Mansell drive with when he was Formula 1 champ?
12 Who was the last Fin before Mika Hakkinen to be Formula 1 champion?
13 Which team did Johnny Herbert move to for the 1999 Grand Prix season?
14 Mika Hakkinen ended up with how many points in becoming 1998 world champion?
15 Which Grand Prix has been held at Mosport and Mont Tremblant?
16 In 1998 the Algerian government claimed that which top driver was in fact an Algerian?
17 James Hunt was born in and died in which city?
18 Who was the first person to clock up over 250 Grand Prix starts?
19 Rod Dennis has been managing director of which team?
20 Who was the first Brit to be Formula 1 champion?
21 In the 90s how many points have been awarded for finishing third in a Grand Prix?
22 What was the last Grand Prix outside Britain in which Damon Hill raced?
23 Which team did Jim Clark drive for at Formula 1?
24 In which year was Nigel Mansell Indy Car champion?
25 When Michael Schumacher was first Formula 1 champ he was with which team?

Answers

Pot Luck 81 (see Quiz 173, page 395)
1 Pittsburgh. **2** Paddington. **3** Foreigner. **4** Mass. **5** Malcolm Rifkind. **6** Milwaukee. **7** Commercial Union. **8** Lionel Bart. **9** Kenneth Clarke. **10** The Third Man. **11** Billiards. **12** IS. **13** Mountain stream. **14** Tobruk. **15** Judo. **16** Alan Alda. **17** One. **18** 70s. **19** Forester. **20** Rex Williams. **21** Stations. **22** Norman Tebbit. **23** 3 million. **24** Bears. **25** Ken Dodd.

Quiz 175 Pot Luck 82

Answers - see Quiz 176, page 398

1 Which politician was involved in charges made by male model Norman Scott?
2 English writer P G Wodehouse took out citizenship in which country?
3 What type of disaster took place in Skopje in 1963?
4 John George Diefenbaker was once PM of where?
5 Under what name did Thomas Hicks become a famous entertainer?
6 What is 50 mph in kilometres per hour?
7 Which musical featured the song My Favourite Things?
8 In WWI according to the Germans, who were the Ladies from Hell?
9 Which drink was advertised with the song I'd Like To Teach The World To Sing?
10 James Braddock was a world champion in which sport?
11 How did Virginia Woolf's life end?
12 What was the surname of underwater film makers Hans and Lotte?
13 What was the title of Dick Francis's first novel set in the horse racing world?
14 In which sport could the Heat take on the Magic?
15 In advertising what type of service was promoted using a giant letter X?
16 Who made No 1 with Killer?
17 Who said, "Talking jaw to jaw is better than going to war"?
18 In which decade did Luxembourg join the European Union?
19 Ian Wright has scored FA Cup Final goals for Arsenal and who else?
20 Who won a Booker Prize for Paddy Clarke Ha Ha Ha?
21 Klagenfurt international airport is in which country?
22 What did the letter A stand for in GATT?
23 Which Red Indian tribe featured in Dances With Wolves?
24 Which golf course includes the Rabbit and the Seal?
25 Father's Day was first celebrated in which country?

Answers

Movie Moguls (see Quiz 176, page 398)
1 Goldie Hawn. **2** Isle of Wight. **3** Francis Ford Coppola. **4** Robert Redford. **5** Woody Allen. **6** Francis Ford Coppola. **7** Tom Hanks. **8** Quentin Tarantino. **9** Three. **10** Bread. **11** Hugh Grant & Liz Hurley. **12** Franco Zeffirelli. **13** Michael Douglas. **14** The Horse Whisperer. **15** Alfred Hitchcock. **16** Barbra Streisand. **17** Clint Eastwood. **18** Pulp Fiction. **19** Robert Redford. **20** Stanley Kubrick. **21** Steve Spielberg. **22** Helen Mirren. **23** Richard Attenborough - for Gandhi. **24** A Passage to India. **25** James Cameron.

Quiz 176 Movie Moguls

Answers - see Quiz 175, page 397

1 Which blonde actress made her debut as a producer in Private Benjamin?
2 On which Isle was Anthony Minghella born?
3 Who directed the first three Godfather films?
4 Which Indecent Proposal star made a directorial debut in Ordinary People?
5 Who wrote and directed Deconstructing Harry?
6 Which director sacked Harvey Keitel from the cast of Apocalypse Now?
7 That Thing You Do was the directorial debut of which double Oscar winner?
8 Who directed Oscar nominated John Travolta in Pulp Fiction?
9 Out of 11 films how many did Grace Kelly make for Hitchcock?
10 Sliding Doors director Peter Howitt starred in which Liverpool sitcom?
11 Which celebrity couple co founded the production company Simian Films?
12 Who directed Tea With Mussolini?
13 Which actor, whose name was linked with Catherine Zeta Jones in 1999, co produced One Flew Over the Cuckoo's Nest?
14 Based on a novel by Nicholas Evans, what was Robert Redford's first film as director and star?
15 Who directed the original Rear Window, remade in the 90s with Christopher Reeve?
16 Which woman starred in and directed The Prince of Tides?
17 Which 'man with no name' directed The Bridges of Madison County?
18 What was Quentin Tarantino's follow up to Reservoir Dogs?
19 Which actor/director founded The Sundance Film Festival?
20 Which director adapted Stephen King's The Shining for the big screen?
21 Which hugely successful director co wrote and produced Poltergeist?
22 Taylor Hackford is the husband of which 50 plus British actress?
23 Who directed Ben Kingsley in his first Oscar winning role as a civil rights hero?
24 Which novel by E M Forster did David Lean make into a film in 1984 with Peggy Ashcroft and Judy Davis?
25 Which director of Titanic gave Arnold Schwarzenegger his big break in The Terminator?

Answers

Pot Luck 82 (see Quiz 175, page 397)

1 Jeremy Thorpe. **2** US. **3** Earthquake. **4** Canada. **5** Tommy Steele. **6** 80. **7** The Sound Of Music. **8** Highland soldiers in kilts. **9** Coca Cola. **10** Boxing. **11** Drowned herself. **12** Hass. **13** Dead Cert. **14** Basketball. **15** Building Society - The Halifax. **16** Adamski. **17** Winston Churchill. **18** 50s. **19** Crystal Palace. **20** Roddy Doyle. **21** Austria. **22** Agreement. **23** Sioux. **24** Troon. **25** USA.

Quiz 177 Pot Luck 83

Answers - see Quiz 178, page 400

1 Which Prize was awarded to Desmond Tutu in 1984?
2 In the musical Oliver which character sings As Long As He Needs Me?
3 In 1994 which Grand Prix saw the controversial Schumacher/Hill collision?
4 Valentina Harris cooks up food particularly from which country?
5 Arthur Griffith founded which political group in 1905?
6 In baseball where do the Orioles come from?
7 In advertising which DIY store claimed that it was "the big one"?
8 Who had an 80s No 1 with Desire?
9 With which sport is Anne Marie Moser-Proll associated?
10 What was Buddy Holly's real first name?
11 Who had a horse called Topper?
12 In which decade was Ralph Fiennes born?
13 Who was the first female member of the Ground Force?
14 Vehicles from which country use the international registration letter T?
15 In the 90s which athlete's autobiography was titled How Long's The Course?
16 Which national company was Ringo Starr's first employer?
17 Michelle Martin has been a 90s world champion in which sport?
18 In which country is the deepwater port of Thunder Bay?
19 Who wrote the thriller The Odessa File?
20 In the 90s how many points have been awarded for finishing fifth in a Grand Prix?
21 In which country was Telly Savalas born?
22 On a computer keyboard which letter on the same line is immediately left of the H?
23 Who wrote, "He who can does. He who cannot, teaches"?
24 Which Bond villain did Gert Frobe play?
25 With which sport was Charles Buchan associated?

Answers

Books (see Quiz 178, page 400)
1 She who must be obeyed. **2** Durham. **3** Salman Rushdie. **4** 40s. **5** Mark Twain. **6** Bram Stoker. **7** Dick Francis. **8** Bertie Wooster. **9** Stephen King. **10** 50s. **11** Billy Bunter. **12** Arthur Hailey. **13** Laurie Lee. **14** Pulitzer. **15** John Le Carre. **16** Tiger. **17** Maigret. **18** Net. **19** Jack London. **20** Arthur Rackham. **21** Ngaio. **22** Hercule Poirot. **23** They are the same person. **24** Nancy. **25** Wales.

Quiz 178 Books

Answers - see Quiz 177, page 399

1 How did the barrister Rumpole refer to his wife Hilda?
2 Which county did Catherine Cookson come from and write about?
3 Who won a Booker Prize for Midnight's Children?
4 In which decade of the 20th century did H G Wells die?
5 Under which name did American author Samuel Langhorne Clemens write?
6 At the very end of the 19th C who wrote the novel that produced the most filmed horror character of the 20th C?
7 Whose sports based novels of the 90s include Comeback and To The Hilt?
8 Aunt Agatha and Bingo Little feature in the escapades of which man about town?
9 Which writer of horrific happenings was himself involved in a road accident while out walking in 1999?
10 In which decade was The Lord Of The Rings first published?
11 Who is Frank Richards' most famous creation?
12 Who penned the airport lounge best seller titled Airport?
13 Which writer was influenced by their upbringing in Slad, Gloucestershire?
14 In 1917 which Joseph endowed an annual literary prize in America?
15 David John Cornell wrote spy stories under which name?
16 What type of jungle animal was Shere Khan?
17 Georges Simenon created which character known by one name?
18 In book selling what does the N stand for in NBA?
19 Which American novelist with an English place surname wrote White Fang?
20 Who wrote the children's classic Swallows And Amazons?
21 What was the first name of New Zealand novelist Ms Marsh?
22 Which fictional detective refers to using the little grey cells?
23 What was the particular link between Jean Plaidy, Phillipa Carr, Victoria Holt?
24 Which of the Mitfords wrote Love In A Cold Climate?
25 In the books as opposed to the TV series, where did Morse's sidekick Lewis come from?

Answers

Pot Luck 83 (see Quiz 177, page 399)
1 Nobel Peace. **2** Nancy. **3** Australian. **4** Italy. **5** Sinn Fein. **6** Baltimore. **7** Texas. **8** U2. **9** Skiing. **10** Charles. **11** Hoppalong Cassidy. **12** 60s. **13** Charlie Dimmock. **14** Thailand. **15** Roger Black. **16** British Railways. **17** Squash. **18** Canada. **19** Frederick Forsyth. **20** 2. **21** USA. **22** G. **23** George Bernard Shaw. **24** Goldfinger. **25** Soccer.

Quiz 179 **Pot Luck 84**

Answers - see Quiz 180, page 402

1 Who was the first MP elected for the SDP?
2 Which song says, "The words of the prophet are written on the subway halls"?
3 In which country did General Jaruzelski impose martial law in 1981?
4 On which channel did Nigel Slater cook up Real Food?
5 Which chair was kidnapped by students from the Cranfield Institute of Technology in 1978?
6 Devon Malcolm took nine wickets in a Test innings against which country?
7 Which musical featured the song The Street Where You Live?
8 Henley has been the 80s and 90s seat of which prominent politician?
9 In cricket which English team became Hawks in the 90s?
10 How is John Virgo known on Big Break?
11 Who sang the title sang for the Bond film A View To A Kill?
12 The Cod War of the 70s was between Britain and which country?
13 Which Desmond wrote the 80s book studying fans behaviour called The Soccer Tribe?
14 What's Alvin Stardust's real name?
15 At which sport did Karen Brown win international success?
16 Which family were the subject of Two Point Four Children?
17 Which Disney film had the theme tune A Whole New World?
18 Hellenikon international airport is in which country?
19 In TV ads who has sung the praises of Kenco Coffee and Renault cars?
20 Who was the target of the failed 'Bomb Plot' of 1944?
21 Who made No 1 with Young At Heart?
22 In basketball where do the Celtics come from?
23 In honours what does the G stand for in GC?
24 Who wrote the novel The Go Between?
25 In which Gloucester Street was the West's House of Horrors?

Answers

Solo Singers (see Quiz 180, page 402)
1 1940s. **2** Curtis Stigers. **3** Detroit. **4** Pierrot. **5** Celine Dion. **6** London. **7** Peter Andre. **8** Michael Bolton. **9** Lionel Richie. **10** Ray Charles. **11** Philadelphia. **12** Snake. **13** Virgin. **14** 42. **15** Encore Une Fois. **16** It's In His Kiss. **17** Bryan Adams. **18** Torn. **19** Cher. **20** Robbie Williams. **21** Peter Andre. **22** 1950s. **23** Light Of My Life. **24** LL Cool J. **25** Army of Me.

Quiz 180 Solo Singers

Answers - see Quiz 179, page 401

1 In which decade was singer Bruce Springsteen born?
2 Who had a hit with You're All That Matters to Me in 1992?
3 Stevie Wonder was given the keys to which city in recognition of his talents in 1984?
4 Which costume was worn by David Bowie on his Ashes to Ashes video?
5 Who, in 1994, did a cover of Jennifer Rush's The Power of Love?
6 George Michael was brought up in which city?
7 Who had a hit with Mysterious Girl in 1996?
8 Whose first album was titled Soul Provider?
9 Who was Dancing on the Ceiling in 1986?
10 Which senior star released an album in 1996 called Strong Love Affair?
11 Which American city links songs by Bruce Springsteen and Elton John?
12 What type of creature is Michael Jackson's pet Muscles?
13 Which record label did David Bowie sign to in 1995?
14 How old was Elvis Presley when he died?
15 What was the first UK top ten hit from March 1997 for Sash!?
16 What is in brackets in the title of Cher's The Shoop Shoop Song?
17 Spice Girl Mel C joined which artist on the hit When You're Gone?
18 Which hit got to No 2 for former Neighbours star Natalie Imbruglia in 1997?
19 Who is the oldest female solo singer to top the UK charts?
20 Who was Old Before I Die in a 1997?
21 Who made it big in 1996 with Flava?
22 In which decade was superstar Michael Bolton born?
23 What was Louise's first solo UK top ten hit?
24 Which American rapper was Loungin' in a UK No 7 from 1996?
25 What was Bjork's first UK top ten hit?

Answers

Pot Luck 84 (see Quiz 179, page 401)
1 Shirley Williams. **2** Sound of Silence. **3** Poland. **4** Channel 4. **5** Mastermind chair. **6** South Africa. **7** My Fair Lady. **8** Michael Heseltine. **9** Hampshire. **10** Mr Trick Shot. **11** Duran Duran. **12** Iceland. **13** Morris. **14** Bernard Jewry. **15** Hockey. **16** The Porters. **17** Aladdin. **18** Greece. **19** Lesley Garrett. **20** Hitler. **21** Bluebells. **22** Boston. **23** George. **24** L P Hartley. **25** Cromwell Street.

Quiz 181 Pot Luck 85

Answers - see Quiz 182, page 404

1 In which decade were LPs first sold in the UK?
2 Peter Mandelson was called in as spin doctor to run whose 1987 campaign?
3 In 1984 who scored the first nine dart 501 finish in a major event?
4 Which new British coin was first issued in the UK in 1983?
5 What is the first name of restaurateur and TV cook Mrs Paul Rankin?
6 Who had an 80s No 1 with You Win Again?
7 In a long running TV series, who had a boss called Dr Gillespie?
8 Which chocolate bar helped you "work, rest and play"?
9 Which musical featured the song Shall We Dance?
10 After 1918 British women were allowed to vote if they were what age?
11 What was Britain's first daily game show for teenagers?
12 What are the international registration letters of a vehicle from Estonia?
13 Which Rugby League team became Rams in the 90s?
14 Who played Whitney Houston's manager in the Bodyguard?
15 In which country did English born US citizen Charlie Chaplin die?
16 In which decade did Finland join the European Union?
17 Who promised that, "You too can have a body like mine"?
18 1993 was the last 20th century Chinese year of the Cock, but when will be the first of the 21st century?
19 Which Boat Race radio commentator said, "I don't know who's ahead - it's either Oxford or Cambridge"?
20 Which famous lady participated in the opening in '92 of Euro Disney Paris?
21 In which decade was Rupert Everett born?
22 On which children's TV show would you visit the Roundabout Stop?
23 In American Football where do the Broncos come from?
24 Who wrote the novel The Cruel Sea?
25 Whose motto is "Per ardua ad astra"?

Answers

Scandals & Disasters (see Quiz 182, page 404)
1 David Mellor. **2** Australian. **3** Canary Islands. **4** Earthquake. **5** Aeroplane. **6** Road rage. **7** Jonathan Aitken. **8** England. **9** Tour de France. **10** Three Mile Island. **11** Tenerife. **12** Richard Nixon. **13** Aberfan. **14** Munich. **15** M1. **16** Cora. **17** Guinness. **18** Nottm Forest. **19** Zeebrugge. **20** Acid bath. **21** Libya. **22** Korean. **23** Horse. **24** 1979. **25** Grand.

Quiz 182 Scandals & Disasters

Answers - see Quiz 181, page 403

1 Which politician got entangled with Antonia de Sancha?
2 Which Open Tennis tournament was John McEnroe expelled from?
3 Robert Maxwell drowned near which islands?
4 Which disaster took place in Kobe, Japan in 1995?
5 Charles Rolls of Rolls Royce fame was actually in what type of vehicle when he died?
6 In 1996 Stephen Cameron became the first fatality of which increasingly violent trend?
7 Whose downfall and disgrace revolved round a stay at the Paris Ritz in September 1993?
8 Bandleader Glenn Miller was last seen in an aircraft leaving which country?
9 In 1998 the Festina team was banned from what over drug allegations?
10 Where was the USA's worst nuclear accident, in 1979?
11 On which of the Canary Islands did a collision of two jumbo jets take place making it one of the worst air disasters in history?
12 Who was the first US President to resign while in office?
13 Where in Wales was a school engulfed by a slag heap in 1966?
14 Which Olympic Games were the scene of a terrorist attack by Palestinian guerrillas?
15 Onto which road did a British Midlands aeroplane crash in 1990?
16 What was the first name of Dr Crippen's wife?
17 Ernest Saunders and Gerald Ronson were convicted for their roles in the scandal in which company?
18 Who were Liverpool's opposition when the Hillsborough disaster took place?
19 The Herald of Free Enterprise capsized outside which port?
20 How did 40s murderer John Haigh dispose of his victims' bodies?
21 Policewoman Yvonne Fletcher was shot outside which London embassy?
22 What was the nationality of the jet shot down in Russian air space in 1983?
23 Who or what was Sefton, injured in a bomb blast in Hyde Park in 1982?
24 Which year was known as the 'winter of discontent'?
25 Which Brighton hotel was bombed during a Tory Party conference in 1984?

Answers

Pot Luck 85 (see Quiz 181, page 403)

1 1950s. **2** Neil Kinnock's. **3** John Lowe. **4** £1. **5** Jeanne. **6** Bee Gees. **7** Dr Kildare. **8** Mars. **9** The King And I. **10** 30. **11** Blockbusters. **12** EST. **13** Dewsbury. **14** Gary Kemp. **15** Switzerland. **16** 90s. **17** Charles Atlas. **18** 2005. **19** John Snagge. **20** Cher. **21** 60s. **22** Playdays. **23** Denver. **24** Nicholas Monsarrat. **25** RAF.

Quiz 183 Pot Luck 86

Answers - see Quiz 184, page 406

1 Who kept saying that it was time for bed in The Magic Roundabout?
2 The sinking of which ship prompted the Sun's "Gotcha!" headline?
3 Who was Sean Penn married to for 27 months before divorce was filed?
4 From which show does Love Changes Everything come?
5 In EastEnders what were Cindy & Ian Beale's twins called?
6 In baseball where do the Royals come from?
7 What colour is Laa Laa?
8 For what did Georgie O'Keefe become famous?
9 St Albans has been the 90s seat of which prominent Tory politician?
10 In economics what does the letter G stand for in GNP?
11 The Spanish soccer team Real Betis play at home in which city?
12 Which character brought the phrase, "You silly old moo" to TV?
13 To the nearest million what is the population of the USA?
14 Who made No 1 with Spaceman?
15 In which country was Michael J Fox born?
16 How much was the top prize on Cilla Black's The Moment of Truth?
17 Under which name did Leonard Slye ride across the silver screen?
18 On which movies soundtrack from the 90s did Brenda Lee feature?
19 Who did Harry Enfield play in the first series of Men Behaving Badly?
20 Which politician said, "He got on his bike and looked for work..."?
21 A-Ha sang the title song for which Bond film?
22 In advertising who or what was "Your flexible friend"?
23 Which German soccer striker was known as The Bomber?
24 Which writer came up with Catch 22 in the 60s?
25 Bourgas international airport is in which country?

Answers

Rich and Famous (see Quiz 184, page 406)
1 Nick Faldo. **2** Alexandra. **3** Madonna. **4** The Queen. **5** Egypt. **6** Bath. **7** Lourdes Maria. **8** Severn. **9** Princess Margaret. **10** Cookery. **11** Margaret Thatcher. **12** Lanfranco. **13** Explorer. **14** Andrew Lloyd Webber. **15** Margaret. **16** Maurice. **17** South Africa. **18** Her mother Linda. **19** Algeria. **20** Prince Albert. **21** Ian Botham. **22** Princess Margaret. **23** Motor racing. **24** Four. **25** The Duchess of Kent.

Quiz 184 Rich & Famous

Answers - see Quiz 183, page 405

1 Which golfer announced he was leaving his wife and three children for Brenna Cepalak in 1996?
2 Marina Mowatt is the daughter of which British Princess?
3 Fitness trainer Carlos Leon was the father of which singer/actress's child?
4 Whose portrait in 1996 was described by Brian Sewell as looking like "a pensioner who is about to lose her bungalow."?
5 In which North African country was Mohammed Al Fayed born?
6 Longleat is the stately home of which Marquess?
7 What is Madonna's daughter called?
8 In addition to be Earl of Wessex Prince Edward became Viscount of where on his marriage?
9 Lady Sarah Chatto is the daughter of which famous lady?
10 Caroline Conran, one time wife of Sir Terence, is a writer in her own right on which subject?
11 In 1996 who did The Spice Girls say was their Girl Power role model?
12 What is Frankie Dettori's real first name?
13 How did Sir Ranulph Twisleton-Wykeham-Fiennes achieve fame?
14 Madeleine Gurdon is the third wife of which millionaire?
15 Who was the first Princess to appear on The Archers?
16 What is the first name of Charles' brother of Saatchi & Saatchi?
17 In which country was Earl Spencer's acrimonious divorce settlement heard?
18 Who did Stella McCartney dedicate her first collection for Chloe to?
19 In which North African country was Yves St Laurent born as Henri Donat Mathieu?
20 Which child of Princess Grace of Monaco competed in the 1988 Olympics?
21 Which former England captain was Viv Richards' best man?
22 Which member of the Royal Family suffered a mild stroke when in the Caribbean in 1998?
23 Which multi million pound sport is Bernie Ecclestone associated with?
24 How many children does Tony Blair have?
25 Which member of the Royal Family converted to Catholicism in the 1990s?

Answers

Pot Luck 86 (see Quiz 183, page 405)
1 Zebedee. **2** General Belgrano. **3** Madonna. **4** Aspects of Love. **5** Peter & Lucy. **6** Kansas City. **7** Yellow. **8** Painting. **9** Peter Lilley. **10** Gross. **11** Seville. **12** Alf Garnett. **13** 265 million. **14** Babylon Zoo. **15** Canada. **16** £20,000. **17** Roy Rogers. **18** Dick Tracy. **19** Dermot. **20** Norman Tebbit. **21** The Living Daylights. **22** Access Card. **23** Gerd Muller. **25** Joseph Heller. **25** Bulgaria.

Quiz 185 Pot Luck 87

Answers - see Quiz 186, page 408

1 Who said 50000 rifles were preferable to 50000 votes?
2 Which fictional hero has been played on TV by Peter Cushing, Alan Badel and Colin Firth?
3 Who is credited with inventing the Tarzan yodel?
4 In cricket what did Middlesex add to their name in the 90s?
5 Which Tory MP lost the Enfield seat in 1997?
6 Who had an 80s No 1 with I Think We're Alone Now?
7 What is Channel 5's quiz without a quizmaster for older contestants called?
8 England soccer captain Billy Wright married one of which singing sisters?
9 Who wrote The Children Of Men?
10 Which British broadcaster talked about an "Up and under!"?
11 Which act banned government employees from disclosing confidential information?
12 What did the S stand for in the name of T S Eliot?
13 Jack Sharkey was a world champion in which sport?
14 The title of an Arnold Wesker play was about what With Everything?
15 Who had a brother in law called Onslow?
16 Who wrote the song MacArthur Park?
17 Which musical featured the song How To Handle A Woman?
18 Which driver gave Jordan their first ever Grand Prix victory?
19 Who was the first man to feature in ads wearing Polly Peck tights?
20 Which gorge is spanned by the Clifton Suspension Bridge?
21 Which British liner was sunk by a German submarine in 1915?
22 Who wrote the novel The Godfather?
23 Vehicles from which country use the international registration letter S?
24 Who was leader of the Liberals from 1967-1976?
25 What was Marilyn Monroe's last film?

Answers

TV Drama (see Quiz 186, page 408)

1 Denzel Washington. **2** City Central. **3** Electrocuted. **4** Baz. **5** Jo. **6** Dublin. **7** Poirot. **8** Pathologist. **9** Stephen Tompkinson. **10** Nigel Havers. **11** Six. **12** Will Preston. **13** Lucy Gannon. **14** Robson Green. **15** Where the Heart Is. **16** Pride & Prejudice. **17** Goodnight Mister Tom. **18** Radio call sign. **19** Agatha Christie. **20** Bergerac's. **21** Sherlock Holmes. **22** School. **23** The Jewel in the Crown. **24** Hampshire. **25** Peak Practice.

Quiz 186 TV Drama

Answers - see Quiz 185, page 407

1 Which TV and Movie actor played Dr Phillip Chandler in St Elsewhere?
2 In which series did Paul Nicholls play Terry Sydenham?
3 How did Assumpta perish in Ballykissangel?
4 Who did Charlie marry in Casualty?
5 In Heartbeat who was Nick's second wife?
6 In which capital city did the action of The Ambassador take place?
7 Which TV detective was obsessed with his little grey cells?
8 What is Sam's profession in Silent Witness?
9 Who co starred with Robson Green in Grafters?
10 Which actor replaced Nigel Le Vaillant in Dangerfield?
11 How many Talking Heads were there in the first series in 1988?
12 What was the name of the doctor played by Simon Shepherd in Peak Practice?
13 Which writer links Soldier, Soldier, Peak Practice and Bramwell?
14 Who played opposite Francesca Annis in Reckless?
15 Which drama series takes place in Skelthwaite in Yorkshire?
16 In which serial did Colin Firth shoot to fame opposite Jennifer Ehle?
17 For which drama did John Thaw win the Best Actor BAFTA in 1999?
18 In Juliet Bravo what was Juliet Bravo?
19 Why Didn't They Ask Evans was the first in a murder mystery series by which famous author?
20 Charlie Hungerford was which detective's ex father in law?
21 Which famous detective did Jeremy Brett play for many years on TV?
22 Lucy Gannon's drama series Hope and Glory was set where?
23 Which 80s drama mini series was based on Paul Scott's Raj Quartet?
24 In which south coast county was Howard's Way set?
25 In which series did Saskia Wickham play Dr Erica Matthews?

Answers

Pot Luck 87 (see Quiz 185, page 407)
1 Mussolini. **2** Mr Darcy. **3** Johnny Weismuller. **4** Crusaders. **5** Michael Portillo. **6** Tiffany. **7** 100 Per Cent Gold. **8** Beverley Sisters. **9** P D James. **10** Eddie Waring. **11** Official Secrets Act. **12** Stearns. **13** Boxing. **14** Chips. **15** Hyacinth Bucket. **16** Jim Webb. **17** Camelot. **18** Damon Hill. **19** Paul Grady as Lily Savage. **20** Avon. **21** Lusitania. **22** Mario Puzo. **23** Sweden. **24** Jeremy Thorpe. **25** The Misfits.

Quiz 187 Pot Luck 88

Answers - see Quiz 188, page 410

1 Dying in 1972, under which name was Emmanuel Goldberg better known?
2 Dave Whatmore left Lancashire to coach which cricket team?
3 Who played the Rev Tony Blair in Sermon From St Albions?
4 What has been the commonest name for Popes through the second millennium?
5 Which great entertainer made his film debut in Pennies From Heaven?
6 Who was David Beckham's best man at his wedding to Posh?
7 Which musical featured the song Ol' Man River?
8 Who wrote The Camomile Lawn, seen on TV starring Felicity Kendal and Tara Fitzgerald?
9 Blackburn has been the 90s seat of which prominent politician?
10 Who sang the theme to One Foot in the Grave?
11 Peter Gilchrist has been a world champion in which sport?
12 Who made No 1 with Return Of The Mack?
13 What was the name of Tom Mix's horse?
14 In which country is the deepwater port of Townsville?
15 Who wrote My Family And Other Animals?
16 Whose one line was "Nice hat" in Friends?
17 In which country was Keanu Reeves born?
18 In which decade did Sweden join the European Union?
19 In which sport could the Knicks take on the Nets?
20 Which politician stated, "Read my lips: no new taxes"?
21 Which famous Michael has promoted Kwik Save in TV ads?
22 The Irish dramatist Samuel Beckett settled in which city?
23 Long Beach airport was built in which US state?
24 Who followed Matt Busby as Man Utd manager?
25 In which decade did Alcatraz close?

Answers

Sporting Chance (see Quiz 188, page 410)

1 Chicago. **2** Cole. **3** Kansas Cannonball. **4** Muhammad Ali. **5** Middlesex. **6** Semi finals. **7** Netball. **8** American golf course. **9** Houston. **10** Mike Denness. **11** Chile. **12** Rallying. **13** Spain. **14** Sugar Ray Robinson. **15** Azharuddin. **16** Flemington Park. **17** Squash. **18** John McEnroe. **19** Knox-Johnson. **20** Bobby Charlton. **21** Northants. **22** Muhammad Ali. **23** Willie Carson. **24** Shot. **25** Spurs.

Quiz 188 Sporting Chance

Answers - see Quiz 187, page 409

1 Which city has a team of Bulls and a team of Bears?
2 Which Man Utd player was replaced by Solskjaer in the 1999 European Champions' Cup Final?
3 What is the nickname of record breaking sprinter Maurice Greene?
4 Who was the first boxer to twice regain the world heavyweight title?
5 At which county did Edmonds and Emburey form a lethal spin attack?
6 What was Sue Barker's best placing in the Wimbledon singles?
7 Which sport do Essex Metropolitan play?
8 Ballustrol, Medinah and Oakmont are all types of what?
9 In basketball where do the Rockets come from?
10 Who was the first Scot to captain England at cricket?
11 Which country does tennis player Marcelo Rios come from?
12 What was the sport of Stirling Moss's sister Pat?
13 Which country does marathon man Abel Anton come from?
14 How was Walker Smith Robinson better known?
15 Who captained India in cricket's 1999 World Cup?
16 The Melbourne Cup is run at which ground?
17 Peter Nichol became the first Brit in 25 years to win the British Open in which sport?
18 Who told a Wimbledon umpire, "You are the pits of the world"?
19 Which Robin was the first yachtsman to sail non stop around the world?
20 Which player has played the most league games for Man Utd?
21 Allan Lamb first played in England for which county?
22 Who fought George Foreman in the Rumble In The Jungle?
23 Who had Derby victories riding Troy, Henbit, Nashwan and Erhaab?
24 With which athletics event was Geoff Capes particularly associated?
25 Teddy Sheringham was with club when he was the top league scorer in England?

Answers

Pot Luck 88 (see Quiz 187, page 409)
1 Edward G Robinson. **2** Sri Lanka. **3** Harry Enfield. **4** John. **5** Louis Armstrong. **6** Gary Neville. **7** Showboat. **8** Mary Wesley. **9** Jack Straw. **10** Eric Idle. **11** Billiards. **12** Mark Morrison. **13** Tony. **14** Australia. **15** Gerald Durrell. **16** Sarah, Duchess of York. **17** Lebanon. **18** 90s. **19** Basketball. **20** George Bush. **21** Barrymore. **22** Paris. **23** California. **24** Wilf McGuinness. **25** 60s.

Quiz 189 Pot Luck 89

Answers - see Quiz 190, page 412

1 Who was Hitler's Minister of Propaganda?
2 In 1998 which Royal appeared on Des O'Connor Tonight?
3 On which mountain did woman climber Alison Hargreaves perish in 1995?
4 Which WWII escapade was led by Guy Gibson?
5 Who had an 80s No 1 with Don't Turn Around?
6 What have Bobby Robson, Graham Taylor and Terry Venables all advertised on TV?
7 Who played plumber Frank Carver in Love Hurts?
8 What does the p in plc stand for?
9 Until its division in the 1990s, what was the capital of Yugoslavia?
10 Which national newspaper did not publish for nearly a year in the late 70s?
11 Which music hall star and radio comic had the catchphrase, "The day that war broke out"?
12 What are the international registration letters of a vehicle from Poland?
13 In which decade did the Sex Discrimination Act come into force in Britain?
14 Where in England was David Hockney born?
15 Princess Margaret plays which musical instrument?
16 On which river was the Tarbela dam built?
17 Which famous sporting figure refused conscription to Vietnam in 1967?
18 Who wrote Farewell My Lovely and the Lady in The Lake?
19 Which politician spoke of a "short, sharp shock" for young offenders?
20 Which country did Idi Amin go to when he fled Uganda?
21 In American Football where do the Browns come from?
22 The first students from where graduated in June 1973?
23 In which decade was Sean Penn born?
24 In economics what does the letter F stand for in IMF?
25 In the Army what is the equivalent of Admiral in the Navy?

Answers

Movie Comedies (see Quiz 190, page 412)
1 Notting Hill. **2** Truman. **3** The Full Monty. **4** La Cage aux Folles. **5** Eddie Murphy. **6** Joan Plowright. **7** Wool. **8** Bus. **9** Diamond. **10** Life of Brian. **11** Jake. **12** Dolly Parton. **13** In bed. **14** Rosanna. **15** Mick. **16** Jack Nicholson. **17** Ted Danson. **18** John Cleese. **19** Melanie Griffith. **20** Married to the Mob. **21** Bob Hoskins. **22** Lawyer. **23** Restaurant. **24** Lego brick. **25** Twins.

Quiz 190 Movie Comedies

Answers - see Quiz 189, page 411

1 What was dubbed 'an equal, not a sequel' to Four Weddings and a Funeral?
2 What was the first name of Truman in The Truman Show?
3 Which 1997 film was the then most successful British movie of all time?
4 Mike Nichols' The Birdcage was a remake of which musical?
5 Who played the Nutty Professor in the 1996 remake of Jerry Lewis's film?
6 Which wife of Laurence Olivier appeared in 101 Dalmatians?
7 What type of shop does Wendowlene own in A Close Shave?
8 Who or what is Priscilla in The Adventures of Priscilla, Queen of the Desert?
9 In the original Pink Panther movie what is the Pink Panther?
10 Which Monty Python film contains 'Always Look on the Bright Side of Life'?
11 Who was Elwood's brother in The Blues Brothers?
12 Which country singer starred in 9 to 5?
13 Where does Goldie Hawn's husband die in Private Benjamin?
14 Which member of the Arquette family starred in Desperately Seeking Susan with Madonna?
15 What is Crocodile Dundee's real first name?
16 Who was the male star of The Witches of Eastwick who famously said "I'm a horny little devil"?
17 Of the Three Men and a Baby who had appeared in Cheers?
18 Who scripted as well as starring in A Fish Called Wanda?
19 Who was the Working Girl of the title in the film in which Harrison Ford also starred?
20 Which 1988 film with Michelle Pfeiffer was about Mafia wives?
21 Who played the private eye hired by Roger Rabbit?
22 What is Jim Carrey's profession in Liar Liar?
23 Where does the most infamous scene in When Harry Met Sally take place?
24 Inside what toy does a love scene in Honey I Shrunk The Kids take place?
25 In which 80s film did Arnold Schwarzenegger play Danny De Vito's brother?

Answers

Pot Luck 89 (see Quiz 189, page 411)
1 Goebbels. **2** Prince Edward. **3** K2. **4** The Dam Busters. **5** Aswad. **6** Yellow Pages. **7** Adam Faith. **8** Public. **9** Belgrade. **10** The Times. **11** Rob Wilton. **12** PL. **13** 70s. **14** Bradford. **15** Piano. **16** Indus. **17** Muhammad Ali. **18** Raymond Chandler. **19** Willie Whitelaw. **20** Saudi Arabia. **21** Cleveland. **22** The Open University. **23** 60s. **24** Fund. **25** General.

Quiz 191 Pot Luck 90

Answers - see Quiz 192, page 414

1 What do Bluebell, Severn Valley and Watercress have in common?
2 Who was Edward VII's Queen?
3 Which country recorded 17 straight wins in Rugby Union in the late 90s?
4 Why were Hope and Crosby 'like Webster's Dictionary'?
5 What is the RAF equivalent to the army rank of Major?
6 In which decade of the 20th century was Jack Nicholson born?
7 Which musical featured the song I Talk To The Trees?
8 What was held for the first time on 11th Nov, 1921?
9 In basketball where do the Kings come from?
10 Who made No 1 with Should I Go Or Should I Stay?
11 What did the second E stand for in Premium Bonds' ERNIE?
12 Which country did tennis playing sisters Katerina and Manuela Maleeva originally come from?
13 In which year did Bill Hayley's Rock Around The Clock top the charts?
14 In advertising which chocolates were said to "Grow on you"?
15 At which sport did Ken Buchanan win international success?
16 Spiro Agnew was vice president to which US President?
17 Who sang the title sang for the Bond film The Spy Who Loved Me?
18 Calgary International airport is in which country?
19 Ansel Adams worked in which field in America?
20 Which politician stated that, "A week is a long time in politics"?
21 Which Liverpool legend was manager of the year six times from 1976 to 1983?
22 Who wrote the novel Doctor Zhivago?
23 In which decade did the Netherlands join the European Union?
24 Who created the, "Ooh, you are awful, but I like you" character Mandy?
25 In which country is the Francorchamps race track?

Answers

Americans (see Quiz 192, page 414)
1 25. **2** 1950s. **3** Porsche. **4** Iceland. **5** Baltimore.
6 Death (although no death penalty in California). **7** Eyes Wide Shut. **8** Louisiana prison.
9 X. **10** Shirley Temple Black. **11** 24th November. **12** Wilson. **13** George Gallup.
14 Hogan. **15** Fred Astaire. **16** Clint Eastwood. **17** Schoolteacher. **18** Irangate.
19 Ingrid Bergman. **20** Dan Quayle. **21** John Lennon. **22** John D Rockefeller.
23 Jake La Motta. **24** Coca Cola. **25** Charles Lindbergh.

Quiz 192 Americans

Answers - see Quiz 191, page 413

1 To the nearest three years, how old was Orson Welles when he made Citizen Kane?
2 In which decade did Berry Gordy set up Tamla Motown?
3 What sort of fast car was James Dean driving when he was killed?
4 In which cold country did Reagan and Gorbachev have their Star Wars summit in October 1986?
5 In which state beginning with a B was Edward VIII's wife Mrs Simpson born?
6 What sentence did Charles Manson receive for the murder of Sharon Tate?
7 What was Stanley Kubrick's final movie with Tom Cruise and Nicole Kidman?
8 In what sort of institution was Leadbelly 'discovered'?
9 Which letter did political activist Malcolm Little adopt for his surname?
10 Which ex film star became Ambassador to Ghana in 1974?
11 President Kennedy was shot on 22nd November; what day was Lee Harvey Oswald shot?
12 What was the surname of the brothers in the Beach Boys?
13 Who founded the American Institution of Public Opinion?
14 Which golfer Ben won all the major world championships in 1953 despite a serious car crash in 1949?
15 Which dancer and movie star married jockey Robyn Smith in 1980?
16 Which actor received $200 per month for his duties as Mayor of Carmel?
17 What was the profession of Christa McAuliffe, who was the first person to fly in the citizen space programme?
18 Which 'gate' scandal was Oliver North involved with?
19 Which Swedish born actress was called by the US Senate a 'powerful force of evil' when she left her husband and child in 1948?
20 Who was chosen as George Bush's Vice President?
21 Which Briton did American Mark Chapman shoot and kill?
22 Who founded Standard Oil?
23 Who was the Bronx Bull who Sugar Ray Robinson defeated in 1951?
24 Which drinks company was founded by Asa Chandler?
25 Which aviation pioneer first flew solo across the Atlantic aged 25?

Answers

Pot Luck 90 (see Quiz 191, page 413)
1 (Preserved) railways. **2** Alexandra. **3** South Africa. **4** They were Morocco bound. **5** Squadron Leader. **6** 30s. **7** Paint Your Wagon. **8** Poppy Day. **9** Sacramento. **10** The Clash. **11** Equipment. **12** Bulgaria. **13** 1955. **14** Roses. **15** Boxing. **16** Nixon. **17** Carly Simon. **18** Canada. **19** Photographer. **20** Harold Wilson. **21** Bob Paisley. **22** Boris Pasternak. **23** 50s. **24** Dick Emery. **25** Belgium.

Quiz 193 Pot Luck 91

Answers - see Quiz 194, page 416

1 What has been the century's best attended exhibition at the British Museum?
2 In the advertising campaign, which drink could be taken "Anytime, any place anywhere"?
3 Which of the four major blood groups is the commonest in the UK?
4 Sarah Fitz-Gerald has been a 90s world champion in which sport?
5 Who directed the classic 30s western Stagecoach?
6 Who had an 80s No 1 with Heart?
7 Which London Palace was destroyed in 1936?
8 Which bandleader had the same name as a British Prime Minister?
9 In cricket which English team became Gladiators in the 90s?
10 Lord Nuffield made his name in which industry?
11 Which school did Billy Bunter attend?
12 Which leader did Hitler meet in the Brenner Pass in WWII?
13 In which musical do the sweeps sing Chim Chim Cheree?
14 In Rugby League what did Leigh add to their name in the 90s?
15 On a computer keyboard which letter on the same line is between C and B?
16 Which band featured Brian Harvey on lead vocals?
17 In which decade did Gary Player last win the British Open?
18 In which city was the peace treaty signed that brought World War I to an end?
19 Which Chinese year follows the year of the Sheep?
20 What does the letter C stand for in OPEC?
21 To the nearest million what is the population of Bombay?
22 Vehicles from which country use the international registration letter C?
23 Which country was Prince Philip born in?
24 Who presented the first edition of Top Of The Pops?
25 Birkdale golf course is in which resort?

Answers

TV Selection (see Quiz 194, page 416)
1 Patrick Wymark. **2** Nick Ross. **3** Dennis Norden. **4** Rolf Harris. **5** The Flintstones. **6** Francis Wilson. **7** Ruth. **8** September 1957. **9** Joanna Lumley. **10** Clarissa Dickson Wright. **11** The Liberator. **12** Aidensfield. **13** Roland Rat. **14** An advertisement broadcast in the guise of a genuine programme. **15** Sir Robert Winston. **16** Lawyers. **17** Napoleon. **18** 1950s. **19** Late Lunch. **20** Michael Parkinson. **21** Pauline Quirke. **22** Lady Jane Felsham. **23** Don Adams. **24** Jan Harvey. **25** Glasgow.

Quiz 194 TV Selection

Answers - see Quiz 193, page 415

1 Who played John Wilder in The Power Game?
2 The original presenters of the BBC'S Breakfast Time were Frank Bough, Selina Scott, and one other. Who?
3 Who introduced It'll be Alright on the Night?
4 Which artist played a digeridoo?
5 The Simpsons became the longest-running cartoon family in 1997, replacing whom?
6 Who was the original weatherman on BBC's Breakfast Time?
7 Which Scottish character in EastEnders was Mark's wife?
8 In which year did the BBC TV schools service begin?
9 Which actress had to survive on her own on a desert isle?
10 Who was Jennifer Paterson's cooking partner?
11 What was the name of the first space ship used by Blake's 7?
12 Which fictional village was Heartbeat set in?
13 Which rodent starred on TVam?
14 What was an Admag, banned by Parliament in 1963?
15 Who presented The Human Body?
16 What was the profession of the major characters in *This Life*?
17 What did the ARP Warden call Captain Mainwaring?
18 In which decade was Hi-De-Hi! first set?
19 Which early evening programme did Mel and Sue introduce?
20 Who is the current host of Going for a Song?
21 Which actress played The Sculptress?
22 Who was Lovejoy's original love interest?
23 Which actor was Maxwell Smart?
24 Who played Tom Howard's wife in Howard's Way?
25 In which city was PI Daniel Pike based?

Answers

Pot Luck 91 (see Quiz 193, page 415)
1 Treasures of Tutankhamen. **2** Martini. **3** O. **4** Squash. **5** John Ford. **6** Pet Shop Boys. **7** Crystal Palace. **8** Edward Heath. **9** Gloucestershire. **10** Motor. **11** Greyfriars. **12** Mussolini. **13** Mary Poppins. **14** Centurions. **15** V. **16** East 17. **17** 70s. **18** Versailles. **19** Monkey. **20** Countries. **21** 10 million. **22** Cuba. **23** Greece. **24** Jimmy Savile. **25** Southport.

Quiz 195 Pot Luck 92

Answers - see Quiz 196, page 418

1 In 1954 what was tested at Bikini Atoll?
2 Who wrote Dinnerladies?
3 Which city is snooker player Willie Thorne's home town?
4 Who was the BBC's royal correspondent at the time of Princess Diana's death?
5 Eurostar will take you to which station in Paris?
6 In which decade of the 20th century did a woman first sit in the Commons?
7 Which musical featured the song Food, Glorious Food?
8 According to the advertising campaign Ian Botham couldn't eat three what?
9 Who was US President when America entered World War II?
10 Who became the first black athlete to captain the British team?
11 Who was appointed Vice President of the European Commission in July 1999?
12 Who made No 1 with Dreams?
13 What was being advertised by Lorraine Chase's Luton Airport character?
14 In which country is the deepwater port of Valparaiso?
15 What was the name of Fitz's wife in Cracker?
16 What was the third Bond film for which Shirley Bassey sang the title song?
17 In the 90s how many points have been awarded for finishing sixth in a Grand Prix?
18 In which decade was Kenneth Branagh born?
19 Who had a No 1 in the 60s with Mike Sarne before becoming a TV actress?
20 Which animal appeared on British eggs in 1957?
21 Which instrument is particularly associated with bandleader Buddy Rich?
22 Which English soccer international was known as 'Crazy Horse'?
23 Findel international airport is in which country?
24 Who wrote East Of Eden?
25 Whose motto is, "Let not the deep swallow me up"?

Answers

Media (see Quiz 196, page 418)
1 Pravda. **2** New York Times. **3** Chris Evans. **4** Women. **5** Bush House. **6** 70s. **7** Fortnightly. **8** Country Music Television. **9** Wapping. **10** Greater. **11** Convenience. **12** Radio 5 Live. **13** 40s. **14** Quarterly. **15** Radio 4 Long Wave. **16** 1990s. **17** S4C. **18** Buckinghamshire. **19** S & SE England. **20** Independent. **21** 1920s. **22** Labour. **23** O.K. **24** Edina & Patsy. **25** 60s.

Quiz 196 Media

Answers - see Quiz 195, page 417

1 Which former Soviet Communist Party newspaper was relaunched as a tabloid in 1996?
2 In 1997 The Duchess of York was signed up by which US newspaper to write a weekly column?
3 Who bought Virgin Radio from Richard Branson in 1997?
4 What was the original target audience for Sky's UK Living?
5 Where is the HQ of the BBC World Service?
6 In which decade was Cosmopolitan magazine launched in the UK?
7 How frequently is Private Eye published?
8 What did CMTV stand for?
9 Where did The Times offices move to in 1986?
10 What did G stand for in GLR?
11 What did C stand for in the shopping channel QVC?
12 Which national radio station was launched by the BBC in the 1990s?
13 In which decade of the 20th century did radio's Desert Island Discs begin ?
14 What does Q stand for in the magazine title GQ?
15 At the end of the 20th century Test Match Special was broadcast on which national radio network?
16 In which decade could Radio Times and TV Times first publish details of programmes on all channels?
17 How is Sianel Pedwar Cymru - Channel 4 in Wales - abbreviated?
18 In which county were Pinewood Studios?
19 Meridian broadcast to which area of the UK ?
20 What does I stand for in ILR?
21 In which decade was Radio Times first published?
22 Tribune supported which political party?
23 Which magazine paid around £1 million for the exclusive rights to David Beckham and Victoria Adams' wedding photos?
24 Which sitcom characters have guest edited Marie Claire?
25 In which decade was The Sun first published?

Answers

Pot Luck 92 (see Quiz 195, page 417)
1 Hydrogen bomb. **2** Victoria Wood. **3** Leicester. **4** Jennie Bond. **5** Gare Du Nord. **6** Second decade. **7** Oliver. **8** Shredded Wheat. **9** Franklin Roosevelt. **10** Kriss Akabusi. **11** Neil Kinnock. **12** Gabrielle. **13** Campari. **14** Chile. **15** Judith. **16** Moonraker. **17** 1. **18** 60s. **19** Wendy Richard. **20** Lion. **21** Drums. **22** Emlyn Hughes. **23** Luxembourg. **24** John Steinbeck. **25** RNLI.

Quiz 197 Pot Luck 93

Answers - see Quiz 198, page 420

1 Which Tory MP lost the Putney seat in 1997?
2 In a one-off performance who appeared with Boyzone on Top of the Pops in 1998?
3 Where in America is the Rockefeller University?
4 In which country was Leo McKern born?
5 In American Football where do the Cardinals come from?
6 Who had an 80s No 1 with I Owe You Nothing?
7 Which musical featured the song Tonight?
8 Sheffield Brightside was the 90s seat of which prominent politician?
9 Which pop singer played Adrian's mother in The Growing Pains of Adrian Mole?
10 In which decade did the Republic of Ireland join the European Union?
11 Which Rugby League team became Tigers in the 90s?
12 What are the international registration letters of a vehicle from Mexico?
13 To the nearest million what is the population of Switzerland?
14 Which character was given The Kabin by Rita in Coronation Street?
15 At which sport did Susan Cheeseborough win international success?
16 Who wrote the novel The French Lieutenant's Woman?
17 Tampa airport was built in which US state?
18 Which football club have a ground with the Matthew Harding stand?
19 Which university is at Uxbridge in Middlesex?
20 In finance what does the letter P stand for in PIN?
21 Which road led Chris Rea to write Road To Hell?
22 What is a young person interested in if they join the YOC?
23 Who announces the results of a parliamentary election?
24 Who had a Morris Minor car named Miriam?
25 What type of animals take part in the Courser's Derby?

Answers

80s Pop Music (see Quiz 198, page 420)

1 Ball. **2** Blue Monday. **3** Sinitta. **4** Mike Read. **5** Bruce Willis. **6** Christians. **7** John Kettley. **8** Level 42. **9** Dire Straits. **10** Battlefield. **11** 69. **12** The Thompson Twins. **13** Wham!. **14** Boy George. **15** Yazz. **16** Bette Midler. **17** Laurie Anderson. **18** Mike and the Mechanics. **19** Black Box. **20** Europe. **21** Odyssey. **22** Pretenders. **23** Sade. **24** The Communards. **25** Air Supply.

Quiz 198 80s Pop Music

Answers - see Quiz 197, page 419

1 Which Michael had a 1989 hit with Love Changes Everything?
2 Which coloured day of the week was a hit for New Order in 1983 and 1988?
3 Who had a man in 1986 who was So Macho?
4 Which Radio 1 DJ would not play Relax by Frankie Goes to Hollywood on his early morning show?
5 Which actor had a hit with Under The Boardwalk in 1987?
6 Which group had a hit in 1988 with Harvest for the World?
7 Which TV weatherperson was celebrated in a 1988 hit for the Tribe of Toffs?
8 Who gave Lessons in Love in 1986?
9 Which group made Private Investigations in a 1982 hit?
10 According to the 1984 hit by Pat Benatar Love is a what?
11 Which Summer gave Bryan Adams a hit in 1985?
12 Who had a hit with You Take Me Up in 1984?
13 Singers of Heartache, Pepsi and Shirley were backing singers to who?
14 Who did a cover of Everything I Own in the 80s?
15 Who had a hit in 1988 with The Only Way Is Up?
16 Which American lady had a hit in 1989 with The Wind Beneath My Wings?
17 Who had a hit in 1981 with Oh Superman?
18 Which group had a hit in 1989 about The Living Years?
19 Who tool Ride On Time to the UK Top Spot for six weeks in 1989?
20 Which rock band had a UK No 1 in 1986 with The Final Count Down?
21 Which group were Going Back To My Roots in a No 4 hit from 1981?
22 Which group asked Don't Get Me Wrong in 1986?
23 Whose only Top Ten UK hit was Your Love Is King from 1984?
24 Who had a hit in 1987 with Never Can Say Goodbye?
25 In 1980 who were All Out of Love?

Answers

Pot Luck 93 (see Quiz 197, page 419)
1 David Mellor. **2** Andrew Lloyd Webber. **3** New York. **4** Australia. **5** Phoenix. **6** Bros. **7** West Side Story. **8** David Blunkett. **9** Lulu. **10** 70s. **11** Castleford. **12** MEX. **13** 7 million. **14** Sharon. **15** Gymnastics. **16** John Fowles. **17** Florida. **18** Chelsea. **19** Brunel. **20** Personal. **21** M25. **22** Birds. **23** Returning officer. **24** Lovejoy. **25** Greyhounds.

Quiz 199 Pioneers

Answers - see Quiz 200, page 422

1 What was the first name of the world's first test tube baby?
2 Jane Couch was the first woman to be granted a professional licence to do what?
3 In which city did the original Wallace and Gromit models get lost in 1996?
4 What sort of radio was designed by British inventor Trevor Baylis?
5 The Ishihara Test is a test for what?
6 Which pioneer in men's appearance had the first names King Camp?
7 Air flight pioneer Amy Johnson vanished over which river?
8 What was the name of Clive Sinclair's electric trike?
9 Reaching which place led to the quote, "Great God, this is an awful place"?
10 Who accompanied Dr Michael Stroud on the first unsupported crossing of the Antarctic?
11 In 1993 Barbara Harmer became the first woman pilot of what?
12 Who was the first racing driver to win the world drivers' championship in his own car?
13 Which country was the first in the world to have a woman Prime Minister?
14 What was the first item of non stick cookware marketed by Teflon?
15 Which flags along with that of the UN were planted on the top of Everest by Hillary and Tensing?
16 In the Whitbread Round the World Race who skippered the all women crew of Maiden?
17 David Scott and James Irwin were the first people to drive where?
18 Who introduced the first personal stereo ?
19 In which decade were camcorders introduced?
20 Which items of sports equipment were developed by US ice hockey players Scott and Brennan Olson?
21 Gro Harlem Brundtland was the first woman PM in which country?
22 Who was the USA's first spacewoman?
23 Who was the first black archbishop of Cape Town?
24 What sort of wave was seen for the first time at a sporting fixture in 1986?
25 Which Scandinavian country was the first to ban aerosol sprays because of the potential damage to the environment?

Answers

Glitterati (see Quiz 200, page 422)
1 Stella McCartney. **2** Rachel Hunter. **3** Surgeon. **4** The Duchess of York. **5** Samantha Shaw. **6** Raymond Blanc. **7** Naomi Campbell. **8** Gucci. **9** Eurovision Song Contest. **10** Yardley. **11** Versace. **12** Camilla Parker-Bowles. **13** David Bowie. **14** Nicky Clarke. **15** Snake. **16** David Bailey. **17** Jasper. **18** Barbara Daly. **19** Czechoslovakia. **20** Pepsi. **21** The Queen. **22** Joan Collins. **23** Jerry Hall. **24** Brookside. **25** Mitford.

Quiz 200 Glitterati

Answers - see Quiz 199, page 421

1 Which famous daughter was made chief designer at Chloe in 1997?
2 Which supermodel was married to Rod Stewart?
3 What was the occupation of Vanessa Feltz's first husband?
4 Which Royal sold her autobiography for $1.3 million to Simon & Schuster?
5 Who designed Sophie Rhys-Jones' wedding dress?
6 Which French chef is famed for his Manoir aux Quat'Saisons restaurant?
7 Flamenco dancer Joaquin Cortes hit the headlines in 1996 over his relationship with which supermodel?
8 Which Italian fashion designer was murdered on the orders of his ex wife?
9 Michael Flatley shot to fame during an interval filler on which programme?
10 Which perfume house did Helena Bonham-Carter advertise?
11 Who designed the see through black dress Caprice wore at the 1996 Narional TV Awards which shot her to stardom?
12 Whose 50th birthday party did Prince Charles host at Highgrove in the summer of 1997?
13 Which pop star did model Iman marry in 1992?
14 Which crimper to the famous launched his Hairomatherapy products in the 90s?
15 What type of creature did Anthea Turner pose nude with on the front of Tatler?
16 Who has been the husband of Catherine Deneuve, Marie Helvin and Catherine Dyer?
17 What is the name of Terence and Shirley Conran's dress designer son?
18 Who did Princess Diana's make up before her wedding in 1981?
19 In which country was Ivana Trump born and brought up?
20 Which drink did The Spice Girls promote?
21 Which Royal did The Beatles mention in Penny Lane?
22 Which soap star launched a perfume called Scoundrel?
23 Which blonde model appeared in Batman?
24 Which TV soap did Russell Grant appear in as himself?
25 The 11th Duke of Devonshire married one of which famous family of sisters?

Answers

Pioneers (see Quiz 199, page 421)
1 Louise. **2** Box. **3** New York. **4** Clockwork radio. **5** Colour blindness. **6** Gillette. **7** Thames. **8** C5. **9** The South Pole. **10** Ranulph Fiennes. **11** Concorde. **12** Jack Brabham. **13** Ceylon later Sri Lanka. **14** Frying pan. **15** Britain & Nepal. **16** Tracey Edwards. **17** Moon. **18** Sony. **19** 80s. **20** Rollerblades. **21** Norway. **22** Sally Ride. **23** Desmond Tutu. **24** Mexican wave. **25** Sweden.

Quiz 201 TV Trivia

Answers - see Quiz 202, page 424

1 Who with Greg Dyke was credited with saving TV am?
2 Which model advertised Pizza Hut with Jonathan Ross?
3 Who found fame in the docu soap about a driving school?
4 Which TV personality appeared on The Archers - as himself - for their 10,000th episode?
5 From which part of her house did Delia Smith present her 90s TV series?
6 Which comedy duo began as stand up comics called The Menopause Sisters?
7 Which airline did Jeremy Spake from Airport work for?
8 In which supermarket ad did Jane Horrocks play Prunella Scales' daughter?
9 Fred Housego shot to fame as a winner on which TV show?
10 Who replaced Danny Baker on Pets Win Prizes?
11 Who provided the music for The Wombles?
12 Who or what did Barbara Woodhouse train?
13 Which Ready Steady Cook regular was also a regular presenter on Breakfast Time?
14 What is the subject of the Quentin Wilson show All the Right Moves?
15 What was Keith Floyd's TV show based on Far East cooking called?
16 Who interviewed Prince Edward and Sophie Rhys Jones in a pre wedding programme?
17 Who wrote and sang the theme music to Spender?
18 Which early presenter of the Big Breakfast wore glasses?
19 Who was the original presenter of Gladiators with Ulrika Jonsson?
20 Which drama series was based on the Constable novels by Nicholas Rhea?
21 Which series had the tag line "The truth is out there...."?
22 Who worked together on The Frost Report and went on to have their own successful series together?
23 Which quiz began with "Your starter for ten.."?
24 Which work of reference do the celebrity and the expert possess in Countdown?
25 Which soap powder did Robbie Coltrane advertise?

Answers

Rugby (see Quiz 202, page 424)
1 Rory Underwood. **2** 80s. **3** Willie John McBride. **4** Rowe. **5** Cricket. **6** Australia. **7** Bill Beaumont. **8** Broke his neck. **9** Wigan. **10** Spain. **11** 1996. **12** S Africa. **13** Hawks. **14** Gavin Hastings. **15** 22. **16** Wales. **17** Scrum half. **18** Leicester. **19** Warrington. **20** Pool B. **21** Brive. **22** New Zealand. **23** Mark Aston. **24** Saracens. **25** 1997.

Quiz 202 Rugby

Answers - see Quiz 201, page 423

1 Who is England's most capped Union player?
2 In which decade did Ireland last win the Five Nations?
3 Who led the British Lions in their all conquering tour of S Africa in the 70s?
4 Which Erica made a clean breast of things at Twickenham in 1982?
5 Apart from Rugby, Rob Andrew captained Cambridge in which other sport?
6 In 1998 against which team did England suffer their worst ever Union defeat?
7 Who led England to their Grand Slam triumph of 1980, the first for nearly a quarter of a century?
8 What injury did Welsh captain Gwyn Jones suffer in Dec 1997 at the Arms Park?
9 Which club thought Wendall Sailor was joining them in 1998?
10 Who did Scotland beat 85-3 to in a 1999 World Cup qualifier?
11 In what year was League's Regal Trophy last contested?
12 Which team played the Welsh in the first game at the Millennium Stadium?
13 Which creature name did Hunslet adopt in the 90s?
14 Who captained the Lions' New Zealand Tour of 1993?
15 At what age did Will Carling first become England skipper?
16 Which country was thrashed 96-13 by South Africa in 1998?
17 What position did Gareth Edwards play?
18 Martin Johnson was at which club when he became England skipper?
19 Jonathan Davies was League's 1994 Man of Steel when playing for which team?
20 In which pool were England drawn for the 1999 World Cup?
21 Which team did Bath beat in 97-98 European Cup?
22 Which country does Wales coach Graham Henry come from?
23 Who was man of the match as Sheffield Eagles sensationally beat Wigan in a Challenge Cup final?
24 Which British club did legendary French player Phillippe Sella join?
25 In which year did Lawrence Dallaglio take over as England's captain?

Answers

TV Trivia (see Quiz 201, page 423)

1 Roland Rat. **2** Caprice. **3** Maureen Rees. **4** Terry Wogan. **5** Conservatory. **6** French & Saunders. **7** Aeroflot. **8** Tesco. **9** Mastermind. **10** Dale Winton. **11** Mike Batt. **12** Dogs. **13** Fern Britton. **14** Property. **15** Far Flung Floyd. **16** Sue Barker. **17** Jimmy Nail. **18** Chris Evans. **19** John Fashanu. **20** Heartbeat. **21** The X Files. **22** The Two Ronnies. **23** University Challenge. **24** Dictionary. **25** Persil.

Quiz 203 The Movies: The Oscars

Answers - see Quiz 204, page 426

1 Which not-so-dizzy blonde won an Oscar for Cactus Flower?
2 Who did Loretta Lynn choose to play her in Coal Miner's Daughter?
3 How tall is an Oscar in centimetres?
4 Whose 1989 Oscar for Glory was the first awarded to a black American for 50 years?
5 Following his True Grit Oscar what did John Wayne's fellow actors and his horse wear while filming a new movie?
6 In which decade of the 20th century were The Oscars born?
7 For which film was Judi Dench nominate for her first Oscar?
8 What is the name of the daughter of Oscar winner Joel Grey who starred in Dirty Dancing?
9 Who was up for an Oscar as Sally Field's daughter in Steel Magnolias?
10 Which actress was the second in history to win an Oscar (for Roman Holiday) and a Tony (for Ondine) in the same year?
11 Which French actor was Oscar nominated for Cyrano de Bergerac?
12 For which movie did Barbra Streisand win an Oscar for Evergreen?
13 Which anniversary did The Oscars celebrate in 1998?
14 Which 1996 multi Oscar winner was based on a novel by Michael Ondaatje?
15 For which film did Robert de Niro win his first Oscar?
16 Which Fonda won an honorary award in 1980?
17 Who won an Oscar for the music of Chariots of Fire?
18 What was the nationality of Sophie in the Oscar winning Sophie's Choice?
19 Dr Haing S Ngor was only the second non professional actor to win an Oscar in which film?
20 Which Stevie Wonder song won an Oscar for The Woman in Red?
21 Which was the first family to boast three generations of Oscar winners including middle generation John?
22 Who won a Best Supporting Actor award for Hannah and her Sisters?
23 Which successful song from Top Gun was a hit for Berlin?
24 In which film did Cher win an Oscar playing Loretta Castorini?
25 1987 was a successful year for Michael Douglas but which movie won him an Oscar?

Answers

On Line (see Quiz 204, page 426)
1 British Telecom. **2** 2nd decade. **3** Pentagon. **4** Shared phone line. **5** Mercury. **6** Timeline. **7** Allows people to touch over long distances. **8** Shopping. **9** Article. **10** Webwise. **11** Oftel. **12** Blue. **13** Bulletin. **14** Tennis. **15** Prestel. **16** Virtual. **17** Eight. **18** Moon. **19** Digital. **20** Phillips. **21** Junkmail. **22** Windows. **23** Design. **24** Telstar. **25** Security barrier.

Quiz 204 On Line

Answers - see Quiz 203, page 425

1 What was BT called before 1991?
2 In which decade of the 20th century were airmail letters first carried?
3 Which Defence Department first set up the messaging system which became the Internet?
4 In telephone terms what was a party line?
5 Which telecommunications company took its name from the Roman messenger of the gods?
6 What was BT's Speaking Clock service called?
7 What is the purpose of a dataglove?
8 BarclaySquare was an early Internet site offering what?
9 What is a message sent to a newsgroup on the Internet called?
10 What was the BBC's introduction to the Internet called?
11 What was set up in 1984 to monitor the telecommunications industry?
12 What colour were special airmail post boxes which used to be seen on city streets?
13 On the Internet what does the first B stand for in BBS?
14 Pong was an early console type game based on which sport?
15 What was the videotext service of BT called?
16 What does V stand for in VR?
17 How many bits are there in a byte?
18 From Earth, where was the destination of the longest long distance telephone call?
19 What does D stand for in ISDN?
20 Which company launched CDi in the early 1990s?
21 On the Internet what is Spam?
22 In the WIMP system of computing what did W stand for?
23 What does D stand for in CAD?
24 What was the name of the first satellite to relay live TV pictures between the USA and Europe?
25 On the Internet what is a firewall?

Answers

The Movies: The Oscars (see Quiz 203, page 425)
1 Goldie Hawn. **2** Sissy Spacek. **3** 30cm. **4** Denzel Washington. **5** Eye patches. **6** 20s. **7** Mrs Brown. **8** Jennifer. **9** Julia Roberts. **10** Audrey Hepburn. **11** Gerard Depardieu. **12** A Star is Born. **13** 70th. **14** The English Patient. **15** The Godfather II. **16** Henry. **17** Vangelis. **18** Polish. **19** The Killing Fields. **20** I Just Called to Say I Love You. **21** Huston. **22** Michael Caine. **23** Take My Breath Away. **24** Moonstruck. **25** Wall Street.

Quiz 205 90s Pop Music

Answers - see Quiz 206, page 428

1 Which country is home to Whigfield?
2 What was Loved by Shanice in 1991 and 1992?
3 Who sang about Black Betty in both 1977 and 1990?
4 Which Wimbledon champion sang with John McEnroe?
5 Which liquid product featured the hit Like A Prayer in its advertisement?
6 Danny, Joe, Sonnie, Jon and Jordan were better known as which group?
7 Who asked you to Please Come Home for Christmas in 1994?
8 Which group took a cover of More Than A Woman to No 2 in 1998?
9 What was Blur's first top ten hit?
10 Who said Let's Get Rocked in a 1992 hit?
11 Who released an album in the 90s called Bilingual?
12 Who recorded the original version of Boyzone's Father and Son?
13 Which group were a Sight For Sore Eyes?
14 Who were Ready Or Not from 1996?
15 Who released an album in 1996 called K?
16 Who had a No.1 in 1991 with his debut single The One and Only?
17 Which Sunday paper featured the audition ads for Upside Down?
18 Which song gave The Corrs their first UK Top Ten hit?
19 Which hit by the Spice Girls gave them their 8th UK No. 1?
20 Which hit gave All Saints their 3rd UK No 1 hit in September 1998?
21 What was Boyzone's first UK Top Ten hit ?
22 Who had a UK No 1 with Gym and Tonic in October 1998?
23 What nationality are the vocal and instrumental group Aqua?
24 What was Jamiroquai's first UK Top Ten hit?
25 Which label do Shamen record on?

Answers

Technology & Industry (see Quiz 206, page 428)
1 Hubble. **2** Heathrow. **3** Baby Buggy. **4** Office of Fair Trading. **5** 20s. **6** Freddie Laker. **7** Paris. **8** Eddie George. **9** Jump jet. **10** Oil. **11** Nautilus. **12** Bank of England. **13** BSB. **14** 30s. **15** Imperial. **16** Rex. **17** Korea. **18** France. **19** Harp. **20** Michelin. **21** Piccadilly. **22** Peter Mandelson. **23** People's car. **24** Midland. **25** Washington.

Quiz 206 Technology & Industry

Answers - see Quiz 205, page 427

1 Which telescope was launched into space on board a space shuttle in 1990?
2 Which UK airport became the first to be connected to a city railway system?
3 In the late 60s Owen Finlay Maclaren pioneered what useful item for parents of small children?
4 What was the OFT?
5 In which decade were windscreen wipers patented in the UK?
6 Who launched the Skytrain air service?
7 Which city was the HQ of the European Space programme?
8 Which Bank of England chief said losses in industry in the north east was a small price to pay for low inflation?
9 What type of aircraft was the Hawker Siddley Harrier?
10 What does the Transalaska Pipeline System transport?
11 What was the name of the world's first nuclear powered submarine?
12 Robin Leigh-Pemberton held the top job at which organisation from 1983 to 1993?
13 Which company linked with Sky Television to form BSkyB?
14 In which decade was the Mersey Tunnel opened?
15 What did the first letter I stand for in ICI?
16 What was Britain's first king size cigarette called?
17 In which country were Daewoo cars originally produced?
18 Which country was the first in the world to introduce a driving test?
19 What did Guinness adopt as its trademark in the 60s?
20 Which Andrei built the first factory to mass produce rubber tyres?
21 Which underground line runs to Heathrow Airport?
22 Which Trade & Industry Secretary resigned in 1998?
23 What does Volkswagen actually mean?
24 The first cheque guarantee card was produced by which British bank?
25 In which city are the headquarters of the IMF?

Answers

90s Pop Music (see Quiz 205, page 427)
1 Denmark. **2** Your Smile. **3** Ram Jam. **4** Pat Cash. **5** Pepsi. **6** New Kids On The Block. **7** Bon Jovi. **8** 911. **9** There's No Other Way. **10** Def Leppard. **11** Pet Shop Boys. **12** Cat Stevens. **13** M People. **14** The Fugees. **15** Kula Shaker. **16** Chesney Hawkes. **17** People. **18** Dreams. **19** Goodbye. **20** Bootie Call. **21** Love Me For A Reason. **22** Spacedust. **23** Danish. **24** Too Young To Die. **25** One Little Indian.

Quiz 207 20th C Leaders

Answers - see Quiz 208, page 430

LEVEL 2

1 Sir Christopher Bland replaced Sir Marmaduke Hussey as Chairman of which corporation in 1996?
2 Paul Keating was a controversial Prime Minister of which country?
3 Which Tory Home Secretary refused an application for British citizenship by the Al Fayed brothers in 1996?
4 Who fought the 1997 election, on behalf of the Referendum Party?
5 Aung San Suu Kyi is a controversial leader in which country?
6 Which Russian leader was buried in 1998 in his family's vault?
7 What was the full name of the trades union which Arthur Scargill led?
8 Who in Tony Blair's Cabinet was a racing tipster for the Glasgow Herald?
9 Who became president of the European Commission in 1995?
10 Which spouse of a party leader deputised for Jimmy Young on Radio 2?
11 Which French Prime Minister funeral's was attended by his wife and his mistress in 1996?
12 Who was only the second heir to the throne to marry in the 20th century?
13 Which Eurovision winner became an MEP in the 1999 elections?
14 Which political party leader's aunt was a big lottery winner in 1998?
15 Which Press Secretary left Downing Street for Radio 5 Live?
16 Which world leader married Graca Machel in 1998?
17 Which royal autographed a Man Utd football on a tour of Malaysia?
18 Bill Clinton was Governor of which US state he became President?
19 Who did William Hague beat in the final round of the contest for the Tory Party leadership after the 1997 election?
20 Earl Spencer appeared on whose US chat show?
21 Who replaced King Hussein as King of Jordan?
22 Which surname of a British leader was Ronald Reagan's middle name?
23 What was the surname of the British Roman Catholic Cardinal who died in June 1999?
24 Which daughter of a Prime Minister was a former girlfriend of convicted ex MP Jonathan Aitken?
25 Michael Cashman became an MEP in the 1999 elections after starring for three years in which TV soap?

Answers

Entertainment (see Quiz 211, page 433)
1 Paul McCartney. **2** 70s. **3** Simon Rattle. **4** Hampstead. **5** English Civil War. **6** Ragamuffins. **7** Ballet. **8** Rank. **9** Puerto Ricans. **10** Nottingham. **11** Beer selling establishment, Munich. **12** Three. **13** Short tennis. **14** Mosaic. **15** Wayne Sleep. **16** Blackpool. **17** Moscow. **18** Films - RKO. **19** Janet. **20** Essex. **21** Salzburg. **22** Daisy. **23** Kyoto. **24** USA. **25** Wireplay.

Quiz 208 On the Box

Answers - see Quiz 211, page 433

1 What was the name of the live weekday programme which Vanessa Feltz fronted in her £2 million deal with the BBC?
2 In which series did Michelle Collins play holiday rep Vicki?
3 What is the first name of the builder in Ground Force?
4 Which broadcaster famously said during the Falklands conflict, "I counted them all out and I counted them all back"?
5 David Wilkinson featured in the docu soap about which West End store?
6 Which song did Robson & Jerome sing on Soldier Soldier which launched their singing career?
7 Sharron Davies aka Gladiator Amazon was an Olympic medallist in which sport?
8 Fred Dibnah found fame on TV as a member of what profession?
9 Which Michael Palin series followed in the steps of Phileas Fogg?
10 In which decade did the BBC's Film review programme with Barry Norman begin?
11 What colour was the chair in the first series of Mastermind?
12 Where are the Pebble Mill studios?
13 At what time of day was Multi Coloured Swap Shop shown?
14 What was the manageress managing in The Manageress?
15 Who played Wooster in the 90s version of Jeeves & Wooster?
16 The action of Sharpe took place during which war?
17 Who was the subject of The Private Man, The Public Role?
18 Who narrated The Wombles?
19 In which drama series were Miles and Egg major characters?
20 Where on a Teletubby is its TV screen?
21 In which US state was Sweet Valley High?
22 Which Coronation Street actress played Jimmy Nail's ex wife in Spender?
23 What was the name of Robson Green's character in Soldier Soldier?
24 Which airline was the subject of the docu soap Airline?
25 In which decade did Newsnight start?

Answers

20th C Leaders (see Quiz 207, page 429)
1 BBC. **2** Australia. **3** Michael Howard. **4** James Goldsmith. **5** Burma.
6 Tsar Nicholas II. **7** National Union Of Mineworkers. **8** Robin Cook. **9** Jacques Santer.
10 Glenys Kinnock. **11** Francois Mitterand. **12** Prince Charles. **13** Dana.
14 William Hague's. **15** Charlie Whelan. **16** Nelson Mandela. **17** The Queen.
18 Arkansas. **19** Kenneth Clarke. **20** Oprah Winfrey. **21** Abdullah. **22** Wilson.
23 Hume. **24** Carol Thatcher. **25** EastEnders.

Quiz 209 Sports Bag

Answers - see Quiz 210, page 432

1 Who said in 1998, "The ball doesn't know how old you are"?
2 Which post war cricketer played his first England game aged 18 and his last aged 45?
3 In which sport was Richard Upton found positive in a drugs test in 1998?
4 In the 1998 play offs, which Sunderland player missed the final penalty?
5 In which sport in 90s Britain did Leopards overcome Sharks in a final?
6 Terry Mancini played soccer for which country?
7 In which decade did Alex Higgins first become snooker world champion?
8 What has been won by Australia II and America 3?
9 In which country and in which sport has a Blackadder played in the 90s?
10 Which Arsenal player scored in the 1998 World Cup Final?
11 Which former England captain added Dylan to his name in honour of Bob Dylan?
12 Where was the Derby held during Word War I and World War II?
13 Who was known as The Manassa Mauler?
14 How many people are there in an official tug of war team?
15 In 1994 who won the US Amateur Championship for the first time?
16 In which sport did Steve Baddeley win 143 caps in the 80s?
17 Who did Damon Hill move to when he was dropped by Williams?
18 Which country does boxer Vitali Klitschko come from?
19 In the 90s in which sport in England did Braves perform at a Craven Park?
20 Who won golf's US Open in 1994 and 1997?
21 Which English club did Daniel Amokachi join after 1994 World Cup success with Nigeria?
22 What is the surname of the first father and son cricket captains of England?
23 In 1998 which British boxer took on Shannon Briggs and Zeljko Mavrovic?
24 Golf star Vijay Singh comes from where?
25 The early days of which sport featured the Renshaw twins, the Baddeley twins and the Doherty brothers?

Answers

Screen Legends (see Quiz 210, page 432)

1 Errol Flynn. **2** Friar. **3** Steve McQueen. **4** Greta Garbo. **5** Audrey Hepburn. **6** Casino Royale. **7** Judy Garland. **8** Katharine Hepburn. **9** Ronald Reagan. **10** Michelle Pfeiffer. **11** Robert Downey Junior. **12** Natalie Wood. **13** Fred Astaire. **14** Bob Hope. **15** WWI. **16** Ingrid Bergman. **17** Clark Gable. **18** Mae West. **19** Bridge. **20** Michael Caine. **21** Bing Crosby. **22** Crawford. **23** James Stewart. **24** Rita Hayworth. **25** Violet.

Quiz 210 Screen Legends

Answers - see Quiz 219, page 431

1 Which swashbuckling hero's autobiography was My Wicked Wicked Ways?
2 What is Sean Connery's profession in The Name of the Rose?
3 Who did Ali McGraw marry after they had made The Getaway together?
4 Who spoke for the first time in Anna Christie?
5 Whose voice did Marni Nixon dub in the classic My Fair Lady?
6 In which film did David Niven play James Bond?
7 I Could Go on Singing was the last film of which screen legend?
8 Who was the first actress to receive four Oscars?
9 John Hinckley's obsession with Jodie Foster led him to attempt to kill who?
10 Who got her first big break in Grease 2?
11 Who played Charlie Chaplin in Richard Attenborough's1992 film?
12 Which star of Gypsy and West Side Story married Robert Wagner twice ?
13 Which legendary dancer was Oscar nominated for The Towering Inferno?
14 Which British born comedian completed a record 60th year of a contract with NBC in 1996?
15 Bogart's trademark sneer was due to an injury sustained in which conflict?
16 Which Swedish actress won the Best Supporting Actress Oscar for Murder on the Orient Express?
17 Who uttered the famous lines "Frankly my dear I don't give a damn"?
18 Who was jailed for her 'obscene' stage play Sex?
19 Omar Sharif is a worldwide expert in which game?
20 Which British actor's autobiography was called 'What's It All About?'?
21 Which screen legend's daughter shot JR in Dallas?
22 Which Joan's career revived in Whatever Happened to Baby Jane??
23 Which much loved US actor won the Best Actor Oscar for The Philadelphia Story?
24 Which red haired actress had the Margarita cocktail named after her as her real name was Margarita Cansino?
25 What colour are Elizabeth Taylor's eyes?

Answers

Sports Bag (see Quiz 209, page 431)
1 Mark O'Meara. **2** Brian Close. **3** Swimming. **4** Michael Gray. **5** Basketball. **6** Republic of Ireland. **7** 70s. **8** America's Cup. **9** New Zealand - Rugby Union. **10** Petit. **11** Bob Willis. **12** Newmarket. **13** Jack Dempsey. **14** Eight. **15** Tiger Woods. **16** Badminton. **17** Arrows. **18** Ukraine. **19** Rugby League. **20** Ernie Els. **21** Everton. **22** Cowdrey. **23** Lennox Lewis. **24** Fiji. **25** Tennis.

Quiz 211 Entertainment

Answers - see Quiz 207, page 429

1 Whose work for orchestra and chorus, Standing Stone was premiered at the Albert Hall in 1997?
2 In which decade of the 20th century did the Gang Show cease to be staged annually in London?
3 Who was made principal conductor of the Birmingham Symphony orchestra in 1980?
4 In which part of London is The Round House?
5 The Sealed Knot Society re enacts battles of which war?
6 Followers of raga music call themselves what?
7 Marie Rambert founded a company in what branch of entertainment?
8 Which J A owned over half British cinemas by the mid 1940s?
9 Which ethnic group popularised salsa dancing in New York in the 1980s?
10 Which home town of Robin Hood has an 'experience' centre in his honour?
11 What and where is the Mathser?
12 How many piers does Blackpool have?
13 What type of tennis is usually played by children on a smaller court?
14 What was the first Web browser called?
15 Which dancer founded the company Dash?
16 Which seaside resort has Britain's largest theatre - and largest stage?
17 Which Russian city was famous for its State Circus?
18 The company whose full name was Radio Keith Orpheum produced what?
19 Who was Michael 'Rage' Hardy and James 'Smarty' Cools' female partner in Virtual Cop 2?
20 In which English county is the longest pleasure pier?
21 In which Austrian city, home of Mozart, has an annual music festival been held since 1920?
22 Who is the Princess in the Super Mario Gang?
23 Where in Japan is the Nintendo company based?
24 In which country did rap music begin?
25 What was BT's online gaming service called?

Answers

On The Box (see Quiz 208, page 430)
1 The Vanessa Show. **2** Sunburn. **3** Tommy. **4** Brian Hanrahan. **5** Selfridges. **6** Unchained Melody. **7** Swimming. **8** Steeplejack. **9** Around the World in 80 Days. **10** 70s. **11** Black. **12** Birmingham. **13** Morning. **14** Football club. **15** Hugh Laurie. **16** Napoleonic. **17** Prince Charles. **18** Bernard Cribbins. **19** This Life. **20** Tummy. **21** California. **22** Denise Welch - Natalie. **23** Dave Tucker. **24** Britannia Airways. **25** 80s.

Hard Questions

These are just the ticket. Especially if you've been slightly caught out by the collective intelligence of your teams. (Possibly not of course!)

But perhaps, just maybe, there are a group of rather smart alecs who seem to be getting absolutely everything ten-out-of-ten spot-on. This could become a little irritating. In which case simply (metaphorically, mind) pop a couple of these questions down on the pub floor, low down and out of sight. Then stand back as your confident contestants come charging in for the next quiz round, and watch as they realize the tremendous trickiness of these teasers, trip up and go flying, completely backside over breast as it were.

However, neither you nor the honourable landlord or landlady want everyone scrambling around on the floor, drunkenly diving about. This could become entirely and shamefully detracting from the purety of mind challenge that is implicit in the pub quiz! But, a light sprinkling of these questions, particularly near the end of your quiz, should help a lot, as well as keeping any clever clogs types at a suitably safe distance.

Quiz 1 Pot Luck 1

Answers - see Quiz 2, page 436

1 Asuncion is the capital of which country?
2 In the 1980s the town of Spitak was destroyed in which disaster?
3 Who had hits with Take Your Time and Got To Have Your Love?
4 What is a paravane used for?
5 Dr James Naismith devised which game?
6 In which decade was Jeremy Paxman born?
7 Which world wide magazine was conceived by DeWitt Wallace?
8 To within two years, when were postcodes introduced to the UK?
9 Waterways Airways operates from which country?
10 Who is the elder – Rowan Atkinson or Clive Anderson?
11 What is prase?
12 Who, in 1890, composed the music for the opera Ivanhoe ?
13 A poniard is a type of what?
14 Who led the Expedition of the Thousand in 1860?
15 Which 60s No 1 was written by Madden and Morse in 1903?
16 Which part of the body is affected by thlipsis?
17 Who was found dead in the first episode of EastEnders?
18 Which Mel Brooks film was a spoof of Hitchcock movies?
19 Which road was part of the title of the TV series based on the true story of the Cavendish Hotel?
20 What did Princess Diana once describe as "hard work and no pay"?
21 Antonio Salazar was dictator for many years in which country?
22 Which US anti-terrorist force is based at Fort Bragg?
23 William Benting was an English pioneer of what?
24 By volume, what makes up about 21% of our atmosphere?
25 Who starred with his wife in the film Mr and Mrs Bridge?
26 Whose one and only hit was I've Never Been To Me in 1982?
27 Whose codename was Pink for This Is Your Life?
28 To which Court are US Ambassadors to Britain officially credited?
29 Which US poet had the middle names Weston Loomir?
30 Which was the first African team to compete in the Cricket World Cup?

Answers

TV Detectives (see Quiz 2, page 436)
1 Lynda La Plante. **2** Maisie Raine. **3** Liverpool One. **4** Adrian Kershaw. **5** Reginald Hill. **6** Eddie Shoestring. **7** Charlie's Angels. **8** R.D.Wingfield. **9** CIB. **10** David Renwick. **11** Rupert Davies. **12** Reilly - Ace of Spies. **13** The Rockford Files. **14** Crime Traveller. **15** Denise Welch. **16** Cadfael. **17** Imogen Stubbs. **18** Jasper Carrott. **19** Taggart. **20** Stanton. **21** Van der Valk. **22** Sexton Blake. **23** Gideon's Way. **24** Cordelia Gray. **25** Chief Inspector Haskins. **26** Hercule Poirot. **27** The Body in the Library. **28** Paul Usher. **29** Henry Crabbe. **30** Simon Templar.

Quiz 2 TV Detectives

Answers - see Quiz 1, page 435

1. Which playwright created the character Jane Tennison?
2. Which TV detective was played by Pauline Quirke?
3. In which series was Samantha Janus transferred from the Met to Merseyside?
4. Who was Morse's sidekick in The Wench is Dead?
5. Which novelist created the characters of Dalziel and Pascoe?
6. Which detective worked for Radio West?
7. Which series centred on Townsend Investigations?
8. Which novelist created Jack Frost?
9. Which acronymic part of the Met did Tony Clark work for in Between The Lines?
10. Which writer created off beat sleuth Jonathan Creek?
11. Who introduced the very first series of Detective?
12. In which series did Inspector Tsientsin appear?
13. Which famous series was introduced with a message on an answering machine?
14. In which series was Slade assisted by Holly?
15. Who played Frances Spender in the Jimmy Nail series?
16. Whose investigations are based in Shrewsbury but often filmed in central Europe?
17. Who played mini skirted detective Anna Lee?
18. Whose real-life daughter plays a nanny in The Archers?
19. Which long running series began with a pilot called Killer in 1983?
20. Where did The Cops take place?
21. What was the full name of TV's most famous Dutch detective?
22. Who had a Rolls Royce called The Grey Panther?
23. Which 60s series had Chief Inspector Keen aiding his Commander?
24. Who is the detective in An Unsuitable Job for a Woman?
25. Who was Regan's boss in The Sweeney?
26. Which detective lived at Whitehaven Mansions?
27. Which was the first Miss Marple adaptation to star Joan Hickson on TV?
28. Which actor linked Brookside with Liverpool One?
29. Who had retired from Barstock CID?
30. Claude Eustace Teal was invariably beaten in his dealings with whom?

Answers

Pot Luck 1 (see Quiz 1, page 435)
1 Paraguay. **2** Armenian earthquake. **3** Mantronix. **4** Mine-sweeping. **5** Basketball. **6** 1950s. **7** Reader's Digest. **8** 1968. **9** New Zealand. **10** Clive Anderson. **11** A type of quartz. **12** Sir Arthur Sullivan. **13** Dagger. **14** Garibaldi. **15** Two Little Boys. **16** The blood vessels. **17** Reg Cox. **18** High Anxiety. **19** Duke Street. **20** Motherhood. **21** Portugal. **22** Delta Force. **23** Slimming diet. **24** Oxygen. **25** Paul Newman. **26** Charlene. **27** Barbara Cartland. **28** St. James. **29** Ezra Pound. **30** East Africa (in 1975).

Quiz 3 Pot Luck 2

Answers - see Quiz 4, page 438

1 Phil Read won several World Championships in which sport?
2 What did an alchemist use an alembic for?
3 What was Eternal's first UK Top Ten hit?
4 In Hindu mythology who was goddess of destruction and death?
5 In which country is the Mackenzie River?
6 Which instrument did Lionel Hampton play?
7 Which character was played by June Allyson in the film The Glenn Miller Story?
8 What was President Carter's wife's first name?
9 Who won the first squash World Open Championship?
10 Where is England's national hockey stadium?
11 Who is the elder – Dame Judi Dench or Barbara Taylor Bradford?
12 Who wrote the novel Rodney Stone?
13 How many times is Annie mentioned in the lyrics of Annie's Song?
14 In Swift's novel what was Gulliver's first name?
15 To which part of the body does the adjective 'cutaneous' refer?
16 In which sport were Hildon and Black Bears British Champions?
17 Whose first Top Ten hit was What A Waste in 1978?
18 Who was James I of England's father?
19 Which record label did Geri Halliwell sign up with when she left the Spice Girls?
20 What was the old name for stamp collecting?
21 In which decade was the Earl of Lichfield born?
22 Alfredo di Stefano of Real Madrid fame was born in which country?
23 What is the name of the police officer in West Side Story?
24 Which language's name means 'one who hopes'?
25 Which public figure resigned over dealings concerning prostitute Monica Coghlan?
26 In The Old Testament which two books are named after women?
27 The Prix Goncourt is awarded for what?
28 Who joined Patrick Macnee on the 1990 No 5 UK hit Kinky Boots?
29 Who or what is a dourousouli?
30 Which broadcaster died in June, 1988, at a Leeds hospital from hepatitis?

Answers

Books 1 (see Quiz 4, page 438)
1 John Cleese. **2** Full Disclosure. **3** Diana Rigg. **4** Martin Amis.
5 Dame Barbara Cartland. **6** Ronnie Spector. **7** Six. **8** Pat Conroy. **9** Clare Francis.
10 Madonna. **11** Isaac Asimov. **12** Ordeal. **13** Pig. **14** Sussex. **15** Richard Noble.
16 Torvill & Dean. **17** South Africa. **18** Her Majesty's Stationery Office.
19 Stephen Hawking. **20** Jilly Cooper. **21** Octaves. **22** Noah Webster. **23** Styles.
24 The Rainbow. **25** The Highway Code. **26** Set. **27** Winston Churchill.
28 Guinness Book of Records. **29** Bridget Jones's. **30** Agatha Christie.

Quiz 4 Books 1

Answers - see Quiz 3, page 437

1 Which comedian wrote Families and How to Survive Them with psychiatrist Robin Skynner?
2 What was Andrew Neil's autobiography called?
3 Who wrote an anthology of critics' anecdotes called No Turn Unstoned?
4 Whose first novel was The Rachel Papers in 1974?
5 Which novelist recorded an Album of Love Songs in 1978?
6 Which pop celebrity wrote Be My Baby?
7 How many Barchester Chronicles are there?
8 Who wrote the novel on which the movie Prince of Tides was based?
9 Who went from Deceit and Betrayal to A Dark Devotion?
10 Whose book Sex, coincided with a dance album Erotica?
11 Which science fiction writer wrote the Foundation Trilogy?
12 In the title of the largely autobiographical 1957 Evelyn Waugh novel, what does the main character experience?
13 Who or what was PG Wodehouse's Empress of Blandings?
14 The founder of Wisden played for which English county?
15 Whose quest for speed is recorded in his book Thrust?
16 Which sports stars' autobiography was called Facing the Music?
17 Rider Haggard's colonial service where influenced his books?
18 Who publishes Hansard?
19 Whose 1998 best seller argued that our universe is a part of a super universe?
20 Which novelist's great great grandfather founded The Yorkshire Post?
21 What did Compton Mackenzie refer to each individual volume of his autobiography as?
22 Whose 19th century dictionary standardised US English?
23 Where was the Mysterious Affair in the first Agatha Christie in Penguin paperback?
24 Which colourful DH Lawrence book was banned because of its sexual content along with Lady Chatterley and Women in Love?
25 First appearing in 1931, what sold out of its new edition in three months in 1996?
26 In the Oxford English Dictionary which word has the longest entry?
27 Whose biography already has 22 volumes and is still being written?
28 What is the best-selling copyright book of all time?
29 Whose Diary was written by Helen Fielding?
30 Who wrote romantic novels as Mary Westmacott?

Answers

Pot Luck 2 (see Quiz 3, page 437)
1 Motor Cycling. **2** To distil liquids. **3** Stay. **4** Kali. **5** Canada. **6** Vibraphone. **7** Glenn Miller's wife. **8** Rosalyn. **9** Geoff Hunt. **10** Milton Keynes. **11** Barbara Taylor Bradford. **12** Sir Arthur Conan Doyle. **13** Never. **14** Lemuel. **15** Skin. **16** Polo. **17** Ian Dury & The Blockheads. **18** Lord Darnley. **19** Chrysalis. **20** Timbrology. **21** 1930s. **22** Argentina. **23** Officer Krupke. **24** Esperanto. **25** Jeffrey Archer. **26** Ruth and Esther. **27** Literature (in France). **28** Honor Blackman. **29** A monkey. **30** Russell Harty.

Quiz 5 Pot Luck 3

Answers - see Quiz 6, page 440

1 Who designed the tapestry behind the altar in Coventry Cathedral?
2 An odalisque is a female what?
3 Who founded the record label Maverick Records?
4 Who won the southern junior and senior cross country titles on the same day?
5 Which English poet had the middle name Chawner?
6 The Russian Revolution began in which year?
7 Which King of Hollywood died on the same day as broadcaster Gilbert Harding?
8 Who is the elder – Zoe Ball or Gary Barlow?
9 In the 1980s Greg Lemond became the first American to do what?
10 Whose one and only hit was Little Things Mean A Lot?
11 Who created the Statue of Zeus about 430 BC?
12 What did Lee Marvin throw in Gloria Grahame's face in The Big Heat?
13 What was film star Edward G Robinson's real name?
14 Who was the husband of cellist Jacqueline du Pre?
15 What is the drink kumiss made from?
16 Who came up with The Book of Heroic Failures?
17 What was discovered in 1930 by Clyde Tombaugh?
18 In The Bible, who was King David's father?
19 In 1865, where did the Confederates surrender?
20 Wellesley is the family name of which Dukes?
21 What is a dhole?
22 Norman Parkinson made his name in which field of art?
23 How many times did Steve Donoghue win the Derby?
24 What was Paula Abdul's first UK Top Ten hit from 1989?
25 Lynn Ripley shone under which name as a pop singer?
26 Which theory was formulated by the German physicist Max Planck?
27 Which poet wrote, "She was a phantom of delight"?
28 Which England soccer manager was born in Burnley, Lancashire?
29 The Haber Process manufactures which gas?
30 Who was Banquo's son in Macbeth?

Answers

Albums (see Quiz 6, page 440)
1 Simon & Garfunkel. **2** If U Can't Dance. **3** Mystery Girl. **4** Vertigo. **5** Innuendo. **6** Alison Moyet (Essex). **7** American Pie. **8** Frank Sinatra. **9** All Things Must Pass. **10** Help! - The Beatles. **11** Sheer Heart Attack. **12** A black dog. **13** Face Value. **14** Tinita Tikaram. **15** Blue. **16** Mark Coyle. **17** The Police. **18** The Sound of Music. **19** Goodbye Yellow Brick Road. **20** As a soloist, with Style Council and the Jam. **21** Chris De Burgh. **22** Fleetwood Mac. **23** Saturday Night Fever. **24** A postal strike. **25** Postcard. **26** Atom Heart Mother. **27** WEA. **28** Transformer. **29** Never For Ever. **30** South Pacific.

Quiz 6 Albums

Answers - see Quiz 5, page 439

1 Who released the biggest-selling album in Britain in the 70s?
2 What was the final track on Spice?
3 Which 1988 album confirmed a comeback by Roy Orbison?
4 Dire Straits first albums came out on which label?
5 Which 6.5 minute hit was the title track of Queen's 7th No 1 album?
6 Who charted with an album named after an English county?
7 Don McLean's Vincent came from which album?
8 Which superstar first charted with Come Fly With Me?
9 What was George Harrison's first solo album after the Beatles?
10 What was the first album to make its debut into the UK chart at No 1?
11 Which album contains the line, "My kingdom for a horse"?
12 Who is not on the front cover of Urban Hymns, but features on an inside cover shot?
13 What was Phil Collins' first solo No 1 album?
14 Whose debut album was Ancient Heart?
15 What was the main colour on the cover of Enya's Shepherd Moons?
16 Who along with Oasis gets production credits on Definitely Maybe?
17 Which group had five consecutive No 1 albums from 1979 to 1986?
18 Which original film soundtrack was on the charts for a staggering 382 weeks?
19 Which album first featured Candle In the Wind?
20 Paul Weller has topped the charts in which three guises?
21 Who was the first artist to enter the Swiss album charts at No 1?
22 What was the last Fleetwood Mac album released before the world smash Rumours?
23 Which double-album film soundtrack was a 30 million seller in 1978?
24 Why weren't the album charts published in 1971 for eight weeks?
25 What was the name of Mary Hopkin's debut album?
26 What was Pink Floyd's first album to top the UK charts?
27 Tubular Bells launched the Virgin label, but which label put out Tubular Bells II?
28 Which album originally featured Perfect Day?
29 Which Kate Bush album featured a song about Delius?
30 Which film soundtrack topped the first UK chart in November 1958?

Answers

Pot Luck 3 (see Quiz 5, page 439)
1 Graham Sutherland. **2** Slave. **3** Madonna. **4** David Bedford. **5** Rupert Brooke. **6** 1917. **7** Clark Gable. **8** Zoe Ball. **9** Win the Tour de France. **10** Kitty Kallen. **11** Phidias. **12** Boiling coffee. **13** Emmanuel Goldenberg. **14** Daniel Barenboim. **15** Milk. **16** Stephen Pile. **17** Pluto. **18** Jesse. **19** Appomattox. **20** Wellington. **21** An Asian wild dog. **22** Photography. **23** Six. **24** Straight Up. **25** Twinkle. **26** Quantum theory. **27** Wordsworth. **28** Ron Greenwood. **29** Ammonia. **30** Fleance.

Quiz 7 Pot Luck 4

Answers - see Quiz 8, page 442

LEVEL 3

1 Who was 'The Radio Doctor' in the 1940s and 50s?
2 What was Golden Earring's first UK Top Ten hit?
3 Started in 1850, what were Children's Temperance Societies called?
4 Which motorcyclist appeared in the film Space Riders?
5 Gravure is a term connected with which industry?
6 Who played the leading role in the film The Stone Killer?
7 To the nearest hundred how many islands make up the Maldives?
8 Who was Prime Minister during the General Strike?
9 What does a mendicant do?
10 Mycology is the study of what?
11 What was the Carla Rosa, existing from 1875 to 1958?
12 Who was the last King of Troy according to legend?
13 What was George Burns real name?
14 The word Ombudsman comes from which language?
15 In which decade was Lord Rothschild born?
16 Who wrote the play The Homecoming?
17 Who was writer and producer for New Kids On the Block?
18 In which American state were Bonnie and Clyde killed in an ambush?
19 The Statue of Liberty's 100th birthday was celebrated in which year?
20 Who is the elder – Jeremy Beadle or Christopher Biggins?
21 What is studied by a pedologist?
22 Spencer Gore was the first winner of what?
23 George Galvin performed in music-hall under what name?
24 Placido Domingo studied music at which National Conservatory?
25 Who was the last Prime Minister during the reign of Queen Victoria?
26 The star Betelgeuse is in which constellation?
27 What does the Thomas Hardy novel The Dynasts deal with?
28 Who was the first woman to be Canadian Prime Minister?
29 What do a tinchel of men do?
30 Ahmed Sukarno was President of which country from 1945-62?

Answers

Cricket (see Quiz 8, page 442)
1 Vengsarkar. **2** Mark Taylor. **3** Leeward Islands. **4** Swansea, Glamorgan.
5 Old Trafford. **6** West Indies. **7** Geoff Boycott. **8** Old Trafford.
9 Cigarettes & Alcohol by Oasis. **10** Warren Hegg. **11** Imperial. **12** Australia.
13 Shell Shield. **14** Sunday Express. **15** New Zealand & India. **16** Charlton Athletic.
17 Steve Bucknor. **18** Ivon. **19** India v New Zealand. **20** India & Pakistan.
21 Bob Taylor. **22** No one. **23** Mike Gatting. **24** Wayne Larkins. **25** Mike Atherton.
26 Six. **27** Alec Stewart. **28** Victoria. **29** Craig McDermott. **30** Surrey.

Quiz 8 Cricket

Answers - see Quiz 7, page 441

1 Who was the first overseas batsman to score three Test centuries at Lord's?
2 Which Aussie equalled Don Bradman's batting record in October 1998 but declared rather than beat it?
3 Which West Indian islands did Viv Richards play for?
4 Where did Sobers hit his 36 runs in one over and against whom?
5 Where did Dennis Amiss score the first century in a one day international?
6 Against whom did Mike Atherton make his first international one-day century?
7 Who deputised for Mike Brearley as England skipper four times in 1977-8?
8 Where did Lance Gibbs take most of his wickets in England?
9 Which song did Phil Tufnell choose to escort him on to the field in the New Zealand test tour?
10 Who scored a maiden first class century in his fourth match in 1987?
11 Until 1965 what did 'I' stand for in ICC?
12 Which was the first women's side to win the World Cup in successive occasions?
13 Which competition in the West Indies was replaced by the Red Stripe Cup?
14 David Gower became which newspaper's cricket correspondent when he retired?
15 Graham Gooch became the first player to score 1000 Test runs in an English summer against which sides?
16 Which football team did Alec Stewart's father play for?
17 Who was the first overseas umpire to umpire a Test Match in England?
18 What is David Gower's middle name?
19 Who was playing when the first hat trick by a bowler was scored in a World Cup?
20 Where was the first World Cup outside England played?
21 In '95 Jack Russell broke whose record for dismissals in a Test match?
22 Who sponsored what became the AXA Equity & Law League in '92?
23 Whose autobiography was called Leading From the Front?
24 Who was the first batsman to score centuries against all the counties?
25 Who was the youngest Lancastrian to score a Test century, in 1990?
26 How old was Graeme Hick when he scored a century for his school?
27 Who was the first Englishman to score a century in each innings against the West Indies in 1994?
28 Which Australian state did Ben Hollioake's father play for?
29 Who was Australia's leading wicket taker on the 1994-5 Ashes tour?
30 Who won the first ever county championship?

Answers

Pot Luck 4 (see Quiz 7, page 441)
1 Charles Hill. **2** Radar Love. **3** Bands of Hope. **4** Barry Sheene. **5** Printing (platemaking). **6** Charles Bronson. **7** 1200 (1196). **8** Stanley Baldwin. **9** Begs. **10** Fungi. **11** An Opera Company. **12** Priam. **13** Nathan Birnbaum. **14** Swedish. **15** 1930s. **16** Harold Pinter. **17** Maurice Starr. **18** Louisiana. **19** 1986. **20** Jeremy Beadle. **21** Soils. **22** Men's singles, Wimbledon. **23** Dan Leno. **24** Mexico. **25** Marquis of Salisbury. **26** Orion. **27** The war with Napoleon. **28** Kim Campbell. **29** Hunt. **30** Indonesia.

Quiz 9 Pot Luck 5

Answers - see Quiz 10, page 444

1 Who was the letter which revealed the Gunpowder Plot addressed to?
2 Which lecturer in philosophy wrote The Second Sex?
3 Which non-metallic element has the atomic number 6?
4 What was Marc Almond's first solo UK Top Ten hit?
5 Made in 1975 with George Segal The Black Bird was a spoof of which screen classic?
6 In surveying, how long is a Gunter's Chain in feet?
7 Susan Godfrey was the first victim of which atrocity?
8 In which city was the infamous Gatting and Rana Test Match flare up?
9 Who was older when they died Jimi Hendrix or Marc Bolan?
10 In which film did Chaplin first tackle dialogue?
11 How did Bruce Lee die?
12 What was a lamia in ancient mythology?
13 What date was the Stock Market's Black Monday of the 1980s?
14 Which saint was shot dead in 288 AD by arrows?
15 In TV's The Six Wives of Henry VIII who played wife number one?
16 The European Economic Community was established in which year?
17 In poetry what was hung around the neck of the Ancient Mariner?
18 In which decade was Greta Scacchi born?
19 Who was the first man to win a Grand Prix in a car he designed himself?
20 Whose one and only hit was Turtle Power in 1990?
21 The sword is the symbol of which of the twelve apostles?
22 Which artist painted Bubbles used by Pears to advertise their soap?
23 What can be a unit of length or a small island in Scotland?
24 Who is the elder – Kenneth Branagh or Rory Bremner?
25 What is the name of America's National Cemetery?
26 Where would you have found Zoroastrianism?
27 Robert, Grattan and Emmett were which famous Wild West outlaw gang?
28 Who wrote the play Old Times?
29 In 1941 which American defined the Four Freedoms?
30 What does Zymurgy magazine deal with?

Answers

Battle Stations (See quiz 10, page 444)
1 Auchinleck. **2** Panmunjom. **3** Madras. **4** Mohne & Eder. **5** Vidkun Quisling.
6 Right arm. **7** MacArthur. **8** Reims. **9** Richthofen's Flying Circus.
10 Gavrilo Princip. **11** Treaty of Sevres. **12** Switzerland & Luxembourg. **13** Anzio.
14 Second Battle of the Somme. **15** Major Johnny Paul Koroma. **16** 29. **17** Contras.
18 Dien Bien Phu. **19** American. **20** Ardennes. **21** Japanese. **22** Tobruk.
23 Near Kiev, Ukraine. **24** Spanish Civil War. **25** Michel Aoun. **26** Boer War.
27 Tutsi v Hutu. **28** Passchendaele. **29** Von Moltke. **30** Vichy France.

Quiz 10 Battle Stations

Answers - see Quiz 9, page 443

1 Who led the British forces in the First Battle of El Alamein?
2 Where was the peace treaty signed after the Korean War?
3 What was the only place in India attacked by foreign forces in WWI?
4 Which dams were destroyed by bouncing bombs in 1943?
5 Which Norwegian leader aided the 1940 invasion of his country through non resistance?
6 Which part of his body did Lord Raglan lose at Waterloo?
7 Who was commander of the US forces in the Pacific from March '42?
8 In which city did the German High Command formally surrender to General Eisenhower?
9 What was the German 11th Chasing Squadron known as in WWI?
10 Who assassinated Archduke Franz Ferdinand in 1914 thus precipitating WWI?
11 What was the last of the treaties which ended WWI?
12 Which countries were on either end of the Maginot Line?
13 Which birthplace of Nero was the site of an Allied beachhead invasion in WWII?
14 How is the battle at St Quentin in 1918 also known?
15 Who led the military coup in Sierra Leone's Civil War in 1997?
16 How many countries made up the coalition v Iraq in the Gulf War?
17 In the Nicaraguan Civil War which faction had US support?
18 Where was France's defeat which brought about the division of Vietnam along the 17th parallel?
19 Hitler's plan 'Watch on the Rhine' was aimed at which troops?
20 In which area of Belgium/Luxembourg was the Battle of the Bulge?
21 Which navy was defeated at the Battle of Midway Island in 1942?
22 The retreat by the British from which port brought about the replacement of Auchinleck by Montgomery?
23 Where is Babi Yar, where 100,000 people were slaughtered in 1941?
24 In which war did the Battle of Ebro take place?
25 Which General declared a 'war of liberation' against Syrian occupation of Lebanon in 1989?
26 Which war was ended with the Peace of Vereeniging?
27 Who were the two opposing factions in the Ruandan Civil War in the mid 90s?
28 How is the third battle of Ypres in WWI also known?
29 Who was in charge of the German troops in the First Battle of the Marne?
30 What name was given to that part of France not occupied by the Germans until 1942?

Answers

Pot Luck 5 (see quiz 9, page 443)
1 Lord Monteagle. **2** Simone de Beauvoir. **3** Carbon. **4** The Days of Pearly Spencer. **5** The Maltese Falcon. **6** 66. **7** Hungerford Massacre. **8** Lahore. **9** Marc Bolan. **10** The Great Dictator. **11** Aneurism. **12** A snake-bodied female demon. **13** October 19th. **14** Sebastian. **15** Annette Crosbie. **16** 1957. **17** An albatross. **18** 1960s. **19** Jack Brabham. **20** Partners In Kryme. **21** St Paul. **22** Millais. **23** Inch. **24** Kenneth Branagh. **25** Arlington. **26** Ancient Persia. **27** The Daltons. **28** Harold Pinter. **29** FD Roosevelt. **30** Brewing.

Quiz 11 Pot Luck 6

Answers - see Quiz 12, page 446

1 What was the original family business of Shell Oil developer Marcus Samuel?
2 What was the middle name of Wallis Simpson, later Duchess of Windsor?
3 Which greedy giant was created by Rabelais?
4 Who is the elder – Tony Blair or Pierce Brosnan?
5 What is sorghum?
6 From what is the writing material true vellum made?
7 What is separated by the oval window and the round window?
8 Whose presidential hopes were ended by model Donna Rice?
9 What fraction of a gold object is a carat as a proportional measure?
10 What is a killick?
11 Which country hosted the first women's world angling championship?
12 What was the name of the cat which retired from 10 Downing Street in 1987?
13 What name is given to an animal that may be slaughtered to provide food under Moslem law?
14 In which county did the Tolpuddle Martyrs form a trade union?
15 What is a bowyang ?
16 Which politician said that northerners die of "ignorance and crisps"?
17 In which decade was actress Kristin Scott Thomas born?
18 Which American duo had a Top Ten 8 hit in 1977 with Oh Lori?
19 Where did Alexander the Great die?
20 What relation was Queen Victoria to George IV?
21 Who won the first WBC cruiserweight title in boxing?
22 Why were the Piccard brothers famous in the 1930s?
23 Which Roman god was the god of beginnings and doors?
24 What is gneiss?
25 What was Florence Nightingale the first woman to receive in 1907?
26 What was a 'quod' in old slang?
27 Who preceded David II as King of the Scots?
28 What was Rainbow's first UK Top Ten hit?
29 The Purple Rose of Cairo was written and directed by which actor?
30 Nim was a type of what?

Answers

Quiz and Games (see Quiz 12, page 446)
1 Chris Tarrant. **2** The Moment of Truth. **3** Patrick Kielty. **4** Alan Coren. **5** Kenny Everett. **6** Fern Britton. **7** Carry on Campus. **8** Vincent Price. **9** Countdown (OED). **10** Ally McCoist. **11** Richard Wilson. **12** Blockbusters. **13** Magnus Magnusson kept it. **14** Pass the Buck. **15** Max Robertson. **16** John Leslie. **17** Gaby Roslin. **18** Newspaper – day of birth. **19** Matthew Kelly. **20** Princess Diana. **21** Blind Date. **22** Max Bygraves. **23** Armand Jammot. **24** Ed Tudor-Pole. **25** Double Your Money. **26** Paul Daniels. **27** Round the World. **28** Leslie Crowther. **29** The Great Garden Game. **30** Anthea Redfern.

Quiz 12 Quiz and Games

Answers - see Quiz 11, page 445

1 Who hosted the show which offered a million pound first prize?
2 Which show has a Dream Directory?
3 Who joined Anthea Turner on The National Lottery's Big Ticket?
4 Who opposed Sandi Toksvig in the 90s Call My Bluff?
5 Who was the first male team captain in That's Showbusiness?
6 Who first hosted Ready Steady Cook?
7 Which student quiz was produced by Ginger Productions?
8 Which horror movie actor was on the first Celebrity Squares?
9 In which show might Mark Nyman adjudicate?
10 Who was the footballing A Question of Sport team captain when Sue Barker took over on a regular basis?
11 Who was the Reverend Green in the second series of Cluedo?
12 In which show were you pleased to be on the Hot Spot?
13 What happened to the black chair after the final Mastermind?
14 Which weekday elimination quiz was hosted by Fred Dinenage?
15 Who presented the original Going For a Song?
16 Which Blue Peter presenter took over Wheel of Fortune?
17 Who presented the show which had a Status Quo hit as its theme tune?
18 What do contestants receive at the end of Today's The Day?
19 Who hosted You Bet before Darren Day?
20 Who was the subject of an entire show of 100% in August 1998?
21 Sue Middleton and Alex Tatham famously followed a TV win on which show with marriage?
22 Who presented Family Fortunes immediately prior to Les Dennis?
23 Who created Countdown?
24 Who replaced Richard O'Brien on The Crystal Maze?
25 The Sky's The Limit was a variation of which show?
26 Who did Bob Monkhouse replace on Wipeout?
27 Where were contestants figuratively taken on the quiz show Anthea Turner presented after leaving GMTV?
28 Who first asked contestants to "Come on down"?
29 What was Channel 5's first gardening quiz called?
30 Who was the female half of the first husband and wife team to present The Generation Game?

Answers

Pot Luck 6 (see Quiz 11, page 445)
1 Importing sea shells. **2** Warfield. **3** Gargantua. **4** Tony Blair. **5** A cereal crop. **6** Calf skin. **7** Middle ear and inner ear. **8** Gary Hart. **9** 1/24th. **10** A small anchor. **11** Italy. **12** Wilberforce. **13** Halal. **14** Dorset. **15** String tied to the knee to hitch trousers up. **16** Edwina Currie. **17** 1960s. **18** Alessi. **19** Babylon. **20** Niece. **21** Marvin Camel. **22** Balloonists. **23** Janus. **24** A type of rock. **25** The Order of Merit. **26** A prison. **27** Robert the Bruce. **28** Since You've Been Gone. **29** Woody Allen. **30** An ancient game.

Quiz 13 Pot Luck 7

Answers - see Quiz 14, page 448

1 Who led the British force in 1898 at Omdurman?
2 What was Adam Ant's first UK Top Ten hit?
3 How many cubic centimetres in a cubic metre?
4 In which decade was Selina Scott born?
5 Which real island, famed in fiction, is some 25 miles south of Elba?
6 Who would use a fyke?
7 Who was the first Irish cyclist to win the Tour de France?
8 What first did Bernard Harris achieve when he did his space walk?
9 Who or what is Katherine Gorge?
10 Which two countries are separated by the Kattegat?
11 In which decade did Picasso die?
12 Houses in Sherwood Crescent were destroyed in which disaster?
13 Which classic film was billed as "The Eighth Wonder of the World"?
14 Which Royal House ruled from 1461 to 1485 in England?
15 What is a gribble?
16 How many books are there in The New Testament?
17 Who narrated the TV series The World at War?
18 Which city is the capital of Tibet?
19 In No Way to Treat a Lady what did the killer leave on the brow?
20 What is bohea?
21 The Greek goddess Nyx was the personification of what?
22 What was Telly Savalas' Christian name?
23 What form did the Yahoos have in Gulliver's Travels ?
24 Who is the elder – Tamara Beckwith or Naomi Campbell?
25 Which Rumanian tennis star appeared in the film Players?
26 Whose one and only hit was First Time in 1988?
27 Which place is in Berkshire in England and Pennsylvania in America?
28 Where did the Great Britain rugby league team tour for the first time in 1984?
29 When George Bush senior was elected president who was his Democrat opponent?
30 Which rock star has children called Rufus Tiger and Tiger Lily?

Answers

50s Films (see Quiz 14, page 448)

1 Giant. **2** St Swithin's. **3** Robert Morley. **4** Kim Novak. **5** Darby O'Gill and the Little People. **6** Richard Burton. **7** George Cole. **8** Danny Kaye. **9** Mount Rushmore. **10** Carry On Nurse. **11** Operation Petticoat. **12** Dorothy Dandridge. **13** George Sanders. **14** High Noon. **15** Mike Todd. **16** Viva Zapata!. **17** Jack Lemmon. **18** Anastasia. **19** The Trouble With Harry. **20** The Swan. **21** Yul Brynner. **22** No Way Out. **23** 1915. **24** The Long Hot Summer. **25** Bewitched Bothered and Bewildered. **26** Green Grow the Rushes. **27** William Wyler. **28** Yves Montand. **29** Larry Adler. **30** Judy Garland.

Quiz 14 50s Films

Answers - see Quiz 13, page 447

1 James Dean died during the filming of which film in 1955?
2 In which hospital would you find Sir Lancelot Spratt?
3 Who played George III in Beau Brummell?
4 Who played the blonde that James Stewart was hired to follow in Vertigo?
5 In which 50s film did Sean Connery sing?
6 Which actor wins Christ's robe in a dice game in The Robe?
7 Who played the younger Scrooge in the classic with Alistair Sim?
8 Who replaced Astaire for the Holiday Inn remake White Christmas?
9 Where does the climax of North By Northwest take place?
10 What was the second Carry On film?
11 What was the only film where Tony Curtis and Cary Grant starred together?
12 Whose voice was dubbed by Marilyn Horne in Carmen Jones?
13 Who won Best Supporting Actor for All About Eve?
14 Which film was based on The Tin Star by John W Cunningham?
15 Which one time husband of Elizabeth Taylor produced Around the World in 80 Days?
16 What was the second of Brando's four consecutive Oscar nominations for between 1951 and 1954?
17 Who contributed a song for his 1957 film Fire Down Below?
18 Ingrid Bergman won a second Oscar for which film, marking her return from Hollywood exile?
19 What was Shirley MacLaine's debut film in 1955?
20 What was the last film Grace Kelly made before becoming a princess?
21 Who played the Pharaoh in The Ten Commandments?
22 What was Sidney Poitier's first film, in 1950?
23 The African Queen, made in 1951, is about events in which year?
24 What was the first film in which Paul Newman and Joanne Woodward appeared together?
25 Which song did Rita Hayworth famously sing in Pal Joey?
26 What was Richard Burton's last UK film before turning to Hollywood?
27 Who won his third Best Director for his third Best Picture in 1959?
28 Which French superstar was the husband of the 1959 Oscar-winning Best Supporting Actress?
29 Who composed and played the music for Genevieve?
30 Who was replaced by Betty Hutton in Annie Get Your Gun?

Answers

Pot Luck 7 (see Quiz 13, page 447)
1 Lord Kitchener. **2** Dog Eat Dog. **3** One million. **4** 1950s. **5** Monte Cristo. **6** A fisherman. **7** Stephen Roche. **8** First black man to walk in space. **9** National Park in Australia. **10** Denmark and Sweden. **11** 1970s. **12** Jumbo jet crash, Lockerbie. **13** King Kong. **14** York. **15** A crustacean. **16** 27. **17** Laurence Olivier. **18** Lhasa. **19** A lipstick kiss. **20** Tea. **21** Night. **22** Aristotle. **23** Human. **24** Tamara Beckwith. **25** Ilie Nastase. **26** Robin Beck. **27** Reading. **28** Papua New Guinea. **29** Michael Dukakis. **30** Roger Taylor.

Quiz 15 Around the UK

Answers - see Quiz 16, page 450

LEVEL 3 

1 The Euroroute E24 is from Birmingham to which county town?
2 Which Scottish university was named after a jeweller and an inventor?
3 Which polo ground is in the park of a burnt down former country house?
4 What is the smallest theatre at the Barbican in London called?
5 Where is Grimsetter Airport?
6 Which inlet of the Clyde was used as a US submarine base from the early 60s?
7 In which part of London is Kenwood?
8 Which shipping area is due north of Trafalgar?
9 In which county was the Open University founded?
10 Where in Berkshire is the Atomic Weapons Research Establishment?
11 How many national parks does the Pennine Way pass through?
12 Which wall runs from the river Forth in the east to Clyde in the west?
13 What is the real name of 'Petticoat Lane'?
14 Which county is due north of Buckinghamshire?
15 Where is the Post Office's main sorting office?
16 What name is given to someone born east of the Medway?
17 Which county is due South of Tyne and Wear?
18 Which colloquial name of the main church in Boston serves as a landmark for ships?
19 Who or what was London's Liverpool Street station named after?
20 Where is the official London residence of the Foreign Secretary?
21 What is the administration centre of Wiltshire?
22 How is London's Collegiate Church of St Peter better known?
23 Which House has an Egyptian Hall for banqueting?
24 Which important collection was given to the city of Glasgow in 1944?
25 Which World Heritage Site was built for the Duke of Marlborough?
26 Which house is headquarters and home to the BBC World Service?
27 What is MOMI on London's South Bank?
28 Which famous House is the only surviving part of Whitehall Palace?
29 Where is Scatsa Airport?
30 Which county is due south of Shropshire?

Answers

Pot Luck 8 (see Quiz 16, page 450)
1 Groove between nose and lip. **2** 1940s. **3** Architecture. **4** Joseph Black. **5** Benjamin Britten. **6** The bowie knife. **7** Russia. **8** Family Plot. **9** Baikonur, Tyuratam. **10** Flushing Meadow, New York. **11** Madonna. **12** A Fairy. **13** Winston. **14** A warship. **15** Lynn Anderson. **16** Marsh Marigold. **17** 100-30. **18** Henry Miller. **19** Rudolf Nureyev. **20** The Road to Hell (Part 2). **21** Julia Carling. **22** Arthur. **23** T S Eliot. **24** Annika Sorenstam. **25** Corpuscles. **26** Stewart Copeland. **27** Edwin Land. **28** Neil Simon. **29** Communism. **30** Thomas Edison.

Quiz 16 Pot Luck 8

Answers - see Quiz 15, page 449

1 Where on your body is your philtrum?
2 In which decade was Delia Smith born?
3 Inigo Jones was famous in which profession?
4 Who discovered carbon dioxide in 1754 and called it "fixed air"?
5 Who was the first musician to be made a life peer?
6 What was the Iron Mistress in the film of the same name?
7 Who defeated Sweden's forces at Poltava in 1709?
8 What was the last film directed by Alfred Hitchcock?
9 Where does Russia launch their space missions from?
10 Where is the Louis Armstrong Stadium?
11 Who wrote Gary Barlow's second solo No 1?
12 What is a peri?
13 What was John Lennon's middle name?
14 The opera Billy Budd is set on what?
15 Whose only UK Top Ten hit from 1971 was called Rose Garden?
16 What is the more common name for the flower called the Kingcup?
17 What odds is a horse if it is "Burlington Bertie" in rhyming slang?
18 Who wrote Tropic of Cancer and Tropic of Capricorn?
19 Which ballet dancer died on the same day as Dizzy Gillespie?
20 What was Chris Rea's first UK Top Ten hit?
21 Who is the elder – Julia Carling or Helena Bonham-Carter?
22 What was Sir John Gielgud's first name?
23 Which poet wrote, "I have measured out my life with coffee spoons"?
24 Who was the first woman golfer to head the money lists in Europe and the US, in 1995?
25 Plasma in blood consists of platelets and red and white what?
26 Who was the drummer in the group Police?
27 Who invented the Polaroid camera in 1947?
28 Barefoot in the Park was written by which US playwright?
29 What is opposed by the John Birch Society in the USA?
30 Which famous inventor had the middle name Alva?

Answers

Around the UK (see Quiz 15, page 449)
1 Ipswich. **2** Heriot-Watt. **3** Cowdray Park. **4** The Pit. **5** Orkney. **6** Holy Loch. **7** Hampstead. **8** Finisterre. **9** Buckinghamshire. **10** Aldermaston. **11** Three. **12** Antonine Wall. **13** Middlesex Street. **14** Northamptonshire. **15** Mount Pleasant. **16** Man of Kent. **17** Durham. **18** The Boston Stump. **19** PM Earl of Liverpool. **20** Carlton House Terrace. **21** Trowbridge. **22** Westminster Abbey. **23** Mansion House. **24** The Burrell Collection. **25** Blenheim Palace. **26** Bush House. **27** Museum of the Moving Image. **28** Banqueting House. **29** Shetlands. **30** Hereford and Worcester.

Quiz 17 Books 2

Answers - see Quiz 18, page 452

1 Which TV presenter published his Unreliable Memoirs in 1980?
2 Whose novel A Time to Dance was adapted into a controversial TV drama?
3 In From One Charlie to Another, who did Charlie Watts write about?
4 Which singer wrote the book Tarantula?
5 What was the colour of the first Penguin paperback?
6 Which blonde wrote The Constant Sinner?
7 Which John Grisham book had a record initial print run of 2.8 million?
8 To be considered for the Booker Prize a book has to be published where first?
9 What according to Dickens was "the best of times, the worst of times"?
10 Whose only novel won the Pullitzer Prize in 1937?
11 Which PM wrote Sybil?
12 For which novel did Tom Clancy receive an advance of $14 million?
13 Which joint 1992 Booker Prize winner had his book made into an Oscar winning film?
14 Which Ian Fleming novel has the shortest title?
15 What was Hercule Poirot's last case called?
16 What did J.M. Barrie give the royalties from Peter Pan to?
17 Who received a record breaking advance of £17 million for three novels in 1992?
18 What was the sequel to D.H. Lawrence's The Rainbow?
19 Who created Pomeroy's wine bar for his hero?
20 Whose early thriller include The Eye of the Needle?
21 Who wrote The House of Stairs under a pseudonym?
22 Which detective novelist wrote the screenplay for Strangers on a Train?
23 What was Charles Dickens second novel, after Pickwick Papers?
24 Who wrote The Exorcist which was made into a successful film?
25 How are Patrick Dannay and Manfred B Lee better known?
26 Who produced The Truth That Leads to Eternal Life?
27 Who wrote the historical romance Micah Clarke?
28 Which novelist once owned a Rolls registration number ANY 1?
29 Whose early novels were Bella, Harriet and Prudence?
30 How is the wife of author Eric Siepmann better known?

Answers

Pot Luck 9 (see Quiz 18, page 452)
1 The Zulus. **2** Phyllis Nelson. **3** Jose Maria Olazabal. **4** Aldeburgh. **5** Jess Yates. **6** Varicella. **7** Baseball. **8** Robbie Coltrane. **9** National Theatre. **10** Georgie Fame. **11** Soot. **12** The tennis Grand Slam. **13** Lloyd Grossman. **14** Toulouse Lautrec. **15** A hangman. **16** Paul Gauguin. **17** Hero. **18** Wear it. **19** Picture Post. **20** Turner. **21** 1970s. **22** Battle of Naseby. **23** 1860. **24** New Zealand. **25** A hoofed mammal. **26** Ipswich. **27** Love In Bloom. **28** Kim Appleby. **29** Margaret Atwood. **30** Land's End.

Quiz 18 **Pot Luck 9**

Answers - see Quiz 17, page 451

1 Cetewayo, Dingaan and Chaka have all led which people?
2 Whose one and only hit was Move Closer in 1985?
3 Which injured player did Ian Woosnam replace in the 1995 European Ryder Cup team?
4 Which Suffolk town was the first in Britain to have a woman mayor?
5 Which 1970s presenter of Stars on Sunday was nicknamed 'The Bishop'?
6 What is the correct name for chickenpox?
7 The film The Stratton Story featured which sport?
8 Who is the elder – Phil Collins or Robbie Coltrane?
9 In the 80s which building did Prince Charles compare to a "nuclear power station"?
10 Under what name did musician Clive Powell find fame and fortune?
11 The brown pigment bistre is prepared from what?
12 Maureen Connolly was the first female to perform what?
13 Which food show presenter once played in a band called Jet Bronx and the Forbidden?
14 Which character was played by Jose Ferrer in the film Moulin Rouge?
15 What did Jack Ketch do for a living?
16 Van Gogh's Sunflowers used to hang in the bedroom of which other famous artist?
17 In mythology, who did Leander swim the Hellespont nightly to see?
18 What would you do with a filibeg?
19 Bert Hardy was a staff photojournalist for which periodical?
20 Who painted Snow Storm – Steamboat off a Harbour's Mouth?
21 In which decade was Mandy Smith born?
22 Which battle was the decisive one in the English Civil War?
23 To ten years, when was the National Rifle Association of Great Britain formed?
24 In which country are the Sutherland Falls?
25 What is an alpaca?
26 At which Crown Court was Lester Piggot's tax evasion case?
27 What was American comedian Jack Benny's signature tune?
28 Who had UK Top Ten hits in the 90s with Don't Worry and G.L.A.D.?
29 Who wrote The Handmaid's Tale?
30 What did businessman Peter de Savray buy for £6.7 million in 1987?

Answers

Books 2 (see Quiz 17, page 451)
1 Clive James. **2** Melvyn Bragg. **3** Charlie Parker. **4** Bob Dylan. **5** Blue. **6** Mae West. **7** The Rainmaker. **8** Britain. **9** French Revolution (Tale of Two Cities). **10** Margaret Mitchell. **11** Disraeli. **12** Without Remorse. **13** Michael Ondaatje. **14** Dr No. **15** Curtain. **16** Children's Hospital. **17** Barbara Taylor Bradford. **18** Women in Love. **19** John Mortimer (Rumpole). **20** Ken Follett. **21** Ruth Rendell as Barbara Vine. **22** Raymond Chandler. **23** Oliver Twist. **24** William Blatty. **25** Ellery Queen. **26** Jehovah's Witnesses. **27** Conan Doyle. **28** Jeffrey Archer. **29** Jilly Cooper. **30** Mary Wesley.

Quiz 19 Musical Greats

Answers - see Quiz 20, page 454

1 Which Pete Ham and Tom Evans song has been at No 1 with two different artists?
2 The Isley Brothers and which other Motown act recorded Grapevine before Marvin Gaye?
3 To the nearest year, how long was there between Sinatra's first and second UK No 1s?
4 Where is the singer's home in the lyrics of On The Dock Of The Bay?
5 What was the first song to be Christmas No 1 in two different versions?
6 Which hit for Sweet was the longest running No 1 of 1973?
7 Which 1970 seven week No 1 was best selling UK single of the year?
8 Who did Billy Joel dedicate his 1983 version of Uptown Girl to?
9 What was Elvis Presley's closing number in his Las Vegas stage act?
10 What was Cliff Richard's first self-produced No 1?
11 What was the chief of the Diddymen's only UK No 1?
12 Which standard has the line, "I see friends shaking hands saying how do you do"?
13 Which Beatles hit stayed in the UK Top 50 for 33 weeks in 1963?
14 Who had the first UK No 1 with Unchained Melody?
15 Which film theme was the biggest selling single of 1979?
16 Who took Led Zeppelin's Stairway To Heaven into the singles charts?
17 Who wrote You'll Never Walk Alone?
18 Which heavenly body is mentioned in the title of the song that gave George Michael his 4th solo and Elton John his 3rd No 1?
19 Who played Buddy Holly in the 1978 movie The Buddy Holly Story?
20 Who wrote Aretha Franklin's first UK hit Respect?
21 Which classic was the Walker Brothers second No 1 hit from 1966?
22 Which 1967 No 1 recorded the longest-ever stay in the UK Top 50?
23 Who is the only French solo male singer to reach No 1?
24 How many weeks in total did Whitney Houston top the US and UK charts with I Will Always Love You?
25 Which hit is the only No 1 for writers Gerry Goffin and Carole King?
26 Which song includes the line, "nothing to kill or die for"?
27 What was the colour mentioned in the title of Tom Jones' final No 1 in the 1960s?
28 What is the biggest international hit from Eurovision Song Contest?
29 What was Sam Cooke's real name?
30 What was the Beatles first No 1 in America?

Answers

Pot Luck 10 (see Quiz 20, page 454)
1 Richard. **2** Physics. **3** Alexander Selkirk. **4** US President. **5** The Strand Magazine. **6** The Verve. **7** Chamonix, France. **8** Albert Reynolds. **9** A fusil. **10** Judge Dredd. **11** Have A Go. **12** Room At The Top. **13** Liquids. **14** Shiny Happy People. **15** Gliders. **16** Sean Connery. **17** Royal Flying Corps. **18** Morgan. **19** Grasmere. **20** The skin that separates the nostrils. **21** Anderson. **22** Ian Woosnam. **23** A seal. **24** Prince Andrew of Greece. **25** Troon. **26** Debussy. **27** 1930s. **28** Paul Channon. **29** Average White Band. **30** St Dominic.

Quiz 20 Pot Luck 10

Answers - see Quiz 19, page 453

1 Which christian name derives from the Germanic for 'strong ruler'?
2 What did the Italian Amedeo Avogadro study?
3 The novel Robinson Crusoe was based on whose experiences?
4 What important post did Millard Fillmore hold?
5 Which magazine serialised The Adventures Of Sherlock Holmes in the 1890s?
6 Which group features Peter Salisbury on drums and Simon Jones on bass?
7 Where were the first Winter Olympics held in 1924?
8 Who preceded John Bruton as Prime Minister of Ireland?
9 What can be a type of musket or a type of rhomboid?
10 Walter, the robot with a lisp, featured in which comic strip?
11 Which long running radio quiz show was hosted by Wilfred Pickles?
12 In which John Braine book is Joe Lampton the central character ?
13 What does a manometer measure the pressure of?
14 What was R.E.M's first UK Top Ten hit?
15 Otto Lilienthal was associated with what form of transport?
16 Who is the elder – Sean Connery or Sir Terence Conran?
17 What amalgamated in 1918 with the Royal Naval Air Service to form the RAF?
18 What did the M stand for in E M Forster's middle name?
19 Where is the poet Wordsworth buried?
20 What is your columella?
21 Which Anna claimed to be Anastasia?
22 Who was the first UK golfer to win the World Match-Play Championship?
23 In folktales a silkie was half man and half what?
24 Who was Prince Philip's father?
25 Which British golf course has a hole called the 'Postage Stamp'?
26 Who composed Clair De Lune?
27 In which decade was the Earl of Snowdon born?
28 Who was Transport Secretary at the time of the King's Cross tube fire disaster?
29 Whose only UK Top Ten hit was Pick Up The Pieces in 1975?
30 Black Friars are members of the religious order established by whom?

Answers

Musicial Greats (see Quiz 19, page 453)
1 Without You. **2** The Miracles. **3** 12 years. **4** Georgia. **5** Mary's Boy Child.
6 Blockbuster. **7** In The Summertime. **8** Christie Brinkley. **9** Can't Help Falling In Love.
10 Mistletoe and Wine. **11** Tears. **12** What A Wonderful World. **13** She Loves You.
14 Jimmy Young. **15** Bright Eyes. **16** Far Corporation. **17** Rodgers and Hammerstein.
18 Sun. **19** Gary Busey. **20** Otis Redding. **21** The Sun Ain't Gonna Shine Anymore.
22 Release Me. **23** Charles Aznavour. **24** 24 weeks. **25** I'm Into Something Good.
26 Imagine. **27** Green. **28** Waterloo by Abba. **29** Cook without an 'e'.
30 I Wanna Hold Your Hand.

Quiz 21 Football

Answers - see Quiz 22, page 456

1 Who preceded Frank O'Farrell as Man Utd manager?
2 How did Joan Bazely make history in 1976?
3 Who were the opponents in Peter Shilton's last game for England?
4 Who coached Cameroon to the latter stages of the 1990 World Cup?
5 Who offered the England and Scotland squads a week on his Caribbean island if they won the World Cup in 1998?
6 Which Mexican player in France 98 ran a chain of sandwich shops?
7 Which club's motto is 'Nil Satis Nisi Optimum'?
8 What was the name of the horse jointly owned by Liverpool's Fowler & McManaman?
9 Apart from Preston, which other team did Alan Ball's father play for?
10 Ray Wilkins was sent off while playing for England against which country?
11 Who did Denis Law play for immediately before Man Utd?
12 Who was the only side to beat England over 90 minutes when Venables was manager?
13 Who appeared in a TV ad for bacon before the 1998 World Cup?
14 Who is Sweden's most capped player of all time?
15 Who led Naples to their first ever Italian championship?
16 Which of the Italian sides David Platt played for had the shortest name?
17 Angus Deayton had a trial with which soccer club?
18 Who was fourth in the 1994 World Cup?
19 Roy Hodgson joined Blackburn Rovers from which club?
20 What was Arsenal tube station called before it was called Arsenal?
21 Who was the first Dutchman to play in an FA Cup Final?
22 Who were Man Utd playing when George Best made his debut?
23 Which sides competed in the first all British UEFA Cup Final?
24 Who were the first winners of the Inter Toto Cup?
25 How many times did Bobby Moore captain England in 108 internationals?
26 Which soccer side does Bank of England Governor Eddie George support?
27 Where did Paul Ince captain England for the first time?
28 Which club side were the first to win the South American Cup?
29 Which two members of the '98 Nigerian squad released rap albums?
30 Who won Olympic gold in Barcelona?

Answers

Pot Luck 11 (see Quiz 22, page 456)
1 James Fenimore Cooper. **2** Monkey. **3** Ailurophobia. **4** Turkey. **5** Rudyard Kipling. **6** One. **7** Senegal. **8** Theme from Harry's Game. **9** John Prescott. **10** Fruits. **11** E102. **12** Catalan. **13** Darby & Joan. **14** Princetown. **15** Newport Jazz Festival. **16** From the beginning. **17** Winston Churchill. **18** Eagle. **19** Azerbaijan. **20** With fire. **21** Black eagle. **22** A. **23** J Danforth Quayle. **24** Newton St Boswells. **25** North and South Islands of New Zealand. **26** 1945. **27** Clout. **28** Equatorial Guinea. **29** Belgium. **30** Dot.

Quiz 22 Pot Luck 11

Answers - see Quiz 21, page 455

1 Who wrote the novel The Red Rover ?
2 Which creature is represented in the year the Chinese call hou?
3 A fear of cats is known as what?
4 Which country ruled Greece until 1830?
5 Who wrote the line: 'The female of the species is more deadly than the male'?
6 How many species of ostrich are there?
7 Dakar is the capital of which country?
8 Which theme gave Clannad their first UK Top Ten hit?
9 Who is the elder – John Prescott or Trevor McDonald?
10 The spice allspice is made from which part of a plant?
11 Which 'E' number is used to represent Tartrazine in products?
12 What is the main language of Andorra?
13 Which elderly couple were immortalised in a poem by Henry Woodfall?
14 Where on Dartmoor is Dartmoor prison?
15 Which jazz festival is held annually in Rhode Island?
16 What does the Latin ab initio mean?
17 Which Prime Minister was offered a dukedom when he retired in '55?
18 The constellation Aquila has which name in English?
19 In which country is the city of Baku?
20 What does the musical term 'con fuoco' mean?
21 Which bird appears with two heads on the Albanian flag?
22 Which letter in Braille comprises a single raised dot?
23 Who was Vice President when George Bush was President of the USA?
24 What is the administrative centre for the Scottish Borders region?
25 What are separated by the Cook Straits?
26 In which year did the UK become a member of the UN?
27 Whose one and only UK hit was Substitute in 1978?
28 Which country has the Ekuele and centimos as units of currency?
29 Prime Minister Wilfried Martens was leader of which country?
30 How would the letter E be formed in Morse Code?

Answers

Football (see Quiz 21, page 455)

1 Wilf McGuinness. **2** First woman ref of men's soccer. **3** Italy (1990). **4** Valeri Nepomaniachi. **5** Richard Branson. **6** Jorge Campos. **7** Everton. **8** Some Horse. **9** Halifax Town. **10** Morocco. **11** Torino. **12** Brazil. **13** Peter Schmeichel. **14** Thomas Ravelli. **15** Diego Maradona. **16** Bari. **17** Crystal Palace. **18** Bulgaria. **19** Inter Milan. **20** Gillespie Road. **21** Arnold Muhren. **22** West Brom. **23** Spurs v Wolves. **24** Ajax. **25** 90. **26** Aston Villa. **27** Boston, USA. **28** Santos. **29** Amokachi & Okocha. **30** Australia.

Quiz 23 TV Sitcoms

Answers - see Quiz 24, page 458

1 Of the elderly trio in the first episode of Last of the Summer Wine who was the first to leave the cast?
2 Thirtysomething was set in which US state?
3 Who did Casualty's George play in May to December?
4 What were Private Godfrey's sisters called in Dad's Army?
5 Which bookie did Vince Pinner work for?
6 Who had a wife, daughter and mother in law who were witches?
7 Which sit com star made the album What Is Going To Become of Us All in 1976?
8 Who sang the theme music for You Rang M'Lord with Bob Monkhouse?
9 What was Richard's mother called in To The Manor Born?
10 Which lead character had the nickname Privet?
11 In which series did George, Kramer and Elaine appear?
12 Which TV husband and wife lived in Lanford Illinois?
13 Who was the first manager of the Bayview Retirement Home?
14 Who in his later years had a black home help called Winston?
15 What was the US series on which The Upper Hand was based?
16 Which property was left to Jim Davidson in Up The Elephant and Round the Castle?
17 In which hospital did Sheila Sabatini work?
18 Which sitcom was first called You'll Never get Rich in the US?
19 What was Reg Varney's character called in On the Buses?
20 What was Thelma's surname before she married Likely Lad Bob?
21 Elaine Nardo was the only female cabbie in which company?
22 In which advertising agency did Caroline work in The Upper Hand?
23 What was Harold Steptoe's middle names?
24 Which character in Soap was later given his own series?
25 Who wrote the original series of Shine on Harvey Moon?
26 Which sit com star played Vera Hopkins in Coronation Street?
27 Who was Roger's wife in Outside Edge?
28 Who was the barman of the Nag's Head as frequented by the Trotters?
29 Who created the theme music for One Foot in the Grave?
30 Which show centred round the 1-2-1 Club?

Answers

Pot Luck 12 (see Quiz 24, page 458)

1 Charles Blondin. **2** Vectis. **3** 38. **4** Fish. **5** Welcome to my World. **6** Emma Thompson. **7** John Williams. **8** Nineveh. **9** July 23rd. **10** The Queen. **11** Mazo De La Roche. **12** Cyril Fletcher. **13** A ship's timber. **14** Fred Astaire. **15** Pewter. **16** 1960s. **17** Nine. **18** Arthur. **19** 1992. **20** The Greek alphabet. **21** Bend. **22** Ruff. **23** Shirley Bassey. **24** Westminster Abbey. **25** Fairground Attraction. **26** Architecture. **27** Yellow River. **28** James Buchanan Brady. **29** To spout rainwater from roof gutters to stop it running down the walls. **30** Frank Capra.

Quiz 24 Pot Luck 12

Answers - see Quiz 23, page 457

1. Who crossed Niagara Falls in 1859 on a tightrope?
2. What did the Romans call the Isle of Wight?
3. How old was George Gershwin when he died?
4. What are gar, wrasse, alewife and blenny?
5. What was Jim Reeves' first UK Top Ten hit?
6. Who is the actress daughter of actress Phillida Law?
7. Who composed the music for Jaws and Star Wars?
8. What was the capital of the ancient empire of Assyria?
9. On what date in 1986 did Prince Andrew marry Fergie?
10. Which part did Prunella Scales play in A Question of Attribution?
11. Who wrote the series about the Whiteoak family?
12. Which presenter of That's Life was famous for his odd odes?
13. What is a futtock?
14. Which film star married Robyn Smith in 1980?
15. Which alloy contains 2% antimony, 8% copper and 90% tin?
16. In which decade was Tomasz Starzewski born?
17. How many No 1 singles did Take That have?
18. Which son of Henry VII married Catherine of Aragon in 1501?
19. In what year did Classic FM begin?
20. What are Lambda, Omicron and Tau all found in?
21. Charing, as in Charing Cross comes from an Old English word meaning what?
22. What can be a trump at cards or a type of sandpiper?
23. Who is the elder – Jilly Cooper or Shirley Bassey?
24. Where is English actor David Garrick buried?
25. Who followed up a No 1 with Find My Love?
26. Walter Gropius was famous in what field?
27. What is the natural water form which the Chinese call Huang Ho?
28. Which American speculator and philanthropist had the nickname Diamond Jim?
29. What is the practical purpose of a gargoyle?
30. Who directed the film You Can't Take It With You?

Answers

TV Sitcoms (see Quiz 23, page 457)
1 Michael Bates. **2** Philadelphia. **3** Hilary. **4** Dolly & Cissy. **5** Eddie Brown's. **6** Darrin Stephens (Bewitched). **7** John Le Mesurier. **8** Paul Shane. **9** Mrs Polouvicka. **10** Bernard Hedges. **11** Seinfeld. **12** Roseanne & Dan Conner. **13** Harvey Bains. **14** Alf Garnett. **15** Whose the Boss?. **16** 17 Railway Terrace. **17** The Gillies Hospital. **18** The Phil Silvers Show. **19** Stan Butler. **20** Chambers. **21** The Sunshine Cab Company. **22** Blake & Hunter. **23** Albert Kitchenere. **24** The butler Benson. **25** Marks & Gran. **26** Kathy Staff. **27** Mim. **28** Mike. **29** Eric Idle. **30** Dear John.

Quiz 25 Animal World

Answers - see Quiz 26, page 460

1 What is the only mammal to live as a parasite?
2 How is a Sibbald's rorqual also known?
3 For how many hours in a period of 24 does a giraffe sleep?
4 What is the world's largest rodent?
5 What gives the sloth its greenish appearance?
6 Which mammal lives at the highest altitude?
7 Which animals are famously sold at Bampton Fair?
8 The mammal which can live at the greatest depth is a species of what?
9 From which part of a sperm whale is ambergris obtained?
10 Where does a cane toad squirt poison from?
11 What is the longest type of worm?
12 Where would you find a shark's denticles?
13 What does the male mouse deer have that no other deer has?
14 Where does a browser find food?
15 What is the only bird which can fly backwards?
16 A Clydesdale was originally a cross between a Scottish draught horse and a what?
17 What colour is a mandrill's beard?
18 The wisent is native to where?
19 Lemurs are only found in their natural habitat where?
20 What is the oldest indigenous breed of cat in the US?
21 What is a koikoi?
22 What is the average life expectancy of the mayfly?
23 Which protein is cartilage made up of?
24 The term monkey refers to all primates except apes, humans and what?
25 Why were Samoyeds originally bred?
26 Falabellas are native to where?
27 What is another name for the aye-aye?
28 Which animal has the longest tail?
29 What name is given to the smaller of a rhino's horns?
30 What does it mean if an animal is homoiothermic?

Answers

Pot Luck 13 (see Quiz 26, page 460)

1 Bowden. **2** Plumber. **3** Vladimir and Estragon. **4** Syphilis. **5** Scotland. **6** 1950s. **7** J.J. Barrie. **8** Rocks. **9** Mozambique. **10** Comet. **11** The Agricultural Hall. **12** Scottish Euro 96 single. **13** A diesel engine. **14** Goat Island. **15** Richard Bacon. **16** Painting **17** Mexico. **18** Bronze. **19** Cloudesley Shovell. **20** He was a horse. **21** Irving Berlin. **22** Belgium. **23** After childbirth. **24** Peter Grimes. **25** Enemy Coast Ahead. **26** Michael Crawford. **27** James and John. **28** Call Up The Groups. **29** Sean Kelly. **30** China.

Quiz 26 Pot Luck 13

Answers - see Quiz 25, page 459

1 What was Arthur Askey's middle name?
2 What was the trade of John Galliano's dad?
3 In the Beckett play which characters were Waiting for Godot?
4 Which disease is diagnosed by the Wasserman Test?
5 The King of Alba ruled in which country?
6 In which decade was Sting born?
7 Whose one and only hit was No Charge in 1976?
8 What does a petrologist study?
9 Which African country lies between the sea and Zimbabwe?
10 What are Temple-Tuttle and Kohoutek both types of?
11 In which London hall was England's first official showjumping event held in 1869?
12 Rod Stewart donated the royalties from which single to the Dunblane fund?
13 The ship Petit Pierre was the first to be driven by what in 1902?
14 Which island is in the middle of Niagara Falls?
15 Who was the first Blue Peter presenter to be sacked?
16 For what did John Singer Sargent achieve fame?
17 In which country is the majority of the Yucatan Peninsula?
18 The statue of Albert opposite the Albert Hall is made from what?
19 Which admiral was thrown ashore from his flagship Association in 1707?
20 Why was the Roman consul Incitatus unusual?
21 Who composed God Bless America?
22 Violinist Arthur Grumiaux came from which country?
23 When can a woman suffer puerperal fever?
24 Which George Crabbe poem was made into an opera?
25 The Dambusters film was based on which book?
26 Who is the elder – Michael Crawford or Eric Clapton?
27 Which of Jesus' disciples were sons of Zebedee?
28 What was the Baron Knights' first UK Top Ten hit?
29 Who won the first cycling World Cup?
30 By tonnage, which country is the world's top fishing nation?

Answers

Animal World (see Quiz 25, page 459)
1 Vampire bat. **2** Blue whale. **3** One. **4** Capybara. **5** Algae which grow on it. **6** Mount Everest pika. **7** Exmoor ponies. **8** Bat. **9** Intestine. **10** Behind its eyes. **11** Bootlace worm. **12** On its skin. **13** Canine teeth. **14** Anywhere above ground. **15** Hummingbird. **16** Flemish horse. **17** Yellow. **18** Europe (bison). **19** Madagascar. **20** Maine coon. **21** Poisonous frog. **22** Couple of hours. **23** Collagen. **24** Tarsiers. **25** Herd reindeer. **26** Argentina. **27** Lemur. **28** Asian elephant. **29** Forehead horn. **30** Warm blooded.

Quiz 27 60s Films

Answers - see Quiz 28, page 462

1 In which 60s film did Richard Attenborough sing?
2 Who became head of production at EMI in 1969?
3 Between which two cities is The Great Race set?
4 Who directed the Civil War sequences of How the West Was Won?
5 Who was Camembert in Carry On – Don't Lose Your Head?
6 Who inspired the David Hemmings role in Antonioni's Blow Up?
7 What is unusual about Christopher Lee's terrifying role in Dracula – Prince of Darkness?
8 What was the sequel to A Million Years BC?
9 Who devised the dance routines in Half A Sixpence?
10 Who is the only American in King Rat?
11 Who was the Doctor in the big screen Doctor Who and the Daleks?
12 Which film classic inspired Billy Wilder to make The Apartment?
13 In which film did Peter Sellers first head the cast as Clouseau?
14 Who took over directing Cleopatra mid way through production?
15 Who was the singing voice of Tony in West Side Story?
16 Who wrote the music for Lawrence of Arabia?
17 In which film of her father's did Anjelica Huston make her screen debut?
18 Which golf course featured in Goldfinger?
19 What was Tracy and Hepburn's final movie together?
20 Which pop star starred in Rag Doll in 1960?
21 Which '62 Best Actor studied medicine at the University of California?
22 Who was Oscar nominated for Pasha in Doctor Zhivago?
23 Which 60s Oscar winner was narrated by Michael MacLiammoir?
24 Who killed Ronald Reagan in his last film The Killers?
25 Who did John Wayne play in North to Alaska?
26 For which film did Elizabeth Taylor win her second Oscar?
27 For which role was Dustin Hoffman nominated in 1969?
28 Which of the Redgrave clan appeared in A Man For All Seasons?
29 Who played opposite then wife Claire Bloom in The Illustrated Man?
30 Who was the older winner of the shared Best Actress Oscar in 1968?

Answers

Food & Drink 1 (see Quiz 28, page 462)
1 Liebfraumilch. **2** Warm. **3** Salsa. **4** Stomach remedy. **5** Ice cream. **6** Tomatoes. **7** Crescent shaped (roll). **8** Steen. **9** Stum. **10** Browned at the edges due to age. **11** Sicily. **12** Semi sparkling, fully sparkling. **13** Calzone. **14** Maize. **15** Grapes are partly sun dried before use. **16** San Lorenzo. **17** Portugal. **18** Barsac, Bommes, Fargues, Preignac. **19** Britain. **20** Jennifer Paterson. **21** Canary Islands. **22** Wine and methylated spirits. **23** Salsify. **24** Remuage. **25** Pomerol. **26** Wine award in Germany. **27** Bechamel. **28** Oenology. **29** Escoffier. **30** Mirin.

Quiz 28 Food & Drink 1

Answers - see Quiz 27, page 461

1 Which wine comes from Worms?
2 How is sake usually drunk?
3 Which food shares its name with Latin American big band music?
4 What were angostura bitters originally used for?
5 In the US if a dessert is served 'a la mode' what is served with it?
6 Which vegetable is a passata made from?
7 What shape is a rugelach?
8 What is chenin blanc wine known as in South Africa?
9 Which term describes the fermented grape juice added to wine that has lost its strength to perk it up?
10 If a wine is madeirized what has happened to it?
11 Where is Marsala, famed for its fortified wine?
12 In wine terms what is the difference between frizzante and spumante?
13 Which folded pizza dough dish takes its name from the Italian for trouser leg?
14 Which cereal is polenta made from?
15 How does Malaga wine achieve its dark colour?
16 Which Kensington restaurant was co founded by Mara Berni in 1963?
17 Where does Dao wine come from?
18 In addition to Sauternes itself which four communes can call their wine Sauternes?
19 Where did balti cooking originate?
20 Who has cooked lunches for The Spectator magazine and written for The Oldie?
21 Other than Spain and Portugal where does sack come from?
22 What is a red biddy?
23 Which food is also called the vegetable oyster?
24 In wine making which term describes turning the bottles so the sediment collects at the cork end?
25 In which district of Bordeaux is Chateau Petrus produced?
26 What is pradikat?
27 Which classic French sauce was named after a courtier of Louis XIV?
28 What is the study of wine called?
29 Which chef created the Bombe Nero and the peche melba?
30 Which sweet rice wine is used in Japanese cookery?

Answers

60s Films (see Quiz 27, page 461)
1 Doctor Dolittle. **2** Bryan Forbes. **3** New York & Paris. **4** John Ford.
5 Kenneth Williams. **6** David Bailey. **7** He has no dialogue.
8 When Dinosaurs Ruled the Earth. **9** Gillian Lynne. **10** George Segal. **11** Peter Cushing.
12 Brief Encounter. **13** A Shot in the Dark. **14** Joseph Mankiewicz. **15** Jimmy Bryant.
16 Maurice Jarre. **17** A Walk With Love and Death. **18** Stoke Poges.
19 Guess Who's Coming to Dinner. **20** Jess Conrad. **21** Gregory Peck. **22** Tom Courtenay.
23 Tom Jones. **24** Lee Marvin. **25** Big Sam. **26** Who's Afraid of Virginia Woolf?.
27 Ratso Rizzo. **28** Corin. **29** Rod Steiger. **30** Katherine Hepburn.

Quiz 29 Pot Luck 14

Answers - see Quiz 30, page 464

1. A zinfandel is used for making what?
2. What separates Alaska from the other 48 US states?
3. How many times is 'Um' sung in the chorus of 60s hit Um Um Um Um Um Um?
4. Which TV personality launched the 1998 poppy appeal?
5. On which island which is also a country is Adam's Peak?
6. In which year did London Underground's Bakerloo Line open?
7. Who won Best Actor Oscar for his part in the musical film Amadeus?
8. If you have comedos, what are you suffering from?
9. What is the third largest city in Britain?
10. Who is the elder – David Bowie or Edwina Currie?
11. What is Warwickshire's county motif?
12. What was Cat Stevens' first UK Top Ten hit?
13. What kind of weapon was an arbalest?
14. Which Austrian physicist gave his name to perceived frequency variations under certain conditions?
15. Imran Khan played cricket for which two English counties?
16. From 1957 to 1985, who was the Russian Foreign Minister?
17. Which optical aid was invented by Benjamin Franklin?
18. What was the Bay City Rollers' first UK Top Ten hit?
19. Where are the ethmoid, vomer and zygomatic bones in your body?
20. In which decade was Peter Stringfellow born?
21. The capital of Japan is an anagram of which former capital?
22. Who rode both Toulon and Moonax to St Leger triumphs?
23. Who wrote All Quiet on the Western Front?
24. Where did John McGregor found the first Canoe Club in 1866?
25. What is the main colour on the cover of Celine Dion's album Let's Talk About Love?
26. Who wrote The Sea Wolf?
27. Which European country lost the battle of Ulm in 1805?
28. Who had hits in the 70s with Love Me and If I Can't Have You?
29. Which country has Guyana to the east and Colombia to the west?
30. How did Emiliano Zapata, the Mexican revolutionary, die in 1919?

Answers

Kings and Queens (see Quiz 30, page 464)

1 17 Bruton St, London. **2** The Delhi Durbar. **3** Edward VII. **4** Adelaide. **5** George I. **6** Hit with a cricket ball. **7** George V. **8** Henry II's wife Eleanor of Aquitaine. **9** Edward I (19). **10** It was his second. **11** The Pope. **12** Dunfermline. **13** Square, she was so obese. **14** Richard II. **15** River Soar. **16** Tax collectors. **17** Charles II. **18** St Stephen's Abbey Caen. **19** Henry I. **20** Edward VIII. **21** George I. **22** William IV. **23** Edward VII. **24** Christian IX of Denmark. **25** William II. **26** Opening Blackfriars Bridge. **27** Norfolk. **28** Two. **29** Jane Seymour & Catherine Parr. **30** Gloucester Cathedral.

Quiz 30 Kings and Queens

Answers - see Quiz 29, page 463

1. At which address was Elizabeth II born?
2. Where were George V and Queen Mary crowned Emperor and Empress of India?
3. Who was the only British monarch from the House of Wettin?
4. Who was William IV's queen?
5. Which monarch's mother was Sophia of Bohemia?
6. How did George II's eldest son die?
7. Who was the first British monarch to make a Christmas Day broadcast?
8. Which English king's wife was a former wife of Louis VII of France?
9. Which British monarch produced the most legitimate children?
10. What was notable about Henry VI's coronation in 1470?
11. Who made Henry VIII Fidei Defensor?
12. Where was Charles I born?
13. What shape was Queen Anne's coffin and why?
14. Which English king is reputed to have invented the handkerchief?
15. Where were Richard III's bones thrown when his grave was desecrated?
16. Why was Henry VIII's execution of Richard Empson and Edmund Dudley a popular move?
17. Who was threatened by the Rye House Plot?
18. Where is William the Conqueror buried?
19. Which king founded the first English zoo?
20. Who was the penultimate Emperor of India?
21. The Duchess of Kendal was mistress of which king?
22. Who was the first monarch born in Buckingham Palace?
23. Who was the first Emperor of India?
24. Who was Edward VII's father in law?
25. Which English king was killed by Walter Tyrel?
26. What was Victoria's only public ceremony in 1870?
27. In which county did George V die?
28. How many shirts did Charles I wear for his execution?
29. Who were Henry VIII's two oldest wives?
30. Where was Henry III crowned?

Answers

Pot Luck 14 (see Quiz 29, page 463)

1 Wine. **2** British Columbia. **3** 24. **4** Des Lynam. **5** Sri Lanka. **6** 1906. **7** F. Murray Abraham. **8** Blackheads. **9** Glasgow. **10** Edwina Currie. **11** A standing bear next to a ragged staff. **12** Matthew and Son. **13** A giant crossbow. **14** Christian Doppler. **15** Worcestershire and Sussex. **16** Gromyko. **17** Bifocal lenses. **18** Keep On Dancing. **19** Skull. **20** 1940s. **21** Kyoto. **22** Pat Eddery. **23** Erich Remarque. **24** Richmond, Surrey. **25** Black. **26** Jack London. **27** Austria. **28** Yvonne Elliman. **29** Venezuela. **30** Assassinated.

Quiz 31 Pot Luck 15

Answers - see Quiz 32, page 466

1 Who directed the1930s film Mr Deeds Goes To Town?
2 Which disease did Prince Albert die from?
3 Shogi is a Japanese form of which game?
4 Who wrote The Seven Pillars of Wisdom?
5 Which bird would you find in a squab pie?
6 Who played the lead character in the film The Loneliness of the Long Distance Runner?
7 In which decade was the Marquis of Tavistock born?
8 What was Rolf Harris' first UK Top Ten hit?
9 Which famous actor played Philo Beddoe in two films?
10 Who did Australia beat when they first won cricket's World Cup?
11 What is the legendary ship The Flying Dutchman doomed to do?
12 Which queen of England had most fingers?
13 Who wrote the novel Fair Stood the Wind for France?
14 Who is the elder – Joan Collins or Michael Caine?
15 Whose one and only hit was Eye Level in 1973?
16 To three years, when did the M1 motorway open?
17 What was found in 1939 at Sutton Hoo, in Suffolk?
18 What is of interest to a thanatologist?
19 Where would you find calderas?
20 Who wrote The Lost World?
21 If something is napiform which vegetable shape is it?
22 What part of the body is studied by a myologist?
23 Which song features the words, "Here am I floating round my tin can"?
24 What was the Triangular Trade mainly concerned with?
25 What, in America, is a cayuse?
26 How many strokes underwater may a competitive breast-stroke swimmer make at the start and turn?
27 The town of Carrara in Italy is famous for what?
28 Who wrote humour books naming Mussolini and Hitler in the titles?
29 Who is thought to be the author of the Acts of the Apostles?
30 The Battle of Antietam was in which war?

Answers

Classic No 1s (see Quiz 33, page 466)
1 Wet Wet Wet. **2** Unchained. **3** My Sweet Lord. **4** Wooden Heart. **5** Maggie May. **6** Frankie Laine. **7** Love. **8** Ticket To Ride. **9** Peter Cetera. **10** Herbert Kretzmer. **11** Girls' School. **12** Elton John. **13** The Fly (U2). **14** The Fleet's In. **15** Slade. **16** I Know Him So Well. **17** Whatever Will Be Will Be. **18** Do They Know It's Christmas? **19** Hello Goodbye. **20** Careless Whisper. **21** Bridge over Troubled Water. **22** Who's Sorry Now? **23** Three Times A Lady. **24** John Travolta. **25** You Wear It Well. **26** Claudette. **27** Mike Read. **28** I'm Not In Love. **29** Bohemian Rhapsody. **30** Living Doll.

Quiz 32 Classic No 1s

Answers - see Quiz 31, page 465

1 Who were the first Scottish group to have three No 1s?
2 Which 1955 American movie had Unchained Melody as theme tune?
3 Which No 1 was the first solo single by George Harrison?
4 Which Elvis hit made him the first artist with three consecutive British No 1s?
5 Which Rod Stewart hit was originally the B-side of Reason to Believe?
6 Who was on top of the charts the week Everest was first climbed?
7 What word appears three times in the title of the Gary Glitter No 1 that was covered by Joan Jett in America?
8 What was the first No 1 from the Beatles' second film Help!?
9 Who wrote Chicago's No 1 classic If You Leave Me Now?
10 Which lyricist of Aznavour's She was a writer on Les Mis?
11 What was on the other side of the double A No 1 Mull of Kintyre?
12 Who co-wrote a No 1 duet song under the pseudonym Ann Orson?
13 What finally knocked (Everything I Do) I Do It For You off the No 1 spot?
14 Which film did Frank Ifield's I Remember You originally come from?
15 Which group holds the record for the most consecutive years in which a song has charted?
16 What became the all time best UK selling single by a female duo?
17 Which Doris Day Oscar-winning song was from The Man Who Knew Too Much in 1956?
18 What was the first debut single to enter straight at No 1?
19 Which No 1 hit by the Beatles equalled 7 weeks at the top with From Me To You?
20 What is the only George Michael song for which Andrew Ridgeley takes equal writing credit?
21 Which album title track gave Simon and Garfunkel their biggest hit?
22 Which 1920s standard gave Concetta Franconero a 6 week No 1 hit?
23 Which Commodores classic became Motown's best UK seller?
24 Who is the male half of the duo that have spent most weeks at No 1?
25 Which No 1 mentions Jackie Onassis?
26 Apart from Cathy's Clown, which other No 1 for the Everly Brothers had a girl's name in the title?
27 Which Radio 1 DJ banned Frankie Goes to Hollywood's Relax?
28 Which 10cc hit was covered by Johnny Logan in 1987?
29 Which 1975 megahit remained at No 1 for 9 weeks?
30 Which No 1 hit was Cliff Richard's first million seller?

Answers

Pot Luck 15 (see Quiz 31, page 465)
1 Frank Capra. **2** Typhoid Fever. **3** Chess. **4** Lawrence of Arabia. **5** Pigeon. **6** Tom Courtenay. **7** 1940s. **8** Tie Me Kangaroo Down Sport. **9** Clint Eastwood. **10** England. **11** Sail forever. **12** Anne Boleyn (11). **13** H.E.Bates. **14** Michael Caine (by 2 months). **15** Simon Park Orchestra. **16** 1959. **17** A Saxon ship. **18** Death. **19** Volcanoes (They are craters). **20** Sir Arthur Conan Doyle. **21** Turnip. **22** Muscles. **23** Space Oddity. **24** Slaves. **25** A horse. **26** One. **27** White marble. **28** Spike Milligan. **29** St Luke. **30** American Civil War.

Quiz 33 Pot Luck 16

Answers - see Quiz 34, page 468

1 What is Kyzyl Kum in Russia?
2 Neville Cardus was associated with which sport?
3 Who played Paul Henreid's wife in the film Casablanca?
4 What was the first woman's magazine to be published in 1693?
5 Where did the Dryad nymphs live in Greek mythology?
6 What sort of creature is a killdeer?
7 What type of music is Ira D Sankey particularly noted for composing?
8 How old was Louis Braille when he invented his reading system for the blind?
9 Which actor starred in the silent films Robin Hood, The Three Musketeers and The Black Pirate?
10 What was Five Star's first UK Top Ten hit?
11 Ficus Elastica is the Latin name for which plant?
12 In which sport is there a bonspiel?
13 Arch, loop and whorl are all parts of what?
14 What is pishogue a form of?
15 Permission was given to whom in 1988 to rebuild London's Globe Theatre?
16 In which decade was Emma Thompson born?
17 A fylfot is better known as a what?
18 Alton Byrd was famous in which sport?
19 Who played the magical Supergran in the 1985 TV series?
20 Whose one and only UK Top Ten hit was called Tarzan Boy?
21 Which actor was The Virginian on TV?
22 Who is the elder – Timothy Dalton or Charles Dance?
23 Richard Meade won Olympic gold in which sport?
24 What is the main difference between squash and rackets?
25 In which year was the CBI set up?
26 Whose first Top Ten hit was House of Love?
27 Where is the Caledonian market held?
28 Which battle in 1813 was the last battle of the Peninsular War?
29 Who would use a trochee?
30 Who wrote the play called A Taste of Honey?

Answers

TV Soaps (see Quiz 34, page 468)
1 Sid Owen. **2** Where Will You Be. **3** General Hospital. **4** Ross Kemp. **5** E20.
6 Jean Alexander. **7** Gordon Clegg. **8** Peggy Mitchell. **9** Brookside. **10** Seven network.
11 Southworth, Ewing, Farlow. **12** Ali and Sue Osman. **13** The Banned.
14 Ida and Frank. **15** Los Barcos. **16** Rodney Harrington. **17** JR & Kristin.
18 Commercial Inn. **19** Desmond Carrington. **20** George Peppard.
21 Braddock County. **22** When I Need You. **23** Mark Torrance. **24** Jacob Sugden.
25 Albion Market. **26** The Fowlers. **27** Larry Hagman. **28** 1942. **29** Michael Grade.
30 Helicopter accident in South America.

Quiz 34 TV Soaps

Answers - see Quiz 33, page 467

1 How is David Sutton better known?
2 Sue Nicholls alias Audrey in Coronation Street made which record?
3 Which soap did Demi Moore appear in?
4 Who played Graham Lodsworth in Emmerdale?
5 What is the post code of the London Borough of Walford?
6 Which former soap star played Christine Keeler's mother in Scandal?
7 Which role did impresario Bill Kenwright play in Coronation Street?
8 Jo Warne played which Albert Square character?
9 Which soap featured the 'Free George Jackson' campaign?
10 On which Australian network was Neighbours first shown?
11 In Dallas what three surnames did Miss Ellie have?
12 Who ran the cafe when EastEnders started?
13 Sharon and Kelvin in EastEnders made a record under what name?
14 What were Ken Barlow's parents called?
15 In which village was the BBC's ill fated Eldorado set?
16 Which role did Ryan O'Neal play in Peyton Place?
17 In Dallas who were the parents of baby Christopher?
18 When Emmerdale was filmed at Esholt which pub was used as The Woolpack?
19 Which Radio 2 regular played Chris Anderson in Emergency Ward 10?
20 Who played Blake Carrington in the pilot for Dynasty?
21 In which county was Southfork ranch?
22 Jambo from Hollyoaks recorded which song as Will Mellor?
23 In Dynasty what name did Blake's supposed son Adam use when he first arrived on the scene?
24 Whose funeral was seen in the first episode of Emmerdale Farm?
25 Where was there a pub called The Waterman's Arms?
26 Who lived at 45 Albert Square?
27 Which soap star directed Son of Blob in 1972?
28 A one off 'prequel' about Albert Square was set in which year?
29 Which BBC 1 controller was responsible for moving Neighbours to a prime time viewing slot?
30 In Dallas, how and where did Jock Ewing die?

Answers

Pot Luck 16 (see Quiz 33, page 467)
1 A desert. **2** Cricket. **3** Ingrid Bergman. **4** The Ladies' Mercury. **5** In trees. **6** A bird (Type of plover). **7** Hymns. **8** 15. **9** Douglas Fairbanks. **10** System Addict. **11** Rubber plant. **12** Curling. **13** Fingerprints. **14** Sorcery. **15** Sam Wanamaker. **16** 1950s. **17** Swastika. **18** Basketball. **19** Gudrun Ure. **20** Baltimora. **21** James Drury. **22** Timothy Dalton. **23** 3 Day Eventing. **24** Squash uses a softer ball. **25** 1965. **26** East 17. **27** East end of London. **28** Battle of Vittoria. **29** A poet. **30** Shelagh Delaney.

Quiz 35 Pot Luck 17

Answers - see Quiz 36, page 470

1 With which police identification system is Francis Galton associated?
2 Which trees mainly produced the fossilised resin which becomes amber?
3 Who was born first – Sarah Brightman or Jill Dando?
4 If a ship is careened, what has happened to it?
5 What did Henry Segrave break at Daytona in 1927 and 1929?
6 What was the Beautiful South's first UK Top Ten hit?
7 Which event is the first in a Decathlon?
8 Which US President died on the same day as Aldous Huxley?
9 When is Haley's Comet predicted to make its next visit in Earth's vicinity?
10 Who wrote the Gormenghast Trilogy?
11 In which county is Chequers?
12 The King of which country was the Prisoner of Zenda?
13 Who was the first jockey to record three consecutive Derby wins?
14 What relation to King Arthur was Mordred?
15 Who designed the first lightning conductor?
16 In which decade was Vivienne Westwood born?
17 What is matzo?
18 Which actor played Captain Bligh, Quasimodo and Henry VIII in films?
19 Which Archbishop of Canterbury was burnt at the stake in 1556?
20 Who is the most capped English hockey player?
21 Which country did Frenchman Patrick Juvet love in his 70s UK hit?
22 Who played King Arthur in First Knight?
23 Whose one and only hit was Michelle in 1966?
24 What can be grapnel, sheet and bower?
25 A trudgen is used in which sport?
26 Which river was first explored by Mungo Park, a Scottish surgeon?
27 To five years, when were Nobel Prizes first awarded?
28 In the poem Beowulf, what kills Beowulf?
29 What would you do with a gigot?
30 The sitcom in which Warren Mitchell made his name took its title from which book?

Answers

Golf (see Quiz 36, page 470)
1 South Africa. **2** Gene Sarazen. **3** Gentleman Golfers of Edinburgh. **4** Sandy Lyle. **5** 1989 PGA. **6** Nick Price. **7** John Jacobs. **8** Nick Faldo. **9** Greg Norman. **10** Ivan Lendl. **11** Carnoustie. **12** Royal Lytham. **13** John Daly in 1991. **14** Worcester, Massachusetts. **15** Willie Park. **16** Bobby Jones (in perpetuity). **17** David Leadbetter. **18** Mark Calcavecchia. **19** Nick Faldo. **20** Walter Hagen. **21** 20. **22** Troon. **23** The Walrus. **24** Seven. **25** British Open. **26** Great Britian & Ireland. **27** Twice. **28** Fred Couples. **29** Laura Davies. **30** Royal Portrush.

Quiz 36 Golf

Answers - see Quiz 35, page 469

1 Who retained golf's Dunhill Cup in 1998?
2 Who was the first man to with the US PGA and the US Open in the same year?
3 What was the world's first golf club called?
4 Which golfer was born on Bernard Gallacher's ninth birthday?
5 What was Payne Stewart's first victory in a major?
6 In 1986 Greg Norman equalled whose record low score of 63 in the US Masters?
7 Who did Tony Jacklin replace as Ryder Cup captain?
8 Who was only the second person after Jack Nicklaus to win two successive US Masters?
9 Who did Nick Faldo sensationally beat to win his third US Masters?
10 In August 1996 who made his debut as a pro in the Czech Open?
11 In 1968 what became the longest course ever used for the British Open?
12 Where did Tom Lehman win his first major?
13 When Steve Jones first won the US Open he was the first qualifier to win a Major since who?
14 Where did the very first Ryder Cup take place?
15 Who won the first ever British Open?
16 Who is the President of Augusta National Golf Club?
17 Who did Nick Faldo sack as his coach at the same time as divorcing wife number two?
18 Who was the last American to win the British Open before John Daly in 1995?
19 Who was the first European to win the US Masters in the 90s?
20 Who was the first US born winner of the British Open?
21 How old was Nick Faldo when he was first in a Ryder Cup team?
22 Which golf course boasts a Postage Stamp?
23 What was Craig Stadler's nickname?
24 By how many strokes did Tony Jacklin win his first US Open?
25 Gary Player won all the Majors but which did he win first?
26 Who were the USA's opponents in the Ryder Cup from '73 to '77?
27 How many times did Jack Nicklaus win the US Amateur title before turning pro?
28 Who was the first American to win the US Masters in the 90s?
29 Who admitted losing half a million gambling in 1996?
30 What is the only Irish course to have staged the British Open?

Answers

Pot Luck 17 (see Quiz 35, page 469)
1 Fingerprints. **2** Coniferous trees. **3** Sarah Brightman. **4** Turned on one side for cleaning. **5** Land Speed record. **6** Song for Whoever. **7** 100 metres. **8** J. F. Kennedy. **9** 2061. **10** Mervyn Peake. **11** Buckinghamshire. **12** Ruritania. **13** Steve Donoghue. **14** Nephew. **15** Benjamin Franklin. **16** 1940s. **17** Unleavened bread. **18** Charles Laughton. **19** Thomas Cranmer. **20** John Potter. **21** America. **22** Sean Connery. **23** Overlanders. **24** Anchors. **25** Swimming. **26** River Niger. **27** 1901. **28** A dragon. **29** Eat it. **30** The Book of Common Prayer.

Quiz 37 Pot Luck 18

Answers - see Quiz 38, page 472

1 What was discovered by Garcia Lopez de Cardenas in 1540?
2 Whose first Top Ten hit was titled September?
3 In the Seven Years War who were Britain's two allies?
4 In which decade was Paula Yates born?
5 Who was the first player to score 100 points in a NBA basketball game?
6 Rose Louise Hovick achieved fame under what name?
7 Who is the father of Marsha Hunt's daughter Karis?
8 What is the final line in the film Gone With the Wind?
9 Which newspaper was featured in the TV series Hot Metal?
10 The gemstone ruby is associated with which month?
11 What is the name of Phil and Jill Archer's farm?
12 Who directed the film It Happened One Night?
13 What was the Tote originally known as?
14 Where on your body are the Mounts of the Sun, Mercury and Venus?
15 Which fungal disease has the name Ceratostomella Ulmi?
16 Who created the cartoon character Colonel Blimp?
17 Where is the village of Skara Brae?
18 Who won the 1989 Best Actor Oscar for the film My Left Foot?
19 Who is the elder – Ian Botham or Jim Davidson?
20 Which actor played the title role in the TV series Dear John?
21 Whose theme was a No 4 UK hit in 1959 for Elmer Bernstein?
22 If you are an encratic person, what do you possess?
23 Who said, "There never was a good war, nor a bad peace"?
24 David Beckham made his league debut on loan at which club?
25 Who wrote The White Company?
26 Which general was the youngest in the American Civil War?
27 What was the Fine Young Cannibals first UK Top Ten hit?
28 With which profession is the organisation RIBA associated?
29 Who founded the record label Respond?
30 Who in 1632 painted The Anatomy Lesson of Dr Tulip?

Answers

Famous Celebs (see Quiz 38, page 472)
1 Marianne Faithfull. **2** Terry O'Neill. **3** Ivana Trump. **4** A handbag.
5 Great grand daughter. **6** Pat van den Hauwe. **7** John Aspinall. **8** Sir Anthony Buck.
9 Tavistock. **10** John Galliano. **11** The Queen Mother. **12** Victor Edelstein.
13 Paula Yates. **14** Countess of Dartmouth. **15** Camilla Parker Bowles.
16 Bianca & Mason. **17** Marquess of Bath. **18** Geri Halliwell. **19** The Earl of Lichfield.
20 Alexandra. **21** Salford. **22** Debbie Moore. **23** David Bailey. **24** Architect.
25 Victoria Lockwood. **26** Barbara Cartland. **27** Camilla Parker Bowles.
28 Stella Tennant. **29** John Galliano. **30** Paula.

Quiz 38 Famous Celebs

Answers - see Quiz 37, page 471

1 Whose first husband was John Dunbar when she was 18?
2 Which photographer married Faye Dunaway in 1981?
3 Who announced her engagement to Riccardo Mazzucchelli in 1995?
4 What did Tara Palmer Tomkinson use to hide her modesty when posing nude with three friends?
5 What relation is Camilla Parker Bowles to Edward VII's mistress Mrs Keppel?
6 Who was Mandy Smith's second husband?
7 Who owns the private zoos, Howletts and Port Lympne?
8 Which Tory MP did Maria-Bienvenida Perez Blanco marry?
9 Former deb Henrietta Tiarks became which Marchioness?
10 Who designed the deep blue, lingerie style dress Diana wore in New York in 1996?
11 Who was Duchess of York before Fergie?
12 Who designed Diana's dress when she danced with John Travolta at the White House?
13 Heller Toren is the mother of which blonde celeb?
14 Which title did Raine have before she married the late Earl Spencer?
15 Whose Regency home is Ray Mill House in Wiltshire?
16 What were Regan Gascoigne's step siblings called?
17 Who is famous for his 'wifelets'?
18 Who is Watford Grammar School's most famous old girl?
19 Who was Mick Jagger's best man when he married Bianca?
20 What is Tiggy Legge-Bourke's real first name?
21 Fergie was appointed Chancellor of which University?
22 Who founded the Pineapple Dance Studios in 1979?
23 Who discovered Jean Shrimpton in the 60s?
24 Queen Noor of Jordan studied for what profession before her marriage?
25 Who was the first wife of the ninth Earl Spencer?
26 Whose husbands were Alexander McCorquodale then his cousin Hugh?
27 Who was the most famous daughter of Major Bruce Shand?
28 Who replaced Claudia Schiffer as the face of Chanel?
29 Who became Dior's chief designer in 1996?
30 Which model Hamilton co founded the elephant charity Tusk Force?

Answers

Pot Luck 18 (see Quiz 37, page 471)
1 The Grand Canyon. **2** Earth, Wind & Fire. **3** Hanover and Prussia. **4** 1960s. **5** Wilt Chamberlain. **6** Gypsy Rose Lee. **7** Mick Jagger. **8** "Tomorrow is another day." **9** Daily Crucible. **10** July. **11** Brookfield. **12** Frank Capra. **13** Paris Mutuel. **14** Your hand. **15** Dutch Elm Disease. **16** David Low. **17** The Orkneys. **18** Daniel Day-Lewis. **19** Jim Davidson. **20** Ralph Bates. **21** Staccato's Theme. **22** Self-control. **23** Benjamin Franklin. **24** Preston. **25** Sir Arthur Conan Doyle. **26** George A Custer. **27** Johnny Come Home. **28** Architects. **29** Paul Weller. **30** Rembrandt.

Quiz 39 Pot Luck 19

Answers - see Quiz 40, page 474

1 Who died in the avalanche in Klosters in 1988 involving Prince Charles' party?
2 Who was chairman of the Joint Chiefs of Staff during the Gulf War?
3 How many hours are there in a fortnight?
4 Which modern day explorer has Twisleton-Wykeham as part of his name?
5 In whose reign was the Chelsea Hospital founded?
6 Who was Elizabeth I's State Secretary from 1573 to 1590?
7 Edward Whymper is associated with which leisure activity?
8 What did alchemists call the imaginary object that would turn base metals to gold?
9 What was the surname of the Lord in the TV series The Buccaneers?
10 Who designed and built the world's first iron bridge?
11 Who took her Toot Toot into the pop charts in the 80s?
12 Who is the elder – Sean Bean or Daniel Day-Lewis?
13 What was Michel Platini's club when he was three times European Footballer of The Year?
14 On the Chinese calendar, what is the only bird?
15 Where are the Padang Highlands?
16 What are you if you are described as being an ectomorph?
17 Where did Indian ink originally come from?
18 In which town is Channel TV based?
19 In which decade was Catherine Zeta Jones born?
20 What bird was the symbol of Persia's monarchy from 1739 to 1979?
21 What is the metal zinc extracted from?
22 Which game uses the expression 'J'adoube'?
23 In London what was the Tyburn?
24 Who attempted the programme of social reform called Fair Deal?
25 Where in England might you do a Furry Dance?
26 What are measured in hadal, abyssal and bathyl zones?
27 The Australian Aborigines' creation legend is told in what stories?
28 The word Eskimo means the eaters of what?
29 If you were banting, what would you be doing?
30 What was the Michael Bolton's first UK Top Ten hit?

Answers

Communications (see Quiz 40, page 474)
1 Atlanta, Georgia. **2** Stephen Wozniak & Steven Jobs. **3** Olympic Games in Atlanta. **4** Fibre-optic Link Around the Globe. **5** Puerto Rico. **6** The Branch Mall. **7** Hand held fax machine. **8** Grote Reber. **9** MERLIN. **10** Analogue Digital Converter. **11** 13. **12** So drivers will concentrate. **13** Siding Spring Mountain. **14** 1866. **15** British Library. **16** Tim Berners-Lee. **17** The Confederation Bridge. **18** The Times. **19** Japan. **20** 1940. **21** BBC & ITV. **22** Betamax. **23** Deep Blue. **24** Leslie Ibsen Rogge. **25** Isaac Newton. **26** Nuffield. **27** The Met Office. **28** Water. **29** Catadioptric. **30** Decca.

Quiz 40 Communications

Answers - see Quiz 39, page 473

1 Where is the HQ of CNN?
2 Who founded the Apple Computer Company?
3 Why was the Bellsouth telephone exchange the world's busiest in 1996?
4 What is FLAG?
5 In which country is the world's largest single dish radio telescope?
6 What was the first shopping mall on the Internet called?
7 What sort of communications device is "Pagentry"?
8 Who built the only purpose built radio telescope before WWII?
9 The Lovell Telescope is part of which network?
10 What is an ADC?
11 On household goods how many lines are there on a bar code?
12 Why was the Confederation Bridge built with so many curves?
13 Which mountain is the site of the Anglo Australian telescope in New South Wales?
14 In which decade of which century was the first transatlantic telegraph cable sent?
15 Where is BLAISE used?
16 Who was the World Wide Web originally created by?
17 Which bridge links Prince Edward Island with New Brunswick?
18 Marconi began a regular news service between the UK and US for which newspaper?
19 Where did the world's first major ISDN centre begin operating in '88?
20 When were the first experimental transmissions of colour TV in the US?
21 Who introduced the world's first teletext systems?
22 What was Sony's video cassette system for domestic viewers called?
23 What was the name of the first computer to beat a world chess champion?
24 Who was the first man to be arrested after having his picture on the Internet?
25 The telescope on La Palma in the Canary Islands is named after which scientist?
26 As which Radio Astronomy Laboratory is Jodrell Bank also known?
27 Who owns the Cray Supercomputer?
28 The New York City West Delaware tunnel is used to supply what?
29 What name is given to a telescope which uses lenses and mirrors?
30 Which company in Britain pioneered the videodisc?

Answers

Pot Luck 19 (see Quiz 39, page 473)
1 Major Hugh Lindsay. **2** Colin Powell. **3** 336. **4** Sir Ranulph Fiennes. **5** Charles II. **6** Sir Francis Walsingham. **7** Mountaineering. **8** Philosopher's Stone. **9** Brightlingsea. **10** Abraham Darby. **11** Denise La Salle. **12** Daniel Day-Lewis. **13** Juventus. **14** Cockerel. **15** Sumatra. **16** Thin. **17** China. **18** St Helier. **19** 1960s. **20** Peacock. **21** Sphalerite. **22** Chess. **23** A stream. **24** President Truman. **25** Helston, Cornwall. **26** Ocean depths. **27** Dreamtime Stories. **28** Raw Meat. **29** Dieting. **30** How Am I Supposed To Live Without You.

Quiz 41 Pot Luck 20

Answers - see Quiz 42, page 476

1 What is a line joining any two points on a curve called in geometry?
2 What was Suzi Quatro's first UK Top Ten hit?
3 Which battle is remembered in the USA in April on Patriots' Day?
4 Who directed the films Marathon Man and Billy Liar?
5 Who was the eldest son of Henry III?
6 Who preceded Douglas Hurd as Foreign Secretary?
7 Which part of the body is affected by chorea?
8 Who was William Shakespeare's mother?
9 Which pop singing duo had the real first names of Reg and Pauline?
10 Who founded the Outward Bound Trust?
11 In which decade was Gary Rhodes born?
12 How old was Klaus Barbie when he was sentenced to life for wartime atrocities?
13 What would you do with a kaki?
14 What are Purple Laver and Devil's Apron types of?
15 Where would ichor supposedly have flowed?
16 Which singing twins were Hal and Herbert?
17 In The Bible, what did Job suffer with?
18 Which straits separate India from Sri Lanka?
19 Who referred to international financiers as "gnomes of Zurich"?
20 Who was the second oldest Goon?
21 What was author John Buchan's real title?
22 Which country do the Hausa people live in?
23 What was the name of Don Quixote's horse?
24 Who wrote the opera The Love for Three Oranges?
25 Christopher Nolan was a Whitbread Book of the Year winner with what?
26 Which fur comes from the coypu?
27 Whose only UK Top ten hit was called Shake You Down. in 1986?
28 Who became Minister of Defence when Churchill became PM in 1940?
29 In which Asian country is there an edition of the FT printed?
30 Who is the elder – Paddy Ashdown or Lord Archer?

Answers

Food & Drink 2 (see Quiz 42, page 476)
1 Type of grape. **2** Buck's Club in London. **3** Doner kebab. **4** Belgium.
5 The Dorchester. **6** Caraway seeds. **7** Australia. **8** Salt cod. **9** John Tovey.
10 Chocolate. **11** Top. (garnish). **12** Chile. **13** Ullage.
14 Madame Harel, a French farmer's wife. **15** Chocolate. **16** Greece. **17** Bucket.
18 VDQS. **19** Cinzano, apricot brandy & angostura bitters. **20** Butter made from coconut.
21 Maths. **22** Biscuit. **23** Asparagus. **24** Tarragon, chervil. **25** Plums.
26 Geese or ducks. **27** Lime juice. **28** Mixed green salad. **29** Kebab.
30 Filled tortilla or pancake.

Quiz 42 Food & Drink 2

Answers - see Quiz 41, page 475

1 What is hanepoot?
2 Who or what was Buck's Fizz named after?
3 Which snack's name comes from the Turkish for rotating?
4 Where is the yeastless beer faro made?
5 Where was Anton Mosimann's first position as chef in the UK?
6 Kummel is a Russian liqueur extracted from what?
7 The macadamia is native to where?
8 What is the main ingredient of a brandade?
9 Who opened the Miller Howe restaurant in 1971?
10 In his diary what did Pepys call 'jucalette'?
11 Where in a dish would you put gremolata?
12 Which country has a wine growing area called O'Higgins?
13 Which term indicates the amount of wine by which a container falls short of being full?
14 Who is credited with creating camembert cheese in about 1790?
15 What is the base of a florentine biscuit made from?
16 Where did malmsey wine originate?
17 Balti is the Indian word for what?
18 Which abbreviation indicates wine between the qualities of vin de pays and appellation controle?
19 What are the ingredients of a Mr Callaghan?
20 What is cocose?
21 What did TV cook Sophie Grigson study at university?
22 In Swiss cooking what is a leckerli?
23 What is added to an omelette to make an omelette Argenteuil?
24 Which herbs are put in a béarnaise sauce?
25 Which fruit is used to make slivovitz?
26 Foie gras is the liver of which creatures?
27 In ceviche raw fish is marinated in what?
28 What is a mesclun?
29 A brochette is another name for what?
30 In Mexican cookery what is a quesadilla?

Answers

Pot Luck 20 (see Quiz 41, page 475)
1 Chord. **2** Can The Can. **3** Lexington. **4** John Schlesinger. **5** Edward I. **6** John Major. **7** The central nervous system. **8** Mary Arden. **9** Elton John and Kiki Dee. **10** Kurt Hahn. **11** 1960s. **12** 73. **13** Eat it . **14** Seaweed. **15** In the veins of Greek gods. **16** Kalin Twins. **17** Boils. **18** Palk Straits. **19** Harold Wilson. **20** Harry Secombe. **21** Lord Tweedsmuir. **22** Nigeria. **23** Rosinante. **24** Prokofiev. **25** Under the Eye Of The Clock. **26** Nutria fur. **27** Gregory Abbot. **28** Churchill. **29** Japan. **30** Lord Archer.

Quiz 43 70s Films

Answers - see Quiz 44, page 478

1 What was Sting's debut movie?
2 What was Justin Henry's surname in a 70s Oscar winner?
3 In which film does railwayman Cleavon Little become sheriff?
4 That's Entertainment was a compilation of clips from which studio?
5 Who played Siegfried to Simon Ward's James in All Creatures Great and Small?
6 Which music plays in the background in 10?
7 What was Alan Parker's first feature film?
8 Who starred in and produced The China Syndrome?
9 What was Tom Selleck's first film, in 1970?
10 Who played Winston's father in Young Winston?
11 Whose was the disembodied voice narrating Agatha Christie's And Then There Were None?
12 Who wrote the music for Shaft?
13 Who was the landlord of 10 Rillington Place?
14 Who sang the title song in The Aristocats?
15 For the trailer of which Hitchcock film was the director seen floating in then Thames?
16 Stacy Keach starred in Fat City after who turned it down?
17 Who directed Death Wish?
18 Who was the first director to cast Goldie Hawn in a non comedy film?
19 Who did Jane Fonda play in Julia?
20 Why did Peter Finch not collect his Oscar for Network?
21 Whose music did Malcolm McDowell like in A Clockwork Orange?
22 Who was the only female Oscar winner for One Flew Over the Cuckoo's Nest?
23 Who played the editor of the Washington Post in All the President's Men?
24 Which club features in Cabaret?
25 Who played the brother in The Railway Children?
26 Who was Maid Marian opposite Sean Connery in Robin and Marian?
27 What was the first film in which Julie Christie and Warren Beatty starred together?
28 What was Peter Ustinov's first film as Hercule Poirot?
29 What was the sequel to Love Story?
30 Which film of a Frederick Forsyth novel starred Jon Voight?

Answers

Pot Luck 21 (see Quiz 44, page 478)
1 Anything (omnivore). **2** Bankers. **3** Areas of equal rainfall. **4** Maria (Seas). **5** Kingston, Ontario. **6** Paranoid. **7** Britain. **8** The Order of the Thistle. **9** Bran. **10** Diphtheria. **11** Woody Harrelson. **12** Smoke it (It's a strong cigar). **13** Hecuba. **14** The Go Between (L. P. Hartley). **15** Copper & nickel. **16** White. **17** 1920s. **18** Ethiopia. **19** The Hopman Cup, Perth, Australia. **20** Cuban Rebel Girls. **21** 1930s. **22** Tivoli gardens in Copenhagen. **23** Officer Barraclough. **24** Gamophobia. **25** Army Of Me. **26** Janet Street-Porter. **27** A ship. **28** Euphemism. **29** Lynsey de Paul. **30** Harley Street doctor.

Quiz 44 Pot Luck 21

Answers - see Quiz 43, page 477

1 What is eaten by a pantophagist?
2 Who were the Fuggers?
3 What do isohyet lines indicate on a map?
4 What are the dark, lowland plains on the moon known as?
5 Where, in 1855, is ice hockey thought to have originated?
6 What was the only UK Top Ten hit for the group Black Sabbath?
7 In which country was musician Leopold Stokowski born?
8 Which Scottish order has the motto 'Nemo me impune lacessit'?
9 What was the name of Fingal's dog in Gaelic legend?
10 The Schich Test can be used to test for which disease?
11 In the Oliver Stone film Natural Born Killers, who played Mickey?
12 What do you do with a maduro?
13 Who was Hector's mother in mythology?
14 Which novel starts "The past is a foreign country: they do things differently there"?
15 Which metals is a 50p piece made from?
16 What is the main colour on the cover of the album Spice?
17 In which decade was Betty Boothroyd born?
18 Coptic Christians are found in Egypt and which one other country?
19 Which 1996 tennis tournament saw the debut of a fluorescent ball?
20 What was Errol Flynn's last film in 1959?
21 In which decade was playwright Sir Alan Ayckbourn born?
22 The Festival Garden in Battersea Park are based on which continental gardens?
23 Which part did Brian Wilde play in the TV series Porridge?
24 Which phobia describes a fear of marriage?
25 What was Bjork's first UK Top Ten hit from 1995?
26 Which female media personality has been President of the Ramblers Association?
27 What was a carrack?
28 What term describes using a gentler expression to soften a hard one?
29 Who is the elder – Lynsey de Paul or Noel Edmonds?
30 What was the profession of Jane Asher's father?

Answers

70s Films (see Quiz 43, page 477)
1 Quadrophenia. **2** Kramer. **3** Blazing Saddles. **4** MGM. **5** Anthony Hopkins. **6** Ravel's Bolero. **7** Bugsy Malone. **8** Michael Douglas. **9** Myra Breckinridge. **10** Robert Shaw. **11** Orson Welles. **12** Isaac Hayes. **13** John Reginald Christie. **14** Maurice Chevalier. **15** Frenzy. **16** Marlon Brando. **17** Michael Winner. **18** Spielberg (The Sugarland Express). **19** Lilian Hellman. **20** He died shortly after it was made. **21** Beethoven. **22** Louise Fletcher. **23** Jason Robards. **24** The Kit Kat Club. **25** Gary Warren. **26** Audrey Hepburn. **27** McCabe and Mrs Miller. **28** Death on the Nile. **29** Oliver's Story. **30** The Odessa File.

Quiz 45 TV Gold

Answers - see Quiz 46, page 480

1 Who played Emperor Nero in I, Claudius?
2 Who was the female presenter of Tiswas?
3 Which presenter once played Sir Julius Berlin in Corrie?
4 Which future Oscar nominee played Samantha Briggs in Dr Who?
5 Who was the only female on the first Top of the Pops?
6 In which TV pub did Vince Hill find fame?
7 On The Golden Shot who famously always got her sums wrong?
8 Who was the housekeeper in All Creatures Great and Small?
9 Who was the first presenter of World of Sport on ITV?
10 What was the booby prize on Crackerjack?
11 Who were the trio in Take Three Girls?
12 Who had the role of George Starling written for him in 1963?
13 Who originally shared a flat with Sandra in The Liver Birds?
14 Which comedian starred as himself in the Northern town of Woodbridge?
15 Who played the shop treasurer in The Rag Trade?
16 The lead singer of Herman's Hermits played whose son on TV?
17 Who was the first Teenage Mutant Hero Turtle alphabetically?
18 Who played Yosser in Boys From the Blackstuff?
19 Who was doing the asking in Ask the Family?
20 Who frequently appeared as Nymphia in Up Pompeii?
21 Who starred as Charley Farley, partner of Piggy Malone?
22 Who was the author played by Elaine Stritch in Two's Company?
23 Which sitcom began with a one off play called The Offer?
24 Who played Nancy Astor's husband in the 80s series Nancy Astor?
25 As which character did David Cassidy shoot to fame in the 70s?
26 In My Wife Next Door which sitcom doyenne played George's mother?
27 Who was the only person the horse Mr Ed would talk to?
28 Which character shot Alan Rickman to fame in The Barchester Chronicles?
29 Who played Tom the tap dancing pimp in Pennies From Heaven?
30 Which corporal in M*A*S*H took to wearing women's clothes in order to be discharged?

Answers

Pot Luck 22 (see Quiz 46, page 480)
1 A group hired to applaud. **2** 1982. **3** A torture device. **4** Fabrics. **5** Margaret Atwood. **6** Japan. **7** A crash. **8** A.J. Cronin. **9** His wife Clytemnestra. **10** Kenya. **11** Daddy Cool. **12** Conscription. **13** Ernest Hemingway. **14** Dawn French. **15** Blucher. **16** Trial of the Pyx. **17** Jennie Lee. **18** Newcastle-upon-Tyne. **19** Goldsbrough Orchestra (after its founder). **20** 1868. **21** Princess Yashara. **22** Tiger. **23** 1970s. **24** Veterinary Surgeon. **25** Big Ben. **26** Blow Monkeys. **27** Lord Nolan. **28** Groucho Marx. **29** Massaging you. **30** The farthing.

Quiz 46 Pot Luck 22

Answers - see Quiz 45, page 479

1 What is a claque?
2 In which year did Channel 4 start to broadcast?
3 What was the Scavenger's Daughter used for in the 16th century?
4 What can be sornick, nainsook and samite?
5 Who wrote Life Before Men and The Edible Woman?
6 Which country launched a strike against Russia's fleet in 1904 at Port Arthur?
7 What is the collective name for a group of rhinoceroses?
8 Who created the character Doctor Finlay?
9 In mythology, who murdered the Greek king Agamemnon?
10 The Flame Trees of Thika was set in which country?
11 What was Boney M's first UK Top Ten hit from 1976?
12 What was the Derby Scheme of 1915?
13 Who wrote A Farewell to Arms?
14 Who is the elder – Dawn French or Jennifer Saunders?
15 What name was given to George Stephenson's first locomotive?
16 At which ceremony are coins of the realm tested?
17 Who was Britain's first Minister for the Arts in 1967?
18 Which Northern city was given the Latin name Pons Aelius?
19 What was the English Chamber Orchestra originally called?
20 When was Exchange & Mart first published?
21 Who did Buddha marry before searching for enlightenment?
22 Alphabetically what is the last of the Chinese Zodiac signs?
23 In which decade was actress Dervla Kirwan born?
24 What was the profession of the pneumatic tyre patentee John Dunlop?
25 What, on 31st December 1923, gave its first broadcast?
26 Whose only UK Top Ten hit was It Doesn't Have To Be This Way?
27 Which Lord headed the investigating committee into 'sleaze' in public life in 1995?
28 Who said, "Don't point that beard at me: it might go off"?
29 If someone was Rolfing you, what would they be doing?
30 What ceased to be legal at midnight, December 31st, 1960?

Answers

TV Gold (see Quiz 45, page 479)

1 Christopher Biggins. **2** Sally James. **3** Leonard Sachs. **4** Pauline Collins. **5** Dusty Springfield. **6** Stars and Garters. **7** Anne Aston. **8** Mrs Edna Hall. **9** Eamonn Andrews. **10** Cabbage. **11** Kate, Avril & Victoria. **12** Richard Briers. **13** Dawn. **14** Harry Worth. **15** Sheila Hancock. **16** Len Fairclough's son in Corrie. **17** Donatello. **18** Bernard Hill. **19** Robert Robinson. **20** Barbara Windsor. **21** Ronnie Corbett. **22** Dorothy McNab. **23** Steptoe & Son. **24** Pierce Brosnan. **25** Keith Partridge. **26** Mollie Sugden. **27** Wilbur Post. **28** Obadiah Slope. **29** Christopher Walken. **30** Maxwell Klinger.

Quiz 47 Girl Power

Answers - see Quiz 48, page 482

1 What are Celine Dion's first two words on My Heart Will Go On?
2 What is Tina Turner's highest ever UK solo singles chart position?
3 What did Geri write by her signature on the cover notes of Spice?
4 Which sisters gave Stock/Aitken/Waterman their first No1 hit?
5 In which year was Diana Ross's first UK solo Top Ten hit?
6 Which hit made Helen Shapiro the youngest British artist to reach No 1?
7 Who sang female vocals on the Beautiful South's first No 1?
8 Belinda Carlisle and Bonnie Tyler both covered which 1970 No 1?
9 Who partnered Janet Jackson on her UK No 3 hit Scream ?
10 Who was the first British female soloist to have three chart No 1 hits?
11 Whose first UK Top Ten hit as a solo artist was Light of My Life?
12 Which character was played by Kylie Minogue in The Delinquents?
13 What is Enya's full name?
14 Which Bananarama star went on to join Shakespear's Sister?
15 What was Madonna's first UK No 1?
16 Whose first UK Top Ten hit was Love Resurrection?
17 When did Shirley Bassey first reach the UK Top Ten?
18 Formed in 1981, girl band The Colours charted under which name?
19 What was Dina Carroll's first solo Top Ten hit?
20 Which UK vocalist released an album in 1974 called Ma?
21 Which film featured the Eternal hit Someday in 1996?
22 Whose first UK Top Ten hit was My One Temptation?
23 Which UK No 3 for Stacy Lattisaw was a No 8 for Dannii Minogue?
24 Which lady recorded the original Midnight Train To Georgia?
25 Which lady was Rockin' Around The Christmas Tree in 1987?
26 What did Belinda Carlisle want in her UK No 6 hit from 1990?
27 Which female star first reached No 1 29 years after her first hit?
28 What was the No 3 hit by Youssou N'Dour featuring Neneh Cherry?
29 What type of girl gave Tori Amos her first UK Top Ten hit in 1994?
30 Who was the first solo female to enter the UK charts at No 1?

Answers

Pot Luck 23 (see Quiz 48, page 482)
1 In a road accident. **2** Jehovah's Witnesses. **3** 1940s. **4** A Lizard. **5** Cain. **6** Laurence Sterne. **7** The Rain. **8** Israel. **9** Virginia. **10** Apollo Creed. **11** Seat placed on the back of an elephant. **12** Velasquez. **13** Amazon. **14** Mariah Carey. **15** A sucker. **16** Chemistry. **17** Max Schmeling (German). **18** Ben Elton. **19** Ted Danson. **20** Mont Blanc. **21** Duke of York. **22** Cheese. **23** Beestings. **24** Mexico. **25** Evelyn Waugh. **26** Estelle. **27** London to Penzance. **28** U-boats. **29** Go Wild In The Country. **30** Tennyson.

Quiz 48 Pot Luck 23

Answers - see Quiz 47, page 481

1 How did Marie Curie's husband Pierre die?
2 Which group of people were once known as Millennial Dawnists?
3 In which decade was musician Mark Knopfler born?
4 What are you like if you are described as being saurian?
5 Who was the father of Enoch in The Bible?
6 Who created the character Tristram Shandy?
7 What was the title of Oran 'Juice' Jones only UK hit from 1986?
8 In which country is there a political party called Likud?
9 What was Tammy Wynette's real first name?
10 Which part did Carl Weathers play in the Rocky movies?
11 Where is a howdah normally found?
12 Which Spaniard painted the picture The Rokeby Venus?
13 Which River mouth was discovered by Amerigo Vespucci in 1499?
14 Who joined Boyz II Men in their 1995 No 6 UK hit One Sweet Day?
15 What did P.T. Barnum allegedly say is born every minute?
16 Richard Kuhn, Jutus Liebig and Harold Urey were famous in which scientific field?
17 Who was the first undisputed heavyweight world champion boxer to be European?
18 Who is the elder – Ben Elton or Harry Enfield?
19 Who played the lead male role in the 1995 film Loch Ness?
20 Horace Saussure made the first ascent of where in 1787?
21 Which title is traditionally given to the second son of the monarch?
22 What sort of food is Dunlop?
23 What is a cow's first milk after calving called?
24 Which country celebrates the National holiday, the 'Day of the Dead'?
25 Who wrote A Handful of Dust?
26 What's Geri Halliwell's middle name?
27 The train the Cornish Riviera ran from where to where?
28 In the Second World War what did the Germans send out in 'wolf packs'?
29 What was Bow Wow Wow's first UK Top Ten hit?
30 Who wrote the poems Maud and Locksley Hall?

Answers

Girl Power (see Quiz 47, page 481)
1 Every Night. **2** Three. **3** Girl Power. **4** Mel and Kim Appleby. **5** 1970.
6 You Don't Know. **7** Briana Corrigan. **8** Freda Payne's Band of Gold.
9 Michael Jackson. **10** Sandie Shaw. **11** Louise. **12** Lola Lovell.
13 Eithne Ni Bhraonain. **14** Siobhan Fahey. **15** Into The Groove. **16** Alison Moyet.
17 1957. **18** The Bangles. **19** Don't Be A Stranger. **20** Lena Zavaroni.
21 Hunchback of Notre Dame. **22** Mica Paris. **23** Jump To The Beat.
24 Cissy Houston. **25** Kim Wilde. **26** (We want) The Same Thing. **27** Lulu.
28 7 Seconds. **29** Cornflake Girl. **30** Mariah Carey.

Quiz 49 Sporting Moments

Answers - see Quiz 50, page 484

1 Which Grand National winner was the first to be trained by a woman?
2 David Broome was the first British showjumping champion on which horse?
3 Which side turned up when the crowd sang "There's only one team in Tallinn"?
4 Who broke the world 5,000m by 11 seconds in 1995?
5 Jesse Owens was part of which university team when he set his three world records?
6 Who was the second player to hit a maximum 36 runs off one over?
7 In which road in Oxford did Roger Bannister run his four minute mile?
8 How many people witnessed Brazil's defeat by Uruguay in the 1950 World Cup Final?
9 Who was the first athlete to break 13 minutes for the 5,000m?
10 Who made Chris Boardman's winning bicycle in Barcelona?
11 Which famous pacemaker founded the London Marathon?
12 Which Grand National horse was the first to cross the line the year the race was abandoned?
13 By what score did Steve Davis lose the World Professional Championship Final in 1985?
14 Who was the first man to break one minute for 100m breaststroke in a 25m pool?
15 With whom did Steve Redgrave take the second of his four Olympic golds?
16 Which British man ran the fastest mile in the 80s?
17 Why did Susan Brown make history in 1981?
18 Which was the last horse before Lammtarra in 1995 to win the classic triple?
19 How many times did Nadia Comaneci score a perfect 10 at Montreal in 1976?
20 To the nearest 10 minutes, how long did it take Brian Lara to score his record 501 against Durham in 1994?
21 Who caddied for Tiger Woods on his first US Masters victory?
22 How many races out of the 16 did Nigel Mansell win to become World Champion?
23 Who was the first player since WWII to score more than 30 goals in three consecutive seasons?
24 Where was Harvey Smith when he made his infamous V sign?
25 Who did Virginia Wade beat to win her Wimbledon Singles title?
26 How many League games had Stanley Matthews played before his final match aged 50?
27 Seb Coe simultaneously held three world records, at which distances?
28 To the nearest 100 what were the odds against Frankie Dettori's seven Ascot wins?
29 Who broke the 1500, 3000 and 5000m records in 1994?
30 Who did Mike Tyson beat to become the youngest WBC champion?

Answers

Pot Luck 24 (see Quiz 50, page 484)
1 50. **2** Polio. **3** A plant. **4** Jack London. **5** Roads. **6** Hobson - the butler/valet. **7** An ornamental hanging in a church. **8** He was shot dead. **9** King Crabbs. **10** Chris Evans. **11** Vanessa Redgrave. **12** A small barrel. **13** Eight. **14** Cliff Richard. **15** Insects. **16** Priests. **17** Four. **18** Win golf's British and US Opens. **19** Toni Braxton. **20** Harold Wilson. **21** 29th February. **22** Donald Coggan. **23** A rainbow bridge. **24** Michael Foot. **25** Parsec. **26** Sir Matt Busby. **27** A silken fabric. **28** Artillery. **29** Athenia. **30** 1940s.

Quiz 50 Pot Luck 24

Answers - see Quiz 49, page 483

1 How many chapters are in the book of Genesis in The Bible?
2 The Salk vaccine was developed against which disease?
3 What is a Venus's Looking Glass?
4 Who wrote White Fang?
5 What were constructed in the Highlands by General Wade in 1724?
6 What was the name of the John Gielgud character in the film Arthur?
7 What is a dossal?
8 What happened in Northern Ireland to Bananarama's road manager?
9 What was the Royal name of the band formed by Jimmy Nail?
10 Who is the elder – Chris Evans or Paul Gascoigne?
11 In the film Isadora who played the role of Isadora Duncan?
12 What is a barrico?
13 How many American colleges and universities are in the Ivy League?
14 Who played the lead role in the film Take Me High?
15 Cicada are types of what?
16 Who are in charge in a theocracy?
17 How many lines has a clerihew?
18 What was Patty Sheehan the first woman to do in the same year?
19 Breathe Again was the first UK Top Ten hit for which female vocalist?
20 Who had been Britain's youngest cabinet member before William Hague?
21 Frederick is born on which day in The Pirates Of Penzance?
22 Who was Archbishop of Canterbury from 1974 to 1980?
23 What was Bifrost in Norse mythology?
24 Which Labour leader was accused by The Sunday Times of being a Russian agent?
25 Which unit of measurement is equal to 3.2616 light years?
26 Which Man Utd manager appeared in a film called Cup Fever?
27 What was sendal?
28 What is a firearm called if it has a calibre over 20mm?
29 Which British liner was the first to be sunk by a U-boat on the first day of the Second World War?
30 In which decade was actor David Jason born?

Answers

Sporting Moments (see Quiz 49, page 483)
1 Corbiere. **2** Beethoven. **3** Scotland. **4** Haile Gebreselassie. **5** Ohio State University. **6** Ravi Shastri. **7** Iffley Road. **8** 200,000. **9** Said Aouita. **10** Lotus. **11** Chris Brasher (pacemaker for Bannister). **12** Esha Ness. **13** 18-17. **14** Adrian Moorhouse. **15** Andrew Holmes. **16** Steve Cram. **17** First woman to take part in the boat race. **18** Mill Reef (1971). **19** Seven. **20** 7hr 54 mins. **21** Mike 'Fluff' Cowan. **22** Nine. **23** Alan Shearer. **24** Hickstead. **25** Betty Stove. **26** 700. **27** 800m, 1000m, 1500m. **28** 25,095-1. **29** Noureddine Morceli. **30** Trevor Berbick.

Quiz 51 20th Century

Answers - see Quiz 52, page 486

LEVEL 3

1 What was the last ruling dynasty of China?
2 Which oil field blow-out caused an 8.2 million gallon spill in April 1977?
3 Who became Europe's youngest head of state at 28 in 1993?
4 Where was Archbishop Makarios exiled by the British in the mid 50s?
5 Which Deputy Ministerial post did Winnie Mandela hold in Nelson Mandela's first government?
6 Which German Chancellor achieved post war reconciliation with France in the 50s and early 60s?
7 Who became the youngest ever member of the GLC in 1969?
8 Which political parties linked in the UK in the 80s to form the Alliance?
9 Which Middle East leaders were awarded the Nobel Peace Prize in 1994?
10 Which film studio released the first talking film?
11 In the Watergate scandal, who or what was CREEP?
12 What was the occupation of Jean Bertrand Aristide of Haiti?
13 Wembley Stadium was completed for which event?
14 Harold Wilson became Baron of where on his elevation to the peerage?
15 Which quotation from Richard III was used to describe the end of 1978 and beginning of 1979?
16 What was nicknamed 'The Flapper Vote' in 1928?
17 Who succeeded the Ayatollah Khomeini as political leader of Iran?
18 Who was the first president of an independent Mozambique?
19 J Arthur Rank entered films in the 30s to promote which cause?
20 In 1987, what did the Tower Commission investigate in the US?
21 Where was the Recruit Scandal of 1988?
22 Which minister in Thatcher's government shared his name with Henry VIII's chaplain?
23 What did the initials of film company RKO stand for?
24 Whose gang did Al Capone's men massacre on Valentine's Day 1929?
25 A shortage of which commodity was a major issue in the 1998 Indian election?
26 At what number Cromwell Street did Rose and Fred West live?
27 King Michael abdicated which throne in 1947?
28 Who did Jacques Santer replace as President of the European Commission?
29 The 1964 Rivonia Trial involved those opposed to what?
30 What was the name of Franco's fascist party in Spain?

Answers

Pot Luck 25 (see Quiz 52, page 486)

1 Vanessa Feltz. **2** Dublin. **3** Bookbinding. **4** Sculling. **5** James Joyce. **6** New York. **7** The flying shuttle. **8** Ken Boothe. **9** Cultivation of plants without soil. **10** Charles II. **11** A whip. **12** Mark Twain. **13** Handsome. **14** Stalin. **15** The Zaire. **16** Four. **17** Horses. **18** Dr Michael Stroud. **19** 1940s. **20** The Victoria Falls. **21** A pine cone. **22** Troops. **23** Muirfield. **24** King Baudouin (Belgium). **25** Esther. **26** September. **27** Ground-hog Day. **28** End Of The Road. **29** Poetry. **30** Salmon.

…z 52 Pot Luck 25

…swers - see Quiz 51, page 485

1 Who is the elder – Paul McKenna or Vanessa Feltz?
2 In which city in 1882 were the Phoenix Park murders?
3 What is Roxburghe a style of?
4 Actor Thomas Doggett is remembered by an award in which sport?
5 Which writer died in Zurich after an operation for an ulcer in 1941?
6 Which city's underground has more stations than any other?
7 Which weaving invention was invented by John Kay?
8 Who was first to take Everything I Own to No 1 ?
9 What is hydroponics?
10 The Rye House Plot of 1683 was aiming to assassinate which king?
11 What is a quirt?
12 Who wrote A Connecticut Yankee in King Arthur's Court?
13 The Christian name Kenneth derives from the Gaelic for what?
14 Which Soviet dictator died on the same day as composer Prokofiev?
15 What is the unit of currency in The People's Republic of Congo?
16 How many No 1 albums did Take That have?
17 Which animals can suffer the disease strangles?
18 Who went with Ranulph Fiennes on his trek across Antarctica in '95?
19 In which decade was Gloria Hunniford born?
20 What were discovered by David Livingstone in 1855?
21 What is a strobilus another name for?
22 The name Commandos comes from an Afrikaans word for what?
23 Where did Nick Faldo win his first British Open?
24 Which European King died in 1993?
25 Which Biblical woman is the Jewish festival Purim a celebration to?
26 In which month is Prince Harry's birthday?
27 In America what is the 2nd February called?
28 What was Boyz II Men's first UK Top Ten hit?
29 Bragi was the Norse god of what?
30 Grilse, Alevins and Kelts are all forms of what?

Answers

20th Century (see Quiz 51, page 485)
1 Manchu or Qing ('Ching'). **2** Ekofisk. **3** Mario Frick of Liechtenstein. **4** Seychelles. **5** Arts & Science. **6** Konrad Adenauer. **7** Jeffrey Archer. **8** Liberals and SDP. **9** Arafat, Rabin, and Peres. **10** Warner Brothers. **11** Committee to RE-Elect the President. **12** Priest. **13** British Empire Exhibition 1924. **14** Rievaulx. **15** Winter of discontent. **16** Vote to women over 21. **17** Rafsanjani. **18** Samora Machel. **19** Methodism. **20** Irangate. **21** Japan. **22** Nicholas Ridley. **23** Radio Keith Orpheum. **24** Bugs Moran. **25** Onions. **26** 25. **27** Romania. **28** Jacques Delors. **29** Apartheid. **30** Falange.

Quiz 53 Hobbies 1

Answers - see Quiz 54, page 488

1 Who owns the Sydney Harbour Casino?
2 Which eating house did Ruthie Rogers found?
3 What was the name of the board game launched by Terry Venables?
4 1949 saw what innovation in the game of badminton?
5 Who founded the Harlem Globetrotters?
6 How many tiles are there in a game of mah-jong?
7 Who designs clothes for younger people under the Emporio label?
8 What type of art was known as Jugenstil in Germany?
9 How long is the rope in water skiing?
10 In the early days of cinema how long would a 'two reeler' last?
11 Serigraphy is also known as what?
12 What name is given to the style of skiing on a single broad ski?
13 Which type of outdoor spectacular was created by Paul Houdin and first shown at the Chateau de Chambord in 1952?
14 Which craft takes its name from the Arabic for 'striped cloth'?
15 Where did canasta originate?
16 What are the two winning numbers made with two dice in craps?
17 Who opened Les Quat' Saisons in 1977?
18 If you follow FINA rules which sport do you practise?
19 How many dominoes are there in a double six set?
20 Southampton boast of having the first sports area of what type in the country?
21 Which sport would interest you if you followed the work of the ACS?
22 Ellem in Scotland is the oldest club of what type?
23 In the Role-Playing Game known as D&D, what does the second D stand for?
24 Where do cycle races called criteriums take place?
25 If you spent your leisure time in a sulky where would you be?
26 If you were spelunking in the US what would you be doing?
27 In 1976 the NBA and the ABA merged in which sport?
28 In sepek takrow you can hit the ball with any part of the body except which?
29 General Choi Hong Hi is responsible for the development of which martial art?
30 What position does the canoeist adopt in Canadian canoeing?

Answers

Pot Luck 26 (see Quiz 54, page 488)
1 Smetana. **2** Mary Peters. **3** Pool. **4** Nine years old. **5** John Wesley. **6** Ballet. **7** Heliopolis. **8** The Mediterranean. **9** T. Rex. **10** Bernard Bresslaw. **11** Second sight. **12** Robin Williams. **13** Robert McClure. **14** Gary Lineker. **15** Nicaragua. **16** Scotland. **17** It is haunted. **18** The Futhark. **19** The eyes. **20** My Prerogative. **21** On the Thames. **22** Ronald Searle. **23** Tannenburg. **24** Horse. **25** 1960s. **26** Clergy. **27** Pact of Steel. **28** Clint Eastwood. **29** Mary O'Brien. **30** Fox.

Quiz 54 Pot Luck 26

Answers - see Quiz 53, page 487

LEVEL 3

1 Who composed the opera The Bartered Bride?
2 Who won the 1972 Olympic pentathlon title?
3 In the film The Baltimore Bullet which game was featured?
4 How old was Henry III when he became King?
5 Who said, "I look upon the world as my parish"?
6 In which performing art was Beryl Grey famous?
7 Where in Egypt did Cleopatra's needle originally stand?
8 The Silk Road ancient trade route ran between China and where?
9 Micky Finn played bongos in which pop group?
10 Whose only UK Top Ten Hit was Mad Passionate Love from 1958?
11 Deuteroscopy is the common name for what?
12 Which actor links Awakenings, Toys and Cadillac Man?
13 Who was the first admiral to pass through the Northwest Passage?
14 Who is the elder – Nicholas Lyndhurst or Gary Lineker?
15 Daniel Ortega was President of which country from 1981-1990?
16 Where was the Encyclopaedia Britannica first published?
17 Why is Chinge Hall in Lancashire famous?
18 What name is given to the Runic alphabet?
19 What are affected by nystagmus?
20 What was Bobby Brown's first UK Top Ten hit?
21 Where were Frost Fairs held in London until 1831?
22 Which illustrator created the girls of St Trinians?
23 Where were the Russians defeated by the Germans from 26-30th August 1914?
24 Which creature is represented in the year the Chinese call 'ma'?
25 In which decade was pop superstar Mick Hucknall born?
26 Crockford's is a register of what?
27 Italy and Germany formed a military alliance in 1939 called what?
28 Who won the Best Director Oscar in 1992 for Unforgiven?
29 What is Dusty Springfield's real name?
30 What's the English name of the constellation Vulpecula?

Answers

Hobbies 1 (see Quiz 53, page 487)
1 Kerry Packer. **2** River Cafe. **3** The Manager. **4** Plastic shuttlecocks. **5** Abraham Saperstein. **6** 144. **7** Armani. **8** Art Nouveau. **9** 23m or 75 feet. **10** 20 minutes. **11** Silk screen printing. **12** Monoboarding. **13** Son et lumiere. **14** Macramé. **15** Uruguay. **16** 7 & 11. **17** Raymond Blanc. **18** Swimming. **19** 28. **20** Bowling green. **21** Cricket. **22** Angling. **23** Dragons. **24** Town or city centres. **25** Small cart in harness racing. **26** Potholing. **27** Basketball. **28** Arms and hands. **29** Taekwondo. **30** Kneeling.

Quiz 55 80s Films

Answers - see Quiz 56, page 490

LEVEL 3

1 In whose stately home was the Tarzan film Greystoke filmed?
2 What was Sharon Stone's first film, in 1980?
3 Uncle Buck was the debut of which movie star?
4 May Day was the Bond girl in which film?
5 What was the occupation of Madame Sousatzka in the Shirley Maclaine film?
6 Who had a lead role in the movie version of Rising Damp who wasn't in the TV sitcom?
7 Who did Alan Rickman play in Die Hard?
8 Who are the two letter writers in 84 Charing Cross Road?
9 Which son of a pop star appears as Jackson's friend in Moonwalker?
10 In which film did Jack Nicholson say the catchphrase "Here's Johnny"?
11 Who played Mrs La Motta in Raging Bull?
12 Which film all but bankrupted United Artist in 1980?
13 Which ailing actor's voice was dubbed by Rich Little in Curse of the Pink Panther?
14 Who played Meryl Streep's eccentric friend in Plenty?
15 Who won an Oscar for his first major role in 1982?
16 Who was Glenn Close's character in Dangerous Liaisons?
17 Which film included the song It Might Be You?
18 Who was the only Cambodian Oscar winner of the 80s?
19 Who was the only winner of an Oscar and a BAFTA for Platoon?
20 Who was nominated as Best Supporting Actress for The Color Purple?
21 In the film A Royal Love Story, who played Princess Diana?
22 The Color of Money recreated the character from which film?
23 Which father and son appeared in Wall Street?
24 Which role did Kevin Kline play in A Fish Called Wanda?
25 Which. presidential candidate's cousin won an Oscar for Moonstruck?
26 Apart from Music and Visual Effects, which other Oscar did E.T. win?
27 Who directed Psycho III?
28 Whose music features on the soundtrack of When Harry Met Sally?
29 Whose novel was Warren Beatty's Reds based on?
30 Who was the aerobics instructor in Perfect?

Answers

TV Times 1 (see Quiz 56, page 490)
1 Prince Edward. **2** Fiona Armstrong & Michael Wilson. **3** Dudley Moore. **4** Sinead O'Connor. **5** Urquhart in House of Cards. **6** French & Saunders. **7** Greta Scacchi. **8** Tumbledown. **9** Frank Skinner. **10** Tony Hart. **11** Tutti Frutti & Fortunes of War. **12** Beavis & Butthead. **13** Ethel Merman. **14** Jack Lemmon. **15** Helen Hewitt. **16** Richard Branson. **17** Jean Marsh. **18** Clive Anderson. **19** Faith, Hope & Charity. **20** Mike Ahearne. **21** Alan Clark. **22** Steve Houghton. **23** Phelan. **24** Westward. **25** Jimmy McGovern. **26** Hotel. **27** Lynne Franks. **28** Alec Baldwin. **29** Timothy Dalton. **30** Frank Muir.

Quiz 56 TV Times 1

Answers - see Quiz 55, page 489

1 Who set up the production company Ardent?
2 Which duo first presented the breakfast show on GMTV?
3 Who appeared in a Tesco ad chasing chickens around France?
4 Who tore up a picture of the Pope on US TV in 1993?
5 Which character said, "You might very well think that, but I couldn't possibly comment"?
6 Who originally appeared in cabaret as the Menopause Sisters?
7 Who had a small role in Bergerac before starring in Heat and Dust?
8 Which play told of Falklands casualty Robert Lawrence?
9 How is comedian Chris Collins better known?
10 Who designed the Blue Peter logo?
11 For which two series did Emma Thompson win best actress BAFTAs two years in succession?
12 Who duetted with Cher on I Got You Babe in 1994?
13 Which Hollywood actress played Lola Lasagne in Batman?
14 Who was Frank Ormand, the Pretzel man in The Simpsons?
15 What was the prison chief called in The Governor?
16 Which British entrepreneur once guested on Friends?
17 Who played Joanna in Dr Who and was the wife of a future Doctor?
18 Who said to Lord Archer, "There's no beginning to your talents, Jeffrey"?
19 Which pop band was Dani Behr a member of before her TV career?
20 What was Gladiator Warrior's real name?
21 Who wrote and presented a History of the Tory Party?
22 Who replaced Craig McLachlan as Ed in Bugs?
23 Which brothers were played by the McGanns in The Hanging Gale?
24 Which TV company was founded by Peter Cadbury?
25 Who wrote the controversial series The Lakes?
26 In which series did Eileen Downey find fame?
27 Ab Fab's Edina was based on which PR lady?
28 Who became narrator for Thomas The Tank Engine in the US in '98?
29 Who played Rhett Butler in the TV sequel to Gone With the Wind?
30 A comedy writing award was introduced in 1998 in whose memory?

Answers

80s Films (see Quiz 55, page 489)
1 Duke of Roxburghe's. **2** Stardust Memories. **3** Macaulay Culkin. **4** A View to a Kill. **5** Piano teacher. **6** Denholm Elliott. **7** Hans Gruber. **8** Helene Hanff & Frank Doel. **9** Sean Lennon. **10** The Shining. **11** Cathy Moriarty. **12** Heaven's Gate. **13** David Niven. **14** Tracey Ullman. **15** Ben Kingsley. **16** Marquise de Merteuil. **17** Tootsie. **18** Haing S. Ngor. **19** Oliver Stone. **20** Oprah Winfrey. **21** Catherine Oxenberg. **22** The Hustler. **23** Martin & Charlie Sheen. **24** Otto. **25** Olympia Dukakis. **26** Sound. **27** Anthony Perkins. **28** Harry Connick Jr. **29** John Reed's. **30** Jamie Lee Curtis.

Quiz 57 Pot Luck 27

Answers - see Quiz 58, page 492

1 Which Saint claimed to have seen the Loch Ness monster in the 6th century?
2 What was Brotherhood of Man's first UK Top Ten hit?
3 In which county did the battle of Edgehill take place?
4 Who directed the films Superman II and Juggernaut?
5 In which decade was TV presenter Eamonn Holmes born?
6 Which theatre foundations were discovered in London in 1988?
7 Who was lead in the films Man of the Moment and The Square Peg?
8 Which ruler led the 7th and 8th Crusades?
9 Which actor won Best Actor Oscar for On Golden Pond aged 76?
10 How many countries surround Botswana?
11 Barbara Trentham was the second wife of which English comic?
12 What is Bordeaux Mixture a blend of?
13 Which Spanish artist painted The Persistence of Memory?
14 Which military group's HQ is at Aubagne near Marseilles?
15 What is the middle name of knighted cricketer Gary Sobers?
16 What was Greta Garbo's last film?
17 The WWSU is the governing body of which sport?
18 What mass is measured in Criths?
19 In which city is the Verrazano Narrows Bridge?
20 Which profession did George Washington start out in?
21 Who was the leading lady in the films McLintock and Rio Grande?
22 Which African country won the 1996 Olympics gold medal for soccer?
23 What was the title of the only UK Top Ten hit for James Brown?
24 Who is the elder – Joanna Lumley or Maureen Lipman?
25 What does the abbreviation 'fz' mean in music?
26 Spaniard Francisco Pizarro founded which city?
27 When was the magazine Cosmopolitan first published?
28 Which city was the first to erect a monument to Lord Nelson in Britain?
29 What was Angel Beast an old type of?
30 What is the county emblem of Lincolnshire?

Answers

Euro Tour (see Quiz 58, page 492)

1 Italy. **2** Romania. **3** Tbilisi. **4** Vienna. **5** Gulf of Riga. **6** Brussels. **7** Austria. **8** Koper. **9** Italy. **10** Baltic. **11** Netherlands. **12** 9 million. **13** Gulf of Finland. **14** Great Britain. **15** Mount Etna and Stromboli. **16** Grande Dizence in Switzerland. **17** Finland. **18** London. **19** Germany. **20** Liechtenstein. **21** Ormeli in Norway. **22** Belarus. **23** Assisi in Central Italy. **24** Germany. **25** Italy. **26** Roman Catholic. **27** Corfu. **28** Tourism and tobacco. **29** Spain. **30** Norway.

Quiz 58 Euro Tour

Answers - see Quiz 57, page 491

1 Which country is Europe's largest wine producer?
2 Tarom Airlines are based in which country?
3 What is the capital of Georgia?
4 Which capital is further north – Budapest or Vienna?
5 Which Gulf is to the west of Estonia and Latvia?
6 Where is the news agency Centre d'Information Presse based?
7 In which country is Kranebitten International airport?
8 What is the chief port of Slovenia?
9 The Pelagian islands belong to which European country?
10 Bornholm is an island in which Sea?
11 Hoge Veluwe National Park is in which country?
12 To the nearest million, what was the population of Moscow in 1995?
13 St Petersburg is at the head of which gulf?
14 What is the largest island in Europe?
15 Which two Italian volcanoes erupted in 1994?
16 What is the world's highest dam?
17 Which country is called Suomen Tasavalta in its own language?
18 Which capital is further north - Berlin or London?
19 Aero Lloyd Airlines are based in which country?
20 Which European country has the highest life expectancy for men and women?
21 What is the highest waterfall in Europe?
22 Brest is a major town in which country other than France?
23 In which town did an earthquake claim nine lives in 1997?
24 In which country is the city of Bochum?
25 To which country do the islands of Stromboli and Vulcano belong?
26 What is the prominent religion of Lithuania?
27 Which is the northernmost and second largest of the Ionian islands?
28 What are Andorra's two main industries?
29 In which country is Sondica International airport?
30 Hardangervidda National Park is in which country?

Answers

Pot Luck 27 (see Quiz 57, page 491)
1 St Columba. **2** United We Stand. **3** Warwickshire. **4** Dick Lester. **5** 1950s. **6** The Rose Theatre. **7** Norman Wisdom. **8** Louis IX. **9** Henry Fonda. **10** Five. **11** John Cleese. **12** Insecticide. **13** Dali. **14** Foreign Legion. **15** St Aubrun. **16** Two-Faced Woman. **17** Water skiing. **18** Mass of gases. **19** New York. **20** A surveyor. **21** Maureen O'Hara. **22** Nigeria. **23** Living In America. **24** Joanna Lumley. **25** Accented (Forzato). **26** Lima. **27** 1972. **28** Glasgow. **29** A card game. **30** An imp.

Quiz 59 Pot Luck 28

Answers - see Quiz 60, page 494

1 What is No in Japan?
2 Who is the elder – David Mellor or Andrew Lloyd Webber?
3 What is a tulwar?
4 Who, with Paul McCartney, composed the Liverpool Oratorio?
5 What were Charles Dickens' two middle names?
6 Which group's only UK Top Ten hit was Word Up from 1986?
7 In which city is Fettes College?
8 Where was the cloth used to make duffle coats first made?
9 On May 21st, 1927, who landed at Le Bourget airport?
10 Where did Joseph of Arimathea's staff take root and bud, in legend?
11 Which song did Frank Sinatra feature in the film Robin And The Seven Hoods?
12 What is a skimmer to an American?
13 What name is given to the Greek letter that is the equivalent of letter O?
14 Which gulf is between the heel and sole of Italy?
15 Which famous leader brought an end to the Pharaohs in Egypt?
16 Which HG Wells' novel is the musical Half a Sixpence based on?
17 To ten years, when was the magazine The Economist founded?
18 What is the final event in a Decathlon?
19 How many unions merged in 1993 to form UNISON?
20 What was Mariah Carey's first UK Top Ten hit?
21 What was Charles De Gaulle's wife known as?
22 Who was the first wicket keeper to claim 50 stumping victims in Tests?
23 Which character was Dustin Hoffman in the film Midnight Cowboy?
24 On which island is Bungee jumping said to have originated?
25 What were the Christian names of the showman Barnum?
26 In mythology what was the special power of Perseus' helmet?
27 Whose one and only hit was Little Things Mean A Lot in 1954?
28 Which monarch introduced the sedan chair into England?
29 What physical property lets a needle float on water?
30 Whom did Dido, the Queen of Carthage, love?

Answers

The Royals (see Quiz 60, page 494)
1 Anthropology. **2** Sir Robert Fellowes. **3** Marie Christine von Reibnitz. **4** Samuel Chatto. **5** Viscount Linley. **6** Marina Olgilvy. **7** Geelong Grammar. **8** Sports Science. **9** The Queen Mother. **10** Duke of Roxburghe. **11** Dame Kiri Te Kanawa. **12** Techno. **13** The Duke of Kent. **14** Diana. **15** Princess Margaret. **16** Eight. **17** Diana, Fergie. **18** Young England. **19** His wedding day. **20** Elizabeth Arden. **21** Les Jolies Eaux. **22** Barbara Daly. **23** The Rottweiler. **24** Sir George Pinker. **25** Ludgrove. **26** To ease traffic congestion. **27** Pulled the coach. **28** Martin Bashir. **29** Andrew and Alice. **30** Page boy to Fergie.

Quiz 60 The Royals

Answers - see Quiz 59, page 493

1 Along with Archaeology, which subject did Prince Edward read at Cambridge?
2 Who became the Queen's Private Secretary in 1990?
3 What was Princess Michael of Kent's maiden name?
4 Who was the third great grandson of the Queen Mother's?
5 Which Royal had a financial interest in a chain of hamburger restaurants called Deal?
6 Who was the first unmarried Royal to announce her pregnancy in 1989?
7 Which school was attended by Prince Charles and Kerry Packer?
8 What did Peter Phillips study at Exeter University?
9 Who was portrayed as a school dinner lady on Spitting Image?
10 At whose home did Prince Andrew propose to Sarah Ferguson?
11 Who sang a Handel aria at Charles and Diana's wedding?
12 In a 16th birthday interview what type of music did Prince William say he preferred?
13 Who has the car registration plate K7?
14 Who was the first Royal bride to include her own family's coat of arms on her marital coat of arms?
15 Who retained the number plate 3 GXM for a new Rolls in 1972?
16 How many Princesses of Wales were there before Diana?
17 Who turned up with Pamela Stephenson at Annabel's on Prince Andrew's stag night dressed as police officers?
18 At which kindergarten did Diana Spencer work?
19 When did Prince Philip become Duke of Edinburgh?
20 The Duchess of Windsor employed a make up artist daily from which cosmetics house?
21 What is Princess Margaret's house on Mustique called?
22 Who did Diana's make up on her wedding day?
23 What was Diana's nickname for Camilla?
24 Who delivered Prince William?
25 What was William and Harry's first boarding school?
26 Why did the Queen change the Birthday Parade from Thursday to Saturday?
27 What part did Lady Penelope and St David play at Charles and Diana's wedding?
28 To which reporter did Diana admit her marriage was "a bit crowded"?
29 What were Prince Philip's parents called?
30 What was Prince William's first public duty?

Answers

Pot Luck 28 (see Quiz 59, page 493)
1 A type of theatre. **2** Lord Lloyd Webber. **3** A sword. **4** Carl Davis. **5** John Huffham. **6** Cameo. **7** Edinburgh. **8** Duffel in Belgium. **9** Charles Lindbergh. **10** Glastonbury. **11** My Kind Of Town. **12** A straw hat. **13** Omicron. **14** Gulf of Taranto. **15** Alexander the Great. **16** Kipps. **17** 1843. **18** 1500 metres. **19** Three. **20** Vision of Love. **21** Tante Yvonne. **22** Bert Oldfield (Australia). **23** Ratso Rizzo. **24** Pentecost Island. **25** Phileas Taylor. **26** Made him invisible. **27** Kitty Kallen. **28** James I. **29** Surface tension. **30** Aeneas.

Quiz 61 Pot Luck 29

Answers - see Quiz 62, page 496

1 The discovery of which plot led to the death of Mary, Queen of Scots?
2 What was Dina Carroll's first UK Top Ten hit?
3 Which Duke commanded the English troops at Culloden?
4 Which letter is one dot and one dash in Morse Code?
5 Which Minister was murdered in 1990 outside his home by an IRA bomb?
6 Which Battle was the first in the Hundred Years War?
7 What is served at a Thyestean feast?
8 Who wrote Goodbye to All That?
9 Who commanded the winning side at the Battle of Marathon?
10 Which eccentric artist is the central character in The Horse's Mouth?
11 Who is the elder – Desmond Lynam or Sir Paul McCartney?
12 In which year did Francis Drake complete the circumnavigation of the world?
13 How do you travel on the Devizes-Westminster race?
14 How old were both Anne Boleyn and Mrs Beeton when they died?
15 Who composed Easter Parade?
16 Which country gained independence in 1908 from Turkey?
17 What is the opening track on the Verve's Urban Hymns?
18 Which hymn was written by Augustus Toplady after sheltering from a storm?
19 In which decade was William Hague born?
20 Who wrote Dr Johnson's biography?
21 Who is the only English monarch to have won a flat race as a jockey?
22 Mary II died of which disease at the age of 32?
23 Whose only UK hit was Patches?
24 What is the correct name for the Ink blot test?
25 Which drill gets women and children into lifeboats first?
26 Which greyhound was the first to win the Greyhound Derby twice?
27 The Sea of Marmara lies between the Bosporus and what?
28 Who designed The Monument in London?
29 Which scale other than the Richter scale measures earthquakes?
30 Who first charted in the UK with Always On My Mind?

Answers

Oldies & Goldies (see Quiz 62, page 496)
1 (How Much Is) That Doggie In The Window? **2** Amazing Grace. **3** Oh Pretty Woman. **4** Honky Tonk. **5** I'm Not In Love. **6** Rosemary Clooney. **7** If you're going. **8** So Gay. **9** Spirit In The Sky. **10** Little Jimmy Osmond. **11** I Can't Stop Loving You. **12** Terry Jacks. **13** Lily the Pink. **14** Adam Faith. **15** My Ding-A-Ling. **16** 1973. **17** Needles and Pins. **18** Tab Hunter. **19** Lee Hazelwood. **20** Johnny Remember Me. **21** Jerry Keller. **22** Roy Wood. **23** Moon River. **24** The Good The Bad and the Ugly. **25** Sunny Afternoon. **26** The Next Time/Bachelor Boy. **27** What A Wonderful World. **28** Land. **29** Ernie. **30** You're My World.

Quiz 62 Oldies & Goldies

Answers - see Quiz 61, page 495

LEVEL 3

1 What was the first UK No 1 in which the title posed a question?
2 Which traditional song provided instrumental and vocal versions that charted for 94 weeks?
3 What was Roy Orbison's final chart topper from 1964?
4 Which 'Women' was the longest ever at No 1 for the Rolling Stones?
5 Graham Gouldman and Eric Stewart wrote which 70s classic No 1?
6 Which 1950s vocalist began singing with the Tony Pastor band?
7 What are the first three words of San Francisco?
8 How were the birds singing in the original title of the No 1 Why Do Fools Fall In Love?
9 Which 1986 No 1 was a cover of a 1970 No 1?
10 Which artist took over the title of the youngest No 1 hitmaker in 1972?
11 What is Ray Charles only UK No 1?
12 Which Canadian was next to No 1 after Paul Anka?
13 Which hit gave producer Norrie Paramour his 27th and final No 1?
14 Emile Ford shared his first week at No 1 with which artist?
15 Which Chuck Berry hit was No 1 at the same time in the UK and US?
16 Steve Miller's The Joker hit No 1 in 1990 but when was it recorded?
17 Which hit gave The Searchers their second No 1?
18 Who had a No 1 with the original version of Young Love?
19 Who wrote and produced Nancy Sinatra's These Boots Are Made For Walking?
20 Which John Leyton hit was covered in 1985 by Bronski Beat and Marc Almond?
21 Whose only UK hit was Here Comes Summer?
22 Who wrote See My Baby Jive?
23 What film theme gave Danny Williams his only No 1 in 1961?
24 What was the first instrumental No 1 after the Shadows Foot Tapper?
25 What was the Kinks' third and final No 1 hit in the summer of 1966?
26 What was the only Cliff Richard & the Shadows No 1 double-A-side?
27 Which 1968 No 1 was revived in the film Good Morning Vietnam?
28 What was Wonderful in the Shadows hit which stayed longest at No 1?
29 Which 1971 No 1 was re-released in 1992 as a tribute to its singer?
30 What was Cilla Black's only US Top 40 hit?

Answers

Pot Luck 29 (see Quiz 61, page 495)
1 Babington Plot. **2** It's Too Late. **3** Duke of Cumberland. **4** A. **5** Ian Gow. **6** Sluys. **7** Human flesh. **8** Robert Graves. **9** Miltiades. **10** Gully Jimson. **11** Sir Paul McCartney. **12** 1580. **13** Canoe. **14** 29 years. **15** Irving Berlin. **16** Bulgaria. **17** Bitter Sweet Symphony. **18** Rock of Ages. **19** 1960s. **20** James Boswell. **21** Charles II. **22** Smallpox. **23** Clarence Carter. **24** Rorschasch Test. **25** Birkenhead Drill. **26** Mick the Miller. **27** The Dardanelles. **28** Christopher Wren. **29** Mercalli Scale. **30** Brenda Lee.

Quiz 63 Pot Luck 30

Answers - see Quiz 64, page 498

1 Which language do the words kiosk, tulip and caviar come from?
2 Whose Drum can be seen at Buckland Abbey in Devon?
3 Where is the Queen's bank account?
4 What do the initials stand for in the name of ghost story writer M.R. James?
5 Which actor played Major Gowen in Fawlty Towers?
6 In which decade was Lloyd Grossman born?
7 Whose hymn book was first published in 1873?
8 A durmast is a variety of what?
9 Whose only UK Top Ten Hit was Blue Is The Colour from 1972?
10 Which Europeans discovered Lake Tanganyika in 1858?
11 Who said, "I never hated a man enough to give him his diamonds back"?
12 Achulophobia is the fear of what?
13 Which brass instrument is wrapped around the player's body?
14 What colour appears with white and green on the Afghanistan flag?
15 In which US state was there a nuclear accident at Three Mile Island in 1979?
16 Who was the first woman to swim the English Channel in 1926?
17 What is the capital of Angola?
18 Where were a set of rules for football drawn up in 1848?
19 What is indium?
20 Who is the elder – Paul Merton or Richard Madeley?
21 Who lived at No. 1, London?
22 Where are the Aventine, Viminal and Quirinal Hills?
23 What nationality was Sir Robert Helpmann?
24 What is a clerihew?
25 To 10 miles, how far was Piper Alpha off Wick when it exploded?
26 In which European country is the province of Brabant?
27 Where, in the Keats' poem, did Ruth stand "in tears"?
28 What was David Cassidy's first UK Top Ten hit?
29 Where did Kun's Red Terror exist in 1919?
30 Who, in 43 AD, led the resistance against the Romans?

Answers

Olympics (see Quiz 64, page 498)
1 Alberto Juantorena. **2** Ice hockey. **3** Yachting. **4** St Moritz. **5** Bars and beam. **6** Michael Johnson. **7** Long jump. **8** Al Oerter. **9** Five. **10** Two. **11** Retained 10,000m and won 5,000m and marathon. **12** Evander Holyfield. **13** Lake Lanier. **14** Simone Jacobs. **15** Michelle Smith. **16** Izzy. **17** Seoul. **18** Allan Wells. **19** Spain. **20** Soling. **21** Poland's Renata Mauer. **22** Tim Henman & Chris Broad. **23** Jayne Torvill. **24** 4 x 400m relay. **25** 1900. **26** Quarantine laws. **27** Denise Lewis. **28** Montreal. **29** Robin Cousins. **30** Japan.

Quiz 64 Olympics

Answers - see Quiz 63, page 497

1 Who won 400m and 800m gold at the '76 Olympics?
2 At which sport did future tennis star Drobny win a medal in 1948?
3 Windsurfing is included in the Olympics as part of which sport's events?
4 Where were the Winter Olympics held in 1928 and 1948?
5 On which apparatus did Nadia Comaneci score perfect tens in 1976?
6 Who was the first man to win Olympic gold at 200m and 400m?
7 In which event did Carl Lewis win his ninth and final gold medal?
8 Who won the first of four discus golds in Melbourne in 1956?
9 How many silver medals did skier Raisa Smetanina win with her four golds and one bronze?
10 How many gold medals did Mark Spitz win in his first Olympics?
11 Which amazing treble did Emil Zatopek achieve at the 1952 Games?
12 Who carried the torch into the stadium at the Atlanta games?
13 On which lake did Steve Redgrave win his record breaking fourth gold medal?
14 Who was the only British woman sprinter to compete in all Olympics between 1984 and 1996?
15 Under what name did Mrs Erik de Bruin win gold at Atlanta?
16 What was the name of the Olympic mascot in Atlanta?
17 Where did Linford Christie run his first Olympic race?
18 Who was the oldest Olympic 100m champion when he won in 1980?
19 Who won women's gold in hockey in Barcelona?
20 Which is the only Olympic yachting event for three person crews?
21 Who won the first medal at the Atlanta games?
22 Who won Britain's first tennis medal since 1924 in Atlanta?
23 Who replaced her partner Michael Hutchinson before winning gold in 1984?
24 Other than 400m hurdles for which event did Sally Gunnell win a medal in Barcelona?
25 In which year did women first compete in the Olympics?
26 Why were equestrian events held in Sweden in 1956 when the Games were held in Australia?
27 Who was Britain's only female medallist at the Atlanta games?
28 Where did Daley Thompson compete in his first Olympics?
29 Which son of a former Millwall goalie won gold in the USA in 1980?
30 What was the first Asian country to have staged the Winter Olympics?

Answers

Pot Luck 30 (see Quiz 63, page 497)
1 Turkish. **2** Francis Drake's. **3** Coutts. **4** Montague Rhodes. **5** Ballard Berkeley. **6** 1950s. **7** Sankey and Moody's. **8** An oak tree. **9** Chelsea F.C. **10** Richard Burton and John Speke. **11** Zsa Zsa Gabor. **12** Darkness. **13** Sousaphone. **14** Black. **15** Pennsylvania. **16** Gertrude Ederle. **17** Luanda. **18** Cambridge University. **19** A metallic element. **20** Richard Madeley. **21** Duke of Wellington. **22** Rome. **23** Australian. **24** A poem. **25** 120. **26** Belgium. **27** 'Amid the alien corn'. **28** Could It Be Forever/Cherish. **29** Hungary. **30** Caractacus.

Quiz 65 Pot Luck 31

Answers - see Quiz 66, page 500

1 Who did the Spice Girls sack as their manager in early 1998?
2 What is a porbeagle?
3 Which bandleader married both Ava Gardner and Lana Turner?
4 What was the family name of artists Jacopo and his sons Gentile and Giovanni?
5 Scottish solicitor William Mitchell drew up the rules for which sport?
6 Which group had a 70s hit with Kiss You All Over?
7 Who was Prince Philip's mother?
8 What two colours go with black and yellow in printing's four-colour process?
9 What did Diana Princess of Wales describe as "a shameful friend"?
10 Who is the elder – Robin Cook or David Blunkett?
11 What was Bad Manners' first UK Top Ten hit?
12 What is a belvedere?
13 In which month is the feast day of St Cuthbert?
14 In which country are the mountains called the Stirling Range?
15 What is tufa?
16 Which soccer club has been managed by both Jimmy Armfield and Brian Clough?
17 Whose one and only hit was Float On in 1977?
18 Who was the first Prime Minister of Israel?
19 Where is New York's Metropolitan Museum of Art?
20 In what year did the London Stock Exchange go computerised?
21 What is a gibus?
22 Who was the first man to hold the post of Astronomer Royal?
23 In which decade was Lord Charles Spencer Churchill born?
24 Who founded the record label Anxious Records?
25 Which Michelangelo statue is in Florence?
26 Vera Caslavska was Olympic and World Champion in which sport?
27 In which year was Wimbledon first televised?
28 Where was the first woman MP to enter the Commons born?
29 Who ceased to be queen when Victoria became queen?
30 What do you do if you siffle?

Answers

Hobbies 2 (see Quiz 66, page 500)
1 0 to 36. **2** Finland, playing football. **3** Chess. **4** Scarlet. **5** 16lb. **6** Bilbao. **7** Steel links. **8** Tintin. **9** Alton Towers. **10** Giverny. **11** Clarice Cliff. **12** Military combat. **13** 10. **14** Baker Street. **15** Caman. **16** Tony Hancock. **17** Curling. **18** Tramp. **19** Aikido. **20** Four (11 and 7 respectively). **21** Stamp collecting. **22** Hang gliding. **23** Harz Mountains (Germany). **24** Mogens Tholstrup. **25** Carry it. **26** Gothenburg, Sweden. **27** Nick Nairn. **28** Bungee jumping. **29** Kung fu. **30** Leiden.

Quiz 66 Hobbies 2

Answers - see Quiz 65, page 499

1 What is the range of numbers on a roulette wheel?
2 Where would you watch FC Jazz and what would they be doing?
3 FIDE is the governing body of which game?
4 If you were watching the Queen's horse race, what colour sleeves would the jockey have?
5 In athletics how much does a hammer weigh?
6 Where in Europe is the Guggenheim Museum?
7 In abseiling what are karabiners?
8 Who first appeared in a strip cartoon 'in the Land of the Soviets'?
9 Which UK tourist attraction is on the site of an 8th century fortress?
10 Where in Normandy would you visit Monet's garden?
11 If you collected Bizarre pottery whose work would you have?
12 Paintball is a simulation of what?
13 How many zones does an archery target have?
14 In which London street was the first artificial ice rink opened?
15 In shinty what is the curved stick called?
16 Which radio star appeared in films such as The Wrong Box?
17 In which sport does a match last for a certain number of heads?
18 John Gold was the owner of which night club for over 30 years?
19 Which activity has two main types, tomiki and uyeshiba?
20 How many more people are there in an outer handball team than there are in an indoor one?
21 John Tomlinson is credited with starting which hobby?
22 Which form of flying was perfected by Francis Rogallo in the 70s?
23 In which mountains is the Brockenbahn steam railway?
24 Which restaurateur owned Daphne's and founded The Collection?
25 In cyclocross what do you do with your bike when you're not riding it?
26 Where is the Liseberg theme park?
27 Who opened the Braeval restaurant in Scotland in 1986?
28 In which activity do you 'dive for the horizon'?
29 Wing Chun is a popular form of which art?
30 In which Botanic Gardens was the tulip first introduced in 1594?

Answers

Pot Luck 31 (see Quiz 65, page 499)
1 Simon Fuller. **2** A shark. **3** Artie Shaw. **4** Bellini. **5** Bowls. **6** Exile.
7 Princess Alice of Battenburg. **8** Cyan, magenta. **9** Bulimia. **10** Robin Cook.
11 Special Brew. **12** A viewing turret. **13** March. **14** Australia. **15** A kind of rock.
16 Leeds. **17** The Floaters. **18** David Ben-Gurion. **19** Central Park. **20** 1986.
21 A top hat. **22** John Flamsteed. **23** 1940s. **24** Dave Stewart. **25** David.
26 Gymnastics. **27** 1937. **28** America. **29** Adelaide. **30** Whistle.

Quiz 67 Pot Luck 32

Answers - see Quiz 68, page 502

1 Bernard Webb was a pseudonym used by which famous song writer?
2 In which country is the royal family the House of Bernadotte?
3 Acrophobia is the fear of what?
4 In which country is the city of Abidjan?
5 What was the only No 1 UK hit for the Clash?
6 What colour is the circle on the Bangladesh flag?
7 A Brazilian Huntsman is a type of what?
8 Who played director Ed Wood in the 1994 film biography?
9 A Nutmegger is an inhabitant of which American state?
10 In which decade did South Africa resign from the Commonwealth?
11 How many locks are there on the Suez Canal?
12 What was the name of Vivienne Westwood's second shop opened in '82?
13 Who composed Rhapsody on a Theme of Paganini for Piano?
14 What was the number of the British Armoured Division nicknamed the 'Desert Rats'?
15 In which year did James Cook land at Botany Bay, Australia?
16 What is the correct form of address to begin a letter to a Baron?
17 In snooker in which year did the Lada Classic have two champions?
18 Who is the elder – Caroline Quentin or Linda Robson?
19 What was Neneh Cherry's first UK Top Ten hit?
20 What was the Christian name of aeroplane manufacturer Mr Boeing?
21 In which European country are the provinces of Sofiya and Burgas?
22 What size is A4 paper in millimetres?
23 Australia hosted the 1956 Olympics but equestrian events were held in which other country?
24 In which decade was Gary Glitter born?
25 Which artist painted The Watering Place in 1777?
26 What are the initials G.B.E an abbreviation of?
27 Who wrote the novel The Last Testament of Oscar Wilde in 1983?
28 Which magazine has been guest edited by Damien Hirst?
29 Clarence House was built for which monarch when he was still Duke of Clarence?
30 What is the capital of Bahrain?

Answers

TV Times 2 (See quiz 68, page 502)

1 Angus Deayton. **2** Po. **3** Andrew Lincoln. **4** Mark Porter and Emma Norman. **5** Tinky Winky. **6** Ascot. **7** Sara. **8** Lakesiders. **9** Duffy (Cathy Shipton). **10** Papa, Bob. **11** Hot Shoe Show. **12** Jane Asher. **13** My Kind of People. **14** Julia Carling. **15** Tantrums and Tiaras. **16** Francesca Annis. **17** Widows. **18** Helen Rollason. **19** James Naughtie. **20** Ian Hislop. **21** Carla Lane. **22** Twin Peaks. **23** Bedrock (The Flintstones). **24** Heineken. **25** Inventor Black. **26** Gomez Addams. **27** Paul McGann. **28** Fiona Phillips. **29** 1313 Mockingbird Heights. **30** The Woodentop twins.

Quiz 68 TV Times 2

Answers - see Quiz 67, page 501

1 Who played Mike Channel in KYTV?
2 Who is the smallest Teletubby?
3 Who found fame as Egg in This Life?
4 Who first hosted The Radio Times Show on Sky?
5 Who is the largest Teletubby?
6 Where did the first outside broadcast on Grandstand come from?
7 Who is Postman Pat's wife?
8 In which docu soap did Emma Boundy find fame?
9 Which Casualty character played a midwife in Spice World?
10 Which two words has Nicole uttered to advertise Renault?
11 What was the name of Wayne Sleep's 80s TV show which he later adapted for the stage?
12 Which TV presenter made the cake when Jemima Goldsmith married Imran Khan?
13 What was Michael Barrymore's talent spotting TV show called?
14 Who replaced Anneka Rice on Carlton's Capital Woman?
15 What was the name of the David Furnish directed documentary about Elton John?
16 Who played the Englishwoman in Parnell and the Englishwoman?
17 In which series did Lynda La Plante introduce Dolly Rawlings?
18 Who was the first woman presenter of Grandstand?
19 Who. replaced Richard Baker as the presenter of the Proms?
20 Who presented Channel 4's religious series Canterbury Tales?
21 How is TV playwright Romana Barrack better known?
22 In which show was Harry S Truman the sheriff?
23 In which town would you read The Daily Slate?
24 The music from Raging Bull was used to advertise which lager?
25 Whose magic ray transformed Supergran?
26 Who had a pet octopus called Aristotle?
27 Who played the title role in Alan Bleasdale's The Monocled Mutineer?
28 Anthea Turner was replaced at GMTV by whom?
29 Where did the Musters live?
30 On a Friday, on children's TV who were Jenny & Willy?

Answers

Pot Luck 32 (see Quiz 67, page 501)
1 Paul McCartney. **2** Sweden. **3** Heights. **4** Ivory Coast.
5 Should I Stay or Should I Go. **6** Red. **7** Spider. **8** Johnny Depp. **9** Connecticut.
10 1960s. **11** None. **12** Nostalgia of Mud. **13** Rachmaninov. **14** 7th. **15** 1770.
16 My Lord. **17** 1980 (Spencer/Davis). **18** Linda Robson. **19** Buffalo Stance.
20 William. **21** Bulgaria. **22** 210mm x 297mm. **23** Sweden. **24** 1940s.
25 Thomas Gainsborough. **26** Knight/Dame Grand Cross of the Order of the British Empire.
27 Peter Ackroyd. **28** The Big Issue. **29** William IV. **30** Manama.

Quiz 69 Pot Luck 33

Answers - see Quiz 70, page 504

1 In which decade was actor John Cleese born?
2 After which American General were sideburns named?
3 Freetown is the capital of which country?
4 Who played Test cricket aged 52 years 165 days?
5 Who directed the 1967 film The Dirty Dozen?
6 What is the main language of Angola?
7 What happened to the Olympic flame during the 1976 games?
8 Hartford is the capital of which American State?
9 Which 18th Century artist painted Peasant Girl Gathering Sticks?
10 To five years, when was the News Of The World founded?
11 What, other than Amazing Grace, was a top ten hit for Judy Collins?
12 A fear of the cold is known as what?
13 In which county is the Rude Man of Cerne?
14 Which country has the dalasi as its currency?
15 What was done in an apodyterium?
16 Emperor Nero was the adopted son of which other emperor?
17 What is the international car index mark for a car from Libya?
18 The spice annatto is made from which part of a plant?
19 Other than Buckingham Palace, which venue sees the daily Changing of the Guard?
20 What is the administrative centre for the Scottish Western Isles?
21 What was the Commodores' first UK Top Ten hit?
22 Who is the elder – George Michael or Anthea Turner?
23 Painter Georges Seurat was born, died and worked in which city?
24 What name is given to elements with atomic numbers 93 to 112?
25 What two colours appear with yellow on the Cameroon flag?
26 Who was the first woman to qualify for the Indy 500 motor race?
27 Which Latin phrase means, 'Let the buyer beware'?
28 In which year did women gain the vote in Switzerland?
29 In which country is the city of Bamako?
30 As a child Jonathan Ross appeared in an ad for which food product?

Answers

90s Films (see Quiz 70, page 504)
1 Wag the Dog. **2** Francis Bacon. **3** Arnold Schwarzenegger. **4** River Phoenix.
5 Spanish Civil War. **6** Jean-Claude Van Damme. **7** That Thing You Do!
8 Pretty Woman. **9** Seal. **10** Ellen Barkin. **11** Frank Drebin. **12** Banker.
13 Julia Roberts. **14** Kevin Kline. **15** Blue Sky. **16** Kennedy & Nixon.
17 James Earl Jones. **18** Abba. **19** Kirsty Alley. **20** Nine Months.
21 Emma Thompson. **22** Elizabeth Taylor. **23** Kevin McCallister.
24 Jim Carrey , who played The Riddler. **25** Mars Attacks! **26** Jude.
27 Christopher Walken. **28** Gonzo. **29** Nil By Mouth. **30** 2000 AD.

Quiz 70 90s Films

Answers - see Quiz 69, page 503

1 Which Barry Levinson film was used to satirise the US presidency during the Lewinsky crisis?
2 Who is the subject of Love is the Devil?
3 Which tough guy directed Christmas in Connecticut?
4 Who died during the filming of Dark Blood in 1993?
5 Which war is depicted in Land and Freedom?
6 Who was Lyon Gaultier in AWOL?
7 In which film did Tom Hanks make his directorial debut?
8 Which film's initial title was $3,000?
9 Who or what is Andre in the film of the same name?
10 Who was Leonardo DiCaprio's mother in This Boy's Life?
11 Who is Leslie Nielsen in the Naked Gun films?
12 What is Jim Carrey's job before he finds the mask in the hit movie?
13 Who was Tinkerbell when Spielberg met JM Barrie?
14 Who was the butler in Princess Caraboo?
15 What was director Tony Richardson's final film?
16 Which US presidents does Gump meet in Forrest Gump?
17 Who was the voice of Mufasa in The Lion King?
18 Muriel is a fan of which band in Muriel's Wedding?
19 Who did Woody Allen cast as his ex wife in Deconstructing Harry?
20 What was Hugh Grant's first Hollywood movie?
21 Who was Oscar winning best screen writer for Sense and Sensibility?
22 Who was John Goodman's mother in law in The Flintstones?
23 What is Macaulay Culkin's full name in the Home Alone movies?
24 Who designed The Riddler's costume in Batman Forever?
25 In which movie did Tom Jones sing It's Not Unusual?
26 In which film did Kate Winslet have her first nude scene?
27 Who played rat catcher Caesar in Mousehunt?
28 Who was the author in The Muppet Christmas Carol?
29 Which film was Gary Oldman's directorial debut?
30 In which comic did Sylvester Stallone's '95 futuristic police character appear?

Answers

Pot Luck 33 (see Quiz 67, page 503)

1 1930s. **2** Ambrose Burnside. **3** Sierra Leone. **4** Wilfred Rhodes (England). **5** Robert Aldrich. **6** Portuguese. **7** Extinguished by a cloudburst. **8** Connecticut. **9** Thomas Gainsborough. **10** 1843. **11** Send In The Clowns. **12** Cheimaphobia. **13** Dorset (figure carved in chalk hillside). **14** Gambia. **15** Clothes were removed before bathing. **16** Claudius. **17** LAR. **18** Seeds. **19** Royal Horse Guards, Whitehall. **20** Stornoway. **21** Easy. **22** Anthea Turner. **23** Paris. **24** Trans-uranic elements. **25** Green and Red. **26** Janet Guthrie. **27** Caveat Emptor. **28** 1971. **29** Mali. **30** Rice Krispies.

Quiz 71 Living World

Answers - see Quiz 72, page 506

1 What is another name for the North American nightjar?
2 Where is the world's greatest discharger of radioactive nuclear waste?
3 How is the disease trypanosomiasis also known?
4 What is meant by a haemorrhage which is 'occult'?
5 Which protein is present in a hair?
6 What does it mean if a cell is haploid?
7 In addition to tea and coffee where is caffeine found?
8 Where is the flexor carpi radialis?
9 What is an erythrocyte?
10 How is the sand hopper also known?
11 Guano is used as fertiliser but what is it made from?
12 Cranes are found on all continents except which two?
13 What is an alternative name for leptospirosis?
14 Carragheen is a type of what?
15 Where is a caterpillar's spinneret?
16 Which bird flies highest?
17 What is an insect's Malpighian tubes?
18 How does a mamba differ from a cobra?
19 Which part of the brain controls muscular movements, balance and co-ordination?
20 Which bird can swim as fast as a seal?
21 An urodele is another name for which reptile?
22 Which bird builds the largest nest?
23 The world's largest spider is named after which Biblical character?
24 What is a bird's furcula?
25 Disulfiram is used in the treatment of what?
26 What is a hairstreak?
27 On which island would you find the bee hummingbird?
28 Which bird produces the largest egg in relation to its body size?
29 Why should you avoid a chigger?
30 How many hearts does an earthworm have?

Answers

Pot Luck 34 (see Quiz 72, page 506)
1 Louis Washkansky. **2** Denmark. **3** Bela Bartok. **4** Cliff Richard. **5** Albania. **6** George Bush. **7** Elephant. **8** Twiggy. **9** Turkey. **10** Mackerel. **11** 1985. **12** Blackheath. **13** Sisserou parrot. **14** 1940s. **15** One Day I'll Fly Away. **16** Bovine Spongiform Encephalopathy. **17** 43,200. **18** Polish. **19** Sexual health in the Third World. **20** Martin Amis. **21** Dot, dot, dot. **22** St Clare. **23** Spencer Perceval (British PM). **24** Trumpet. **25** Edo. **26** Excessive growth. **27** New Zealand. **28** Indiana. **29** Kid Creole and the Coconuts. **30** Touch.

Quiz 72 Pot Luck 34

Answers - see Quiz 71 , page 505

1 Who was the first person to receive a heart transplant?
2 In which European country are the counties of Viborg and Aarhus?
3 Who composed the music for the ballet The Wooden Prince?
4 Who played the lead role in the film Two A Penny?
5 Which country has the lek as its unit of currency?
6 Who was Vice President when Ronald Reagan was President?
7 Which animal head represents the Hindu god Ganesa?
8 Who is the elder – Julie Walters or Twiggy?
9 In which country is the city of Adana?
10 Which type of fish gives its name to a particular patterning of the sky?
11 In which year did Roy Plomley last present Desert Island Discs?
12 The first men's hockey club in England was founded in which London suburb?
13 Which bird stands in the centre of the national flag of Dominica?
14 In which decade was Michael Gambon born?
15 What was Randy Crawford's first UK Top Ten hit?
16 What are the initials BSE an abbreviation of?
17 How many seconds are there in half a day?
18 What was the nationality of the astronomer Nicolaus Copernicus?
19 Geri Halliwell became a UN ambassador specialising in what?
20 Who wrote the novels London Fields and Time's Arrow?
21 How is the letter S formed in Morse Code?
22 Who is the patron Saint of television?
23 Which public figure was shot dead by John Bellingham?
24 Bandleader Quincy Jones chiefly plays which instrument?
25 Changed in 1868 what was the former name of Tokyo?
26 What do you suffer from if you have acromegaly?
27 The yacht Black Magic won the America's Cup for which country?
28 A Hoosier is an inhabitant in which American state?
29 Who had hits with Stool Pigeon and I'm A Wonderful Thing, Baby?
30 Haphephobia is the fear of what?

Answers

Living World (see Quiz 71, page 505)
1 Whippoorwill. **2** Sellafield. **3** Sleeping sickness. **4** Internal. **5** Keratin. **6** Single set of chromosomes. **7** Kola nuts. **8** Human's forearm. **9** Red blood cell. **10** Beachflea. **11** Bird droppings. **12** South America & Antarctica. **13** Weil's disease. **14** Seaweed. **15** Head. **16** Ruppell's vulture. **17** Excretory organs. **18** Not hooded. **19** Cerebellum. **20** Penguin. **21** Salamander. **22** Male malle fowl. **23** Goliath. **24** Wishbone. **25** Alcoholism. **26** Butterfly. **27** Cuba. **28** Kiwi. **29** Harvest mite (which bites). **30** Ten.

Quiz 73 Who Was Who?

Answers - see Quiz 74, page 508

1 Who was known as the 'father of the Soviet H-bomb'?
2 In which shipyards did Lech Walesa work before becoming Polish president?
3 Terry Waite was the envoy of which Archbishop of Canterbury when he was kidnapped?
4 Who founded the Police Memorial Trust after PC Yvonne Fletcher's death?
5 Who was the first US Ambassador in London?
6 Who recorded with the Hot Five and the Hot Seven in the 1920s?
7 Who became the youngest ever member of the GLC in 1969?
8 Who was the 20th Prince of Wales?
9 Who succeeded Len Murray as TUC general secretary in 1984?
10 Who was the first Archbishop of Canterbury to be appointed by the Church Crown Appointments Commission?
11 Which children's author was Russian correspondent for the Daily News during WWI and the Revolution?
12 Which advocate of black rights left the US to live in England in the late 50s?
13 Who was the last British monarch to refuse royal assent of a Bill through Parliament?
14 Who was UK Deputy PM between 1942 and 1945?
15 Which UK PM was responsible for the purchase of US Polaris missiles?
16 Who did Douglas Hurd replace as Foreign Secretary in 1989?
17 Who became President of the ANC in 1997?
18 Which Chancellor of the Exchequer introduced old age pensions?
19 Which Fine Gael candidate did Mary McAleese defeat in the 1997 election for Irish President?
20 Which invention improved on Alexander Cummings invention a century earlier?
21 What was Mikhail Gorbachev's wife called?
22 Who founded Standard Oil in 1870?
23 How was entrepreneur Roland Fuhrhop better known?
24 Which son of Findlaech was killed at Lumphanan?
25 Who was the first Archbishop of Canterbury?
26 Which former Enfield MP has the middle names Denzil Xavier?
27 The name of which UK PM was Ronald Reagan's middle name?
28 Who was shot at a rally in the US in 1972 while campaigning for the Democrats?
29 Which Baron began a continental pigeon post in 1849?
30 Who was German foreign minister during WWII?

Answers

Pot Luck 35 (see Quiz 74, page 508)

1 Fruit pods. **2** Nebraska. **3** Weather With You. **4** His height. (World's tallest man). **5** Eight. **6** RB. **7** 1930s. **8** Vulcan. **9** Mold. **10** Arithmetic and logic unit. **11** Edgar Rice Burroughs. **12** Three. **13** Andrew Bonar Law. **14** Paul Cezanne. **15** 1642. **16** Warren Beatty. **17** Traffic Wardens. **18** Zambia. **19** When he gives up his seat. **20** If You Let Me Stay. **21** My Lord Duke. **22** 1989. **23** Indonesia. **24** David Hockney. **25** Henry VIII. **26** Michael Heseltine. **27** Peacock. **28** 148mm x 210 mm. **29** French. **30** Trumpet.

Quiz 74 **Pot Luck 35**

Answers - see Quiz 73, page 507

1 The spice cayenne is made from which part of a plant?
2 Lincoln is the capital of which US state?
3 What was the only UK Top Ten hit from 1992 for Crowded House?
4 What was special about Robert Pershing Wadlow?
5 How many singles had Take That released before their first No 1 Pray?
6 What is the international car index mark for a car from Botswana?
7 In which decade was Sir David Frost born?
8 Who was the Roman God of fire?
9 What is the administrative centre for the Welsh county of Clwyd?
10 Mathematically speaking, what is an ALU?
11 In the 1920s who wrote The Land That Time Forgot?
12 How many stripes are on the national flag of Estonia?
13 Who is the only British prime minister to have been born outside the UK?
14 Which artist painted Le Jardinier in 1906?
15 In which year was the Battle of Edgehill?
16 Who directed the 1990 film Dick Tracy?
17 A Chief Constable is responsible for which uniformed force other than the police?
18 Lusaka is the capital of which country?
19 When does an MP apply for the Chiltern Hundreds?
20 What was Terence Trent D'Arby's first UK Top Ten hit?
21 What is the correct form of address to begin a letter to a Duke?
22 In which year did Frank Bruno first fight with Mike Tyson?
23 In which country is the city of Banjarmasin?
24 Who painted The Rake's Progress and A Bigger Splash in the 1960s?
25 Saint John Fisher was martyred during the reign of which English king?
26 Who is the elder – Lester Piggott or Michael Heseltine?
27 What's the English name of the constellation Pavo?
28 What size is A5 paper in millimetres?
29 What is the main language of the Republic of Benin?
30 Miles Davis is associated with which musical instrument?

Answers

Who Was Who? (see Quiz 73, page 507)
1 Andrei Sakharov. **2** Gdansk. **3** Robert Runcie. **4** Michael Winner. **5** John Adams. **6** Louis Armstrong. **7** Jeffrey Archer. **8** The future Edward VIII. **9** Norman Willis. **10** Robert Runcie. **11** Arthur Ransome. **12** Paul Robeson. **13** Queen Anne. **14** Attlee. **15** Macmillan. **16** John Major. **17** Thabo Mbeki. **18** Asquith. **19** Mary Bannotti. **20** Flushing toilet. **21** Raisa. **22** John D Rockefeller. **23** Tiny Rowland. **24** Macbeth. **25** St Augustine. **26** Michael Portillo. **27** Wilson. **28** George Wallace. **29** Paul Julius Reuter. **30** Joachim von Ribbentrop.

Quiz 75 Rockers

Answers - see Quiz 76, page 510

1 What was Eddie Cochrane's next UK single after Three Steps To Heaven?
2 Who played Jerry Lee Lewis in the 1989 biopic of his life?
3 How does Roger Peterson figure in rock history?
4 What was Billy Fury's first UK Top Ten hit from 1960?
5 In which city were R.E.M. formed?
6 As a teenager Morrissey ran a fan club for which group?
7 Who wrote the Holly classic It Doesn't Matter Anymore?
8 Which Elvis No 1 is the only one written solely by Lieber and Stoller?
9 Which hard-rock band did the Scottish Young brothers form in Australia?
10 Rock Around The Clock came out on which label?
11 Who did Keith Richard work for before coming a full-time Stone?
12 Which Slade hit was No 1 when US soldiers left Vietnam in 1973?
13 What did Rick Allen of Def Leppard lose in 1984?
14 What did an electrician fitting a burglar alarm find in Seattle in 1984?
15 Who first charted with Rip It Up?
16 James Jewel Osterberg took the stage under which name?
17 At which studio did the 'Million Dollar Quartet' get together in the 50s?
18 In which month did Jim Morrison die in 1971?
19 Where in London was the Sex Pistols first concert?
20 Which Dickie Valentine hit replaced Rock Around The Clock at No 1?
21 Which place used to form part of The Stranglers name?
22 Who was Francis Rossi's school mate and long time bass player in Status Quo?
23 How were the Rolling Stones billed for their first live concert?
24 Which Jerry Lee Lewis hit is the only version of the Ray Charles' classic to reach the British charts?
25 Who ran the Clovis, New Mexico studio where Buddy Holly recorded?
26 Who was Phil Lynott's father in law?
27 Who recorded the album Ma Kelly's Greasy Spoon?
28 Which Led Zeppelin drummer died in 1980?
29 Who ran the Chelsea clothes shop called Let It Rock?
30 Which 1955 Glenn Ford movie featured Rock Around The Clock?

Answers

Pot Luck 36 (see Quiz 76, page 510)
1 Wales. **2** Jeffrey Archer. **3** Court of Chief Pleas. **4** Blue. **5** Divine Brown. **6** Belmopan. **7** Cygnus. **8** Eloise. **9** 8000. **10** A fish. **11** Knight/Dame Grand Cross of the Royal Victorian Order. **12** Cat. **13** US Civil War. **14** Kazakhstan. **15** Australia. **16** 1960s. **17** Nepal. **18** Madame Tussaud's (In 1997). **19** Fog. **20** Patricia Hodge. **21** A small pail. **22** 1969. **23** Chris Evans. **24** Charlie Daniels Band. **25** Chilterns. **26** Benjamin Britten. **27** Evelyn Waugh. **28** Billy Ocean. **29** Philadelphia. **30** With fun.

Quiz 76 Pot Luck 36

Answers - see Quiz 75, page 509

1 Which part of the UK does not receive Channel 4?
2 In the 1980s, who wrote the novel A Twist in the Tale ?
3 What is the Parliament of Sark called?
4 What colour appears with white and red on the Faroe Islands flag?
5 In 1995 Hugh Grant got into trouble for performing a lewd act with whom?
6 What is the capital of Belize?
7 The North American Nebula is a region in which constellation?
8 What was The Damned's one and only UK Top Ten hit?
9 To the nearest thousand, how many different species of ant are there?
10 What is a golomyanka?
11 What are the initials GCVO an abbreviation of?
12 Bombay, Chartreux and Japanese bobtail are all types of what?
13 Which war is Stephen Crane's novel The Red Badge of Courage set in?
14 In which country is the city of Alma-Ata?
15 The writer Thomas Keneally comes from which country?
16 In which decade was actor Colin Firth born?
17 Prithwi Narayan Shah was the first King of which kingdom?
18 Where were William Hague, Jesse Owens and Pele brought together?
19 Homichlophobia is the fear of what?
20 Who is the elder – Patricia Hodge or Judy Finnigan?
21 Who or what was a piggin?
22 In which year was the Women's International Bowling Board formed?
23 Which media presenter left his wife Carol McGiffin in 1993?
24 Which band had a 70s UK hit with The Devil Went Down to Georgia?
25 Among which hills does Chequers lie?
26 Who composed the opera Noye's Fludde?
27 Who wrote Decline and Fall?
28 Under which name did Leslie Charles sail to pop success?
29 Which city has the oldest stock exchange in the USA?
30 What does the musical term 'giocoso' mean?

Answers

Rockers (see Quiz 75, page 509)
1 Sweetie Pie. **2** Dennis Quaid. **3** Pilot in the crash that killed Holly. **4** Colette. **5** Athens, USA. **6** The New York Dolls. **7** Paul Anka. **8** Jailhouse Rock. **9** AC/DC. **10** Decca. **11** The Post Office. **12** Cum On Feel The Noize. **13** An arm (in a car crash). **14** Kurt Cobain's body. **15** Little Richard. **16** Iggy Pop. **17** Sun Studio, Memphis. **18** July. **19** St Martin's School Of Art. **20** Christmas Alphabet. **21** Guildford. **22** Alan Lancaster. **23** Rollin' Stones. **24** What'd I Say. **25** Norman Petty. **26** Leslie Crowther. **27** Status Quo. **28** John Bonham. **29** Malcolm McLaren. **30** Blackboard Jungle.

Quiz 77 Hobbies 3

Answers - see Quiz 78, page 512

1 CIPS regulates which sport?
2 Where were Haagen-Daz ice creams first sold?
3 Where is Rick Stein's famous seafood restaurant?
4 What is octopush?
5 Where is the world's largest nightclub, Gilley's Club?
6 Who jointly opened La Gavroche in 1967?
7 Which venue was designed by George London and Henry Wise?
8 What colour might your balls be in croquet?
9 What is the nearest town to the Lightwater Valley Theme Park?
10 Which game was originally called Lexico?
11 The Toucan Terribles are prolific champions at what?
12 What is the name of England's smallest pub in Bury St Edmunds?
13 Which UK town has the longest shopping mall?
14 Where was the Grand National run during WWI?
15 Who founded the London restaurants Quaglino's and Mezzo?
16 In judo which Dan grades are awarded a red belt?
17 How many points is the gold circle on an archery target worth?
18 In 1848 William Mitchell drew up the rules to which modern game?
19 In shinty what is the opponent's goal called?
20 Which musical instrument was the creation of Charles Wheatstone?
21 Which soccer club has a fanzine called Fly Me to the Moon?
22 Who opened his first restaurant Harveys in 1987?
23 In paddle tennis what is the ball made from?
24 Which game was derived from baggataway?
25 What is important dress code at France's Domaine de Lambetran?
26 What is a gricer?
27 Where is the UK's largest amusement park?
28 What name is given to the circular target in curling?
29 What is Denmark's Rutschebahnen?
30 What do you wear on your feet in street hockey?

Answers

Pot Luck 37 (see Quiz 78, page 512)
1 Francis Ford Coppola. **2** Earl Of Liverpool. **3** The Valley of the Queens. **4** Alexander. **5** John Constable. **6** New Orleans. **7** Fruits. **8** 1969. **9** The Ivy League (US colleges). **10** RC. **11** Doctor. **12** Yasmin Le Bon. **13** String. **14** Walter F Mondale. **15** Sir William Walton. **16** Lord Lovat (1747). **17** 1970s. **18** Sugarbush. **19** The Hob. **20** Ecuador. **21** The Milan - San Remo (Primavera). **22** Fred Titmus. **23** Solomon Islands. **24** Gordonstoun. **25** A black star. **26** Four. **27** Milk and Alcohol. **28** Buenos Aires. **29** Gordon setter. **30** Madagascar.

Quiz 78 Pot Luck 37

Answers - see Quiz 77, page 571

LEVEL 3 

1 Who directed the 1992 film Bram Stoker's Dracula?
2 Robert Banks Jenkinson was British PM under which title?
3 Which cemetery is to the south of the Valley of the Kings?
4 What is Nick Faldo's middle name?
5 Which artist painted The White Horse in 1819?
6 The Lake Pontchartrain Causeway links Mandeville, Louisiana with where?
7 The spice coriander is made from which part of a plant?
8 When was The Sun newspaper founded?
9 Brown, Cornell and Dartmouth are all members of what?
10 What is the international car index mark for a car from Taiwan?
11 Neil Diamond started to train – but didn't qualify – as what?
12 Who is the elder – Liz Hurley or Yasmin Le Bon?
13 What type of musical instrument is the Japanese koto?
14 Who was Vice President when Jimmy Carter was President of USA?
15 Which British composer died on the island of Ischia in 1983?
16 Who was the last person to be executed by beheading in the UK?
17 In which decade did Agatha Christie die?
18 What was Doris Day's first UK Top Ten hit?
19 In quoits, what name is given to the target at which the rings are thrown?
20 Which country had a guerrilla group whose name translated as 'Alfaro lives, dammit'?
21 In cycling what is the first major classic of the season?
22 Which England cricketer lost four toes in a swimming accident while touring the West Indies?
23 In which island group is Guadalcanal?
24 Prince Charles, Prince Edward and Prince Philip were all head boys at which school?
25 What appears in the centre of the national flag of Ghana?
26 How many symphonies did Brahms compose?
27 What was the title of Dr. Feelgood's only Top Ten hit?
28 Which South American city has a name meaning 'fair winds'?
29 Alexander Gordon 1743-1827 gave his name to what?
30 In which country is the city of Antananarivo?

Answers

Hobbies 3 (see Quiz 77, page 571)
1 Angling. **2** New York. **3** Padstow, Cornwall. **4** Underwater hockey. **5** Houston, Texas. **6** The Roux Brothers. **7** Hampton Court maze. **8** Blue, red, yellow or black. **9** Ripon. **10** Scrabble. **11** Marbles. **12** The Nutshell. **13** Milton Keynes. **14** Gatwick. **15** Terence Conran. **16** 9th to 11th. **17** 10. **18** Bowls. **19** Hail. **20** Harmonica. **21** Middlesbrough. **22** Marco Pierre White. **23** Sponge. **24** Lacrosse. **25** None (it's a naturist site). **26** Trainspotter. **27** Blackpool. **28** House. **29** Roller coaster. **30** Roller skates.

Quiz 79 TV Times 3

Answers - see Quiz 80, page 514

1 What is the real name of Renault's Nicole?
2 Mrs Peter Hook is best known on TV as whom?
3 Who co presented The Big Breakfast with Zoe Ball?
4 Who played Kadi Toura in the drama series Roots?
5 Who was the antiques dealer in the Paddington stories?
6 Who used to say, "The next Tonight will be tomorrow night"?
7 Which was the English port in the Triangle drama series?
8 Mrs Robert Powell was a member of which famous dance group?
9 Who was the first Teletubby to have its alter ego sacked?
10 Who composed the Barcarolle which advertised Bailey's Irish Cream?
11 In which series did Charles Dance play Guy Perron?
12 Who does the daughter of Band of Gold's creator play in Coronation Street?
13 Who directed a documentary called Genderquake after leaving a top soap?
14 Who followed Phillip Schofield as link man on Children's BBC?
15 Whose final TV role was as Daniel Reece?
16 In May to December what was Zoe's name before she married Alec?
17 Who composed the music for ITV's coverage of Grand Prix racing?
18 Who are the parents of Live & Kicking's first female presenter?
19 What is the profession of Postman Pat's Mrs Goggins?
20 Which series took place in Lochdubh?
21 Who was Bamm Bamm's dad?
22 What was Alan B'Stard's constituency?
23 Which magazine did Amanda work for in Girls On Top?
24 Who were Father Ted's colleagues?
25 Which disgraced ex MP is the uncle of Jack Davenport from This Life?
26 What did Angela Rippon dance to on The Morecambe and Wise Show?
27 George Baker aka Inspector Wexford appeared as which special agent in Up Pompeii?
28 What were the goldfish on Playschool called?
29 Who played Liz Shaw in Bodyguards?
30 What did Peter do in The Peter Principle?

Answers

Pot Luck 38 (see Quiz 80, page 514)
1 Shetlands. **2** Bob Monkhouse. **3** Plum. **4** Colombia. **5** Lawrence Durrell. **6** Brazil. **7** My Lord Mayor. **8** Three Coins In The Fountain. **9** Crowds. **10** Dog. **11** Bromley. **12** Piracy. **13** Benjamin Britten. **14** Gin and beer. **15** 1880s. **16** Archbishop of Canterbury. **17** Argentina. **18** Witch (Tam O'Shanter). **19** Chess. **20** Aestivation. **21** Carl Douglas. **22** International Phonetic Alphabet. **23** Waterloo & City Line. **24** Germany. **25** Melvyn Bragg. **26** Francis Coppola. **27** Peas. **28** Ireland. **29** Volto subito. **30** Blue and White.

Quiz 80 Pot Luck 38

Answers - see Quiz 79, page 513

1 Where is Baltasound Airport?
2 Who is the elder – Bob Monkhouse or Princess Margaret?
3 Grand Duke, Stanley and Lombard are all varieties of which fruit?
4 In which country is the city of Cali?
5 Who wrote The Alexandria Quartet novels?
6 Against which country did David Platt make his first full England appearance?
7 What is the correct form of address to begin a letter to a Lady Lord Mayor?
8 What was Frank Sinatra's first UK No 1?
9 Demophobia is the fear of what?
10 Which creature is represented in the year the Chinese call gou?
11 What is the most southerly London borough?
12 Anne Bonney and Mary Read famously carried out which trade?
13 Who composed the opera Death In Venice?
14 What have you had if you've just had a dog's nose?
15 During which decade did the Orient Express first run?
16 The Court of Arches is the chief court of whom?
17 Which country has the austral as a unit of currency?
18 Who was the ship Cutty Sark named after?
19 Emanuel Lasker was undisputed world champion for over 26 years at what?
20 What is the summer equivalent of hibernation?
21 Whose one and only UK Top Ten hit was Kung Fu Fighting?
22 What are the initials IPA an abbreviation of, as well as being an ale?
23 Which part of the London Underground is called the Drain?
24 The landau carriage takes its name from a town in which country?
25 Who wrote the novel A Time to Dance?
26 Talia Shire is the sister of which film director?
27 What have you got with a plateful of Pisum satvium?
28 Which country left the Commonwealth in 1949?
29 In music what does the abbreviation VS stand for?
30 Which two colours appear on the national flag of Honduras?

Answers

TV Times 3 (see Quiz 79, page 513)
1 Estelle Skornik. **2** Mrs Merton. **3** Mark Little. **4** O.J. Simpson. **5** Mr Gruber. **6** Cliff Michelmore. **7** Felixstowe. **8** Pan's People. **9** Tinky Winky. **10** Offenbach. **11** Jewel in the Crown. **12** Judy Mallett. **13** Susan Tully. **14** Andy Crane. **15** Rock Hudson in Dynasty. **16** Angell. **17** Jay Kay of Jamiroquai. **18** Bryan Forbes & Nanette Newman. **19** Postmistress. **20** Hamish Macbeth. **21** Barney Rubble. **22** Haltemprice. **23** Spare Cheeks. **24** Douglas & Jack. **25** Jonathan Aitken. **26** Let's Face the Music and Dance. **27** Jamesus Bondus. **28** Bit & Bot. **29** Louise Lombard. **30** Bank Manager.

Quiz 81 Rugby

Answers - see Quiz 82, page 516

1 Who has been an Irish international and the head of HJ Heinz?
2 In which decade of which century did the first league varsity match take place?
3 In which city were Barbarians RFC founded?
4 Which was the first league side to score 1,000 points in a season?
5 Who was Wales' youngest ever captain?
6 Rob Andrew is qualified in what profession?
7 Where did Brian Moore begin his career?
8 How old was Will Carling when he played for Terra Nova Under 11s?
9 Against which side did Jeremy Guscott make his international debut?
10 Which league side was the first to win all its league games in a season?
11 Which of Wigan's 1994-5 trophies is no longer played for?
12 In 1986 St Helens beat Carlisle 112-0 in which competition?
13 Who was the first union player to kick eight penalties in an international?
14 What was Jason Leonard's first club?
15 Who were the beaten finalists in the first league Knockout Trophy?
16 Who captained Ireland in their centenary season?
17 Who did the All Blacks beat 106-4 in 1987?
18 Where was the first floodlit rugby union match played?
19 What name was given to the breakaway clubs from the Rugby Union in 1895?
20 Which club won the first Middlesex Sevens at Twickenham?
21 What position did J.J. Williams play for Llanelli?
22 Who in 1998 held the world record for the most capped hooker?
23 Who recorded the then highest score draw 46-46 in 1994?
24 Who sponsored the rugby league before Courage?
25 In which country was the first rugby league World Cup held?
26 Who was the first UK rugby league club side to play in Australia?
27 Who played a record 17 appearances on five tours with the British Lions?
28 What was the score when Salford beat Wigan's unbeaten 43 game run?
29 Who made the lowest score (0-0) in the BBC's Floodlit Rugby League competition?
30 Who were the first Scottish rugby union club champions?

Answers

Pot Luck 39 (see Quiz 82, page 516)
1 Hungary. **2** Oneirophobia. **3** Kiss Me. **4** 100 miles (161 km). **5** Armoured Fighting Vehicle. **6** The Chicken Song. **7** I. **8** 1960s. **9** Swaziland. **10** Marquis of Granby. **11** Green. **12** God willing. **13** Matthew Broderick. **14** North Carolina. **15** 250mm x 353mm. **16** Salvador Dali. **17** Hyde Park. **18** Llandrindod Wells. **19** Liam Neeson. **20** Under the Coronation Chair. **21** RCH. **22** 1897. **23** Joe Dante. **24** China. **25** Orcus. **26** Winston Churchill's. **27** Seeds. **28** Love's Gotta Hold On Me. **29** A dolphin. **30** Joe DiMaggio.

Quiz 82 **Pot Luck 39**

Answers - see Quiz 81, page 515

1 Which country has the forint as its unit of currency?
2 A fear of dreams is known as what?
3 What was Stephen 'Tin Tin' Duffy's only Top Ten hit?
4 How long is the Suez Canal?
5 In the military, what is an AFV?
6 Which UK No 1 was written by Red Dwarf creators Robert Grant and Doug Naylor?
7 Which letter is two dot in Morse Code?
8 In which decade was Rory Bremner born?
9 Mbabane is the capital of which country?
10 What popular pub name comes from the title held by soldier John Manners?
11 What colour are the stars on the national flag of the Republic of Iraq?
12 What does the Latin deo volente mean?
13 Which actor is married to actress Sarah Jessica Parker?
14 Raleigh is the capital of which US state?
15 What size is B4 paper in millimetres?
16 Which artist painted Christ of St John of the Cross in 1951?
17 Where was the Prince's Trust charity Party In The Park held in 1998?
18 What is the administrative centre for the Welsh county of Powys?
19 Who is the elder – Jimmy Nail or Liam Neeson?
20 Where in Westminster Abbey was the Stone of Scone?
21 What is the international car index mark for a car from Chile?
22 To five years when was the magazine Country Life founded?
23 Who directed the 1990 film Gremlins 2: The New Batch?
24 In which country is the city of Dalian?
25 Who was the Roman God of death?
26 Whose top hat sold for £22,000 at Sotheby's in 1988?
27 The spice fenugreek is made from which part of a plant?
28 What was Dollar's first UK Top Ten hit in 1979?
29 In the film Ace Ventura: Pet Detective Ace is hired to find what?
30 Who was known as 'Joltin Joe' and 'the Yankee Clipper'?

Answers

Rugby (see Quiz 81, page 515)
1 Tony O'Reilly. **2** 1981. **3** Bradford. **4** St Helens. **5** Gareth Edwards.
6 Chartered surveyor. **7** Nottingham. **8** Six. **9** Romania. **10** Hull. **11** Regal Cup.
12 Lancashire Cup. **13** Canada's Mark Wyatt. **14** Barking. **15** Wakefield Trinity.
16 Willie John McBride. **17** Japan. **18** Rodney Parade, Newport. **19** Northern Union.
20 Harlequins. **21** Right wing. **22** New Zealand's Sean Fitzpatrick.
23 Sheffield Eagles & Leeds. **24** Slalom lager. **25** France. **26** St Helens.
27 Willie John McBride. **28** 26-16. **29** Salford & Warrington. **30** Hawick.

Quiz 83 World Tour

Answers - see Quiz 84, page 518

LEVEL 3 

1. What is the currency of Bolivia?
2. Between which two rivers does Manhattan lie?
3. To the nearest million, what was the population of Seoul in 1995?
4. In which country is the city of Curitiba?
5. What is the capital of Brunei?
6. In which country is the deep-water port of Lobito?
7. The islands of Taipa and Coloane are part of which possession?
8. Pluna Airlines are based in which country?
9. Which capital is further north – Khartoum or Addis Ababa?
10. What is the official language of Bhutan?
11. In which country is Kakadu National Park?
12. Which country is due north of Uruguay?
13. Which two countries border Morocco?
14. Which desert lies between the Kalahari and the Atlantic Ocean?
15. Where is the news agency Colprensa based?
16. What is Madison Square Garden situated over?
17. On which island is Nassau, the capital of the Bahamas?
18. In which US state was the first National Park?
19. How is Denali in Alaska also known?
20. The Negev desert tapers to which port?
21. Who designed New Delhi?
22. What is the third longest river in Africa?
23. Which country has the largest oil resources in Africa?
24. To the nearest million, what was the population of the largest US city in 1994?
25. In which country is the city of Medan?
26. What is the capital of Burundi?
27. What is South Africa's judicial capital?
28. What is the most north-eastern US state?
29. SAHSA Airlines are based in which country?
30. Which island is situated between Sumatra and Bali?

Answers

Blockbusters (see Quiz 84, page 518)
1 It Happened One Night. **2** Elwood P Dowd. **3** Lewis Gilbert. **4** Miracle on 34th Street. **5** Philadelphia Story. **6** A Night at the Opera. **7** Walter Pidgeon. **8** Dodi Fayed. **9** Robert Newton. **10** Dances With Wolves. **11** James Cameron. **12** Busby Berkeley. **13** Waterworld. **14** Gary Oldman. **15** Blenheim. **16** Amon Goeth. **17** Bruce Springsteen & Neil Young. **18** Ben Hur. **19** Gandhi. **20** Ellen Burstyn. **21** King Kong, 1933. **22** Bolivia. **23** Endora in Bewitched. **24** The Shadows. **25** Costume. **26** Liv Ullmann. **27** Cary Grant. **28** Mammy (Gone With the Wind). **29** The Full Monty. **30** How to paint.

Quiz 84 Blockbusters

Answers - see Quiz 83, page 517

1 Which 30s classic was originally called Night Bus?
2 Who does James Stewart play in Harvey?
3 Who did Carol Reed replace at the last minute on Oliver!?
4 In which 40s classic did Edward Gwenn play Kris Kringle?
5 Katharine Hepburn bought the rights to a Philip Barry play to make which movie?
6 What was the Marx Brother's first film for MGM?
7 Who played Mr Miniver in the Greer Garson Oscar winner?
8 Which film producer who died in 1997 co produced Chariots of Fire?
9 Who played Bill Sikes when Alec Guinness was Fagin?
10 What was the first Western to win a Best Picture Oscar after a 60 year gap?
11 Who directed the first Terminator films?
12 Who choreographed 42nd Street?
13 Titanic overtook which movie as the most costly ever made?
14 Which actor kidnapped Harrison Ford in Air Force One?
15 Which palace was used for Kenneth Branagh's Hamlet?
16 What is the name of Ralph Fiennes' character in Schindler's List?
17 Whose songs were on the soundtrack of Philadelphia?
18 Which 50s film cost $4 million, twice the maximum of the time?
19 Which film begins with "No man's life can be encompassed in one telling"?
20 Which star of The Exorcist also used the name Edna Rae?
21 Which film has the quote, "It wasn't the airplanes. It was beauty killed the beast"?
22 Where were Butch Cassidy and Sundance finally tracked down?
23 What is the most famous TV role of actress Agnes Moorhead?
24 The composer of the only Oscar nominated song from Grease was from which famous quartet?
25 John Mollo won an Oscar in Star Wars for what?
26 Who was the only woman to have top billing in A Bridge Too Far?
27 Who was originally sought for the role of Shears in The Bridge on the River Kwai?
28 Hattie McDaniel was the first black actress to win an Oscar, but for which role?
29 Which movie did Titanic overtake as a record UK earner?
30 The ex GI is in Paris to learn what in An American in Paris?

Answers

World Tour (see Quiz 83, page 517)
1 Boliviano. **2** Hudson & East. **3** Ten million. **4** Brazil. **5** Bandar Seri Begawan. **6** Angola. **7** Macao. **8** Uruguay. **9** Khartoum. **10** Dzongkha. **11** Australia. **12** Brazil. **13** Algeria and Mauritania. **14** Namib desert. **15** Bogota. **16** Pennsylvania Station. **17** New Providence Island. **18** Wyoming. **19** Mount McKinley. **20** Eilat. **21** Edwin Lutyens. **22** Niger. **23** Nigeria. **24** 7 million - New York. **25** Indonesia. **26** Bujumbura. **27** Bloemfontein. **28** Maine. **29** Honduras. **30** Java.

Quiz 85 Pot Luck 40

Answers - see Quiz 86, page 520

1 Both Emma Bunton's dad and Robert Redford's dad worked as what?
2 London's Royal College of Music is in which regal sounding road?
3 Which actress starred in Thelma and Louise and Lorenzo's Oil?
4 In which European country are the regions of Kitaa and Tunu?
5 In which decade was Lord Archer born?
6 What name is given to the Greek letter that is the equivalent of letter M?
7 What is the Scottish equivalent of the Countryside Commission in England?
8 Who joined the European Union in 1995 with Finland and Sweden?
9 Which sea would you cross if you sailed from Corfu to Cephalonia?
10 Who is the elder – Paula Yates or the Duke of York?
11 What are the initials KCVO an abbreviation of?
12 What was Celine Dion's first solo UK Top Ten hit?
13 Which US state is called the Bullion State?
14 What name did former Mayfair hairdresser Nigel Davies adopt in the 1960s?
15 What colours appear with black and red on the Jordanian flag?
16 In which year did Dennis the Menace first appear in the Beano?
17 Which British army officer invented shells containing bullets to inflict more casualties?
18 Who was the longest serving British PM?
19 What is a cutty sark according to Robert Burns?
20 What is the capital of Djibouti?
21 Which English seaside resort is associated with Count Dracula?
22 What was Donny Osmond's last UK No 1?
23 Who wrote Chicken Soup With Barley?
24 Doraphobia is the fear of what?
25 What was the pirate Blackbeard's real name?
26 What is the name Blimp derived from in the character Colonel Blimp?
27 Which fund pays the Queen's private expenses as sovereign?
28 What is tattooed on Robert Mitchum's knuckles in the film The Night of the Hunter?
29 Where was Captain James Cook killed in 1779?
30 Who composed the opera Billy Budd?

Answers

Plant World (see Quiz 86, page 520)
1 Ginkgo. **2** Oxalic. **3** Callus. **4** Cherokee leader. **5** It dissolves blood corpuscles. **6** Italy. **7** Rockies. **8** North & South Carolina. **9** Blue. **10** Ferns & mosses. **11** Pacific coast of North America. **12** Stalk. **13** African violet. **14** From insects. **15** It loses its green colour. **16** Matchbox bean. **17** Rose of Jericho. **18** Fungi. **19** Cactus. **20** Poppy. **21** General Sherman. **22** Lettuce. **23** On dung. **24** Sierra Nevada. **25** Belladonna. **26** Stalk. **27** By the sea. **28** Silver Fir. **29** Praslin & Curiense. **30** Giant waterlily.

Quiz 86 Plant World

Answers - see Quiz 85, page 519

1 How is the maidenhair tree also known?
2 Which acid makes rhubarb leaves poisonous?
3 What is a tissue which forms on a damaged plant surface called?
4 The Sequoia takes its name from what?
5 What makes the death cap mushroom so toxic?
6 Which European country produces more than half of Europe's rice?
7 Where would you find the home of the bristlecone pine?
8 The Venus flytrap is found naturally in which US states?
9 A meadow clary has flowers of what colour?
10 What sort of plants are cryptogams?
11 The world's tallest tree is native only to where?
12 If a leaf is sessile what is missing?
13 What is another name for the Saintpaulia?
14 How does a bladderwort receive its nourishment?
15 If a plant suffers from chlorosis what happens to it?
16 How is the entada known in Australia?
17 What is the only plant which can change its shape?
18 What does a mycologist study?
19 What type of plant is a saguaro?
20 To which family does the greater celandine belong?
21 The largest known giant redwood is named after whom?
22 How is the plant lactuca sativa better known?
23 If something is coprophilous where does it grow?
24 The tree sometimes known as Wellingtonia is native to which mountains?
25 Atropine is derived from which plant?
26 Which part of the flax plant is used to make linen?
27 If a plant is halophytic where does it grow?
28 Which tree is the tallest native to Europe?
29 On which two islands would you find the sea coconut?
30 Which plant has the largest leaves?

Answers

Pot Luck 40 (see Quiz 85, page 519)

1 Milkmen. **2** Prince Consort Road. **3** Susan Sarandon. **4** Greenland. **5** 1940s. **6** Mu. **7** Scottish Natural Heritage. **8** Austria. **9** Ionian. **10** Duke of York. **11** Knight Commander of the Royal Victorian Order. **12** The Power of Love. **13** Missouri. **14** Justin de Villeneuve. **15** White and green. **16** 1951. **17** Shrapnel (Sir Henry). **18** Earl of Liverpool. **19** Short shirt. **20** Djibouti. **21** Whitby. **22** Young Love. **23** Arnold Wesker. **24** Fur. **25** Edward Teach. **26** The word for an airship in WWI. **27** Privy Purse. **28** Love and Hate. **29** Hawaii. **30** Benjamin Britten.

Quiz 87 Pot Luck 41

Answers - see Quiz 88, page 522

LEVEL 3 

1 A sentence containing all the alphabet's letters is known as a what?
2 What is the international car index mark for a car from Singapore?
3 Who is the elder – Terry Wogan or Bill Wyman?
4 What are Tony Blair's middle names?
5 In which decade did Fiji leave the Commonwealth?
6 Who wrote the novel The Pathfinder?
7 Columbus is the capital of which US state?
8 Who directed the 1991 film The Silence of the Lambs?
9 What was Duran Duran's first UK Top Ten hit?
10 Which post was held by William Gilbert at the courts of Elizabeth I and James I?
11 Which poet was awarded an Order of Merit in 1953, three years before his death?
12 A fear of dust is known as what?
13 Which river was explored by Scotsman Mungo Park?
14 Bill Robertie became the first person to win which World Championship twice?
15 Mogadishu is the capital of which country?
16 Where did the married Princess Elizabeth live before she came to the throne?
17 In music what does the expression 'pesante' mean?
18 Who was the Greek goddess of victory?
19 On the first of which month is Canada Day celebrated?
20 What is the title of the head of the College of Arms?
21 Which mathematician wrote the book The Elements?
22 Which TV character drove a yellow car called Bessie?
23 In which country is the city of Douala?
24 Whose only UK Top Ten hit was Jeans On?
25 For which film did Geena Davis first win an Oscar?
26 In 1860 Willie Park became the first winner of which sporting trophy?
27 What is the correct form of address to begin a letter to a Rabbi?
28 What colour separates the black, red and green bands on the Kenyan flag?
29 What part of your body is initialised as the ANS?
30 Which artist painted Dancer at the Bar around 1900?

Answers

Music Superstars (see Quiz 88, page 522)
1 Jumping Jack Flash. **2** David Cassidy. **3** Neil Diamond. **4** Girls! Girls! Girls! **5** Sorry Seems To Be the Hardest Word. **6** When I Need You. **7** 1960s. **8** Bohemian Rhapsody. **9** Bob Dylan. **10** Eleven. **11** Kate Bush. **12** Dancing Queen. **13** Turandot. **14** Barry, Robin & Maurice Gibb. **15** Let's Dance. **16** Jean Terrell. **17** The Wonder of You. **18** Madonna. **19** Epic. **20** 1962. **21** Mick Jagger. **22** Roxy Music. **23** Rod Stewart. **24** Thunderclap Newman. **25** Celine Dion and Peabo Bryson. **26** Love Me For A Reason. **27** Zubin Mehta. **28** Hot Chocolate. **29** Blinded By The Light. **30** Rock On.

Quiz 88 Music Superstars

Answers - see Quiz 87, page 521

1 What did the Rolling Stones sing to close their 1981 USA shows?
2 Who replaced Cliff Richard in the West End Musical Time in 1987?
3 Who wrote I'm A Believer for The Monkees?
4 From which film was Elvis Presley's 1962 No 1 Return to Sender?
5 What was Elton John's first solo hit on his own Rocket label?
6 Which Leo Sayer hit gave the Chrysallis label their first No1?
7 In which decade did Barbra Streisand first make the UK charts?
8 Which hit was the first to be No 1 over two separate Christmases?
9 Which singer/songwriter penned the lines, "The carpet, too, is moving under you"?
10 How many consecutive UK No 1 hits did the Beatles have?
11 Who duetted with Peter Gabriel on Games Without Frontiers?
12 What was Abba's only No 1 in the USA?
13 Which opera does Pavarotti's anthem Nessun Dorma come from?
14 Which of the Gibb brothers wrote their first UK No 1 Massachusetts?
15 Which David Bowie hit was his fourth UK and second US No 1 in '83?
16 Who replaced Diana Ross when she left The Supremes?
17 What was Elvis Presley's penultimate UK No 1 hit?
18 Stephen Bray and Patrick Leonard have both co-written No 1s with which singer?
19 Michael Jackson's Thriller and Bad came out on which label?
20 When did Tony Bennett first record I Left My Heart In San Francisco?
21 Which group singer put out a solo album called Primitive Cool?
22 A John Lennon song gave which group their only UK No 1?
23 Which singing superstar once had a trial for Brentford FC?
24 Pete Townshend first No 1 as a producer was for which group?
25 Who sang the theme song to the film Beauty and the Beast?
26 What was the final No 1 by any of the Osmond family?
27 Who conducted the Three Tenors for their Italia 90 concert?
28 Who is the only group to appear in the charts in every year of the 70s?
29 Which Springsteen song was a hit for Manfred Mann's Earth Band?
30 Which David Essex hit was the sound track for That'll Be The Day?

Answers

Pot Luck 41 (see Quiz 87, page 521)

1 Pangram. **2** SGP. **3** Bill Wyman. **4** Charles Lynton. **5** 1980s. **6** James Fenimore Cooper. **7** Ohio. **8** Jonathan Demme. **9** Girls On Film. **10** Royal Physician. **11** Walter de la Mare. **12** Amathophobia. **13** River Niger. **14** Backgammon. **15** Somalia. **16** Clarence House. **17** Heavy, ponderous. **18** Nike. **19** July. **20** Earl Marshall. **21** Euclid. **22** Dr Who. **23** Cameroon. **24** David Dundas. **25** The Accidental Tourist. **26** Golf's British Open. **27** Dear Sir. **28** White. **29** Autonomic Nervous System. **30** Edgar Degas.

Quiz 89 Pot Luck 42

Answers - see Quiz 90, page 524

1. Which US state is called the Gopher State?
2. From which musical is the song June is Bustin' Out All Over?
3. In which decade was Frankie Dettori born?
4. The French physician Laennec invented which medical aid?
5. Nelophobia is the fear of what?
6. Who wrote Death In The Afternoon?
7. In which country is the city of Fortaleza?
8. Which French rugby union player holds the record for the most tries for his country?
9. Which tree appears on the Lebanese flag?
10. What's the English name of the constellation Dorado?
11. Whose only UK Top Ten hit was The Final Countdown?
12. Who is the most photographed person to attend Riddlesdown High school, Croydon?
13. In which country are the regions of Liguria and Calabria?
14. Which artist painted the famous painting The Ambassadors?
15. The majority of tourists to the USA are from which country?
16. Who composed the opera The Golden Cockerel?
17. What type of roses were in Lady Diana Spencer's wedding bouquet?
18. Which country has the ngultrum as a unit of currency?
19. Who is the elder – Ruby Wax or Victoria Wood?
20. How old was James Herriot when he began writing books?
21. Which King of Spain was known as Charles the Mad?
22. Who joined the European Union in the same year as Portugal?
23. What is the Swedish plattar?
24. Which media celeb founded a magazine called Passing Wind?
25. Who wrote the novel The Sound and the Fury?
26. What was Earth, Wind and Fire's first UK Top Ten hit?
27. The wall, bar and frog are all part of a horse's what?
28. What is the capital of the Dominican Republic?
29. What is Julie Andrews' full real name?
30. In which decade was the first Archery World Championship?

Answers

TV Times 4 (see Quiz 90, page 524)
1 Colin Firth. **2** AA. **3** Robert Lindsay. **4** Boyzone. **5** Nero. **6** Eric Idle. **7** British Rail. **8** Robert de Niro. **9** Crossroads, King's Oak. **10** TISWAS. **11** Cedric Charlton. **12** Cricket St Thomas. **13** No one, he was never seen. **14** A moose. **15** Play Your Cards Right. **16** Letitia Dean. **17** The Winchester. **18** Michael Cole. **19** Alan Alda. **20** World's biggest one man band. **21** Fleur. **22** Geoffrey Lancashire. **23** Charlie Gimbert. **24** Seymour Utterthwaite. **25** Susan Hampshire. **26** Crimewatch UK. **27** Rathouse International. **28** It Ain't Half Hot Mum. **29** Purple. **30** Bill Treacher (aka Arthur Fowler).

Quiz 90 TV Times 4

Answers - see Quiz 89, page 523

1 Who played John McCarthy in Hostages?
2 Which emergency service did Anthea Turner work for before her media career?
3 Who played the scheming city council chief in GBH?
4 Who did Andrew Lloyd Webber appear on Top of the Pops with in 1998?
5 What was the caterpillar called in Dangermouse?
6 Who founded Rutland Weekend Television?
7 Which company did Colin work for in Colin's Sandwich?
8 In a Comic Strip Hollywood spoof of the miners' strike Peter Richardson played which actor supposedly playing Arthur Scargill?
9 What did Crossroads change its name to in 1987?
10 Which show had a punk dog called Spit?
11 In The Darling Buds of May what was Charley's real name?
12 To The Manor Born was set in which village?
13 Who played Joe Maplin in Hi De Hi!?
14 What strolled across the opening title in Northern Exposure?
15 How was the US series Card Sharks known when it transferred to the UK?
16 Who played Lucinda in Grange Hill?
17 What was the name of the pub in Minder?
18 Who left the employ of Mohammed Fayed to host a daytime chat show on satellite TV?
19 Who hosted That Was the Week That Was in the US?
20 What record did Roy Castle break on the very first Record Breakers?
21 What was Zoe and Alec's baby called in May to December?
22 Which father of a former Corrie barmaid wrote The Lovers?
23 In Lovejoy who bough Felsham Manor after Lady Jane left?
24 Who replaced Foggy Dewhurst when Michael Aldridge joined the Last of the Summer Wine cast?
25 Which TV actress became President of the Dyslexia Institute?
26 Which series was based on Germany's File XY Unsolved?
27 Which company did Terence 'Twiggy' Rathbone own in Hot Metal?
28 In which series were jungle sequences shot in Norfolk and desert scenes in Sussex?
29 What colour hair did Crystal Tipps have?
30 Which actor was digging an allotment to advertise BT?

Answers

Pot Luck 42 (see Quiz 89, page 523)
1 Minnesota. **2** Carousel. **3** 1970s. **4** Stethoscope. **5** Glass. **6** Ernest Hemingway. **7** Brazil. **8** Serge Blanco with 38. **9** Cedar tree. **10** Swordfish. **11** Europe. **12** Kate Moss. **13** Italy. **14** Holbein. **15** Canada. **16** Rimsky-Korsakov. **17** Mountbatten roses. **18** Bhutan. **19** Ruby Wax. **20** 50 years old. **21** Charles II. **22** Spain. **23** Pancake. **24** Ian Hislop. **25** William Faulkner. **26** September. **27** Hoof. **28** Santo Domingo. **29** Julia Elizabeth Wells. **30** 1930s.

Quiz 91 Pot Luck 43

Answers - see Quiz 92, page 526

LEVEL 3

1 In which country is the city of Ibadan?
2 What do the initials for the chemical DDT stand for?
3 Who directed the film trilogy Lethal Weapon?
4 Arthur Scargill and the Duchess of York were removed from where in 1996?
5 What was Pigmeat Markham's only UK Top Ten hit?
6 What is the main language of the Republic of Chad?
7 Douroucouli, de Brazza's guenon and red colobus are types of what?
8 Which artist painted Black Paintings in the 1820s?
9 Who invented the word 'frabjous'?
10 Salem is the capital of which US state?
11 What is Robson Green's middle name?
12 In which decade was Comtesse Raine de Chambrun born?
13 Windhoek is the capital of which country?
14 A fear of fear is known as what?
15 What invaded the town of San Antonio de los Caballeros in June '98?
16 What was Rod Stewart's last UK No 1?
17 Who was the Roman goddess of horses?
18 What does the green pentacle on the Moroccan flag depict?
19 What is the international car index mark for a car from Burundi?
20 What did the M stand for in J.M.W. Turner's name?
21 Where are the headquarters of the French Foreign Legion?
22 What is the drug thiopental used for?
23 Desmond Tutu's middle name is Mpilo, which means what?
24 How is Patricia Andrejewski better known?
25 Who had an 80s hit with She Means Nothing To Me?
26 Fergie was made Chancellor of which university?
27 In 1998 Tommy Dixon was arrested at home after what was mistaken for a gunshot?
28 In which city is the 305 metre long cable braced Erskine bridge?
29 The spice sassafras is made from which part of a plant?
30 Who is the elder – Earl Spencer or Sinead O'Connor?

Answers

Performing Arts (see Quiz 92, page 526)
1 French & English. **2** Michael Crawford. **3** English National Ballet. **4** A cappella. **5** Cell Mates. **6** Vanessa Mae. **7** Louis B Mayer. **8** John Ogdon. **9** Rowan Atkinson. **10** Quintet du Hot Club de France. **11** Dash. **12** Mississippi. **13** Placido Domingo. **14** Phil Collins. **15** Popcorn. **16** Maureen Lipman. **17** Laurence Olivier. **18** Bournemouth Sinfonietta. **19** Tony Richardson. **20** Jerome Robbins. **21** Alan Ayckbourn. **22** Napoleon III. **23** Jim Steinman. **24** Steve Coogan. **25** Jim Davidson. **26** Hello Dolly. **27** Arpeggio. **28** Leslie Bricusse. **29** South Pacific. **30** Sir Peter Hall.

Quiz 92 Performing Arts

Answers - see Quiz 91, page 525

1 In which languages did Irishman Samuel Beckett write his plays?
2 Who performed his one man show EFX in Las Vegas?
3 Princess Diana was patron of which ballet company?
4 Which type of singing means 'in the style of the chapel'?
5 Which play did Stephen Fry walk out of in 1995?
6 Who went on a Red Hot world tour in 1996?
7 Who founded the American Academy of Motion Picture Arts and Sciences?
8 Who won the 1962 Tchaikovsky competition with Ashkenazy?
9 Who, in '81, became the youngest star of a West End one-man show?
10 Grappelli and Reinhardt were leaders of which Quintet?
11 What was the name of Wayne Sleep's 1980 dance company?
12 Tennessee Williams was born in which US state?
13 Which opera singer sang with Sarah Brightman in Requiem?
14 Who played the Artful Dodger in the first stage production of Oliver!?
15 Which Ben Elton novel was the first to be adapted into a West End play?
16 Who had a one woman show called Live and Kidding?
17 Who shared management of the Old Vic between 1944 and 1950 with Ralph Richardson?
18 With which orchestra did Simon Rattle make his professional debut?
19 Who established the English Stage Company with George Devine at the Royal Court in 1955?
20 Who choreographed West Side Story and Fiddler on the Roof?
21 Who was in the Guinness Book of Records for having five plays running in the West End at one time?
22 Which leader is the subject of the play L'Aiglon by Edmond Rostand?
23 Who wrote the lyrics for Lloyd Webber's Whistle Down the Wind?
24 Whose was the star of The Man Who Thinks He's It?
25 Who became the youngest comedian to appear at the London Palladium, in 1977?
26 Thornton Wilder's The Matchmaker was made into which musical?
27 Which musical term means 'like a harp'?
28 Who wrote the songs for Doctor Dolittle?
29 Sean Connery's first West End appearance was in which chorus line?
30 Who founded the RSC aged 30?

Answers

Pot Luck 43 (see Quiz 91, page 525)

1 Nigeria. **2** Dichloro-diphenyl-trichloroethane. **3** Richard Donner. **4** Madame Tussaud's displays. **5** Here Comes The Judge. **6** French. **7** Monkey. **8** Goya. **9** Lewis Carroll. **10** Oregon. **11** Golightly. **12** 1920s. **13** Namibia. **14** Phobophobia. **15** Butterflies. **16** Baby Jane. **17** Epona. **18** The Seal of Solomon. **19** RU. **20** Mallord. **21** Corsica. **22** General anaesthetic. **23** Life. **24** Pat Benatar. **25** Phil Everly and Cliff Richard. **26** Salford. **27** A balloon bursting. **28** Glasgow. **29** Root bark. **30** Earl Spencer.

Quiz 93 Pot Luck 44

Answers - see Quiz 94. page 528

1. In which Hawaiian island is Pearl Harbor?
2. What was Cliff Richard's first 1980s No 1?
3. JF Kennedy was one of how many children?
4. Under what name did Helen Porter Mitchell sing her way to success?
5. What was John Schlesinger's first US film?
6. In which month is the US holiday President's Day?
7. In which European country are the areas of Telemark and Troms?
8. Joe Fagin's 80s hit was a theme tune for which TV series?
9. Which country has the pula as a unit of currency?
10. What is the correct form of address to begin a letter to an Earl?
11. Which US state is called the Bay State?
12. Who is the elder – Michael Flatley or Stephen Fry?
13. Hypegiaphobia is the fear of what?
14. Who did Joe Louis beat to first become world heavyweight champ?
15. What was Eva Braun working as when she met Adolf Hitler?
16. What does the second S stand for in the initials SSSI?
17. Which Battle was the last in the Hundred Years War?
18. Who joined the European Union in the same year as UK and Denmark?
19. Who composed the opera Punch and Judy?
20. What was American hero Paul Revere's day job?
21. Who founded the Pakistan People's Party?
22. In which country is the city of Guayaquil?
23. What was the name of the Queen's first corgi?
24. Who played Sally Bowles in the 1955 film I am a Camera?
25. What did Rajiv Gandhi study at the University of Cambridge?
26. Kurt Weill and Henrik Ibsen were born in which month?
27. Who was the first Austrian to top the UK charts?
28. Which country has the only national flag which is not rectangular?
29. Who played the lead role in the film Finders Keepers?
30. To five either way, how many weeks did Sinatra's My Way spend in the UK charts between 1969 and 1971?

Answers

Tennis (see Quiz 94, page 528)

1 Borotra, Brugnon, Cochet & Lacoste. **2** Vijay Amritraj. **3** Martina Navratilova. **4** Arthur Ashe. **5** Gabriela Sabatini. **6** Pete Sampras. **7** French Open. **8** Margaret Smith. **9** Plus an Olympic gold medal. **10** Karen Hantze. **11** 1968. **12** Michael Stich. **13** Richard Krajicek. **14** Jensen brothers. **15** Cyril Suk & Helena Sukova. **16** Chris Evert. **17** The Queen. **18** Men's doubles. **19** French. **20** Martina Navratilova. **21** Michael Stich. **22** Lindsay Davenport. **23** Kevin Curren. **24** Tony Pickard. **25** Stefan Edberg. **26** Tim Gullikson. **27** Roger Taylor. **28** Kosice, Slovakia. **29** Sue Barker. **30** Sukova.

Quiz 94 **Tennis**

Answers - see Quiz 93, page 527

1 Who were tennis's 'Four Musketeers'?
2 Which tennis player appeared in Octopussy?
3 Who had the car number plate X CZECH?
4 Who won the first US Men's Open?
5 Who, in 1986, became the youngest woman semi finalist at Wimbledon for 99 years?
6 Who won the inaugural Grand Slam Cup in Munich in 1990?
7 What was Monica Seles's first Grand Slam title?
8 Who was the first Australian woman to win the Wimbledon Singles?
9 How does a Golden Grand Slam differ from a Grand Slam?
10 With whom did Billie Jean Moffitt win her first Wimbledon Doubles title?
11 What year was the world's first Open tournament?
12 Who was the first German to win the Wimbledon Men's Singles after reunification?
13 At Wimbledon who won an unseeded Men's final in the 90s?
14 Which brothers asked to wear England shirts on Centre Court during the 1996 championships?
15 Which brother and sister won the Wimbledon Mixed Doubles in successive years in the 90s?
16 Who was the first woman to win $1 million in prize money?
17 Who gave Virginia Wade her trophy when she won Wimbledon?
18 Which new competition was included in the Wimbledon championships in 1884 along with the Women's Singles?
19 Which Grand Slam title has Boris Becker never won?
20 Who did Miss Kiyomura beat in the Wimbledon Junior Final in 1973?
21 In 1992 John McEnroe won the Wimbledon Doubles title with whom?
22 Who replaced Martina Hingis as World No 1 in October 1998?
23 Who did Boris Becker beat to become Wimbledon's youngest Men's Singles winner?
24 Who did Greg Rusedski sack as his coach during Wimbledon 98?
25 Who won his first Open title in 1985 two years after winning the Junior Grand Slam?
26 Which mentor of Pete Sampras died in May 1996?
27 Who was the last British man before Tim Henman to reach a Wimbledon quarter final?
28 Where was Martina Hingis born?
29 How is Wimbledon semi finalist Mrs Lampard better known?
30 Which Helena won two titles in one day at Wimbledon 96?

Answers

Pot Luck 44 (see Quiz 93, page 527)
1 Oahu. **2** Mistletoe and Wine. **3** Nine. **4** Nellie Melba. **5** Midnight Cowboy. **6** February. **7** Norway. **8** Auf Wiedersehen, Pet. **9** Botswana. **10** My Lord. **11** Massachusetts. **12** Stephen Fry. **13** Responsibility. **14** James Braddock. **15** Photographer's assistant. **16** Special. **17** Castillon. **18** Republic of Ireland. **19** Harrison Birtwistle. **20** Silversmith. **21** Zulfikar Ali Bhutto. **22** Ecuador. **23** Susan. **24** Julie Harris. **25** Engineering. **26** March. **27** Falco (Rock Me Amadeus). **28** Nepal. **29** Cliff Richard. **30** 122.

Quiz 95 Pot Luck 45

Answers - see Quiz 96, page 530

1 What was the christian name of chocolate founder Mr Cadbury?
2 In which country is the city of Gwangju?
3 Bill Perks the son of a bricklayer became known as who?
4 What does the Latin mea culpa mean?
5 Which creature is represented in the year the Chinese call 'long'?
6 Which country has the rufiyaa as a unit of currency?
7 Who was Willie Vernon to James Cagney?
8 Where does the Symphony of the Stars take place annually in Hollywood?
9 What was Foreigner's first UK Top Ten hit in 1981?
10 Who is the elder – Bob Geldof or Nigel Kennedy?
11 Which Hitchock film title ties in with his father's field of work?
12 Which three colours make up the Sultanate of Oman flag?
13 Whose nickname was 'Stormin' Norman'?
14 Who directed the 1987 film Good Morning Vietnam?
15 Columbia is the capital of which US state?
16 What is a honey locust?
17 Born Marie Grosholtz, under what name is this French lady remembered?
18 Who were Waiting For a Train in their only UK Top Ten hit?
19 Which saints share their names with three of the five inhabited Scilly Isles?
20 Maputo is the capital of which country?
21 What does the medical term D & C stand for?
22 A fear of floods is known as what?
23 Which artist painted Toledo Landscape around 1610?
24 How is the letter O formed in Morse Code?
25 How many square chains make one hectare in surveying?
26 In which county was Sir Humphry Davy, inventor of the miner's safety lamp, born?
27 What did Terry Wogan study at Belvedere College, Dublin?
28 Who was the Greek god of vegetation and re-birth?
29 Which seasonal rose is from the genus Helleborus?
30 What is the international car index mark for a car from Lebanon?

Answers

Famous Names (see Quiz 96, page 530)
1 Earl of Lichfield. **2** West Green. **3** Robin. **4** George Michael. **5** Helen Mirren. **6** Vic Reeves. **7** His hair was too long. **8** Duchess of Kent. **9** Mountbatten's. **10** Bernard Ingham. **11** Roger Moore. **12** Catherine Walker. **13** Marco Pierre White. **14** Malcolm McLaren. **15** Jane and Jonathan Ross. **16** Fascinating Aida. **17** Samira Khashoggi. **18** Duke Of Westminster. **19** Ryan Giggs. **20** Michael Grade. **21** Sir Peregrine Worsthorne. **22** Gary & Michelle Lineker. **23** Sean Bean. **24** Soft drinks. **25** Chloe. **26** First cousin. **27** Her favourite restaurant. **28** Ralph Fiennes. **29** Swansea. **30** Alexander McQueen.

Quiz 96 Famous Names

Answers - see Quiz 95, page 529

1 Whose stately home is Shugborough Hall?
2 Lord McAlpine is Lord of where?
3 What is the first name of the person who preceded Eddie George as Governor of the Bank of England?
4 Who is known to his family as 'Yog'?
5 Who became Mrs Taylor Hackford in 1997?
6 Who changed his name from Jim Moir so it didn't clash with the BBC's Head of Light Entertainment?
7 Why was Cliff Richard banned from entering Singapore in 1972?
8 How is the former Miss Katharine Worsley better known?
9 In whose family home did Charles and Diana spend the first night of their honeymoon?
10 Who was Margaret Thatcher's Press Secretary when she resigned?
11 Who aged 19 married fellow drama student Doorn van Steyn?
12 Who founded the Chelsea Design Company in 1976?
13 Which Leeds born chef won three Michelin stars by his early thirties?
14 Who opened the punk boutique Seditionaries in the 70s with Vivienne Westwood?
15 Who has children called Betty Kitten, Harvey Kirby and Honey Kinny?
16 How were Issy Van Randwyck, Dillie Keane and Adele Anderson known collectively?
17 Who was Mohammed Fayed's first wife and Dodi Fayed's mother?
18 Who is London's largest landowner?
19 Who is the son of former rugby league international Danny Wilson?
20 Who was raised by his grandmother Olga Winogradsky?
21 Which former editor is Lady Lucinda Lambton's third husband?
22 Who are the parents of George, Harry, Tobias and Angus?
23 Who has '100% Blades' tattooed on his left arm?
24 William Hague's father's business produced what?
25 In '98 Stella McCartney designed for which fashion house?
26 What relation is Natasha Richardson to Jemma Redgrave?
27 After who or what did Lady Helen Taylor (nee Windsor) name her first son?
28 Which Hamlet ran off with his mother Gertrude in 1995?
29 Where was Michael Heseltine born?
30 Who succeeded John Galliano at Givenchy in 1996?

Answers

Pot Luck 45 (see Quiz 95, page 529)
1 John. **2** South Korea. **3** Bill Wyman (Rolling Stones). **4** Through my fault. **5** Dragon. **6** Maldives. **7** His wife. **8** Hollywood Bowl. **9** Waiting For A Girl Like You. **10** Bob Geldof. **11** The Birds (Dad a poultry trader). **12** Red, white and green. **13** US General Norman Schwarzkopf. **14** Barry Levinson. **15** South Carolina. **16** A tree. **17** Madame Tussaud. **18** Flash and the Pan. **19** Agnes, Mary & Martin. **20** Mozambique. **21** Dilation and Curettage. **22** Antlophobia. **23** El Greco. **24** Dash, dash, dash. **25** Ten. **26** Cornwall. **27** Philosophy. **28** Adonis. **29** Christmas Rose. **30** RL.

Quiz 97 Pot Luck 46

Answers - see Quiz 98, page 532

1 Which occupation was shared by the fathers of Roger Moore and Burt Reynolds?
2 What are the two colours of the national flag of Pakistan?
3 Who is the elder – Liam Gallagher or Ryan Giggs?
4 What is Gerald Ford's middle name?
5 What was the profession of escapologist Harry Houdini's father?
6 Over 700 people died in Greece in July 1987 due to what?
7 Who composed the opera The Rape of Lucretia?
8 What are the initials TARDIS an abbreviation of?
9 Whose one and only UK hit which reached No 1 was Float On ?
10 Which writer is actress Rudi Davies' mother?
11 Which prince was born in the year Ted Hughes became Poet Laureate?
12 If a wine is said to be flabby what does it lack?
13 What is the capital of Greenland?
14 In music, what does the expression 'strepitoso' mean?
15 For a role in which film did Vanessa Redgrave shave her head?
16 Which country has the lev as a unit of currency?
17 For what offence did Sophia Loren spend 17 days in prison in 1982?
18 In which decade was Richard Branson born?
19 In which European country are the regions of Beja and Guarda?
20 Which playwright was born in Whiston on Merseyside in 1947?
21 Which American state is called the Hawkeye State?
22 Which vitamin is also known as biotin?
23 Astraphobia is the fear of what?
24 What common factor links children of Cheryl Baker and children of Mollie Sugden?
25 Who played Ron Jenkins in Coronation Street?
26 DJ Jimmy Young was what sort of instructor in the army?
27 Which hit got to No 2 simultaneously in November 1995 with two separate groups?
28 Who created The Simpsons on TV?
29 Who in Gilbert and Sullivan is 'a dealer in magic and spells'?
30 Which soccer side does Eamonn Holmes support?

Answers

Screen Greats (see Quiz 98, page 532)
1 None. **2** Betty Grable. **3** Peter Lorre. **4** Goldfinger. **5** Errol Flynn. **6** 20th Century Fox. **7** Charles Bronson. **8** Tony Curtis. **9** Barbara Stanwyck's. **10** Bela Lugosi. **11** Gene Kelly. **12** Audrey Hepburn. **13** Marlon Brando. **14** Ingrid Bergman. **15** Rita Hayworth. **16** Rebecca. **17** Sophia Loren. **18** One Night in the Tropics. **19** Dustin Hoffman. **20** George C Scott. **21** Julie Andrews. **22** Lola-Lola. **23** His wife Carole Lombard. **24** Ginger Rogers. **25** Charlotte Bronte. **26** Twenty. **27** Anchors Aweigh. **28** The Big Broadcast. **29** The Barkleys of Broadway. **30** Making A Living.

Quiz 98 Screen Greats

Answers - see Quiz 97, page 531

1 What is the total number of Oscars won by Errol Flynn, Peter Cushing and Richard Burton?
2 Who once had her name changed to Frances Dean by Goldwyn?
3 Who is mentioned by name in Al Stewart's song The Year of the Cat?
4 Which Bond film did Sean Connery make prior to Hitchcock's Marnie?
5 Eric Porter played Soames on TV but who played Soames in That Forsyte Woman?
6 Which was the first US studio Richard Burton worked for?
7 Who is known in Italy as 'Il Brutto'?
8 Who changed Bernie for Tony in his first film Criss Cross?
9 Bette Midler recreated whose 30s role in Stella?
10 Which screen great did Martin Landau play in Ed Wood?
11 Who was lent to Columbia by MGM for Cover Girl?
12 Sean Ferrer was the son of which Hollywood Oscar winner?
13 Whose first Oscar was for playing Terry Malloy in a 50s classic?
14 Who was the mother of actress Isabella Rossellini?
15 Whose pin up was pinned to the atomic bomb dropped on Bikini?
16 What was Hitchcock's first Hollywood film?
17 Who was the first performer to win an Oscar for a performance entirely in a foreign language?
18 What was Abbot and Costello's first feature film?
19 Who played Sean Connery's son in Family Business?
20 Who was the first actor ever to refuse an Oscar?
21 Who was the first British born British actress of British parents to win an Oscar?
22 What was the name of Marlene Dietrich in The Blue Angel?
23 Whose death in 1942 spurred Clark Gable to join the US Air Corps?
24 Whose first film was Campus Sweethearts with Rudy Vallee?
25 Which author did Olivia de Havilland play in Devotion?
26 How old was Debbie Reynolds when she made Singin' in the Rain?
27 What was the first film which teamed Gene Kelly with Frank Sinatra?
28 In which film did Bob Hope find his theme tune?
29 In which 1949 film were Rogers and Astaire reunited after a 10 year break?
30 In which film did Chaplin make his screen debut, in 1914?

Answers

Pot Luck 46 (see Quiz 97, page 531)
1 Police officers. **2** White and green. **3** Liam Gallagher. **4** Rudolph. **5** A Rabbi. **6** Heatwave. **7** Benjamin Britten. **8** Time and Relative Dimensions in Space. **9** Floaters. **10** Beryl Bainbridge. **11** Prince Harry. **12** Acidity. **13** Godthab. **14** Noisy, boisterous. **15** Playing For Time. **16** Bulgaria. **17** Tax evasion. **18** 1950s. **19** Portugal. **20** Willy Russell. **21** Iowa. **22** B6. **23** Lightning. **24** Twins. **25** Ben Kingsley. **26** Physical training. **27** Wonderwall. **28** Matt Groening. **29** John Wellington Wells (The Sorcerer). **30** Manchester United.

Quiz 99 World History

Answers - see Quiz 100, page 534

1 What was the last ruling dynasty of China?
2 The Isle of Man belonged to which two countries before it came under UK administration in 1765?
3 What name meaning 'achievement of universal peace' is given to the reign of Emperor Akihito?
4 How did the former Princess Alix of of Hessen meet her death?
5 Who did not seek re election as Austrian President in 1991 after revelations about his activities in WWII?
6 Who was the first President of Israel?
7 How many days after Waterloo did Napoleon resign?
8 Which governor of Sumatra was responsible for the founding of Singapore?
9 What did the Rarotonga Treaty secure in 1987?
10 What does Rasputin mean, as a name given to Grigory Efimovich?
11 Where were all but six French kings crowned?
12 Which country had a secret police force called the securitate which was replaced in 1990?
13 Which President Roosevelt was Republican?
14 What name was given to the incorporation of Austria into the Third Reich?
15 What did Haile Selassie's title Ras Tafari mean?
16 Who was Nazi minister of eastern occupied territories from '41-44?
17 Who was secretary of state to Kennedy and Johnson?
18 Who was the first president of an independent Mozambique?
19 In which country was the Rosetta Stone found in in 1799?
20 What name was given to the socialist movement which carried out the Nicaraguan Revolution?
21 Which Conference drew up the United Nations Charter?
22 Where was the explosive Semtex manufactured?
23 Which city has the oldest university in the world?
24 Who succeeded Ian Smith as Prime Minister of Rhodesia which then became known as Zimbabwe?
25 Where was the first Marxist state in Africa created?
26 Where was the Maoist guerrilla group Sendero Luminoso active in the 80s?
27 Who became New Zealand PM in December 1997?
28 Who was joint secretary general of the ANC with Mandela in 1964?
29 Who were the first three states to break away from Yugoslavia in '91?
30 Where did the Hundred Flowers Movement encourage government criticism in the 50s?

Answers

Pot Luck 47 (see Quiz 100, page 534)
1 When I Fall In Love - Rick Astley and Nat 'King' Cole. **2** Brighton & Hove Albion. **3** South Dakota. **4** Joan Crawford. **5** Johnny Briggs (Mike Baldwin). **6** Boa snakes. **7** Rosemary Conley. **8** Anita Lonsborough. **9** She fell down a flight of stairs. **10** Ouranophobia. **11** Ben E King. **12** MC. **13** Henri Matisse. **14** Maroon. **15** Myalgic Encephalitis. **16** Eltham. **17** Steven Spielberg. **18** Mali. **19** Barry Humphries. **20** Catherine Zeta Jones. **21** Delia Smith. **22** Terry Waite. **23** Mauritania. **24** Samuel. **25** From New York to L.A. **26** Lewis Carroll. **27** Taiwan. **28** American. **29** Winifred Holtby. **30** 2197.

Quiz 100 Pot Luck 47

Answers - see Quiz 99, page 533

1 Which two versions of the same song were in the Top Ten simultaneously in December 1987?
2 Which football team does Des Lynam support?
3 Pierre is the capital of which American State?
4 Which actress was also known as Lucille Le Sueur?
5 Which member of the Coronation Street cast has sung in the chorus of an Italian opera company?
6 Which reptiles come from the family Boidae?
7 Who produced a fitness video called Ultimate Fat Burner?
8 Who was the first female winner of the BBC Sports Personality of the Year?
9 How did fashion empress Laura Ashley die?
10 A fear of heaven is known as what?
11 Which singer's real name is Benjamin Earl Nelson?
12 What is the international car index mark for a car from Monaco?
13 Which artist painted La Desserte in 1908?
14 What colour appears with white on the State of Qatar flag?
15 What is the full name for the medical condition known as ME?
16 Where in the UK did Bob Hope have a theatre named after him?
17 Who directed the 1992 film Hook?
18 Bamako is the capital of which country?
19 Who is the elder – Barry Humphries or Eddie George?
20 Who duetted with David Essex on True Love Ways in 1994?
21 Whose first book was How to Cheat at Cooking?
22 Who is taller – Terry Waite or Frank Bruno?
23 Which country has the ouguiya as a unit of currency?
24 What was the christian name of shipowner Cunard?
25 Where was Patsy Gallant going from in her 70s UK Top Ten hit?
26 Which children's author appeared on the cover of Sergeant Pepper?
27 In which country is the city of Kaohsiung?
28 What is the nationality of writer and chef Ken Hom?
29 Testament of Friendship is about Vera Brittain's friendship with which author?
30 What is 13 cubed?

Answers

World History (see Quiz 99, page 533)
1 Manchu or Qing ('Ching'). **2** Norway & Scotland. **3** Heisei.
4 Shot with her husband Tsar Nicholas II. **5** Kurt Waldheim. **6** Chaim Weizmann.
7 Four. **8** Thomas Stanford Raffles. **9** Nuclear-free South Pacific. **10** Dissolute.
11 Reims. **12** Romania. **13** Theodore. **14** Anschluss. **15** Lion of Judah.
16 Alfred Rosenberg. **17** Dean Rusk. **18** Samora Machel. **19** Egypt. **20** Sandanista.
21 San Francisco Conference. **22** Czechoslovakia. **23** Cairo (El Azhar).
24 Bishop Abel Muzorewa. **25** Congo. **26** Peru. **27** Jenny Shipley. **28** Walter Sisulu.
29 Slovenia, Macedonia & Croatia. **30** China.

Quiz 101 TV - Who's Who?

Answers - see Quiz 102, page 536

LEVEL 3 

1 Who starred with Steve Coogan on The Dead Good Show?
2 Who was the real life husband of the first girl in the famous Nescafe commercials?
3 How was comedy writer Gerald Wiley better known?
4 Who found fame with Emma Thompson playing Danny McGlone?
5 Who starred in and produced a mini series called Sins?
6 Who was a regular in Crown Court as barrister Jeremy Parsons QC?
7 In which series has Philip Franks been a tax inspector and a policeman?
8 Who stormed out of a TV interview when Robin Day called him a "here today gone tomorrow politician"?
9 Whose first pop TV series was called The Power Station?
10 Which Moll Flanders lost husband Ralph to Francesca Annis?
11 Who was the first male presenter of Live & Kicking?
12 What was Lenny Henry's Rastafarian community police officer called?
13 Who came to fame as 'Q' of The Little Ladies?
14 Who was Cherie Lunghi's character in The Manageress?
15 Who played Fletch's son Raymond in Going Straight?
16 Who runs the Amy International production company with wife Susan George?
17 Who are the two youngest McGann brothers?
18 Who was the first female presenter of Top Gear?
19 Who wrote the Magic Roundabout scripts when they were first broadcast in the UK?
20 Which actresses created The House of Eliot?
21 Who appeared in Dixon of Dock Green aged 10 and found fame as Mrs Theodopolopoudos?
22 What is the real name of the comedian who had a No 1 with a cover version of Tommy Roe's Dizzy and wanted a One-2-One with Terry-Thomas?
23 Which EastEnders star used to be better known by his catchphrase 'Terr-i-fic'?
24 Who played Marjory in The Outside Dog in the Talking Heads series?
25 Who won New Faces and went on to present it?
26 Who is the real life mum of Grace and Henry Durham?
27 Who left Sherwood Forest for oil in Denver?
28 Who adapted his novel of the same name into Men Behaving Badly?
29 Who played the seventh Doctor Who?
30 Who was the only female presenter at the Live Aid concert?

Answers

Pot Luck 48 (see Quiz 102, page 536)

1 Betty Joan Perske. **2** Margaret Thatcher. **3** Tennyson. **4** Jeweller. **5** Harvey Goldsmith. **6** Scilly Isles. **7** RM. **8** Queen Margarethe of Denmark. **9** Oops Up Side Your Head. **10** Conakry. **11** Karpov. **12** Oriental rug. **13** Liberator. **14** Bolivia & Peru v Chile. **15** Little Sioux River. **16** Children. **17** Conservatives. **18** Michael Ramsey. **19** Brighton. **20** Jane Seymour. **21** (I Was Made For) Dancin'. **22** Kris Kristofferson & Rita Coolidge. **23** Complete works of Shakespeare. **24** Maine. **25** Phil Collins. **26** Myanmar. **27** Yellow. **28** Gannex. **29** Romania. **30** Glenn Hoddle and Chris Waddle.

Quiz 102 Pot Luck 48

Answers - see Quiz 101, page 535

1 What is Lauren Bacall's full real name?
2 About whom did Cliff Richard say, "She really is a woman just like my Mum"?
3 Who wrote the poem The Idylls of the King?
4 What was the profession of fizzy drinks maker Jacob Schweppes?
5 Who is the elder – Harvey Goldsmith or Sir Elton John?
6 Saint Mary's airport serves which Isles?
7 What is the international car index mark for a car from Madagascar?
8 Who opened Europe's longest suspension bridge in 1998?
9 What was the Gap Band's first UK Top Ten hit?
10 What is the capital of Guinea?
11 Who did Kasparov beat to become world chess champion in 1985?
12 What is a kelim?
13 What was the by-name for the B24 bomber?
14 Which countries fought the Pacific War in the 19th century?
15 On which river does the US city of Cherokee lie?
16 What or who does UNICEF benefit?
17 Which political party did Mrs Pankhurst join in 1925?
18 Who was the first Archbishop of Canterbury to meet a Pope since the 16th century?
19 The first Bodyshop opened in which town?
20 Who was Elizabeth I's first stepmother?
21 What was Leif Garrett made for in his only UK Top Ten hit from 1979?
22 Which husband and wife team had a hit with A Song I'd Like to Sing?
23 What was the first text to be 'bowdlerised' by Thomas Bowdler?
24 Which American state is called the Pine Tree State?
25 Who is taller – Mick Jagger or Phil Collins?
26 Which country has the kyat as a unit of currency?
27 What colour appears with red and blue on the Romanian flag?
28 What make of raincoat did Harold Wilson popularise?
29 In which European country are the counties of Arad, Arges and Cluj?
30 Which duo got to No 30 with the hit Diamond Lights in 1987?

Answers

TV - Who's Who? (see Quiz 101, page 535)
1 Caroline Aherne. **2** Trevor Eve. **3** Ronnie Barker. **4** Robbie Coltrane.
5 Joan Collins. **6** Richard Wilson. **7** The Darling Buds of May, Heartbeat.
8 John Nott. **9** Chris Evans. **10** Alex Kingston. **11** Andi Peters. **12** PC Ganja.
13 Rula Lenska. **14** Gabriella Benson. **15** Nicholas Lyndhurst. **16** Simon MacCorkindale.
17 Mark & Stephen. **18** Angela Rippon. **19** Eric Thompson.
20 Jean Marsh & Eileen Atkins. **21** Pauline Quirke. **22** Jim Moir (Vic Reeves).
23 Mike Reid. **24** Julie Walters. **25** Marti Caine. **26** Victoria Wood. **27** Michael Praed.
28 Simon Nye. **29** Sylvester McCoy. **30** Janice Long.

Quiz 103 The Media

Answers - see Quiz 104, page 538

1 What was Bob Geldof's TV production company called?
2 What is Kerry Packer's media company called?
3 Which mag did Jennifer Saunders and Joanna Lumley guest edit?
4 What was the first INR radio station?
5 Kelly's Directories catalogue what?
6 What is the signature tune of the BBC World Service?
7 What was the first magazine in the UK in 1691?
8 In which magazine did the Addams Family first appear?
9 Which American syndicated a newspaper column called 'My Day'?
10 Who founded the Daily Mail?
11 Where is the newspaper ABC from?
12 Which two UK national newspaper were founded in 1990?
13 Apart from the Tribune, which other US newspaper has Chicago in its name?
14 Which press agency has the abbreviation IRNA?
15 Which newspaper proprietor was born Jan Ludvik Hoch?
16 In '89 Richard Murdoch bought a 50% stake in which Hungarian tabloid?
17 Which Sunday Times editor made headline news himself regarding details of his affair with Pamella Bordes?
18 Lloyd Grossman was restaurant critic of which magazine in the 80s?
19 Who took over The Observer in 1981?
20 Apart from the Guardian, which other newspaper did James Naughtie work for before joining the BBC?
21 What type of correspondent for the BBC was Michael Cole before he went to work for Mohammed Fayed?
22 Who was chairman of Saatchi & Saatchi when they took over the Tory Party account?
23 Which agency did the Saatchi brothers found in 1995?
24 Which famous columnist is married to Lady Camilla Harris?
25 Whose affair with David Mellor brought media man Max Clifford into the public gaze?
26 Which media man's sons all have the middle name Paradine?
27 Which soccer side does Tony Blair's press Secretary support?
28 Which co founder of TV am was married to a future Leader of the House of Lords?
29 What was Ted Turner's family business before he turned to TV?
30 Which media magnate has owned AC Milan and been his country's PM?

Answers

Pot Luck 49 (see Quiz 104, page 538)
1 Blue and white. **2** Maldives. **3** 20th. **4** BDS. **5** Rob Reiner. **6** Record collection. **7** Paradise. **8** Paramount Studios. **9** Angola. **10** Mona Lisa. **11** Debbie Gibson. **12** Mongolia. **13** Lyndon Baines Johnson. **14** Prince Edward Island. **15** Jacopo Robusti. **16** Ulrika Jonsson. **17** Arabian Sea. **18** Sierra Leone & Liberia. **19** Iris. **20** British United Provident Association. **21** House painting. **22** David Thewlis. **23** Texas. **24** Securities and Investments Board. **25** Reptiles. **26** Sea. **27** Games Without Frontiers. **28** Sylvia Syms. **29** John Osborne. **30** Spanish.

Quiz 104 Pot Luck 49

Answers - see Quiz 103, page 537

LEVEL 3

1 What two colours appear on the flag of San Marino?
2 Male is the capital of which country?
3 In which century was Dame Barbara Cartland born?
4 What is the international car index mark for a car from Barbados?
5 Who directed the 1992 film A Few Good Men?
6 What did Paul Gambaccini sell at auction in 1997?
7 Which Persian word means 'pleasure garden'?
8 Which film production company began as the Famous Players Film Company?
9 In which country is the port of Lubango?
10 Which painting did Arthur Scargill choose as his luxury on Desert Island Discs?
11 Which vocalist had Top Ten hits with Shake Your Love and Foolish Beat?
12 Which country has the tugrik as a unit of currency?
13 Who was President of the USA before Richard Nixon?
14 In which Canadian province is the novel Anne of Green Gables set?
15 What was painter Tintoretto's real name?
16 Who is the elder – Patsy Kensit or Ulrika Jonsson?
17 Which Sea, after the Coral Sea, is the largest in area in the world?
18 From which countries do the Mende people originate?
19 Who was the Greek Goddess of the rainbow?
20 What does BUPA stand for?
21 What trade did playwright Brendan Behan learn on leaving school?
22 Who played Paul Verlaine in the film Total Eclipse to Leonardo DiCaprio's Rimbaud?
23 What is the only US state to have been an independent republic?
24 In monetary and banking terms, what do the initials SIB stand for?
25 The Gladys Porter Zoo in Texas is noted for its collection of what?
26 Thalassophobia is a fear of what?
27 What was Peter Gabriel's first UK Top Ten hit?
28 Which actress is the mother of actress Beatie Edney?
29 Who wrote the screen play for the 1963 film Tom Jones?
30 What is the main language of the Dominican Republic?

Answers

The Media (see Quiz 103, page 537)
1 Planet 24. **2** Consolidated Press. **3** Marie Claire (UK). **4** Classic FM. **5** Towns and cities. **6** Lilliburlero. **7** Compleat Library. **8** New Yorker. **9** Eleanor Roosevelt. **10** Lord Northcliffe. **11** Madrid. **12** The Independent on Sunday & The European. **13** Chicago Sun-Times. **14** Islamic Republic News Agency. **15** Robert Maxwell. **16** Reform. **17** Andrew Neil. **18** Harpers and Queen. **19** Tiny Rowland. **20** The Scotsman. **21** Royal. **22** Tim Bell. **23** M & C Saatchi. **24** Nigel Dempster. **25** Antonia de Sancha. **26** David Frost. **27** Burnley. **28** Peter Jay. **29** Advertising. **30** Silvio Berlusconi.

Quiz 105 Music Who's Who?

Answers - see Quiz 106, page 540

1. Who was knocked off No 1 position by Wannabe?
2. Whose record has the longest playing time of any to make No 1?
3. Who was Mike McGear's famous elder brother?
4. Whose one hit wonder replaced Honky Tonk Women at No 1 in US and Britain?
5. Which singer left school in 1961 to appear in the film It's Trad, Dad?
6. Which No 1 singer was born Arnold George Dorsey in Madras?
7. Which top musician produced Shakin' Stevens Merry Christmas Everyone?
8. Who sang lead vocal on the chart topper Babe?
9. Who wrote the lines, "All alone, without a telephone"?
10. Who has recorded singles with Paul McCartney, Julio Iglesias and Diana Ross?
11. Who was the first drummer with The Stone Roses?
12. Joyce Vincent and Thelma Hopkins were the girls in which 70s group?
13. Who joined Wendy Richard in the No 1 from 1962 Come Outside?
14. Which female singer did Peter Skellern ask to join his Oasis in 1983?
15. Which chart topper started life at Leigh, Lancashire as Clive Powell?
16. Who set up the DEP record label?
17. Which 60s artist was the first British born artist with three No 1 hits?
18. How is James Michael Aloysious Bradford better known?
19. Who wrote Chain Reaction for Diana Ross?
20. Who joined the Beatles on their first hit to enter the charts at No 1?
21. Who recorded the 1993 No 1 written and produced by Shaw and Rogers?
22. Which actor was talking to the trees on the B side of Wand'rin' Star?
23. Who was No 1 in the UK and US singles and album charts at the same time in 1971?
24. Who covered the Searchers' No 1 Sweets for My Sweet in 1994?
25. Which Creation Records boss signed Oasis?
26. Which duo made up the Righteous Brothers?
27. Who joined the Beautiful South after being roadie for The Housemartins?
28. Whose death moved Don McLean to write American Pie?
29. The Beatles apart, who first took a Lennon & McCartney song to No 1, with the Dakotas?
30. In the 1950s who was the first instrumentalist to achieve two No 1s?

Answers

Pot Luck 50 (see Quiz 106, page 540)

1 Liberia. **2** Arnold Wesker. **3** Man City. **4** Five.
5 A tiny diamond studded golden horseshoe. **6** Thomas Middleton. **7** God. **8** Alaska.
9 John Donne. **10** Dreams. **11** Physics. **12** Spain. **13** An antelope.
14 Harrison Birtwistle. **15** 1900. **16** The Red House Mystery. **17** Five. **18** Jim Gilstrap.
19 European Coal and Steel Community. **20** Charles Buchinski. **21** MA.
22 San Quentin prison. **23** Rho. **24** Veterans Day. **25** Great Ultimate Boxing.
26 Princess Michael of Kent. **27** Mozambique. **28** Brian Johnston.
29 Michael Tippett. **30** Derby County.

Quiz 106 Pot Luck 50

Answers - see Quiz 105, page 539

1 Which country has the ports of Buchanan and Grenville?
2 Who wrote Chips With Everything?
3 Who were the first English team outside London to claim the European Cup Winners' Cup?
4 In Scrabble what would the word DOG score without any bonus points?
5 What was sewn into the hem of Princess Diana's wedding dress for luck?
6 Who co-wrote The Changeling with William Rowley around 1622?
7 Theophobia is the fear of what?
8 Which American state is called the Last Frontier?
9 "For whom the bell tolls" is a quote from whom?
10 What was Gabrielle's first UK Top Ten hit?
11 What did Olivia Newton-John's grandfather win a Nobel Prize for in 1954?
12 In which European country are the regions of Vigo and Murcia?
13 What type of animal is a kudu?
14 Who composed the opera Mask of Orpheus?
15 In which year did Michelin produce the first of its Red Guides?
16 Which detective novel did A A Milne write in 1922?
17 How many stripes are there on the Thai flag?
18 Whose first UK Top Ten hit was Swing Your Daddy?
19 What does ECSC stand for in European Community Organisations?
20 What is Charles Bronson's full real name?
21 What is the international car index mark for a car from Morocco?
22 Where had Jim Rockford been in the years preceding The Rockford Files?
23 What name is given to the Greek letter that is the equivalent of letter R?
24 What is Remembrance Sunday called in the US?
25 What does 'tai chi chuan' mean in Chinese?
26 Who is the elder – Princess Michael of Kent or Felicity Kendal?
27 In which country is the city of Maputo?
28 Which cricket commentator was awarded the Military Cross in WWII for his 'cheerfulness under fire'?
29 Who wrote the opera The Knot Garden?
30 Which soccer side does actor Robert Lindsay support?

Answers

Music Who's Who? (see Quiz 105, page 539)
1 Gary Barlow. **2** Meat Loaf. **3** Paul McCartney. **4** Zager and Evans - In the Year 2525. **5** Helen Shapiro. **6** Engelbert Humperdinck. **7** Dave Edmunds. **8** Mark Owen. **9** Marc Bolan (Metal Guru). **10** Stevie Wonder. **11** Alan 'Remi' Wren. **12** Dawn. **13** Mike Sarne. **14** Mary Hopkin. **15** Georgie Fame. **16** UB40. **17** Frank Ifield. **18** Jimmy Nail. **19** The Gibb Brothers. **20** Billy Preston on Get Back. **21** Mr Blobby. **22** Clint Eastwood. **23** Rod Stewart. **24** C.J.Lewis. **25** Alan McGhee. **26** Bill Medley and Bobby Hatfield. **27** Dave Stead. **28** Buddy Holly. **29** Billy J. Kramer. **30** Eddie Calvert.

Quiz 107 Sport Who's Who?

Answers - see Quiz 108, page 542

LEVEL 3

1 Who beat Jahangir Khan's five year unbeaten record in 1986?
2 Who had the car number plate 1 CUE?
3 How was Walker Smith better known?
4 What was boxer Paul Ryan's nickname?
5 Who won the Oaks and the St Leger for the Queen in 1978 on Dunfermline?
6 What was the nickname of baseball player Ty Cobb?
7 Which woman was undefeated over 400m between 1977 and 1981?
8 Which horse did Willie Shoemaker ride in his last race?
9 Who was the only person to beat Sugar Ray Leonard in a professional fight?
10 Which athlete was nicknamed 'The Flying Finn'?
11 Who beat Babe Ruth's long standing record of 714 home runs in '74?
12 Who was the first jockey to saddle more than 8,000 winners?
13 Who was the first skier to overtake Pirmin Zurbriggen's four overall world championship titles?
14 Which American football player was nicknamed 'Sweetness'?
15 Who in 1985 was the first man for 30 years to hold the 1500m and 5000m world records at the same time?
16 Whose Triple Jump World Record did Jonathan Edwards break?
17 Who was the first South African to win the Benson & Hedges Masters snooker title?
18 Where did Nelson Piquet win his first Grand Prix?
19 Who did Giancarlo Fisichella drive for in 1998?
20 Who won the Moto Cross des Nations for the first time in 1975?
21 Who was dubbed the Louisville Lip?
22 Whose record of 24 Grand Prix wins was broken by Jim Clark?
23 Who was the first non European to win the Tour de France?
24 Who won the 1988 Jesse Owens Award as the year's most outstanding athlete?
25 Fiona May represents which country at which sport?
26 Who won the Fosters World Doubles with Stephen Hendry in 1989?
27 Which French cyclist's nickname means 'The Badger'?
28 Gene Tunney was only beaten once, by whom?
29 Who was the first Australian to win the Women's World Open Snooker Championship?
30 Who was the first racing driver to win 500 points in Formula 1?

Answers

Pot Luck 51 (see Quiz 108, page 542)
1 Five. **2** E101. **3** Richard Attenborough. **4** Venezuela. **5** 1920s. **6** George Bernard Shaw. **7** Spanish Civil War. **8** My Lord Archbishop. **9** White & yellow. **10** Madison. **11** John of Gaunt. **12** Nick Faldo. **13** Triskaidekaphobia. **14** Mel B. **15** Easel. **16** The Tide Is High. **17** United Arab Emirates. **18** Milk. **19** EAT. **20** Tennessee. **21** Ken Dodd. **22** Amharic. **23** Richard Roundtree. **24** Peace. **25** Goombay Dance Band. **26** Kate Moss. **27** James Fenimore Cooper. **28** Honduras. **29** Clarence. **30** Oliver Stone.

Quiz 108 Pot Luck 51

Answers - see Quiz 107, page 541

1 What's the most number of raised dots in a single letter of Braille?
2 Which 'E' number is used to represent riboflavin in products?
3 Who was actress Jane Seymour's first father in law?
4 In which country is the city of Maracaibo?
5 In which decade was Mohammed Fayed born?
6 Who, on the cover of Sergeant Pepper, was known by his three names?
7 Picasso's Guernica is a comment on what?
8 What is the correct form of address to begin a letter to a Roman Catholic Archbishop?
9 Which two colours form the background for the Vatican City flag?
10 What is the capital of the American state of Wisconsin?
11 Who was Henry IV's father?
12 Who has larger feet – Gladiator Hunter or Nick Faldo?
13 A fear of the number thirteen is known as what?
14 Which Spice Girl once appeared as an extra in Emmerdale?
15 What's the English name of the constellation Pictor?
16 What was Blondie's last UK No 1 of the 1980s?
17 Which country has the dirham as a unit of currency?
18 What is the main food of baby whales?
19 What is the international car index mark for a car from Tanzania?
20 In which US state is a university endowed by Cornelius Vanderbilt?
21 Which comedian played Tollmaster in Doctor Who in 1987?
22 What is the main language of Ethiopia?
23 Who played the black film detective Shaft?
24 Which Nobel Prize was won in 1975 by Andrei Sakharov?
25 Who had a No 1 UK hit with Seven Tears in 1982?
26 Who is the elder – Jemima Khan or Kate Moss?
27 Who wrote the Leatherstocking Tales?
28 Tegucigalpa is the capital of which country?
29 What was the Christian name of frozen food man Mr Birdseye?
30 Who directed the 1991 film JFK?

Answers

Sport Who's Who? (see Quiz 107, page 541)
1 Ross Norman. **2** Jimmy White. **3** Sugar Ray Robinson. **4** Scrap Iron. **5** Willie Carson. **6** The Georgia Peach. **7** Marita Koch. **8** Patchy Groundfog. **9** Roberto Duran. **10** Paavo Johannes Nurmi. **11** Hank Aaron. **12** Willie Shoemaker. **13** Marc Girardelli. **14** Walter Paynton. **15** Said Aouita. **16** Willie Banks. **17** Perrie Mans. **18** Long Beach USA. **19** Benetton. **20** Czechoslovakia. **21** Muhammad Ali. **22** Juan Manuel Fangio. **23** Greg LeMond. **24** Florence Griffith-Joyner. **25** Italy, long jump. **26** Mike Hallett. **27** Bernard Hinault. **28** Harry Greb. **29** Lesley McIlraith. **30** Alain Prost.

Quiz 109 Exploration

Answers - see Quiz 110, page 544

1 What is chiefly grown in Alabama's Canebrake country?
2 The Julian and Dinaric Alps extend into which two countries?
3 The Amur river forms much of the boundary between which two countries?
4 What is the Maori name for New Zealand?
5 Which two main metals are found in the Atacama Desert in Chile?
6 What is the currency of Malaysia?
7 Which country has the highest density of sheep in the world?
8 Which African country takes its name from the Shona for 'House of Stone'?
9 Which volcanic peak is west of Cook inlet in Alaska?
10 San Miguel is the main island of which group?
11 What is the capital of the Lazio region of Italy?
12 What is the former name of the capital of Dominica?
13 Which Brazilian state is the centre of Amazonian tin and gold mining?
14 Aqaba is which country's only port?
15 On which island of the Philippines is Manila?
16 What is the world's flattest continent?
17 Which former fort in New York State is the home of the US Military Academy?
18 Which US state capital lies on the river Jordan?
19 In which country is Africa's lowest point?
20 What is the largest primeval forest left in Europe?
21 The Red Sea is the submerged section of which valley?
22 Regina in Saskatchewan was originally called what?
23 How many countries do the Andes pass through?
24 In which country do the Makua live?
25 What is the highest peak of the Apennines?
26 Which city south east of St Malo was the old capital of Brittany?
27 Which Alps lie north east of the Sea of Showers?
28 Robben Island is a prison in which Bay?
29 What is Malawi's largest city?
30 Which south American port's name means River of January?

Answers

Pot Luck 52 (see Quiz 110, page 544)
1 New Delhi. **2** Wood not metal resonators. **3** Indonesia. **4** Tippett. **5** Dick Tracy. **6** Amy Grant. **7** Tea. **8** Freud. **9** Six. **10** Henry. **11** Crimean. **12** Doris Kappelhoff. **13** Kansas. **14** Z. **15** Jawaharlal (Pandit) Nehru. **16** Lieutenant of the Royal Victorian Order. **17** Sousaphone. **18** Journalism, literature & music. **19** Turkey. **20** Ghosts. **21** Czech Republic. **22** Elaine Paige. **23** Max. **24** Ice cream. **25** Muscat. **26** The Phantom. **27** Ecuador. **28** Puppetry. **29** Kidney. **30** William I.

Quiz 110 Pot Luck 52

Answers - see Quiz 109, page 543

1 Where was Paddy Ashdown born?
2 How does a marimba differ from a xylophone?
3 In which country is the city of Surabaya?
4 Who composed the opera The Ice Break?
5 Which comic strip character was played by Warren Beatty?
6 Whose first UK Top Ten hit was Baby Baby?
7 What would you drink from a cha-no-yu?
8 Whose theories did Jeffrey Masson attack in Against Therapy?
9 How many stripes are there on the Ugandan national flag?
10 What did the last emperor of China Hsuan Tung ask to be called after he was deposed?
11 In which war was the Battle of Inkerman?
12 What is Doris Day's full real name?
13 Which American state is called the Sunflower State?
14 Which letter is two dashes and two dots in Morse Code?
15 Who preceded Lal Shastri as Prime Minister of India?
16 What are the initials LVO an abbreviation of?
17 According to the Bonzo Dog Doo-Dah Band's The Intro and the Outro what is Princess Anne playing?
18 The Pulitzer Prize is awarded in which three categories?
19 In which European country is the region of Anatolia?
20 Phasmophobia is the fear of what?
21 Which country has the koruna as a unit of currency?
22 Who is the elder – Elaine Paige or Lily Savage?
23 Who is the male hero of the children's book Where the Wild Things Are?
24 What is cassata a type of?
25 What is the capital of Oman?
26 In the first Pink Panther film what was the professional jewel thief called?
27 In which country is the sculpture Monument to the Equator?
28 In Japan what type of entertainment is bunraku?
29 Pyelitis affects which organ of the body?
30 Which king of England was crowned on Christmas Day?

Answers

Exploration (see Quiz 109, page 543)
1 Cotton. **2** Albania & Yugoslavia. **3** China & Russia. **4** Aotearoa. **5** Silver & copper. **6** Ringgit. **7** Wales. **8** Zimbabwe. **9** Mount Redoubt. **10** Azores. **11** Rome. **12** Charlotte Town. **13** Rondonia. **14** Jordan. **15** Luzon. **16** Australia. **17** West Point. **18** Salt Lake City. **19** Djibouti. **20** Hainburg in Austria. **21** Great Rift Valley. **22** Pile of Bones. **23** Seven. **24** Mozambique. **25** Gran Sasso d'Italia. **26** Rennes. **27** Lunar Alps. **28** Table Bay. **29** Blantyre. **30** Rio de Janeiro.

Quiz 111 Transport

Answers - see Quiz 112, page 546

1 What was the name of Helen Sharman's space craft?
2 Over which part of Paris was the first successful balloon flight?
3 What was Boeing's first sea plane made from?
4 Who built the oil tanker Jahre Viking?
5 In which craft did Kenneth Warby set a water speed record in 1978?
6 The space probe Magellan went into orbit where in 1990?
7 What are the terminal cities of Japan's Hikari trains?
8 Why were Britain's first traffic lights built?
9 Which was the last country in Europe to change from driving on the left to the right?
10 Who produced the first mass produced four wheel drive saloon car?
11 The world's highest railway line runs between which countries?
12 Who designed and owned the eight engine Spruce Goose in the '40s?
13 What are the two termini of the Volga-Baltic Waterway?
14 Where is Narita airport?
15 In which craft did Charles Yeager first break the sound barrier in the air?
16 Who built Concorde with BAC?
17 What was the first ocean-going oil tanker called?
18 What was the first space station called?
19 Who built the B17 Flying Fortress in WWII?
20 How many passengers did the first hovercraft carry?
21 What was the name of the first nuclear powered ship?
22 Where was the Volkswagen factory before WWII?
23 In which country was the launch site of the European Ariane rocket?
24 How many people can ride a Frankencycle?
25 What was the cruise ship Norway called before a Norwegian bought it?
26 How many capital cities do you pass through on the Pan American Highway?
27 What was the name of the first balloon to cross the Atlantic?
28 If you took the India Pacific train where would you be?
29 Where did the Hindenberg explode in May 1937?
30 What was the first ship launched by Queen Elizabeth II?

Answers

Movie People (see Quiz 112, page 546)
1 Michael J Fox. **2** Charles Laughton & Noel Coward. **3** Bryan Forbes. **4** Max Shreck. **5** Jill Balcon. **6** Jack Lemmon. **7** David Duchovny. **8** George Segal. **9** John Travolta. **10** Writer Jonathan Lynn. **11** Rowan Atkinson. **12** Betty Grable's. **13** Michael Keaton. **14** Robin Williams (Flubber). **15** John Huston. **16** Going My Way. **17** Steve Martin. **18** Sofia Coppola. **19** Woody Allen. **20** Tony Curtis. **21** Meryl Streep. **22** Anthony Shaffer. **23** Simian Films. **24** John Quincy Adams. **25** Rupert Everett. **26** Timothy Leary. **27** Anjelica Huston's. **28** Jason Gould. **29** Cuba Gooding Jr. **30** Chris Columbus.

Quiz 112 Movie People

Answers - see Quiz 111, page 545

1 Who duetted with Joan Jett on Light of Day in 1986?
2 Which two actors rejected Bridge on the River Kwai before Alec Guinness got the lead role?
3 How is actor/director Nobby Clarke better known?
4 Who played the first cinema vampire in Nosferatu?
5 Who was Daniel Day-Lewis' actress mother?
6 Who has a production company called Edited?
7 Which TV hero played a movie villain in Beethoven?
8 Who walked off the set of 10 and gave Dudley Moore a movie break?
9 Who did Schwarzenegger's love interest in Twins marry after the movie was made?
10 Who links TV's Yes Minister and the film Nuns on the Run?
11 Who was the voice of Zazu in The Lion King?
12 Whose legs were insured for more – Fred Astaire's or Betty Grable's?
13 Who did Val Kilmer replace as Batman?
14 Who had the title role in the remake of The Absent Minded Professor?
15 Which director was an amateur lightweight boxing champion in the early 20s?
16 In which film did Bing Crosby first play Father O'Malley?
17 Who adapted the play Cyrano de Bergerac into the movie Roxanne?
18 Who appeared in her father's Godfather Part III?
19 Who directed the first two films in which Dianne Wiest won Oscars?
20 After landing a weekend with which actor the winner said she really wanted the second prize of a fridge?
21 Who did Kristin Scott Thomas beat to win the role in The Horse Whisperer?
22 Who adapted Agatha Christie's Evil Under the Sun for the big screen?
23 Which production company was set up by Hugh Grant and Elizabeth Hurley?
24 Who is the president played by Anthony Hopkins in Amistad?
25 Who played Prinny in The Madness of King George?
26 Which 60s activist was the godfather of Winona Ryder?
27 Which actress's husband designed the Olympic Gateway in LA. '84?
28 Who played Streisand's son in Prince of Tides?
29 Who won supporting actor Oscar for Jerry Maguire?
30 Who directed Mrs Doubtfire?

Answers

Transport (see Quiz 111, page 545)
1 Soyuz TM-12. **2** Bois de Boulogne. **3** Spruce. **4** Japan. **5** The Spirit of Australia. **6** Venus. **7** Tokyo & Osaka. **8** To make access easier to the Palace of Westminster. **9** Sweden. **10** Audi. **11** Peru & Bolivia. **12** Howard Hughes. **13** Astrakhan to St Petersburg. **14** Tokyo. **15** Bell X-1 rocket plane. **16** Aerospatiale. **17** Gluckauf. **18** Salyut 1. **19** Boeing. **20** Three. **21** Lenin. **22** Wolfsburg. **23** French Guiana. **24** Four. **25** France. **26** 17. **27** Double Eagle II . **28** Australia. **29** Lakehurst, New Jersey. **30** Britannia.

Quiz 113 80s Music

Answers - see Quiz 114, page 548

LEVEL 3 

1 Somewhere In My Heart was the only Top Ten hit for which group?
2 Who asked you to Kiss Me in 1985?
3 What was Amazulu's only UK Top Ten hit?
4 Whose Harbour was taken to No 10 in 1988 by All About Eve?
5 Who were on the Road to Nowhere in 1985?
6 Whose first UK Top Ten hit was The Look?
7 Who had a No 4 hit with (Something Inside) So Strong?
8 What was the first Top Ten UK hit for Heart?
9 What was the Pretenders first Top Ten hit of the 80s?
10 Which Soft Cell No 1 from 1981 got to No 5 in 1991?
11 Who did some Wishful Thinking in their only UK Top Ten hit?
12 Which successful 80s band was fronted by Graham McPherson?
13 Which duo had a Top 20 hit from 1983 with First Picture Of You?
14 Who was Right Here Waiting on their first UK Top Ten hit from 1989?
15 Who was the only US act to achieve three successive UK No 1s in the 80s?
16 Which vocalist had a No 8 hit in 1987 with the Moonlighting theme?
17 Who had a US No1 and a UK No 2 with Funkytown in 1980?
18 Which group had a No 5 in 1987 with It Doesn't Have To Be This Way?
19 Which female vocalist expressed Self Control in 1984?
20 Which artist spent the most number of weeks in the UK chart in 1989?
21 Which Pet Shop Boys video featured Sir Ian McKellen as Dracula?
22 Which song gave Steve Winwood his highest UK chart position?
23 What was the Oscar-winning song from Working Girl?
24 Who had a hit with Captain Beaky and Wilfred the Weasel in 1980?
25 Who requested "If you'll be my bodyguard" in his No 4 from 1986?

Answers

Pot Luck 53 (see Quiz 114, page 548)
1 Take A Chance On Me. **2** Leo XIII. **3** Shark Tank. **4** Capricorn. **5** 17. **6** Taunton. **7** The English Patient. **8** Half Crown. **9** Sir John Gielgud. **10** Canada. **11** Bette Davis. **12** AND. **13** Jimmy Hill. **14** Kansas. **15** Patrick. **16** Richard Adams. **17** Leo. **18** Jan Kodes. **19** Iran. **20** 127. **21** General Hospital. **22** Belize. **23** The Mauritania. **24** Robert Aldrich. **25** William Bailey.

Quiz 114 Pot Luck 53

Answers - see Quiz 113, page 547

LEVEL 3 

1 What was Abba's last UK No 1 of the 70s?
2 Who was Pope at the beginning of the 20th C?
3 In which unusual place were Nick Anderson and Julie Boone married?
4 What star sign is David Bellamy?
5 How many storeys are there in the circular tower of Strasbourg's new Euro parliament building?
6 Where in England was Jenny Agutter born?
7 What was awarded Best Film at the Motion Picture Academy Awards in '96?
8 Which coin ceased to be legal tender at midnight on 31st December 1969?
9 Which actor played the Mock Turtle in a 1966 BBC screened version of Alice In Wonderland?
10 In which country is the Alex Fraser bridge?
11 Who is attributed to have described a starlet as "the original good time that was had by all"?
12 What are the international registration letters of a vehicle from the Yemen?
13 Who became LWT's Deputy Controller of Programmes after a career in football management?
14 Wichita international airport is in which US state?
15 What is Ryan O'Neal's real first name?
16 Whose autobiography was called The Day Gone By?
17 What star sign is shared by Robert De Niro and Sean Penn?
18 Who was the defending champion when Jimmy Connors first won Wimbledon singles?
19 Abadan International airport is in which country?
20 How many Grand Prix had Eddie Jordan's team entered before they won?
21 In which soap did Demi Moore find fame?
22 Which country does the airline Island Air come from?
23 Which liner launched in 1907 was called the Grand Old Lady of the Atlantic?
24 Who directed The Dirty Dozen?
25 What is Axl Rose's real name?

Answers

80s Music (see Quiz 113, page 547)
1 Aztec Camera. **2** Stephen Tin Tin Duffy. **3** Too Good To Be Forgotten. **4** Martha's. **5** Talking Heads. **6** Roxette. **7** Labi Siffre. **8** Alone. **9** Talk of The Town. **10** Tainted Love. **11** China Crisis. **12** Madness. **13** Lotus Eaters. **14** Richard Marx. **15** Blondie. **16** Al Jarreau. **17** Lipps Inc.. **18** Blow Monkeys. **19** Laura Branigan. **20** Bobby Brown. **21** Heart. **22** Higher Love. **23** Let The River Run. **24** Keith Michell. **25** Paul Simon

Quiz 115 The Royals

Answers - see Quiz 116, page 550

1 Which monarch said, "The thing that impresses me most about America is the way parents obey their children"?
2 Who said that pregnancy was, "an occupational hazard of being a wife"?
3 Who wrote the words to "I Vow to Thee My Country" which was sung at Princess Diana's wedding and at her funeral?
4 Who had the Queen for tea in her Glasgow council house in July 1999?
5 What is Princess Margaret's eldest grandson called?
6 Who was the first fund raising manager of the Diana Memorial Fund?
7 How old was Elizabeth Taylor when she first danced in front of George V?
8 In which year was the TV film Royal Family made?
9 Who was George V's doctor who announced in 1936 "The King's life is moving peacefully to its close"?
10 Which Earl owned a restaurant called Deals with Viscount Linley?
11 What was the name of the intruder found in the Queen's bedroom in 1982?
12 Where did the Queen, as Princess Elizabeth, spend her 21st birthday?
13 Which monarch asked a party leader to form the first Labour government?
14 Which Royal said "I should like to be a horse" when asked her ambition?
15 Where was Princess Anne when she famously told journalists to "Naff off!"?
16 What did Queen Mary reputedly describe to Stanley Baldwin as "a pretty kettle of fish"?
17 Which Olympic athlete was born on the same day as Princess Diana?
18 What was Princess Michael of Kent's maiden name?
19 Which hospital was Princess Diana taken to after her tragic car accident?
20 In which city did the Queen say, "I sometimes sense that the world is changing almost too fast for its inhabitants"?
21 Which lawyer presided over the divorce of Charles and Diana?
22 How old will the Queen be if she becomes the longest reigning monarch in British history?
23 Who was described by the Queen as, "more royal than the rest of us"?
24 Who said, "I don't feel relaxed at Buckingham Palace.... I don't expect anyone does when they visit their mother in law"?
25 For how long were Charles and Diana divorced?

Answers

***Pot Luck* 54** (see Quiz 116, page 550)
1 Noddy. **2** 8 million. **3** Capricorn. **4** Youssou N'Dour. **5** Athens. **6** Siberia. **7** Sydney Greenstreet. **8** Fighting well. **9** Queensland. **10** 1930s. **11** Julian Clary. **12** Indonesia. **13** Grand Hotel. **14** Wisconsin. **15** Dog. **16** A computer (in the Sci-Fi Tv show Blake's Seven). **17** 32. **18** Gloria Hunniford. **19** W H Davies. **20** Daily Express. **21** John Buchan. **22** Australia. **23** 48. **24** Petula Clark. **25** Lee.

Quiz 116 Pot Luck 54

Answers - see Quiz 115, page 549

1 Which character opened the New York Stock Exchange on June 8th 99?
2 What is the population of Austria to the nearest million?
3 What star sign is shared by Steve Bruce and Alex Ferguson?
4 Who had a UK No 3 hit with 7 Seconds in 1994?
5 Where are the 2004 Summer Olympic Games being held?
6 In which country was Yul Brynner born?
7 Which British character actor made his film debut in The Maltese Falcon?
8 According to the modern Olympics founder Baron de Coubertin, "The essential thing is not conquering but..." what?
9 Who were England playing when David Gower did his Biggles impression?
10 In which decade was the Sydney Harbour bridge opened?
11 Which comedian has four initials, J P M S?
12 Vehicles from which country use the international registration letter RI?
13 In which movie did Garbo say, "I want to be alone"?
14 Truax Field international airport is in which US state?
15 In the cartoon characters Pip, Squeak and Wilfred, what kind of creature was Pip?
16 What was ORAC?
17 When she died how old was Karen Carpenter?
18 Which TV personality married hairdresser Stephen Way in 1998?
19 Who wrote, "What is this life if full of care, We have no time to stand and stare?"?
20 Which paper's 17 June 1977 headline was (Prince) 'Charles To Marry Astrid - Official!'?
21 Which writer said, "An atheist is a man who has no invisible means of support."?
22 Which country does the airline Ansett come from?
23 How many goals did Gary Lineker score for his country?
24 Which singer/actress began her career in the film Here Come the Huggetts?
25 What is Alexander McQueen's real first name?

Answers

The Royals (see Quiz 115, page 549)

1 Edward VIII. **2** Princess Anne. **3** Cecil Spring-Rice. **4** Susan McCarron. **5** Samuel. **6** Paul Burrel. **7** Three. **8** 1969. **9** Viscount Dawson. **10** Lichfield. **11** Michael Fagin. **12** South Africa. **13** George V. **14** The Queen. **15** Badminton. **16** The abdication. **17** Carl Lewis. **18** Von Reibnitz. **19** La Pitie Salpetriere. **20** Islamabad. **21** Anthony Julius. **22** 89. **23** Princess Michael of Kent. **24** Mark Phillips. **25** One year.

Quiz 117 20th C Who's Who?

Answers - see Quiz 118, page 552

1 Who was Jeremy Thorpe talking about when he said, "Greater love hath no man than this than he lay down his friends for his life"?
2 Which major event was covered by war correspondent, Martha Gellhorn?
3 Who said, "When you marry your mistress you create a job vacancy"?
4 Who was Tony Blair's first President of the Board of Trade?
5 Which title did Tony Benn relinquish to sit in the House of Commons?
6 What did Jorge Luis Borges refer to as "a fight between two bald men over a comb"?
7 Who said, "How can you rule a country which produces 246 different kinds of cheese?"?
8 To whom was Nancy Astor speaking when she said, "You'll never get on in politics my dear, with that hair"?
9 Who wrote a book on disarmament called In Place of Fear?
10 Who planned to be the Gromyko of the Labour Party for the next 30 years?
11 Whose last words were, "Now it's on to Chicago and let's win there"?
12 Which woman was President of the Oxford Union in 1977?
13 Who put forward the industrial relations legislation In Place of Strife?
14 Who was the last emperor of Vietnam?
15 Who did Neil Kinnock say was "a ditherer, a dodger, a ducker and a weaver"?
16 Who was the first freely elected Marxist president in Latin America?
17 Paddy Ashdown was in which military unit before entering politics?
18 Who was the official British observer of the atomic bomb at Nagasaki?
19 Who said, "History is littered with wars which everybody 'knew' would never happen"?
20 Which US committee won the Nobel Peace Prize in 1997?
21 Who was First Secretary of State in John Major's last government?
22 Whose help in an election "was like being measured by an undertaker"?
23 Who held the post of Minister of Technology from 1966-1970?
24 Who was runner up to John Major in the Personality of the Year award for 1996 organised by the Today programme?
25 Who said, "There cannot be a crisis next week, my schedule is already full"?

Answers

Pot Luck 55 (see Quiz 118, page 552)

1 Keith. **2** Tony Pawson. **3** Douglas Adams. **4** Steve Davis. **5** Herbert Hoover. **6** Newcastle Upon Tyne. **7** Torvill & Dean's Olympic Dance. **8** Rhode Island. **9** William Broad. **10** Goody Two Shoes. **11** Arthritis. **12** AFG. **13** Christopher Timothy. **14** Beach rugby. **15** Pisces. **16** C Day Lewis. **17** Kevin Curren. **18** Queen Elizabeth. **19** Algeria. **20** Duke of York. **21** Richardson. **22** Colombia. **23** Robert Altman. **24** Freuder. **25** Band Aid II.

Quiz 118 Pot Luck 55

Answers - see Quiz 117, page 551

1 What is Rupert Murdoch's real first name?
2 Who was the first Britain to become World Fly Fishing Champion?
3 Who wrote the novel Mostly Harmless?
4 Who did Jimmy White lose to in his first World Championship snooker final?
5 Who followed Calvin Coolidge as US President?
6 Where in England was Rowan Atkinson born?
7 Which sports event had the most viewers in 1994?
8 Theodore Francis international airport is in which US state?
9 What is Billy Idol's real name?
10 What was Adam Ant's last UK No 1 of the 80s?
11 In 1999 super athlete Carl Lewis revealed that he was suffering from what?
12 What are the international registration letters of a vehicle from Afghanistan?
13 Which actor wrote a book called Vet Behind the Ears?
14 What sport did Lawrence Dallaglio play in June 99 while England played in Australia?
15 What star sign is Patsy Kensit?
16 Who replaced John Masefield as Poet Laureate?
17 Who did Boris Becker beat when he won his first Wimbledon men's singles?
18 What was the largest passenger ship ever built who made her last voyage in 1968?
19 Ain el Bay International airport is in which country?
20 Which British battleship sank the German battlecruiser The Scharnhorst in 1943?
21 What was the first surname of Jane Rossington in Crossroads?
22 Which country does the airline Avianca come from?
23 Who directed M*A*S*H?
24 What is Mark Knopfler's middle name?
25 Who was the last group to have a Xmas No 1 in the 80s?

Answers

20th C Who's Who? (see Quiz 117, page 551)
1 Harold Macmillan. **2** D Day landings. **3** James Goldsmith. **4** Margaret Beckett. **5** Viscount Stansgate. **6** Falklands conflict. **7** Charles de Gaulle. **8** Shirley Williams. **9** Aneurin Bevan. **10** Denis Healey. **11** Bobby Kennedy. **12** Benazir Bhutto. **13** Barbara Castle. **14** Bao Dai. **15** John Major. **16** Allende. **17** Royal Marines. **18** Sir Leonard Cheshire. **19** Enoch Powell. **20** Land Mines. **21** Michael Heseltine. **22** Edward Heath. **23** Tony Benn. **24** Lisa Potts. **25** Henry Kissinger.

Quiz 119 Soccer

Answers - see Quiz 120, page 554

1. Denis Irwin joined Man Utd from which club?
2. What was the first London club that David Seaman played for?
3. Who was the first England player born after the World Cup triumph to become a full international?
4. In how many games did Mick Channon captain England?
5. Which country was the first to lose in two World Cup finals?
6. When did Scotland make their first appearance in the World Cup?
7. Who said, "You're not a real manager until you've been sacked"?
8. In Germany in which decade was the Bundesliga formed?
9. Against which country was England's Ray Wilkins sent off?
10. What would Ryan Giggs' surname have been if he had used his father's name instead of his mother's?
11. Which club did Peter Beardsley join when he left Liverpool in 1991?
12. Steve Davis became a director of which soccer club in 1997?
13. Emmanuel Petit joined Arsenal from which soccer club?
14. When did Arsenal move to Highbury?
15. How many minutes of extra time were played in the Euro 96 final before Germany's Golden Goal winner?
16. Which team did Aberdeen beat in the 1983 European Cup Winners' Cup final?
17. Who did Billie Hampson play for in an FA Cup Final when aged nearly 42?
18. How many goals did Brian Kidd score for England?
19. In what decade was Scotland's first abandoned international match?
20. Who was the first Englishman to play for A C Milan?
21. How many of Gordon Banks's 73 England games ended in clean sheets?
22. Which Arsenal manager signed Dennis Bergkamp?
23. In which year did Wales make it to the World Cup final stages for the only time in the 20th century?
24. Which team has played at home at Pound Park, Selhurst Park and Upton Park during the 20th century?
25. Turek played in goal for which World Cup winning country?

Answers

Pot Luck 56 (see Quiz 120, page 554)
1 South Africa. **2** Taurus. **3** Queen's corgis. **4** 40s. **5** Richard Crossman - in his diaries. **6** 10 million. **7** Tams. **8** Sibelius. **9** Siouxsie Sioux. **10** Australia. **11** Howard Hawks. **12** Grenada. **13** Cliff Richard. **14** He robbed them. **15** 1927. **16** Bath. **17** George Harrison. **18** And that's the way it is. **19** Denmark. **20** Robert. **21** Seattle. **22** Costa Rica. **23** David Platt. **24** Edward Elgar. **25** John Le Mesurier.

Quiz 120 Pot Luck 56

Answers - see Quiz 119, page 553

1 In which country was Cyril Cusack born?
2 What star sign is shared by Maureen Lipman and Glenda Jackson?
3 Who or what are Pharos, Kelpe, Swift and Emma?
4 In which decade was the London Philharmonic Orchestra founded?
5 TV's Yes Minister took its title from the real-life writings of which Labour politician?
6 What is the population of Belgium to the nearest million?
7 Who had a UK No 1 hit with Hey Girl Don't Bother Me?
8 Who wrote the first theme music used in The Sky at Night?
9 Susan Ballion is better known by which name?
10 In which country is the Gladesville bridge?
11 Who directed The Big Sleep and Gentlemen Prefer Blondes?
12 Vehicles from which country use the international registration letter WG?
13 Who sang the theme song for Trainer?
14 What's the link between a certain Peter Scott and Lauren Bacall, Liz Taylor and Sophia Loren?
15 In which year was the talkie The Jazz Singer released?
16 In which city is the Burrows Toy Museum?
17 Who said, "The great thing about the Spice Girls is that you can listen to them with the sound off"?
18 What was CBS TV news broadcaster Walter Cronkite's stock closing phrase?
19 Alborg Roedslet International airport is in which country?
20 What was Oliver Reed's real first name?
21 Tacoma international airport is in which US state?
22 Which country does the airline Sansa come from?
23 Who was England skipper in Terry Venables' first game in charge?
24 Who is the first composer to appear on a British banknote?
25 Which Dad's Army actor said he had conked out in the Times in 1983?

Answers

Soccer (see Quiz 119, page 553)
1 Oldham. **2** QPR. **3** Tony Adams. **4** Two. **5** Hungary. **6** 1954. **7** Malcolm Allison. **8** 60s. **9** Morocco. **10** Wilson. **11** Everton. **12** Leyton Orient. **13** Monaco. **14** 1913. **15** Five. **16** Real Madrid. **17** Aston Villa. **18** One. **19** 60s. **20** Jimmy Greaves. **21** 35. **22** Bruce Rioch. **23** 1958. **24** Charlton. **25** W Germany.

Quiz 121 Film Classics

Answers - see Quiz 122, page 556

1 Which film classic took its name from Ernest Dowson's Cynara?
2 In Casablanca who played Sam, who was asked to "play it again"?
3 What was the first word in Citizen Kane?
4 Which 60s film told of the exploits of Robert Gold and Diana Scott?
5 In which film did Groucho Marx say, "Either this man is dead or my watch has stopped"?
6 What was the motto of MGM?
7 What was Melissa Mathison's contribution to E.T.?
8 What are the final words of The Face of Fu Manchu?
9 The title of the movie In Which We Serve comes from which book?
10 "It was beauty killed the beast" was the last line of which film?
11 In which film did Bacall say to Bogart, "If you want me just whistle"?
12 "Mean, moody, magnificent." was the slogan used to advertise which film?
13 In which film does the heroine say, "I am big, It's the pictures that got small"?
14 Which character said, "Love means never having to say you're sorry"?
15 What was the name of the very first sci fi movie made in 1902?
16 Who directed The Day of the Jackal in 1973?
17 About which film did Victor Fleming say, "This picture is going to be one of the biggest white elephants of all time"?
18 In which film did Mae West say, "Why don't you come up some time and see me."?
19 In Bringing Up Baby, what is Baby?
20 Whose recording of a Bond theme reached highest in the UK's charts?
21 Which film finishes with Joe E. Brown saying "Nobody's perfect" to Jack Lemmon?
22 What is the name of Katharine Hepburn's character in The African Queen?
23 About which film did Bob Hope say, "I thought it was about a giraffe."?
24 Which company used the slogan A Diamond is Forever which Ian Fleming used for the book turned film Diamonds Are Forever?
25 In which film did Bette Davis say, "fasten your seatbelts it's going to be a bumpy night"?

Answers

Pot Luck 57 (see Quiz 122, page 556)
1 Acrobat. **2** Lyndon Johnson. **3** Tragedy. **4** John. **5** Brian Aldiss. **6** Colorado. **7** Cody Jarrett. **8** Tony Blair. **9** Brixton. **10** W B Yeats. **11** Badminton. **12** AND. **13** White. **14** Andrew. **15** Colombia. **16** Newcastle. **17** The Wailers. **18** Salvador Dali. **19** 58. **20** Westminster Abbey. **21** Charlotte Lamb. **22** Australia. **23** Taurus. **24** Warren Beatty. **25** Terry Nelhams.

Quiz 122 Pot Luck 57

Answers - see Quiz 121, page 555

1 What was Burt Lancaster's profession when he worked in the circus?
2 Which politician said, "You let a bully come into your front yard, and the next day he'll be on your porch"?
3 What was the Bee Gees' last UK No 1 of the 70s?
4 What is Anthony Quayle's real first name?
5 Who wrote the novel The Detached Retina?
6 Stapleton International airport is in which US state?
7 Which character did James Cagney play in White Heat?
8 In housemaster Eric Anderson's words who was "maddening, pretty full of himself and very argumentative"?
9 Where in England was David Bowie born?
10 Which poet has "Under Ben Bulben" carved on his gravestone?
11 Actor Gary Webster was a county player in which sport?
12 What are the international registration letters of a vehicle from Andorra?
13 What colour were the horses for Edward and Sophie's wedding carriage ride?
14 What is David Seaman's middle name?
15 Alfonso Bonilla Aragon International airport is in which country?
16 Rowan Atkinson attended which university?
17 Junior Braithwaite was the original lead singer with which group?
18 Who said "There's only one difference between a madman and me. I am not mad."?
19 How old was Charlie Watts when he took part in the Rolling Stones 1999 tour?
20 Where was the Stone of Scone stolen from on 25th December 1950?
21 Under which name does Sheila Holland write romantic fiction?
22 Which country does the airline Augusta come from?
23 What star sign is Sir David Attenborough?
24 Who directed the movie Heaven Can Wait?
25 What is Adam Faith's real name?

Answers

Film Classics (see Quiz 121, page 555)
1 Gone With the Wind. **2** Dooley Wilson. **3** Rosebud. **4** Darling. **5** A Day at the Races. **6** Ars Gratia Artis. **7** Scriptwriter. **8** The world shall hear from me again. **9** Book of Common Prayer. **10** King Kong. **11** To Have and Have Not. **12** The Outlaw. **13** Sunset Boulevard. **14** Oliver. **15** Voyage to the Moon. **16** Fred Zimmerman. **17** Gone With the Wind. **18** She Done Him Wrong. **19** Leopard. **20** Duran Duran. **21** Some Like It Hot. **22** Rose Sayer. **23** Deep Throat. **24** De Beers. **25** All About Eve.

Quiz 123 TV Soaps

Answers - see Quiz 124, page 558

1 Which 60s pop star played a hairdresser in Albion Market?
2 Which ex soap star used to host The Saturday Banana?
3 Which EastEnders actress recorded the song Little Donkey?
4 Who was the head of the sect which Zoe joined in Coronation Street?
5 Which soap actress switched on the Oxford Street Christmas lights in 1983?
6 Who played Mrs Eckersley in Emmerdale before becoming more famous in EastEnders?
7 As well as Liz McDonald which other character has Beverley Callard played in Coronation Street?
8 Who played Malcolm Nuttall in Coronation Street?
9 Rosa di Marco in EastEnders was which assistant of Dr Who in a previous life?
10 Who did Angie leave Albert Square with as she headed for Majorca?
11 In which soap did Chris Lowe of The Pet Shop Boys appear as himself?
12 Which EastEnders character was played by David Scarboro until the actor's early death?
13 Which soap actress played Marsha Stubbs in Soldier Soldier?
14 What was the second surname Valene had in Knot's Landing?
15 Which actor who found fame as a soap star played DI Monk in the first series of Birds of a Feather?
16 Who left EastEnders and appeared in the drama Real Women?
17 What did Bill Roache alias Ken Barlow study at university?
18 The scorer Charles of Telly Addicts has been a regular in which soap for many years?
19 What was the name of the EastEnders video about the Mitchell brothers released in 1998?
20 In EastEnders what football team did Simon Wicks support?
21 What was Kylie Minogue's character's profession in Neighbours?
22 In what type of vehicle did Fallon leave at the end of The Colbys?
23 Which Coronation Street actor conducted the Halle Orchestra in 1989?
24 What is Sinbad's real name in Brookside?
25 In which soap was soap's first test tube baby born?

Answers

Pot Luck 58 (see Quiz 124, page 558)

1 Caine. **2** Portcullis House. **3** I'm No Angel. **4** Arizona. **5** Pope John Paul II. **6** Rowan Atkinson. **7** Sometimes. **8** Jason 1. **9** Doctor. **10** Jasper Carrott. **11** Manfred Mann. **12** Venezuela. **13** Capricorn. **14** Madagascar. **15** The Daleks. **16** 158 million. **17** Germaine Greer. **18** James. **19** Terry Jacks. **20** Berkelium. **21** Arizona. **22** Paris. **23** 60. **24** H G Wells. **25** 1957.

Quiz 124 Pot Luck 58

Answers - see Quiz 123, page 557

1 What is Ben Hollioake's middle name?
2 What is the name of the Westminster building near Big Ben designed to provide extra accommodation for MPS?
3 In which film did Mae West say, "Beulah, peel me a grape"?
4 Sky Harbour international airport is in which US state?
5 Under what name did Karol Wojtyla become known to millions?
6 Who said, "People who meet me for the first time leave thinking 'What a miserable git'"?
7 What's the first word of Stand By Your Man?
8 What name did Amy Johnson's De Haviland Gipsy Moth have?
9 Star Trek actor DeForest Kelley wanted to train as what?
10 Actress Lucy Davis is the daughter of which comedian?
11 Michael Lubowitz is better known by which name?
12 Vehicles from which country use the international registration letter YV?
13 What star sign is shared by Dennis Taylor and Brendan Foster?
14 Amborovy International airport is in which country?
15 What is the most popular creation of Terry Nation's?
16 What is the population of Brazil to the nearest million?
17 Who co presented Nice Time with Kenny Everett and Jonathan Routh?
18 What was Harold Wilson's real first name?
19 Who had a UK No 1 hit with Seasons In The Sun?
20 Which element symbol Bk was discovered in 1950?
21 Sky Harbour international airport is in which US state?
22 In which city did Rudolf Nureyev seek asylum and defect to the West?
23 How many years were between Sir Harold Macmillan's maiden speeches in the Houses of Lords and Commons?
24 Who wrote the story The Country Of The Blind?
25 When did the Queen present her first Christmas Day TV broadcast?

Answers

TV Soaps (see Quiz 123, page 557)
1 Helen Shapiro. **2** Susan Tully. **3** June Brown. **4** Nirab. **5** Pat Phoenix. **6** Pam St Clement. **7** June Dewhurst. **8** Michael Ball. **9** Leela. **10** Sonny. **11** Neighbours. **12** Mark Fowler. **13** Denise Welch. **14** Gibson. **15** Ross Kemp. **16** Michelle Collins. **17** Medicine. **18** The Archers. **19** Naked Truths. **20** West Ham. **21** Car mechanic. **22** Flying saucer. **23** William Tarmey. **24** Thomas. **25** Crossroads.

Quiz 125 Around The UK

Answers - see Quiz 126, page 560

LEVEL 3 

1 Which UK holiday resort had the motto "It's so bracing" from 1909?
2 Who created the Angel of the North?
3 What did the National Trust ban on its land in 1997?
4 Who designed Liverpool's Roman Catholic Cathedral?
5 Which London building designed by Alfred Waterhouse in the 19th century remains one of the most visited today?
6 In which city is the Bate Collection of Historical Instruments?
7 In which year was the first Mersey tunnel completed?
8 Where is the English end of the English Channel where it reaches its widest point?
9 Lots of people visit Alton Towers, but which county is it in?
10 Which architect was responsible for London's National Theatre?
11 In which county is the longest cave system in the UK?
12 Which London borough has the most blue plaques?
13 Who designed the eastern facade of Buckingham Palace early this century?
14 Edward Maddrell was the last Briton this century to have which language as his native tongue?
15 In which city is the world's oldest surviving passenger station?
16 In which Park are the Yorkshire based gardens of Tropical World?
17 Which city are you in if you visit the East Midlands Gas Museum?
18 To the nearest quarter of a million, how many people visited London Zoo in 1990?
19 In which city was the International Garden Festival held in 1984?
20 Which was the first of the UK cathedrals to charge admission?
21 How often does the Leeds International Pianoforte Competition take place?
22 Ben Nevis is the highest mountain in the UK, but which mountain comes next in height?
23 In which English county did Sir Robert Baden Powell hold his first Scout camp in 1907?
24 Which city has the oldest public library in England?
25 In which country was Coventry Cathedral architect Basil Spence born?

Answers

Pot Luck 59 (see Quiz 126, page 560)

1 Won Wimbledon men's singles. **2** Capricorn. **3** Marie. **4** 1903. **5** Orson Welles. **6** Nanu Nanu. **7** Texas. **8** Eric Ambler. **9** 42. **10** Venezuela. **11** Weston Super Mare. **12** BD. **13** Sidney Weighell. **14** Switzerland. **15** Love is. **16** Hospital. **17** Fulham restaurant. **18** Christmas Day. **19** Cape Verde. **20** The Times. **21** Kevin Whately. **22** Wisconson. **23** Eleanor Gow. **24** Francis Ford Coppola. **25** Norway.

Quiz 126 Pot Luck 59

Answers - see Quiz 125, page 559

1 What have Americans Bobby Riggs, Bob Falkenberg and Ted Schroeder all done?
2 What star sign is Freddie Starr?
3 What is Dionne Warwick's real first name?
4 When was the Daily Mirror founded?
5 Who described a Hollywood studio set as, "The biggest train set a boy ever had"?
6 In Mork and Mindy, what was the Orkan phrase for 'Goodbye'?
7 San Antonio international airport is in which US state?
8 Who wrote the novel The Story So Far?
9 How old was Dodi Fayed at the time of his death in 1997?
10 In which country is the Angostura bridge?
11 Where in England was John Cleese born?
12 What are the international registration letters of a vehicle from Bangladesh?
13 Which union leader said in the 70s, "Come on (lads) get your snouts in the trough"?
14 In which country did Basil Hume study theology?
15 Which cartoons are associated with Kim Casalli?
16 Where was William Kellogg working when he decided to sell cornflakes?
17 In Robin's Nest what was Robin's Nest?
18 On which special day did Charlie Chaplin die in 1977?
19 Amilcar Cabral International airport is in which country?
20 Which national newspaper reappeared in 1979 following a year-long strike?
21 Who was Sgt Fletcher in the Miss Marple series with Joan Hickson before becoming another detective's assistant?
22 Senator Joe McCarthy represented which state?
23 What is Elle Macpherson's real name?
24 Who directed Apocalypse Now?
25 Which country does the airline Braathens SAFE come from?

Answers

Around The UK (see Quiz 125, page 559)
1 Skegness. **2** Antony Gormley. **3** Deer Hunting. **4** Edwin Lutyens. **5** Natural History Museum. **6** Oxford. **7** 1934. **8** Lyme Bay. **9** Staffordshire. **10** Denys Lasdun. **11** West Yorkshire. **12** Westminster. **13** Aston Webb. **14** Manx. **15** Manchester. **16** Roundhay Park. **17** Leicester. **18** 1,250,000. **19** Liverpool. **20** St Paul's. **21** Every three years. **22** Ben Macdhui. **23** Dorset. **24** Manchester. **25** India.

Quiz 127 90s Music

Answers - see Quiz 128, page 562

1 What finally knocked (Everything I Do) I Do It For You off the No 1 position?
2 How many singles had the Manic Street Preachers put out before releasing a single that made the top three?
3 Before B*Witched who last made the top twenty with a song called Rollercoaster?
4 Which UK male vocalist had a Peacock Suit at No 5 in 1996?
5 What was the first UK No 1 in the 1990s by Wet Wet Wet?
6 The theme from Friends was a No 3 hit for which group in 1995?
7 Who partnered Whitney Houston on When You Believe?
8 Which hit for D:Ream gave them their first Top Ten hit?
9 Which country was Rozalla from?
10 What was Snaps' first UK Top Ten hit?
11 What was the first record of the 90s to enter the charts at No 1?
12 Who was featured on Puff Daddy's Come with Me?
13 What was the second successive No 1 for Aqua?
14 Who covered You Might Need Somebody to No 4 in 1997?.
15 Who had a UK No 1 hit with Please Don't Go in 1992?
16 Who joined Cher, Chrissie Hynde and Neneh Cherry on Love Can Build A Bridge?
17 What was the follow up to Saturday Night for Whigfield?
18 What nationality is Tina Arena?
19 Which Ace of Base hit was first to get into the Top Ten after All That She Wants?
20 Who sang with Elton John on his only Top Ten of 1996?
21 Who was the featured vocalist on the No 1 Killer by Adamski?
22 Whose first UK No 1 was Ice Ice Baby?
23 Who joined Debbie Gibson on You're The One That I Want?
24 What was Gina G's follow up to her Eurovision entry?
25 Which airline banned Liam Gallagher for life?

Answers

Pot Luck 60 (see Quiz 128, page 562)
1 First scoring sub in an English soccer game. **2** Bobby Kennedy. **3** Elvis Costello. **4** Figueres. **5** Buster Keaton. **6** Wales. **7** One-Upmanship. **8** Joanna Lumley. **9** Monster Raving Loony Party. **10** 1950s. **11** Aquarius. **12** Nigeria. **13** Keith Chegwin. **14** Jo Stafford. **15** 48 times. **16** Marie. **17** Pennsylvania. **18** Panorama. **19** Nigeria. **20** 1949. **21** Painting. **22** Frank Hampson. **23** 14 million. **24** Panama. **25** Turandot.

Quiz 128 Pot Luck 60

Answers - see Quiz 127, page 561

1 What first did Bobbie Knox achieve on Aug 21st 1965?
2 Which US politican said, "Always forgive your enemies, but never forget their names."?
3 Declan McManus is better known by which name?
4 Where in Spain is the Dali Museum?
5 Who starred in the films Our Hospitality and The Navigator?
6 In which country was Timothy Dalton born?
7 What was Stephen Potter's word for letting someone know things weren't quite right?
8 Who wrote an autobiography called Stare Back and Smile?
9 Alan Hope was the first person to win an election for which British political party?
10 In which decade was the Greater New Orleans bridge opened?
11 What star sign is shared by Sandy Lyle and Colin Jackson?
12 Vehicles from which country use the international registration letter WAN?
13 Which TV presenter was lead singer with Kenny?
14 Who was the first female to have a UK No 1 hit?
15 How many times did Valenina Tereshkova orbit the Earth in her 1963 space flight?
16 What is actress Debra Winger's real first name?
17 Which of the US state did Arnold Palmer come from?
18 Which continuing TV programme made its debut on 11th November 1953?
19 Aminu International airport is in which country?
20 In which year were the twin Gibb brothers, Maurice and Robin, born?
21 For what was Georgia O'Keefe noted?
22 Who created Dan Dare?
23 What is the population of Chile to the nearest million?
24 Which country does the airline COPA come from?
25 Which Puccini opera was first performed in 1926?

Answers

90s Music (see Quiz 127, page 561)
1 The Fly. **2** 14. **3** Grid. **4** Paul Weller. **5** Goodnight Girl. **6** Rembrandts. **7** Mariah Carey. **8** Things Can Only Get Better. **9** Zimbabwe. **10** The Power. **11** Bring Your Daughter To The Slaughter. **12** Jimmy Page. **13** Doctor Jones. **14** Shola Ama. **15** KWS. **16** Eric Clapton. **17** Another Day. **18** Australian. **19** The Sign. **20** Luciano Pavarotti. **21** Seal. **22** Vanilla Ice. **23** Craig McLachlan. **24** I Belong To You. **25** Cathay Pacific.

Quiz 129 Famous Names

Answers - see Quiz 130, page 564

1 Who said, "An alcoholic is someone you don't like who drinks as much as you do"?
2 Who created the Mars bar?
3 What would Diane Keaton's surname have been if she had used her father's name instead of her mother's?
4 Who had the catchphrase "nicky nokky, noo!"?
5 Who is the wife of Brian Blosil and father of their seven children?
6 Arnold Bax said one should try everything once except incest and what?
7 Who was dubbed the Brazilian Bombshell?
8 In 1998 who did Vanity Fair describe as "simply the world's biggest heart throb"?
9 Whose business motto was 'Pile it high, sell it cheap'?
10 Who said "I became one of the stately homos of England"?
11 Journalist Dawn Alford was responsible for 'trapping' which famous in name in the late 90s?
12 How many days after Princess Diana's death was the death of Mother Teresa announced?
13 Which fellow politician was Kenneth Clarke's best man?
14 Which actor owned the restaurant Langan's Brasserie?
15 In which High Street store did Glenda Jackson work?
16 Which ex MP and broadcaster has a daughter called Aphra Kendal?
17 Which playwright went to the same school as Adrian Edmondson?
18 Michael Grade became a director of which soccer club in 1997?
19 Which American said, "Boy George is all England needs; another Queen who can't dress"?
20 What do kd lang's initials stand for?
21 Whose portrait was removed form an exhibition called Sensation at the Royal Academy in 1997?
22 Which singer wrote the novel Amy The Dancing Bear?
23 Jeffrey Archer became Lord Archer of where on elevation to the peerage?
24 Who was John Major's last heritage Secretary?
25 What part of his body did Keith Richards insure for £1 million?

Answers

Pot Luck 61 (see Quiz 130, page 564)
1 Eleanor Roosevelt. **2** Ross Norman. **3** Bath salts. **4** Triumph and Disaster. **5** California. **6** Clement Attlee. **7** 1991. **8** Martin Amis. **9** Harlem Globetrotters. **10** Richard. **11** Don Johnson. **12** BDS. **13** Dancing In The Street. **14** Hull. **15** Kikuyu. **16** Pisces. **17** Finland. **18** Arthur Ashe. **19** Sweden. **20** 1929. **21** The Move. **22** Angola. **23** A crossword. **24** Jonathan Demme. **25** Primrose.

Quiz 130 Pot Luck 61

Answers - see Quiz 129, page 563

1. Which US First Lady said, "No one can make you feel inferior unless you consent."?
2. Who brought to an end Jahangir Khan's long unbeaten run of success in squash in the 80s?
3. Which luxury did Esther Rantzen choose on Desert Island Discs?
4. According to Rudyard Kipling what were the "two impostors" to meet and treat the same?
5. Peninsula international airport is in which US state?
6. Who was British Prime Minister when independence was granted to India, Pakistan and Ceylon?
7. When was the Scrabble world championshiop first held?
8. Who wrote the novel The Information?
9. What did Abraham Saperstein start in January 1927?
10. What is Geoffrey Howe's real first name?
11. Who duetted with Barbra Streisand on Till I Loved You in 1988?
12. What are the international registration letters of a vehicle from Barbados?
13. What was David Bowie's last UK No. 1 of the 80s?
14. Where in England was Tom Courtenay born?
15. Jomo Kenyatta was born into which tribe?
16. What star sign is Prince Andrew?
17. Which European country was the first to allow women the vote?
18. Who was the defending champion when Bjorn Borg first won Wimbledon singles?
19. Arlanda International airport is in which country?
20. In which year was Grace Kelly born?
21. Which group recorded the first record played on Radio 1?
22. Which country does the airline TAAG come from?
23. What was first published on 21st December 1913 in the New York World?
24. Who directed The Silence of the Lambs?
25. What is Bob Wilson's middle name?

Answers

Famous Names (see Quiz 129, page 563)
1 Dylan Thomas. **2** Forrest Mars. **3** Hall. **4** Ken Dodd. **5** Marie Osmond.
6 Folk dancing. **7** Carmen Miranda. **8** Leonardo DiCaprio. **9** Jack Cohen.
10 Quentin Crisp. **11** William Straw. **12** Five. **13** John Selwyn Gummer.
14 Michael Caine. **15** Boots. **16** Gyles Brandreth. **17** Tom Stoppard.
18 Charlton Athletic. **19** Joan Rivers. **20** Kathryn Dawn. **21** Myra Hindley.
22 Carly Simon. **23** Weston Super Mare. **24** Virginia Bottomley. **25** Third finger, left hand.

Quiz 131 US Presidents

Answers - see Quiz 132, page 566

1 Which US President did Guiseppe Zangara attempt to assassinate?
2 Who was vice president directly before Spiro Agnew?
3 Who used the line "Randy, where's the rest of me?" as the title of an early autobiography?
4 Which US President had the middle name Wilson?
5 What day of the week was Kennedy assassinated?
6 Dean Acheson was US Secretary of State under which President?
7 Which US President was the heaviest?
8 Which President is credited with the quote, "If you can't stand the heat get out of the kitchen"?
9 Who was the first assassin of a US President this century?
10 Who was the first US President to have been born in a hospital?
11 Which President conferred honorary US citizenship on Winston Churchill?
12 What did Ronald Reagan describe as a shining city on a hill?
13 Who said, "A radical is a man with both feet planted firmly in the air"?
14 In 1996 who was Bob Dole's Vice Presidential candidate?
15 Which US President was described as looking like "the guy in a science fiction movie who is first to see the Creature"?
16 Who described Ronald Reagan's policies as "Voodoo economics"?
17 What type of car was Kennedy travelling in when he was shot?
18 Which aristocratic title is one of Jimmy Carter's Christian names?
19 Al Gore was Senator of which state before becoming Bill Clinton's Vice President in 1992?
20 How old was John F Kennedy's assassin?
21 Who was the Democrat before Clinton to be elected for a second term?
22 Who was Richard Nixon named after?
23 What was the name of the report into J F Kennedy's assassination?
24 What was the name of Kitty Kelley's biography of Jackie Kennedy Onassis?
25 Which president's campaign slogan was "Why not the best"?

Answers

Pot Luck 62 (see Quiz 132, page 566)
1 John Le Mesurier. **2** 61 million. **3** Ernestine. **4** Perrie Mans. **5** Warren Harding. **6** Colorado. **7** Carl Douglas. **8** Aquarius. **9** Fly fishing. **10** Germany. **11** AA. **12** Sierra Leone. **13** Bjorn Borg. **14** 20s. **15** Alan Jay Lerner. **16** 105. **17** Lynsey de Paul. **18** Warwick. **19** Chile. **20** 1919. **21** 80. **22** USA. **23** Grandad. **24** Fire-eater. **25** Edvard Shevardnadze.

Quiz 132 Pot Luck 62

Answers - see Quiz 131, page 565

1 Which popular actor's last words were, "It's all been rather lovely"?
2 What is the population of Egypt to the nearest million?
3 What is Jane Russell's real first name?
4 Who did Ray Reardon beat in the final in his last snooker World Championship triumph?
5 Who followed Woodrow Wilson as US President?
6 Peterson Field international airport is in which US state?
7 Who had a UK No 1 hit with Kung Fu Fighting?
8 What star sign is shared by Vanessa Redgrave and Bobby Robson?
9 Which sporting world championship has been held at the Kuusinski and Kitka Rivers in Finland?
10 In which country is the Bendorf bridge?
11 Who did Anthea Turner work for before she began her TV career?
12 Vehicles from which country use the international registration letter WAL?
13 Who was the last man to win Wimbledon and the French Open singles in the same year?
14 In which decade was insulin first used to treat a diabetic sufferer?
15 Who wrote the words to Thank Heaven For Little Girls?
16 The fabulous Cullinan diamond was cut into how many separate gems?
17 Who wrote the theme song for Hearts of Gold?
18 Simon Mayo and Timmy Mallet studied at which university?
19 Arturo Marino Benitez International airport is in which country?
20 In which year was the first two-minute silence commemorating the Great War held?
21 Gun toting Wyatt Earp survived to what age?
22 Which country does the airline Tower Air come from?
23 Which song by a solo singer stopped T Rex's classic Ride A White Swan from getting to No 1?
24 What was Bob Hoskins' profession when he worked in the circus?
25 Who resigned in December 1990 as Soviet Foreign Minister?

Answers

US Presidents (see Quiz 131, page 565)
1 Roosevelt. **2** Hubert Humphrey. **3** Ronald Reagan. **4** Reagan. **5** Friday. **6** Truman. **7** William Taft. **8** Harry S Truman. **9** Leon Czolgosz. **10** Jimmy Carter. **11** Kennedy. **12** USA. **13** Roosevelt. **14** Jack Kemp. **15** Gerald Ford. **16** George Bush. **17** Lincoln. **18** Earl. **19** Tennessee. **20** 24. **21** FD Roosevelt. **22** Richard the Lionheart. **23** Warren Report. **24** Jackie Oh! **25** Jimmy Carter.

Quiz 133 Sport: 90s Action Replay

Answers - see Quiz 134, page 568

1 Who was the first driver in the 90s to win the first F1 race and not end the season as champion?
2 How many century breaks did John Higgins make in the 1998 World Championship?
3 At which ground did Brian Lara make his record innings of 375?
4 What was the score when England met Uruguay at Wembley in 1990?
5 Who won the first all American French Open Men's Singles final for almost 40 years?
6 How many points did Damon Hill score in his season for Arrows?
7 In which sport did Eric Navet of France become a 1990 world champion?
8 Where did Jonathan Edwards set his 1995 triple jump world record?
9 Which jockey went flat out on the flat to set a record with 1068 rides in the 1992 season?
10 Who was Jeremy Bates' partner in winning the Australian mixed doubles?
11 After six consecutive finals, how many frames did Stephen Hendry win in the 1998 World Championship?
12 Up to his departure in Nov 98, how many years had Roy Evans been with Liverpool?
13 Who finally beat Bob Beaman's 20 plus year long jump record?
14 Who hit a century in some 22 minutes in a county game in July, 1993?
15 Jim Leighton retired after winning how many Scottish soccer caps?
16 Which horse was Henry Cecil's first Oaks winner of the 90s?
17 Alec Stewart was captain for how many Tests?
18 Which horse finished second when Oath won the 1999 Derby?
19 Against which country did Ryan Giggs make his international debut?
20 Who were the first team in the 90s to bat first in a Nat West Final and win?
21 What is Linford Christie's best time for 100m?
22 In which sport have Uhlenhorst Mullheim dominated 90s Europe?
23 Which snooker star made a witnessed practice break of 149 in 1995?
24 Which American state renewed Mike Tyson's boxing licence in 1998?
25 Sanath Jayasuriya belted a limited overs century v Pakistan in 1996 off how many balls?

Answers

Pot Luck 63 (see Quiz 134, page 568)
1 Campbell-Bannerman. **2** Terry Wogan. **3** Figaro. **4** Russell Roberts. **5** Portugal. **6** Pride and Prejudice. **7** First traffic lights. **8** Ayatollah Khomeini. **9** Pisces. **10** Maeve Binchy. **11** Loyd Grossman. **12** BH. **13** Insulin. **14** Cooking. **15** York. **16** 30s. **17** Eritrea. **18** 1957. **19** Norway. **20** Four. **21** John. **22** Fiji. **23** Eamonn Andrews. **24** Coniston. **25** Federico Fellini.

Quiz 134 Pot Luck 63

Answers - see Quiz 133, page 567

1 Who was the next British Prime Minister after Arthur Balfour?
2 Who narrated Stoppit and Tidyup?
3 What was Brotherhood Of Man's last UK No 1 of the 70s?
4 What is Russ Abbot's real name?
5 From which country did Angola achieve independence in 1975?
6 Which novel written in 1813 was adapted into one of TV's hits of the 90s?
7 What first appeared in Ohio in 1914 to affect transport?
8 Who said, "Anybody wishing to banish theft from the world must cut off the thief's hands"?
9 What star sign is Michael Caine?
10 Who wrote the novel Evening Class?
11 Which TV presenter was once in a group called Jet Bronx and the Forbidden?
12 What are the international registration letters of a vehicle from Belize?
13 Banting and Best pioneered the use of what?
14 What did Emma Forbes present on Going Live!?
15 Where in England was Dame Judi Dench born?
16 In which decade did Billboard magazine first publish an American hit chart?
17 Asmara International airport is in which country?
18 In which year did Andy Capp first appear in the Daily Mirror?
19 Which was the first European country to abolish capital punishmnent?
20 How many soccer World Cup campaigns was Walter Winterbottom involved with for England?
21 What was Enoch Powell's real first name?
22 Which country does the airline Air Pacific come from?
23 Which Irish TV celebrity received a Papal knighthood for charitable works?
24 On which lake was Donald Campbell killed?
25 Who directed the movie La Dolce Vita?

Answers

Sport: 90s Action Replay (see Quiz 133, page 567)
1 David Coulthard - in 1997. **2** 14. **3** Recreation Ground. **4** 2-1 to Uruguay. **5** Jim Courier. **6** 7. **7** Show jumping. **8** Sweden. **9** Michael Roberts. **10** Jo Durie. **11** 4. **12** 35. **13** Mike Powell. **14** Glen Chapple - of Lancashire. **15** 91. **16** Lady Carla. **17** 11. **18** Daliapour. **19** Germany. **20** Lancashire. **21** 9.87. **22** Hockey. **23** Tony Drago. **24** Nevada. **25** 48.

Quiz 135 Movies - Who's Who?

Answers - see Quiz 136, page 570

LEVEL 3

1 Who described his acting range as "left eyebrow raised, right eyebrow raised"?
2 Which actor became playwright Arthur Miller's son in law in 1997?
3 Who played the King of Messina in the 90s Much Ado About Nothing?
4 Who said, "I squint because I can't take too much light"?
5 Who was Geena Davis's husband when they made the loss maker Cutthroat Island?
6 In 1993 who tried to buy the rights of his first movie Sizzle Beach USA?
7 Which star of The Krays wrote a prose and poetry book called America?
8 Who owned the LA nightclub The Viper Room at the time of River Phoenix's death there in 1993?
9 Which future First Lady had walk on parts in Becky Sharp and Small Town Girl in the 30s?
10 Who was described by co star Nick Nolte as, "... a ball buster. Protect me from her"?
11 Which sportsman appeared as himself in the 1964 film The Beauty Jungle?
12 Which actress was Roger Moore's first Bond girl?
13 Who was the star of the film based on the record Harper Valley PTA by Jeannie C Riley?
14 Which actress is ex beauty queen Miss Orange County 1976?
15 Which actress perished in the shower in the remake of Psycho?
16 Which film director was Anthony Quinn's father in law?
17 Who wrote the screenplay for The Crying Game?
18 Which novelist appeared in the film Day For Night?
19 What is Barbra Streisand's middle name?
20 How many films had Christopher Reeve made before Superman in 1978?
21 Who starred in Roger Vadim's remake of And God Created Woman?
22 Which actress wrote the novel The Last of the Really Great Whangdoodles?
23 Which film maker's first film was Pather Panchali?
24 Who did Winona Ryder replace on the set of Mermaids?
25 How is Paul Reubens also known in the film and TV world?

Answers

Pot Luck 64 (see Quiz 136, page 570)
1 Bunty. **2** Alan Smith. **3** Adam Ant. **4** Pisces. **5** Woodrow Wilson. **6** Marvin. **7** The City Varieties Theatre, Leeds. **8** Tymes. **9** 58 million. **10** Denmark. **11** USA. **12** Uruguay. **13** Ray and Deirdre Langton's. **14** Rik Mayall. **15** Great Yarmouth. **16** Leon Spinks. **17** Italy. **18** Marwood. **19** Nicaragua. **20** Catherine Zeta Jones. **21** North Carolina. **22** France. **23** Nike. **24** Clement Attlee. **25** Angus.

Quiz 136 Pot Luck 64

Answers - see Quiz 135, page 569

1 What is Lily Savage's 'daughter' called?
2 Who came on when Gary Lineker was controversially pulled off in his last international?
3 Stewart Goddard is better known by which name?
4 What star sign is shared by Prince Andrew and Princess Michael of Kent?
5 Who was the US President during World War I?
6 What is Neil Simon's real first name?
7 Which theatre was home to the final edition of TV's The Good Old Days?
8 Who had a UK No 1 hit with Ms. Grace?
9 What is the population of France to the nearest million?
10 In which country is the Great Belt East bridge?
11 In which country was Emilio Estevez born?
12 Vehicles from which country use the international registration letter ROU?
13 Which Corrie wedding took place the same year as Meg & Hugh Mortimer?
14 Which comedian said of his wild image, "... really I am Mr Mortgage"?
15 Where in Britain were the first deaths caused by an air raid?
16 Who was the last undisputed boxing world heavyweight champion before Mike Tyson?
17 Which country's invasion of Ethiopia in 1935 forced Haile Selassie to flee?
18 What is John Cleese's middle name?
19 Augusto C Sandino International airport is in which country?
20 Which star duetted with David Essex on True Love Ways in 1994?
21 Raleigh international airport is in which US state?
22 Which country does the airline Air Littoral come from?
23 Which brand had to apologise for a logo said to be like the Arabic for Allah?
24 King George VI conferred an Order of Merit on which former PM in 1951?
25 What was Hudson's first name in the TV series Upstairs Downstairs?

Answers

Movies - Who's Who? (see Quiz 135, page 569)
1 Roger Moore. **2** Daniel Day-Lewis. **3** Richard Briers. **4** Clint Eastwood. **5** Renny Harlin. **6** Kevin Costner. **7** Steven Berkoff. **8** Johnny Depp. **9** Patricia Nixon. **10** Barbra Streisand. **11** Stirling Moss. **12** Jane Seymour. **13** Barbara Eden. **14** Michelle Pfeiffer. **15** Anne Heche. **16** Cecil B de Mille. **17** Neil Jordan. **18** Graham Greene. **19** Joan. **20** One. **21** Rebecca de Mornay. **22** Julie Andrews. **23** Satyajit Ray. **24** Emily Lloyd. **25** Pee Wee Herman.

Quiz 137 Famous Faces

Answers - see Quiz 138, page 572

1. Which former Gladiator presented Finders Keepers?
2. What is Rowan Atkinson's middle name?
3. Which part of Dave Allen's body is partly missing?
4. Which TV interviewer was South of England show jumping champion in 1964?
5. Who designed the original Blue Peter badge?
6. Which Brit won the American Sportscasters' Association International Award in 1989?
7. Who played Pte Mick Hopper in Lipstick on Your Collar before shooting to film superstardom?
8. How old was Twiggy when she appeared on This Is Your Life?
9. Who was the first sports presenter on Newsnight?
10. What luxury did Bob Monkhouse choose on Desert Island Discs?
11. Whose TV debut was presenting Hippo on Sky's Superchannel?
12. Where does Roseanne have a tattoo of a pink rose?
13. Which star of EastEnders appeared on a Sammy Davis Jr Special along with Mandy Rice-Davies?
14. What was the Earl of Wessex's TV programme about his great uncle called?
15. What was Jo Brand's profession before being a successful comic?
16. For which series did Emma Thompson win her second successive best actress BAFTA?
17. Which TV detective had received the George Cross?
18. Des O'Connor had a football trial with which club?
19. What was Zoe Ball's first children's show on terrestrial TV?
20. What relation is Jon to Peter Snow?
21. Which famous TV face was part of the girl band Faith, Hope and Charity?
22. Jim Davidson became a director of which soccer club in 1981?
23. Who presented the first edition of News At Ten?
24. Which character did Anthony Andrews play in The Pallisers before finding fame in Brideshead Revisited?
25. What was Trevor McDonald's codename for This Is Your Life?

Answers

***Pot Luck* 65** (see Quiz 138, page 572)

1 Ruth. **2** 1900s. **3** Taurus. **4** Bonar Law. **5** Texas. **6** Joanna Lumley. **7** Henry. **8** 69. **9** Indonesia. **10** Richard Noble. **11** Pat Barker. **12** BRN. **13** Ice skating. **14** Wrexham. **15** Bros. **16** Daydreamer. **17** Salford. **18** Ian Callaghan. **19** Poland. **20** Colombia. **21** 27. **22** Barbara Hepworth. **23** John Ford. **24** Christian Hawkins. **25** Release Me.

Quiz 138 Pot Luck 65

Answers - see Quiz 137, page 571

1 What was Bette Davis' real first name?
2 In which decade was Alzheimer's disease first clinically described?
3 What star sign is Glenda Jackson?
4 Who was the first British Prime Minister to be born overseas?
5 Robert Mueller Municipal Airport is in which US state?
6 Which sitcom star was married to script writer Jeremy Lloyd for only four months?
7 What was the first name of the original food manufacturer Mr Heinz?
8 How old was Ronald Reagan when he became US President?
9 Which country does the airline Garuda come from?
10 Which Brit broke the land speed record in 1990 in Thrust 2?
11 Who wrote The Ghost Road?
12 What are the international registration letters of a vehicle from Bahrain?
13 In which sport did Hollywood star Sonja Henie win Olympic Gold?
14 Which soccer side does Tim Vincent support?
15 In which brothers pop group was Craig Logan not a brother?
16 What was David Cassidy's last UK No 1 of the 70s?
17 Where in England was Albert Finney born?
18 In soccer, who holds Liverpool's league appearance record?
19 Balice International airport is in which country?
20 Panama proclaimed independence in 1903 from which country?
21 How old was Jimi Hendrix when he died?
22 Which sculptor died in a fire in a studio in the 70s?
23 Who directed How The West Was Won?
24 What is Christian Slater's real name?
25 Which song by a solo singer stopped Penny Lane from getting to No 1?

Answers

Famous Faces (see Quiz 137, page 571)
1 Diane Youdale. **2** Sebastian. **3** Finger. **4** Jonathan Dimbleby. **5** Tony Hart. **6** Harry Carpenter. **7** Ewan McGregor. **8** 20. **9** David Davies. **10** Picture of Marilyn Monroe. **11** Gaby Roslin. **12** Foot. **13** Wendy Richard. **14** Edward on Edward. **15** Psychiatric nurse. **16** The Fortunes of War. **17** Frost. **18** Northampton Town. **19** The O Zone. **20** Cousin. **21** Dani Behr. **22** Bournemouth. **23** Alastair Burnet. **24** Lord Stockbridge. **25** Burger.

Quiz 139 Euro Tour

Answers - see Quiz 140, page 574

1 In which city is the Glynn Vivian Art Gallery and Museum?
2 Which city did Truman Capote describe as "eating an entire box of chocolate liqueurs in one go"?
3 Where in Europe is the Sikkens Museum of Signs?
4 Which monarch popularised the Homburg which came from the German town of the same name?
5 What is Switzerland's largest city?
6 Which city was the cultural capital of Europe in 1990?
7 Which architect designed the Pompidou Centre in Paris?
8 In which European city would you go to the Bardini Museum and the Bargello Museum?
9 What is the name of the lake which remained when the Zuider Zee was closed and reclaimed in 1932?
10 Which country was the first to break away from Yugoslavia after Tito's death?
11 Where is the Optimisticeskaja cave, the second longest in the world?
12 How many countries does the Danube pass through?
13 Which European country saw one of the major avalanches of the 20th century in December 1916?
14 What is the second largest of the Ionian Islands?
15 Where is Tingwall airport?
16 Where would you be if the Parliament was called The Althing?
17 Down which valley does the Mistral blow?
18 Inishmor is part of which island group?
19 Syracuse is part of New York, but where does it exist in Europe?
20 Which European country was first this century to give women the vote?
21 What is Europe's second largest city in terms of population?
22 Where would you spend stotinki?
23 Which French phrase described an innovative movement in the cinema?
24 Which was the first European city this century to open an underground railway system?
25 What is the longest river in Portugal, and the fifth longest in Europe?

Answers

Pot Luck 66 (see Quiz 140, page 574)
1 Groucho Marx. **2** Donna Summer. **3** Gillingham. **4** 1970s. **5** 82 million. **6** Bee keeping. **7** Massachusetts. **8** Milan. **9** Leonard Martin. **10** 1930s. **11** 26. **12** Madagascar. **13** Ainsley Harriott. **14** Peru. **15** Curium. **16** Pisces. **17** Quincy. **18** Parachute jump. **19** Libya. **20** Borley. **21** Giles Villeneuve. **22** Bahrain. **23** Alfred. **24** 100. **25** Willy Brandt.

Quiz 140 Pot Luck 66

Answers - see Quiz 139, page 573

1 Who said "A man is only as old as the woman he feels."?
2 Donna Gaines is better known by which name?
3 Which team were at home when Matthew Fox died in an after match street brawl?
4 In which decade was the Academy of Ancient Music orchestra founded?
5 What is the population of Germany to the nearest million?
6 What had Edmund Hillary worked at before taking up mountain climbing?
7 In which American state is the Isabella Stewart Gardner Museum?
8 Which group was Martine McCutcheon in before finding fame in EastEnders?
9 Who first read the football results on Grandstand?
10 In which decade was the Kincardine bridge opened?
11 How old was Bjorn Borg when he decide to retire?
12 Vehicles from which country use the international registration letter RM?
13 Who was resident chef on Good Morning With Anne & Nick?
14 Which country did Thor Heyerdahl's Kon-Tiki set sail from on its journey to Eastern Polynesia?
15 Which element is named after Pierre and Marie Curie?
16 What star sign is shared by Leslie Ash and Lynn Redgrave?
17 What was Mr Magoo's first name?
18 In 1912 Albert Berry made the first successful what?
19 Benina International airport is in which country?
20 Which rectory burned down in 1939 was said to be the most haunted place in Britain?
21 Who was runner up when Jody Scheckter won the F1 championship?
22 Which country does the airline Gulf Air come from?
23 What is Alistair Cooke's real first name?
24 How old was Laurel and Hardy producer Hal Roach when he died in 1992?
25 Who was West German Chancellor from 1969 to 1974?

Answers

Euro Tour (see Quiz 139, page 573)
1 Swansea. **2** Venice. **3** The Hague. **4** Edward VII. **5** Zurich. **6** Glasgow. **7** Richard Rodgers. **8** Florence. **9** Ijsselmeer. **10** Slovenia. **11** Ukraine. **12** Seven. **13** Italy. **14** Corfu. **15** Lerwick. **16** Iceland. **17** Rhone. **18** Aran. **19** Sicily. **20** Finland. **21** London. **22** Bulgaria. **23** Nouvelle vague. **24** Paris. **25** Tagus.

Quiz 141 Charts

Answers - see Quiz 142, page 576

1 Who was the first female with two UK million-selling singles?
2 Which was the first Spice Girls hit which did not reach No 1?
3 Whose debut album Ten Good Reasons was the UK's top seller in '89?
4 Which female artist was the first to achieve 32 consecutive UK Top 10 hits?
5 Who was the first act to put his first eleven hits into the UK Top Ten?
6 Who topped the US chart in 1976 with the triple-platinum album Breezin'?
7 Who sang on at least one hit every year for 33 years?
8 Which band released the chart topping album Steeltown in 1984?
9 Which hit reached No 1 in the UK and US for Phil Collins?
10 Who was the first UK male to score two US Top Ten hits?
11 Whose debut single was How Do I Live?
12 Who had a UK No 1 in 1998 with You Make Me Wanna?
13 Who was the first act to release eight singles which entered at No 1?
14 Which group achieved the UK's biggest selling album of 1994?
15 What was on the original double A side of Prince's No 1 hit 1999?
16 What was the title of U2's third UK No 1?
17 Who was the first UK group to top the US chart after The Beatles?
18 Who was the first female to score twelve hits in the American Top Five?
19 Who, after Gerry and the Pacemakers, were first to reach No 1 with their first three releases?
20 Who had a UK No 10 hit in 1987 with Walk The Dinosaur?
21 What was the Monkees' first Top Ten UK hit after their first No 1?
22 What was the top selling single of 1998?
23 What was the Manic Street Preachers' second UK Top Ten hit?
24 Whose first UK Top Ten hit was You're Still The One?
25 What was the first Top Ten hit of the 90s for Michael Jackson?

Answers

Pot Luck 67 (see Quiz 142, page 576)
1 A Groovy Kind of Love. **2** Emerson Carlyle. **3** Edward Appleton. **4** John Parrot. **5** Oracle. **6** 1919. **7** Petula Clark. **8** Electrocuted with a hair dryer. **9** Ronald Searle. **10** India. **11** Lionel Twiss. **12** BRU. **13** Norvell. **14** A.S. Byatt. **15** Mexico. **16** Underwater. **17** Coventry. **18** William Scale. **19** Susan Weaver. **20** Welsh. **21** 1924. **22** Greenland. **23** Taurus. **24** William Friedkin. **25** Ringmaster.

Quiz 142 Pot Luck 67

Answers - see Quiz 141, page 575

1 What was Phil Collins' last UK No 1 of the 80s?
2 What are Paul Ince's middle names?
3 Who discovered the layer of electrically charged particles in the upper atmosphere which now bears his name?
4 Since the first to 18 frames began in snooker's World Championship who recorded the lowest losing score in a final?
5 What was replaced by Teletext Ltd in 1993?
6 In which year did Alcock and Brown make their Atlantic crossing?
7 Which singer wrote the musical Someone Like You?
8 In Coronation Street how did Ken Barlow's first wife die?
9 Who created the St Trinians schoolgirls?
10 In which country is the Howrah bridge?
11 Who was the first person to fly at over 100 miles an hour?
12 What are the international registration letters of a vehicle from Brunei?
13 What was Oliver Hardy's real first name?
14 Who wrote Babel Tower?
15 Benito Juarez International airport is in which country?
16 Otis Barton was a pioneer in exploring where?
17 Where in England was Nigel Hawthorne born?
18 What would the Kelvin Scale have been called if it had adopted the originator's first name?
19 What is Sigourney Weaver's real name?
20 In which principal language did TV station S4C begin transmitting in 1982?
21 In which year were the first Winter Olympics?
22 Which country does the airline Gronlandsfly come from?
23 What star sign is Bob Carolgees?
24 Who directed The Exorcist?
25 What was Jeremy Beadle's profession when he worked in the circus?

Answers

Charts (see Quiz 141, page 575)
1 Celine Dion. **2** Stop. **3** Jason Donovan. **4** Madonna. **5** Gary Glitter. **6** George Benson. **7** Diana Ross. **8** Big Country. **9** A Groovy Kind of Love. **10** Lonnie Donegan. **11** LeAnn Rimes. **12** Usher. **13** Take That. **14** Bon Jovi. **15** Little Red Corvette. **16** Discotheque. **17** Animals. **18** Olivia Newton-John. **19** Frankie Goes to Hollywood. **20** Was (Not Was). **21** A Little Bit of Me A Little Bit of You. **22** Never Ever. **23** A Design For Life. **24** Shania Twain. **25** Black or White.

Quiz 143 **20th C Celebs**

Answers - see Quiz 144, page 578

1 Who said, "Some women get excited about nothing - and then they marry him"?
2 What was the occupation of Roger Moore's father?
3 Which newspaper did Lord Linley sue in 1990?
4 What breed of dog was Barry Manilow's Bagel?
5 Who was fashion designer of the year in 1990?
6 Which White House resident's book was a bestseller in the late 80s?
7 Who was the fourth successive PM this century to go to a state school?
8 Who became Paul Mowatt's mother in law when he joined the Royal Family in the 90s?
9 Pamela Stephenson stood for Parliament for which party?
10 Which TV presenter owned a restaurant called Midsummer House?
11 Who was Jeremy Irons' best man?
12 What is the name of Dave Stewart and Siobhan Fahey's son?
13 Who said, "I'd rather have a cup of tea than go to bed with someone – any day"?
14 Who is the famous mother of Elijah Blue?
15 Who designed Victoria Adams' wedding dress?
16 Which rock star did Cindy Crawford name her first son after?
17 What did Michael Jackson say instead of "I do" when he married Lisa Marie Presley?
18 Who said, "The only place a man wants depth in a woman is in her decolletage"?
19 In which Sydney cathedral did Michael Hutchence's funeral take place?
20 Who became chief designer at Givenchy in 1996?
21 Whose first West End club was the Hanover Grand?
22 Who was Axl Rose's famous singer father in law?
23 Who was Joaquim Cortes' girlfriend, who was rushed to hospital after a suspected overdose in 1997?
24 Who designed the dress which made the most at Diana's dress auction?
25 Richard Gere won a scholarship to the University of Massachusetts in which sport?

Answers

Pot Luck 68 (see Quiz 144, page 578)
1 Order Of Merit. **2** Campbell-Bannerman. **3** Richard Gere. **4** Hoover. **5** North Pole. **6** David. **7** Texas. **8** Just the one!. **9** French. **10** California. **11** 1915. **12** Lebanon. **13** Mike Read. **14** Sub four minute mile. **15** Ireland. **16** 10 million. **17** Henry Cooper. **18** Daily Bugle. **19** Mozambique. **20** Ralph Reader. **21** 60s. **22** Netherlands. **23** Big Bird. **24** Pisces. **25** Slik.

Quiz 144 Pot Luck 68

Answers - see Quiz 143, page 577

1. Florence Nightingale was the first and chemist Dorothy Hodgkin was the second woman to be awarded what?
2. Who was the only British PM to die at No 10 Downing Street?
3. What is Richard Gere's real name?
4. How is J Murray Spangler's invention known today?
5. South Pole explorer Roald Amundsen vanished flying over where?
6. What is the name of Sophie Rhys-Jones' elder brother?
7. In which US state was Buddy Holly born?
8. In On the Up how did Mrs Wembley respond when offered a drink?
9. Pioneering doctor Elizabeth Garrett Anderson took her medical exams in which language?
10. Oakland international airport is in which US state?
11. In what year were passport photos first required in Britain?
12. Vehicles from which country use the international registration letter RL?
13. Who was General Manager of the Saturday Superstore?
14. John Landy became the first Australian to do what?
15. In which country was Michael Gambon born?
16. What is the population of Greece to the nearest million?
17. Who was the first person to win the BBC Sports Personality of the Year twice?
18. In his day job which paper does Spiderman work for?
19. Beira International airport is in which country?
20. Who presented the first Gang Show for Scouts in 1932?
21. In which decade did Honda start to manufacture cars?
22. Which country does the airline Transavia Airlines come from?
23. What was West Indian fast bowler Joel Garner's nickname?
24. What star sign is shared by Roger Daltrey and Quincy Jones?
25. Who had a UK No 1 hit with Forever and Ever?

Answers

20th C Celebs (see Quiz 143, page 577)
1 Cher. **2** Policeman. **3** Today. **4** Beagle. **5** Vivienne Westwood. **6** Millie the dog. **7** Thatcher. **8** Princess Alexandra. **9** Blancmange Thrower. **10** Chris Kelly. **11** Christopher Biggins. **12** Django. **13** Boy George. **14** Cher. **15** Vera Wang. **16** Presley. **17** Why not?. **18** Zsa Zsa Gabor. **19** St Andrew's. **20** Alexander McQueen. **21** Piers Adam. **22** Don Everly. **23** Naomi Campbell. **24** Victor Edelstein. **25** Gymnastics.

Quiz 145 20th C: First 50 Years

Answers - see Quiz 146, page 580

1 The British police adopted fingerprinting after it had been used where?
2 In what month was the attack on Pearl Harbor?
3 Which magazine ran the "Your country needs you!" ad which was then used widely for recruitment?
4 What did the Labour Party change its name from after the 1906 Election?
5 Who was British PM when independence was granted to India and Pakistan?
6 In 1939 who described the actions of Russia as "a riddle wrapped in a mystery inside an enigma"?
7 Whose epitaph reads "Hereabouts died a very gallant gentleman"?
8 In which month did the 1951 election take place?
9 Who became mayor of Cologne in 1945?
10 At which Embassy did Kim Philby work with Guy Burgess after WWII?
11 In 1910 Paul Ehrlich developed a cure for which disease?
12 Who was Churchill referring to when he said "never was so much owed by so many to so few"?
13 In Nazi Germany what was Endl slung?
14 Who founded the American Institution of Public Opinion in 1935?
15 Who was the first President of the National Union of Women's Suffrage Societies?
16 Who did L S Amery say "In the name of God go!" to in 1940?
17 Which writer and politician became Lord Tweedsmuir?
18 At which British airport did Neville Chamberlain wave the Munich agreement in 1938 believing he had averted war?
19 "A bridge too far" referred to airborne landings in which country?
20 Which future MP was president of the Oxford Union in 1947?
21 On whose tomb are the words "They buried him among Kings because he had done good toward God and toward his house"?
22 Tora tora tora was the signal to attack Pearl Harbor but what does it mean?
23 Who said Chamberlain was "a good mayor of Birmingham in an off year"?
24 The Rotary Club was founded in 1905 in which American city?
25 Who was Hitler's Prime Minister in Prussia?

Answers

Pot Luck 69 (see Quiz 146, page 580)
1 Emiliano Zapata. **2** 40s. **3** Isaac. **4** July 20th. **5** Leo. **6** Builder. **7** 4th. **8** Linda Evangelista. **9** Poet Laureate. **10** Mel B. **11** Albanian. **12** BS. **13** Sealed With A Kiss. **14** 1964. **15** Barbara Cartland. **16** Brunei. **17** David Icke. **18** Bury St Edmunds. **19** Swam underwater. **20** Diane Hall. **21** Nebraska. **22** Switzerland. **23** 13. **24** Gerald Ford. **25** George Roy Hill.

Quiz 146 Pot Luck 69

Answers - see Quiz 145, page 579

1 Who said, "It is better to die on your feet than live on your knees"?
2 In which decade did motor car pioneer Henry Ford die?
3 What is Viv Richard's real first name?
4 On what date in 1969 did Neil Armstrong first set foot on the moon?
5 What star sign is Barry Norman?
6 What was the day job that Boris Yeltsin started out with?
7 Where did Tessa Sanderson finish in the 1992 Olympics?
8 Which supermodel said. "I look very scary in the mornings"?
9 What position did Alfred Austin hold from 1896 to 1913?
10 Which Spice Girl appeared in Emmerdale as an extra?
11 What nationality were Mother Teresa's parents?
12 What are the international registration letters of a vehicle from The Bahamas?
13 What was Jason Donovan's last UK No 1 of the 80s?
14 In which year did Tanganyika and Zanzibar merge to form Tanzania?
15 Who wrote the novel Love Solves The Problem?
16 Bandar Seri Begawan International airport is in which country?
17 Who presented sport on Saturday Superstore?
18 Where in England was Bob Hoskins born?
19 What was special about Fred Balasare's 1962 Channel swim?
20 What is Diane Keaton's real name?
21 Lincoln international airport is in which US state?
22 Which country hosted the very first Eurovision Song Contest?
23 How many teams contested the first World Cup held in 1930?
24 Who was Richard Nixon's Vice President from 1973 to 1974?
25 Who directed The Sting?

Answers

20th C: First 50 Years (see Quiz 145, page 579)
1 India. **2** December. **3** London Opinion. **4** Labour Representative Committee. **5** Attlee. **6** Churchill. **7** Captain Oates. **8** October. **9** Konrad Adenauer. **10** Washington. **11** Syphilis. **12** RAF pilots in the Battle of Britain. **13** The Final Solution. **14** Gallup. **15** Millicent Fawcett. **16** Neville Chamberlain. **17** John Buchan. **18** Heston. **19** Netherlands. **20** Tony Benn. **21** Unknown Soldier. **22** Tiger. **23** Lloyd George. **24** Chicago. **25** Goering.

Quiz 147 Sporting Who's Who?

Answers - see Quiz 148, page 582

1 Who was the last person to score for both teams in an FA Cup Final?
2 Which England cricket captain has played hockey for London University?
3 Who was the oldest British Open winner of the century?
4 Which sportswoman wrote the novel Total Zone?
5 Who was the first winner of the first to18 frames format in snooker's World Championship?
6 Who was the only American Wimbledon men's singles champion of the 60s?
7 Who said, "The atmosphere is so tense you could cut it with a cricket stump"?
8 Who was the first National Hunt jockey to reach 1000 wins?
9 Who was the winner of the last Open at Carnoustie before Paul Lawrie?
10 Bill Beaumont established the then record for captaining England how many times?
11 Who is the youngest ever Wightman Cup player?
12 Who was hacked down when Scholes got his second England booking v Sweden?
13 Roberto Rempi was the doctor of which sportsperson in a 90s drugs row?
14 Who won the Oaks on Dunfermline, Sun Princess and Unite?
15 Which record breaker became Master of Pembroke College, Oxford in the 80s?
16 Arnaud Massey is the only Frenchman to have won what?
17 Which snooker champion was a torch-bearer at the 1956 Melbourne Olympics?
18 John Potter has been England's most capped player in which sport?
19 Who was the British soccer manager sacked by Real Madrid in 1990?
20 Who was champion jockey on the flat five times in the 50s?
21 Who was Ole Gunnar Solskjaer playing for before he joined Man Utd?
22 Who scored England's winner in Italia 90 v Egypt?
23 Who was runner up when Niki Lauda won his last F1 championship?
24 What is Brian Lara's middle name?
25 Who rode Arkle to a hat trick of Cheltenham Gold Cup triumphs?

Answers

Pot Luck 70 (see Quiz 148, page 582)
1 Aries. **2** Big Eggo - an ostrich. **3** 953 million. **4** Ruz. **5** Groote Schuur. **6** Deniece Williams. **7** Trevor McDonald. **8** TV. **9** Baldwin. **10** China. **11** John Paul II. **12** Congo. **13** Matthew. **14** Tony Parkes. **15** Tony Warren. **16** Papua New Guinea. **17** Bill Wyman. **18** Joanne Whalley. **19** Ethiopia. **20** 20. **21** Vivienne Westwood. **22** Lyndon Johnson. **23** Golightly. **24** USA. **25** 1958.

Quiz 148 Pot Luck 70

Answers - see Quiz 147, page 581

1 What star sign is shared by John Major and Sir David Frost?
2 Which character was on the first cover of the Beano?
3 What is the population of India to the nearest million?
4 What is Fidel Castro's real first name?
5 At which hospital did the first heart transplant take place?
6 Who had a UK No 1 hit with Free?
7 Which British news reader interviewed Saddam Hussein just before the Gulf War?
8 What did Anne Robinson's report on on Breakfast Time?
9 Who was the next British Prime Minister after Ramsay Macdonald?
10 In which country is the Humen bridge?
11 Who has been Pope longest in the 20th C?
12 Vehicles from which country use the international registration letter RCB?
13 What did the M stand for in J M Barrie's name?
14 Who was in charge at Blackburn after Roy Hodgson's sacking and before Brian Kidd's arrival?
15 Who wrote an autobiography called I Was Ena Sharples' Father?
16 Bill Skate and Julius Chan had been 90s Prime Ministers of which country?
17 Which veteran rock musician said, "If I had my time again I would like to take up archaeology"?
18 Which future film star played Angela Reid in Emmerdale?
19 Bole International airport is in which country?
20 How many caps did Bobby Robson gain as an England player?
21 Which British fashion designer received her OBE on 15th December 1992?
22 Hubert Humphrey was Vice President to which US President?
23 What is Robson Green's middle name?
24 Which country does the airline Kiwi International Airlines come from?
25 In which year was the State Opening of Parliament televised for the first time?

Answers

Sporting Who's Who? (see Quiz 147, page 581)
1 Gary Mabbutt. **2** David Gower. **3** Robert de Vincenzo - 44 years 93 days. **4** Martina Navratilova. **5** Cliff Thorburn. **6** Chuck McKinley. **7** Murray Walker. **8** Stan Mellor. **9** Tom Watson. **10** 21. **11** Jennifer Capriati. **12** Schwarz. **13** Marco Pantani. **14** Willie Carson. **15** Roger Bannister. **16** Golf's British Open. **17** Eddie Charlton. **18** Hockey. **19** John Toshack. **20** Doug Smith. **21** Molde. **22** Mark Wright. **23** Alain Prost. **24** Charles. **25** Pat Taffe.

Quiz 149 Musical Movies

Answers - see Quiz 150, page 584

1 Who directed Finian's Rainbow, his first film for a major studio?
2 Who played a character based on Bob Fosse in a 1979 Oscar winning film?
3 Where in Europe was much of Evita filmed?
4 Who directed the film version of Hair?
5 Which musical was Victor Fleming making the same time as he was making Gone With the Wind?
6 What was Xanadu in the title of the film?
7 Who was the voice of O'Malley in The Aristocats?
8 In which 70s musical did Paul Michael Glaser star?
9 How many different hats does Madonna wear in Evita?
10 Who played the title role in the film version of Jesus Christ Superstar?
11 In Cabaret, what was the profession of Sally Bowles' father?
12 In which film was chorus girl Peggy Sawyer told to "come back a star!"?
13 What are the last lines of My Fair Lady?
14 What was the name of the brothel in The Best Little Whorehouse in Texas?
15 Which musical includes the lines "Got no cheque books, got no banks. Still I'd like to express my thanks"?
16 What was the name of the butler in The Rocky Horror Picture Show?
17 Which Club featured in cabaret?
18 "The corn is as high as an elephant's eye" is in which musical?
19 Who was the male star of the movie The Man of La Mancha?
20 What was the name of Bob Fosse's character in All That Jazz?
21 In Saturday Night Fever where does Tony work by day?
22 A Little Night Music was based on which non musical film?
23 What was the name of the sax player in New York New York who fell for Francine?
24 Who was the father in law of the male star of Grease 2?
25 In The Muppet Movie what was the name of the restaurant Doc Hopper wanted to open?

Answers

Pot Luck 71 (see Quiz 150, page 584)
1 Leslie Charles. **2** Congo. **3** Gowan Avenue. **4** Edwin Hubble. **5** Snooker. **6** Massachusetts. **7** Rock'n'roll. **8** The Reflex. **9** Advanced Dungeons and Dragons. **10** Family Channel. **11** May. **12** CDN. **13** Cancer. **14** 1978. **15** Peter. **16** Alice Thomas Ellis. **17** Michael Stich. **18** 750. **19** Morocco. **20** Stan Smith. **21** Vienna. **22** South Africa. **23** Chesterfield. **24** John Huston. **25** Peter.

Quiz 150 Pot Luck 71

Answers - see Quiz 149, page 583

1 What is Billy Ocean's real name?
2 What was The Zaire River called before 27th October 1971?
3 In which London street was Jill Dando murdered?
4 Who is credited with the discovery of galaxies outside of our own?
5 Tom Dennis was the first runner up in a world ranking final in which sport?
6 Logan international airport is in which US state?
7 Alan Freed is usually credited for popularising which expression?
8 What was Duran Duran's last UK No 1 of the 80s?
9 In the 80s, what did AD&D stand for?
10 Which satellite channel was originally called CBN Satellite Service in the US?
11 In which month of the year did Bing Crosby record White Christmas?
12 What are the international registration letters of a vehicle from Canada?
13 What star sign is Suzanne Dando?
14 When was the Daily Star founded?
15 In the early days of Grange Hill what was Tucker Jenkins real first name?
16 Who wrote the novel Fairy Tale?
17 Who was the defending champion when Andre Agassi first won Wimbledon singles?
18 How many people was Howard Hughes' Spruce Goose meant to carry?
19 Boukhalef International airport is in which country?
20 Who beat Ilie Nastase in the 1972 Men's Singles Final at Wimbledon?
21 In which European city is the Belvederen Gallery?
22 Which country does the airline Transkei Airways come from?
23 Where in England was John Hurt born?
24 Who directed the movie The African Queen?
25 What is Sir Norman Fowler's real first name?

Answers

Musical Movies (see Quiz 149, page 583)
1 Francis Ford Coppola. **2** Roy Scheider. **3** Hungary. **4** Milos Forman. **5** The Wizard of Oz. **6** Roller disco. **7** Phil Harris. **8** Fiddler on the Roof. **9** 39. **10** Ted Neeley. **11** US diplomat. **12** 42nd Street. **13** Where the devil are my slippers. **14** Chicken Ranch. **15** Annie Get Your Gun. **16** Riff Raff. **17** Kit Kat. **18** Oklahoma. **19** Peter O'Toole. **20** Joe Gideon. **21** DIY store. **22** Smiles of a Summer Night. **23** Jimmy. **24** John Mills - star was Maxwell Caulfield. **25** Frogs' Legs.

Quiz 151 Quiz & Game Shows

Answers - see Quiz 152, page 586

1. What were Neil and Christine Hamilton presented with when they appeared on Have I Got News For You?
2. What was the name of the quiz show on Crackerjack?
3. Which record was broken on the first Record Breakers?
4. Who presented the first edition of The Golden Shot?
5. Mastermind champion Christopher Hughes followed which profession?
6. Which quiz of the 80s was hosted by Angela Rippon?
7. Which US show was University Challenge based on?
8. Which show was based on a Dutch programme called One From Eight?
9. In the very first University Challenge Reading played who?
10. Which Radio 5 Live presenter was the first UK host of Wheel of Fortune?
11. Who is acknowledged as the Creator of Countdown?
12. For how many years were there female winners of Mastermind before the programme had its first male winner?
13. On which part of Double Your Money could you win the £1,000?
14. Who hosted ITV's early rival to Telly Addicts, We Love TV?
15. Which female joined Jeremy Beadle on Game For A Laugh after Sarah Kennedy?
16. Which show offered losers a Dusty Bin?
17. What was the junior version of Big Break called?
18. Who presented Ice Warriors?
19. What surname did Malandra Burrows, later of Emmerdale, use when she appeared on New Faces aged nine?
20. Who replaced Terry Wogan on Blankety Blank?
21. Who first presented The Price is Right in the UK?
22. Which celebrity chef produced the first recipe book spin off from Ready Steady Cook with Brian Turner?
23. Who was the very first woman to be a Call My Bluff team captain, albeit for a one off special?
24. Who hosted What's My Line? when it was revived yet again in 1994?
25. Who did Carol Smillie replace on Wheel of Fortune?

Answers

Pot Luck 72 (see Quiz 152, page 586)

1 Trapeze artist. **2** 38. **3** Barcelona - in 1992. **4** Peru. **5** William McKinley. **6** 1920. **7** Helen Mirren. **8** Stanley Baldwin. **9** Guillotined. **10** Sweden. **11** Sir Paul McCartney. **12** Chile. **13** Desmond. **14** Anita Ward. **15** Brenda Gilhooly. **16** Aries. **17** 62 million. **18** Interceptor. **19** Sweden. **20** 1965. **21** Buddy Boy. **22** 1960s. **23** Ice Cream Cone. **24** Belgium. **25** Keanu Reeves.

Quiz 152 Pot Luck 72

Answers - see Quiz 151, page 585

1 What was John Major's father's profession in the circus?
2 How old was George Gershwin when he died?
3 Who won the 90s European Cup Final staged at Wembley?
4 In which country did Paris born Paul Gaugin spend his childhood?
5 Who was US President at the start of the 20th C?
6 Here we ask what was the year, when Rupert Bear did first appear?
7 Which actress's real name is Ilynea Lydia Mironoff?
8 Which ex Prime Minister became the first Earl of Bewdley?
9 Eugene Wiedmann was the last person to meet his death how in 1939?
10 Which country does the airline Linjeflyg come from?
11 Which knight has appeared on Baywatch?
12 Vehicles from which country use the international registration letter RCH?
13 What is John Humphry's real first name?
14 Who had a UK No 1 hit with Ring My Bell?
15 Whose alter ego was Gayle Tuesday?
16 What star sign is shared by William Shatner and Marlon Brando?
17 What is the population of Iran to the nearest million?
18 Which game show did Annabel Croft star in after Treasure Hunt?
19 Bromma International airport is in which country?
20 On 26th October in which year did the Beatles receive their MBEs?
21 In the classic sitcom Mr Ed, what did Mr Ed call Wilbur?
22 In which decade was the Tay road bridge opened?
23 What was patented in 1903 by Italian merchant Italio Marcione?
24 In which country was Audrey Hepburn born?
25 What is Keanu Reeves' real name?

Answers

Quiz and Game Shows (see Quiz 151, page 585)
1 Brown envelopes. **2** Double or Drop. **3** Biggest one man band. **4** Jackie Rae. **5** Train driver. **6** Masterteam. **7** College Bowl. **8** The Generation Game. **9** Leeds. **10** Nicky Campbell. **11** Armand Jammot. **12** Three. **13** Treasure Trail. **14** Gloria Hunniford. **15** Rustie Lee. **16** 3-2-1. **17** Big Break - Stars of the Future. **18** Dani Behr. **19** Newman. **20** Les Dawson. **21** Leslie Crowther. **22** Anthony Worrall Thompson. **23** Joanna Lumley. **24** Emma Forbes. **25** Angela Ekaette.

Quiz 153 On The Road

Answers - see Quiz 154, page 588

1 Which tree features most frequently in London street names?
2 In which year was the National Parks and Access to the Countryside Act passed?
3 In 1983 which car company ran an April Fool's day ad for an open top car that kept out the rain?
4 The fastest man on land at the beginning of the 20th century came from which country?
5 Which town did Britain's first motorway bypass?
6 Which was the last country in mainland Europe to switch to driving on the left?
7 In what year did the millionth Volkswagen roll of the assembly line?
8 In which country were motorised ambulances first used?
9 By the end of the 80s, what percentage of British households had two cars?
10 When did the first Morris car appear?
11 Which work designed by Aston Webb do people drive under in London?
12 Which Asian country has the longest road network?
13 Where was the world's first production line producing Model T Fords?
14 According to a 50s ad what was the loudest noise in the new Rolls Royce?
15 Where was Stenson Cooke's signature seen by motorists in the early years of the century?
16 What was the starting price for a Morris Cowley when it came of the production line in 1920?
17 Who was the President of the AA at the beginning of the 1990s?
18 When were yellow lines used as parking restrictions on Britain's roads?
19 How old must you be to accompany a learner driver?
20 In which city was the first Model T produced outside the USA?
21 Which celebrity chose a motorway service station as a luxury when he appeared on Desert Island Discs?
22 In which city is the Blackfriars Museum of Antiquities?
23 What animal appears on a road sign to show there are wild animals?
24 Where were London's first traffic lights installed in 1926?
25 Which company manufactured the first car to run on diesel?

Answers

Pot Luck 73 (see Quiz 154, page 588)
1 Lee Trevino. **2** John. **3** Millicent. **4** Liz Dawn - Vera Duckworth. **5** 30s. **6** American football. **7** High Street. **8** Virgo. **9** The Power of Love. **10** USA. **11** 36 years. **12** CL. **13** Bryan Mosley. **14** Wrestling. **15** Ione. **16** Diana Dors. **17** Francis King. **18** Georgina. **19** Burundi. **20** Oslo. **21** Michelle Wallen. **22** Burnley. **23** Elia Kazan. **24** Liverpool. **25** Texas.

Quiz 154 Pot Luck 73

Answers - see Quiz 153, page 587

1 Which golfer said, "Grey hair is great. Ask anyone who's bald."?
2 What was Rambo's first name?
3 What is Anthea Turner's middle name?
4 Which Coronation Street actress is patron of the Manchester Taxi Drivers Association?
5 In which decade did Oor Wullie appear in the Sunday Post?
6 Bill Cosby had a professional trial in which sport?
7 What is the most common street name in the UK?
8 What star sign is Michael Jackson?
9 What was Frankie Goes To Hollywood's last UK No. 1 of the 80s?
10 In which country is the Lake Pontchartrain Causeway bridge?
11 How long had Perez Prado been out of the pop charts before his 90s return?
12 What are the international registration letters of a vehicle from Sri Lanka?
13 Which former Coronation Street actor was a skilled stuntman?
14 What did Kent Walton commentate on on World of Sport?
15 What is Tessa Sanderson's middle name?
16 Which actress made her film debut in The Shop at Sly Corner?
17 Who wrote Ash on an Old Man's Sleeve?
18 What is Davina Murphy's real first name?
19 Bujumbura International airport is in which country?
20 Where was the painting The Scream stolen from on 12th December 1994?
21 What is Mica Paris' real name?
22 Who were the first soccer club to have a royal spectator?
23 Who directed the movie East of Eden?
24 Where in England was Glenda Jackson born?
25 Lubbock international airport is in which US state?

Answers

On the Road (see Quiz 153, page 587)
1 Elm. **2** 1949. **3** BMW. **4** Belgium. **5** Preston. **6** Sweden. **7** 1955. **8** France. **9** 20%. **10** 1913. **11** Admiralty Arch. **12** India. **13** Detroit. **14** Electric clock. **15** First AA badge - he was its secretary. **16** £165. **17** Duke of Kent. **18** 1958. **19** 21. **20** Manchester. **21** Noel Edmonds. **22** Newcastle. **23** Stag. **24** Piccadilly Circus. **25** Mercedes Benz.

Quiz 155 Pop Legends

Answers - see Quiz 156, page 590

1 Who has accumulated the most UK and US Top 10 albums and grossed most income from foreign touring?
2 Who was Elton John's early idol?
3 Which superstar fronted The Nomads and Blackjack before going solo?
4 Who was posthumously awarded a Lifetime Achievement Grammy in 1996?
5 Who compered Buddy Holly's only UK tour?
6 Which artist has spent most weeks in the UK Top Ten?
7 Who married Julianne Phillips in May 1985 in Oregon?
8 Who issued bonds in his name for people to invest in in 1997?
9 Who was the first group to hold the top two US and UK album places on the week of release?
10 Which duo were joined by Tammy Wynette on their No 2 in 1991?
11 Who won the BRIT award for Outstanding Contribution to British Music in 1996?
12 Who had a record eight albums simultaneously in the UK chart three months after his death?
13 Which name links Whitney Houston's childhood nickname with her TV Production company?
14 Who made his stage debut in a 1960 production of The Pyjama Game?
15 What honour was awarded to Eric Clapton in January 1995?
16 Who duetted on the 1992 version of Crying with Roy Orbison?
17 How many UK Top Ten hits has Marvin Gaye had since his death?
18 Who jumped off the top of a moving bus during a Swedish tour and broke a foot?
19 Who was awarded a Lifetime Achievement Award at the 1993 Brit Awards?
20 Who collaborated with Michael Bolton on Bolton's Steel Bars hit?
21 Who did Celine Dion support in his Canadian tour in 1991?
22 Who is the sister of the drummer of the Dakotas during their 60s heyday?
23 Whose autobiography was titled Laughter in the Rain?
24 Which group sponsored Clydebank Football Club in 1993?
25 Who had a rabies jab after biting a rat on stage?

Answers

Pot Luck 74 (see Quiz 156, page 590)
1 The Lone Ranger. **2** Taurus. **3** Fern Kinney. **4** 58 million. **5** Olive. **6** Joe Louis. **7** Marquis of Salisbury. **8** Sculptor. **9** Sue Johnston. **10** John Glenn. **11** Dale Robertson the actor. **12** Botswana. **13** Anita Loos. **14** Mr Rusty. **15** Madame Tussaud's. **16** Wolfsburg. **17** 15.4%. **18** Kiri Te Kanawa. **19** Nigeria. **20** Frank Skinner. **21** Nevada. **22** Poland. **23** Doctor. **24** Allan Wells. **25** 1992.

Quiz 156 Pot Luck 74

Answers - see Quiz 155, page 589

1 Which TV series intro said, "Return with us now to those thrilling days of yesteryear..."?
2 What star sign is shared by Peter Gabriel and Stevie Wonder?
3 Who had a UK No 1 hit with Together We Are Beautiful?
4 What is the population of Italy to the nearest million?
5 What is Marie Osmond's real first name?
6 Which boxer is quoted as saying, "He can run, but he can't hide"?
7 Who was Prime Minister at the beginning of the 20th century?
8 Albert Giacometti found fame as what?
9 Which actress's autobiography was called Hold on to the Messy Times?
10 Who first flew in Friendship 7?
11 Who or what was Dale Winton named after?
12 Vehicles from which country use the international registration letter RB?
13 Who wrote the novel Gentlemen Prefer Blondes?
14 Whose barrel organ played the music for The Magic Roundabout?
15 Where did Brad Pitt, Darcey Bussell and William Hague appear together?
16 In which German city was the original Volkswagen factory?
17 What were mortgage rates in Feb 1990 - an all time high?
18 Who sang a solo at Prince Charles and Lady Di's wedding?
19 Calabar International airport is in which country?
20 Who wrote the Channel 4 sitcom Blue Heaven?
21 McCarran international airport is in which US state?
22 Which country does the airline LOT come from?
23 What was W.G. Grace's profession other than a cricketer?
24 Which British gold medallist had the middle name Wipper?
25 In which year did Wimbledon's famous commentator Dan Maskell die?

Answers

Pop Legends (see Quiz 155, page 589)
1 Rolling Stones. **2** Winifred Atwell. **3** Michael Bolton. **4** Marvin Gaye. **5** Des O'Connor. **6** Elvis Presley. **7** Bruce Springsteen. **8** David Bowie. **9** Guns 'N'Roses. **10** KLF. **11** David Bowie. **12** Jim Reeves. **13** Nippy. **14** David Cassidy. **15** OBE. **16** k.d.lang. **17** One. **18** Liam Gallagher. **19** Rod Stewart. **20** Bob Dylan. **21** Michael Bolton. **22** Elkie Brooks. **23** Neil Sedaka. **24** Wet Wet Wet. **25** Ozzy Osbourne.

Quiz 157 Heroes & Villains

Answers - see Quiz 158, page 592

LEVEL 3

1. Which prison did Jonathan Aitken go to after he was convicted in 1999?
2. What was the official occupation of Sir Anthony Blunt who was unmasked as a Soviet spy in 1979?
3. Which fictional character was based on Scottish soldier William Ironside?
4. Who said, "Being a thief is a terrific life, but the trouble is they do put you in the nick for it"?
5. Under who did Joseph McCarthy carry out his 'witch hunts'?
6. Where did Ferdinand Marcos live in exile?
7. Which MP wrote The Young Meteors?
8. Which medal did Robert Maxwell win in WWII?
9. Which terrorist group murdered Italian PM Aldo Moro?
10. Which was the first party Oswald Mosley was in Parliament with?
11. Which American was nicknamed Old Blood and Guts?
12. Who was Jeremy Thorpe accused of attempting to murder in 1976?
13. Which Conservative MP was killed by an IRA bomb in 1990?
14. Which organisation handed over Brian Keenan in Beirut after 1600 days?
15. Which stockbroker was given an 18 month prison sentence for his role in the Guinness scandal?
16. According to Neil Kinnock whose principles "produce martyrdom for the followers and never sacrifice the leaders"?
17. Which company headed by Asil Nadir collapsed in 1990?
18. In 1985 Terry Waite returned to Beirut after securing the release of four British hostages where?
19. Which little boy who appeared on TV screens with Saddam Hussein as one of his 'guests' during the Gulf crisis?
20. Where did the Pope land on his arrival in Britain in 1982?
21. General Boris Gromov was the last Soviet soldier to leave where in 1989?
22. In the Profumo scandal which Russian had an affair with Christine Keeler?
23. Who referred to drawing "a line in the sand" about the Gulf War?
24. What was Ronald Biggs official occupation when he was convicted of the Great Train Robbery?
25. What was Mother Teresa's real first name?

Answers

***Pot Luck* 75** (see Quiz 158, page 592)

1 Scorpio. **2** Leytonstone. **3** Always Yours. **4** 14th. **5** Pauline Matthews. **6** Jimmy Tarbuck. **7** Heidelberg. **8** 32. **9** Clergyman. **10** Posh Spice. **11** Helicopter accident. **12** Costa Rica. **13** Dresses. **14** Tim Rice. **15** Walter. **16** Windscreen wipers. **17** Joan Rivers. **18** William Golding. **19** Helicopter. **20** Brian Moore. **21** Florida. **22** DZ. **23** Sunset Boulevard. **24** Stanley Kubrick. **25** Gloria Hunniford.

Quiz 158 Pot Luck 75

Answers - see Quiz 157, page 591

1 What star sign is Jamie Lee Curtis?
2 Where in England was Derek Jacobi born?
3 What was Gary Glitter's last UK No. 1 of the 70s?
4 To become PM Alec Douglas-Home renounced his peerage as what number Earl of Home?
5 What is Kiki Dee's real name?
6 Who played Johnny McKenna in The Detectives?
7 At which university did Joseph Goebbels become a doctor of philosophy?
8 How old was Damon Hill when he started Formula 1 racing?
9 What was the profession of Sir David Frost's father?
10 Who was the only Spice Girl not to have a middle name?
11 How did Jock die in Dallas?
12 Which country does the airline LACSA come from?
13 What did Janet Street Porter sell at auction in 1997?
14 Which songwriter sang backing lyrics on Lily the Pink by Scaffold?
15 What is Bruce Willis' real first name?
16 Which innovation for the car was developed by Prince Henry of Prussia in 1911?
17 How is Joan Molinsky better known?
18 Which British writer won the Nobel Prize for Literature in 1983?
19 The VS-300 was a type of what?
20 Who wrote the novel The Statement?
21 McCoy international airport is in which US state?
22 What are the international registration letters of a vehicle from Algeria?
23 Which Lloyd Webber musical premiered in the US on 10th December 1993?
24 Who directed 2001 : A Space Odyssey?
25 Which TV presenter shares a birth date with Bobby Hatfield of The Righteous Brothers?

Answers

Heroes & Villains (see Quiz 157, page 591)
1 Standford Hill. **2** Art historian. **3** Richard Hannay. **4** John McVicar. **5** Truman. **6** Hawaii. **7** Jonathan Aitken. **8** Military Cross. **9** Red Brigade. **10** Conservative. **11** Patton. **12** Norman Scott. **13** Ian Gow. **14** Islamic Dawn. **15** Tony Parnes. **16** Arthur Scargill. **17** Polly Peck. **18** Libya. **19** Stuart Lockwood. **20** Cardiff. **21** Afghanistan. **22** Ivanov. **23** George Bush. **24** Carpenter. **25** Agnes.

Quiz 159 90s News

Answers - see Quiz 160, page 594

1 Which David headed the Cult which staged a 1993 mass suicide in Waco?
2 How many Northern Ireland MP's were there at the 1997 General Election?
3 Who won Miss World the first time it was held in India?
4 Who won Taiwan's first democratic Presidential election?
5 Where was the UN Earth summit held in 1992?
6 What number TWA flight exploded shortly after take off in July 1996?
7 What was the name of the mother of the Iowa septuplets born in 1997?
8 Who did Grant Ferrie marry in prison in 1997?
9 Where in the USA was there a total eclipse in 1991?
10 What was O J Simpson driving in the famous police chase?
11 Britain's worst rail disaster involved a train travelling from where to London in 1997?
12 Who went on trial for the Oklahoma bombing after Timothy McVeigh was sentenced to death for the crime?
13 Who was the brother of the nurse Deborah Parry was accused of murdering in Saudi Arabia?
14 What was the name of the judge in the Louise Woodward trial?
15 Who was investigated with Neil Hamilton in the cash for questions affair?
16 Which prominent Nigerian writer was executed in 1996?
17 Name the car in which Andy Green broke the land speed record in 1997?
18 Whose sacking caused an attack on Michael Howard by Ann Widdecombe?
19 Which company won a libel action against Dave Morris and Helen Street?
20 In which city did Princess Diana have her last meeting with Mother Teresa?
21 Which charity along with the Aids Crisis Trust chiefly benefited from the sale of Diana's dresses at Christie's in 1997 ?
22 Which Kennedy was due to marry when John F Kennedy's plane crashed on its way to the wedding?
23 In September 1996 who pledged a £1 million making it the then largest donation to the Labour Party by any individual?
24 The advertising of which products was banned on Guernsey in 1996?
25 On what did the Queen sign her autograph on a tour of Kuala Lumpur in September 1998?

Answers

Pot Luck 76 (see Quiz 160, page 594)

1 Mississippi. **2** Su Pollard. **3** Gerd Muller. **4** Charles. **5** Germany. **6** 50s. **7** Superman. **8** Taurus. **9** Vancouver. **10** Odyssey. **11** 126 million. **12** Argentina. **13** Florence Nightingale. **14** Julian Clary. **15** Margaret Drabble. **16** Nevada. **17** Anthea Turner. **18** Elaine Paige. **19** Uruguay. **20** Glass of water. **21** Mull Of Kintyre. **22** Ireland. **23** Vienna. **24** Golda Meir. **25** Bruno Nero.

Quiz 160 Pot Luck 76

Answers - see Quiz 159, page 593

1 In which US state was Tennessee Williams born?
2 Which Hi De Hi star was a member of a group called Midnight News?
3 Who won soccer's World Cup with his last international goal?
4 What is Robert Redford's real first name?
5 Which country does the airline LTU International Airways come from?
6 In music, in which decade was the Academy of St Martin-in-the-Fields founded?
7 Who was the son of Jor-El and Lara Lor-Van?
8 What star sign is shared by Sir David Attenborough and Paula Yates?
9 Where in Canada is the Lion's Gate bridge?
10 Who had a UK No. 1 hit with Use It Up and Wear It Out?
11 What is the population of Japan to the nearest million?
12 Vehicles from which country use the international registration letter RA?
13 Who was pictured for the first time on new £10 notes isssued in 1975?
14 What is Julian Clary's real name?
15 Which writer was married to actor Clive Swift aka Richard Bucket?
16 In which American state is the Harrah's Auto Collection situated?
17 Who did Eamonn Holmes nickname Miss Tippy Toes?
18 Which musical star played Caroline Winthrop in Crossroads?
19 Carrasco International airport is in which country?
20 What did Richard Branson once pour over Clive Anderson?
21 What was the first single to sell over 2 million copies in the UK?
22 In which country was Anjelica Huston born?
23 What was the name of Rigsby's cat in TV's Rising Damp?
24 Who was Israeli Prime Minister from 1969 to 1974?
25 What are Lawrence Dallaglio's middle names?

Answers

90s News (see Quiz 159, page 593)
1 Koresh. **2** 17. **3** Irene Skliva. **4** Lee Teng-Hui. **5** Rio. **6** 800. **7** Bobbi McCaughey. **8** Lucille McLauchlan. **9** Hawaii. **10** Ford Bronco. **11** Swansea. **12** Terry Nichols. **13** Frank Gilford. **14** Hiller Zobel. **15** Tim Smith. **16** Ken Saro Wiwa. **17** Thrust. **18** Derek Lewis. **19** McDonalds. **20** New York. **21** Royal Marsden Cancer Fund. **22** Rory. **23** Matthew Harding. **24** Cigarettes. **25** Man Utd football.

Quiz 161 Summer Sports

Answers - see Quiz 162, page 596

1 How many times was Wes Hall named as Wisden Cricketer of the Year?
2 At which venue did Tony Jacklin win the US Open?
3 Who was the defending champion when Stefan Edberg first won the Wimbledon singles?
4 Who ended Graham Gooch's mammoth 333 England innings at Lord's?
5 Which horse landed the Derby and the Irish Derby in 1993?
6 Who was the last man out in England's 1999 World Cup campiagn?
7 What were the initials of W G Grace's brother who played for England?
8 What was the total prize money for the British Open in 1945?
9 Which country does sprinter David Ezinwa come from?
10 By the end of the 20th century which country has had the most Men's Singles winners at Wimbledon?
11 How many members joined the original International Amateur Athletic Federation?
12 Which assistant manager of England's cricket team sadly died of a heart attack on the 1981 tour of W Indies?
13 At which venue did Greg Norman first win the British Open?
14 In the summer of 98 Jap Stam joined Man Utd from which club?
15 Which golden girl athlete married comedian Bobby Knut?
16 Which Brit won the doubles at Wimbledon in 1987 and in Australia in 1991?
17 Who was the first lady golfer to land the British and US Open in the same year?
18 Which country did 70s French Open women's singles winner Virginia Rusici come from?
19 What is the nickname of cycling's Marco Pantani?
20 What was Sue Barker's highest world ranking?
21 Why was Kiernon Fallon fined £1000 at the 1999 Derby?
22 Gary Sobers' then record Test score of 365 was made against which team?
23 Who was Britian's first Singles winner at Wimbledon in the second half of the 20th century?
24 What is the lowset total for the British Open in the century?
25 In which country was Ted Dexter born?

Answers

Pot Luck 77 (see Quiz 162, page 596)
1 Dagenham. **2** Leonard. **3** 76. **4** Capricorn. **5** Carol Vorderman. **6** One Moment In Time. **7** First official 147 snooker break. **8** Morris Minor. **9** Mother's Union. **10** Elephant attendant. **11** Nicholas Witchell. **12** EAK. **13** All had roses named after them. **14** Black Panthers. **15** Bill Maynard. **16** Philippines. **17** Henry VIII. **18** Cathleen Collins. **19** The Queen. **20** Ronnie Peterson. **21** Mouse trap. **22** South Africa. **23** Nicholas Mosley. **24** Akira Kurosawa. **25** George Bernard Shaw.

Quiz 162 Pot Luck 77

Answers - see Quiz 161, page 595

1 Where in England was Dudley Moore born?
2 What is James Callaghan's real first name?
3 How old was Pope John XXIII when he took office in 1958?
4 What star sign is Annie Lennox?
5 Who co presented Notes and Queries with Clive Anderson?
6 What was Whitney Houston's last UK No 1 of the 80s?
7 Willie Smith was left standing as which sporting first happened in 1955?
8 What was Sophie Rhys-Jones' first car?
9 In 1999 Reg Bailey became chief executive of which Union?
10 What was W.C.Fields' profession when he worked in the circus?
11 Which news journalist has written a book called The Loch Ness Story?
12 What are the international registration letters of a vehicle from Kenya?
13 What links Anna Ford, Geoff Boycott and Paul McCartney?
14 Power to the People was originally a slogan for which movement?
15 Which Heartbeat star played Mickey Malone in Coronation Street?
16 Cebu International airport is in which country?
17 Which British monarch ruled the last time a non Italian pope was in office before John Paul II in Elizabeth II's reign?
18 What is Bo Derek's real name?
19 Who opened the Sydney Opera House in 1973?
20 Who was runner up when Mario Andretti won the F1 championship?
21 Which form of pest control was developed by James Atkinson in 1910?
22 Which country does the airline Theron Airways come from?
23 Who wrote the novel Children of Darkness And Light?
24 Who directed The Seven Samurai?
25 Which person with three names is on the cover of Sgt Pepper's Lonely Hearts Club Band?

Answers

Summer Sports (see Quiz 161, page 595)
1 Never. **2** Hazeltine. **3** Pat Cash. **4** Prabhakar. **5** Commander In Chief. **6** Alan Mullally. **7** E C. **8** £1,000. **9** Nigeria. **10** UK. **11** 17. **12** Ken Barrington. **13** Turnberry. **14** PSV. **15** Donna Hartley. **16** Jeremy Bates. **17** Patty Sheehan. **18** Romania. **19** The Pirate. **20** 6th. **21** Breaking early from the parade. **22** Pakistan. **23** Angela Mortimer. **24** 267. **25** Italy.

Quiz 163 1990s Movies

Answers - see Quiz 164, page 598

1 On whose life was the film Reversal of Fortune based?
2 Which sitcom did the director of Sliding Doors appear in in the 80s?
3 In which US state is The Horse Whisperer with Redford & Scott Thomas largely set?
4 Which writer directed Sleepless in Seattle?
5 What was the name of the Miss Haversham figure played by Anne Bancroft in the 90s Great Expectations?
6 Which 90s film was a remake of the 1987 German film Wings of Desire?
7 Who had a No 1 hit with the theme from Buddy's Song?
8 What was the name of Bruce Willis's character in Armageddon?
9 Where in Florida was Wild Things set?
10 What year was it in The Fifth Element?
11 Which 1997 film held the record at the time for the biggest opening for a British film, taking £2.5 million in three days?
12 In which film is Elliot Carver the villain?
13 Ten Things I Hate About You is based on which Shakespeare play?
14 Which original Picasso picture was used in Titanic, as one of Rose's possessions?
15 In the 'human' version of 101 Dalmatians what is Roger's occupation?
16 Who played the delicate daughter in Little Women?
17 What is the name of the Sikh bomb disposal expert in The English Patient?
18 What was the eighth Star Trek film called?
19 What is the name of the President in Independence Day?
20 In which film did Morgan Freeman play cop William Somerset?
21 Which studio worked with Disney on Toy Story?
22 What was the first film to have a budget of over $100 million?
23 Which Derek Jarman film was based on a Christopher Marlowe play?
24 What was the name of the weather girl played by Nicole Kidman in To Die For?
25 Which Pennsylvania town is the setting for Groundhog Day?

Answers

Pot Luck 78 (see Quiz 164, page 598)
1 Roberta. **2** Graham Taylor. **3** Battleships. **4** Whiz. **5** Gordon Burns. **6** 1985. **7** Lassie's Rescue Rangers. **8** Ohio. **9** Lloyd George. **10** 1930s. **11** Tarrant. **12** Nicaragua. **13** Alaska. **14** Gemini. **15** Lowestoft. **16** Kelly Marie. **17** 93 million. **18** PE instructor. **19** Brazil. **20** C Day Lewis. **21** 1924. **22** Women. **23** Virginia Slims. **24** Bergerac. **25** 250.

Quiz 164 Pot Luck 78

Answers - see Quiz 163, page 597

1 What is Joni Mitchell's real first name?
2 Which England soccer boss saved his last game for his biggest victory?
3 "We want eight and we won't wait" was a call for more what?
4 In which comic did Captain Marvel first appear?
5 Who hosted the Searchline spot on Surprise Surprise for five years?
6 The Titanic sank in 1912 but when was the wreck of the ship discovered?
7 What was the first animated series of Lassie called?
8 James M Cox international airport is in which US state?
9 Who was the next British Prime Minister after Asquith?
10 In which decade was the Transbay bridge in San Francisco opened?
11 Which fictional place did Howard's Way take place in?
12 Vehicles from which country use the international registration letter NIC?
13 The electric shaver was invented by a soldier stationed where?
14 What star sign is shared by Liz McColgan and Zola Budd?
15 Where did Reg Holdsworth head for when he left Coronation Street?
16 Who had a UK No 1 hit with Feels Like I'm In Love?
17 What is the population of Mexico to the nearest million?
18 What did Mick Jagger's father do for a living?
19 Congonhas International airport is in which country?
20 Who was Poet Laureate from 1968-1972?
21 In what year did a crossword appear in a British newspaper for the first time?
22 In 1934 a Test match involved who for the first time?
23 Which cigarette company ran the ad "You've come a long way baby"?
24 Which TV detective series made its debut on 18th October 1981?
25 How many years had 10 Downing Street been an official home on 4th December 1985?

Answers

1990s Movies (see Quiz 163, page 597)
1 Claus Von Bulow. **2** Bread. **3** Montana. **4** Nora Ephron. **5** Ms Dinsmoor. **6** City of Angels. **7** Chesney Hawkes. **8** Harry Stamper. **9** Blue Bay. **10** 2259. **11** Bean: The Ultimate Disaster Movie. **12** Tomorrow Never Dies. **13** The Taming of the Shrew. **14** The Guitar Player. **15** Computer games programmer. **16** Claire Danes. **17** Kip. **18** The First Contact. **19** Whitmore. **20** Se7en. **21** Pixar. **22** True Lies. **23** Edward II. **24** Suzanne Stone. **25** Punxsutawney.

Quiz 165 20th C TV Classics

Answers - see Quiz 166, page 600

1 In what year was the famous Spaghetti Harvest April Fool's Day prank shown on BBC TV?
2 What was the first name of the person The Fugitive was accused of killing?
3 Whose song provided the music for In Sickness and In Health?
4 Who famously announced "Heeeere's Johnny" on the Johnny Carson show from the early 60s?
5 From whose diaries did Jonathan Lynn and Anthony Jay come up with the title Yes Minister?
6 Who presented the first edition of Come Dancing?
7 Which series produced the catchphrase, "Excuse me sir, do you think that's wise?"?
8 Which classic TV series had the catchphrase "Kookie, Kookie lend me your comb"?
9 Who wrote the original scripts of Dr Who?
10 Stuebenville was a US pilot based on which UK classic?
11 In Friday Night Live what football team did Stavros support?
12 Which of Kenny Everett's characters said, "It's all done in the best possible taste"?
13 Which comedy programme won The Golden Rose of Montreux in 1967?
14 On which show was the catchphrase "I'm in charge" first used?
15 Which show had the Flying Fickle Finger of Fate?
16 Who created the drama series Minder?
17 On which TV show did Janice Nicholls regularly appear?
18 Which show had the slogan "The weekend starts here"?
19 What is the longest running children's programme?
20 Who played The Siren in the original Batman TV series?
21 In Upstairs Downstairs where did Lady Marjorie die?
22 What name did Reginald Perrin use when he went his own funeral?
23 Who was the sixth Dr Who?
24 Which role did Colin Welland play in Z Cars for many years?
25 Who played Dixon's daughter in the early years of Dixon of Dock Green?

Answers

Pot Luck 79 (see Quiz 166, page 600)
1 John Landis. **2** Three. **3** Donald Wayne. **4** Sheffield. **5** Morgan Fairchild.
6 Michigan. **7** Mark Wingett. **8** William. **9** Holland. **10** Canada/USA.
11 Rupert Bear. **12** EAT. **13** Stanley Matthews. **14** Paris. **15** Mike Smith. **16** Surtsey.
17 Jonathan Ross. **18** Tax evasion. **19** Sardinia. **20** Tom Stoppard. **21** Libra.
22 Canada. **23** I Just Can't Stop Loving You. **24** Dickson. **25** Harold Robbins.

Quiz 166 Pot Luck 79

Answers - see Quiz 165, page 599

1 Who directed the movie The Blues Brothers?
2 How many years after the end of the Great War was the first 'Poppy Day' held?
3 What is Don Johnson's real name?
4 Where in England was Michael Palin born?
5 Which US soap actress's real name is Patsy McClenny?
6 Kent County international airport is in which US state?
7 Which long time star of The Bill is a qualified scuba diving instructor?
8 What is Brad Pitt's real first name?
9 You Bet! was based on a game show from which country?
10 Which two countries are joined by the Rainbow bridge?
11 Who is the most famous creation of Mary Tourtel?
12 What are the international registration letters of a vehicle from Tanzania?
13 Who became the first European Player Of The Year?
14 In which city was the peace treaty ending the Vietnam war signed?
15 Who hosted Trick or Treat with Julian Clary?
16 What was the name of the island off Iceland which appeared in 1963 as a result of an underwater volcano?
17 Who is dad to Betty Kitten and Honey Kinny?
18 Why was Al Capone sent to prison in 1931?
19 Costa Smeralda International airport is in which country?
20 Which playwright said, "I think age is a very high price to pay for maturity."?
21 What star sign is Chris Tarrant?
22 Which country does the airline Norontair come from?
23 What was Michael Jackson's last UK No 1 of the 80s?
24 What is Jeremy Paxman's middle name?
25 Who wrote the novel Tycoon in 1996?

Answers

20th C TV Classics (see Quiz 165, page 599)
1 1957. **2** Helen. **3** Chas & Dave. **4** Ed McMahon. **5** Richard Crossman. **6** Sylvia Peters. **7** Dad's Army. **8** 77 Sunset Strip. **9** Terry Nation. **10** The Likely Lads. **11** Arsenal. **12** Cupid Stunt. **13** The Frost Report. **14** Sunday Night at the London Palladium. **15** Rowan & Martin's Laugh In. **16** Leon Griffiths. **17** Thank Your Lucky Stars. **18** Ready Steady Go. **19** Sooty. **20** Joan Collins. **21** On the Titanic. **22** Martin Wellbourne. **23** Peter Davison. **24** David Graham. **25** Billie Whitelaw.

Quiz 167 World Tour

Answers - see Quiz 168, page 602

1 In what year did the first McDonald's open in Moscow?
2 In which city was the Olympic stadium designed by Pier Luigi Nervi?
3 What was the name by which Lesotho used to be known?
4 Who designed New York's Gugenheim Museum?
5 Which US mountains gave their name to a fever discovered in that area in the early 20th century?
6 Where was Ian Botham talking about when he said everyone should send his mother in law there all expenses paid?
7 In which American state is the Rockefeller Folk Art Collection?
8 In which US state is the only major military academy founded this century?
9 Who designed the Mile High Centre, Boston, and The Glass Pyramids at the Louvre?
10 What would an American be talking about if he mentioned a scallion?
11 Lassa fever is so called as it was first reported in 1970 in Lassa in which country?
12 In which American city would you go to see the Frick Collection?
13 Who designed the Hiroshima Peace Centre?
14 Who said, "Concorde is great. It gives you three extra hours to find your luggage"?
15 In the 50s who designed The Museum of Modern Art in Tokyo?
16 Where did the Pope consecrate the world's biggest church in 1990?
17 In which city was the Olympic stadium designed by Felix Candela?
18 How is Tenochtitlan now known?
19 During which marathon do runners cross the Verrazano Bridge?
20 Whose tomb was opened to the public in Egypt for the first time in 1996?
21 The architect who designed the Sydney Opera House came from which country?
22 In California Suite which city is described as "not Mecca. It just smells like it"?
23 Which airport was opened in 1994 on a specially made island?
24 What is the English title of the new South African National Anthem?
25 Where did the largest rollercoaster in the world open in 1994?

Answers

Pot Luck 80 (see Quiz 168, page 602)
1 Harry S Truman. **2** 27 million. **3** Gemini. **4** Aneka. **5** George. **6** Samuel Goldwyn. **7** Timothy Dalton. **8** Germany. **9** Cardiff. **10** Work together. **11** South Africa. **12** Macedonia. **13** Llaniog. **14** Cobb. **15** February. **16** Clint Eastwood. **17** Lee Martin. **18** Paramount News. **19** Tobago. **20** Metal detector. **21** New York. **22** Mongolia. **23** Bank Of England. **24** The Onedin Line. **25** 1967.

Quiz 168 Pot Luck 80

Answers - see Quiz 167, page 601

1 Alben Barkley was Vice President to which US President?
2 What is the population of Morocco to the nearest million?
3 What star sign is shared by Jackie Stewart and Mike Gatting?
4 Who had a UK No 1 hit with Japanese Boy?
5 What is Van Morrison's real first name?
6 Who said, "Include me out"?
7 Who played Rhett Butler in the TV film sequel to Gone With the Wind?
8 In which country was Nastassja Kinski born?
9 Which city did the first Songs of Praise come from?
10 What does the Chinese expression Gung ho mean, which was adopted by US Marines in WWII?
11 Which country does writer Nadine Gordimer come from?
12 Vehicles from which country use the international registration letter MK?
13 In Ivor the Engine, what was the name of the station?
14 Which British John has held the land speed record?
15 In which calendar month was Prince Charles and Lady Di's engagement announced?
16 What is Clint Eastwood's real name?
17 Who scored Man Utd's FA Cup Final winner v Crystal Palace in 1990?
18 What was dubbed "the eyes and ears of the world"?
19 Crown Point International airport is in which country?
20 Which luxury did Leslie Grantham, aka Dirty Den, choose on Desert Island Discs?
21 La Guardia international airport is in which US state?
22 Which country does the airline MAIT come from?
23 Where in London did The Wind In the Willows writer Kenneth Grahame carry out his day job ?
24 Khatchaturians's Spartacus introduced the first episode of which TV drama in 1971?
25 In which year did Dr Christian Barnard perform the first heart transplant?

Answers

World Tour (see Quiz 167, page 601)
1 1990. **2** Rome. **3** Basutoland. **4** Frank Lloyd Wright. **5** Rocky Mountains. **6** Pakistan. **7** Virginia. **8** Colorado USAF. **9** Leah Meng Pei. **10** Spring onion. **11** Nigeria. **12** New York. **13** Kenzo Tange. **14** Bob Hope. **15** Le Corbusier. **16** Ivory Coast. **17** Mexico. **18** Mexico City. **19** New York. **20** Queen Nefertiti. **21** Denmark - It was Jorn Utzon. **22** New York. **23** Kansai. **24** God Bless Africa. **25** Blackpool.

Quiz 169 Sounds of the 60s & 70s

Answers - see Quiz 170, page 604

1 Who said I was Made For Dancing in a 70s No 4 hit?
2 Who released an album in 1961 called 21 Today?
3 What was the follow up to Fleetwood Mac's first No 1?
4 What was the first UK No 1 by KC and The Sunshine Band?
5 What was the first Top Ten Hit for The Kinks in the 70s?
6 Where was yodeller Frank Ifield born?
7 What was the second 70s No 1 by Mud?
8 Who was the UK's biggest-selling artist in 1967?
9 What UK chart position was achieved by the original release of Je t'aime?
10 Which group did Steve Marriott form after leaving the Small Faces?
11 Which No 1 group from 1974 were recognised by their white berets?
12 Who was On The Rebound in 1961?
13 Which group were fronted by Dennis Locorriere and Ray Sawyer?
14 Which female vocalist said Yes My Darling Daughter in '62 ?
15 How many Top Ten hits had Lindisfarne had before Run For Home?
16 What was the only UK No 1 for the Dave Clark Five?
17 Which group achieved their 4th successive Top Ten hit with Belfast?
18 Which rock group was voted World's Top Band in 1972?
19 Which band consisted of the Cluskeys and John Stokes?
20 What was Brotherhood of Man's first Top Ten hit after Save Your Kisses?
21 Who got to No 10 with Sunshine After The Rain in Jubilee Year?
22 Which Top Ten hit followed Mr Tambourine Man for the Byrds?
23 Who released an album in the 60s called Please Get My Name Right?
24 Who had most weeks in the charts in 1974?
25 Who danced a Morning Dance in 1979?

Answers

Pot Luck 81 (see Quiz 170, page 604)
1 Hammond Innes. **2** David Sutton. **3** Anwar El-Sadat. **4** Beat Surrender. **5** Listerine mouthwash. **6** Cambridge. **7** Virginia Wade. **8** $200 plus expenses. **9** Eve Pollard. **10** Gugnuncs. **11** Barry Crocker. **12** EAU. **13** Passport Agency. **14** Gliding. **15** St Lawrence. **16** Frozen peas. **17** Hearing aid. **18** Penguin. **19** El Salvador. **20** John Paul I. **21** Wisconsin. **22** Uruguay. **23** David Lean. **24** Cancer. **25** Eldred.

Quiz 170 Pot Luck 81

Answers - see Quiz 169, page 603

1 Who wrote the novel Delta Connection?
2 What is Sid Owen's real name?
3 Who preceeded Hosni Mubarak as President of Egypt?
4 What was the Jam's last UK No. 1 of the 80s?
5 "Even your best friends won't tell you" was part of an ad to promote what?
6 Where in England was Emma Thompson born?
7 Who was the defending champion when Martina Navratilova first won Wimbledon singles?
8 In The Rockford Files what was Jim Rockford's daily fee?
9 How is Lady Nicholas Lloyd better known?
10 What name was given to followers of cartoon characters Pip, Squeak and Wilfred?
11 Who first sang the Neighbours theme song?
12 What are the international registration letters of a vehicle from Uganda?
13 What was the first organisation to have its charter mark withdrawn?
14 In the 70s George Lee was a world champion in which sport?
15 Which river is spanned by the world's longest cantilever bridge?
16 Toothpaste was the first ever TV ad in the UK but what was the first TV ad in colour for?
17 What type of aid was developed by Miller Hutchinson in the early years of the 20th century?
18 In the cartoon characters Pip, Squeak and Wilfred what kind of creature was Squeak?
19 Cuscatlan International airport is in which country?
20 Who was Pope for the shortest length of time in the 20th C?
21 General Mitchell international airport is in which US state?
22 Which country does the airline Pluna come from?
23 Who directed A Passage to India?
24 What star sign is Pauline Quirke?
25 What is Gregory Peck's real first name?

Answers

Sounds of the 60s and 70s (see Quiz 169, page 603)
1 Leif Garrett. **2** Cliff Richard. **3** Man Of The World. **4** Give It Up. **5** Lola. **6** Coventry. **7** Lonely This Christmas. **8** Engelbert Humperdinck. **9** 2. **10** Humble Pie. **11** The Rubettes. **12** Floyd Cramer. **13** Dr Hook. **14** Eydie Gorme. **15** Two. **16** Glad All Over. **17** Boney M. **18** Alice Cooper. **19** Bachelors. **20** Oh Boy - The Mood I'm In. **21** Elkie Brooks. **22** All I Really Want To Do. **23** Twiggy. **24** The Wombles. **25** Spyro Gyra.

Quiz 171 Headline Makers

Answers - see Quiz 172, page 606

1 How much did Vivian Nicholson win on the pools in 1961?
2 Which boat capsized in the 1997 Vendee Globe round the world race?
3 Who was Mandy Rice-Davies referring to when she said, "Well he would wouldn't he?"?
4 How old was the man who was granted the first divorce in Irish history?
5 How old was Ruth Lawrence when she passed A level maths?
6 Who investigated the cash for questions affair involving Neil Hamilton?
7 In the painting by Michael Browne featuring Eric Cantona who was Alex Ferguson depicted as?
8 What description did Dr Desmond Morris give of a city as opposed to a concrete jungle?
9 Princess Diana made a public apology after underage William and Harry saw which 15 certificate film?
10 Sue Ryder became Baroness Ryder of where along with Cavendish?
11 Which university did Andrew Morton represent on University Challenge?
12 Who founded Gordonstoun school in 1934?
13 What were Bomber Harris's real first names?
14 How many years elapsed between DH Lawrence's writing of Lady Chatterley's Lover and the book's publication?
15 In which city were the 'Chariots Of Fire' Olympic Games?
16 Lindbergh wrote about his New York to Paris flight in which book?
17 Maria Montessori was the first woman in Italy to be awarded a degree in which subject?
18 Rudolf Nureyev took citizenship of which country in 1982?
19 In which country was Pasternak's Dr Zhivago first published?
20 Which Peter co founded the Aldeburgh Festival?
21 Which seat did Cherie Booth unsuccessfully contend in 1983?
22 Child expert Dr Spock won an Olympic gold medal in what event?
23 In 1990 a cinema owner was fined for refusing to remove what from the roof of his house?
24 Which British nurse was imprisoned in Iraq in 1990 for spying?
25 Which athlete sued Mirror Newspapers for libel?

Answers

***Pot Luck* 82** (see Quiz 172, page 606)
1 Perrie Mans. **2** 7p. **3** Ireland. **4** Daniel. **5** Soap. **6** David Suchet. **7** 1958. **8** Qatar. **9** Francoise Durr. **10** Brazil. **11** 165 Eaton Square. **12** Monaco. **13** Avon. **14** 1986. **15** Cyprus. **16** Frasier. **17** Patrick Duffy. **18** Australia. **19** Paula Yates. **20** Kraftwerk. **21** Hurricanes. **22** Paraguay. **23** Ernest Deveraux. **24** Cancer. **25** 16 million.

Quiz 172 Pot Luck 82

Answers - see Quiz 171, page 605

1 Who was the first South African to win snooker's Benson & Hedges Masters?
2 How much did the Dandy cost by the time issue 2000 came out in 1980?
3 Who beat England in their first home defeat in soccer?
4 What is Patrick Macnee's real first name?
5 The rationing of which non food product ended in 1950?
6 Who played Inspector Tsientsin in Reilly Ace of Spies?
7 When did the Chinese TV service begin broadcasting?
8 Doha International airport is in which country?
9 Who was the last Frenchwoman to win a Grand Slam event before Mary Pierce?
10 In which country is the Rio-Niteroi bridge?
11 What was the Bellamy's address in the first episode of Upstairs, Downstairs?
12 Vehicles from which country use the international registration letter MC?
13 Ex PM Anthony Eden became the first Earl of where?
14 In which year was the Independent first published?
15 Enosis was a slogan calling for the unfication of which island with the mainland?
16 In which series was there the Cafe Nervosa?
17 Which Dallas star sang with the Seattle Opera?
18 Gough Whitlam became Prime Minister of which country in 1972?
19 Which TV star wrote a book called Rock Stars in their Underpants?
20 Who had a UK No 1 hit with The Model?
21 In 1954 girls names were first applied to identify what?
22 Which country does the airline LAP come from?
23 What are Damon Hill's middle names?
24 What star sign is shared by Meryl Streep and Lindsay Wagner?
25 What is the population of the Netherlands to the nearest million?

Answers

Headline Makers (see Quiz 171, page 605)

1 £152,000. **2** Exide Challenger. **3** Lord Astor. **4** 68. **5** Nine. **6** Gordon Downey. **7** Julius Caesar. **8** Human zoo. **9** The Devil's Own. **10** Warsaw. **11** Sussex. **12** Kurt Hahn. **13** Arthur Travers. **14** 32. **15** Paris. **16** Spirit of St Louis. **17** Medicine. **18** Austria. **19** Italy. **20** Pears. **21** Thanet East. **22** Rowing. **23** A fibreglass shark. **24** Daphne Parish. **25** Tessa Sanderson.

Quiz 173 World Leaders

Answers - see Quiz 174, page 608

1 Who was described by his foreign minister as having "a nice smile, but he has got iron teeth"?
2 Who became president of Zambia in 1991?
3 Who succeeded Brezhnev as President of the USSR?
4 Who was Nigeria's first president and has been described as the father of modern Nigeria?
5 Who was born Karl Herbert Frahm?
6 Who was chairman of the Organisation of African Unity from 1975-76?
7 Errol Flynn's last film was a documentary tribute to which world leader?
8 Gorbachev introduced the expression perestroika but what does it mean?
9 Who was the first PM of South Africa?
10 Who said of Margaret Thatcher, "She adds the diplomacy of Alf Garnett to the economics of Arthur Daley"?
11 In what year did Hussein become King of Jordan?
12 How was Papa Doc also known?
13 Which leader did Churchill say was like a "female llama surprised in her bath"?
14 Who was the last leader of Communist East Germany?
15 Who did Lionel Jospin replace as French PM?
16 What name was given to the period of rule of Emperor Hirohito?
17 Which part of Lenin was preserved after his death?
18 Who said, "We are not at war with Egypt. We are in armed conflict"?
19 In what year was the world's first woman Prime Minister elected?
20 Who was the leader of ZAPU?
21 Which British Prime Minister was Rudyard Kipling's cousin?
22 Who said, "We have the happiest Africans in the world"?
23 What did Mao Tse Tung call the 'great leap forward'?
24 Which newspaper originally coined the term Iron Lady about Margaret Thatcher?
25 Which role did Harold Macmillan say was, "forever poised between a cliche and an indiscretion"?

Answers

***Pot Luck* 83** (see Quiz 174, page 608)
1 Turn on, tune in. **2** Clive Branson. **3** Joanna Trollope. **4** 1967. **5** Gordon. **6** New York. **7** Worked in insurance. **8** Tantrums and Tiaras. **9** Birmingham. **10** Cancer. **11** Architect. **12** ETH. **13** Tom Lehrer. **14** Two. **15** Let's Party. **16** Stabbed Monica Seles. **17** James Osterberg. **18** Canada. **19** Will Mellor. **20** Special Christmas stamps. **21** 1990. **22** Gary Kasparov. **23** Edward Elgar. **24** Barry Levinson. **25** Peru.

Quiz 174 Pot Luck 83

Answers - see Quiz 173, page 607

1 According to hippy guru Dr Timothy Leary what did you do before you "drop out"?
2 Who was the first Welshman to become angling's World Freshwater Champion?
3 Who wrote the novel The Rector's Wife?
4 In which year were breathalyser tests introduced in Britain?
5 What is Angus Deayton's real first name?
6 Hancock Field international airport is in which US state?
7 What did Franz Kafka do for a day job?
8 What was the name of the TV profile of Elton John made by his partner David Furnish?
9 Where in England was Julie Walters born?
10 What star sign is Harrison Ford?
11 Which profession did Janet Street-Porter study for before her media career?
12 What are the international registration letters of a vehicle from Ethiopia?
13 Which entertainer said, "He was into animal husbandry - until they caught him at it"?
14 How many policewomen went on duty when women first went on the beat?
15 What was Jive Bunny and the Mastermixers' last UK No 1 of the 80s?
16 How did Guenter Parche leave his mark on sport in the 90s?
17 What is Iggy Pop's real name?
18 Dorval International airport is in which country?
19 Which soap star recorded When I Need You in 1998?
20 What could be bought at the Post Office in late 1966 which had not been available before?
21 In which year were both sides of the Channel Tunnel linked by the service tunnel?
22 Harry Weinstein became a world champion under which name?
23 Whose face appeared for the first time on a bank note in June 1999?
24 Who directed Good Morning Vietnam?
25 Where did the Shining Path terrorists operate?

Answers

World Leaders (see Quiz 173, page 607)

1 Mikhail Gorbachev. **2** Chiluba. **3** Andropov. **4** Nnamdi Azikiwe. **5** Willy Brandt. **6** Idi Amin. **7** Castro. **8** Reconstruction. **9** Louis Botha. **10** Denis Healey. **11** 1952. **12** Francois Duvalier. **13** Charles de Gaulle. **14** Egon Krenz. **15** Alain Juppe. **16** Showa. **17** Brain. **18** Anthony Eden. **19** 1960. **20** Joshua Nkomo. **21** Stanley Baldwin. **22** Ian Smith. **23** Enforced industrialisation. **24** Red Star. **25** Foreign Secretary.

Quiz 175 20th C Olympics

Answers - see Quiz 176, page 610

1 Which country broke the India/Pakistan 50 year monopoly of men's hockey tournaments?
2 Who won Great Britain's first medal of the Atlanta Games?
3 Who last won the 100m gold for Canada before Donovan Bailey?
4 In which sport did Mike Agassi, father of Andre, compete in the 1948 and 1952 Olympics?
5 In which event did Great Britain's Henry Taylor land eight Golds?
6 Ralph Craig ran the 100 metres for the US in 1912; when did he next compete in the Olympics?
7 Who won Silver when Tessa Sanderson won Gold in the javelin?
8 Which was the first city to host the Summer Olympics twice?
9 In which event did Michelle Smith win bronze in 1996?
10 What did Paavo Nurmi always carry with him during his gold medal winning races?
11 Who won the 400m hurdles in the games sandwiched between Ed Moses' two triumphs?
12 Which country did 70s star Lassie Virren come from?
13 Who wore a T shirt saying "Thank You America For A Wonderful Games"?
14 Why was Finn Volmari Iso-Hollo's 1932 steeplechase win exceptional?
15 In 1956 Australia hosted the Games except for equestrian events which were held in which country?
16 Charles Bennett and Arnold Jackson have both taken gold for Britain in which athletic event?
17 Who came second when Donovan Bailey won 100m Gold?
18 How many Gold medals did Great Britain win in 1996?
19 In which event did an individual first won four successive Golds?
20 At which venue did Steve Redgrave first win Gold?
21 Britain and which other country have won Gold in every Summer Games?
22 In what year did baseball become a medal sport?
23 In which sporting event did John Huish claim 1996 Olympic Gold?
24 Tessa Sanderson first competed in the Olympics in which country?
25 Which country had its only Gold in men's basketball in 1980?

Answers

Pot Luck 84 (see Quiz 176, page 610)
1 Oprah Winfrey. **2** Kashmir. **3** Michel Vaucaire. **4** Cairo. **5** Tony Slattery. **6** Davis Cup. **7** Don Lockwood. **8** Daily Sketch. **9** USA. **10** 4 million. **11** Cancer. **12** Malaysia. **13** Goombay Dance Band. **14** James. **15** Lisbon. **16** Nigel Planer. **17** Windsurfing. **18** Lancaster. **19** Cameroon. **20** Derek Jameson. **21** Baby crocodile. **22** 1970s. **23** Barbara Castle. **24** Dean Martin. **25** Vostok 6.

Quiz 176 Pot Luck 84

Answers - see Quiz 175, page 609

1 What is Oprah Winfrey's real name?
2 In which country was Joanna Lumley born?
3 Who wrote the lyrics to "Je ne regrette rien"?
4 Which capital city has the fewest cinemas in relation to its population?
5 Which star of Whose Line Is It Anyway? is a black belt at judo?
6 Dwight Filley were the first names of the presenter of which sporting cup?
7 What was the name of the UK's Lovejoy in US soap Dallas?
8 Which Daily Paper ran the strip cartoon Pop?
9 Which country does the airline Horizon Air come from?
10 What is the population of New Zealand to the nearest million?
11 What star sign is shared by Virginia Wade and Glenys Kinnock?
12 Vehicles from which country use the international registration letter MAL?
13 Who had a UK No. 1 hit with Seven Tears?
14 What is Gordon Brown's real first name?
15 In which European city is the Calouste Gulbenkian Museum?
16 Who narrated The Magic Roundabout when it resumed in the 90s?
17 Capt Webb was a pioneer swimming the Channel but how did Jonathan Webb cross the Channel in 1977?
18 What is Yorkshireman Timothy West's middle name?
19 Douala International airport is in which country?
20 Which ex editor of the Daily Express and News of the World went into broadcasting?
21 What were the Queen and Prince Philip given as a present for baby Prince Andrew while on a visit to the Gambia?
22 In which decade was the New River George bridge West Virginia opened?
23 Which Transport Minister introduced breathalyser tests in the UK?
24 Who said, "You're not drunk if you can lie on the floor without holding on."?
25 In which craft did Valentina Tereshkova make her historic space flight?

Answers

20th C Olympics (see Quiz 175, page 609)
1 Germany. **2** Paul Palmer. **3** Percy Williams. **4** Boxing. **5** Swimming. **6** 1948 - yachting team. **7** Tiina Lillak. **8** Paris. **9** 200m butterfly. **10** Stopwatch. **11** Volker Beck. **12** Finland. **13** Daley Thompson. **14** He ran an extra lap by mistake. **15** Sweden. **16** 1500m. **17** Frankie Fredericks. **18** One. **19** Discus. **20** Los Angeles. **21** France. **22** 1992. **23** Archery. **24** Canada. **25** Yugoslavia.

Quiz 177 Hollywood

Answers - see Quiz 178, page 612

1 In how many countries did A Few Good Men open simultaneously making it the largest premiere on record?
2 In which film is Vince LaRocca the gangster boyfriend of Deloris?
3 What was the third sequel to Child's Play?
4 The documentary Hearts of Darkness told of the making of which film?
5 Who said, "I knew that with a mouth like mine I just had to be a star or something"?
6 How many years after Terminator was Terminator 2 released?
7 Which director of Madonna's Vogue video directed Alien 3?
8 Which Clint Eastwood film had the highest stuntman ratio?
9 In Reversal of Fortune what is the name of Claus's wife whom he is found guilty of attempting to murder?
10 Which Hollywood couple called one of their children Dakota Mayi?
11 Whose slogan was 'More stars than there are in heaven'?
12 In which 1990 Robert de Niro film did the director's parents both appear?
13 Who played Judy, Doralee and Violet's boss in 9 to 5?
14 What was the name of the first sci fi movie to cost more than $1 million?
15 During the making of which film did Grace Kelly meet Prince Rainier of Monaco thus ending her Hollywood career?
16 Which actor said of Hollywood, "If you say what you mean in this town, you're an outlaw"?
17 What was included inside the wooden horse for Helen of Troy to make the actors more comfortable?
18 Which 50s film held the record for the most number of animals in a film?
19 Who said, "I'm old. I'm young. I'm intelligent. I'm stupid"?
20 What was John Cazale's last film?
21 Who was Tatum O'Neal's equestrian coach in International Velvet?
22 Who directed Eyes Wide Shut?
23 Who won the Best Actress Oscar the year Princess Diana died?
24 How old was Richard Gere when starred in An Officer and a Gentleman?
25 Although Anthony Hopkins starred in the film of Shadowlands who had played it on Broadway and the West End?

Answers

Pot Luck 85 (see Quiz 178, page 612)

1 Fly fishing. **2** 50s. **3** John Mungo. **4** Attorney General. **5** None. **6** James Clavell. **7** 15. **8** Georgia. **9** Gemini. **10** Cambridge. **11** Woman. **12** FJI. **13** Yvon Petra. **14** Moscow. **15** Camille Javal. **16** 1905. **17** Four. **18** Portugal. **19** Police. **20** 1965. **21** Prokofiev. **22** Brazil. **23** George. **24** George Lucas. **25** Kenneth Connor.

Quiz 178 Pot Luck 85

Answers - see Quiz 177, page 611

1 Lake Echternach was the first venue for which world championship?
2 In which decade did Dennis the Menace start his menacing?
3 What are Hugh Grant's middle names?
4 Which senior post did Nigel Havers' father hold in Margaret Thatcher's government?
5 How many games did England lose in soccer's 1982 World Cup in Spain?
6 Who wrote the best seller Shogun?
7 How old was Stacey Hillyard when she first became snooker's World Amateur Champion?
8 Hartsfield international airport is in which US state?
9 What star sign is George Best?
10 Where in England was Sir Richard Attenborough born?
11 What was John Lennon's last UK No 1 of the 80s?
12 What are the international registration letters of a vehicle from Fiji?
13 Who was the first Wimbledon men's singles champion after World War II?
14 In 1957 an air service was set up between London and which city?
15 What is Brigitte Bardot's real name?
16 In what year was the ambulance service introduced in London?
17 In all how many England managers did Kevin Keegan play for?
18 In which country is the Salazar bridge?
19 "Dull it isn't" was part of an ad to promote which profession?
20 In which year was the then tallest building the Post Office Tower opened?
21 Greg Lake's I Believe in Father Christmas was based an a suite by which composer?
22 Which country does the airline Varig come from?
23 What was Anthony Newley's real first name?
24 Who directed American Graffiti?
25 Who played Monsieur Alfonse in the TV comedy 'Allo 'Allo?

Answers

Hollywood (see Quiz 177, page 611)

1 51. **2** Sister Act. **3** Bride of Chucky. **4** Apocalypse Now. **5** Barbra Streisand. **6** Seven. **7** David Fincher. **8** The Rookie. **9** Sunny. **10** Don Johnson & Melanie Griffith. **11** MGM. **12** Goodfellas. **13** Dabney Coleman. **14** Forbidden Planet. **15** To Catch a Thief. **16** Kevin Costner. **17** Air conditioning. **18** Around the World in 80 Days. **19** Warren Beatty. **20** The Deer Hunter. **21** Marcia Williams. **22** Stanley Kubrick. **23** Helen Hunt. **24** 30. **25** Nigel Hawthorne.

Quiz 179 Sitcoms

Answers - see Quiz 180, page 614

1 Which Deputy Party leader appeared in an episode of Chef!?
2 What was the provisional title of Last of the Summer Wine?
3 Empty Nest was a spin off from which sitcom?
4 Which Seinfeld star was the voice of Hugo in The Hunchback of Notre Dame?
5 Whose song provided the music for Girls On Top?
6 In Man About the House what football team did Robin Tripp support?
7 What was the business owned by Ted Simcock called in A Bit of a Do?
8 What was Jean Boht's codename for This Is Your Life?
9 What was the name of the singles club in Dear John by John Sullivan?
10 In May to December Miss Flood became Mrs Who?
11 What was Polly's surname in Fawlty Towers?
12 On which UK sitcom special did Fergie make a guest appearance?
13 In what type of hospital was Get Well Soon set?
14 In 1979, which sitcom netted the highest audience of the year of 24 million viewers?
15 What was the surname of Rhoda in the sitcom spin off from the Mary Tyler Moore show?
16 When Fawlty Towers was shown in Spain, Manuel became what nationality in order to avoid offence to the Spaniards?
17 Which star of a popular sitcom made a fitness video called Let's Dance?
18 In which state was Roseanne set?
19 Which sitcom star released a solo album called What Is Going to Become of Us All in 1976?
20 Which star of Barbara was mayoress of her home town Blackburn?
21 Which show was originally called These Friends of Mine?
22 What was the name of the house Hester and William rented in French Fields?
23 What was the name of the housekeeper in Father Ted?
24 Who sang the theme music for You Rang M'Lord along with one its stars Paul Shane?
25 Alf Garnett was originally to have had what name?

Answers

Pot Luck 86 (see Quiz 180, page 614)
1 Agatha Christie. **2** Bonar Law. **3** Ohio. **4** First of the 20th century. **5** Kenneth Baker. **6** Jean Batten. **7** Lichfield. **8** Nicole. **9** Female Grand National rider. **10** Leo. **11** Victoria Wood. **12** Morocco. **13** 10. **14** Medical student. **15** 42 million. **16** 1900. **17** Cliff Richard. **18** Robert Bridges. **19** Italy. **20** Harry Secombe. **21** Radioactivity. **22** Oscar Wilde. **23** The Oval. **24** KLM. **25** Shirley Bassey.

Quiz 180 Pot Luck 86

Answers - see Quiz 179, page 613

1 Whose second husband was Max Mallowan?
2 Who was the next British Prime Minister after Lloyd George?
3 Hopkins international airport is in which US state?
4 In which decade was the London Symphony Orchestra founded?
5 On Spitting Image who was seen as a slug?
6 Which pioneering aviator had a plane called Percival Gull?
7 Which Earl has presented Miss World?
8 Who had a UK No 1 hit with A Little Peace?
9 What was Charlotte Brew's famous first?
10 What star sign is shared by Danny La Rue and Roy Walker?
11 Which magician's wife wrote songs on That's Life?
12 Vehicles from which country use the international registration letter MA?
13 How old was Elizabeth Taylor when she appeared in National Velvet?
14 Educationalist Maria Montessori was Italy's first ever female what?
15 What is the population of South Africa to the nearest million?
16 When was the Daily Express founded?
17 Who was the first person in the 90s to have a solo Christmas No 1 hit?
18 Who was Poet Laureate from 1913-1930?
19 Elmas International airport is in which country?
20 Whose autobiography was called Arias and Raspberries?
21 Henri Becquerel shared a Nobel prize for his work in discovering what?
22 Who took the assumed name Sebastian Melmoth when living in Paris?
23 At which ground did Muralitharan take nine wickets v England?
24 Established in 1919 which is the world's oldest surviving airline?
25 Which personality had her shoe replaced by an army boot in a classic Morecambe and Wise sketch?

Answers

Sitcoms (see Quiz 179, page 613)
1 Roy Hattersley. **2** Last of the Summer Wine. **3** The Golden Girls. **4** Jason Alexander. **5** Squeeze. **6** Southampton. **7** Jupiter Foundry. **8** Yeast. **9** 1-2-1. **10** Tipple. **11** Sherman. **12** The Vicar of Dibley. **13** TB sanatorium. **14** To The Manor Born. **15** Morgenstern. **16** Italian. **17** Richard Wilson. **18** Illinois. **19** John LeMesurier. **20** Madge Hindle - Doreen. **21** Ellen. **22** Les Hirondelles. **23** Mrs Doyle. **24** Bob Monkhouse. **25** Alf Ramsey.

Quiz 181 Books

Answers - see Quiz 182, page 616

1 In which Ian Fleming novel did the dog Edison appear?
2 Which MP wrote The Smile on the Face of the Tiger?
3 Which country's national anthem was used by John Steinbeck for his book The Grapes of Wrath?
4 Which British novelist said, "Fame is a powerful aphrodisiac"?
5 Which writer did Sean O'Casey describe as English Literature's performing flea?
6 Which novelist was the cousin of actor Christopher Lee?
7 Ten Days That Shook the World is about what?
8 How was H H Munro better known?
9 Who completed his novel Omerta shortly before his death?
10 What was DH Lawrence's Lady Chatterley's Lover originally to have been called?
11 In Peter Pan, what are Hook's last words?
12 Which novelist wrote The ABC of French Food?
13 What was Ian Fleming's first novel?
14 Which sit com actress was a judge for the Booker Prize in 1985?
15 What was Robert Graves autobiography called?
16 Which opera singer's memoirs were called Full Circle?
17 John Betjeman's book Ghastly Good Taste was on the subject of what?
18 Which country banned Black Beauty for its supposed racist title?
19 Which novelist is the mother of actress Rudi Davies?
20 What was the first volume of Dirk Bogarde's autobiography called?
21 Which actress wrote the children's book Nibbles & Me?
22 Which children's author's autobiography was called Boy?
23 What was William Golding's follow up to The Lord of the Flies?
24 What is the first name of P G Wodehouse's character Cheesewright?
25 Which French novelist played in goal for Algeria?

Answers

Pot Luck 87 (see Quiz 182, page 616)

1 Michael Dumble-Smith. **2** Yamaha. **3** D W Griffith. **4** Sir Michael Hopkins. **5** America's Cup. **6** Athens. **7** Arthur C Clarke . **8** Edmonton Oilers. **9** 15th. **10** The Beano Comic. **11** Liverpool. **12** FL. **13** Cardiff. **14** Turkey. **15** Vicky Licorish. **16** Pisces. **17** Liz Hurley. **18** Ferry 'Cross The Mersey. **19** Niki Lauda. **20** Doctor. **21** Even. **22** Honduras. **23** 1925. **24** Roman Polanski. **25** Melvyn Bragg.

Quiz 182 Pot Luck 87

Answers - see Quiz 181, page 615

1 What is Michael Crawford's real name?
2 Which company sponsored snooker's British Gold Cup from 1981-1984?
3 Who directed the three hour silent movie epic The Birth Of A Nation?
4 Who designed the Westminster building to provide MPs with more office space from 2000 onwards?
5 What did Dennis Connor win three times in the 80s?
6 In which European city is the Goulandis Natural History Museum?
7 Who wrote the book The Hammer of God?
8 Wayne Gretzky first played league ice hockey with which team?
9 What was the date of the October 1987 gales that hit Britain?
10 What was launched on Tuesday 30 July, 1938 and kept going to the end of the century?
11 Where in England was actor Tom Baker born?
12 What are the international registration letters of a vehicle from Liechtenstein?
13 Ex PM James Callaghan became Baron Callaghan of where?
14 Esenboga International airport is in which country?
15 Which female was in the coffee shop in Saturday Superstore?
16 What star sign is Mikhail Gorbachev?
17 Who made her TV debut in Dennis Potter's Christabel?
18 What was the last UK No 1 of the 80s featuring Paul McCartney?
19 Who was runner up when James Hunt was F1 champion?
20 What did Che Guevara train to be?
21 What single word did boxer Joe Louis want on his tombstone?
22 Which country does the airline Sahsa come from?
23 In which year was TV personality Ernie Wise born?
24 Who directed the movie Tess?
25 Which TV presenter wrote the novel A Time To Dance?

Answers

Books (see Quiz 181, page 615)
1 Chitty Chitty Bang Bang. **2** Douglas Hurd. **3** USA. **4** Graham Greene. **5** P.G.Wodehouse. **6** Ian Fleming. **7** Russian Revolution. **8** Saki. **9** Mario Puzo. **10** Tenderness. **11** Floreat Etona. **12** Len Deighton. **13** Casino Royale. **14** Joanna Lumley. **15** Goodbye to All That. **16** Janet Baker. **17** Architecture. **18** Namibia. **19** Beryl Bainbridge. **20** A Postilion Struck By Lightning. **21** Elizabeth Taylor. **22** Roald Dahl. **23** The Inheritors. **24** Stilton. **25** Albert Camus.

Quiz 183 Pop: Who's Who?

Answers - see Quiz 184, page 618

1 Who partnered Patti Austin on Baby Come To Me?
2 Which artist was the biggest-selling singles artist in the UK in 1991?
3 Which male singer fronted the group Change before his solo career took off?
4 Which London based group featured two Davies brothers?
5 What nationality is Peter Andre?
6 Who sang with R Kelly on I'm Your Angel?
7 Who featured on You Got The Love with Source?
8 How many members were in the Mancunian band The Smiths?
9 Who partnered Michael McDonald with On My Own?
10 Which act were voted Best British Dance Act at the 1994 BRIT awards?
11 Who was born Gloria Fajarda?
12 Which member of Def Leppard died in 1991?
13 Vince Clarke and Andy Bell achieved chart success as who?
14 Who won a record four BRIT awards in 1995?
15 Who was the lead vocalist for The Go-Gos?
16 How is Douglas Trendle better known?
17 Who was the first British female to win a Grammy award?
18 Who featured on If You Ever by East 17?
19 Who was the oldest solo female singer to have a No 1 in the 20th century?
20 Which artist has had the most UK Top Ten hits in the 1990s?
21 What relationship was Brian Connolly of Sweet to Mark McManus aka Taggart?
22 Who played the heavy metal guitar on Michael Jackson's Beat It?
23 Which Manic Street Preacher has been missing presumed dead since '95?
24 Which artist has achieved the most consecutive UK Top Ten hits?
25 What nationality were Rednex?

Answers

Pot Luck 88 (see Quiz 184, page 618)
1 Charlene. **2** Nebraska. **3** Edwin. **4** Rodney Harrington. **5** 39 million. **6** Rev J C du Plessis. **7** Dwight Eisenhower. **8** Fiji. **9** Tracey Austin. **10** Canada. **11** Darius Perkins. **12** Lithuania. **13** N. Ireland. **14** Gene Hackman. **15** Lenin. **16** Dallas. **17** Soccer. **18** 1974. **19** Hungary. **20** Chris Evert. **21** Leo. **22** 80. **23** Chocolate. **24** Crosby. **25** Ciaran.

Quiz 184 Pot Luck 88

Answers - see Quiz 183, page 617

LEVEL 3

1 Who had a UK No. 1 hit with I've Never Been To Me?
2 Eppley Airfield international airport is in which US state?
3 What is Hardy Amies' real first name?
4 Which role did John McEnroe's ex father in law play in Peyton Place?
5 What is the population of Spain to the nearest million?
6 Who first coined the phrase apartheid?
7 Richard Nixon was Vice President to which US President?
8 Which country of islands was declared a republic in 1987?
9 Who is the youngest female tennis player to win the US Open?
10 In which country is the Sky Train Rail bridge?
11 Who played Scott Robinson before Jason Donovan in Neighbours?
12 Vehicles from which country use the international registration letter LT?
13 In which country was Sam Neill born?
14 What is Gene Hackman's real name?
15 What was the world's first atomic powered ship called?
16 Which soap boasted a cafe called the Hot Biscuit?
17 Veteran presenter Frank Bough won an Oxbridge blue for which sport?
18 In which year did Dennis the Menace push Biffo off the Beano's front cover?
19 Ferihegy International airport is in which country?
20 Who was the defending champion when Virginia Wade won the Wimbledon singles?
21 What star sign is shared by Kate Bush and Daley Thompson?
22 How many 'victories' did The Red Baron claim in aerial dogfights?
23 "Desperation, Pacification, Expectation, Acclamation, Realization" was part of an ad to promote what?
24 Which by-election was won by Shirley Williams in November 1981 to become the first SDP MP?
25 What is Michael Barrymore's middle name?

Answers

Pop: Who's Who? (see Quiz 183, page 617)
1 James Ingram. **2** Bryan Adams. **3** Luther Vandross. **4** Kinks. **5** English. **6** Celine Dion. **7** Candi Staton. **8** 4. **9** Patti Labelle. **10** M People. **11** Gloria Estefan. **12** Steve Clark. **13** Erasure. **14** Blur. **15** Belinda Carlisle. **16** Buster Bloodvessel. **17** Petula Clark. **18** Gabrielle. **19** Cher. **20** Madonna. **21** Brother. **22** Eddie Van Halen. **23** Richey Edwards. **24** Madonna. **25** Swedish.

Quiz 185 20th C Rich & Famous

Answers - see Quiz 186, page 620

1 Whose marriage was headlined in Variety as "Egghead weds Hourglass"?
2 At whose castle did Elizabeth Taylor spend her 60th birthday?
3 Who launched her own perfume called White Diamonds?
4 Josie Borain was the partner of which rich and famous person during his difficult divorce settlement?
5 What is Jose Carreras' middle name?
6 Marion and Tito were two members of which famous family group?
7 What breed of dog was Madonna's Chiquita?
8 Whose funeral caused Sam Goldwyn to say, "The only reason people showed up was to make sure he was dead"?
9 From which year did Martina Navratilova compete officially as an American rather than a Czech player?
10 Lady Elizabeth Anson is the sister of which Lord?
11 Chevy Chase was a professional in which sport?
12 Which woman was head of Sock Shop?
13 What was the name of John Gummer's daughter photographed burger munching in the early days of the BSE scare?
14 Who was the first British royal to visit the Soviet Union after 1917?
15 Who said, "I'd rather go mad than see a psychiatrist"?
16 Where was the wedding of David Beckham and Victoria Adams held?
17 Prince Charles said, "Diana only married me so that she could . . ." what?
18 Who said, "I never really hated a man enough to give him his diamonds back"?
19 What did Elvis's widow Priscilla call her child by a different partner?
20 Which disease did Lord Snowdon suffer from as a child?
21 Which ex MP had the car registration plate ANY 1 on his Rolls Royce?
22 Which name is shared by the daughters of Tony Curtis and Vanessa Feltz?
23 What type of car was Isadora Duncan test driving when her scarf caught in the wheel spokes and strangled her?
24 Who said, "I'm into pop because I want to get rich, famous and laid"?
25 Which sportsman said of his autobiography, "I can honestly say I have written one more book than I have read"?

Answers

Pot Luck 89 (see Quiz 186, page 620)
1 Like A Prayer. **2** Amy Johnson. **3** Mary. **4** 1980. **5** Franklin D Roosevelt. **6** Provident. **7** Gary Owen. **8** J P Donleavy. **9** Barbara Edwards. **10** North Carolina. **11** Italy. **12** GCA. **13** Belfast. **14** 1921. **15** Nine. **16** Rita Crudgington. **17** 1919. **18** Engineer. **19** Norway. **20** Clairol. **21** Mark Twain. **22** Aries. **23** 1952. **24** Sydney Pollack. **25** Mozambique.

Quiz 186 Pot Luck 89

Answers - see Quiz 185, page 619

1 What was Madonna's last UK No 1 of the 80s?
2 Who was the famous wife of pilot Jim Mollison?
3 What is Dame Barbara Cartland's real first name?
4 In which year did Carry On star Hattie Jacques die?
5 Who was the first US President to be re-elected for a fourth term of office?
6 What does the P stand for in BUPA?
7 Who did John Spencer defeat in snooker's first knockout World Championship final?
8 Who wrote The Lady Who Liked Clean Rest Rooms?
9 Who was the first woman weather presenter on BBC TV?
10 Which university did Michael Jordan play basketball for?
11 Which were the first country to win soccer's World Cup on foreign soil?
12 What are the international registration letters of a vehicle from Guatemala?
13 Where was Kenneth Branagh born?
14 In what year did the first woman qualify as a barrister in the UK?
15 How many years after her death were Garbo's ashes returned to her Swedish homeland?
16 What is Cheryl Baker's real name?
17 In what year was Australia reached by air from England?
18 Cricketer Anil Kumble has qualified as what?
19 Fornebu International airport is in which country?
20 Which company first advertised "Is it true blondes have more fun?"?
21 Which writer described newspaper reports of his own death as being "greatly exaggerated"?
22 What star sign is Omar Sharif?
23 In which year did the world's longest-running stage play The Mousetrap open?
24 Who directed Out Of Africa?
25 Which country does the airline LAM come from?

Answers

20th C Rich & Famous (see Quiz 185, page 619)
1 Arthur Miller & Marilyn Monroe. **2** Sleeping Beauty's. **3** Elizabeth Taylor. **4** Earl Spencer. **5** Maria. **6** Jackson Five. **7** Chihuahua. **8** Louis B Mayer. **9** 1981. **10** Lichfield. **11** Tennis. **12** Sophie Mirman. **13** Cordelia. **14** Princess Anne. **15** Michael Caine. **16** Luttrellstown Castle. **17** Go through red lights. **18** Zsa Zsa Gabor. **19** Navarone. **20** Polio. **21** Jeffrey Archer. **22** Allegra. **23** Bugatti. **24** Bob Geldof. **25** Merv Hughes.

Quiz 187 Murder Most Foul

Answers - see Quiz 188, page 622

1 Who was murdered along with O J Simpson's estranged wife Nicole?
2 Who was nicknamed the Vampire of Dusseldorf?
3 Who was the first woman to be executed for murder in Texas after 1863?
4 The Sicilian Specialist by Norman Lewis is a thinly disguised fictional account of which assassination plot?
5 Where was Martin Luther King assassinated?
6 What was the real name of Butch Cassidy?
7 Who was convicted with Jon Venables of the murder of Jamie Bulger?
8 Which famous name was killed by Kenneth Halliwell?
9 Under what name did Dr Crippen leave the country after the murder of his wife?
10 In which Lake did Peter Hogg dump the body of his wife in 1976 although it was 11 years before he was jailed?
11 Keith Blakelock was killed in riots where?
12 Where did Michael Ryan carry out an horrific massacre?
13 How many men did Dennis Nilsen admit to killing between 1978 and 1983?
14 Where did John Christie live?
15 Who did Gaetano Bresci assassinate?
16 What was gangster Lucky Luciano's real first name?
17 What was the name of Ruth Ellis's lover whom she murdered?
18 How was murderer Pedro Alonzo Lopez nicknamed?
19 How old was the Yorkshire Ripper when he was captured?
20 What was the name of the Captain who sent the first wireless telegraphy message which brought about the capture of Dr Crippen?
21 Who was convicted of the murder of aviator Charles Lindbergh's son?
22 On which island did Martin Bryant massacre 34 people in 1996?
23 What was the name of the rally which Yitzhak Rabin had attended just before his assassination?
24 What was the name of the man killed in the A6 Murder, for which James Hanratty was hanged?
25 Who did the Boston Strangler say he worked for in order to gain his victims' confidence?

Answers

Pot Luck 90 (see Quiz 188, page 622)
1 Hepler. **2** Atlanta. **3** Toy theatres. **4** 9 million. **5** Martyn Lewis. **6** Achille Lauro. **7** Virginia. **8** Chickens. **9** Musical Youth. **10** 1970s. **11** Paris. **12** Lesotho. **13** Andrew Bonar Law. **14** Arts Council of Great Britain. **15** Lady Chatterley's Lover. **16** Ernie Wise. **17** 9. **18** Bristol. **19** The Bahamas. **20** Andrew Glenn. **21** 163. **22** Portugal. **23** Dancing. **24** Sergeant. **25** Virgo.

Quiz 188 Pot Luck 90

Answers - see Quiz 187, page 621

1 What is Rob Lowe's middle name?
2 Where were the 1996 Summer Olympic Games held?
3 What sort of toys does Peter Baldwin, the former Derek Wilton of Coronation St, collect?
4 What is the population of Sweden to the nearest million?
5 Which newsreader wrote Cats in the News, and Dogs in the News?
6 What was the name of the Italian cruise ship hijacked by Palestinian terrorists in October 1985?
7 In which US state is John F Kennedy buried?
8 What was Dudley Moore chasing in France in Tesco ads?
9 Who had a UK No 1 hit with Pass The Dutchie?
10 In which decade was London Southwark bridge opened?
11 What did Big Bertha shell in 1918?
12 Vehicles from which country use the international registration letter LS?
13 Which Prime Minister was quoted as saying, "I must follow them; I am their leader"?
14 How is the Council for Encouragement for Music and the Arts now known?
15 Which controversial book contained the line, "You can't ravish a tin of sardines"?
16 Whose 1991 autobiography was called Still On My Way to Hollywood?
17 John F Kennedy was one of how many children?
18 In which English city was Cary Grant born?
19 Freeport International airport is in which country?
20 In comic strip what was the name of Black Bob's owner?
21 What was blonde bombshell Jayne Mansfield's IQ measured at?
22 Which country does the airline TAP come from?
23 What did George Bernard Shaw describe as "a perpendicular expression of a horizontal desire"?
24 What was the title of the first Carry On film - Carry On?
25 What star sign is shared by Elvis Costello and Julio Iglesias?

Answers

Murder Most Foul (see Quiz 187, page 621)
1 Ronald Goldman. **2** Peter Kurten. **3** Karla Faye Tucker. **4** JF Kennedy. **5** Memphis. **6** Robert LeRoy Parker. **7** Robert Thompson. **8** Joe Orton. **9** Robinson. **10** Wast Water. **11** Tottenham. **12** Hungerford. **13** 15. **14** 10 Rillington Place. **15** King Umberto I of Italy. **16** Salvatore. **17** David Blakely. **18** The Monster of the Andes. **19** 34. **20** Kendall. **21** Bruno Hauptmann. **22** Tasmania. **23** Peace Yes Violence No. **24** Michael Gregsten. **25** Model agency.

Quiz 189 Sporting Chance

Answers - see Quiz 190, page 624

1 Why does the leader of the Tour de France wear a yellow jersey?
2 Where did golfer Mark Calcavecchia win his only British Open?
3 In the season Damon Hill was F1 champion how many races did he win?
4 Who was Czechoslovakia's only Wimbledon Men's Singles winner of the 20th century, playing as a Czech?
5 As well as Red Rum which other Red did Brian Fletcher ride to a Grand National victory?
6 How many games had Steve Davis won before Denis Taylor opened his account in the classic 1985 World Snooker final?
7 How many times did Terry Venables play for England?
8 In which country did Lynn Davies set the British long jump record that has stood for 30 years?
9 What was the first sport shown on ITV?
10 What was Jack Dempsey's nickname?
11 Brian Barnes played golf for Scotland in the 70s but where was he born?
12 What do JPR Williams initials stand for?
13 Who went airborne during a cricket match with David Gower in the Gooch led Australia tour?
14 How old was Stephen Hendry when he appeared on This Is Your Life?
15 Who has won the Badminton Horse Trials on Priceless and Master Craftsman?
16 Which boxer appeared in the film Spirit of Youth?
17 In which year did none of the four golf majors go to an American?
18 Who was team leader of Williams when Damon Hill was promoted to No 2?
19 What was the name of the horse on which Pat Eddery first won the Derby?
20 Who were the first winners of hockey's English National Cup?
21 What breed of dog was Steffi Graf's Ben?
22 In what year was snooker's World Championship first contested?
23 What is the middle name of golfer Mark James?
24 In how many games did Ray Wilkins captain England?
25 At which race circuit did Ayrton Senna lose his life?

Answers

Pot Luck 91 (see Quiz 190, page 624)

1 1999 royal wedding horses. **2** Instant coffee. **3** Five. **4** Suzanne Lenglen. **5** Omar Sharif. **6** Diamond. **7** Bermuda. **8** Alex Higgins. **9** Carol Shields. **10** Arthur. **11** Canada. **12** GUY. **13** Excursion 2-1 Match. **14** Aries. **15** John Paul I. **16** Glasgow. **17** Hand On My Heart. **18** John Masefield. **19** Paul Hewson. **20** Orby. **21** Connecticut. **22** Star Trek. **23** Ian Wright. **24** Ridley Scott. **25** 1991.

Quiz 190 Pot Luck 91

Answers - see Quiz 189, page 623

1 Who or what were Alderney, Aukland, Hillsborough, Twilight?
2 Which convenience food did Joel Cheek develop?
3 How many Royal Variety shows did Morecambe and Wise both appear in?
4 Who was the first non English speaking winner of Wimbledon women's singles?
5 Who was on stage with Wogan in 1990 when George Best appeared to be drunk?
6 Discovered in the 30s, Jonker and President Vargas were types of what?
7 Hamilton Kindley Field International airport is in which country?
8 Who did Cliff Thorburn beat in the final in his only snooker World Championship triumph?
9 Who wrote The Stone Dairies?
10 What is Nigel Davenport's real first name?
11 In which country is the Trois-Rivieres bridge?
12 What are the international registration letters of a vehicle from Guyana?
13 What appeared in the destination display on Man Utd's double decker bus after the 1999 European triumph?
14 What star sign is Gloria Hunniford?
15 Which Pope died in 1978 after a mere 33 days in office?
16 Where in the UK was Robert Carlyle born?
17 What was Kylie Minogue's last UK No. 1 of the 80s?
18 Who was Poet Laureate at the time of the Queen's Coronation?
19 What is Bono's real name?
20 What is Sir Terence Conran's middle name?
21 Bradley International airport is in which US state?
22 Jeffrey Hunter was the lead in the original pilot for which successful series?
23 Who scored England's last goal under Graham Taylor?
24 Who directed the blockbusting movie Alien?
25 Freddie Mercury died in which year?

Answers

Sporting Chance (see Quiz 189, page 623)
1 Its sponsor printed its newspaper on yellow paper. **2** Troon. **3** 8. **4** Jan Kodes. **5** Red Alligator. **6** 8. **7** Twice. **8** Switzerland. **9** Boxing. **10** Manassa Mauler. **11** London. **12** John Peter Rhys. **13** John Morris. **14** 21. **15** Virginia Leng - nee Holgate. **16** Joe Louis. **17** 1993. **18** Alain Prost. **19** Grundy. **20** Hounslow. **21** Boxer. **22** 1927. **23** Hugh. **24** Ten. **25** Imola.

Quiz 191 Movies - Comedies

Answers - see Quiz 192, page 626

1 Who wrote the lyrics for the song from Notting Hill sung by Elvis Costello?
2 What was Michael Palin's occupation in A Private Function?
3 Which boxer appeared in the film Carry On Constable?
4 Which film tells of the exploits of singer Deco Duffe?
5 What was the name of the orphanage where The Blues Brothers were brought up?
6 Airplane! was triggered off by which movie?
7 How old was Macaulay Culkin when he was cast for his role in Home Alone?
8 In Private Benjamin what is the name of Benjamin's captain?
9 What was the name of the High School in Porky's?
10 What was Tootsie's name before he turned into Tootsie?
11 Who was the leader of the band that appeared in The Brady Bunch Movie?
12 Who directed The Cable Guy?
13 What type of drug is Sherman Klump trying to perfect in The Nutty Professor?
14 In what year does Demolition Man take place?
15 Which comedy contained the song A Wink and a Smile?
16 What was Steve Martin's first film?
17 In which category was Mrs Doubtfire Oscar nominated?
18 On which film was Three Men and a Baby based?
19 Which canine caper had the song The Day I Fall in Love?
20 Whose poems returned to the best sellers list after Four Weddings and a Funeral?
21 Who was both Oscar and BAFTA nominated for When Harry Met Sally?
22 What was the third Road movie?
23 What was the signal for an angel getting its wings in It's A Wonderful Life?
24 Who was Louise Lasser's husband when she starred with him in What's Up Tiger Lily?
25 What was the first sequel to The Pink Panther called?

Answers

Pot Luck 92 (see Quiz 192, page 626)
1 April 30th. **2** Val Kilmer. **3** Charles Darrow. **4** Baldwin. **5** Helen Keller. **6** A.C.Benson. **7** Pennsylvania. **8** Do your best. **9** Lili Marlene. **10** Dave Stewart. **11** Vienna. **12** Algeria. **13** The Commercial. **14** Virgo. **15** Wal-Mart. **16** Afghanistan. **17** Heart. **18** Warren. **19** Liberia. **20** 1906. **21** Colorado. **22** Chile. **23** 60 million. **24** Alden. **25** New Edition.

Quiz 192 Pot Luck 92

Answers - see Quiz 191, page 625

1 On which date in 1945 did Hitler take cyanide then shoot himself?
2 What is Val Kilmer's real name?
3 Who devised Monopoly?
4 Who did Neville Chamberlain follow as British Prime Minister?
5 Who was Anne Sullivan's most famous pupil?
6 Who wrote the words to Land of Hope and Glory?
7 Which state was particularly threatened by the leak on Three Mile Island in 1979?
8 What does dyb dyb dyb mean?
9 Which wartime classic was the title of a 1980 film with Hanna Schygulla & Mel Ferrer?
10 Who composed the music played by the Royal Philarmonic to launch the Rover 75?
11 Where was the UN Atomic Energy Agency based when it was set up in 1957?
12 Oran International airport is in which country?
13 Which Esholt inn was originally used as The Woolpack?
14 What star sign is shared by Tommy Lee Jones and Oliver Stone?
15 Which retailing operation was started by Sam Walton?
16 In the 90s Babrak Karmal and Sultan Ali Keshtmond have been Prime Minister in which country?
17 Which Pet Shop Boys video did Sir Ian McKellen appear in ?
18 Which Commission reported on the death of John F Kennedy in 1964?
19 Vehicles from which country use the international registration letter LB?
20 In what year was the Kellogg Company set up to manufacture cornflakes?
21 In which river is the Boulder Dam?
22 Which country does the airline Ladeco come from?
23 What is the population of Thailand to the nearest million?
24 What is Gene Hackman's middle name?
25 Who had a UK No 1 hit with Candy Girl?

Answers

Movies – Comedies (see Quiz 191, page 625)
1 Herbert Kretzmer. **2** Chiropodist. **3** Freddie Mills. **4** The Commitments.
5 Saint Helen of the Blessed Shroud. **6** Zero Hour!. **7** Nine. **8** Lewis. **9** Angel Beach.
10 Michael Dorsey. **11** Davy Jones. **12** Ben Stiller. **13** Weight loss. **14** 2032.
15 Sleepless in Seattle. **16** The Jerk. **17** Best Make up. **18** Trois Hommes et un Couffin.
19 Beethoven's 2nd. **20** W H Auden. **21** Nora Ephron - writer. **22** Road to Morocco.
23 Bell ringing. **24** Woody Allen. **25** A Shot in the Dark.

Quiz 193 TV Ads

Answers - see Quiz 194, page 628

1 Which actor famous for a series of TV ads writes poetry under the pseudonym Robert Williams?
2 Toothpaste was famously the first ad on ITV. What was the second?
3 "Nice one Cyril" was the slogan to advertise what?
4 What did the Hoddles advertise when they performed in a TV ad?
5 Which drink suitable for children was advertised by Sharron Davies?
6 Who famously threw away her ring and fur coat but kept her VW Golf?
7 Which Dynasty character is 'worth it' in the hair ads?
8 Who played Prunella Scales daughter in the Tesco ads?
9 Who wrote Adiemus which was used by BA to advertise their services?
10 Characters from which soap were used to advertise BT?
11 Which company said, "Never forget you have a choice"?
12 Which supermarket chain sacked John Cleese because customers found his ads very unfunny?
13 Which personality famous for voiceovers described this way of earning money as the late 20th century equivalent of taking in washing?
14 Which wine store used Pachelbel's Canon as an advertising theme?
15 Which lager was advertised to the accompaniment of Verdi's La forza del destino?
16 Which female writer is credited with coming up with the slogan "Go to work on an egg"?
17 Which theme music did BT use to promote their Internet services?
18 When did Guinness first say their drink was "good for you"?
19 "Does she or doesn't she..?" was a slogan used to advertise what?
20 Which make of car had the slogan Vorsprung durch Technik?
21 When did the word pinta enter the English language via an ad for milk?
22 What was advertised as the chocolate bar you could eat "without ruining your appetite"?
23 Who made over 50 ads for Schh you know who in nine years?
24 According to the ad, what put the T in Britain?
25 When did the first anti drink driving campaign start?

Answers

Pot Luck 93 (see Quiz 194, page 628)
1 Texas. **2** Pius. **3** Virgo. **4** Caryn Johnson. **5** Oh Boy. **6** Monster Raving Loony Party. **7** Steve Wright. **8** I Heard It Through The Grapevine. **9** Gemma Jones. **10** Kirk. **11** Nicaragua. **12** HKJ. **13** Edna O'Brien. **14** Fairbanks. **15** Esso petrol. **16** 1973. **17** Columcille. **18** India. **19** Wimbledon. **20** Joseph. **21** Nevada. **22** Venezuela. **23** 4.5 hours. **24** Robert Zemeckis. **25** Chicago.

Quiz 194 Pot Luck 93

Answers - see Quiz 193, page 627

1 In which American state is the Merril Collection and the Burke Museum of Fine Arts?
2 From 1903 to 1958 all the Popes bar one had which name?
3 What star sign is Pauline Collins?
4 What is Whoopi Goldberg's real name?
5 What was Mud's last UK No 1 of the 70s?
6 Which political party had the Golden Lion in Ashburton, Devon as its meeting place?
7 Who hosted the quiz show Home Truths?
8 What was the first oldies pop song used in a Levi's TV ad?
9 Which actress played a hotel manager in The Duchess of Duke Street?
10 What was the name of William Shatner's Doberman Pinscher dog?
11 Which nation was the first to ratify the United Nations charter in 1945?
12 What are the international registration letters of a vehicle from Jordan?
13 Who wrote the novel Time and Tide?
14 What is the Alaskan terminus of the Alaskan Highway?
15 Put a tiger in your tank was originally an advertising slogan for what?
16 In which year did David Bedford set a new 10,000m record?
17 What is Mel Gibson's middle name?
18 In which country was Julie Christie born?
19 In the 60s the last London trolleybus journey started where?
20 What was Buster Keaton's actual first name?
21 Cannon international airport is in which US state?
22 Which country does the airline VIASA come from?
23 To the nearest 30 minutes how long was the longest speech ever made at the United Nations?
24 Who directed Back To The Future?
25 Richard Daley was mayor of which city for 21 years?

Answers

TV Ads (see Quiz 193, page 627)

1 Bob Hoskins. **2** Drinking chocolate. **3** Wonderloaf bread. **4** Breakfast cereal. **5** Ribena Toothkind. **6** Paula Hamilton. **7** Sammy Jo. **8** Jane Horrocks. **9** Carl Jenkins. **10** EastEnders. **11** British Caledonian Airways. **12** Sainsbury's. **13** John Peel. **14** Thresher. **15** Stella Artois. **16** Fay Weldon. **17** E.T. **18** 1930. **19** Hair colour. **20** Audi. **21** 1958. **22** Milky Way. **23** William Franklin. **24** Typhoo. **25** 1964.

Quiz 195 Media

Answers - see Quiz 196, page 630

LEVEL 3 

1 All human life is there was a slogan used to advertise which newspaper?
2 Which newspaper published detailed photographs of Diana's car crash?
3 In 1980 which radio station ran an April Fool's day prank saying Big Ben's clockface would be replaced by a digital one?
4 Who founded the Pergamon Press?
5 Who drew Felix the Cat?
6 In what profession did Bruce Bairnsfather find fame?
7 In radio's Beyond Our Ken which Kenneth Williams character's catchphrase was, "The answer lies in the soil"?
8 Which newspaper was launched in January 1990?
9 When he was on Desert Island Discs, which newspaper did Des O'Connor ask to have delivered regularly as his luxury?
10 Tessa Sanderson won libel damages in 1990 against which newspapers?
11 Who was DC Thomson's first cartoonist allowed to sign his name?
12 Who found fame on radio as Lady Beatrice Counterblast?
13 Who created the line from a cartoon, "Happiness is a warm puppy"?
14 Whose poem For the Fallen was printed in The Times in 1914?
15 When did the Popeye cartoon begin?
16 What percentage of the US TV audience saw Elvis on the Ed Sullivan Show?
17 Which group of people did radio producer D G Bridson describe as "The wriggling ponces of the spoken word"?
18 Who said, "When a journalist enters the room, your privacy ends and his begins"?
19 Which radio DJ said, "And don't forget on Sunday you can hear the two minute silence on Radio One"?
20 Who was Little Jim in The Goons?
21 "Good girls go to heaven, bad girls go everywhere" was the slogan used to launch which magazine?
22 Which journalist took the name Cassandra?
23 Who scripted The Navy Lark?
24 Who launched the news magazine Now! around 1980?
25 Which classic radio show had the line, "Can I do you now sir"?

Answers

Pot Luck 94 (see Quiz 196, page 630)
1 Germany. **2** 1964. **3** Libra. **4** Radio's Listen with Mother. **5** Prince Charming. **6** Norbridge High. **7** Woodrow Wilson. **8** Law. **9** 63 million. **10** Venezuela. **11** Arte Johnson. **12** Libya. **13** Yaw. **14** ANC. **15** Europe. **16** Cartoons. **17** Accountancy. **18** Billy Sherrill. **19** Spain. **20** Dudley Watkins. **21** Air hostess. **22** Howards' Way. **23** 197. **24** Alastair. **25** Queen Mary.

Quiz 196 Pot Luck 94

Answers - see Quiz 195, page 629

1 In which country was the Zoo Bridge constructed?
2 The Windmill Theatre which "never closed" in World War II shut down in which year?
3 What star sign is shared by Meatloaf and Luciano Pavarotti?
4 In what context was Julia Lang's voice often heard from the 50s onwards?
5 Which Adam and the Ants video did Diana Dors appear in?
6 Which school featured in Press Gang?
7 Thomas Marshal was Vice President to which US President?
8 What did the French artist Henri Matisse begin a career in?
9 What is the population of Turkey to the nearest million?
10 Which country does the airline Avensa come from?
11 Who was the German soldier in Rowan and Martin's Laugh In?
12 Vehicles from which country use the international registration letter LAR?
13 What is Paul Boateng's middle name?
14 Spear of the Nation was an armed wing of which group?
15 Who had a UK No. 1 hit with The Final Countdown?
16 What is Osbert Lancaster best known for producing?
17 According to Dateline figures, the highest percentage of male clients are in which profession?
18 Who co-wrote Stand by Your Man with Tammy Wynette?
19 Santander International airport is in which country?
20 Who created Desperate Dan?
21 Ellen Church is recognised as being the first female what?
22 Actress Dulcie Gray played Kate in which TV drama series?
23 How many nations took part in the 1996 Olympics?
24 What is Brian Walden's real first name?
25 Which liner launched in 1934 was the largest of her time?

Answers

Media (see Quiz 195, page 629)
1 The News of the World. **2** Bild. **3** BBC World Service. **4** Robert Maxwell. **5** Otto Messmer. **6** Cartoonist. **7** Arthur Fallowfield. **8** The Independent on Sunday. **9** The Sporting Life. **10** Sunday Mirror/People. **11** Dudley Watkins. **12** Betty Marsden. **13** Charles Schultz. **14** Laurence Binyon. **15** 1933. **16** 82%. **17** Disc jockeys. **18** Warren Beatty. **19** Steve Wright. **20** Spike Milligan. **21** Cosmopolitan. **22** William Connor. **23** Lawrie Wyman. **24** James Goldsmith. **25** ITMA.

Quiz 197 Words & Music

Answers - see Quiz 198, page 632

1 Who was the first female to top the singles chart with a self-composed song?
2 Whose album Fat of the Land debuted at No 1 in more than 20 countries?
3 What was the first UK No 1 written by Shakin' Stevens himself?
4 What was the first TV theme to top the UK charts?
5 Who used and wrote under the pseudonym Bernard Webb?
6 Whose book of poems was called Songs for While I'm Away?
7 Who won Grammys for Best Album, Male Vocalist and Producer in 1986?
8 Lennon and McCartney wrote Goodbye for which vocalist?
9 Who was described as "a woman who pulled herself up by her bra straps"?
10 How many times was "Walk On By" sung by Gabrielle in the first chorus?
11 What type of vehicle were Reo Speedwagon named after?
12 What was Barry Manilow's Mandy originally titled in the US?
13 What was Sir Cliff Richard's first self produced UK No 1?
14 What was the first UK No 1 with "rock and roll" in the title?
15 Which song by Paul Simon begins "Wish I Was a Kellogg's Corn Flake"?
16 In the film Grease, who sang Beauty School Dropout?
17 On what date did Elton John first sing his biggest selling single in public?
18 What was the average age of a soldier in World War II in the UK No 1 hit 19?
19 Which artist was the subject of a 1991 biography by Randy Taraborelli?
20 Which Kenny Rogers song was written by Lionel Richie?
21 Which song by Lisa Stansfield featured in Indecent Proposal?
22 Who co-wrote Fame with David Bowie?
23 Who was Michael Jackson's massive hit Ben originally intended for?
24 Whose 1991 autobiography was called And The Beat Goes On?
25 Who was Willy Russell's co-writer on the musical Tallulah Who?

Answers

Pot Luck 95 (see Quiz 198, page 632)
1 France. **2** 1964. **3** Rudyard Kipling. **4** Derby County. **5** Russia. **6** Michael Browne. **7** Four. **8** Christopher. **9** Trevor Lock. **10** Gemini. **11** North Carolina. **12** Bob Hope. **13** Henry Ford. **14** Yellow. **15** Summer Nights. **16** Nigel Godwin Tranter. **17** Dana. **18** Bobby Kennedy. **19** Dorothy Parker. **20** Japan. **21** Agatha Christie. **22** Fred Zinnemann. **23** Brazil. **24** 1984. **25** Margaret Hyra.

Quiz 198 Pot Luck 95

Answers - see Quiz 197, page 631

LEVEL 3

1 Cardinal Basil Hume's father was Scottish but which country was his mother from?
2 In which year was the Sun first published?
3 Who wrote that the female of the species is more deadly than the male?
4 Which soccer side does Robert Lindsay support?
5 In which country did Frank and Tessa finally marry in Love Hurts?
6 Who painted The Art of the Game which depicted Eric Cantona as Christ?
7 How many times was Stirling Moss runner up in the F1 championship?
8 What is Nicholas Parsons' real first name?
9 Which Police Constable was taken prisoner in the 1980 London Iranian embassy siege?
10 What star sign is Gladys Knight?
11 Charlotte international airport is in which US state?
12 Which celebrity was born in Craighton Road, Eltham in 1903?
13 Who said ,"Money is like an arm or a leg, use it or lose it."?
14 What colour were the covers of the crime novels published in the 1930s by Victor Gollancz?
15 What was Olivia Newton-John's last UK No 1 of the 70s?
16 Who wrote the novel Honours Even?
17 Rosemary Brown is better known by which name?
18 The 'girl in the polka dot dress' was a key witness in whose assassination?
19 Who said, "Brevity is the soul of lingerie.."?
20 In which country was Olivia De Havilland born?
21 Which writer said, "Where large sums of money are involved, it is advisable to trust nobody."?
22 Who directed the classic movie High Noon?
23 Which country does the airline VASP come from?
24 In which year was Indira Gandhi assassinated by Sikh extremists?
25 What is Meg Ryan's real name?

Answers

Words & Music (see Quiz 197, page 631)
1 Kate Bush. **2** Prodigy. **3** Oh Julie!. **4** Eye Level. **5** Paul McCartney. **6** Phil Lynott. **7** Phil Collins. **8** Mary Hopkin. **9** Madonna. **10** 3. **11** A fire engine. **12** Brandy. **13** Mistletoe and Wine. **14** Rock and Roll Waltz. **15** Punky's Dilemma. **16** Frankie Avalon. **17** 6th Sept 1997. **18** 26. **19** Michael Jackson. **20** Lady. **21** In All The Right Places. **22** John Lennon. **23** Donny Osmond. **24** Sonny Bono. **25** Suzy Quatro.

Quiz 199 Unforgettables

Answers - see Quiz 200, page 634

LEVEL 3 

1 What would Pablo Picasso's surname have been if he had used his father's name instead of his mother's?
2 In what country was British choreographer Sir Frederick Ashton born?
3 Who made the film Renaldo and Clara with Bob Dylan?
4 Who said, "The hardest thing to understand in the world is income tax"?
5 Four minute miler Dr Roger Bannister has published papers on what?
6 Which orchestral conductor was married to one of the subjects of the film Hilary and Jackie?
7 Groucho Marx resigned from where as he didn't care to belong to any club that would have him as a member?
8 Which of the Barrymores wrote the memoir We Barrymores?
9 Which British composer wrote the theme music for the film Murder on the Orient Express?
10 Who said, "Middle age is when your age starts to show around your middle"?
11 What was Humphrey Bogart's middle name?
12 Which director's autobiography was called The Name Above the Title?
13 About whom did Kenneth Tynan say, "What one sees in other women drunk, one sees in... sober"?
14 Who designed the WRAC uniform?
15 The expression Great White Hope was used to describe which black boxer's opponents?
16 Where did Anne Frank die?
17 Who created Bugs Bunny?
18 What was Buster Keaton's real first name?
19 Whose famous teacher was Anne Sullivan?
20 In which craft did Bernard Leach find fame?
21 Where was blues singer Leadbelly when he was 'discovered' musically?
22 In which film did Harold Lloyd hang from a clockface?
23 Which Marx brother was not in Duck Soup?
24 How many England caps did Stanley Matthews win in 22 years?
25 Which political party did Emmeline Pankhurst join in 1926?

Answers

Pot Luck 96 (see Quiz 200, page 634)

1 12 million. **2** Sebastian. **3** Sagittarius. **4** 30s. **5** Intruder in the Queen's bedroom. **6** Snap. **7** Vidal Sassoon. **8** Marks & Spencer. **9** Zimbabwe cricket team. **10** 1920s. **11** Paul Anka - in My Way. **12** Kuwait. **13** Kathy and Me. **14** Ramsay MacDonald. **15** Ernie The Fastest Milkman in the West. **16** 15. **17** London. **18** Worrals of the WAAF. **19** France. **20** Southampton. **21** Christine Keeler. **22** Australia. **23** James Whale. **24** Harrison Ford. **25** Middleweight.

Quiz 200 Pot Luck 96

Answers - see Quiz 199, page 633

1 What is the population of Zimbabwe to the nearest million?
2 What is Rowan Atkinson's middle name?
3 What star sign is shared by Ian Botham and Billy Idol?
4 In which decade was the BBC Scottish Symphony Orchestra founded?
5 What did Elizabeth Andrews find in the 80s that posed important security questions?
6 Who had a UK No 1 hit with Rhythm Is A Dancer?
7 Which hairdresser said "The only place where success comes before work is in the dictionary"?
8 Sir Richard Greenbury resigned in June 99 as chairman of which big company?
9 Which international team was captained by Alistair Campbell in 1999?
10 In which decade was the Benjamin Franklin suspension bridge opened?
11 Who wrote the karaoke classic line, "And now the end is near.."?
12 Vehicles from which country use the international registration letter KWT?
13 What was Gillian Taylforth's autobiography called?
14 Which ex Prime Minister went on a cruise to improve his health, and died?
15 Which song by a solo singer stopped T Rex's Jeepster from getting to No 1?
16 How many years did Petra the dog appear on Blue Peter?
17 Pollock's Toy Museum is in which city?
18 What was the name of the female version of Biggles created by EW Johns?
19 Satolas International airport is in which country?
20 As a player what was Alf Ramsey's first club?
21 Who said "Discretion is a polite word for hypocrisy."?
22 Which country does the airline Rottnest Airbus come from?
23 Which TV and radio star set a world record for kissing in 1978?
24 What is Harrison Ford's real name?
25 At what weight did Chris Eubank win the WBO title in 1990?

Answers

Unforgettables (see Quiz 199, page 633)
1 Ruiz. **2** Ecuador. **3** Joan Baez. **4** Albert Einstein. **5** Neurology. **6** Daniel Barenboim. **7** Friars Club. **8** Lionel. **9** Richard Rodney Bennett. **10** Bob Hope. **11** De Forrest. **12** Frank Capra. **13** Greta Garbo. **14** Norman Hartnell. **15** Jack Johnson. **16** Belsen. **17** Chuck Jones. **18** Joseph. **19** Helen Keller. **20** Pottery. **21** Prison. **22** Safety Last. **23** Gummo. **24** 54. **25** Conservative.

Quiz 201 Famous Firsts

Answers - see Quiz 202, page 636

1 Who was the first person to make a solo trek to the South Pole on foot?
2 In what year was the first external heart pacemaker fitted?
3 Who was the first woman to sail around the world?
4 SRN1 was the first what?
5 The first Miss World came from which country?
6 What did Carlton Magee devise in the US for motorists?
7 What was first revealed at Lord's in 1975?
8 What was the name of the first long lasting perfume, launched in Japan in 1993?
9 Which two national teams made the first flight over Everest in a hot air balloon?
10 In which country was the first kidney transplant carried out?
11 What was Lester Piggott's first Derby winner back in 1954?
12 Which British bank was the first to issue cash dispenser cards?
13 Which orchestra was the first in London to be conducted by a woman?
14 Which support group was founded in Ohio in 1935?
15 Who founded the Cubism movement with Picasso?
16 Joseph Mornier patented which building material?
17 Who was the first black American to win the Nobel Peace prize?
18 In what year did Plaid Cymru win its first seat in the House of Commons?
19 Jacqui Mofokeng was the first black woman to win what?
20 At what mph did Malcolm Campbell set the land speed record in 1931?
21 In which category did Marie Curie win her second Nobel Prize, becoming the first person to win a Nobel Prize twice?
22 Where was the first nuclear reactor built, by Enrico Fermi?
23 Who led the team which made the first successful overland crossing of Antarctica?
24 Who was the first Governor General of Pakistan?
25 After record breaking flights to Australia and Cape Town where was Amy Johnson's plane lost?

Answers

Pot Luck 97 (see Quiz 202, page 636)
1 Salt Lake City. **2** Jennifer Morrow. **3** Frank Skinner. **4** Margaret Smith. **5** Cancer. **6** 6d. **7** Heart. **8** Ice cream. **9** Thomas. **10** USA. **11** Richard Kimble. **12** K. **13** Heinz-Harald Frentzen. **14** Dylan Thomas. **15** Andrea Jaeger. **16** Horseradish sauce. **17** Argentina. **18** Henrietta. **19** Jordan. **20** The Penguin. **21** New Mexico. **22** Germany. **23** John Landis. **24** Hobart. **25** John Le Carre.

Quiz 202 Pot Luck 97

Answers - see Quiz 201, page 635

1 Where are the 2002 Winter Olympic Games being held?
2 What is Jennifer Jason Leigh's real name?
3 Chris Collins took a show biz name from someone in a local pub dominoes team; what was it?
4 Who was the defending champion when Billie Jean King first won Wimbledon singles?
5 What star sign is actress Kathy Staff?
6 How much were the first Penguin books?
7 What was the Pet Shop Boys' last UK No 1 of the 80s?
8 Stop me and buy one was originally an advertising slogan for what?
9 What is Richard Dunwoody's real first name?
10 In which country was the Verrazano Narrows bridge built?
11 What is the name of the Doctor played by Harrison Ford in The Fugitive?
12 What are the international registration letters of a vehicle from Cambodia?
13 Who replaced Damon Hill at Williams?
14 Who wrote the line, "Do not go gentle into that good night"?
15 Which ex tennis player has run a foundation for terminally ill children through the 90s?
16 What was the first product made by Heinz?
17 In which country did Argentina first win soccer's World Cup?
18 What is Joan Collins' middle name?
19 Queen Alia International airport is in which country?
20 Which part was played by Burgess Meredith in the '60s Batman TV series?
21 Albuquerque international airport is in which US state?
22 Which country does the airline Aero Lloyd come from?
23 Who directed the movie Trading Places?
24 Where in Australia was swashbuckling Errol Flynn born?
25 Who wrote the novel The Tailor of Panama?

Answers

Famous Firsts (see Quiz 201, page 635)
1 Erling Kagge. **2** 1952. **3** Naomi James. **4** Cross channel Hovercraft. **5** Sweden. **6** Parking meter. **7** A streaker. **8** Shiseido. **9** Australia/UK. **10** USA. **11** Never Say Die. **12** Barclays. **13** Royal Philharmonic. **14** Alcoholics Anonymous. **15** Braque. **16** Reinforced concrete. **17** Ralph Bunche. **18** 1966. **19** Miss South Africa. **20** 246. **21** Chemistry. **22** Chicago. **23** Fuchs. **24** Jinnah. **25** Thames Estuary.

Quiz 203 Horse Racing

Answers - see Quiz 204, page 638

1 Which horse gave Lester Piggott his 30th victory in an English Classic?
2 On the flat what is the most number of winners achieved by a jockey in a season in the 20th century?
3 Which horse finished first in the abandoned 1993 Grand National?
4 The Coronation Cup celebrates which coronation?
5 In the 1989 Oaks which 'winning' horse was later disqualified after a post-race test?
6 Who rode Red Rum for the third Grand National triumph?
7 Who was the first National Hunt jockey to employ an agent?
8 How many winners did Frankie Dettori ride in his 1994 super season?
9 Which of the English Classics has Lester Piggott won least times?
10 At the beginning of last century what did Sceptre achieve in 1902?
11 Which horse gave Richard Dunwoody his first Grand National success?
12 What's the only Derby winner of the 20th century to have a date as its name?
13 In which year did the Grand National witness Devon Loch's sensational fall 50 yards from home?
14 Which was the first English Classic to be raced in Scotland?
15 Which horse was the first on which Lester Piggott won two Classics?
16 Who sponsored the 1000 Guineas from 1984 to 1992?
17 What was the last Grand National winner ridden by an amateur before Mr Fisk?
18 Who trained the prolific winner Brigadier Gerard?
19 What was the name of the horse on which Geoff Lewis won his only Derby?
20 To the nearest 1,000, how many rides did the legendary Willie Shoemaker make?
21 Which horse gave Mick Kinane his first 2000 Guineas success?
22 Who was the youngest jockey to win the Grand National in the 20th century?
23 What did Golden Miller win five years in a row back in the 30s?
24 Who won the Oaks on Oh So Sharp and on Diminuendo?
25 How many times has Lester Piggott ridden over 200 winners in a season?

Answers

The Oscars (see Quiz 204, page 638)
1 Ben Kingsley. **2** Vivienne Leigh. **3** Rain Man. **4** Morning Glory. **5** Max Cady. **6** Imogen Stubbs. **7** A Star is Born - the song. **8** Maggie Smith. **9** Emma Thompson. **10** Jessica Tandy. **11** The Adventures of Priscilla Queen of the Desert. **12** Deborah Kerr. **13** Seven. **14** Ghost. **15** Mickey Rooney. **16** Who's Afraid of Virginia Woolf? **17** Creature Comforts. **18** Chariots of Fire. **19** Diane Ladd. **20** Amadeus. **21** Daniel Day Lewis. **22** The Color Purple. **23** Walter & John Huston. **24** Sophia Loren. **25** Thelma and Louise.

Quiz 204 The Oscars

Answers - see Quiz 203, page 637

1 Who was the only British actor to win the best Actor Oscar in the 80s?
2 Whose Oscar was sold in 1994 for over half a million dollars?
3 Which film won the Best Film Oscar on the 60th anniversary of the awards?
4 For which film did Katharine Hepburn win the first of her four 20th century Oscars?
5 Robert de Niro was Oscar nominated for his portrayal of which ex con in Cape Fear?
6 Who eventually played the part Kate Winslet went for in Sense & Sensibility?
7 For which film did Barbra Streisand win her second Oscar?
8 Who was the first actress to win an Oscar for playing the role of an Oscar nominee?
9 Who was the first woman to receive an Oscar for acting and scripting?
10 Who was the oldest winner of the Best Actress Oscar in the 20th century?
11 Which 1994 film won the Oscar for best costume design?
12 Who failed to win an Oscar after six nominations but received an honorary award in 1993?
13 How many times was Richard Burton nominated for an Oscar, though he never won?
14 For which 1990 film did Bruce Joel Rubin win Best Screenplay Oscar?
15 In 1982 who won a special award for 50 years of film making?
16 What was the first film to have its whole cast Oscar nominated?
17 In 1990 which short cartoon won Nick Park an Oscar?
18 Which movie won Best Film the year Charles and Diana were married?
19 Who was Oscar nominated in the same year as her daughter?
20 What was Best Picture the year of the Los Angeles Olympics?
21 Who was the first British actor in the 90s to win the Best Actor Oscar?
22 In 1986 which film had 11 nominations and won nothing?
23 Who were the first father and son to win acting Oscars for the same film?
24 In 1990 who won an achievement Oscar with Myrna Loy?
25 For which film did Callie Khouri win an Oscar in 1991 for screenplay?

Answers

Horse Racing (see Quiz 203, page 637)
1 Rodrigo de Triano. **2** 269. **3** Esha Ness. **4** Edward VII. **5** Aliyssa. **6** Tommy Stack. **7** Jonjo O'Neill. **8** 233. **9** 1000 Guineas. **10** Won four Classics. **11** West Tip. **12** April the Fifth. **13** 1956. **14** St Leger - in 1989. **15** Crepello. **16** General Accident. **17** Grittar. **18** John Hislop. **19** Mill Reef. **20** 40,000. **21** Tirol. **22** Bruce Hobbs. **23** Cheltenham Gold Cup. **24** Steve Cauthen. **25** Never.

Quiz 205 TV Times

Answers - see Quiz 206, page 640

1 Which celebrity couple had the number plate 8 DEB?
2 Which TV cook went to the same school as Jeffrey Archer?
3 What was William Shatner's codename for This Is Your Life?
4 Which TV detective wrote A Cook For All Seasons under his own name?
5 Which British programme won The Golden Rose of Montreux in 1995?
6 Who wrote the song which launched Channel 5?
7 Which former Breakfast Time presenter is a former Miss Great Britain?
8 Who was the first woman on This is Your Life when it transferred to ITV in 1969?
9 Who was the first BBC Sports Personality of the Year of the 1990s?
10 Which actor wrote the show Mac and Beth?
11 Who was described by an interviewee as "the thinking woman's crumpet gone stale"?
12 Who hosted the BBC version of You've Been Framed, Caught In the Act?
13 Which 80s medical drama had the same production company as Hill Street Blues?
14 Which West End show starring ex EastEnder Anita Dobson closed after just three weeks in 1993?
15 Which TV writer was born Romana Barrack?
16 Eileen Downey shot to fame in a docu soap about what?
17 Whose song provided the music for The Seven Faces of Woman?
18 What is the name of cafe owned by Hayley's husband in Coronation Street?
19 How much was Seinfeld offered for each episode of his comedy show when he announced in 1998 he wanted to quit?
20 What was Michael Barrymore's occupation before becoming a TV star?
21 Who was the third soccer player to win BBC Sports Personality of the year?
22 Which Gilbert & Sullivan opera was playing on Derek Wilton's car radio as he suffered his fatal heart attack in Coronation Street?
23 Which character opened the first ever episode of Crossroads and closed the last ever one?
24 What was Tosh Lines' real first name in The Bill?
25 Wilma's vacuum cleaner in The Flintstones was which animal?

Answers

Technology (see Quiz 206, page 640)
1 Altair. **2** Minitel. **3** Sanford. **4** Clockwork. **5** Wounds. **6** Olfactory. **7** Art teacher. **8** Plant movements. **9** R.U.R.. **10** Polaroid. **11** Polio. **12** Guy's. **13** Buildings. **14** Marshall Islands. **15** Abdus Salam. **16** The Branch Mall. **17** The Internet. **18** Shockley. **19** Little Boy. **20** 77. **21** Harness maker. **22** Schick. **23** 43 minutes. **24** French. **25** Austria.

Quiz 206 Technology

Answers - see Quiz 205, page 639

1 What was the name of the first home computer to be manufactured?
2 What was France's on line telecom service called?
3 Who developed the Gaia Theory?
4 How was Trevor Baylis's revolutionary radio powered?
5 Alan Roberts' special super glue was used to join what?
6 What does O stand for in the equipment NOSE which imitates the human nose?
7 What was the occupation of Bruce Rushin who designed the £2 coin to symbolize the progress of technology in British history?
8 Sir Jagadis Chandra Bose's invention the crescograph measures what?
9 Which play by Capek introduced the word robot?
10 What type of camera did Edwin Land develop?
11 Edward Salk developed a vaccine against what?
12 Which hospital performed the first heart surgery on a baby in its mother's womb?
13 Adolf Loos was a designer of what?
14 In which islands is Bikini Atoll where the first atomic bombs were tested?
15 Who was the first Nobel Prize winner to come from Pakistan?
16 What was the first shopping mall on the Internet called?
17 Leslie Rogge was the first person to be arrested due to what?
18 Who led the team which invented transistors in the 1940s?
19 What was the codename of the first atomic bomb dropped on Hiroshima?
20 In 1908 Wilbur Wright travelled what record breaking number of miles in 2 hours 20 minutes?
21 William Henry Hoover started making vacuum cleaners because his original trade was dying out; what was it?
22 Which company manufactured the first electric razor?
23 How long did Bleriot's first cross channel flight last?
24 What nationality of plane first broke the 100mph sound barrier?
25 The first air collision took place over which country?

Answers

TV Times (see Quiz 205, page 639)

1 Paul Daniels & Debbie McGee. **2** Keith Floyd. **3** Beam. **4** George Baker. **5** Don't Forget Your Toothbrush. **6** The Spice Girls. **7** Debbie Greenwood. **8** Twiggy. **9** Paul Gascoigne. **10** Michael Praed. **11** Melvyn Bragg. **12** Shane Richie. **13** St Elsewhere. **14** Eurovision. **15** Carla Lane. **16** Hotel. **17** Charles Aznavour. **18** Roy's Rolls. **19** $5 million. **20** Hairdresser. **21** Michael Owen. **22** The Mikado. **23** Jill. **24** Alfred. **25** Elephant.

Quiz 207 20th C Leaders

Answers - see Quiz 208, page 642

LEVEL 3

1 Paddy Ashdown is fluent in which oriental language?
2 How is Tenzin Gyatso better known?
3 Roy Jenkins became Lord Jenkins of where?
4 Which politician was a judge for the Booker Prize in 1988?
5 Neil Kinnock became MP for which constituency when he entered Parliament in 1970?
6 Who was the first leader of the Belgian Congo?
7 Who replaced Geoffrey Howe as Foreign Secretary in Thatcher's government?
8 Who was Greece's first socialist Prime Minister?
9 Canadian leader Lester Pearson won the Nobel Peace prize for his mediation role in which conflict?
10 Who was Pope during WWII?
11 Which former Tory Party Chairman wrote I Have No Gun But I Can Spit?
12 What was Ronald Reagan's last film?
13 Who formulated his Sinatra Doctrine - foreign policy to be constructed on a My Way basis?
14 Vaclav Havel and George VI both lost what part of their bodies?
15 Which former leader wrote the novel The Cardinal's Hat?
16 Which 'stalking horse' stood for the Tory leadership against Margaret Thatcher in 1989?
17 Where was Nelson Mandela's first foreign trip to after his release from prison?
18 Who did Jonathan Sacks replace as Chief Rabbi in 1990?
19 In 1990 Transport Minister Cecil Parkinson called for a new inquiry into the sinking of what ship?
20 Which leader has played in goal for Polish soccer side Wotsyla?
21 Who became first President of Israel?
22 In 1990 who faced banners saying Goodbye Pineapple Face?
23 Who took over as President of Romania after Ceaucescu was executed?
24 Who did Lord McNally describe as the Kevin Keegan of politics?
25 Who did Thatcher describe as "a man we can do business with"?

Answers

Space – The Final Frontier (see Quiz 208, page 642)
1 Ham. **2** Five hours. **3** The Sun. **4** Tranquillity base here. **5** First fare paying passenger. **6** 4th July. **7** Virgil Grissom. **8** 1930. **9** Galileo. **10** Mark Lee. **11** Hornet. **12** Merritt. **13** Clyde Tombaugh. **14** 1995. **15** James Lovell. **16** Alden. **17** Muses-A. **18** Polyakov. **19** Titov. **20** Japanese. **21** Viking. **22** Ten months. **23** Launch director. **24** Eileen Collins. **25** 10.

Quiz 208 Space - The Final Frontier

Answers - see Quiz 207, page 641

LEVEL 3

1 What was the name of the first chimpanzee the Americans sent in space?
2 How long did the record breaking space walk from space shuttle Endeavour last in 1993?
3 Where did the European space probe Ulysses set off for in 1991?
4 What did Neil Armstrong say immediately before "the eagle has landed"?
5 Which space first was achieved by Toyohiro Akiyama in 1991?
6 On what date in 1997 did Pathfinder land on Mars right on schedule?
7 Who was the next American in space after Shephard?
8 In which year were all three astronauts on the first moon landing expedition born?
9 Which probe sent back the first major pictures of Jupiter in 1995?
10 Who made the first untethered space walk of the 1990s?
11 On which ship did President Nixon welcome the astronauts back from the Moon?
12 On which island is the Kennedy Space centre?
13 Which scientist located Pluto?
14 In what year was Hale Bopp first seen?
15 Which astronaut said, "Houston we have a problem"?
16 What is Neil Armstrong's middle name?
17 What was the name of the Japanese Moon orbiter launched in 1990?
18 Which cosmonaut returned to Earth in 1996 after spending a record breaking 438 days in space?
19 Who was the second Soviet cosmonaut?
20 What was the nationality of the journalist who accompanied a docking mission to MIR in 1990?
21 What was the name of the first probe to send back pictures from Mars?
22 How long did Sergei Krikalyev spend on Mir in the early 90s?
23 What was the role of Rocco Petrone in the Apollo XI project?
24 Who was the first woman to captain a space shuttle crew?
25 How many orbits of the moon were there on the first manned orbit?

Answers

20th C Leaders (see Quiz 207, page 641)
1 Mandarin. **2** The Dalai Lama. **3** Hillhead. **4** Michael Foot. **5** Bedwelty. **6** Lumumba. **7** John Major. **8** Papandreou. **9** Suez. **10** Pius XII. **11** Kenneth Baker. **12** The Killers. **13** Eduard Shevardnadze. **14** Lung. **15** Mussolini. **16** Sir Anthony Meyer. **17** Zambia. **18** Lord Jakobovits. **19** Titanic. **20** The Pope. **21** Chaim Weizmann. **22** Manuel Noriega. **23** Ion Iliescu. **24** Paddy Ashdown. **25** Gorbachev.

Quiz 209 Sports Bag

Answers - see Quiz 210, page 644

1 At which venue did Sandy Lyle win the British Open?
2 In women's hockey which country has won the World Cup most times?
3 In which sport did actor Noel Harrison compete in the 1952 Olympics?
4 In which year did Graham Hill win the Le Mans 24 hour race?
5 Who did Terry Griffiths beat in the final in his only snooker World Championship triumph?
6 Great Britain's Rugby League side toured where for the first time in 1984?
7 The Stoke Poges golf club was used for location shots for which film?
8 In Red Rum's first Grand National triumph which 9 -1 favourite had led the field until the final dash?
9 In how many games did Bobby Charlton captain England?
10 Anton Geesink was the first person out of Japan to win a judo world championship, but which country did he come from?
11 Who played Harlequins in the first Rugby Union game at Twickenham?
12 How many of his 45 races did Mike Hawthorn, F1 world champion, win?
13 In which decade were the Badminton Horse Trials first held?
14 In how many of his 39 Tests was Mike Brearley not the captain?
15 Name France's last Wimbledon Men's Singles winner of this century.
16 Who did Spurs meet in the first all British European final?
17 In which soap did Fred Trueman appear as himself?
18 Which was the last horse before Nijinsky to win the triple of Derby, 2000 Guineas and St Leger?
19 In which UK event did Tony Jacklin make the first live TV hole in one?
20 When Wimbledon became Open in 1968 what was the men's singles prize money?
21 Britain's William Lane became a world champion in which sport?
22 In which events did Gert Frederiksson win six Olympic Golds?
23 Who was the defending champion when Chris Evert first won Wimbledon singles?
24 Which first is held by the New Zealander E J 'Murt' O'Donoghue?
25 Which British Open winner's dad was a professional at Hawkstone Park, Shropshire?

Answers

Film Legends (see Quiz 210, page 644)
1 Woman of the Year. **2** Tallulah Bankhead. **3** Blonde Crazy. **4** Rowing. **5** Charlie Chaplin. **6** Robert Newton - in Treasure Island. **7** Erich Von Stroheim. **8** Prissy. **9** He was allergic to the make up. **10** 1991. **11** Mexico. **12** Kirk Douglas. **13** Utah. **14** Six. **15** Cansino. **16** Jean Harlow. **17** Tony Curtis. **18** Making Cleopatra. **19** Ginger Rogers. **20** Who's Afraid of Virginia Woolf? **21** Angelo Maggio. **22** 85. **23** Playtex. **24** Sophia Loren. **25** Groucho Marx.

Quiz 210 Film Legends

Answers - see Quiz 209, page 643

1 What was Katharine Hepburn and Spencer Tracy's first film together?
2 Which actress said, "I'm as pure as driven slush"?
3 In which film did James Cagney say "You dirty double crossing rat" which led to his catchphrase?
4 In which sport did John Kelly compete in the 1920 Olympics?
5 Who said, "All I need to make a comedy is a park, a policeman and a pretty girl"?
6 Which actor was Tony Hancock impersonating with his "Ha harr Jim lad" routine?
7 Who was "the man you love to hate"?
8 Which famous character was played by Butterfly McQueen in Gone With the Wind?
9 Why was Buddy Ebsen forced to quit his role as the Tin Man in The Wizard of Oz?
10 In what year did David Lean die?
11 In which country did Steve McQueen die?
12 Whose autobiography was called The Ragman's Son?
13 In which state did Robert Redford found the Sundance Institute?
14 How old was Shirley Temple when she received an honorary Oscar?
15 What would Rita Hayworth's surname have been if she had used her father's name instead of her mother's?
16 On which 30s screen legend was Catwoman in Batman based?
17 Which Marilyn Monroe co star said, "Kissing her is like kissing Hitler"?
18 About who or what did Elizabeth Taylor say, "It was like an illness one had a very difficult time recuperating from"?
19 Which musical star was a cousin of Rita Hayworth?
20 For which film did Elizabeth Taylor win her second Oscar?
21 Which character did Frank Sinatra play in From Here to Eternity?
22 How old was Mae West when she starred in the film Sextet?
23 Which lingerie company did Jane Russell work for in the 1970s?
24 Who has the nickname 'The Stick' as a child?
25 Who said, "I never forget a face, but in your case I'll make an exception"?

Answers

Sports Bag (see Quiz 209, page 643)
1 Sandwich. **2** Netherlands. **3** Alpine skiing. **4** 1972. **5** Dennis Taylor. **6** Papua New Guinea. **7** Goldfinger. **8** Crisp. **9** Three. **10** Holland. **11** Richmond. **12** 3. **13** 40s. **14** 8. **15** Yvon Petra. **16** Wolves. **17** Emmerdale. **18** Bahram. **19** Dunlop Masters. **20** £2,000. **21** Angling. **22** Canoeing. **23** Billie Jean King. **24** 147 snooker break. **25** Sandy Lyle.

Quiz 211 TV Trivia

Answers - see Quiz 212, page 646

1 Who was the first sportsman to appear on This Is Your Life?
2 What was the first feature film shown on BBC2?
3 In Tutti Frutti, who was bass player with The Majestics?
4 Which TV presenter once held the title Miss Parallel Bars?
5 Which newsreader was a judge for the Booker Prize in 1987?
6 Margo Turner's life was researched for This Is Your Life and then became the basis for which drama series?
7 Which Coronation Street star played Christine Keeler's mother in Scandal?
8 Which TV presenter produced a fitness video called Fit For Life?
9 In which real life store did Wendy Richard used to work?
10 What was Winston Churchill referring to when he said, "Why do we need this peep show?"?
11 In which event did Bill Nankeville, father of Bobby Davro, compete in the 1948 Olympics?
12 What was the first Dr Who series called in which The Daleks appeared?
13 In Minder what football team did Terry McCann support?
14 Which show of the 50s used the catchphrase 'Goody goody gumdrops'?
15 Where was Brian Hanrahan when he "counted them all out, and counted them all back"?
16 Which TV presenter wrote The Hired Man with Howard Goodall?
17 Which building designed by Norman Shaw in the 19th C appeared on TV screens throughout the 20th C?
18 What was Nigel Kennedy's codename for This Is Your Life?
19 What did Harry Enfield study at university?
20 Which music was used for the BBC's 1998 World Cup coverage?
21 Who was the only woman in the 1980s to win the BBC Sports Personality of the Year single handed?
22 Which newsreader advertised Cow & Gate baby food as a child?
23 What was the occupation of Noel Edmonds' father?
24 Who was the first soap star to receive an honour from the Queen?
25 Who presented Channel 4's religious series Canterbury Tales?

Answers

Entertainment (see Quiz 212, page 646)
1 Royal Court. **2** Oh Calcutta. **3** A psychiatrist. **4** Mike Read. **5** Stephen Joseph Theatre. **6** Circus. **7** Scott. **8** Balanchine. **9** Barbirolli. **10** Arthur Askey. **11** Butter. **12** Early Morning. **13** TV. **14** 1926. **15** Pilton. **16** Winston Churchill. **17** Bing Crosby. **18** Pinewood. **19** 13. **20** Oh! Calcutta. **21** Mary Hayley Bell. **22** Bangladesh. **23** Cynthia. **24** 1947. **25** Coliseum.

Quiz 212 Entertainment

Answers - see Quiz 211, page 645

1 Which London theatre saw the premiere of Look Back in Anger?
2 Which show made critic Robert Helpmann say, "The trouble with nude dancing is that not everything stops when the music does"?
3 According to bishop Mervyn Stockwood who would "go to the Folies Bergere and look at the audience"?
4 Who wrote the music for the show Betjeman with words by the poet himself?
5 What is the name of the theatre in Scarborough linked with Alan Ayckbourn?
6 The slogan "The Big One" was originally used to advertise what?
7 Which brothers bought Shepperton studios in 1994?
8 Who founded the New York City ballet in 1928?
9 To which conductor did Vaughan Williams dedicate his 8th Symphony to?
10 Who was known as big hearted Arthur?
11 What food has sexual overtones in Bertolucci's Last Tango in Paris?
12 Which stage play was the last to be banned by the Lord Chamberlain in the UK?
13 What did critic John Mason Brown describe as "chewing gum for the eyes"?
14 In what year did Elstree studios open?
15 Where is the location of the Glastonbury Festival?
16 On whose life was the short lived musical Winnie based?
17 Which singer had the first names Harry Lillis?
18 Which studios did the Rank Organisation open in 1936?
19 How many Gilbert & Sullivan operas are there?
20 Which show made critic Clive Barnes say, "It gives pornography a bad name"?
21 Who wrote the book on which the musical Whistle Down the Wind was based?
22 The first great rock charity show was in aid of the people of which country?
23 What was the name of Hylda Baker's silent friend?
24 In what year did the first Edinburgh Festival take place?
25 Which London theatre is home to the ENO?

Answers

TV Trivia (see Quiz 211, page 645)
1 Stanley Matthews. **2** Kiss Me Kate. **3** Fud O'Donnell. **4** Carol Smillie. **5** Trevor McDonald. **6** Tenko. **7** Jean Alexander. **8** Gloria Hunniford. **9** Fortnum & Mason. **10** Commercial TV. **11** 1500 metres. **12** The Dead Planet. **13** Fulham. **14** Whirligig. **15** Port Stanley. **16** Melvyn Bragg. **17** New Scotland Yard. **18** Bow. **19** Politics. **20** Faure's Pavane. **21** Fatima Whitbread. **22** Martyn Lewis. **23** Headmaster. **24** Violet Carson. **25** Ian Hislop.

HOW TO SET UP YOUR OWN PUB QUIZ

It isn't easy, get that right from the start. This isn't going to be easy. Think instead of words like; 'difficult', 'taxing', 'infuriating'. Consider yourself with damp palms and a dry throat and then, when you have concentrated on that, put it out of your mind and think of the recognition you will receive down the local, imagine all the regulars lifting you high upon their shoulders dancing and weaving their way around the pub. It won't help but it's good to dream every once in a while.

What you will need:

- A good selection of biros (never be tempted to give your own pen up, not even to family members)
- A copy of *The Biggest Pub Quiz Book Ever! 2*
- A set of answer sheets photocopied from the back of the book
- A good speaking voice and possibly a microphone and an amp
- A pub
- At least one pint inside you
- At least one more on your table
- A table

What to do:

Choose your local to start with, there is no need to get halfway through your first quiz and decide you weren't cut out for all this and then find yourself in the roughest pub in Christendom, 30 miles and a long run from home.

Chat it through with the landlord and agree on whether you will be charging or not. If you don't then there is little chance of a prize for the winners other than a free pint each and this is obviously at the landlord's discretion – if you pack his pub to bursting then five free pints won't worry him, but if it's only you and two others then he may be less than unwilling, as publicans tend to be.

If you decide on a payment entry keep it reasonable. You don't

want to take the fun out of the quiz; some people will be well aware that they have very little hope of winning and so will be reluctant to celebrate the fact by mortgaging their house.

Once location and prize are all sorted then advertising the event is paramount, get people's attention, sell, sell, sell or, alternatively, stick up a gaudy looking poster on the door of the bogs. Be sure to specify all the details, time, prize and so on – remember you could be selling to people whose tiny attention span is being whittled down to nothing by alcohol.

After this it is time for the big night. If you are holding the event in the 'snug' which seats ten or so you can rely on your voice, if not you should get hold of a good microphone and an amplifier so that you can boom out your questions across the length and breadth of the pub (once again, clear this with the landlord and don't let liquid anywhere near the electrical equipment). Make sure to practise, and get comfortable with the sound of your own voice and relax as much as possible. Try not to rely on alcohol too much or "round one" will be followed by "rown' too", which will eventually give way to "run-free". Relax with your voice so that you can handle any queries from the teams, and any venomous abuse from the 'lively' bar area.

When you enter the pub make sure you take everything listed above. Also, make sure you have a set of tie-break questions and that you instruct everybody who is taking part of the rules – and be firm. It will only upset people if you start handing out impromptu solutions and, let's face it, the wisdom of Solomon is not needed when you are talking pub quiz rules; 'no cheating' is a perfectly healthy stance to start with.

Finally, keep the teams to a maximum of five members, hand out your answer papers and pens and, when everybody is good and settled, start the quiz. It might not be easy and it might not propel you to international stardom or pay for a life of luxury but you will enjoy yourself. No, really.

ANSWERS

Round One

1 ____________________

2 ____________________

3 ____________________

4 ____________________

5 ____________________

6 ____________________

7 ____________________

8 ____________________

9 ____________________

10 ____________________

11 ____________________

12 ____________________

13 ____________________

14 ____________________

15 ____________________

16 ____________________

17 ____________________

18 ____________________

19 ____________________

20 ____________________

21 ____________________

22 ____________________

23 ____________________

24 ____________________

25 ____________________

26 ____________________

27 ____________________

28 ____________________

29 ____________________

30 ____________________

ANSWERS Round One

1 ______

2 ______

3 ______

4 ______

5 ______

6 ______

7 ______

8 ______

9 ______

10 ______

11 ______

12 ______

13 ______

14 ______

15 ______

16 ______

17 ______

18 ______

19 ______

20 ______

21 ______

22 ______

23 ______

24 ______

25 ______

26 ______

27 ______

28 ______

29 ______

30 ______

ANSWERS

Round Two

1 ______

2 ______

3 ______

4 ______

5 ______

6 ______

7 ______

8 ______

9 ______

10 ______

11 ______

12 ______

13 ______

14 ______

15 ______

16 ______

17 ______

18 ______

19 ______

20 ______

21 ______

22 ______

23 ______

24 ______

25 ______

26 ______

27 ______

28 ______

29 ______

30 ______

ANSWERS — Round Two

1 ______

2 ______

3 ______

4 ______

5 ______

6 ______

7 ______

8 ______

9 ______

10 ______

11 ______

12 ______

13 ______

14 ______

15 ______

16 ______

17 ______

18 ______

19 ______

20 ______

21 ______

22 ______

23 ______

24 ______

25 ______

26 ______

27 ______

28 ______

29 ______

30 ______

ANSWERS Round Three

1 ______

2 ______

3 ______

4 ______

5 ______

6 ______

7 ______

8 ______

9 ______

10 ______

11 ______

12 ______

13 ______

14 ______

15 ______

16 ______

17 ______

18 ______

19 ______

20 ______

21 ______

22 ______

23 ______

24 ______

25 ______

26 ______

27 ______

28 ______

29 ______

30 ______

ANSWERS — Round Three

1 ______________________

2 ______________________

3 ______________________

4 ______________________

5 ______________________

6 ______________________

7 ______________________

8 ______________________

9 ______________________

10 ______________________

11 ______________________

12 ______________________

13 ______________________

14 ______________________

15 ______________________

16 ______________________

17 ______________________

18 ______________________

19 ______________________

20 ______________________

21 ______________________

22 ______________________

23 ______________________

24 ______________________

25 ______________________

26 ______________________

27 ______________________

28 ______________________

29 ______________________

30 ______________________

NOTES